File Structures

SECOND EDITION

MICHAEL J. FOLK
University of Illinois

BILL ZOELLICK
Avalanche Development Company

 Addison-Wesley Publishing Company, Inc.

Reading, Massachusetts • Menlo Park, California • New York
Don Mills, Ontario • Wokingham, England • Amsterdam
Bonn • Sydney • Singapore • Tokyo • Madrid
San Juan • Milan • Paris

Sponsoring Editor   Peter Shepard
Production Administrator   Juliet Silveri
Copyeditor   Patricia Daly
Text Designer   Melinda Grosser for *silk*
Cover Designer   Peter Blaiwas
Technical Art Consultant   Dick Morton
Illustrator   Scot Graphics
Manufacturing Supervisor   Roy Logan

Photographs on pages 126 and 187 courtesy of S. Sukumar. Figure 10.7 on page 470 courtesy of International Business Machines Corporation.

Library of Congress Cataloging-in-Publication Data

Folk, Michael J.
   File structures / Michael J. Folk, Bill Zoellick.—2nd ed.
      p.   cm.
   Includes bibliographical references and index.
   ISBN 0-201-55713-4
   1. File organization (Computer science)   I. Zoellick, Bill.
   II. Title.
   QA76.9.F5F65   1992
   005.74—dc20   91-16314
                                                                       CIP

Reprinted with corrections June, 1992

13 DOC 97

To Pauline and Rachel

and

To Karen, Joshua, and Peter

Preface

We wrote the first edition to promote file structure literacy. Literacy implies familiarity with the tools used to organize files. It also means knowing the story of how the different tools have evolved. Knowing the story is the basis for using the tools appropriately.

The first edition told the story of file structures up to about 1980. This second edition continues the story, examining developments such as extendible hashing and optical disc storage that have moved from being a research topic at the start of the last decade to a mature technology by its end.

While the history of file structures provides the key organizing principle for much of this text, we also find ourselves compelled, particularly in this second edition, to attend to developments in computing hardware and system software. In the last twenty years computers have evolved from being expensive monoliths, maintained by a priesthood of specialists, to being appliances as ubiquitous as toasters. No longer do we need to confront a corps of analysts to get information in and out of a computer. We do it ourselves. Today, more often than yesterday, programmers design and build their own file structures.

This text shows you how to design and build efficient file structures. All you need is a good programming language, a good operating system, and the conceptual tools that enable you to think through alternative file structure designs that apply to the task at hand. The first six chapters of this book give you the basic tools to design simple file structures from the ground up. We provide examples of program code and, if you are a UNIX user, we show you, whenever possible, how to use this operating system to help with much of the work. Building on the first six chapters of foundation work, the last five chapters introduce you to the most important high-level file structure designs, including sequential access, B-trees and B$^+$trees, and hashing and extendible hashing.

The last ten years of development in software design are reason enough for this second edition, but we have also used this edition to discuss the decreased cost and increased availability of computer storage hardware. For instance, one of the most dramatic changes in computer configurations over the past decade is the increase in the amount of available RAM on computers of all sizes. In 1986, when we completed the first edition of this book, it was rare that a personal computer had more than 640 Kbytes of RAM. Now, even for many mundane applications, four Mbytes is common, and sometimes even mandatory. A decade ago, a sophisticated mainframe system that was used extensively for sorting large files typically had two to four Mbytes of primary memory; now 32 to 64 Mbytes is common on workstations, and there are some computers with several *giga*bytes of RAM.

When more RAM is available we can approach file structures problems differently. For example, most earlier file structure texts deal with the sorting of large files assuming it is always done on tape. One reason for this is that, when RAM is scarce, sorting on tape is much more viable than sorting on disk. Now that RAM is much cheaper and more readily available, sorting on disk is not only viable, it is usually preferable. This second edition reflects this change and others that arise from changes in computer hardware.

Using the Book as a College Text

The first edition has been used extensively as a text for many different kinds of students in many different kinds of universities. Because the book is quite readable, students typically are expected to read the entire book over the course of a semester. The text covers the basics; class lectures can expand and supplement the material presented in the text. The lecturer is free to explore more complex topics and applications, relying on the text to supply the fundamentals.

A word of caution: It is easy to spend too much time on the low-level issues presented in the first six chapters. Move quickly through this material. The relatively large number of pages devoted to these matters is not a reflection of the percentage of the course that should be spent on them. The intent, instead, is to provide thorough coverage in the text so that the instructor can simply assign these chapters as background reading, saving precious lecture time for more important topics.

It is important to get students involved in writing file processing programs early in the semester. Consider starting with a file reading and writing assignment that is due after the first week of class. The inclusion in the text of sample programs in both C and Pascal makes it easier to work in this hands-on style. We recommend that, by the time the students encounter the B-tree chapter, they should have already written programs that access a data set through a simple index structure. Since the students then already have first-hand experience with the fundamental organizational issues, it is possible for lectures to focus on the conceptual issues involved in B-tree design.

Finally, we suggest that instructors adhere to a close approximation of the sequence of topics used in the book, especially through the first six chapters. We have already stressed that we wrote the book so that it can be read from cover to cover. It is not a reference work. Instead, we develop ideas as we proceed from chapter to chapter. Skipping around in the book makes it difficult for students to follow this development.

A Book for Computing Professionals

Both authors used to teach, but we now design and write programs for a living. We wrote and revised this book with our colleagues in mind. The style is conversational; the intent is to provide a book that you can read over a number of evenings, coming away with a good sense of how to approach file structure design problems. If you are already familiar with basic file structure design concepts, skim through the first six chapters and begin reading about cosequential access methods in Chapter 7. Subsequent chapters introduce you to B-trees, B$^+$trees, hashing, and extendible hashing. These are key design tools for any practicing programmer who is building file structures. We have tried to present them in a way that is both thorough and readable.

If you are not already a serious UNIX user, the UNIX material in the first seven chapters will give you a feel for why UNIX is a powerful environment in which to work with files. Similarly, the C programs in several of the chapters provide an introduction to the use of C with files. Also, if you need to build and access file structures similar to the ones in the text, you may be able to use these programs as a source code toolkit that you can adapt to your needs.

Finally, we know that an increasing number of computing professionals are confronted with the need to understand and use CD-ROM. Appendix A not only provides an example of how the design principles introduced in this text are applied to this important medium, but it also gives you a good introduction to the medium itself.

Acknowledgements

There are a number of people we would like to thank for help in preparing this second edition. Peter Shepard, our editor at Addison-Wesley, initiated the idea of a new edition, kept after us to get it done, and saw the production through to completion. We thank our reviewers; James Canning, Jan Carroll, Suzanne Dietrich, Terry Johnson, Theodore Norman, Gregory Riccardi, and Cliff Shaffer. We also thank Deebak Khanna for comments and suggestions for improving the code.

Since the publication of the first edition, we have received a great deal of feedback from readers. Their suggestions and contributions have had a major effect on this second edition, and in fact are largely responsible for our completely rewriting several of the chapters.

Colleagues with whom we work have also contributed to the second edition, many without knowing they were doing so. We are grateful to them for information, explanations, and ideas that have improved our own understanding of many of the topics covered in the book. These colleagues include Chin Chau Low, Tim Krauskopf, Joseph Hardin, Quincey Koziol, Carlos Donohue, S. Sukumar, Mike Page, and Lee Fife.

Thanks are still outstanding to people who contributed to the initial edition: Marilyn Aiken, Art Crotzer, Mark Dalton, Don Fisher, Huey Liu, Gail Meinert, and Jim Van Doren.

We thank J.S. Bach, whose magnificent contribution of music to work by makes this work possible.

Most important of all, we thank Pauline, Rachel, Karen, Joshua and Peter for putting up with fathers and husbands who get up too early to write, are tired all day, and stay up too late at night to write some more. It's the price of fame.

Boulder, Colorado   **B.Z.**

Urbana, Illinois   **M.F.**

Contents

3   Secondary Storage and System Software   35

4

Fundamental File Structure Concepts 93

5   Organizing Files for Performance 183

8   B-Trees and Other Tree-structured File Organizations   333

9 The B$^+$ Tree Family and Indexed Sequential File Access   405

10 Hashing 445

11 Extendible Hashing 503

Appendix A: File Structures on CD-ROM 541

Introduction to File Structures

1

CHAPTER OBJECTIVES

- Introduce the primary design issues that characterize file structure design.
- Survey the history of file structure design, since tracing the developments in file structures teaches us much about how to design our own file structures.
- Introduce the notions of file structure literacy and of a *conceptual toolkit* for file structure design.

1.1 The Heart of File Structure Design

Disks are slow. They are also technological marvels, packing hundreds of megabytes on disks that can fit into a notebook computer. Only a few years ago, disks with that kind of capacity looked like small washing machines. However, relative to the other parts of a computer, disks are slow.

How slow? The time it takes to get information back from even relatively slow electronic random access memory (RAM) is about 120 nanoseconds, or 120 billionths of a second. Getting the same information from a typical disk might take 30 milliseconds, or 30 thousandths of a second. To understand the size of this difference, we need an analogy. Assume that RAM access is like finding something in the index of this book. Let's say that this local, book-in-hand access takes 20 seconds. Assume that disk access is like sending to a library for the information you cannot find here in this book. Given that our "RAM access" takes 20 seconds, how long does the "disk access" to the library take, keeping the ratio the same as that of a real RAM access and disk access? The disk access is a quarter of a million times longer than the RAM access. This means that getting information back from the library takes 5,000,000 seconds, or almost 58 days. Disks are *very* slow compared to RAM.

On the other hand, disks provide enormous capacity at much less cost than RAM. They also keep the information stored on them when they are turned off. The tension between a disk's relatively slow access time and its enormous, nonvolatile capacity is the driving force behind file structure design. Good file structure design will give us access to all the capacity without making our applications spend a lot of time waiting for the disk. This book shows you how to develop such file designs.

1.2   A Short History of File Structure Design

Put another way, our goal is to show you how to think creatively about file structure design problems. Part of our approach to doing this is based on history: After introducing basic principles of design in the first part of this book, we devote the last part to studying some of the key developments in file design over the last 30 years. The problems that researchers struggle with reflect the same issues that you confront in addressing any substantial file design problem. Working through the approaches used to address major file design issues shows you a lot about how to approach new design problems.

The general goals of research and development in file structures can be drawn directly from our library analogy:

☐   Ideally, we would like to get the information we need with one access to the disk. In terms of our analogy, we do not want to issue a series of 58-day requests before we get what we want.

☐   If it is impossible to get what we need in one access, we want structures that allow us to find the target information with as few accesses as possible. For example, you may remember from your studies of data structures that a binary search allows us to find a particular record among 50,000 other records with no more than 16 comparisons. But having to look 16 places on a disk before finding what we want takes too much time. We need file structures that allow us to find what we need with only two or three trips to the disk.

☐   We want our file structures to group information so we are likely to get everything we need with only one trip to the disk. If we need a client's name, address, phone number, and account balance, we would prefer to get all that information at once, rather than having to look in several places for it.

It is relatively easy to come up with file structure designs that meet these goals when we have files that never change. Designing file structures that maintain these qualities as files change, growing and shrinking as information is added and deleted, is much more difficult.

Early work with files presumed that files were on tape, since most files were. Access was sequential, and the cost of access grew in direct proportion to the size of the file. As files grew intolerably large for unaided sequential access and as storage devices like disk drives became available, indexes were added to files. The indexes made it possible to keep a list of keys and pointers in a smaller file that could be searched more quickly; given the key and pointer, the user had direct access to the large, primary file.

Unfortunately, simple indexes had some of the same, sequential flavor as the data files themselves, and as the indexes grew they too became difficult to manage, especially for dynamic files in which the set of keys changes. Then, in the early 1960s, the idea of applying tree structures emerged as a potential solution. Unfortunately, trees can grow very unevenly as records are added and deleted, resulting in long searches requiring many disk accesses to find a record.

In 1963 researchers developed the AVL tree, an elegant, self-adjusting binary tree structure for data in RAM. Other researchers began to look for ways to apply AVL trees, or something like them, to files. The problem was that even with a balanced binary tree, dozens of accesses are required to find a record in even moderate-sized files. A way was needed to keep a tree balanced when each node of the tree was not a single record, as in a binary tree, but a file block containing dozens, perhaps even hundreds, of records.

It took nearly 10 more years of design work before a solution emerged in the form of the *B-tree*. Part of the reason that finding a solution took so long was that the approach required for file structures was very different from the approach that worked in RAM. Whereas AVL trees grow from the top down as records are added, B-trees grow from the bottom up.

B-trees provided excellent access performance, but there was a cost: No longer could a file be accessed sequentially with efficiency. Fortunately, this problem was solved almost immediately by adding a linked list structure at the bottom level of the B-tree. The combination of a B-tree and a sequential linked list is called a B^+tree.

Over the following 10 years B-trees and B^+ trees became the basis for many commercial file systems, since they provide access times that grow in proportion to $\log_k N$, where N is the number of entries in the file and k is the number of entries indexed in a single block of the B-tree structure. In practical terms, this means that B-trees can guarantee that you can find one file entry among millions of others with only three or four trips to the disk. Further, B-trees guarantee that as you add and delete entries, performance stays about the same.

Being able to get information back with just three or four accesses is pretty good. But how about our goal of being able to get what we want with a single request? An approach called *hashing* is a good way to do that with files that do not change size greatly over time. From early on, hashed indexes were used to provide fast access to files. However, until recently, hashing did not work well with volatile, dynamic files that changed greatly in size. After the development of B-trees, researchers turned to work on systems for extendible, dynamic hashing that could retrieve information with one or, at most, two disk accesses no matter how big the file becomes. We close this book with a careful look at this work, which took place from the late 1970s through the first part of the 1980s.

1.3   A Conceptual Toolkit: File Structure Literacy

As we move through the developments in file structures over the last three decades, watching file structure design evolve as it addresses dynamic files first sequentially, then through tree structures, and finally through direct access, we see that the same design problems and design tools keep emerging. We decrease the number of disk accesses by collecting data into buffers, blocks, or buckets; we manage the growth of these collections by splitting them, which requires that we find a way to increase our address or index space, and so on. Progress takes the form of finding new ways to combine these basic tools of file design.

We think of these tools as *conceptual* tools. They are ways of framing and addressing a design problem. Our own work in file structures has shown us that by understanding the tools thoroughly, and by studying how the tools have been combined to produce such diverse approaches as B-trees and extendible hashing, we develop mastery and flexibility in our own use of the tools. In other words, we acquire literacy with regard to file structures. This text is designed to help readers acquire file structure literacy. Chapters 1 through 6 introduce the basic tools; Chapters 7 through 11 introduce readers to the highlights of the past several decades of file structure design, showing how the basic tools are used to handle efficient sequential access, B-trees, B^+ trees, hashed indexes, and extendible, dynamic hashed files.

■ SUMMARY

The key design problem that shapes file structure design is the relatively large amount of time that is required to get information from disk. All file structure designs focus on minimizing disk accesses and maximizing the likelihood that the information the user will want is already in RAM.

This text begins by introducing the basic concepts and issues associated with file structures. The last half of the book tracks the development of file structure design as it has evolved over the last 30 years. The key problem addressed throughout this evolution is finding ways to minimize disk accesses for files that keep changing in content and size. Tracking these developments takes us first through work on sequential file access, then through developments in tree-structured access, and finally to relatively recent work on direct access to information in files.

Our experience has been that the study of the principal research and design contributions to file structures, focusing on how the design work uses the same tools in new ways, provides a solid foundation for thinking creatively about new problems in file structure design.

■ KEY TERMS

AVL tree. A self-adjusting binary tree structure that can guarantee good access times for data in RAM.

B-tree. A tree structure that provides fast access to data stored in files. Unlike binary trees, in which the branching factor from a node of the tree is two, the descendents from a node of a B-tree can be a much larger number. We introduce B-trees in Chapter 8.

B$^+$ tree. A variation on the B-tree structure that provides sequential access to the data as well as fast-indexed access. We discuss B$^+$ trees at length in Chapter 9.

Extendible hashing. An approach to hashing that works well with files that undergo substantial changes in size over time.

File structures. The organization of data on secondary storage devices such as disks.

Hashing. An access mechanism that transforms the search key into a storage address, thereby providing very fast access to stored data.

Sequential access. Access that takes records in order, looking at the first, then the next, and so on.

Fundamental File
Processing Operations

2

CHAPTER OBJECTIVES

▪ Describe the process of linking a *logical file* within a program to an actual *physical file* or device.

▪ Describe the procedures used to create, open, and close files.

▪ Describe the procedures used for reading from and writing to files.

▪ Introduce the concept of *position* within a file and describe procedures for *seeking* different positions.

▪ Provide an introduction to the organization of the UNIX file system.

▪ Present the UNIX view of a file, and describe UNIX file operations and commands based on this view.

2.1 Physical Files and Logical Files

When we talk about a file on a disk or tape, we refer to a particular collection of bytes stored there. A file, when the word is used in this sense, physically exists. A disk drive might contain hundreds, even thousands, of these *physical files*.

From the standpoint of an application program, the notion of a file is different. To the program, a file is somewhat like a telephone line connected to a telephone network. The program can receive bytes through this phone line, or send bytes down it, but knows nothing about where these bytes actually come from or where they go. The program knows only about its own end of the phone line. Moreover, even though there may be thousands of physical files on a disk, a single program is usually limited to the use of only about 20 files.

The application program relies on the operating system to take care of the details of the telephone switching system, as illustrated in Fig. 2.1. It could be that bytes coming down the line into the program originate from an actual physical file, or they might come from the keyboard or some other input device. Similarly, the bytes that the program sends down the line might end up in a file, or they could appear on the terminal screen. Although the program often doesn't know where bytes are coming from or where they are going, it does know which line it is using. This line is usually referred to as the *logical file* to distinguish this view from the *physical files* on the disk or tape.

Before the program can open a file for use, the operating system must receive instructions about making a hookup between a logical file (e.g., a phone line) and some physical file or device. When using operating systems such as IBM's OS/MVS, these instructions are provided through job control language (JCL). On minicomputers and microcomputers, more modern operating systems such as UNIX, MS-DOS, and VMS provide the instructions within the program. For example, in Turbo Pascal[†] the association between a logical file called *inp_file* and a physical file called *myfile.dat* is made with the following statement:

```
assign(inp_file,'myfile.dat')
```

This statement asks the operating system to find the physical file named *myfile.dat* and then to make the hookup by assigning a logical file (phone line) to it. The number identifying the particular phone line that is assigned is returned through the FILE variable *inp_file,* which is the file's *logical name.* This logical name is what we use to refer to the file inside the program. Again, the telephone analogy applies: My office phone is connected to six telephone lines. When I receive a call I get an intercom message such as, "You have a call on line three." The receptionist does not say, "You have a call from 918-123-4567." I need to have the call identified *logically,* not *physically.*

2.2 Opening Files

Once we have a logical file identifier hooked up to a physical file or device, we need to declare what we intend to do with the file. In general, we have two options: (1) open an *existing* file or (2) create a *new* file, deleting any existing contents in the physical file. Opening a file makes it ready for use by the program. We are positioned at the beginning of the file and are ready to start reading or writing. The file contents are not disturbed by the open statement. Creating a file also opens the file in the sense that it is ready for use after creation. Since a newly created file has no contents, writing is initially the only use that makes sense.

[†]Different Pascal compilers vary widely with regard to I/O procedures, since standard Pascal contains little in the way of I/O definition. Throughout this book we use the term *Pascal* when discussing features common to most Pascal implementations. When we refer to the features of a specific implementation, such as Turbo Pascal, we say so.

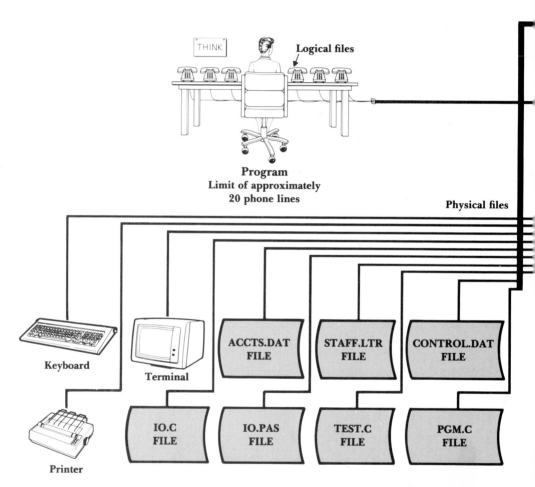

FIGURE 2.1 The program relies on the operating system to make connections between logical files and physical files and devices.

In Pascal the *reset( )* statement is used to open existing files and the *rewrite( )* statement is used to create new ones. For example, to open a file in Turbo Pascal we might use a sequence of statements such as:

```
assign(inp_file, 'myfile.dat');
reset (inp_file)
```

Operating system switchboard
Can make connections to thousands
of files or I/O devices

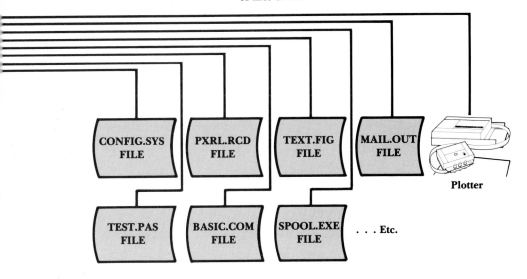

Plotter

Note that we use the logical file name, not the physical one, in the *reset()* statement. To *create* a file in Turbo Pascal, the statements might read:

```
assign(out_file, 'myfile.dat');
rewrite (inp_file)
```

We can open an existing file or create a new one in C through the UNIX system function *open( )*. This function takes two required arguments and a third argument that is optional:

```
fd = open(filename, flags, [pmode]);
```

The return value *fd* and the arguments *filename, flags,* and *pmode* have the following meanings:

fd	The *file descriptor.* Using our earlier analogy, this is the phone line (logical file identifier) used to refer to the file within the program. It is an integer. If there is an error in the attempt to open the file, this value is negative.
filename	A character string containing the physical file name. (Later we discuss *pathnames* that include directory information about the file's location. This argument can be a pathname.)
flags	The *flags* argument is an integer that controls the operation of the *open* function, determining whether it opens an existing file for reading or writing. It can also be used to indicate that you want to create a new file, or open an existing file but delete its contents. The value of *flags* is set by performing a bitwise OR of the following values, among others.[†]

O_APPEND	Append every write operation to the end of the file.
O_CREAT	Create and open a file for writing. This has no effect if the file already exists.
O_EXCL	Return an error if O_CREATE is specified and the file exists.
O_RDONLY	Open a file for reading only.
O_RDWR	Open a file for reading and writing.
O_TRUNC	If the file exists, truncate it to a length of zero, destroying its contents.
O_WRONLY	Open a file for writing only.

Some of these flags cannot be used in combination with one another. Consult your documentation for details, as well as for other options.

pmode	If O_CREAT is specified, *pmode* is required. This integer argument specifies the *protection mode* for the file. In UNIX, the *pmode* is a three-digit octal number that indicates how the file can be used by the owner (first digit), by members of the owner's group (second digit), and by everyone else (third

---

[†]These values are defined in an "include" file packaged with your UNIX system or C compiler. The name of the include file is often *fcntl.h* or *file.h,* but it can vary from system to system.

digit). The first bit of each octal digit indicates read permission, the second write permission, and the third execute permission. So, if *pmode* is the octal number 0751, the file's owner has read, write, and execute permission for the file; the owner's group would have read and execute permission; and everyone else has only execute permission:

```
                    r w e   r w e   r w e
PMODE = 0751 =      1 1 1   1 0 1   0 0 1
                    owner   group   world
```

Given this description of the *open( )* function, we can develop some examples to show how it can be used to open and create files in C. The following function call opens an existing file for reading and writing, or creates a new one if necessary. If the file exists it is opened without change; reading or writing would start at the file's first byte.

```
fd = open(filename, O_RDWR | O_CREAT, 0751);
```

The following call creates a new file for reading and writing. If there is already a file with the name specified in *filename,* its contents are truncated.

```
fd = open(filename, O_RDWR | O_CREAT | O_TRUNC, 0751);
```

Finally, here is a call that will create a new file only if there is not already a file with the name specified in *filename*. If a file with this name exists, it is not opened and the function returns a negative value to indicate an error.

```
fd = open(filename, O_RDWR | O_CREAT | O_EXCL,  0751);
```

File protection is tied more to the host operating system than to a specific language. For example, implementations of Pascal running on systems that support file protection, such as VAX/VMS, often include extensions to standard Pascal that let you associate a protection status with a file when you create it.

2.3 Closing Files

In terms of our telephone line analogy, closing a file is like hanging up the phone. When you hang up the phone, the phone line is available for taking or placing another call; when you close a file, the logical file name or file descriptor is available for use with another file. Closing a file that has been used for output also ensures that everything has been written to the file. As you will learn in a later chapter, it is more efficient to move data to and from secondary storage in blocks than it is to move data one byte at a time.

Consequently, the operating system does not immediately send off the bytes we write, but saves them up in a buffer for transfer as a block of data. Closing a file makes sure that the buffer for that file has been flushed of data and that everything we have written has actually been sent to the file.

Files are usually closed automatically by the operating system when a program terminates normally. Consequently, the explicit use of a CLOSE statement within a program is needed only as protection against data loss in the event of program interruption and to free up logical filenames for reuse. Some languages, including Standard Pascal, do not even provide a CLOSE statement. However, explicit file closing is possible in the C language, VAX Pascal, PL/I, and most other languages used for serious file processing work.

Now that you know how to connect and disconnect programs to and from physical files and how to open the files, you are ready to start sending and receiving data.

2.4   Reading and Writing

Reading and *writing* are fundamental to file processing; they are the actions that make file processing an *input/output* (I/O) operation. The actual form of the read and write statements used in different languages varies. Some languages provide very high-level access to reading and writing and automatically take care of details for the programmer. Other languages provide access at a much lower level. Our use of Pascal and C allows us to explore some of these differences.[†]

2.4.1 Read and Write Functions

We begin here with reading and writing at a relatively low level. It is useful to have a kind of systems-level understanding of what happens when we send and receive information to and from a file.

A low-level read call requires three pieces of information, expressed here as arguments to a generic READ( ) function.

```
READ(Source_file,Destination_addr,Size)
```

Source_file	The READ( ) call must know from where it is to read. We specify the source by logical file name (phone line) through which data is re-

---

[†]To accentuate these differences and provide a look at I/O operations at something closer to a systems level, we use the *read( )* and *write( )* system calls in C rather than higher-level functions such as *fgetc( )*, *fgets( )*, and so on.

ceived. (Remember, before we do any reading we must have already opened the file, so the connection between a logical file and a specific physical file or device already exists.)

Destination_addr   READ( ) must know where to place the information it reads from the input file. In this generic function we specify the destination by giving the first address of the memory block where we want to store the data.

Size   Finally, READ( ) must know how much information to bring in from the file. Here the argument is supplied as a byte count.

A *WRITE* statement is similar; the only difference is that the data moves in the other direction:

```
WRITE(Destination_file,Source_addr,Size)
```

Destination_file   The logical file name we use for sending the data.

Source_addr   WRITE( ) must know where to find the information that it will send. We provide this specification as the first address of the memory block where the data is stored.

Size   The number of bytes to be written must be supplied.

2.4.2 A Program to Display the Contents of a File

Let's do some reading and writing to see how these functions are used. This first simple file processing program, which we call LIST, opens a file for input and reads it, character by character, sending each character to the screen after it is read from the file. LIST includes the following steps:

1. Display a prompt for the name of the input file.
2. Read the user's response from the keyboard into a variable called *filename*.
3. Open the file for input.
4. While there are still characters to be read from the input file,
   a. read a character from the file and
   b. write the character to the terminal screen.
5. Close the input file.

Figures 2.2 and 2.3 are, respectively, C and Pascal language implementations of this program. It is instructive to look at the differences between these implementations.

```
/* list.c--program to read characters from a file and write them
**            to the terminal screen
*/
#include <stdio.h>
#include <fcntl.h>

main( )
{

        char c;
        int  fd;    /* file descriptor */
        char filename[20];

        printf("Enter the name of the file: ");    /* Step 1 */
        gets(filename);                             /* Step 2 */
        fd =open(filename, O_RDONLY);               /* Step 3 */

        while (read(fd, &c, 1) != 0)                /* Step 4a */
                write(STDOUT, &c, 1);               /* Step 4b */

        close(fd);                                  /* Step 5 */
```

FIGURE 2.2 The LIST program in C.

Steps 1 and 2 of the program involve writing and reading, but in each of the implementations this is accomplished through the usual functions for handling the screen and keyboard. Step 4a, where we read from the input file, is the first instance of actual file I/O. Note that the *read( )* call in the C language parallels the low-level, generic READ( ) statement we described earlier; in truth, we used the *read( )* system call in C as the model for our low-level READ( ). The function's first argument gives the file descriptor (C's version of a logical file name) as the *source* for the input, the second argument gives the *address* of a character variable used as the *destination* for the data, and the third argument specifies that only one byte will be read.

The arguments for the Pascal *read( )* call communicate the same information at a higher level. Once again, the first argument is the logical file name for the input source. The second argument gives the *name* of a character variable used as a destination; given the name, Pascal can find the address. Because of Pascal's strong emphasis on variable types, the third argument of the generic READ( ) function is not required. Pascal assumes that since we are reading data into a variable of type *char,* we must want to read only one byte.

After a character is read, we write it out to the screen in Step 4b. Once again the differences between C and Pascal indicate the range of approaches to I/O used in different languages. Everything must be stated explicitly in the C *write( )* call. Using the special, assigned file descriptor of *STDOUT* to identify the terminal screen as the destination for our writing,

```
write( STDOUT, &c, 1 );
```

means: "Write to the screen the contents from memory starting at the address &c. Write only one byte." Beginning C programmers should pay special attention to the use of the & symbol in the *write( )* call here; this particular C call, as a very low-level call, requires that the programmer provide the starting *address* in RAM of the bytes to be transferred.

STDOUT, which stands for "standard output," is an integer value defined in the file *stdio.h,* which has been included at the top of the program. The actual value of *STDOUT* that is set in *stdio.h* is, by convention, always 1. The concept of standard output and its counterpart "standard input" are covered later in the section "Physical and Logical Files in UNIX."

FIGURE 2.3 The LIST program in Pascal.

```
PROGRAM list (INPUT, OUTPUT);

{ reads input from a file and writes it to the terminal screen }

VAR

        c        : char;
        infile   : file of char;                    { logical file name }

        filename : packed array [1..20] of char; { physical file name }

BEGIN {main}

        write('Enter the name of the file: ');    { Step 1 }
        readln(filename);                          { Step 2 }
        reset(infile, filename);                   { Step 3 }
        while not (eof(infile)) DO

        BEGIN

            read(infile,c);                        { Step 4a }
            write(c)                               { Step 4b }

        END;

        close(infile)                              { Step 5 }

END.
```

Again the Pascal code operates at a higher level.[†] When no logical file name is specified in a *write( )* statement, Pascal assumes that we are writing to the terminal screen. Since the variable *c* is of type *char,* Pascal assumes we are writing a single byte. The statement becomes simply

```
write(c)
```

As in the *read( )* statement, Pascal takes care of finding the *address* of the bytes; the programmer need specify only the name of the variable *c* that is associated with that address.

2.4.3 Detecting End-of-File

The programs in Figs. 2.2 and 2.3 have to know when to end the *while* loop and stop reading characters. Pascal and C signal the end-of-file condition differently, illustrating two of the most commonly used approaches to end-of-file detection.

Pascal supplies a Boolean function, *eof( ),* which can be used to test for end-of-file. As we read from a file, the operating system keeps track of our location in the file with a *read/write pointer.* This is necessary so when the next byte is read, the system knows where to get it. The *eof( )* function queries the system to see whether the read/write pointer has moved past the last element in the file. If it has, *eof( )* returns *true*; otherwise it returns *false.* As Fig. 2.3 illustrates, we use the *eof( )* call before trying to read the next byte. For an empty file, *eof( )* immediately returns *true* and no bytes are read.

In the C language, the *read( )* call returns the number of bytes read. If *read( )* returns a value of zero, then the program has reached the end of the file. So, rather than using an *eof( )* function, we construct the *while* loop to run as long as the *read( )* call finds something to read.

2.5   Seeking

In the preceding sample programs we read through the file *sequentially,* reading one byte after another until we reach the end of the file. Every time a byte is read, the operating system moves the read/write pointer ahead, and we are ready to read the next byte.

[†]This is not to say that C does not have similar high-level functions. In fact, the standard C library provides a panoply of higher-level I/O functions, including *putc( ),* which functions for characters exactly like the Pascal *write( )* shown here. We have chosen to emphasize the use of the lower-level C functions mainly for pedagogical reasons. They provide opportunities for us to understand more fully the way file I/O works.

Sometimes we want to read or write without taking the time to go through every byte sequentially. Perhaps we know that the next piece of information we need is 10,000 bytes away, and so we want to jump there to begin reading. Or perhaps we need to jump to the end of the file so we can add new information there. To satisfy these needs we must be able to control the movement of the read/write pointer.

The action of moving directly to a certain position in a file is often called *seeking*. A *seek* requires at least two pieces of information, expressed here as arguments to the generic pseudocode function SEEK( ):

```
SEEK(Source_file,Offset)
```

Source_file   The logical file name in which the seek will occur.

Offset   The number of positions in the file the pointer is to be moved from the start of the file.

Now, if we want to move directly from the origin to the 373rd position in a file called *data,* we don't have to move sequentially through the first 372 positions first. Instead, we can say

```
SEEK( data, 373 )
```

2.5.1 Seeking in C

One of the features of UNIX that has been incorporated into many implementations of the C language is the ability to view a file as a potentially very large *array of bytes* that just happens to be kept on secondary storage. In an array of bytes in RAM, we can move to any particular byte through the use of a subscript. The C language seek function, called *lseek( )*, provides a similar capability for files. It lets us set the read/write pointer to any byte in a file.

The *lseek( )* function has the following form:

```
pos = lseek(fd, byte_offset, origin)
```

where the variables have the following meanings:

pos   A long integer value returned by *lseek( )* equal to the position (in bytes) of the read/write pointer after it has been moved.

fd   The file descriptor of the file to which the *lseek( )* is to be applied.

byte_offset The number of bytes to move from some *origin* in the file. The byte offset must be specified as a long integer, hence the name *lseek* for long seek. When appropriate, the *byte_offset* can be negative.

> *origin*   A value that specifies the starting position from which the
>   *byte_offset* is to be taken. The *origin* can have the value 0, 1,
>   or 2:[†]
>
>   0—*lseek( )* from the beginning of the file;
>
>   1—*lseek( )* from the current position;
>
>   2—*lseek( )* from the end of the file.

The following program fragment shows how you could use *lseek( )* to
move to a position that is 373 bytes into a file.

```
long pos,lseek(int fd, long offset, int origin);
int fd;
.
.
pos=lseek(fd, 373L, 0);
```

2.5.2 Seeking in Pascal

The view of a file as presented in Pascal differs from the C view in at least
two important respects:

□ In C a file is a sequence of bytes, so addressing within the file is on a
   byte-by-byte basis. When we seek to a position, we express the address in terms of bytes. In Pascal a file is a sequence of "records" of
   some particular type. A record can be a simple scalar such as a character or integer, or it may be a more complex structure. Addressing
   within a file in Pascal is in terms of these records. For example, if a
   file is made up of 100-byte records, and we want to refer to the
   fourth record, we would do so in Pascal simply by referencing
   record number 4. In C, where the view is solely and always in terms
   of bytes, we would have to address the fourth record as byte address
   400.

□ Standard Pascal actually does not provide for seeking. The model for
   I/O for standard Pascal is magnetic tape, which must be read sequentially. In standard Pascal, adding data to the end of a file requires
   reading the entire file from beginning to end, writing out the data
   from the input file to a second, output file, and then adding the new
   data to the end of the output file. However, many implementations
   of Pascal such as VAX Pascal and Turbo Pascal have extended the
   standard and do support seeking.

[†]Although the values 0, 1, and 2 are almost always used here, they are not guaranteed to
work for all C implementations. Consult your documentation.

There is an extension to Pascal proposed by the Joint ANSI/IEEE Pascal Standards Committee (1984) that may be included in the Pascal standard in the future. It includes the following procedures and functions that permit seeking:

SeekWrite(f,n) A procedure that positions the file f on the element with index n and places the file in write mode, so the selected and following elements may be modified.

SeekRead(f,n) A procedure that positions the file f on the element with index n and places the file in read mode, so the selected and following elements may be examined. If SeekRead( ) attempts to position beyond the end of the file, then the file is positioned at the end of the file.

Position(f) A function that returns the index value representing the position of the current file element.

EndPosition(f) A function that returns the index value representing the position of the last file element.

Many Pascal implementations, recognizing the need to provide seeking capabilities, had already implemented seeking functions before these proposals were set forth. Consequently, the mechanisms for handling seeking vary widely among implementations.

2.6 Special Characters in Files

As you create the file structures described in this text, you may encounter some difficulty with extra, unexpected characters that turn up in your files, with characters that disappear, and with numeric counts that are inserted into your files. Here are some examples of the kinds of things you might encounter:

☐ On many small computers you may find that a Control-Z (ASCII value of 26) is appended at the end of your files. Some applications use this to indicate end-of-file even if you have not placed it there. This is most likely to happen on MS-DOS systems.

☐ Some systems adopt a convention of indicating end-of-line in a text file[†] as a pair of characters consisting of a carriage return (CR: ASCII value of 13) and a line feed (LF: ASCII value of 10). Sometimes I/O

[†]When we use the term *text file* in this text, we are referring to a file consisting entirely of characters from a specific standard character set, such as ASCII or EBCDIC. Unless otherwise specified, the ASCII character set will be assumed. Appendix A contains a table that describes the ASCII character set.

procedures written for such systems automatically expand single CR characters or LF characters into CR-LF pairs. This unrequested addition of characters can cause a great deal of difficulty. Again, you are most likely to encounter this phenomenon on MS-DOS systems.

☐ Users of larger systems, such as VMS, may find that they have just the opposite problem. Certain file formats under VMS *remove* carriage return characters from your file without asking you, replacing them with a *count* of the characters in what the system has perceived as a line of text.

These are just a few examples of the kinds of uninvited modifications that record management systems or I/O support packages might make to your files. You will find that they are usually associated with the concepts of a line of text or end of a file. In general, these modifications to your files are an attempt to make your life easier by doing things for you automatically. This might, in fact, work out for users who want to do nothing more than store some text in a file. Unfortunately, however, programmers building sophisticated file structures must sometimes spend a lot of time finding ways to disable this automatic assistance so they can have complete control over what they are building. Forewarned is forearmed; readers who encounter these kinds of difficulties as they build the file structures described in this text can take some comfort from the knowledge that the experience they gain in disabling automatic assistance will serve them well, over and over, in the future.

2.7 The UNIX Directory Structure

No matter what computer system you have, even if it is a small PC, chances are there are hundreds or even thousands of files you have access to. To provide convenient access to such large numbers of files, your computer has some method for organizing its files. In UNIX this is called the *filesystem*.

The UNIX filesystem is a tree-structured organization of *directories,* with the *root* of the tree signified by the character '/'. All directories, including the root, can contain two kinds of files: regular files with programs and data, and directories (Fig. 2.4). Since devices such as tape drives are also treated like files in UNIX, directories can also contain references to devices, as shown in the *dev* directory in Fig. 2.4. The file name stored in a UNIX directory corresponds to what we call its physical name.

Since every file in a UNIX system is part of the filesystem that begins with root, any file can be uniquely identified by giving its *absolute pathname*. For instance, the true, unambiguous name of the file "addr" in Fig. 2.4 is

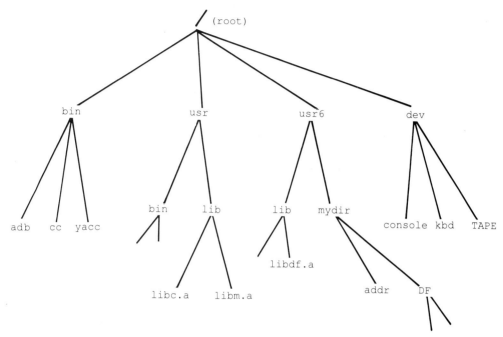

FIGURE 2.4 Sample UNIX directory structure.

/usr6/mydir/addr. (Note that the '/ ' is used both to indicate the root directory and to separate directory names from the file name.)

When you issue commands to a UNIX system, you do so within some directory, which is called your *current directory*. A pathname for a file that does not begin with a '/ ' describes the location of a file relative to the current directory. Hence, if your current directory in Fig. 2.4 is mydir, *addr* uniquely identifies the file */usr6/mydir/addr.*

The special filename "." stands for the current directory, and ".." stands for the parent of the current directory. Hence, if your current directory is */usr6/mydir/DF,* "*../addr*" refers to the file */usr6/mydir/addr.*

2.8   Physical and Logical Files in UNIX

2.8.1 Physical Devices as UNIX Files

One of the most powerful ideas in UNIX is reflected in its notion of what a file is. In UNIX, a file is a sequence of bytes, without any implication of how or where the bytes are stored or where they originate. This simple conceptual view of a file makes it possible in UNIX to do with a very few operations what might require many times as many operations on a different operating system. For example, it is easy to think of a magnetic disk as the source of a file, because we are used to the idea of storing such things on disks. But in UNIX, devices like the keyboard and the console are also files—in Fig. 2.4, */dev/kbd* and */dev/console,* respectively. The keyboard produces a sequence of bytes that are sent to the computer when keys are pressed; the console accepts a sequence of bytes and displays their corresponding symbols on a screen.

How can we say that the UNIX concept of a file is simple when it allows so many different physical things to be called files? Doesn't this make the situation more complicated, not simpler? The trick in UNIX is that no matter what physical representation a file may take, the logical view of a UNIX file is the same. In its simplest form, a UNIX file is represented logically by an integer—the file descriptor. This integer is an index to an array of more complete information about the file. A keyboard, a disk file, and a magnetic tape are all represented by integers. Once the integer that describes a file is identified, a program can access that file. If it knows the logical name of a file, a program can access that file without knowing whether the file comes from a disk, a tape, or a telephone.

2.8.2 The Console, the Keyboard, and Standard Error

We see an example of the duality between devices and files in the LIST program in Fig. 2.2:

```
printf("Enter the name of the file: "); /* Step 1 */
gets(filename);                          /* Step 2 */
fd =open(filename, O_RDONLY);            /* Step 3 */

while (read(fd, &c, 1) > 0)              /* Step 4a */
write(STDOUT, &c, 1);                    /* Step 4b */
```

The logical file *fd* is some small integer value returned by the *open( )* call. We assign this integer to the variable *fd* in Step 3. In Step 4b, we use the integer *STDOUT,* defined as 1 earlier in the program, to identify the console as the file to be written to.

There are two other file descriptors that are special in UNIX: The keyboard is called *STDIN (standard input)* and the error file is called *STDERR (standard error)*. Hence, *STDIN* is the keyboard on your terminal. The statement

```
read(STDIN, &c, 1);
```

reads a single character from your terminal. *STDERR* is an error file which, like *STDOUT,* is usually just your console. When your compiler detects an error, it generally writes the error message to this file, which means normally that the error message turns up on your screen. As with *STDIN,* the values *STDIN* and *STDERR* are usually defined in *stdio.h.*

Steps 1 and 2 of the LIST program also involve reading and writing from *STDIN* or *STDOUT.* Since an enormous amount of I/O involves these devices, most programming languages have special functions to perform console input and output—in LIST, the C functions *printf* and *gets* are used. Ultimately, however, *printf* and *gets* send their output through *STDOUT* and *STDIN,* respectively. But these statements hide important elements of the I/O process. For our purposes, the second set of read and write statements is more interesting and instructive.

2.8.3 I/O Redirection and Pipes

Suppose you would like to change the LIST program so it writes its output to a regular file, rather than to *STDOUT.* Or suppose you wanted to use the output of LIST as input to another program. Because it is common to want to do both of these, UNIX provides convenient shortcuts for switching between standard I/O (*STDIN* and *STDOUT*) and regular file I/O. These shortcuts are called *I/O redirection* and *pipes.*[†]

I/O redirection lets you specify at execution time alternate files for input or output. The notations for input and output redirection are

```
< file          (redirect STDIN to "file")
> file          (redirect STDOUT to "file")
```

For example, if the executable LIST program is called "list," we redirect the output from *STDOUT* to a file called "myfile" by entering the line

```
list > myfile
```

What if, instead of storing the output from the list program in a file, you wanted to use it immediately in another program to sort the results? UNIX pipes let you do this. The notation for a UNIX pipe is '|'. Hence,

```
program1 | program2
```

[†]Strictly speaking, I/O redirection and pipes are part of a UNIX shell, which is the command interpreter that sits on top of the core UNIX operating system, the kernel. For the purpose of this discussion, this distinction is not important.

means take any *STDOUT* output from program1 and use it in place of any *STDIN* input to program2. Since UNIX has a special program called *sort,* which takes its input from *STDIN,* you can sort the output from the list program, without using an intermediate file, by entering

```
list | sort
```

Since *sort* writes its output to *STDOUT,* the sorted listing appears on your terminal screen unless you use additional pipes or redirection to send it elsewhere.

2.9   File-related Header Files

UNIX, like all operating systems, has special names and values that you must use when performing file operations. For example, some C functions return a special value indicating end-of-file (EOF) when you try to read beyond the end of a file.

Recall the flags that you use in an *open( )* call to indicate whether you want read-only, write-only, or read/write access. Unless we know just where to look, it is often not easy to find where these values are defined. UNIX handles the problem by putting such definitions in special header files such as /usr/include, which can be found in special directories.

Three header files relevant to the material in this chapter are *stdio.h, fcntl.h,* and *file.h.* EOF, for instance, is defined on many UNIX systems in */usr/include/stdio.h,* as are the file pointers STDIN, STDOUT, and STDERR. And the flags O_RDONLY, O_WRONLY, and O_RDWR can usually be found in */usr/include/sys/file.h* or possibly one of the files that it includes.

It would be instructive for you to browse through these files, as well as others that pique your curiosity.

2.10   UNIX Filesystem Commands

UNIX provides many commands for manipulating files. We list a few that are relevant to the material in this chapter. Most of them have many options, but the simplest uses of most should be obvious. Consult a UNIX manual for more information on how to use them.

`cat` *filenames*	Print the contents of the named text files.
`tail` *filename*	Print the last 10 lines of the text file.

c p *file1 file2*	Copy *file1* to *file2*.
m v *file1 file2*	Move (rename) *file1* to *file2*.
r m *filenames*	Remove (delete) the named files.
c h m o d *mode filename*	Change the protection mode on the named files.
l s	List the contents of the directory.
m k d i r *name*	Create a directory with the given name.
r m d i r *name*	Remove the named directory.

■ SUMMARY

This chapter introduces the fundamental operations of file systems: OPEN( ), CREATE( ), CLOSE( ), READ( ), WRITE( ), and SEEK( ). Each of these operations involves the creation or use of a link between a *physical file* stored on a secondary device and a *logical file* that represents a program's more abstract view of the same file. When the program describes an operation using the *logical file name,* the equivalent physical operation gets performed on the corresponding physical file.

The six operations appear in programming languages in many different forms. Sometimes they are built-in commands, sometimes they are functions, and sometimes they are direct calls to an operating system. Not all languages provide the user with all six operations. The operation SEEK( ), for instance, is not available in standard Pascal.

Before we can use a physical file, we must link it to a logical file. In some programming environments we do this with a statement (e.g., *assign* in Turbo Pascal) or with instructions outside of the program (e.g., job control language [JCL] instructions). In other languages the link between the physical file and a logical file is made with OPEN( ) or CREATE( ).

The operations CREATE( ) and OPEN( ) make files ready for reading or writing. CREATE( ) causes a new physical file to be created. OPEN( ) operates on an already existing physical file, usually setting the read/write pointer to the beginning of the file. The CLOSE( ) operation breaks the link between a logical file and its corresponding physical file. It also makes sure that the file buffer is flushed so everything that was written is actually sent to the file.

The I/O operations READ( ) and WRITE( ), when viewed at a low, systems level, require three items of information:

■ The *logical name* of the file to be read from or written to;

- An *address* of a memory area to be used for the "inside of the computer" part of the exchange; and

- An indication of *how much data* is to be read or written.

These three fundamental elements of the exchange are illustrated in Fig. 2.5.

READ( ) and WRITE( ) are sufficient for moving sequentially through a file to any desired position, but this form of access is often very inefficient. Some languages provide seek operations that let a program move directly to a certain position in a file. C provides direct access by means of the *lseek( )* operation. The *lseek( )* operation lets us view a file as a kind of large array, giving us a great deal of freedom in deciding how to organize a file. Standard Pascal does not support direct file access, but many dialects of Pascal do.

One other useful file operation involves knowing when the end of a file has been reached. End-of-file detection is handled in different ways by different languages.

Much effort goes into shielding programmers from having to deal with the physical characteristics of files, but inevitably there are little details about the physical organization of files that programmers must know. When we try to have our program operate on files at a very low level (as we do a great deal in this text), we must be on the lookout for little surprises inserted in our file by the operating system or applications.

The UNIX file system, called the *filesystem,* organizes files in a tree structure, with all files and subdirectories expressable by their *pathnames.* It is possible to navigate around the filesystem as you work with UNIX files.

UNIX views both physical devices and traditional disk files as files, so, for example, a keyboard (*STDIN*), a console (*STDOUT*), and a tape drive all are considered files. This simple conceptual view of files makes it possible in UNIX to do with a very few operations what might require many times the operations on a different operating system.

I/O redirection and *pipes* are convenient shortcuts provided in UNIX for transferring file data between files and *standard I/O. Header files* in UNIX, such at *stdio.h,* contain special names and values that you must use when

FIGURE 2.5 The exchange between memory and external device.

performing file operations. It is important to be aware of the most common of these in use on your system.

The following section lists a sampling of UNIX commands for manipulating files.

■ KEY TERMS

Access mode. Type of file access allowed. The variety of access modes permitted varies from operating system to operating system.

Buffering. When input or output is saved up rather than sent off to its destination immediately, we say that it is *buffered*. In later chapters, we find that we can dramatically improve the performance of programs that read and write data if we buffer the I/O.

Byte offset. The distance, measured in bytes, from the beginning of the file. The very first byte in the file has an offset of 0, the second byte has an offset of 1, and so on.

CLOSE( ). A function or system call that breaks the link between a logical file name and the corresponding physical file name.

CREATE( ). A function or system call that causes a file to be created on secondary storage and may also bind a logical name to the file's physical name—see OPEN( ). A call to CREATE( ) also results in the generation of information used by the system to manage the file, such as time of creation, physical location, and access privileges for anticipated users of the file.

End-of-file (EOF). An indicator within a file that the end of the file has occurred, a function that tells if the end of a file has been encountered (e.g., *eof( )* in Pascal), or a system-specific value that is returned by file-processing functions indicating that the end of a file has been encountered in the process of carrying out the function (e.g., EOF in UNIX).

File descriptor. A small, non-negative integer value returned by a UNIX *open( )* or *creat( )* call that is used as a logical name for the file in later UNIX system calls.

Filesystem. The name used in UNIX to describe a collection of files and directories organized into a tree-structured hierarchy.

Header file. A file in a UNIX environment that contains definitions and declarations commonly shared among many other files and applications. In C, header files are included in other files by means of the "#include" statement (see Fig. 2.2). The header files *stdio.h, file.h,* and *fcntl.h* described in this chapter contain important declarations and definitions used in file processing.

I/O redirection. The redirection of a stream of input or output from its normal place. For instance, the operator '>' can be used to redirect to a file output that would normally be sent to the console.

Logical file. The file as seen by the program. The use of logical files allows a program to describe operations to be performed on a file without knowing what actual physical file will be used. The program may then be used to process any one of a number of different files that share the same structure.

OPEN( ). A function or system call that makes a file ready for use. It may also bind a logical file name to a physical file. Its arguments include the logical file name and the physical file name and may also include information on how the file is expected to be accessed.

Pathname. A character string that describes the location of a file or directory. If the pathname starts with a '/', then it gives the *absolute pathname*—the complete path from the root directory to the file. Otherwise it gives the *relative pathname*—the path relative to the current working directory.

Physical file. A file that actually exists on secondary storage. It is the file as known by the computer operating system and that appears in its file directory.

Pipe. A UNIX operator specified by the symbol '|' that carries data from one process to another. The originating process specifies that the data is to go to *STDOUT,* and the receiving process expects the data from *STDIN.* For example, to send the standard output from a program *makedata* to the standard input of a program called *usedata,* use the command "makedata | usedata".

Protection mode. An indication of how a file can be accessed by various classes of users. In UNIX, the protection mode is a three-digit octal number that indicates how the file can be read, written to, and executed by the owner, by members of the owner's group, and by everyone else.

READ( ). A function or system call used to obtain input from a file or device. When viewed at the lowest level, it requires three arguments: (1) a Source_file logical name corresponding to an open file; (2) the Destination_address for the bytes that are to be read; and (3) the Size or amount of data to be read.

SEEK( ). A function or system call that sets the read/write pointer to a specified position in the file. Languages that provide seeking functions allow programs to access specific elements of a file *directly,* rather than having to read through a file from the beginning (*sequen-*

tially) each time a specific item is desired. In C, the *lseek( )* system call provides this capability. Standard Pascal does not have a seeking capability, but many nonstandard dialects of Pascal do.

Standard I/O. The source and destination conventionally used for input and output. In UNIX, there are three types of standard I/O: *standard input (STDIN), standard output (STDOUT),* and *STDERR (standard error).* By default *STDIN* is the keyboard, and *STDOUT* and *STDERR* are the console screen. I/O redirection and pipes provide ways to override these defaults.

WRITE( ). A function or system call used to provide output capabilities. When viewed at the lowest level, it requires three arguments: (1) a Destination_file name corresponding to an open file; (2) the Source_address of the bytes that are to be written; and (3) the Size or amount of the data to be written.

■ EXERCISES

1. Look up operations equivalent to *OPEN( ), CLOSE( ), CREATE( ), READ( ), WRITE( ),* and *SEEK* in other high-level languages, such as PL/I, COBOL, and Fortran. Compare them with the C or Pascal versions.

2. If you use C:
a) Make a list of the different ways to perform the file operations CREATE( ), OPEN( ), CLOSE( ), READ( ), and WRITE( ). Why is there more than one way to do each operation?
b) How would you use *lseek( )* to find the current position in a file?
c) Show how to change the permissions on a file *myfile* so the owner has read and write permissions, group members have execute permission, and others have no permission.
d) What is the difference between *pmode* and O_RDWR? What *pmodes* and O_RDWR are available on your system?
e) In some typical C environments, such as UNIX and MS-DOS, all of the following represent ways to move data from one place to another:

```
scanf( )    fgetc( )  read( )  cat (or type)
fscanf( )   gets( )   <        main (argc,argv)
getc( )     fgets( )  |
```

Describe as many of these as you can, and indicate how they might be useful. Which belong to the C language, and which belong to the operating system?

3. If you use Pascal:
a) What ways are provided in your version of Pascal to perform the file operations CREATE( ), OPEN( ), CLOSE( ), READ( ), and WRITE( )? If there is more than one way to do a certain operation, tell why. If an operation is missing, how are its functions carried out?
b) Implement a SEEK( ) function in your Pascal, if it does not already have one.

4. A couple of years ago a company we know of bought a new COBOL compiler. One difference between the new compiler and the old one was that the new compiler did not automatically close files when execution of a program terminated, whereas the old compiler did. What sorts of problems did this cause when some of the old software was executed after having been recompiled with the new compiler?

5. Look at the two LIST programs in the text. Each has a *while* loop. In Pascal, the sequence of steps in the loop is test, read, write. In C, it is read, test, write. Why the difference? What would happen in Pascal if we used the loop construction used for C? What would happen in C if we used the Pascal loop construction?

6. In Fig. 2.4:
a. Give the full pathname for a file in directory *DF*.
b. Suppose your current directory is *bin*. Show how to copy the file *libdf.a* to the directory *DF* without changing your current directory.

7. What is the difference between *STDOUT* and *STDERR?* Find how to direct error messages from a compilation on your system to *STDERR*.

8. Look up the UNIX command *wc*. Execute the following in a UNIX environment, and explain why it gives the number of files in the directory.

```
ls | wc -w
```

9. Find *stdio.h* on your system, and find what value is used to indicate end-of-file. Also examine *file.h* or *fcntl.h* and describe in general what its contents are for.

Programming Exercises

10. Make the LIST program we provide in this chapter work with your compiler on your operating system.

11. Write a program to create a file and store a string in it. Write another program to open the file and read the string.

12. Try setting the *protection mode* on a file to read-only, then opening the file with an access mode of read/write. What happens?

13. Implement the UNIX command *tail -n,* where *n* is the number of lines from the end of the file to be copied to *STDOUT.*

14. Change the program LIST so it reads from the *STDIN,* rather than a file, and writes to a file, rather than the *STDOUT.* Show how to execute the new version of the program in a UNIX environment, given that the input is actually in a file called *instuff.* (You can also do this in most MS-DOS environments.)

15. Write a program to read a series of names, one per line, from standard input, and write out those names spelled in reverse order to standard output. Use I/O redirection and pipes to do the following:

    a. Input a series of names that are typed in from the keyboard and write them out, reversed, to a file called *file1.*

    b. Read the names in from *file1;* then write them out, re-reversed, to a file called *file2.*

    c. Read the names in from *file2,* reverse them again, and then sort the resulting list of reversed words using *sort.*

■ FURTHER READINGS

Introductory textbooks on C and Pascal tend to treat the fundamental file operations only briefly, if at all. This is particularly true with regard to C, since there are higher-level standard I/O functions in C, such as the read operations *fgets( )* and *fgetc( ).* Some books on C and/or UNIX that do provide treatment of the fundamental file operations are Bourne (1984), Kernighan and Pike (1984), and Kernighan and Ritchie (1978, 1988). These books also provide discussions of higher-level I/O functions that we omitted from our text.

As for UNIX specifically, as of this writing there are two dominant flavors of UNIX: UNIX System V from AT&T, the originators of UNIX, and 4.3BSD (Berkeley Software Distribution) UNIX from the University of California at Berkeley. The two versions are close enough that learning about either will give you a good understanding of UNIX generally. However, as you begin to use UNIX, you will need reference material on the specific version that you are using. There are many accessible texts on both versions, including Morgan and McGilton (1987) on System V, and Wang (1988) on 4.3BSD. Less readable but absolutely essential to a serious UNIX user is the 4.3BSD *UNIX Programmers Reference Manual* (U.C. Berkeley, 1986) or the *System V Interface Definition* (AT&T, 1986).

For Pascal, these operations vary so greatly from one implementation to another that it is probably best to consult user's manuals and literature relating to your specific implementation. Cooper (1983) covers the ISO standard Pascal, as well as some extensions. Jensen and Wirth (1974) is the definition of Pascal on which all others are based. Wirth (1975) discusses some difficulties with standard Pascal and file operations in the section, "An Important Concept and a Persistent Source of Problems: Files."

Secondary Storage and System Software

3

CHAPTER OBJECTIVES

- Describe the organization of typical disk drives, including basic units of organization and their relationships.

- Identify and describe the factors affecting disk access time, and describe methods for estimating access times and space requirements.

- Describe magnetic tapes, identify some tape applications, and investigate the implications of block size on space requirements and transmission speeds.

- Identify fundamental differences between media and criteria that can be used to match the right medium to an application.

- Describe in general terms the events that occur when data is transmitted between a program and a secondary storage device.

- Introduce concepts and techniques of buffer management.

- Illustrate many of the concepts introduced in the chapter, especially system software concepts, in the context of UNIX.

CHAPTER OUTLINE

Good design is always responsive to the constraints of the medium and to the environment. This is as true for file structure design as it is for designs in wood and stone. Given the ability to create, open, and close files, and to seek, read, and write, we can perform the fundamental operations of file *construction*. Now we need to look at the nature and limitations of the devices and systems used to store and retrieve files, preparing ourselves for file design.

If files were stored just in RAM, there would be no separate discipline called file structures. The general study of data structures would give us all the tools we would need to build file applications. But secondary storage devices are very different from RAM. One difference, as already noted, is that accesses to secondary storage take much more time than do accesses to RAM. An even more important difference, measured in terms of design impact, is that not all accesses are equal. Good file structure design uses knowledge of disk and tape performance to arrange data in ways that minimize access costs.

In this chapter we examine the characteristics of secondary storage devices, focusing on the constraints that shape our design work in the chapters that follow. We begin with a look at the major media used in the storage and processing of files, magnetic disks, and tapes. We follow this with an overview of the range of other devices and media used for secondary storage. Next, by following the journey of a byte, we take a brief look at the many pieces of hardware and software that become involved when a byte is sent by a program to a file on a disk. Finally, we take a closer look at one of the most important aspects of file management—buffering.

3.1   Disks

Compared to the time it takes to access an item in RAM, disk accesses are always expensive. However, not all disk accesses are *equally* expensive. The reason for this has to do with the way a disk drive works. Disk drives[†] belong to a class of devices known as *direct access storage devices* (DASDs) because they make it possible to access data *directly*. DASDs are contrasted with *serial devices,* the other major class of secondary storage devices. Serial devices use media such as magnetic tape that permit only serial access—a particular data item cannot be read or written until all of the data preceding it on the tape have been read or written in order.

Magnetic disks come in many forms. So-called *hard disks* offer high capacity and low cost per bit. Hard disks are the most common disk used in everyday file processing. *Floppy* disks are inexpensive, but they are slow and hold relatively little data. Floppies are good for backing up individual files or other floppies and for transporting small amounts of data. Removable disk packs are hard disks that can be mounted on the same drive at different times, providing a convenient form of backup storage that also makes it possible to access data directly.

Nonmagnetic disk media, especially optical discs, are becoming increasingly important for secondary storage. (See Appendix A for a full treatment of optical disc storage and its applications.)

3.1.1 The Organization of Disks

The information stored on a disk is stored on the surface of one or more platters (Fig. 3.1). The arrangement is such that the information is stored in successive *tracks* on the surface of the disk (Fig. 3.2). Each track is often

---

[†]When we use the terms *disks* or *disk drives,* we are referring to *magnetic* disk media.

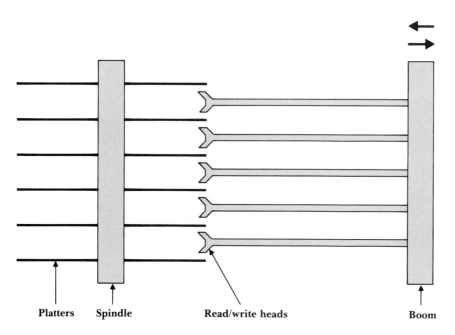

FIGURE 3.1 Schematic illustration of disk drive.

divided into a number of *sectors*. A sector is the smallest addressable portion of a disk. When a *READ( )* statement calls for a particular byte from a disk file, the computer operating system finds the correct surface, track, and sector, reads the entire sector into a special area in RAM called a *buffer,* and then finds the requested byte within that buffer.

If a disk drive uses a number of platters, it may be called a *disk pack.* The tracks that are directly above and below one another form a *cylinder* (Fig. 3.3). The significance of the cylinder is that all of the information on a single cylinder can be accessed without moving the arm that holds the read/write heads. Moving this arm is called *seeking.* This arm movement is usually the slowest part of reading information from a disk.

3.1.2 Estimating Capacities and Space Needs

Disks range in width from 2 to about 14 inches. They range in storage capacity from less than 400,000 bytes to billions of bytes. In a typical disk pack, the top and bottom platter each contribute one surface, and all other

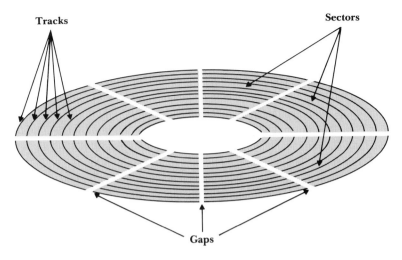

FIGURE 3.2 Surface of disk showing tracks and sectors.

FIGURE 3.3 Schematic illustration of disk drive viewed as a set of seven cylinders.

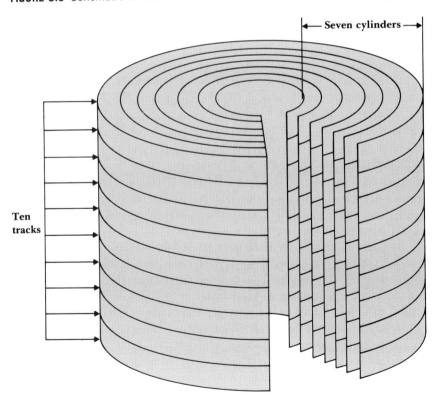

platters contribute two surfaces to the pack, so the number of tracks per cylinder is a function of the number of platters.

The amount of data that can be held on a track depends on how densely bits can be stored on the disk surface. (This in turn depends on the quality of the recording medium and the size of the read/write heads.) An inexpensive, low-density disk can hold about 4 kilobytes on a track, and 35 tracks on a surface. A top-of-the-line disk can hold about 50 kilobytes on a track, and more than 1,000 tracks on a surface. Table D.1 in Appendix D shows how a variety of disk drives compare in terms of capacity, performance, and cost.

Since a cylinder consists of a group of tracks, a track consists of a group of sectors, and a sector consists of a group of bytes, it is easy to compute track, cylinder, and drive capacities:

Track capacity = number of sectors per track × bytes per sector

Cylinder capacity = number of tracks per cylinder × track capacity

Drive capacity = number of cylinders × cylinder capacity.

If we know the number of bytes in a file, we can use these relationships to compute the amount of disk space the file is likely to require. Suppose, for instance, that we want to store a file with 20,000 fixed-length data records on a "typical" 300-megabyte small computer disk with the following characteristics:

Number of bytes per sector = 512

Number of sectors per track = 40

Number of tracks per cylinder = 11

Number of cylinders = 1,331.

How many cylinders does the file require if each data record requires 256 bytes? Since each sector can hold two records, the file requires

$$\frac{20,000}{2} = 10,000 \text{ sectors.}$$

One cylinder can hold

$$40 \times 11 = 440 \text{ sectors}$$

so the number of cylinders required is approximately

$$\frac{10,000}{440} = 22.7 \text{ cylinders.}$$

Of course, it may be that a disk drive with 22.7 cylinders of available space does not have 22.7 *physically contiguous* cylinders available. In this likely case, the file might in fact have to be spread out over dozens, perhaps even hundreds, of cylinders.

3.1.3 Organizing Tracks by Sector

There are two basic ways to organize data on a disk: by sector and by user-defined block. So far, we have only mentioned sector organizations. In this section we examine sector organizations more closely. In the following section we look at block organizations.

The Physical Placement of Sectors   There are several views that one can have of the organization of sectors on a track. The simplest view, one that suffices for most users most of the time, is that sectors are adjacent, fixed-sized segments of a track that happen to hold a file (Fig. 3.4a). This is often a perfectly adequate way to view a file *logically,* but it may not be a good way to store sectors *physically.*

When you want to read a series of sectors that are all in the same track, one right after the other, you often cannot read *adjacent* sectors. That is

FIGURE 3.4 Two views of the organization of sectors on a 32-sector track.

(a)

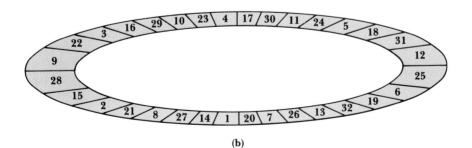

(b)

because, after reading the data, it takes the disk controller a certain amount of time to process the received information before it is ready to accept more. So, if *logically* adjacent sectors were placed on the disk so they were also *physically* adjacent, we would miss the start of the following sector while we were processing the one we had just read in. Consequently, we would be able to read only one sector per revolution of the disk.

I/O system designers usually approach this problem by *interleaving* the sectors, leaving an interval of several physical sectors between logically adjacent sectors. Suppose our disk had an *interleaving factor* of 5. The assignment of logical sector content to the 32 physical sectors in a track is illustrated in Fig. 3.4(b). If you study this figure, you can see that it takes five revolutions to read the entire 32 sectors of a track. That is a big improvement over 32 revolutions.

Over the last year or two, controller speeds have improved so high-performance disks can now offer 1:1 interleaving. This means that successive sectors actually are physically adjacent, making it possible to read an entire track in a single revolution of the disk.

Clusters   A third view of sector organization, also designed to improve performance, is the view maintained by that part of a computer's operating system that we call the *file manager*. When a program accesses a file, it is the file manager's job to map the logical parts of the file to their corresponding physical locations. It does this by viewing the file as a series of *clusters* of sectors. A cluster is a fixed number of contiguous sectors.[†] Once a given cluster has been found on a disk, all sectors in that cluster can be accessed without requiring an additional seek.

To view a file as a series of clusters and still maintain the sectored view, the file manager ties logical sectors to the physical clusters that they belong to by using a *file allocation table* (FAT). The FAT contains a list of all the clusters in a file, ordered according to the logical order of the sectors they contain. With each cluster entry in the FAT is an entry giving the physical location of the cluster (Fig. 3.5).

On many systems, the system administrator can decide how many sectors there should be in a cluster. For instance, in the standard physical disk structure used by VAX systems, the system administrator sets the cluster size to be used on a disk when the disk is initialized. The default value is three 512-byte sectors per cluster, but the cluster size may be set to any value between 1 and 65,535 sectors. Since clusters represent physically contiguous groups of sectors, larger clusters guarantee the ability to read

[†]It is not always *physically* contiguous; the degree of physical contiguity is determined by the interleaving factor.

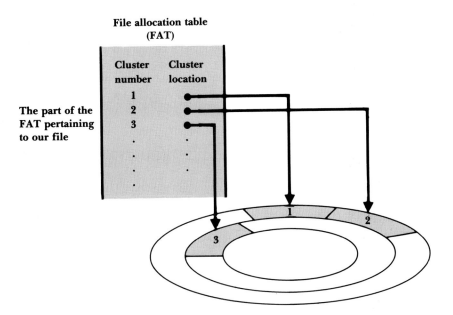

FIGURE 3.5 The file manager determines which cluster in the file has the sector that is to be accessed.

more sectors without seeking, so the use of large clusters can lead to substantial performance gains when a file is being processed sequentially.

Extents Our final view of sector organization represents a further attempt to emphasize physical contiguity of sectors in a file, hence minimizing seeking even more. (If you are getting the idea that the avoidance of seeking is an important part of file design, you are right.) If there is a lot of free room on a disk, it may be possible to make a file consist entirely of contiguous clusters. When this is the case, we say that the file consists of one *extent:* All of its sectors, tracks, and (if it is large enough) cylinders form one contiguous whole (Fig. 3.6a). This is a good situation, especially if the file is to be processed sequentially, because it means that the whole file can be accessed with a minimum amount of seeking.

If there is not enough contiguous space available to contain an entire file, the file is divided into two or more noncontiguous parts. Each part is an extent. When new clusters are added to a file, the file manager tries to make them physically contiguous to the previous end of the file, but if space is unavailable for this, it must add one or more extents (Fig. 3.6b). The

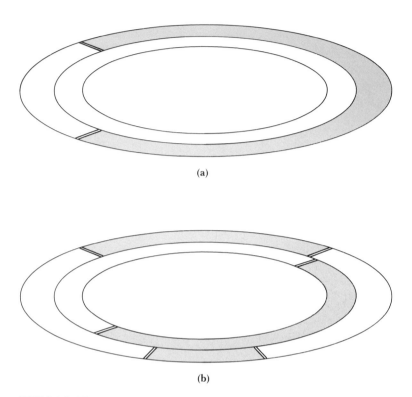

(a)

(b)

FIGURE 3.6 File extents (shaded area represents space on disk used by a single file).

most important thing to understand about extents is that as the number of extents in a file increases, the file becomes more spread out on the disk, and the amount of seeking required to process the file increases.

Fragmentation   Generally, all sectors on a given drive must contain the same number of bytes. If, for example, the size of a sector is 512 bytes and the size of all records in a file is 300 bytes, there is no convenient fit between records and sectors. There are two ways to deal with this situation: Store only one record per sector, or allow records to *span* sectors, so the beginning of a record might be found in one sector and the end of it in another (Fig. 3.7).

The first option has the advantage that any record can be retrieved by retrieving just one sector, but it has the disadvantage that it might leave an enormous amount of unused space within each sector. This loss of space within a sector is called *internal fragmentation*. The second option has the advantage that it loses no space from internal fragmentation, but it has the disadvantage that some records may be retrieved only by accessing two sectors.

Another potential source of internal fragmentation results from the use of clusters. Recall that a cluster is the smallest unit of space that can be allocated for a file. When the number of bytes in a file is not an exact multiple of the cluster size, there will be internal fragmentation in the last extent of the file. For instance, if a cluster consists of three 512-byte sectors, a file containing one byte would use up 1,536 bytes on the disk; 1,535 bytes would be wasted due to internal fragmentation.

Clearly, there are important trade-offs in the use of large cluster sizes. A disk that is expected to have mainly large files that will often be processed sequentially would usually be given a large cluster size, since internal fragmentation would not be a big problem and the performance gains might be great. A disk holding smaller files or files that are usually accessed only randomly would normally be set up with small clusters.

3.1.4 Organizing Tracks by Block

Sometimes disk tracks are *not* divided into sectors, but into integral numbers of user-defined *blocks* whose size can vary. (*Note:* The word *block*

FIGURE 3.7 Alternate record organization within sectors (shaded areas represent data records, and unshaded areas represent unused space).

(a)

(b)

FIGURE 3.8 Sector organization versus block organization.

has a different meaning in the context of the UNIX I/O system. See section 3.7 for details.) When the data on a track is organized by block, this usually means that the amount of data transferred in a single I/O operation can vary depending on the needs of the software designer, not the hardware. Blocks can normally be either fixed or variable in length, depending on the requirements of the file designer. As with sectors, blocks are often referred to as physical records. (Sometimes the word *block* is used as a synonym for a sector or group of sectors. To avoid confusion, we do not use it in that way here.) Figure 3.8 illustrates the difference between one view of data on a sectored track and that of a blocked track.

A *block* organization does not present the sector-spanning and fragmentation problems of sectors because blocks can vary in size to fit the logical organization of the data. A block is usually organized to hold an integral number of logical records. The term *blocking factor* is used to indicate the number of records that are to be stored in each block in a file. Hence, if we had a file with 300-byte records, a block-addressing scheme would let us define a block to be some convenient multiple of 300 bytes, depending on the needs of the program. No space would be lost to internal fragmentation, and there would be no need to load two blocks to retrieve one record.

Generally speaking, blocks are superior to sectors when it is desirable to have the physical allocation of space for records correspond to their logical organization. (There are disk drives that allow both sector-addressing and block-addressing, but we do not describe them here. See Bohl, 1981.)

In block-addressing schemes, each block of data is usually accompanied by one or more *subblocks* containing extra information about the data block. Typically there is a *count subblock* that contains (among other things) the number of bytes in the accompanying data block (Fig. 3.9a). There may also be a *key subblock* containing the key for the last record in the data block

(Fig. 3.9b). When *key* subblocks are used, a track can be searched by the disk controller for a block or record identified by a given key. This means that a program can ask its disk drive to search among all the blocks on a track for a block with a desired key. This approach can result in much more efficient searches than are normally possible with sector-addressable schemes, in which keys cannot generally be interpreted without first loading them into primary memory.

3.1.5 Nondata Overhead

Both blocks and sectors require that a certain amount of space be taken up on the disk in the form of *nondata overhead.* Some of the overhead consists of information that is stored on the disk during *preformatting,* which is done before the disk can be used.

On sector-addressable disks, preformatting involves storing, at the beginning of each sector, such information as sector address, track address, and condition (whether the sector is usable or defective). Preformatting also involves placing gaps and synchronization marks between fields of information to help the read/write mechanism distinguish between them. This nondata overhead usually is of no concern to the programmer. When the sector size is given for a certain drive, the programmer can assume that this is the amount of actual data that can be stored in a sector.

On a block-organized disk, some of the nondata overhead is invisible to the programmer, but some of it must be accounted for by the programmer. Since subblocks and interblock gaps have to be provided with every block,

FIGURE 3.9 Block addressing requires that each physical data block be accompanied by one or more subblocks containing information about its contents.

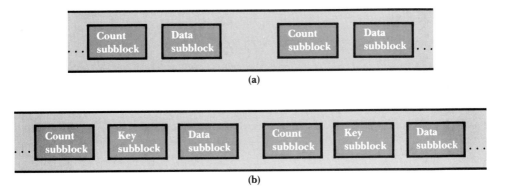

there is generally more nondata information provided with blocks than with sectors. Also, since the number and sizes of blocks can vary from one application to another, the relative amount of space taken up by overhead can vary when block addressing is used. This is illustrated in the following example.

Suppose we have a block-addressable disk drive with 20,000 bytes per track, and the amount of space taken up by subblocks and interblock gaps is equivalent to 300 bytes per block. We want to store a file containing 100-byte records on the disk. How many records can be stored per track if the blocking factor is 10, or if it is 60?

1. If there are 10 100-byte records per block, each block holds 1,000 bytes of data and uses 300 + 1,000, or 1,300, bytes of track space when overhead is taken into account. The number of blocks which can fit on a 20,000-byte track can be expressed as

$$\left\lfloor \frac{20,000}{1,300} \right\rfloor = \lfloor 15.38 \rfloor = 15.$$

So 15 blocks, or 150 records, can be stored per track. (Note that we have to take the *floor* of the result because a block cannot span two tracks.)

2. If there are 60 100-byte records per block, each block holds 6,000 bytes of data and uses 6,300 bytes of track space. The number of blocks per track can be expressed as

$$\left\lfloor \frac{20,000}{6,300} \right\rfloor = 3.$$

So 3 blocks, or 180 records, can be stored per track.

Clearly, the larger blocking factor can lead to more efficient use of storage. When blocks are larger, fewer blocks are required to hold a file, so there is less space consumed by the 300 bytes of overhead that accompany each block.

Can we conclude from this example that larger blocking factors always lead to more efficient storage utilization? Not necessarily. Since we can put only an integral number of blocks on a track, and since tracks are fixed in length, we almost always lose some space at the end of a track. Here we have the internal fragmentation problem again, but this time it applies to fragmentation within a *track*. The greater the block size, the greater potential amount of internal track fragmentation. What would have happened if we had chosen a blocking factor of 98 in the preceding example? What about 97?

The flexibility introduced by the use of blocks, rather than sectors, can result in savings in time and efficiency, since it lets the programmer determine to a large extent how data are to be organized physically on a disk. On the negative side, blocking schemes *require* the programmer and/or operating system to do the extra work of determining the data organization. Also, the very flexibility introduced by the use of blocking schemes precludes the synchronization of I/O operations with the physical movement of the disk, which sectoring permits. This means that strategies such as sector interleaving cannot be used to improve performance.

3.1.6 The Cost of a Disk Access

To give you a feel for the factors contributing to the total amount of time needed to access a file on a fixed disk, we calculate some access times. A disk access can be divided into three distinct physical operations, each with its own cost: *seek time, rotational delay,* and *transfer time*.

Seek Time   Seek time is the time required to move the access arm to the correct cylinder. The amount of time spent seeking during a disk access depends, of course, on how far the arm has to move. If we are accessing a file sequentially and the file is packed into several consecutive cylinders, seeking needs to be done only after all of the tracks on a cylinder have been processed, and even then the read/write head needs to move the width of only one track. At the other extreme, if we are alternately accessing sectors from two files that are stored at opposite extremes on a disk (one at the innermost cylinder, one at the outermost cylinder), seeking is very expensive.

Seeking is likely to be more costly in a multiuser environment, where several processes are contending for use of the disk at one time, than in a single-user environment, where disk usage is dedicated to one process.

Since seeking can be very costly, system designers often go to great extremes to minimize seeking. In an application that merges three files, for example, it is not unusual to see the three input files stored on three different drives and the output file stored on a fourth drive, so no seeking need be done as I/O operations jump from file to file.

Since it is usually impossible to know exactly how many tracks will be traversed in every seek, we usually try to determine the *average seek time* required for a particular file operation. If the starting and ending positions for each access are random, it turns out that the average seek traverses one third of the total number of cylinders that the read/write head ranges over.[†] Manufacturers' specifications for disk drives often list this figure as the

---

[†]Derivations of this result, as well as more detailed and refined models, can be found in Wiederhold (1983), Knuth (1973b), Teory and Fry (1982), and Salzberg (1988).

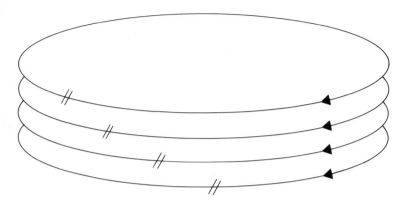

FIGURE 3.10 When a single file can span several tracks on a cylinder, we can stagger the beginnings of the tracks to avoid rotational delay when moving from track to track during sequential access.

average seek time for the drives. Most hard disks available today (1991) have average seek times of less than 40 milliseconds (msec), and high-performance disks have average seek times as low as 10 msec.

Rotational Delay   Rotational delay refers to the time it takes for the disk to rotate so the sector we want is under the read/write head. Hard disks usually rotate at about 3,600 rpm, which is one revolution per 16.7 msec. On average, the rotational delay is half a revolution, or about 8.3 msec. On floppy disks, which often rotate at only 360 rpm, average rotational delay is a sluggish 83.3 msec.

As in the case of seeking, these averages apply only when the read/write head moves from some random place on the disk surface to the target track. In many circumstances, rotational delay can be much less than the average. For example, suppose that you have a file that requires two or more tracks, that there are plenty of available tracks on one cylinder, and that you write the file to disk sequentially, with one write call. When the first track is filled, the disk can immediately begin writing to the second track, without any rotational delay. The "beginning" of the second track is effectively staggered by just the amount of time it takes to switch from the read/write head on the first track to the read/write head on the second. Rotational delay, as it were, is virtually nonexistent. Furthermore, when you read the file back, the position of data on the second track ensures that there is no rotational delay in switching from one track to another. Figure 3.10 illustrates this staggered arrangement.

Transfer Time Once the data we want is under the read/write head, it can be transferred. The transfer time is given by the formula

$$\text{Transfer time} = \frac{\text{number of bytes transferred}}{\text{number of bytes on a track}} \times \text{rotation time.}$$

If a drive is sectored, the transfer time for one sector depends on the number of sectors on a track. For example, if there are 32 sectors per track, the time required to transfer one sector would be 1/32nd of a revolution, or 0.5 msec.

Some Timing Computations Let's look at two different file processing situations that show how different types of file access can affect access times. We will compare the time it takes to access a file *in sequence* with the time it takes to access all of the records in the file *randomly*. In the former case, we use as much of the file as we can whenever we access it. In the random-access case, we are able to use only one record on each access.

The basis for our calculations is a "typical" 300-megabyte fixed disk described in Table 3.1. This particular disk is typical of one that might be used with a workstation in 1991. Although it is typical only of a certain class of fixed disk, the observations we draw as we perform these calculations are quite general. The disks used with larger, more expensive computers are bigger and faster than this disk, but the nature and relative costs of the factors contributing to total access times are essentially the same.

TABLE 3.1 Specifications of disk drive used in examples in text

Minimum (track-to-track) seek time	6 msec
Average seek time	18 msec
Rotational delay	8.3 msec
Maximum transfer rate ( )	16.7 msec/track, or 1,229 bytes/msec
Bytes per sector	512
Sectors per track	40
Tracks per cylinder	11
Tracks per surface	1,331
Interleave factor	1
Cluster size	8 sectors
Smallest extent size	5 clusters

Since our drive uses a cluster size of 8 sectors (4,096 bytes) and the smallest extent is 5 clusters, space is allocated for storing files in one-track units. Sectors are interleaved with an interleave factor of 1, so data on a given track can be transferred at the stated transfer rate.

Let's suppose that we wish to know how long it will take, using this drive, to read a 2,048-K-byte file that is divided into 8,000 256-byte records. First we need to know how the file is distributed on the disk. Since the 4,096-byte cluster holds 16 records, the file will be stored as a sequence of 500 4,096-byte clusters. Since the smallest extent size is 5 clusters, the 500 clusters are stored as 100 extents, occupying 100 tracks.

This means that the disk needs 100 tracks to hold the entire 2,048 K bytes that we want to read. We assume a situation in which the 100 tracks are randomly dispersed over the surface of the disk. (This is an extreme situation chosen to dramatize the point we want to make. Still, it is not so extreme that it could not easily occur on a typical overloaded disk that has a large number of small files.)

Now we are ready to calculate the time it would take to read the 2,048-K-byte file from the disk. We first estimate the time it takes to read the file sector by sector *in sequence*. This process involves the following operations for each track:

Average seek	18	msec
Rotational delay	8.3	msec
Read one track	16.7	msec
Total	43	msec.

We want to find and read 100 tracks, so the

Total time = 100 × 43 msec = 4,300 msec = 4.3 seconds.

Now let's calculate the time it would take to read in the same 8,000 records using *random access* rather than sequential access. In other words, rather than being able to read one sector right after another, we assume that we have to access the records in some order that requires jumping from track to track every time we read a new sector. This process involves the following operations for each record:

Average seek	18	msec
Rotational delay	8.3	msec
Read one cluster $\left(\frac{1}{5} \times 16.7\right)$	3.3	msec
Total	29.6	msec

Total time = 8,000 × 29.6 msec = 236,800 msec = 236.8 seconds.

This difference in performance between sequential access and random access is very important. If we can get to the right location on the disk and read a lot of information sequentially, we are clearly much better off than we are if we have to jump around, *seeking* every time we need a new record. Remember that seek time is very expensive; when we are performing disk operations we should try to minimize seeking.

3.1.7 Effect of Block Size on Performance: A UNIX Example

In deciding how best to organize disk storage allocation for several versions of BSD UNIX, the Computer Systems Research Group (CSRG) in Berkeley investigated the trade-offs between block size and performance in a UNIX environment (Leffler et al., 1989). The results of their research provide an interesting case study involving trade-offs between block size, fragmentation, and access time.

The CSRG research indicated that minimum block size of 512 bytes, standard at the time on UNIX systems, was not very efficient in a typical UNIX environment. Files that were several blocks long often were scattered over many cylinders, resulting in frequent seeks and thereby significantly decreasing throughput. The researchers found that doubling the block size to 1,024 bytes improved performance by more than a factor of 2. But even with 1,024-byte blocks, they found that throughput was only about 4% of the theoretical maximum. Eventually, they found that 4,096-byte blocks provided the fastest throughput, but this led to large amounts of wasted space due to internal fragmentation. These results are summarized in Table 3.2.

TABLE 3.2   The amount of wasted space as a function of block size

Space Used (Mbyte)	Percent Waste	Organization
775.2	0.0	Data only, no separation between files
807.8	4.2	Data only, each file starts on 512-byte boundary
828.7	6.9	Data + inodes, 512-byte block UNIX file system
866.5	11.8	Data + inodes, 1,024-byte block UNIX file system
948.5	22.4	Data + inodes, 2,048-byte block UNIX file system
1,128.3	45.6	Data + inodes, 4,096-byte block UNIX file system

From *The Design and Implementation of the 4.3BSD UNIX Operating System,* Leffler et al., p. 198.

To gain the advantages of both the 4,096-byte and the 512-byte systems, the Berkeley group implemented a variation of the cluster concept (see section 3.1.3). In the new implementation, they allocate 4,096-byte blocks for files that are big enough to need them; but for smaller files, they allow the large blocks to be divided into one or more fragments. With a fragment size of 512 bytes, as many as eight small files can be stored in one block, greatly reducing internal fragmentation. With the 4,096/512 system, wasted space was found to decline to about 12%.

3.1.8 Disk as Bottleneck

Disk performance is increasing steadily, even dramatically, but disk speeds still lag far behind local network speeds. A high-performance disk drive with 50 K bytes per track can transmit at a peak rate of about 3 megabytes per second, and only a fraction of that under normal conditions. High-performance networks, in contrast, can transmit at rates of as much as 100 megabytes per second. The result can often mean that a process is *disk bound*—the network and the CPU have to wait inordinate lengths of time for the disk to transmit data.

A number of techniques are used to solve this problem. One is multiprogramming, in which the CPU works on other jobs while waiting for the data to arrive. But if multiprogramming is not available, or if the process simply cannot afford to lose so much time waiting for the disk, ways must be found to speed up disk I/O.

One technique that is now offered on many high-performance systems is called *striping*. Disk striping involves splitting the parts of a file on several different drives, then letting the separate drives deliver parts of the file to the network simultaneously.

For example, suppose we have a 10-megabyte file spread across 20 high-performance (3 megabytes per second) drives that hold 50 K per track. The first drive has the first 50 K of the file, the second drive has the second 50 K, etc., through the twentieth drive. The first drive also holds the twenty-first 50 K, and so forth until 10 megabytes are stored. Collectively, the 20 drives can deliver to the network 250 K per revolution, a combined rate of 60 megabytes per second.

Disk striping exemplifies an important concept that we see more and more in system configurations—*parallelism*. Whenever there is a bottleneck at some point in the system, consider duplicating the thing that is the source of the bottleneck, and configure the system so several of them operate in parallel.

Another approach to solving the disk bottleneck is to avoid accessing the disk at all. As the cost of RAM steadily decreases, more and more users are using RAM to hold data that a few years ago had to be kept on a disk. Two effective ways in which RAM can be used to replace secondary storage are RAM disks and disk caches.

A *RAM disk* is a large part of RAM configured to simulate the behavior of a mechanical disk in every respect except speed and volatility. Since data can be located in RAM without a seek or rotational delay, RAM disks can provide much faster access than mechanical disks. Since RAM is normally volatile, the contents of a RAM disk are lost when the computer is turned off. RAM disks are often used in place of floppy disks because they are much faster than floppies and because relatively little RAM is needed to simulate a typical floppy disk.

A *disk cache*[†] is a large block of RAM configured to contain *pages* of data from a disk. A typical disk-caching scheme might use a 256-K cache with a disk. When data is requested from secondary memory, the file manager first looks into the disk cache to see if it contains the page with the requested data. If it does, the data can be processed immediately. Otherwise, the file manager reads the page containing the data from disk, replacing some page already in the disk cache.

Cache memory can provide substantial improvements in performance, especially when a program's data access patterns exhibit a high degree of *locality*. Locality exists in a file when blocks that are accessed in close temporal sequence are stored close to one another on the disk. When a disk cache is used, blocks that are close to one another on the disk are much more likely to belong to the page or pages that are read in with a single read, diminishing the likelihood that extra reads are needed for extra accesses.

RAM disks and cache memory are examples of *buffering,* a very important and frequently used family of I/O techniques. We take a closer look at buffering in section 3.6.

In these three techniques we see once again examples of the need to make trade-offs in file processing. With RAM disks and disk caches, there is tension between the cost/capacity advantages of disk over RAM, on the one hand, and the speed of RAM on the other. Striping provides opportunities to increase throughput enormously, but at the cost of a more complex and sophisticated disk management system. Good file design balances these tensions and costs creatively.

[†]The term *cache* (as opposed to *disk cache*) generally refers to a very high-speed block of primary memory that performs the same types of performance-enhancing operations with respect to RAM that a disk cache does with respect to secondary memory.

3.2 Magnetic Tape

Magnetic tape units belong to a class of devices that provide no direct accessing facility but that can provide very rapid sequential access to data. Tapes are compact, stand up well under different environmental conditions, are easy to store and transport, and are less expensive than disks.

3.2.1 Organization of Data on Tapes

Since tapes are accessed sequentially, there is no need for addresses to identify the locations of data on a tape. On a tape, the logical position of a byte within a file corresponds directly to its physical position relative to the start of the file. We may envision the surface of a typical tape as a set of parallel tracks, each of which is a sequence of bits. If there are nine tracks (see Fig. 3.11), the nine bits that are at corresponding positions in the nine respective tracks are taken to constitute one byte, plus a *parity bit*. So a byte can be thought of as a one-bit-wide slice of tape. Such a slice is called a *frame*.

The parity bit is not part of the data but is used to check the validity of the data. If *odd parity* is in effect, this bit is set to make the number of 1 bits in the frame *odd*. Even parity works similarly but is rarely used with tapes.

Frames (bytes) are grouped into data blocks whose size can vary from a few bytes to many kilobytes, depending on the needs of the user. Since tapes are often read one block at a time, and since tapes cannot stop or start instantaneously, blocks are separated by *interblock gaps,* which contain no

FIGURE 3.11 Nine-track tape.

information and are long enough to permit stopping and starting. When tapes use odd parity, no valid frame can contain all 0 bits, so a large number of consecutive 0 frames is used to fill the interrecord gap.

Tape drives come in many shapes, sizes, and speeds. Performance differences among drives can usually be measured in terms of three quantities:

☐ Tape density—commonly 800, 1,600, or 6,250 bits per inch (bpi) per track, but recently as much as 30,000 bpi;
☐ Tape speed—commonly 30 to 200 inches per second (ips); and
☐ Size of interblock gap—commonly between 0.3 inch and 0.75 inch.

Note that a 6,250-bpi nine-track tape contains 6,250 bits per inch per track, and 6,250 *bytes* per inch when the full nine tracks are taken together. Thus, in the computations that follow, 6,250 bpi is usually taken to mean 6,250 bytes of data per inch.

3.2.2 Estimating Tape Length Requirements

Suppose we want to store a backup copy of a large mailing list file with one million 100-byte records. If we want to store the file on a 6,250-bpi tape that has an interblock gap of 0.3 inches, how much tape is needed?

To answer this question we first need to determine what takes up space on the tape. There are two primary contributors: interblock gaps and data blocks. For every data block there is an interblock gap. If we let

$$b = \text{the physical length of a data block,}$$

$$g = \text{the length of an interblock gap, and}$$

$$n = \text{the number of data blocks,}$$

then the space requirement s for storing the file is

$$s = n \times (b + g).$$

We know that g is 0.3 inch, but we do not know what b and n are. In fact, b is whatever we want it to be, and n depends on our choice of b. Suppose we choose each data block to contain one 100-byte record. Then b, the length of each block, is given by

$$b = \frac{\text{block size (bytes per block)}}{\text{tape density (bytes per inch)}} \quad \frac{100}{6,250} = 0.016 \text{ inch,}$$

and n, the number of blocks, is one million (one per record).

The number of records stored in a physical block is called the *blocking factor*. It has the same meaning that it had when it was applied to the use of blocks for disk storage. The blocking factor we have chosen here is 1 because each block has only one record. Hence, the space requirement for the file is

$$s = 1,000,000 \times (0.016 + 0.3) \text{ inch}$$
$$= 1,000,000 \times 0.316 \text{ inch}$$
$$= 316,000 \text{ inches}$$
$$= 26,333 \text{ feet}.$$

Magnetic tapes range in length from 300 feet to 3,600 feet, with 2,400 feet being the most common length. Clearly, we need quite a few 2,400-foot tapes to store the file. Or do we? You may have noticed that our choice of block size was not a very smart one from the standpoint of space utilization. The interblock gaps in the physical representation of the file take up about *19 times* as much space as the data blocks do. If we were to take a snapshot of our tape, it would look something like this:

| Data | Gap | Data | Gap | Data | Gap | Data |

Most of the space on the tape is not used!

Clearly, we should consider increasing the relative amount of space used for actual data if we want to try to squeeze the file onto one 2,400-foot tape. If we increase the blocking factor, we can *decrease* the number of blocks, which decreases the number of interblock gaps, which in turn decreases the amount of space consumed by interblock gaps. For example, if we increase the blocking factor from 1 to 50, the number of blocks becomes

$$n = \frac{1,000,000}{50} = 20,000,$$

and the space requirement for interblock gaps decreases from 300,000 inches to 6,000 inches. The space requirement for the data is of course the same as it was previously. What has changed is the *relative* amount of space occupied by the gaps, as compared to the data. Now a snapshot of the tape would look much different:

| Data | Gap | Data | Gap | Data | Gap | Data | Gap | Data |

We leave it to you to show that the file can fit easily on one 2,400-foot tape when a blocking factor of 50 is used.

When we compute the space requirements for our file, we produce numbers that are quite specific to our file. A more general measure of the effect of choosing different block sizes is *effective recording density*. The effective recording density is supposed to reflect the amount of actual data that can be stored per inch of tape. Since this depends exclusively on the relative sizes of the interblock gap and the data block, it can be defined as

$$\frac{\text{number of bytes per block}}{\text{number of inches required to store a block}}.$$

When a blocking factor of 1 is used in our example, the number of bytes per block is 100, and the number of inches required to store a block is 0.316. Hence, the effective recording density is

$$\frac{100 \text{ bytes}}{0.316 \text{ inches}} = 316.4 \text{ bpi},$$

which is a far cry from the *nominal* recording density of 6,250 bpi.

Either way you look at it, space utilization is sensitive to the relative sizes of data blocks and interblock gaps. Let us now see how they affect the amount of *time* it takes to transmit tape data.

3.2.3 Estimating Data Transmission Times

If you understand the role of interblock gaps and data block sizes in determining effective recording density, you can probably see immediately that these two factors also affect the rate of data transmission. Two other factors that affect the rate of data transmission to or from tape are the nominal recording density and the speed with which the tape passes the read/write head. If we know these two values, we can compute the *nominal data transmission rate:*

$$\text{Nominal rate} = \text{tape density (bpi)} \times \text{tape speed (ips)}.$$

Hence, our 6,250-bpi, 200-ips tape has a nominal transmission rate of

$$6,250 \times 200 = 1,250,000 \text{ bytes/sec}$$
$$= 1,250 \text{ kilobytes/sec}.$$

This rate is competitive with most disk drives.

But what about those interblock gaps? Once our data gets dispersed by interblock gaps, the *effective transmission rate* certainly suffers. Suppose, for example, that we use our blocking factor of 1 with the same file and tape drive discussed in the preceding section (1,000,000 100-byte records, 0.3-inch gap). We saw that the effective recording density for this tape organization is 316.4 bpi. If the tape is moving at a rate of 200 ips, then its effective transmission rate is

$$316.4 \times 200 = 63,280 \text{ bytes/sec}$$

$$= 63.3 \text{ kilobytes/sec},$$

a rate that is about *one twentieth* of the nominal rate!

It should be clear that a blocking factor larger than 1 improves on this result, and that a substantially larger blocking factor improves on it substantially.

Although there are other factors that can influence performance, block size is generally considered to be the one variable with the greatest influence on space utilization and data transmission rate. The other factors we have included—gap size, tape speed, and recording density—are often beyond the control of the user. Another factor that can sometimes be important is the time it takes to start and stop the tape. We consider start/stop time in the exercises at the end of this chapter.

3.2.4 Tape Applications

Magnetic tape is an appropriate medium for sequential processing applications *if* the files being processed are not likely also to be used in applications that require direct access. For example, consider the problem of updating a mailing list for a monthly periodical. Is it essential that the list be kept absolutely current, or is a monthly update of the list sufficient?

If information must be up-to-the-minute, then the medium must permit direct access so individual updates can be made immediately. But if the mailing list needs to be current only when mailing labels are printed, all of the changes that occur during the course of a month can be collected in one batch and put into a transaction file that is sorted in the same way that the mailing list is sorted. Then a program that reads through the two files simultaneously can be executed, making all the required changes in one pass through the data.

Since tape is relatively inexpensive, it is an excellent medium for storing data offline. At current prices, a removable disk pack that holds 150 megabytes costs about 30 times as much as a reel of tape that, properly blocked, can hold the same amount. Tape is a good medium for archival storage and for transporting data, as long as the data does not have to be available on short notice for direct processing.

A special kind of tape drive, a *streaming tape drive,* is used widely for nonstop, high-speed dumping of data to and from disks. Generally less expensive than general-purpose tape drives, it is also less suited for processing that involves much starting and stopping.

3.3   Disk versus Tape

In the past, magnetic tape and magnetic disk accounted for the lion's share of all secondary storage applications. Disk was excellent for random access and storage of files for which immediate access was desired; tape was ideal for processing data sequentially and for long-term storage of files. Over time, these roles have changed somewhat in favor of disk.

The major reason that tape was preferable to disk for sequential processing is that tapes are dedicated to one process, while disk generally serves several processes. This means that between accesses a disk read/write head tends to move away from the location where the next sequential access will occur, resulting in an expensive seek; while the tape drive, being dedicated to one process, pays no such price in seek time.

This problem of excessive seeking has gradually diminished, and disk has taken over much of the secondary storage niche previously occupied by tape. This change is largely due to the continued dramatic decreases in the cost of disk and RAM storage. To fully understand this change, we need to understand the role of RAM buffer space in performing I/O.[†] Briefly, it is that performance depends largely on how big a chunk of a file we can transmit at any time; as more RAM space becomes available for I/O buffers, the number of accesses decreases correspondingly, which means that the number of seeks required goes down as well. Most systems now available, even small systems, have enough RAM available to decrease the number of accesses required to process most files to a level that makes disk quite competitive with tape for sequential processing. This change, added to the superior versatility and decreasing costs of disks, has resulted in use of disk for most sequential processing, which in the past was primarily the domain of tape.

This is not to say that tapes should not be used for sequential processing. If a file is kept on tape, and there are enough drives available to use them for sequential processing, it may be more efficient to process the file directly from tape than to stream it to disk and then process it sequentially.

Although it has lost ground to disk in sequential processing applications, tape remains important as a medium for long-term archival storage. Tape is still far less expensive than magnetic disk, and it is very easy and fast

[†]Techniques for RAM buffering are covered in section 3.6.

to stream large files or sets of files between tape and disk. In this context, tape has emerged as one of our most important media (along with CD-ROM) for *tertiary* storage.

3.4 Storage as a Hierarchy

Although the best mixture of devices for a computing system depends on the needs of the system's users, we can imagine any computing system as a hierarchy of storage devices of different speed, capacity, and cost. Figure 3.12 summarizes the different types of storage found at different levels in

FIGURE 3.12 Approximate comparisons of types of storage, circa 1991.

Types of memory	Devices and media	Access times (sec)	Capacities (bytes)	Cost (cents/bit)
Primary				
Registers RAM RAM disk and disk cache	Core and semiconductors	$10^{-9}-10^{-5}$	$10^{0}-10^{9}$	$10^{0}-10^{-3}$
Secondary				
Direct-access	Magnetic disks	$10^{-3}-10^{-1}$	$10^{4}-10^{9}$	$10^{-2}-10^{-5}$
Serial	Tape and mass storage	$10^{1}-10^{2}$	$10^{0}-10^{11}$	$10^{-5}-10^{-7}$
Offline				
Archival and backup	Removable magnetic disks, optical discs, and tapes	$10^{0}-10^{2}$	$10^{4}-10^{12}$	$10^{-5}-10^{-7}$

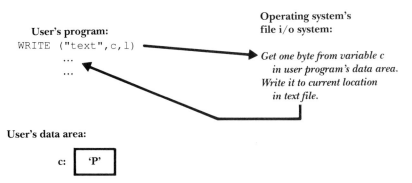

User's program:
```
WRITE ("text",c,l)
    ...
    ...
```

Operating system's file i/o system:

*Get one byte from variable c
    in user program's data area.
Write it to current location
    in text file.*

User's data area:

c: ‘P’

FIGURE 3.13 The WRITE( ) statement tells the operating system to send one character to disk and gives the operating system the location of the character. The operating system takes over the job of doing the actual writing and then returns control to the calling program.

such hierarchies and shows approximately how they compare in terms of access time, capacity, and cost.

3.5   A Journey of a Byte

What happens when a program writes a byte to a file on a disk? We know what the program does (it says WRITE(. . .)), and we now know something about how the byte is stored on a disk, but we haven't looked at what happens *between* the program and the disk. The whole story of what happens to data between program and disk is not one we can tell here, but we can give you an idea of the many different pieces of hardware and software involved and the many jobs that have to be done by looking at one example of a journey of one byte.

Suppose we want to append a byte representing the character ‘*P*’ stored in a character variable *c* to a file named in the variable TEXT stored somewhere on a disk. From the program's point of view, the entire journey that the byte will take might be represented by the statement

```
WRITE(TEXT, c, 1)
```

but the journey is much longer than this simple statement suggests.

The *WRITE( )* statement results in a call to the computer's operating system, which has the task of seeing that the rest of the journey is completed successfully (Fig. 3.13). Often our program can provide the operating system with information that helps it carry out this task more effectively, but once the operating system has taken over, the job of overseeing the rest of the journey is largely beyond our program's control.

3.5.1 The File Manager

An operating system is not a single program, but a collection of programs, each one designed to manage a different part of the computer's resources. Among these programs are ones that deal with file-related matters and I/O devices. We call this subset of programs the operating system's *file manager*. The file manager may be thought of as several layers of procedures (Fig. 3.14), with the upper layers dealing mostly with symbolic, or *logical,* aspects of file management, and the lower layers dealing more with the *physical* aspects. Each layer calls the one below it, until, at the lowest level, the byte is actually written to the disk.

The file manager begins by finding out whether the logical characteristics of the file are consistent with what we are asking it to do with the file. It may look up the requested file in a table, where it finds out such things as whether the file has been opened, what type of file the byte is being sent to (a binary file, a text file, some other organization), who the file's owner is, and whether WRITE( ) access is allowed for this particular user of the file.

The file manager must also determine where in the file TEXT the 'P' is to be deposited. Since the 'P' is to be appended to the file, the file manager needs to know where the end of the file is—the physical location of the last sector in the file. This information is obtained from the file allocation table (FAT) described earlier. From the FAT, the file manager locates the drive, cylinder, track, and sector where the byte is to be stored.

3.5.2 The I/O Buffer

Next, the file manager determines whether the sector that is to contain the 'P' is already in RAM or needs to be loaded into RAM. If the sector needs to be loaded, the file manager must find an available *system I/O buffer* space for it, then read it from the disk. Once it has the sector in a buffer in RAM, the file manager can deposit the 'P' into its proper position in the buffer (Fig. 3.15). The system I/O buffer allows the file manager to read and write data in sector-sized or block-sized units. In other words, it enables the file manager to ensure that the organization of data in RAM conforms to the organization it will have on the disk.

Instead of sending the sector immediately to the disk, the file manager usually waits to see if it can accumulate more bytes going to the same sector

Logical

1. The program asks the operating system to write the contents of the variable *c* to the next available position in TEXT.

2. The operating system passes the job on to the file manager.

3. The file manager looks up TEXT in a table containing information about it, such as whether the file is open and available for use, what types of access are allowed, if any, and what physical file the logical name TEXT corresponds to.

4. The file manager searches a file allocation table for the physical location of the sector that is to contain the byte.

5. The file manager makes sure that the last sector in the file has been stored in a system I/O buffer in RAM, then deposits the '*P*' into its proper position in the buffer.

6. The file manager gives instructions to the I/O processor about where the byte is stored in RAM and where it needs to be sent on the disk.

7. The I/O processor finds a time when the drive is available to receive the data and puts the data in proper format for the disk. It may also buffer the data to send it out in chunks of the proper size for the disk.

8. The I/O processor sends the data to the disk controller.

9. The controller instructs the drive to move the read/write head to the proper track, waits for the desired sector to come under the read/write head, then sends the byte to the drive to be deposited, bit-by-bit, on the surface of the disk.

Physical

FIGURE 3.14 Layers of procedures involved in transmitting a byte from a program's data area to a file called TEXT on disk.

before actually transmitting anything. Even though the statement WRITE-(TEXT,c,1) seems to imply that our character is being sent immediately to the disk, it may in fact be kept in RAM for some time before it is sent. (There are many situations in which the file manager cannot wait until a buffer is filled before transmitting it. For instance, if TEXT were closed, it would have to *flush* all output buffers holding data waiting to be written to TEXT so the data would not be lost.)

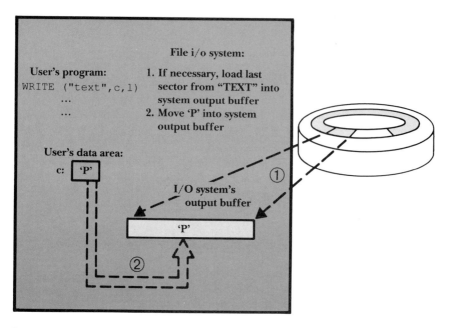

FIGURE 3.15 The file manager moves *P* from the program's data area to a system output buffer, where it may join other bytes headed for the same place on the disk. If necessary, the file manager may have to load the corresponding sector from the disk into the system output buffer.

3.5.3 The Byte Leaves RAM: The I/O Processor and Disk Controller

So far, all of our byte's activities have occurred within the computer's primary memory and have probably been carried out by the computer's central processing unit (CPU). The byte has travelled along data paths that are designed to be very fast and that are relatively expensive. Now it is time for the byte to travel along a data path that is likely to be slower and narrower than the one in primary memory. (A typical computer might have an internal data-path width of four bytes, whereas the width of the path leading to the disk might be only two bytes.)

Because of bottlenecks created by these differences in speed and data-path widths, our byte and its companions might have to wait for an external data path to become available. This also means that the CPU has extra time on its hands as it deals out information in small enough chunks and at slow enough speeds that the world outside can handle them. In fact, the differences between the internal and external speeds for transmitting data are often so great that the CPU can transmit to several external devices simultaneously.

The processes of disassembling and assembling groups of bytes for transmission to and from external devices are so specialized that it is unreasonable to ask an expensive, general-purpose CPU to spend its valuable time doing I/O when a simpler device could do the job as well, freeing the CPU to do the work that it is most suited for. Such a special-purpose device is called an *I/O processor*.

An I/O processor may be anything from a simple chip capable of taking a byte and, on cue, just passing it on; to a powerful, small computer capable of executing very sophisticated programs and communicating with many devices simultaneously. The I/O processor takes its instructions from the operating system, but once it begins processing I/O, it runs independently, relieving the operating system (and the CPU) of the task of communicating with secondary storage devices. This allows I/O processes and internal computing to overlap.[†]

In a typical computer, the file manager might now tell the I/O processor that there is data in the buffer that is to be transmitted to the disk, how much data there is, and where it is to go on the disk. This information might come in the form of a little program that the operating system constructs and the I/O processor executes (Fig. 3.16).

The job of actually controlling the operation of the disk is done by a device called a *disk controller*. The I/O processor asks the disk controller if the disk drive is available for writing. If there is much I/O processing, there is a good chance that the drive will not be available and that our byte will have to wait in its buffer until the drive becomes available.

What happens next often makes the time spent so far seem insignificant in comparison: The disk drive is instructed to move its read/write head to the track and sector on the drive where our byte and its companions are to be stored. For the first time, a device is being asked to do something mechanical! The read/write head must seek to the proper track (unless it is already there), and then wait until the disk has spun around so the desired sector is under the head. Once the track and sector are located, the I/O processor (or perhaps the controller) can send out bytes, one at a time, to the drive. Our byte waits until its turn comes, then travels, alone, to the drive, where it probably is stored in a little one-byte buffer while it waits to be deposited on the disk.

[†]On many systems the I/O processor can take data directly from RAM, without further involvement from the CPU. This process is called *direct memory access* (DMA). On other systems, the CPU must place the data in special I/O registers before the I/O processor can have access to it.

FIGURE 3.16 The file manager sends the I/O processor instructions in the form of an I/O processor program. The I/O processor gets the data from the system buffer, prepares it for storing on the disk, and then sends it to the disk controller, which deposits it on the surface of the disk.

Finally, as the disk spins under the read/write head, the eight bits of our byte are deposited, one at a time, on the surface of the disk (Fig. 3.16). There the '*P*' remains, at the end of its journey, spinning about at a leisurely 50 to 100 miles per hour.

3.6   Buffer Management

Any user of files can benefit from some knowledge of what happens to data travelling between a program's data area and secondary storage. One aspect of this process that is particularly important is the use of buffers. Buffering involves working with large chunks of data in RAM so the number of accesses to secondary storage can be reduced. We concentrate on the operation of *system* I/O buffers, but be aware that the use of buffers within programs can also substantially affect performance.

3.6.1 Buffer Bottlenecks

We know that a file manager allocates I/O buffers that are big enough to hold incoming data, but we have said nothing so far about *how many* buffers are used. In fact, it is common for file managers to allocate several buffers for performing I/O.

To understand the need for several system buffers, consider what happens if a program is performing both input and output on one character at a time, and only one I/O buffer is available. When the program asks for its first character, the I/O buffer is loaded with the sector containing the character, and the character is transmitted to the program. If the program then decides to output a character, the I/O buffer is filled with the sector into which the output character needs to go, destroying its original contents. Then when the next input character is needed, the buffer contents have to be written to disk to make room for the (original) sector containing the second input character, and so on.

Fortunately, there is a simple and generally effective solution to this ridiculous state of affairs, and that is to use more than one system buffer. For this reason, I/O systems almost always use at least two buffers — one for input and one for output.

Even if a program transmits data in only one direction, the use of a single system I/O buffer can slow it down considerably. We know, for instance, that the operation of reading a sector from a disk is extremely slow compared to the amount of time it takes to move data in RAM, so we can guess that a program that reads many sectors from a file might have to spend much of its time waiting for the I/O system to fill its buffer every time a read operation is performed before it can begin processing. When this happens, the program that is running is said to be *I/O bound*—the CPU spends much of its time just waiting for I/O to be performed. The solution to this problem is to use more than one buffer and to have the I/O system filling the next sector or block of data while the CPU is processing the current one.

3.6.2 Buffering Strategies

Multiple Buffering   Suppose that a program is only writing to a disk and that it is I/O bound. The CPU wants to be filling a buffer at the same time that I/O is being performed. If *two* buffers are used and I/O-CPU overlapping is permitted, the CPU can be filling one buffer while the contents of the other are being transmitted to disk. When both tasks are finished, the roles of the buffers can be exchanged. This technique of swapping the roles of two buffers after each output (or input) operation is called *double buffering*. Double buffering allows the operating system to be operating on one buffer while the other buffer is being loaded or emptied (Fig. 3.17).

The idea of swapping system buffers to allow processing and I/O to overlap need not be restricted to two buffers. In theory, any number of buffers can be used, and they can be organized in a variety of ways. The actual management of system buffers is usually done by the operating system and can rarely be controlled by programmers who do not work at the systems level. It is common, however, for users to be able to control the *number* of system buffers assigned to jobs.

Some file systems use a buffering scheme called *buffer pooling:* When a system buffer is needed, it is taken from a pool of available buffers and used. When the system receives a request to read a certain sector or block, it looks to see if one of its buffers already contains that sector or block. If no buffer contains it, then the system finds from its pool of buffers one that is not currently in use and loads the sector or block into it.

FIGURE 3.17 Double buffering: (a) The contents of system I/O buffer 1 are sent to disk while I/O buffer 2 is being filled; and (b) the contents of buffer 2 are sent to disk while I/O buffer 1 is being filled.

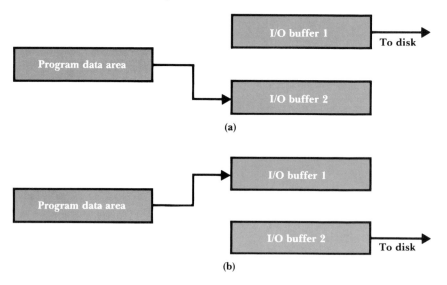

Several different schemes are used to decide which buffer to take from a buffer pool. One generally effective strategy is to take from the pool that buffer that is *least recently used*. When a buffer is accessed, it is put on a least-recently-used queue, so it is allowed to retain its data until all other less-recently-used buffers have been accessed. The least-recently-used (LRU) strategy for replacing old data with new data has many applications in computing. It is based on the assumption that a block of data that has been used recently is more likely to be needed in the near future than one that has been used less recently. (We encounter LRU again in later chapters.)

It is difficult to predict the point at which the addition of extra buffers ceases to contribute to improved performance. As the cost of RAM continues to decrease, so does the cost of using more and bigger buffers. On the other hand, the more buffers there are, the more time it takes for the file system to manage them. When in doubt, consider experimenting with different numbers of buffers.

Move Mode and Locate Mode Sometimes it is not necessary to distinguish between a program's data area and system buffers. When data must always be copied from a system buffer to a program buffer (or vice versa), the amount of time taken to perform the move can be substantial. This way of handling buffered data is called *move mode,* since it involves moving chunks of data from one place in RAM to another before they can be accessed.

There are two ways that move mode can be avoided. If the file manager can perform I/O directly between secondary storage and the program's data area, no extra move is necessary. Alternatively, the file manager could use system buffers to handle all I/O, but provide the program with the *locations,* through the use of pointer variables, of the system buffers. Both techniques are examples of a general approach to buffering called *locate mode.* When locate mode is used, a program is able to operate directly on data in the I/O buffer, eliminating the need to transfer data between an I/O buffer and a program buffer.

Scatter/Gather I/O Suppose you are reading in a file with many blocks, where each block consists of a header followed by data. You would like to put the headers in one buffer and the data in a different buffer so the data can be processed as a single entity. The obvious way to do this is to read the whole block into a single big buffer, and then move the different parts to their own buffers. Sometimes we can avoid this two-step process using a technique called *scatter input.* With scatter input, a single READ call identifies not one, but a collection of buffers into which data from a single block is to be scattered.

The converse of scatter input is *gather output*. With gather output, several buffers can be gathered and written with a single WRITE call, avoiding the need to copy them to a single output buffer. When the cost of copying several buffers into a single output buffer is high, scatter/gather can have a significant effect on the running time of a program.

It is not always obvious when features like scatter/gather, locate mode, and buffer pooling are available in an operating system. You often have to go looking for them. Sometimes you can invoke them by communicating with your operating system, and sometimes you can cause them to be invoked by organizing your program in ways that are compatible with the way the operating system does I/O. Throughout this text we return many times to the issue of how to enhance performance by thinking about how buffers work and adapting programs and file structures accordingly.

3.7   I/O in UNIX

We see in the journey of a byte that we can view I/O as proceeding through several layers. UNIX provides a good example of how these layers occur in a real operating system, so we conclude this chapter with a look at UNIX. It is of course beyond the scope of this text to describe the UNIX I/O layers in detail. Rather, our objective here is just to pick a few features of UNIX that illustrate points made in the text. A secondary objective is to familiarize you with some of the important terminology used in describing UNIX systems. For a comprehensive, detailed look at how UNIX works, plus a thorough discussion of the design decisions involved in creating and improving UNIX, see Leffler et al. (1989).

3.7.1 The Kernel

In Fig. 3.14 we see how the process of transmitting data from a program to an external device can be described as proceeding through a series of layers. The topmost layer deals with data in *logical,* structural terms. We store in a file a name, a body of text, an image, an array of numbers, or some other logical entity. This reflects the view that an application has of what goes into a file. The layers that follow collectively carry out the task of turning the logical object into a collection of bits on a *physical* device.

Likewise, the topmost I/O layer in UNIX deals with data primarily in logical terms. This layer in UNIX consists of *processes* that impose certain logical views on files. Processes are associated with solving some problem,

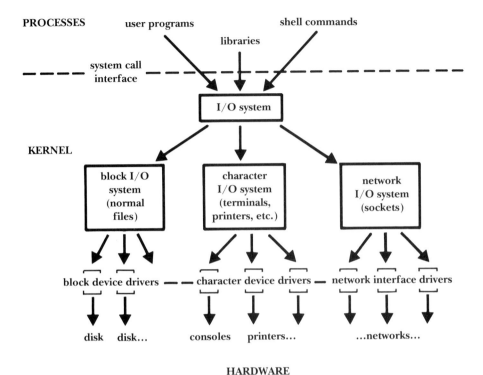

FIGURE 3.18 Kernel I/O structure.

such as counting the words in the file or searching for somebody's address. Processes include *shell routines* like cat and tail, *user programs* that operate on files, and *library routines* like scanf( ) and fread( ) that are called from programs to read strings, numbers, etc.

Below this layer is the UNIX *kernel,* which incorporates all the rest of the layers.[†] The components of the kernel that do I/O are illustrated in Fig. 3.18. The kernel views all I/O as operating on a sequence of bytes, so once we pass control to the kernel all assumptions about the logical view of a file are gone. The decision to design UNIX in this way—to make all operations below the top layer independent of an application's logical view of a file—is unusual. It is also one of the main attractions in choosing UNIX as a focus for this text, for UNIX lets us make all of the decisions

---

[†]It is beyond the scope of this text to describe the UNIX kernel in detail. For a full description of the UNIX kernel, including the I/O system, see Leffler et al. (1989).

about the logical structure of a file, imposing no restrictions on how we think about the file beyond the fact that it must be built from a sequence of bytes.

Let's illustrate the journey of a byte through the kernel, as we did earlier in this chapter by tracing the results of an I/O statement. We assume in this example that we are writing a character to disk. This corresponds to the left branch of the I/O system in Fig. 3.18.

When your program executes a system call such as

```
write (fd, &c, 1);
```

the kernel is invoked immediately.[†] The routines that let processes communicate directly with the kernel make up the *system call interface*. In this case, the system call instructs the kernel to write a character to a file.

The kernel I/O system begins by connecting the file descriptor *(fd)* in your program to some file or device in the filesystem. It does this by proceeding through a series of four tables that enable the kernel to find its way from a process to the places on the disk that will hold the file that they refer to. The four tables are

- □   a file descriptor table;
- □   an open file table, with information about open files;
- □   a file allocation table, which is part of a structure called an index node; and
- □   a table of index nodes, with one entry for each file in use.

Although these tables are managed by the kernel's I/O system, they are, in a sense, "owned" by different parts of the system:

- □   The file descriptor table is owned by the process (your program).
- □   The open file table and index node tables are owned by the kernel.
- □   The index node itself is part of the filesystem.

The four tables are invoked in turn by the kernel to get the information it needs to write to your file on disk. Let's see how this works by looking at the functions of the tables.

The *file descriptor table* (Fig. 3.19a) is a simple table that associates each of the file descriptors used by a process with an entry in another table, the open file table. Every process has its own descriptor table, which includes entries for all files it has opened, including the "files" *STDIN, STDOUT,* and *STDERR.*

[†]This should not be confused with a *library* call, such as *fprintf( )*, which invokes the standard library to perform some additional operations on the data, such as converting it to an ASCII format, and *then* makes a corresponding system call.

(a) *descriptor* table

(b) *open file* table

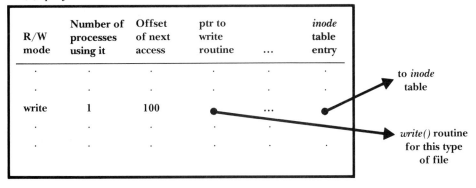

FIGURE 3.19 Descriptor table and open file table.

The *open file* table (Fig. 3.19b) contains entries for every open file. Every time a file is opened or created, a new entry is added to the open file table. These entries are called *file structures,* and they contain important information about how the corresponding file is to be used, such as the read/write mode used when it was opened, the number of processes currently using it, and the offset within the file to be used for the next read or write. The open file table also contains an array of pointers to generic functions that can be used to operate on the file. These functions will differ depending on the type of file.

It is possible for several different processes to refer to the same open file table entry, so one process could read part of a file, another process could read the next part, and so forth, with each process taking over where the previous one stopped. On the other hand, if the same file is opened by two separate *open ( )* statements, two separate entries are made in the table, and the two processes operate on the file quite independently.[†]

The information in the open file table is transitory. It tells the kernel what it can do with a file that has been opened in a certain way and provides information on how it can operate on the file. The kernel still needs more information about the file itself, such as where the file is stored on disk, how big the file is, and who owns it. This information is found in an *index node,* more commonly referred to as an *inode* (Fig. 3.20).

An inode is a more permanent structure than an open file table's file structure. A file structure exists only while a file is open for access, but an inode exists as long as its corresponding file exists. For this reason, a file's inode is kept on disk *with* the file (though not physically adjacent to the file). When a file is opened, a copy of its inode is usually loaded into RAM where it is added to the aforementioned *inode table* for rapid access.

For the purposes of our discussion, the most important component of the inode is a list (index) of the disk blocks that make up the file. This list is the UNIX counterpart to the *file allocation table* that we described earlier in this chapter.[‡] Once the kernel's I/O system has the inode information, it knows all that it needs to know about the file. It then invokes an I/O processor program that is appropriate for the type of data, the type of operation, and the type of device that is to be written. In UNIX, this program is called a *device driver.*

The device driver sees that your data is moved from its buffer to its proper place on disk. Before we look at the role of device drivers in UNIX, it is instructive to look at how the kernel distinguishes among the different kinds of file data that it must deal with.

3.7.2 Linking File Names to Files

It is instructive to look a little more closely at how a file name is actually linked to the corresponding file. All references to files begin with a

---

[†]Of course, there are risks in letting this happen. If you are writing to a file with one process at the same time that you are independently reading from the file with another, the meaning of these may be difficult to determine.

[‡]This might not be a simple linear array. To accommodate both large and small files, this table often has a dynamic, tree-like structure.

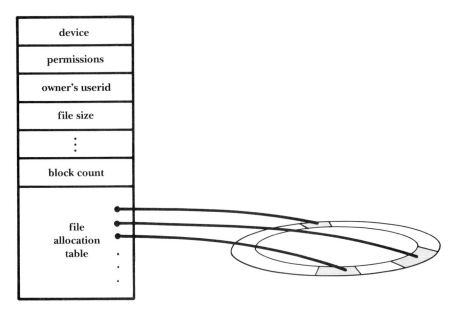

FIGURE 3.20 An inode. The inode is the data structure used by UNIX to describe the file. It includes the device containing the file, permissions, owner and group IDs, and file allocation table, among other things.

directory, for it is in directories that file names are kept. In fact, a directory is just a small file that contains, for each file, a file name together with a pointer to the file's inode on disk.[†] This pointer from a directory to the inode of a file is called a *hard link*. It provides a direct reference from the file name to all other information about the file. When a file is opened, this hard link is used to bring the inode into RAM and to set up the corresponding entry in the open file table.

It is possible for several file names to point to the same inode, so one file can have several different names. A field in the inode tells how many hard links there are to the inode. This means that if a file name is deleted and there are other file names for the same file, the file itself is not deleted; its inode's hard-link count is just decremented by one.

There is another kind of link, called a *soft link*, or *symbolic link.* A symbolic link links a file name to another file name, rather than to an actual file. Instead of being a pointer to an inode, a soft link is a pathname of some

---

[†]The actual structure of a directory is a little more complex than this, but these are the essential parts. See Leffler, et al. (1989) for details.

file. Since a symbolic link does not point to an actual file, it can refer to a directory or even to a file in a different file system. Symbolic links are not supported on all UNIX systems. UNIX System 4.3BSD supports symbolic links, but System V does not.

3.7.3 Normal Files, Special Files, and Sockets

The "everything is a file" concept in UNIX works only when we recognize that some files are quite a bit different from others. We see in Fig. 3.18 that the kernel distinguishes among three different types of files. *Normal files* are the files that this text is about. *Special files* almost always represent a stream of characters and control signals that drive some device, such as a line printer or a graphics device. The first three file descriptors in the descriptor table (Fig. 3.19a) are special files. *Sockets* are abstractions that serve as endpoints for interprocess communication.

At a certain conceptual level, these three different types of UNIX files are very similar, and many of the same routines can be used to access any of them. For instance, you can establish access to all three types by opening them, and you can write to them with the *write( )* system call.

3.7.4 Block I/O

In Fig. 3.18, we see that the three different types of files access their respective devices via three different I/O systems, the *block I/O system,* the *character I/O system,* and the *network I/O system*. Henceforth we ignore the second and third categories, since it is normal file I/O that we are most concerned with in this text.[†]

The block I/O system is the UNIX counterpart of the file manager in the journey of a byte. It concerns itself with how to transmit normal file data, viewed by the user as a sequence of bytes, onto a block-oriented device like a disk or tape. Given a byte to store on a disk, for example, it arranges to read in the sector containing the byte to be replaced, to replace the byte, and to write the sector back to the disk.

The UNIX view of a block device most closely resembles that of a disk. It is a randomly addressable array of fixed blocks. Originally all blocks were 512 bytes, which was the common sector size on most disks. No other organization (such as clusters) was imposed on the placement of files on

---

[†]This is not entirely true. Sockets, for example, can be used to move normal files from place to place. In fact, high-performance network systems bypass the normal file system in favor of sockets to squeeze every bit of performance out of the network.

disk. (In section 3.1.7 we saw how the design of later UNIX systems dealt with this convention.)

3.7.5 Device Drivers

For each peripheral device there is a separate set of routines, called a *device driver,* that performs the actual I/O between the I/O buffer and the device. A device driver is roughly equivalent to the I/O processor program described in the journey of a byte.

Since the block I/O system views a peripheral device as an array of physical blocks, addressed as block 0, block 1, etc., a block I/O device driver's job is to take a block from a buffer, destined for one of these physical blocks, and see that it gets deposited in the proper physical place on the device. This saves the block I/O part of the kernel from having to know anything about the specific device it is writing to, other than its identity and that it is a block device. A thorough discussion of device drivers for block, character, and network I/O can be found in Leffler et al. (1989).

3.7.6 The Kernel and Filesystems

In Chapter 2 we described the UNIX concept of a *filesystem.* A UNIX filesystem is a collection of files, together with secondary information about the actual files in the system. A filesystem includes the directory structure, the directories, ordinary files, and the inodes that describe the files.

In our discussions we talk about the filesystem as if it is part of the kernel's I/O system, which it is, but it is also in a sense separate from it. All parts of a filesystem reside on disk, rather than in RAM where the kernel does its work. These parts are brought into RAM by the kernel as needed. This separation of the filesystem from the kernel has many advantages. One important advantage is that we can tune a filesystem to a particular device or usage pattern independently of how the kernel views files. The discussions in section 3.1.7 of 4.3BSD block organization are file-system concerns, for example, and need not have any effect on how the kernel works.

Another advantage of keeping the filesystem and I/O system distinct is that we can have separate filesystems that are organized differently, perhaps on different devices, but are accessible by the same kernel. In Appendix A, for instance, we describe the design of a filesystem on CDROM that is organized quite differently from a typical disk-based file system yet looks just like any other filesystem to the user and to the I/O system.

3.7.7 Magnetic Tape and UNIX

Important as it is to computing, magnetic tape is somewhat of an orphan in the UNIX view of I/O. A magnetic tape unit has characteristics similar to both block I/O devices (being block oriented) and character devices (being primarily used for sequential access), but does not fit nicely into either category. Character devices read and write streams of data, not blocks, and block devices in general access blocks randomly, not sequentially.

Since block I/O is generally the least inappropriate of the two inappropriate paradigms for tape, a tape device is normally considered in UNIX to be a block I/O device and hence is accessed through the block I/O interface. But because the block I/O interface is most often used to write to random-access devices, disks, it does not require blocks to be written in sequence, as they must be written to a tape. This problem is solved by allowing only one write request at a time per tape drive. When high-performance I/O is required, the character device interface can be used in a raw mode to stream data to tapes, bypassing the stage that requires the data to be collected into relatively small blocks before or after transmission.

■ SUMMARY

In this chapter we look at the software environment in which file processing programs must operate and at some of the hardware devices on which files are commonly stored, hoping to understand how they influence the ways we design and process files. We begin by looking at the two most common storage media: magnetic disks and tapes.

A disk drive consists of a set of read/write heads that are interspersed among one or more platters. Each platter contributes one or two surfaces, each surface contains a set of concentric tracks, and each track is divided into sectors or blocks. The set of tracks that can be read without moving the read/write heads is called a cylinder.

There are two basic ways to address data on disks: by sector and by block. Used in this context, the term *block* refers to a group of records that are stored together on a disk and treated as a unit for I/O purposes. When blocks are used, the user is better able to make the physical organization of data correspond to its logical organization, and hence can sometimes improve performance. Block-organized drives also sometimes make it possible for the disk drive to search among blocks on a track for a record with a certain key without first having to transmit the unwanted blocks into RAM.

Three possible disadvantages of block-organized devices are the danger of internal track fragmentation, the burden of dealing with the extra complexity that the user has to bear, and the loss of opportunities to do some of the kinds of synchronization (such as sector interleaving) that sector-addressing devices provide.

The cost of a disk access can be measured in terms of the time it takes for seeking, rotational delay, and transfer time. If sector interleaving is used, it is possible to access logically adjacent sectors by separating them physically by one or more sectors. Although it takes much less time to access a single record directly than sequentially, the extra seek time required for doing direct accesses makes it much slower than sequential access when a series of records is to be accessed.

Despite increasing disk performance, network speeds have improved to the point that disk access is often a significant bottleneck in an overall I/O system. A number of techniques are available for addressing this problem, including striping, the use of RAM disks, and disk caching.

Research done in connection with BSD UNIX shows that block size can have a major effect on performance. By increasing the default block size from 512 bytes to 4,096 bytes, throughput was improved enormously, especially for large files, because eight times as much data could be transferred in a single access. A negative consequence of this reorganization was that wasted storage increased from 6.9% for 512-byte blocks to 45.6% for 4,096-byte blocks. It turned out that this problem of wasted space could be dealt with by treating the 4,096-byte blocks as clusters of 512-byte blocks, which could be allocated to different files.

Though not as important as disks, magnetic tape has an important niche in file processing. Tapes are inexpensive, reasonably fast for sequential processing, compact, robust, and easy to store and transport. Data are usually organized on tapes in one-bit-wide parallel tracks, with a bit-wide cross-section of tracks interpreted as one or more bytes. When estimating processing speed and space utilization, it is important to recognize the role played by the interblock gap. Effective recording density and effective transmission rate are useful measurements of the performance one can expect to achieve for a given physical file organization.

In comparing disk and tape as secondary storage media, we see that disks are replacing tape in more and more cases. This is largely because RAM is becoming less expensive, relative to secondary storage, which means that one of the earlier advantages of tape over disk, the ability to do sequential access without seeking, has diminished significantly.

This chapter follows a journey of a byte as it is sent from RAM to disk. The journey involves the participation of many different programs and devices, including

- a user's program, which makes the initial call to the operating system;

- the operating system's file manager, which maintains tables of information that it uses to translate between the program's logical view of the file and the physical file where the byte is to be stored;
- an I/O processor and its software, which transmit the byte, synchronizing the transmission of the byte between an I/O buffer in RAM and the disk;
- the disk controller and its software, which instruct the drive about how to find the proper track and sector, then send the byte; and
- the disk drive, which accepts the byte and deposits it on the disk surface.

Next, we take a closer look at buffering, focusing mainly on techniques for managing buffers to improve performance. Some techniques include double buffering, buffer pooling, locate-mode buffering, and scatter/gather buffering.

We conclude with a second look at I/O layers, this time concentrating on UNIX. We see that every I/O system call begins with a call to the UNIX kernel, which knows nothing about the logical structure of a file, treating all data essentially the same—as a sequence of bytes to be transmitted to some external device. In doing its work the I/O system in the kernel invokes four tables: a file descriptor table, an open file table, an inode table, and a file access table in the file's inode. Once the kernel has determined which device to use and how to access it, it calls on a device driver to carry out the actual accessing.

Although it treats every file as a sequence of bytes, the kernel I/O system deals differently with three different types of I/O: block I/O, character I/O, and network I/O. In this text we concentrate on block I/O. We look briefly at the special role of the file system within the kernel, describing how it uses links to connect file names in directories to their corresponding inodes. Finally, we remark on the reasons that magnetic tape does not fit well into the UNIX paradigm for I/O.

■ KEY TERMS

bpi. Bits per inch per track. On a disk, data is recorded serially on tracks. On a tape, data are recorded in parallel on several tracks, so a 6,250-bpi nine-track tape contains 6,250 bytes per inch, when all nine tracks are taken into account (one track being used for parity).

Block. Unit of data organization corresponding to the amount of data transferred in a single access. *Block* often refers to a collection of records, but it may be a collection of sectors (see *cluster*) whose size has no correspondence to the organization of the data. A block is sometimes called a physical record; a sector is sometimes called a block.

Block device. In UNIX, a device such as a disk drive that is organized in blocks and accessed accordingly.

Block I/O. I/O between a computer and a block device.

Block organization. Disk drive organization that allows the user to define the size and organization of blocks, and then access a block by giving its block address or the key of one of its records. (See *sector organization*.)

Blocking factor. The number of records stored in one block.

Character device. In UNIX, a device such as a keyboard or printer (or tape drive when stream I/O is used) that sends or receives data in the form of a stream of characters.

Character I/O. I/O between a computer and a character device.

Cluster. Minimum unit of space allocation on a sectored disk, consisting of one or more contiguous sectors. The use of large clusters can improve sequential access times by guaranteeing the ability to read longer spans of data without seeking. Small clusters tend to decrease internal fragmentation.

Controller. Device that directly controls the operation of one or more secondary storage devices, such as disk drives and magnetic tape units.

Count subblock. On block-organized drives, a small block that precedes each data block and contains information about the data block, such as its byte count and its address.

Cylinder. The set of tracks on a disk that are directly above and below each other. All of the tracks in a given cylinder can be accessed without having to move the access arm; that is, they can be accessed without the expense of seek time.

Descriptor table. In UNIX, a table associated with a single process that links all of the file descriptors generated by that process to corresponding entries in an open file table.

Device driver. In UNIX, an I/O processor program invoked by the kernel that performs I/O for a particular device.

Direct access storage device (DASD). Disk or other secondary storage device that permits access to a specific sector or block of data without first requiring the reading of the blocks that precede it.

Direct memory access (DMA). Transfer of data directly between RAM and peripheral devices, without significant involvement by the CPU.

Disk cache. A segment of RAM configured to contain pages of data from a disk. Disk caches can lead to substantial improvements in access time when access requests exhibit a high degree of locality.

Disk pack. An assemblage of magnetic disks mounted on the same vertical shaft. A pack of disks is treated as a single unit consisting of a number of cylinders equivalent to the number of tracks per surface. If disk packs are removable, different packs can be mounted on the same drive at different times, providing a convenient form of offline storage for data that can be accessed directly.

Effective recording density. Recording density after taking into account the space used by interblock gaps, nondata subblocks, and other space-consuming items that accompany data.

Effective transmission rate. Transmission rate after taking into account the time used to locate and transmit the block of data in which a desired record occurs.

Extent. One or more adjacent clusters allocated as part (or all) of a file. The number of extents in a file reflects how dispersed the file is over the disk. The more dispersed a file, the more seeking must be done in moving from one part of the file to another.

File allocation table (FAT). A table that contains mappings to the physical locations of all the clusters in all files on disk storage.

File manager. The part of an operating system that is responsible for managing files, including a collection of programs whose responsibilities range from keeping track of files to invoking I/O processes that transmit information between primary and secondary storage.

File structure. In connection with the open file table in a UNIX kernel, the term *file structure* refers to a structure that holds information the kernel needs about an open file. File structure information includes such things as the file's read/write mode, number of processes currently using it, and the offset within the file to be used for the next read or write.

Filesystem. In UNIX, a hierarchical collection of files, usually kept on a single secondary device, such as a hard disk or CD-ROM.

Fixed disk. A disk drive with platters that may not be removed.

Formatting. The process of preparing a disk for data storage, involving such things as laying out sectors, setting up the disk's file allocation table, and checking for damage to the recording medium.

Fragmentation. Space that goes unused within a cluster, block, track, or other unit of physical storage. For instance, track fragmentation occurs when space on a track goes unused because there is not enough space left to accommodate a complete block.

Frame. A one-bit-wide slice of tape, usually representing a single byte.

Hard link. In UNIX, an entry in a directory that connects a file name to the inode of the corresponding file. There can be several hard links to a single file; hence a file can have several names. A file is not deleted until all hard links to the file are deleted.

Index node. In UNIX, a data structure associated with a file that describes the file. An index node includes such information as a file's type, its owner and group IDs, and a list of the disk blocks that comprise the file. A more common name for index node is *inode*.

Inode. See *index node*.

Interblock gap. An interval of blank space that separates sectors, blocks, or subblocks on tape or disk. In the case of tape, the gap provides sufficient space for the tape to accelerate or decelerate when starting or stopping. On both tapes and disks the gaps enable the read/write heads to tell accurately when one sector (or block or subblock) ends and another begins.

Interleaving factor. Since it is often not possible to read physically adjacent sectors of a disk, logically adjacent sectors are sometimes arranged so they are not physically adjacent. This is called interleaving. The interleaving factor refers to the number of physical sectors the next logically adjacent sector is located from the current sector being read or written.

I/O processor. A device that carries out I/O tasks, allowing the CPU to work on non-I/O tasks.

Kernel. The central part of the UNIX operating system.

Key subblock. On block-addressable drives, a block that contains the key of the last record in the data block that follows it, allowing the drive to search among the blocks on a track for a block containing a certain key, without having to load the blocks into primary memory.

Mass storage system. General term applied to storage units with large capacity. Also applied to very high-capacity secondary storage systems that are capable of transmitting data between a disk and any of several thousand tape cartridges within a few seconds.

Nominal recording density. Recording density on a disk track or magnetic tape without taking into account the effects of gaps or non-data subblocks.

Nominal transmission rate. Transmission rate of a disk or tape unit without taking into account the effects of such extra operations as seek time for disks and interblock gap traversal time for tapes.

Open file table. In UNIX, a table owned by the kernel with an entry, called a file structure, for each open file. See *file structure*.

Parity. An error-checking technique in which an extra parity bit accompanies each byte and is set in such a way that the total number of 1 bits is even (even parity) or odd (odd parity).

Platter. One disk in the stack of disks on a disk drive.

Process. An executing program. In UNIX, several instances of the same program can be executing at the same time, as separate processes. The kernel keeps a separate file descriptor table for each process.

RAM disk. Block of RAM configured to simulate a disk.

Rotational delay. The time it takes for the disk to rotate so the desired sector is under the read/write head.

Scatter/gather I/O. Buffering techniques that involve, on input, scattering incoming data into more than one buffer, and, on output, gathering data from several buffers to be output as a single chunk of data.

Sector. The fixed-sized data blocks that together make up the tracks on certain disk drives. Sectors are the smallest addressable unit on a disk whose tracks are made up of sectors.

Sector organization. Disk drive organization that uses sectors.

Seek time. The time required to move the access arm to the correct cylinder on a disk drive.

Sequential access device. A device, such as a magnetic tape unit or card reader, in which the medium (e.g., tape) must be accessed from the beginning. Sometimes called a serial device.

Socket. In UNIX, a socket is an abstraction that serves as an endpoint of communication within some domain. For example, a socket can be used to provide direct communication between two computers. Although in some ways the kernel treats sockets like files, we do not deal with sockets in this text.

Soft link. See *symbolic link*.

Special file. In UNIX, the term *special file* refers to a stream of characters and control signals that drive some device, such as a line printer or a graphics device.

Streaming tape drive. A tape drive whose primary purpose is dumping large amounts of data from disk to tape or from tape to disk.

Subblock. When blocking is used, there are often separate groupings of information concerned with each individual block. For example, a count subblock, a key subblock, and a data subblock might all be present.

Symbolic link. In UNIX, an entry in a directory that gives the pathname of a file. Since a symbolic link is an indirect pointer to a file, it is not as closely associated with the file as a hard link. Symbolic links can point to directories, or even to files in other filesystems.

Track. The set of bytes on a single surface of a disk that can be accessed without seeking (without moving the access arm). The surface of a disk can be thought of as a series of concentric circles, with each circle corresponding to a particular position of the access arm and read/write heads. Each of these circles is a track.

Transfer time. Once the data we want is under the read/write head, we have to wait for it to pass under the head as we read it. The amount of time required for this motion and reading is the transfer time.

■ EXERCISES

1. Determine as well as you can what the journey of a byte would be like on your system. You may have to consult technical reference manuals that describe your computer's file management system, operating system, and peripheral devices. You may also want to talk to local gurus who have experience using your system.

2. Suppose you are writing a list of names to a text file, one name per write statement. Why is it not a good idea to close the file after every write, and then reopen it before the next write?

3. Find out what utility routines are available on your computer system for monitoring I/O performance and disk utilization. If you have a large computing system, there are different routines available for different kinds of users, depending on what privileges and responsibilities they have.

4. When you create or open a file in C or Pascal, you must provide certain information to your computer's file manager so it can handle your file properly. Compared to certain languages, such as PL/I or COBOL, the amount of information you must provide in C or Pascal is very small. Find a text or manual on PL/I or COBOL and look up the ENVIRONMENT file description attribute, which can be used to tell the file manager a great deal about how you expect a file to be organized and used. Compare PL/I or COBOL with C or Pascal in terms of the types of file specifications available to the programmer.

5. Much is said in section 3.1 about how disk space is organized physically to store files. Assume that no such complex organization is used and that every file must occupy a single contiguous piece of a disk, somewhat the way a file is stored on tape. How does this simplify disk storage? What problems does it create?

6. A disk drive uses 512-byte sectors. If a program requests that a 128-byte record be written to disk, the file manager may have to read a sector from the disk before it can write the record. Why? What could you do to decrease the number of times such an extra read is likely to occur?

7. We have seen that some disk operating systems allocate storage space on disks in clusters and/or extents, rather than sectors, so the size of any file must be a multiple of a cluster or extent.

  a. What are some advantages and potential disadvantages of this method of allocating disk space?

  b. How appropriate would the use of large extents be for an application that mostly involves sequential access of very large files?

  c. How appropriate would large extents be for a computing system that serves a large number of C programmers? (C programs tend to be small, so there are likely to be many small files that contain C programs.)

  d. The VAX record management system uses a default cluster size of three 512-byte sectors but lets a user reformat a drive with any cluster size from 1 to 65,535 sectors. When might a cluster size larger than three sectors be desirable? When might a smaller cluster size be desirable?

8. In early UNIX systems, inodes were kept together on one part of a disk, while the corresponding data was scattered elsewhere on the disk. Later editions divided disk drives into groups of adjacent cylinders called cylinder groups, in which each cylinder group contains inodes and their corresponding data. How does this new organization improve performance?

9. In early UNIX systems, the minimum block size was 512 bytes, with a cluster size of one. The block size was increased to 1,024 bytes in 4.0BSD, more than doubling its throughput. Explain how this could occur.

10. Draw pictures that illustrate the role of fragmentation in determining the numbers in Table 3.2, section 3.1.7.

11. The IBM 3350 disk drive uses block addressing. The two subblock organizations described in the text are available:

☐ Count-data, where the extra space used by count subblock and inter-block gaps is equivalent to 185 bytes; and

☐ Count-key-data, where the extra space used by the count and key subblocks and accompanying gaps is equivalent to 267 bytes, plus the key size.

An IBM 3350 has 19,069 usable bytes available per track, 30 tracks per cylinder, and 555 cylinders per drive. Suppose you have a file with 350,000

80-byte records that you want to store on a 3350 drive. Answer the following questions. Unless otherwise directed, assume that the blocking factor is 10 and that the count-data subblock organization is used.

a. How many blocks can be stored on one track? How many records?

b. How many blocks can be stored on one track if the count-key-data subblock organization is used and key size is 13 bytes?

c. Make a graph that shows the effect of block size on storage utilization, assuming count-data subblocks. Use the graph to help predict the best and worst possible blocking factor in terms of storage utilization.

d. Assuming that access to the file is always sequential, use the graph from the preceding question to predict the best and worst blocking factor. Justify your answer in terms of efficiency of storage utilization and processing time.

e. How many cylinders are required to hold the file (blocking factor 10 and count-data format)? How much space will go unused due to internal track fragmentation?

f. If the file were stored on contiguous cylinders and if there were no interference from other processes using the disk drive, the average seek time for a random access of the file would be about 12 msec. Use this rate to compute the average time needed to access one record randomly.

g. Explain how retrieval time for random accesses of records is affected by increasing block size. Discuss trade-offs between storage efficiency and retrieval when different block sizes are used. Make a table with different block sizes to illustrate your explanations.

h. Suppose the file is to be sorted and a shell sort is to be used to sort the file. Since the file is too large to read into memory, it will be sorted in place, on the disk. It is estimated (Knuth, 1973b, p. 380) that this requires about $15N1.25$ moves of records, where N represents the total number of records in the file. Each move requires a random access. If all of the preceding is true, how long does it take to sort the file? (As you will see, this is not a very good solution. We provide much better ones in Chapter 7, which deals with cosequential processing.)

12. A sectored disk drive differs from one with a block organization in that there is less of a correspondence between the logical and physical organization of data records or blocks.

For example, consider the Digital RM05 disk drive, which uses sector addressing. It has 32 512-byte sectors per track, 19 tracks per cylinder, and 823 cylinders per drive. From the drive's (and drive controller's) point of view, a file is just a vector of bytes divided into 512-byte sectors. Since the drive knows nothing about where one record ends and another begins, a record can span two or more sectors, tracks, or cylinders.

One common way that records are formatted on the RM05 is to place a two-byte field at the beginning of each block, giving the number of bytes of data, followed by the data itself. There is no extra gap and no other overhead. Assuming that this organization is used, and that you want to store a file with 350,000 80-byte records, answer the following questions:

a. How many records can be stored on one track if one record is stored per block?

b. How many cylinders are required to hold the file?

c. How might you block records so each physical record access results in 10 actual records being accessed? What are the benefits of doing this?

13. Suppose you have a collection of 500 large images stored in files, one image per file, and you wish to "animate" these images by displaying them in sequence on a workstation at a rate of at least 15 images per second over a high-speed network. Your secondary storage consists of a disk farm with 30 disk drives, and your disk manager permits striping over as many as 30 drives, if you request it. Your drives are guaranteed to perform I/O at a steady rate of 2 megabytes per second. Each image is 3 megabytes in size. Network transmission speeds are not a problem.

a. Describe in broad terms the steps involved in doing such an animation in real time from disk.

b. Describe the performance issues that you have to consider in implementing the animation. Use numbers.

c. How might you configure your I/O system to achieve the desired performance?

14. Consider the 1,000,000-record mailing list file discussed in the text. The file is to be backed up on 2,400-foot reels of 6,250-bpi tape with 0.3-inch interblock gaps. Tape speed is 200 inches per second.

a. Show that only one tape would be required to back up the file if a blocking factor of 50 is used.

b. If a blocking factor of 50 is used, how many extra records could be accommodated on a 2,400-foot tape?

c. What is the effective recording density when a blocking factor of 50 is used?

d. How large does the blocking factor have to be to achieve the maximum effective recording density? What negative results can result from increasing the blocking factor? (*Note:* An I/O buffer large enough to hold a block must be allocated.)

e. What would be the minimum blocking factor required to fit the file onto the tape?

f. If a blocking factor of 50 is used, how long would it take to read one block, including the gap? What would the effective transmission rate be? How long would it take to read the entire file?

g. How long would it take to perform a binary search for one record in the file, assuming that it is not possible to read backwards on the tape? (Assume that it takes 60 seconds to rewind the tape.) Compare this with the expected average time it would take for a sequential search for one record.

h. We implicitly assume in our discussions of tape performance that the tape drive is always reading or writing at full speed, so no time is lost by starting and stopping. This is not necessarily the case. For example, some drives automatically stop after writing each block.

Suppose that the extra time it takes to start before reading a block and to stop after reading the block totals 1 msec, and that the drive must start before and stop after reading each block. How much will the effective transmission rate be decreased due to starting and stopping if the blocking factor is 1? What if it is 50?

15. Why are there interblock gaps on tapes? In other words, why do we not just jam all records into one block?

16. The use of large blocks can lead to severe internal fragmentation of tracks on disks. Does this occur when tapes are used? Explain.

■ FURTHER READINGS

Many textbooks contain more detailed information on the material covered in this chapter. In the area of operating systems and file management systems, we have found the operating system texts by Deitel (1984), Peterson and Silberschatz (1985), and Madnick and Donovan (1974) useful. Hanson (1982) has a great deal of material on blocking and buffering, secondary storage devices, and performance. Flores's book (1973) on peripheral devices may be a bit dated, but it contains a comprehensive treatment of the subject.

Bohl (1981) provides a thorough treatment of mainframe-oriented IBM DASDs. Chaney and Johnson (1984) wrote a good article on maximizing hard disk performance on small computers. Ritchie and Thompson (1974), Kernighan and Ritchie (1978), Deitel (1984), and McKusick et al. (1984) provide information on how file I/O is handled in the UNIX operating system. The latter provides a good case study of ways in which a filesystem can be altered to provide substantially faster throughput for certain applications. A comprehensive coverage of UNIX I/O from the design perspective can be found in Leffler et al. (1989).

Information on specific systems and devices can often be found in manuals and documentation published by manufacturers. (Unfortunately, information about how software actually works is often proprietary and therefore not available.) If you use a VAX, we recommend the manuals *Introduction to the VAX Record Management Services* (Digital, 1978), *VAX Software Handbook* (Digital, 1982), and *Peripherals Handbook* (Digital, 1981). UNIX users will find it useful to look at the Bell Laboratories' monograph *The UNIX I/O System* by Dennis Ritchie (1979). Users of IBM PCs will find the *Disk Operating System* (Microsoft, 1983 or later) manual useful.

Fundamental File Structure Concepts

4

CHAPTER OBJECTIVES

■ Introduce file structure concepts dealing with

- □ Stream files;
- □ Field and record boundaries;
- □ Fixed-length and variable-length fields and records;
- □ Search keys and canonical forms;
- □ Sequential search;
- □ Direct access; and
- □ File access and file organization.

■ Examine other kinds of file structures in terms of

- □ Abstract data models;
- □ Metadata;
- □ Object-oriented file access; and
- □ Extensibility.

■ Examine issues of portability and standardization.

4.1 Field and Record Organization

When we build file structures we are imposing order on data. In this chapter we investigate the many forms that this ordering can take. We begin by looking at the base case: a file organized as a stream of bytes.

4.1.1 A Stream File

Suppose the file we are building contains name and address information. A program to accept names and addresses from the keyboard, writing them out as a stream of consecutive bytes to a file with the logical name OUTPUT, is described in the pseudocode shown in Fig. 4.1.

Implementations of this program in both C and Pascal, called *writstrm.c* and *writstrm.pas,* are provided in the C and Pascal Programs sections at the end of this chapter. You should type in this program, working in either C or Pascal, compile it, and run it. We use it as the basis for a number of experiments, and you can get a better feel for the differences between

```
PROGRAM: writstrm

    get output file name and open it with the logical name OUTPUT

    get LAST name as input
    while ( LAST name has a length > 0)
        get FIRST name, ADDRESS, CITY, STATE and ZIP as input

        write LAST     to the file OUTPUT
        write FIRST    to the file OUTPUT
        write ADDRESS  to the file OUTPUT
        write CITY     to the file OUTPUT
        write STATE    to the file OUTPUT
        write ZIP      to the file OUTPUT

        get LAST name as input
    endwhile

    close OUTPUT

end PROGRAM
```

FIGURE 4.1 Program to write out a name and address file as a stream of bytes.

the file structures we are discussing if you perform the experiments your-self.

The following names and addresses are used as input to the program:

```
John Ames                Alan Mason
123 Maple                90 Eastgate
Stillwater, OK 74075     Ada, OK 74820
```

When we list the output file on our terminal screen, here is what we see:

```
AmesJohn123 MapleStillwaterOK74075MasonAlan90 EastgateAdaOK74820
```

The program writes the information out to the file precisely as specified: as a stream of bytes containing no added information. But in meeting our specifications, the program creates a kind of "reverse Humpty-Dumpty" problem. Once we put all that information together as a single byte stream, there is no way to get it apart again.

We have lost the integrity of the fundamental organizational units of our input data; these fundamental units are not the individual characters, but meaningful aggregates of characters, such as "John Ames" or "123 Maple."

When we are working with files, we call these fundamental aggregates *fields*. A field is *the smallest logically meaningful unit of information in a file.*[†]

A field is a logical notion; it is a *conceptual tool*. A field does not necessarily exist in any physical sense, yet it is important to the file's structure. When we write out our name and address information as a stream of undifferentiated bytes, we lose track of the fields that make the information meaningful. We need to organize the file in some way that lets us keep the information divided into fields.

4.1.2 Field Structures

There are many ways of adding structure to files to maintain the identity of fields. Four of the most common methods are

- Force the fields into a predictable length.
- Begin each field with a length indicator.
- Place a *delimiter* at the end of each field to separate it from the next field.
- Use a "keyword = value" expression to identify each field and its contents.

Method 1: Fix the Length of Fields   The fields in our sample file vary in their length. If we force the fields into predictable lengths, then we can pull them back out of the file simply by counting our way to the end of the field. We can define a structure in C or a record in Pascal to hold these fixed-length fields, as shown in Fig. 4.2.

Using this kind of fixed-field length structure changes our output so it looks like that shown in Fig. 4.3(a). Simple arithmetic is sufficient to let us recover the data in terms of the original fields.

One obvious disadvantage of this approach is that adding all the padding required to bring the fields up to a fixed length makes the file much larger. Rather than using 4 bytes to store the last name *Ames,* we use 10. We can also encounter problems with data that is too long to fit into the allocated amount of space. We could solve this second problem by fixing all the fields at lengths that are large enough to cover all cases, but this would just make the first problem of wasted space in the file even worse.

[†]Readers should not confuse the term *field* and *record* with the meanings given to them by some programming languages, including Pascal. In Pascal, a record is an aggregate data structure that can contain members of different types, where each member is referred to as a field. As we shall see, there is often a direct correspondence between these definitions of the terms and the fields and records that are used in files. However, the terms *field* and *record* as we use them have much more general meanings than they do in Pascal.

In C:	In Pascal:

```
In C:
struct {
    char last[10];
    char first[10];
    char address[15];
    char city[15];
    char state[2];
    char zip[9];
} set_of_fields;
```

```
In Pascal:
TYPE
    set_of_fields = RECORD
        last    : packed array [1..10] of char;
        first   : packed array [1..10] of char;
        address : packed array [1..15] of char;
        city    : packed array [1..15] of char;
        state   : packed array [1..2]  of char;
        zip     : packed array [1..9]  of char;
    END;
```

FIGURE 4.2 Fixed-length fields.

Because of these difficulties, the fixed-field approach to structuring data is often inappropriate for data that inherently contain a large amount of variability in the length of fields, such as names and addresses. But there are kinds of data for which fixed-length fields are highly appropriate. If every field is already fixed in length, or if there is very little variation in field lengths, using a file structure consisting of a continuous stream of bytes organized into fixed-length fields is often a very good solution.

Method 2: Begin Each Field with a Length Indicator Another way to make it possible to count to the end of a field involves storing the field length just ahead of the field, as illustrated in Fig. 4.3(b). If the fields are not too long (length less than 256 bytes), it is possible to store the length in a single byte at the start of each field.

Method 3: Separate the Fields with Delimiters We can also preserve the identity of fields by separating them with delimiters. All we need to do is choose some special character or sequence of characters that will not appear within a field and then *insert* that delimiter into the file after writing each field.

The choice of a delimiter character can be very important since it must be a character that does not get in the way of processing. In many instances *white-space characters* (blank, new line, tab) make excellent delimiters because they provide a clean separation between fields when we list them on the console. Also, most programming languages include I/O statements that, by default, assume that fields are separated by white space.

Unfortunately, white space would be a poor choice for our file since blanks often occur as legitimate characters within an address field.

```
Ames        John      123 Maple    Stillwater  OK74075377-1808
Mason       Alan       90 Eastgate Ada         OK74820
```

(a) Field lengths fixed. Place blanks in the spaces where the phone number would go.

```
Ames|John|123 Maple|Stillwater|OK|74075|377-1808|
Mason|Alan|90 Eastgate|Ada|OK|74820||
```

(b) Delimiters are used to indicate the end of a field. Place the delimiter for the "empty" field immediately after the delimiter for the previous field.

```
Ames|…|Stillwater|OK|74075|377-1808|#Mason|… 90Eastgate|Ada|OK|74820|#…
```

(c) Place the field for business phone at the end of the record. If the end-of-record mark is encountered, assume that the field is missing.

```
SURNAME=Ames|FIRSTNAME=John|STREET=123 Maple|…|ZIP=74075|PHONE=377-1808|#…
```

(d) Use a keyword to identify each field. If the keyword is missing, the corresponding field is assumed to be missing.

FIGURE 4.3 Four methods for organizing fields within records to account for possible missing fields. In the examples, the second record is missing the phone number.

Therefore, instead of white space we use the vertical bar character as our delimiter, so our file appears as in Fig. 4.3(c). Readers should modify the original stream-of-bytes programs, *writstrm.c* and *writstrm.pas* (found in the C and Pascal Programs sections at the end of this chapter), changing them so they place a delimiter after each field. We use this delimited field format in the next few sample programs.

Method 4: Use a "Keyword = Value" Expression to Identify Fields
This option, illustrated in Fig. 4.2(d), has an advantage that the others do not: It is the first structure in which a field provides information about itself. Such *self-describing* structures can be very useful tools for organizing files

in many applications. It is easy to tell what fields are contained in a file, even if we don't know ahead of time what fields the file is supposed to contain. It is also a good format for dealing with missing fields. If a field is missing, this format makes it obvious, because the keyword is simply not there.

You may have noticed in Fig. 4.3(d) that this format is used in combination with another format, a delimiter to separate fields. While this may not always be necessary, in this case it is helpful because it shows the division between each value and the keyword for the following field.

Unfortunately, for the address file this format also wastes a lot of space. Fifty percent or more of the file's space could be taken up by the keywords. But there are applications in which this format does not demand so much overhead. We discuss some of these applications in section 4.5.

4.1.3 Reading a Stream of Fields

Given modified versions of *writstrm.c* and *writstrm.pas* that use delimiters to separate fields, we can write a program called *readstrm* that reads the stream of bytes back in, breaking the stream into fields. It is convenient to conceive of the program on two levels, as shown in the pseudocode description provided in Fig. 4.4. The outer level of the program opens the file and then calls the function *readfield( )* until *readfield( )* returns a field length of zero, indicating that there are no more fields to read. The *readfield( )* function, in turn, works through the file, character by character, collecting characters into a field until the function encounters a delimiter or the end of the file. The function returns a count of the characters that are found in the field. Implementations of *readstrm* in both C and Pascal are included with the programs at the end of this chapter.

When this program is run using our delimited-field version of the file containing data for John Ames and Alan Mason, the output looks like this:

```
Field #  1: Ames
Field #  2: John
Field #  3: 123 Maple
Field #  4: Stillwater
Field #  5: OK
Field #  6: 74075
Field #  7: Mason
Field #  8: Alan
Field #  9: 90 Eastgate
Field # 10: Ada
Field # 11: OK
Field # 12: 74820
```

```
Define Constant: DELIMITER = '¦'

PROGRAM: readstrm

    get input file name and open as INPUT
    initialize FIELD_COUNT

    FIELD_LENGTH := readfield (INPUT, FIELD_CONTENT)
    while ( FIELD_LENGTH > 0 )

        increment the FIELD_COUNT
        write FIELD_COUNT and FIELD_CONTENT to the screen
        FIELD_LENGTH := readfield (INPUT, FIELD_CONTENT)

    endwhile

    close INPUT
end PROGRAM


FUNCTION: readfield (INPUT, FIELD_CONTENT)

    initialize I
    initialize CH

    while (not EOF (INPUT) and CH does not equal DELIMITER)

        read a character from INPUT into CH
        increment I
        FIELD_CONTENT [I] := CH

    endwhile
    return (length of field that was read)

end FUNCTION
```

FIGURE 4.4 Program to read fields from a file and display them on the screen.

Clearly, we now preserve the notion of a field as we store and retrieve these data. But something is still missing. We do not really think of this file as a stream of fields. In fact, the fields need to be grouped into sets. The first six fields are a set associated with someone named John Ames. The next six are a set of fields associated with Alan Mason. We call these sets of fields *records*.

4.1.4 Record Structures

A *record* can be defined as *a set of fields that belong together when the file is viewed in terms of a higher level of organization*. Like the notion of a field, a record is another conceptual tool. It is another level of organization that we impose on the data to preserve meaning. Records do not necessarily exist in the file in any physical sense, yet they are an important logical notion included in the file's structure.

Here are some of the most often used methods for organizing a file into records:

☐ Require that the records be a predictable number of bytes in length.

☐ Require that the records be a predictable number of fields in length.

☐ Begin each record with a length indicator consisting of a count of the number of bytes that the record contains.

☐ Use a second file to keep track of the beginning byte address for each record.

☐ Place a delimiter at the end of each record to separate it from the next record.

Method 1: Make Records a Predictable Number of Bytes (Fixed-length Records) ˙ A *fixed-length record file* is one in which each record contains the same number of bytes. This method of recognizing records is analogous to the first method we discussed for making fields recognizable. As we will see in the chapters that follow, fixed-length record structures are among the most commonly used methods for organizing files.

The C structure *set_of_fields* (or the Pascal RECORD of the same name) that we define in our discussion of fixed-length fields is actually an example of a fixed-length *record* as well as an example of fixed-length fields. We have a fixed number of fields, each with a predetermined length, which combine to make a fixed-length record. This kind of field and record structure is illustrated in Fig. 4.5(a).

It is important to realize, however, that fixing the number of bytes in a record does not imply that the sizes or number of fields in the record must be fixed. Fixed-length records are frequently used as containers to hold variable numbers of variable length fields. It is also possible to mix fixed- and variable-length fields within a record. Figure 4.5(b) illustrates how variable-length fields might be placed in a fixed-length record.

Method 2: Make Records a Predictable Number of Fields   Rather than specifying that each record in a file contain some fixed number of bytes, we can specify that it will contain a fixed number of fields. This is a good way to organize the records in the name and address file we have been

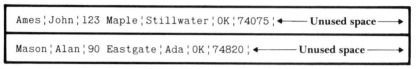

| Ames | John | 123 Maple | Stillwater | 0K74075 |
| Mason | Alan | 90 Eastgate | Ada | 0K74820 |

(a)

Ames¦John¦123 Maple¦Stillwater¦0K¦74075¦ ◄——— Unused space ———►

Mason¦Alan¦90 Eastgate¦Ada¦0K¦74820¦ ◄——— Unused space ———►

(b)

Ames¦John¦123 Maple¦Stillwater¦0K¦74075¦Mason¦Alan¦90 Eastgate¦Ada¦0K . . .

(c)

FIGURE 4.5 Three ways of making the lengths of records constant and predictable. (a) Counting bytes: fixed-length records with fixed-length fields. (b) Counting bytes: fixed-length records with variable-length fields. (c) Counting fields: six fields per record.

looking at. The *writstrm* program asks for six pieces of information for every person, so there are six contiguous fields in the file for each record (Fig. 4.5c). We could modify *readstrm* to recognize fields simply by counting the fields *modulo* six, outputting record boundary information to the screen every time the count starts over.

Method 3: Begin Each Record with a Length Indicator   We can communicate the length of records by beginning each record with a field containing an integer that indicates how many bytes there are in the rest of the record (Fig. 4.6a). This is a commonly used method for handling variable-length records. We look at it more closely in the next section.

Method 4: Use an Index to Keep Track of Addresses   We can use an *index* to keep a byte offset for each record in the original file. The byte offsets allow us to find the beginning of each successive record and also let us compute the length of each record. We look up the position of a record in the index and then seek to the record in the data file. Figure 4.6(b) illustrates this two-file mechanism.

Method 5: Place a Delimiter at the End of Each Record   This option, at a record level, is exactly analogous to the solution we used to keep the *fields* distinct in the sample program we developed. As with fields, the delimiter character must not get in the way of processing. Because we often want to read files directly at our console, a common choice of a record delimiter for files that contain readable text is the end-of-line character (carriage return/new-line pair or, on UNIX systems, just a new-line character—'\n'). In Fig 4.6(c) we use a '#' character as the record delimiter.

4.1.5 A Record Structure That Uses a Length Indicator

Not one of these approaches to preserving the idea of a *record* in a file is appropriate for all situations. Selection of a method for record organization depends on the nature of the data and on what you need to do with it. We begin by looking at a record structure that uses a record–length field at the beginning of the record. This approach lets us preserve the *variability* in the length of records that is inherent in our initial stream file.

Writing the Variable-length Records to the File   We call the program that builds this new, variable-length record structure *writrec*. The set of programs at the end of this chapter contains versions of this program in C and Pascal. Implementing this program is partially a matter of building on

FIGURE 4.6 Record structures for variable-length records. (a) Beginning each record with a length indicator. (b) Using an index file to keep track of record addresses. (c) Placing the delimiter '#' at the end of each record.

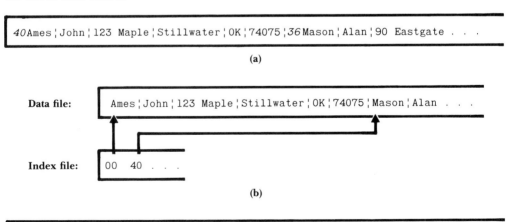

the *writstrm* program that we created earlier in this chapter, but also involves addressing some new problems:

☐ If we want to put a length indicator at the *beginning* of every record (before any other fields), we must know the sum of the lengths of the fields in each record before we can begin writing the record to the file. We need to accumulate the entire contents of a record in a *buffer* before writing it out.

☐ In what form should we write the record-length field to the file? As a binary integer? As a series of ASCII characters?

The concept of buffering is one we run into again and again as we work with files. In the case of *writrec*, the buffer can simply be a character array into which we place the fields and field delimiters as we collect them. Resetting the buffer length to zero and adding information to the buffer can be handled using the loop logic provided in Fig. 4.7.

Representing the Record Length   The question of how to represent the record length is a little more difficult. One option would be to write the length in the form of a two-byte binary integer before each record. This is a natural solution in C, since it does not require us to go to the trouble of converting the record length into character form. Furthermore, we can represent much bigger numbers with an integer than we can with the same number of ASCII bytes (e.g., 32,767 versus 99). It is also conceptually

FIGURE 4.7 Main program logic for *writrec*.

```
get LAST name as input
while ( LAST name has a length > 0 )
    set length of string in BUFFER to zero
    concatenate: BUFFER + LAST name + DELIMITER

    while ( input fields exist for record )
        get the FIELD
        concatenate: BUFFER + FIELD + DELIMITER
    endwhile

    write length of string in BUFFER to the file
    write the string in BUFFER to the file

    get LAST name as input
endwhile
```

interesting, since it illustrates the use of a fixed-length, binary field in combination with variable-length character fields.

Although we could use this same solution for a Pascal implementation, we might choose, instead, to account for some important differences between C and Pascal:

☐ Unlike C, Pascal automatically converts binary integers into character representations of those integers if we are writing to a text file. Consequently, it is no trouble at all to convert the record length into a character form: It happens automatically.

☐ In Pascal, a file is defined as a sequence of elements of a single type. Since we have a file of variable-length strings of characters, the natural type for the file is that of a character.

In short, the easiest thing to do in C is to store the integers in the file as fixed-length, two-byte fields containing integers. In Pascal it is easier to make use of the automatic conversion of integers into characters for text files. File structure design is always an exercise in flexibility. Neither of these approaches is correct; good design consists of choosing the approach that is most *appropriate* for a given language and computing environment. In the programs included at the end of this chapter, we have implemented our record structure both ways, using integer-length fields in C and character representations in Pascal. The output from the Pascal implementation is shown in Fig. 4.8. Each record now has a record-length field preceding the data fields. This field is delimited by a blank. For example, the first record (for John Ames) contains 40 characters, counting from the first 'A' in "Ames" to the final delimiter after "74075," so the characters '4' and '0' are placed before the record, followed by a blank.

Since the C version of *writrec* uses binary integers for the record length, we cannot simply print it to a console screen. We need a way to interpret the noncharacter portion of the file. For this, we introduce in the next section the file dump, a valuable tool for viewing the contents of files. But first, let's look at a program that will read in any file that is written by *writrec*.

Reading the Variable-length Records from the File Given our file structure of variable-length records preceded by record-length fields, it is

FIGURE 4.8 Records preceded by record-length fields in character form.

```
40 Ames¦John¦123 Maple¦Stillwater¦OK¦74075¦36 Mason¦Alan¦90
Eastgate¦Ada¦OK¦74820:
```

```
PROGRAM: readrec

    open input file as INP_FILE
    initialize SCAN_POS to 0
    RECORD_LENGTH := get_rec(INP_FILE, BUFFER)
    while (RECORD_LENGTH > 0)
        SCAN_POS := get_fld(FIELD,BUFFER,SCAN_POS,RECORD_LENGTH)
        while (SCAN_POS > 0)
            print FIELD on the SCREEN
            SCAN_POS := get_fld(FIELD,BUFFER,SCAN_POS,RECORD_LENGTH)
        endwhile

        RECORD_LENGTH := get_rec(INP_FILE, BUFFER)
    endwhile
end PROGRAM


FUNCTION: get_rec(INP_FILE, BUFFER)

    if EOF (INP_FILE) then return 0

    read the RECORD_LENGTH
    read the record contents into the BUFFER
    return the RECORD_LENGTH

end FUNCTION


FUNCTION: get_fld(FIELD,BUFFER,SCAN_POS,RECORD_LENGTH)

    if SCAN_POS == RECORD_LENGTH then return 0

    get a character CH at the SCAN_POS in the BUFFER
    while (SCAN_POS < RECORD_LENGTH and CH is not a DELIMITER)
        place CH into the FIELD
        increment the SCAN_POS
        get a character CH at the SCAN_POS in the BUFFER
    endwhile


    return the SCAN_POS

end FUNCTION
```

FIGURE 4.9 Main program logic for *readrec*, along with functions *get_rec( )* and *get_fld( )*.

easy to write a program that reads through the file, record by record, displaying the fields from each of the records on the screen. The program logic is shown in Fig. 4.9. The main program calls the function *get_rec( )* that reads records into a buffer; this call continues until *get_rec( )* returns a value of 0. Once *get_rec( )* places a record's contents into a buffer, the buffer is passed to the function *get_fld( )*. The call to *get_fld( )* includes a scanning position (SCAN_POS) in the argument list. Starting at the SCAN_POS, *get_fld( )* reads characters from the buffer into a field until either a delimiter or the end of the record is reached. Function *get_fld( )* returns the SCAN_POS for use on the next call. Implementations of *writrec* and *readrec* in both C and Pascal are included along with the other programs at the end of this chapter.

4.1.6 Mixing Numbers and Characters: Use of a File Dump

File dumps give us the ability to look inside a file at the actual bytes that are stored there. Consider, for instance, the record-length information in the Pascal program output that we were examining a moment ago. The length of the Ames record, which is the first one in the file, is 40 characters, including delimiters. In the Pascal version of *writrec,* where we store the ASCII character representation of this decimal number, the actual bytes stored *in the file* look like the representation in Fig. 4.10(a). In the C implementation, where we choose to represent the length field as a two-byte integer, the bytes look like the representation in Fig. 4.10(b).

As you can see the *number* 40 is not the same as the set of characters '4' and '0'. The hex value of the *binary integer* 40 is 0x28; the hex values of the *characters* '4' and '0' are 0 x 34 and 0 x 30. (We are using the C language convention of identifying hexadecimal numbers through the use of the prefix 0x.) So, when we are storing a number in ASCII form, it is the hex

FIGURE 4.10 The number 40, stored as ASCII characters and as a short integer.

	Decimal value of number	Hex value stored in bytes		ASCII character form
(a) 40 stored as ASCII chars:	40	34	30	'4' '0'
(b) 40 stored as a 2-byte integer:	40	00	28	'\0' "("

values of the *ASCII characters* that go into the file, not the hex value of the number itself.

Figure 4.10(b) shows the byte representation of the number 40 stored as an integer (this is called storing the number in *binary* form, even though we usually view the output as a hexadecimal number). Now the hexadecimal value stored in the file is that of the number itself. The ASCII characters that happen to be associated with the number's actual hexadecimal value have no obvious relationship to the number. Here is what the version of the file that uses binary integers for record lengths looks like if we simply print it on a terminal screen:

```
(Ames | John | 123 Maple | Stillwater | OK | 74075 |  $Mason|Alan|...
```

0x28 is ascii code for '('

Blank, since '\0' is unprintable.

0x28 is ascii code for '('

Blank; '\0' is unprintable.

The ASCII representations of characters and numbers in the actual record come out nicely enough, but the binary representations of the length fields are displayed cryptically. Let's take a different look at the file, this time using the UNIX dump utility od. Entering the UNIX command

```
        od -xc <filename>
```

produces the following:

```
Offset                 Values
0000000 \0   (   A   m   e   s   |   J   o   h   n   |   1   2   3     ←ASCII
        0028    416d    6573    7c4a    6f68    6e7c    3132    3320  ←Hex
0000020  M   a   p   l   e   |   S   t   i   l   l   w   a   t   e   r
        4d61    706c    657c    5374    696c    6c77    6174    6572
0000040  |   O   K   |   7   4   0   7   5   |  \0   $   M   a   s   o
        7c4f    4b7c    3734    3037    357c    0024    4d61    736f
0000060  n   |   A   l   a   n   |   9   0     E   a   s   t   g   a
        6e7c    416c    616e    7c39    3020    4561    7374    6761
0000100  t   e   |   A   d   a   |   O   K   |   7   4   8   2   0   |
        7465    7c41    6461    7c4f    4b7c    3734    3832    307c
```

As you can see, the display is divided into three different kinds of data. The column on the left labeled *Offset* gives the offset of the first byte of the row that is being displayed. The byte offsets are given in octal form; since each line contains 16 (decimal) bytes, moving from one line to the next adds 020 to the range. Every pair of lines in the printout contains interpretations of the bytes in the file in hexadecimal and ASCII. These representations were requested on the command line with the -xc flag (x = "hex;" c = "character").

Let's look at the first row of ASCII values. As you would expect, the data placed in the file in ASCII form appears in this row in a readable way. But there are hexadecimal values for which there is no printable ASCII representation. The only such value appearing in this file is 0 x 00. But there could be many others. For example, the hexadecimal value of the number 500,000,000 is 0x1DCD6500. If you write this value out to a file, an *od* of the file with the option *-xc* looks like this:

```
0000000  \035\315  e  \0
         1dcd 6500
```

The only printable byte in this file is the one with the value 0x65 ('e'). *Od* handles all of the others by listing their equivalent octal values in the ASCII representation.

The hex dump of this output from the C version of *writrec* shows how this file structure represents an interesting mix of a number of the organizational tools we have encountered. In a single record we have both binary and ASCII data. Each record consists of a fixed-length field (the byte count) and several delimited, variable-length fields. This kind of mixing of different data types and organizational methods is common in real-world file structures.

A Note about Byte Order   If the computer you are using is an IBM PC or a computer from DEC, such as a VAX, your octal dump for this file will probably be different from the one we see here. These machines store the values of numbers in reverse order from the way we think of them. For example, if this dump were executed on an IBM PC, the hex representation of the first two-byte value in the file would be 0x2800, rather than 0x0028. This reverse order also applies to long, four-byte integers on these machines. This is an aspect of files that you need to be aware of if you expect to make sense out of dumps like this one. A more serious consequence of the byte-order differences among machines occurs when we move files from a machine with one type of byte ordering to one with a different byte ordering. We discuss this problem and ways to deal with it in section 4.6, "Portability and Standardization."

4.2   Record Access

4.2.1 Record Keys

Since our new file structure so clearly focuses on the notion of a record as the quantity of information that is being read or written, it makes sense to think in terms of retrieving just one specific record rather than having to read all the way through the file, displaying everything. When looking for an individual record, it is convenient to identify the record with a *key* based on the record's contents. For example, in our name and address file we might want to access the "Ames record" or the "Mason record" rather than thinking in terms of the "first record" or "second record." (Can you remember which record comes first?) This notion of a *key* is another fundamental conceptual tool. We need to develop a more exact idea of what a key is.

When we are looking for a record containing the last name *Ames,* we want to recognize it even if the user enters the key in the form "AMES", "ames", or "Ames". To do this, we must define a standard form for keys, along with associated rules and procedures for converting keys into this standard form. A standard form of this kind is often called a *canonical form* for the key. One meaning of the word *canon* is rule, and the word *canonical* means conforming to the rule. A canonical form for a search key is the *single* representation for that key that conforms to the rule.

As a simple example, we could state that the canonical form for a key requires that the key consist solely of uppercase letters and have no extra blanks at the end. So, if a user enters "Ames", we would convert the key to the canonical form "AMES" before searching for it.

It is often desirable to have *distinct keys,* or keys that uniquely identify a single record. If there is not a one-to-one relationship between the key and a single record, then the program has to provide additional mechanisms to allow the user to resolve the confusion that can result when more than one record fits a particular key. Suppose, for example, that we are looking for John Ames's address. If there are several records in the file for several different people named John Ames, how should the program respond? Certainly it should not just give the address of the first John Ames that it finds. Should it give all the addresses at once? Should it provide a way of scrolling through the records?

The simplest solution is to *prevent* such confusion. The prevention takes place as new records are added to the file. When the user enters a new record, we form a unique canonical key for that record and then search the file for that key. This concern about uniqueness applies only to *primary keys.* A primary key is, by definition, the key that is used to identify a record uniquely.

It is also possible, as we see later, to search on *secondary keys.* An example of a secondary key might be the city field in our name and address file. If we wanted to find all the records in the file for people who live in towns named Stillwater, we would use some canonical form of "Stillwater" as a secondary key. Typically, secondary keys do not uniquely identify a record.

Although a person's name might at first seem to be a good choice for a primary key, a person's name runs a high risk of failing the test for uniqueness. A name is a perfectly fine secondary key, and in fact is often an important secondary key in a retrieval system, but there is too great a likelihood that two names in the same file will be identical.

The reason a name is a risky choice for a primary key is that it contains a real data value. In general, *primary keys should be dataless.* Even when we think we are choosing a unique key, if it contains data there is a danger that unforeseen identical values could occur. Sweet (1985) cites an example of a file system that used a person's Social Security number as a primary key for personnel records. It turned out that, in the particular population that was represented in the file, a large number of people who were not U.S. citizens were included, and in a different part of the organization all of these people had been assigned the Social Security number 999–99–9999!

Another reason, other than uniqueness, that a primary key should be dataless is that a primary key should be *unchanging.* If information that corresponds to a certain record changes, and that information is contained in a primary key, what do you do about the primary key? You probably cannot change the primary key itself, in most cases, because there are likely to be reports, memos, indexes, or other sources of information that refer to the record by its primary key. As soon as you change the key, those references become useless.

A good rule of thumb is to avoid trying to put data into primary keys. If we want to access records according to data content, we should assign this content to secondary keys. We give a more detailed look at record access by primary and secondary keys in Chapter 6. For the rest of this chapter, we suspend our concern about whether a key is primary or secondary and concentrate simply on finding things by key.

4.2.2 A Sequential Search

Now that you know about keys, you should be able to write a program that reads through the file, record by record, looking for a record with a particular key. Such *sequential searching* is just a simple extension of our *readrec* program, adding a comparison operation to the main loop to see if the key for the record matches the key we are seeking. We leave the actual program as an exercise.

Evaluating Performance of Sequential Search   In the chapters that follow, we find ways to search for records that are faster than the sequential search mechanism. We can use sequential searching as a kind of baseline against which to measure the improvements that we make. It is important, therefore, to find some way of expressing the amount of time and work expended in a sequential search.

Developing a performance measure requires that we decide on a unit of work that usefully represents the constraints on the performance of the whole process. When we describe the performance of searches that take place in electronic RAM, where comparison operations are more expensive than fetch operations to bring data in from memory, we usually use the *number of comparisons* required for the search as the measure of work. But, given that the cost of a comparison in RAM is so small compared to the cost of a disk access, comparisons do not fairly represent the performance constraints for a search through a file on secondary storage. Instead, we count low-level READ( ) calls. We assume that each READ( ) call requires a seek and that any one READ( ) call is as costly as any other. We know from the discussions of matters such as system buffering in Chapter 3 that these assumptions are not strictly accurate. But, in a multiuser environment where many processes are using the disk at once, they are close enough to correct to be useful.

Suppose we have a file with 1,000 records and we want to use a sequential search to find Al Smith's record. How many READ( ) calls are required? If Al Smith's record is the first one in the file, the program has to read in only a single record. If it is the last record in the file, the program makes 1,000 READ( ) calls before concluding the search. For an average search, 500 calls are needed.

If we double the number of records in a file, we also double both the average and the maximum number of READ( ) calls required. Using a sequential search to find Al Smith's record in a file of 2,000 records, requires, on the average, 1,000 calls. In other words, the amount of work required for a sequential search is directly proportional to the number of records in the file.

In general, the work required to search sequentially for a record in a file with n records is proportional to n; it takes at most n comparisons; on average it takes approximately $n/2$ comparisons. A sequential search is said to be of the order $O(n)$ because the time it takes is proportional to n.[†]

Improving Sequential Search Performance with Record Blocking
It is interesting and useful to apply some of the information from Chapter 3 about disk performance to the problem of improving sequential search performance. We learned in Chapter 3 that the major cost associated with a disk access is the time required to perform a seek to the right location on the disk. Once data transfer begins, it is relatively fast, although still much slower than a data transfer within RAM. Consequently, the cost of seeking

---

[†]If you are not familiar with this "big-oh" notation, you should look it up. Knuth (1973a) is a good source.

and reading a record and then seeking and reading another record is greater than the cost of seeking just once and then reading two successive records. (Once again, we are assuming a multiuser environment in which a seek is required for each separate READ( ) call.) It follows that we should be able to improve the performance of sequential searching by reading in a *block* of several records all at once and then processing that block of records in RAM.

We began this chapter with a stream of bytes. We grouped the bytes into fields, and then grouped the fields into records. Now we are considering a yet higher level of organization, grouping records into blocks. This new level of grouping, however, differs from the others. Whereas fields and records are ways of maintaining the logical organization within the file, blocking is done strictly as a performance measure. As such, the block size is usually related more to the physical properties of the disk drive than to the content of the data. For instance, on sector-oriented disks the block size is almost always some multiple of the sector size.

Suppose we have a file of 4,000 records and that the average length of a record is 512 bytes. If our operating system uses sector-sized buffers of 512 bytes, then an unblocked sequential search requires, on the average, 2,000 READ( ) calls before it can retrieve a particular record. By blocking the records in groups of 16 per block, so each READ( ) call brings in 8 kilobytes worth of records, the number of reads required for an average search comes down to 125. Each READ( ) requires slightly more time, since more data is transferred from the disk, but this is a cost that is usually well worth paying for such a large reduction in the number of reads.

There are several things to note from this analysis and discussion of record blocking:

□   Although blocking can result in substantial performance improvements, it does not change the order of the sequential search operation. The cost of searching is still $O(n)$, increasing in direct proportion to increases in the size of the file.

□   Blocking clearly reflects the differences between RAM access speed and the cost of accessing secondary storage.

□   Blocking does not change the number of comparisons that must be done in RAM, and it probably increases the amount of data transferred between disk and RAM. (We always read a whole block, even if the record we are seeking is the first one in the block.)

□   Blocking saves time because it decreases the amount of seeking. We find, again and again, that this differential between the cost of seeking and the cost of other operations, such as data transfer or RAM access, is the force that drives file structure design.

When Sequential Searching Is Good   Much of the remainder of this text is devoted to identifying better ways to access individual records; sequential searching is just too expensive for most serious retrieval situations. This is unfortunate, because sequential access has two major practical advantages over other types of access: It is extremely easy to program, and it requires the simplest of file structures.

Whether sequential search is advisable depends largely on how the file is to be used, how fast the computer system is that is performing the search, and structural aspects of the file. There are many situations in which a sequential search is often reasonable. Here are some examples:

☐ ASCII files in which you are searching for some pattern (see *grep* in the next section);
☐ Files with few records (e.g., 10 records);
☐ Files that hardly ever need to be searched (e.g., tape files usually used for other kinds of processing); and
☐ Files in which you want all records with a certain secondary key value, where a large number of matches is expected.

Fortunately, these sorts of applications do occur often in day-to-day computing—so often, in fact, that operating systems provide many utilities for performing sequential processing. UNIX is one of the best examples of this, as we see in the next section.

4.2.3 UNIX Tools for Sequential Processing

Recognizing the importance of having a standard file structure that is simple and easy to program, the most common file structure that occurs in UNIX is *an ASCII file with the new-line character as the record delimiter and, when possible, white space as the field delimiter.* Practically all files that we create using UNIX editors use this structure. And since most of the built-in C and Pascal functions that perform I/O write to this kind of file, it is common to see data files that consist of fields of numbers or words separated by blanks or tabs, and records separated by new-line characters. Such files are simple and easy to process. We can, for instance, generate an ASCII file with a simple program, and then use an editor to browse through it or alter it.

UNIX provides a rich array of tools for working with files in this form. Since this kind of file structure is inherently sequential (records are variable in length, so we have to pass from record to record to find any particular field or record), many of these tools process files sequentially.

Suppose, for instance, that we choose the white-space/new-line structure for our address file, ending every field with a tab and ending every record with a new line. While this causes some problems in distinguishing fields (a blank is white space, but it doesn't separate a field), and in that sense is not an ideal structure, it buys us something very valuable: the full use of those UNIX tools that are built around the white-space/new-line structure. For example, we can print the file on our console using any of a number of utilities, such as

```
cat:

>cat myfile
Ames    John 123 Maple    Stillwater OK 74075
Mason   Alan 90 Eastgate Ada        OK 74820
```

Or we can use tools like wc and grep for processing the files.

wc The command wc ("word count") reads through an ASCII file sequentially and counts the number of lines (delimited by new lines), words (delimited by white space), and characters in a file:

```
>wc myfile
      2   14   76
```

grep It is common to want to find out if a text file has a certain word or character string in it. For ASCII files that can reasonably be searched sequentially, UNIX provides an excellent filter for doing this called *grep* (and its variants egrep and fgrep). The word *grep* stands for "generalized regular expression," which describes the type of pattern that grep is able to recognize. In its simplest form, grep searches sequentially through a file for a pattern, and then returns to standard output (the console) all the lines in the file that contain the pattern.

```
>grep Ada myfile
Mason    Alan    90 Eastgate Ada    OK    74820
```

We can also combine tools to create, on the fly, some very powerful file processing software. For example, to find the number of words in all records containing the word Ada:

```
>grep Ada | wc
      1   7   36
```

As we move through the text we will encounter a number of other powerful UNIX commands that sequentially process files with the basic white-space/new-line structure.

4.2.4 Direct Access

The most radical alternative to searching sequentially through a file for a record is a retrieval mechanism known as *direct access*. We have direct access to a record when we can seek directly to the beginning of the record and read it in. Whereas sequential searching is an $O(n)$ operation, direct access is $O(1)$; no matter how large the file is, we can still get to the record we want with a single seek.

Direct access is predicated on knowing where the beginning of the required record is. Sometimes this information about record location is carried in a separate index file. But, for the moment, we assume that we do not have an index. We assume, instead, that we know the *relative record number* (RRN) of the record that we want. The idea of an RRN is an important concept that emerges from viewing a file as a collection of records rather than a collection of bytes. If a file is a sequence of records, then the RRN of a record gives its position relative to the beginning of the file. The first record in a file has RRN 0, the next has RRN 1, and so forth.[†]

In our name and address file, we might tie a record to its RRN by assigning membership numbers that are related to the order in which we enter the records in the file. The person with the first record might have a membership number of 1001, the second a number of 1002, and so on. Given a membership number, we can subtract 1001 to get the RRN of the record.

What can we do with this RRN? Not much, given the file structures we have been using so far, which consist of variable-length records. The RRN tells us the relative position of the record we want in the sequence of records, but we still have to read sequentially through the file, counting records as we go, to get to the record we want. An exercise at the end of this chapter explores a method of moving through the file called *skip sequential* processing, which can improve performance somewhat, but looking for a particular RRN is still an $O(n)$ process.

To support direct access by RRN, we need to work with records of fixed, known length. If the records are all the same length, then we can use a record's RRN to calculate the *byte offset* of the start of the record relative to the start of the file. For instance, if we are interested in the record with an RRN of 546 and our file has a fixed-length record size of 128 bytes per record, we can calculate the byte offset as follows:

$$\text{Byte offset} = 546 \times 128 = 69{,}888.$$

In general, given a fixed-length record file where the record size is r, the byte offset of a record with an RRN of n is

$$\text{Byte offset} = n \times r.$$

Programming languages and operating systems differ with regard to where this byte offset calculation is done and even with regard to whether

---

[†]In keeping with the conventions of C and Turbo Pascal, we assume that the RRN is a *zero-based* count. In some file systems, the count starts at 1 rather than 0.

byte offsets are used for addressing within files. In C (and the UNIX and MS-DOS operating systems), where a file is treated as just a sequence of bytes, the application program does the calculation and uses the *lseek( )* command to jump to the byte that begins the record. All movement within a file is in terms of bytes. This is a very low-level view of files; the responsibility for translating an RRN into a byte offset belongs wholly to the application program.

The PL/I language and the operating environments in which PL/I is often used (OS/MVS, VMS) are examples of a much different, higher-level view of files. The notion of a sequence of bytes is simply not present when you are working with record-oriented files in this environment. Instead, files are viewed as collections of records that are accessed by keys. The operating system takes care of the translation between a key and a record's location. In the simplest case, the key is, in fact, just the record's RRN, but the determination of actual location within the file is still not the programmer's concern.

If we limit ourselves to the use of standard Pascal, the question of seeking by bytes or seeking by records is not an issue: There is no seeking at all in standard Pascal. But, as we said earlier, many implementations of Pascal extend the standard definition of the language to allow direct access to different locations in a file. The nature of these extensions varies according to the differences in the host operating systems around which the extensions were developed. All the same, one feature that is consistent across implementations is that a file in Pascal always consists of elements of a single type. A file is a sequence of integers, characters, arrays, or records, and so on. Addressing is always in terms of this fundamental element size. For example, we might have a *file of datarec,* where *datarec* is defined as

```
TYPE datarec = packed array [0..64] of char;
```

Seeking within this file is in terms of multiples of the elementary unit *datarec,* which is to say in multiples of a 65-byte entity. If I ask to jump to *datarec* number 3 (zero-based count), I am jumping 195 bytes ($3 \times 65 = 195$) into the file.

4.3   More about Record Structures

4.3.1 Choosing a Record Structure and Record Length

Once we decide to fix the length of our records so we can use the RRN to give us direct access to a record, we have to decide on a record length. Clearly, this decision is related to the size of the fields we want to store in the record. Sometimes the decision is easy. Suppose we are building a file of sales transactions that contain the following information about each transaction:

☐   A six-digit account number of the purchaser;
☐   Six digits for the date field;
☐   A five-character stock number for item purchased;
☐   A three-digit field for quantity; and
☐   A 10-position field for total cost.

These are all fixed-length fields; the sum of the field lengths is 30 bytes. Normally, we would simply stick with this record size, but if performance is so important that we need to squeeze every bit of speed out of our retrieval system, we might try to fit the record size to the block organization of our disk. For instance, if we intend to store the records on a typical sectored disk (see Chapter 3) with a sector size of 512 bytes or some other power of 2, we might decide to pad the record out to 32 bytes so we can place an integral number of records in a sector. That way, records will never span sectors.

The choice of a record length is more complicated when the lengths of the fields can vary, as in our name and address file. If we choose a record length that is the sum of our estimates of the largest possible values for all the fields, we can be reasonably sure that we have enough space for everything, but we also waste a lot of space. If, on the other hand, we are conservative in our use of space and fix the lengths of fields at smaller values, we may have to leave information out of a field. Fortunately, we can avoid this problem to some degree through appropriate design of the field structure *within* a record.

In our earlier discussion of record structures, we saw that there are two general approaches we can take toward organizing fields within a fixed-length record. The first, illustrated in Fig. 4.11(a), uses fixed-length fields inside the fixed-length record. This is the approach we took for the sales transaction file previously described. The second approach, illustrated in Fig. 4.11(b), uses the fixed-length record as a kind of standard-sized container for holding something that looks like a variable-length record.

The first approach has the virtue of simplicity: It is very easy to "break out" the fixed-length fields from within a fixed-length record. The second approach lets us take advantage of an averaging-out effect that usually occurs: The longest names are not likely to appear in the same record as the longest address field. By letting the field boundaries vary, we can make more efficient use of a fixed amount of space. Also, note that the two approaches are not mutually exclusive. Given a record that contains a number of truly fixed-length fields and some fields that have variable-

Ames	John	123 Maple	Stillwater	OK74075
Mason	Alan	90 Eastgate	Ada	OK74820

(a)

Ames ¦ John ¦ 123 Maple ¦ Stillwater ¦ OK ¦ 74075 ¦ ◀────── **Unused space** ──────▶

Mason ¦ Alan ¦ 90 Eastgate ¦ Ada ¦ OK ¦ 74820 ¦ ◀────── **Unused space** ──────▶

(b)

FIGURE 4.11 Two fundamental approaches to field structure within a fixed-length record. (a) Fixed-length records with fixed-length fields. (b) Fixed-length records with variable-length fields.

length information, we might design a record structure that combines these two approaches.

The programs *update.c* and *update.pas,* which are included in the set of programs at the end of this chapter, use direct access to allow a user to retrieve a record, change it, and then write it back. These programs create a file structure that uses variable-length fields within fixed-length records. Given the variability in the length of the fields in our name and address file, this is an appropriate choice.

One of the interesting questions that must be resolved in the design of this kind of structure is that of distinguishing the real-data portion of the record from the unused-space portion. The range of possible solutions parallels that of the solutions for recognizing variable-length records in any other context: We can place a record-length count at the beginning of the record, we can use a special delimiter at the end of the record, we can count fields, and so on. Because both *update.c* and *update.pas* use a character string buffer to collect the fields, and because we are handling character strings differently in C than in Pascal (strings are null-terminated in C; we keep a byte count of the string length at the beginning of the Pascal strings), it is convenient to use a slightly different file structure for the two implementations. In the C version we fill out the unused portion of the record with null characters. In the Pascal version we actually place a fixed-length field (an integer) at the start of the record to tell how many of the bytes in the record are valid. As usual, there is no single right way to implement this file structure; instead we seek the solution that is most appropriate for our needs and situation.

Figure 4.12 shows the hex dump output from each of these programs. The output introduces a number of other ideas, such as the use of *header records,* which we discuss in the next section. For now, however, just look at the structure of the data records. We have italicized the length fields at the start of the records in the output from the Pascal program. Although we filled out the records created by the Pascal program with blanks to make the output more readable, this blank fill is unnecessary. The length field at the start of the record guarantees that we do not read past the end of the data in the record.

4.3.2 Header Records

It is often necessary or useful to keep track of some general information about a file to assist in future use of the file. A *header record* is often placed at the beginning of the file to hold this kind of information. For example, in some versions of Pascal there is no easy way to jump to the end of a file, even though the implementation supports direct access. One simple solution to this problem is to keep a count of the number of records in the file and to store that count somewhere. We might also find it useful to include information such as the length of the data records, the date and time of the file's most recent update, and so on. Header records can help make a file a self-describing object, freeing the software that accesses the file from having to know *a priori* everything about its structure, and hence making the file-access software able to deal with more variation in file structures.

The header record usually has a different structure than the data records in the file. The output from *update.c,* for instance, uses a 32-byte header record, whereas the data records each contain 64 bytes. Furthermore, the data records created by *update.c* contain only character data, whereas the header record contains an integer that tells how many data records are in the file.

Implementing a header record presents more of a challenge for the Pascal programmer. Recall that the Standard Pascal view of a file is one of a repeated collection of components, all of which are the same component type. Since a header record is fundamentally a different kind of record than the other records in a file, Pascal does not naturally support header records. In some cases, Pascal lets us get around this problem by using *variant records.* A variant record in Pascal is one that can have different meanings, depending on context. Unfortunately, a variant record cannot vary in size, so its use as a header record is constrained by the fact that it must be the same size as all other records in the file.

When faced with a language like Standard Pascal that strictly proscribes the types of records we can use in a file, we often find ourselves resorting

```
0000000   0002 0000 0000 0000 0000 0000 0000 0000    ................    Header record
0000020   0000 0000 0000 0000 0000 0000 0000 0000                        Record count in
                                                                          first two bytes
0000040   416d 6573 7c4a 6f68 6e7c 3132 3320 4d61    Ames|John|123 Ma    First record
0000060   706c 657c 5374 696c 6c77 6174 6572 7c4f    ple|Stillwater|O
0000100   4b7c 3734 3037 357c 0000 0000 0000 0000    K|74075|.........
0000120   0000 0000 0000 0000 0000 0000 0000 0000
0000140   4d61 736f 6e7c 416c 616e 7c39 3020 4561    Mason|Alan|90 Ea    Second record
0000160   7374 6761 7465 7c41 6461 7c4f 4b7c 3734    stgate|Ada|OK|74
0000200   3832 307c 0000 0000 0000 0000 0000 0000    820|..........
0000220   0000 0000 0000 0000 0000 0000 0000 0000

                              (a)

0000000   0002 0000 0000 0000 0000 0000 0000 0000    ................    Header record
0000020   0000 0000 0000 0000 0000 0000 0000 0000                        Record count in
                                                                          first two bytes
0000040   0000 0000 0000 0000 0000 0000 0000 0000    ................
0000060   0000 0000 0000 0000 0000 0000 0000 0000
0000100   0000 0000
0000102   0028 416d 6573 7c4a 6f68 6e7c 3132         (.Ames|John|12      First record
0000120   3320 4d61 706c 657c 5374 696c 6c77         3 Maple|Stillwat    Integer in first
0000140   6572 7c4f 4b7c 3734 3037 357c              er|OK|74075|        two bytes contains
0000160   2020 2020 2020 2020 2020 2020 2020                             the number of
0000200   2020 2020                                                      bytes of data in
                                                                          the record
0000204   0024 4d61 736f 6e7c 416c 616e              $.Mason|Alan        Second record
0000220   7c39 3020 4561 7374 6761 7465 7c41 6461    |90 Eastgate|Ada
0000240   7c4f 4b7c 3734 3832 307c 2020 2020 2020    |OK|74820|
0000260   2020 2020 2020 2020 2020 2020 2020 2020
0000300   2020 2020 2020

                              (b)
```

FIGURE 4.12 Two different record structures that carry variable-length fields in a fixed-length record. (a) Record structure created by *update.c*: fixed-length records containing variable-length fields that are terminated by a null character. (b) Record structure created by *update.pas*: fixed-length records beginning with a fixed-length (integer) field that indicates the number of usable bytes in the record's variable-length fields.

121

to tricks. We use such a trick in *update.pas:* We just use the initial integer field in the record for a different purpose in the header record. In the data records this field holds a count of the bytes of valid data within the record; in the header record it holds a count of the data records in the file.

Header records are a widely used, important file design tool. For example, when we reach the point where we are discussing the construction of tree-structured indexes for files, we see that header records are often placed at the beginning of the index to keep track of matters such as the RRN of the record that is the root of the index. We investigate some more elaborate uses of header records later in this chapter and also in subsequent chapters.

4.4   File Access and File Organization

In the course of our discussions in this chapter, we have looked at

- Variable-length records;
- Fixed-length records;
- Sequential access; and
- Direct access.

The first two of these relate to aspects of *file organization*. The second pair has to do with *file access*. The interaction between file organization and file access is a useful one; we need to look at it more closely before continuing with this chapter.

Most of what we have considered so far falls into the category of file organization:

- Can the file be divided into fields?
- Is there a higher level of organization to the file that combines the fields into records?
- Do all the records have the same number of bytes or fields?
- How do we distinguish one record from another?
- How do we organize the internal structure of a fixed-length record so we can distinguish between data and extra space?

We have seen that there are many possible answers to these questions and that the choice of a particular file organization depends on many things, including the file-handling facilities of the language you are using and the *use you want to make of the file.*

Using a file implies access. We looked first at sequential access, ultimately developing a *sequential search.* So long as we did not know where individual records began, sequential access was the only option open to us.

When we wanted *direct access,* we fixed the length of our records, and this allowed us to calculate precisely where each record began and to seek directly to it.

In other words, our desire for direct *access* caused us to choose a fixed-length record file *organization.* Does this mean that we can equate fixed-length records with direct access? Definitely not. There is nothing about our having fixed the length of the records in a file that precludes sequential access; we certainly could write a program that reads sequentially through a fixed-length record file.

Not only can we elect to read through the fixed-length records sequentially, but we can also provide direct access to *variable-length* records simply by keeping a list of the byte offsets from the start of the file for the placement of each record. We chose a fixed-length record structure in *update.c* and *update.pas* because it is simple and adequate for the data that we want to store. Although the lengths of our names and addresses vary, the variation is not so great that we cannot accommodate it in a fixed-length record.

Consider, however, the effects of using a fixed-length record organization to provide direct access to records that are documents ranging in length from a few hundred bytes to over a hundred kilobytes. Fixed-length records would be disastrously wasteful of space, so some form of variable-length record structure would have to be found. Developing file structures to handle such situations requires that you clearly distinguish between the matter of *access* and your options regarding *organization.*

The restrictions imposed by the language and file system used to develop your applications do impose limits on your ability to take advantage of this distinction between access method and organization. For example, the C language provides the programmer with the ability to implement direct access to variable-length records, since it allows access to any byte in the file. On the other hand, Pascal, even when seeking is supported, imposes limitations related to Pascal's definition of a file as a collection of elements that are all of the same *type* and, consequently, size. Since the elements must all be of the same size, direct access to variable-length records is difficult, at best, in Pascal.

4.5 Beyond Record Structures

Now that we have a grip on the concepts of organization and access, we look at some interesting new file organizations and more complex ways of accessing files. We want to extend the notion of a file beyond the simple idea of records and fields.

We begin with the idea of abstract data models. Our purpose here is to put some distance between the physical and the logical organization of files, to allow us to focus more on the information content of files and less on physical format.

4.5.1 Abstract Data Models

The history of file structures and file processing parallels the history of computer hardware and software. When file processing first became common on computers, magnetic tape and punched cards were the primary means used to store files, RAM space was dear, and programming languages were primitive. Programmers as well as users were compelled to view file data exactly as it might appear on a tape or cards—as a sequence of fields and records. Even after data was loaded into RAM, the tools for manipulating and viewing the data were unsophisticated and reflected the magnetic tape metaphor. Data processing meant processing fields and records in the traditional sense.

Gradually, computer users began to recognize that computers could process more than just fields and records. Computers could, for instance, process and transmit sound, and they could process and display images and documents (Fig. 4.13). These kinds of applications deal with information that does not nicely fit the metaphor of data stored as sequences of records that are divided into fields, even if, ultimately, the data might be stored physically in the form of fields and records. It is easier, in the mind's eye, to envision data objects such as documents, images, and sound as objects that we manipulate in ways that are specific to the objects themselves, rather than simply as fields and records on a disk.

The notion that we need not view data only as it appears on a particular medium is captured in the phrase *abstract data model,* a term that encourages

FIGURE 4.13 Data such as sound, images, and documents do not fit the traditional metaphor of data stored as sequences of records that are divided into fields.

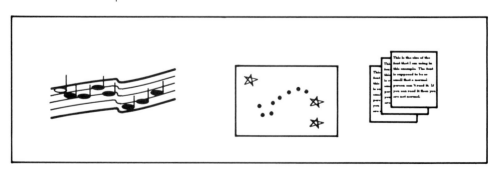

an application-oriented view of data, rather than a medium-oriented view. The organization and access methods of abstract data models are described in terms of how an application views the data, rather than how the data might physically be stored.

One way that we save a user from having to know about objects in a file is to keep information in the file that file-access software can use to "understand" those objects. A good example of how this might be done is to put file structure information in a header.

4.5.2 Headers and Self-Describing Files

We have seen how a header record can be used to keep track of how many records there are in a file. If our programming language permits it, we can put much more elaborate information about a file's structure in the header. When a file's header contains this sort of information, we say the file is *self-describing*. Suppose, for instance, that we store in a file the following information:

☐   A name for each field;
☐   The width of each field; and
☐   The number of fields per record.

We can now write a program that can read and print a meaningful display of files with any number of fields per record and any variety of fixed-length field widths. In general, the more file structure information we put into a file's header, the less our software needs to know about the specific structure of an individual file.

As usual, there is a trade-off: If we do not hard-code the field and record structures of files in the programs that read and write them, the programs themselves must be more sophisticated. They must be flexible enough to interpret the self-descriptions that they find in the file headers.

4.5.3 Metadata

Suppose you are an astronomer interested in studying images generated by telescopes that scan the sky, and you want to design a file structure for the digital representations of these images (Fig. 4.14). You expect to have many images, perhaps thousands, that you want to study, and you want to store one image per file. While you are primarily interested in studying the images themselves, you will certainly need information *about* each image: where in the sky the image is from, when it was made, what telescope was used, references to related images, and so forth.

This kind of information is called *metadata*—data that describes the primary data in a file. Metadata can be incorporated into any file whose

FIGURE 4.14 To make sense of this two-Mbyte image, an astronomer needs such metadata as the kind of image it is, the part of the sky it is from, and the telescope that was used to view it. Astronomical metadata is often stored in the same file as the data itself. (This image shows polarized radio emission from the southern spiral galaxy NGC 5236 [M83] as observed with the Very Large Array radio telescope in New Mexico.)

primary data requires supporting information. If a file is going to be shared by many users, some of whom might not otherwise have easy access to its metadata, it may be most convenient to store the metadata in the file itself. A common place to store metadata in a file is the header record.

Typically, a community of users of a particular kind of data agrees on a standard format for holding metadata. For example, a standard format called FITS (Flexible Image Transport System) has been developed by the International Astronomers' Union for storing the kind of astronomical data just described in a file's header.[†] A FITS header is a collection of 2,880-byte blocks of 80-byte ASCII records, in which each record contains a single piece of metadata. Figure 4.15 shows part of a FITS header. In a FITS file, the header is followed by the actual numbers that describe the image, one binary number per observed point of the image.

Note that the designers of the FITS format chose to use ASCII in the header, but binary values for the image. ASCII headers are easy to read and process and, since they occur only once, take up relatively little extra space. Since the numbers that make a FITS image are rarely read by humans, but rather are first processed into a picture and then displayed, binary format is the preferred choice for them.

[†]For more details on FITS, see the references listed at the end of this chapter in "Further Readings."

```
SIMPLE   =                 T / CONFORMS TO BASIC FORMAT
BITPIX   =                16 / BITS PER PIXEL
NAXIS    =                 2 / NUMBER OF AXES
NAXIS1   =               256 / RA AXIS DIMENSION
NAXIS2   =               256 / DEC AXIS DIMENSION
EXTEND   =                 F / T MEANS STANDARD EXTENSIONS EXIST
BSCALE   =      0.000100000 / TRUE = [TAPE*BSCALE]+BZERO
BZERO    =      0.000000000 / OFFSET TO TRUE PIXEL VALUES
MAP_TYPE= 'REL_EXPOSURE'/ INTENSITY OR RELATIVE EXPOSURE MAP
BUNIT    = '            '/ DIMENSIONLESS PEAK EXPOSURE FRACTION
CRVAL1   =            0.625 / RA    REF POINT VALUE (DEGREES)
CRPIX1   =          128.500 / RA    REF POINT PIXEL LOCATION
CDELT1   =      -0.006666700 / RA   INCREMENT ALONG AXIS (DEGREES)
CTYPE1   = 'RA---TAN'       / RA    TYPE
CROTA1   =            0.000 / RA    ROTATION
CRVAL2   =           71.967 / DEC   REF POINT VALUE (DEGREES)
CRPIX2   =          128.500 / DEC   REF POINT PIXEL LOCATION
CDELT2   =      0.006666700 / DEC   INCREMENT ALONG AXIS (DEGREES)
CTYPE2   = 'DEC--TAN'       / DEC   TYPE
CROTA2   =            0.000 / DEC   ROTATION
EPOCH    =           1950.0 / EPOCH OF COORDINATE SYSTEM
ARR_TYPE=                 4 / 1=DP, 3=FP, 4=I
DATAMAX  =            1.000 / PEAK INTENSITY (TRUE)
DATAMIN  =            0.000 / MINIMUM INTENSITY (TRUE)
ROLL_ANG=          -22.450 / ROLL ANGLE (DEGREES)
BAD_ASP  =                0 / 0=good, 1=bad(Do not use roll angle)
TIME_LIV=           5649.6 / LIVE TIME (SECONDS)
OBJECT   = 'REM6791    ' / SEQUENCE NUMBER
AVGOFFY  =            1.899 / AVG Y OFFSET IN PIXELS, 8 ARCSEC/PIXEL
AVGOFFZ  =            2.578 / AVG Z OFFSET IN PIXELS, 8 ARCSEC/PIXEL
RMSOFFY  =            0.083 / ASPECT SOLN RMS Y PIXELS, 8 ARCSC/PIX
RMSOFFZ  =            0.204 / ASPECT SOLN RMS Z PIXELS, 8 ARCSC/PIX
TELESCOP= 'EINSTEIN    ' / TELESCOPE
INSTRUME= 'IPC         ' / FOCAL PLANE DETECTOR
OBSERVER= '2          ' / OBSERVER #: 0=CFA; 1=CAL; 2=MIT; 3=GSFC
GALL     =          119.370 / GALACTIC LONGITUDE OF FIELD CENTER
GALB     =            9.690 / GALACTIC LATITUDE OF FIELD CENTER
DATE_OBS= '80/238     ' / YEAR & DAY NUMBER FOR OBSERVATION START
DATE_STP= '80/238     ' / YEAR & DAY NUMBER FOR OBSERVATION STOP
TITLE    = 'SNR SURVEY: CTA1                                     '
ORIGIN   = 'HARVARD-SMITHSONIAN CENTER FOR ASTROPHYSICS          '
DATE     = '22/09/1989 ' / DATE FILE WRITTEN
TIME     = '05:26:53   ' / TIME FILE WRITTEN
END
```

FIGURE 4.15 Sample FITS header. On each line, the data to the left of the '/' is the actual metadata (data about the raw data that follows in the file). For example, the second line ("BITPIX = 16") indicates that the raw data in the file will be stored in 16-bit integer format. Everything to the right of a '/' is a comment, describing for the reader the meaning of the metadata that precedes it. Even a person uninformed about the FITS format can learn a great deal about this file just by reading through the header.

A FITS image is a good example of an abstract data model. The data itself is meaningless without the interpretive information contained in the header, and FITS-specific methods must be employed to convert FITS data into an understandable image. Another example is the raster image, which we look at next.

4.5.4 Color Raster Images

From a user's point of view, a modern computer is as much a graphical device as it is a data processor. Whether we are working with documents, spreadsheets, or numbers, we are likely to be viewing and storing pictures in addition to whatever other information we work with. Let's examine one type of image, the color raster image, as a means to filling in our conceptual understanding of data objects.

A color raster image is a rectangular array of colored dots, or *pixels,*[†] that are displayed on a screen. A FITS image is a raster image in the sense that the numbers that make up a FITS image can be converted to colors and then displayed on a screen. There are many different kinds of metadata that can go with a raster image, including

☐ The dimensions of the image: the number or pixels per row and the number of rows.

☐ The number of bits used to describe each pixel. This determines how many colors can be associated with each pixel. A 1-bit image can display only two colors, usually black and white. A 2-bit image can display four colors (2^2), an 8-bit image can display 256 colors (2^8), and so forth.

☐ A *color lookup table,* or *palette,* indicating which color is to be assigned to each pixel value in the image. A 2-bit image uses a color lookup table with 4 colors, an 8-bit image uses a table with 256 colors, and so forth.

If we think of an image as an abstract data type, what are some methods that we might associate with images? There are the usual ones associated with getting things in and out of a computer: a *read_image* routine and *store_image* routine. Then there are those that deal with images as special objects; for example,

☐ Display an image in a window on a console screen;
☐ Associate an image with a particular color lookup table;
☐ Overlay one image onto another to produce a composite image; and
☐ Display several images in succession, producing an animation.

[†]*Pixel* stands for "picture element."

The color raster image is an example of a type of data object that requires more than the traditional field/record file structure. This is particularly true when more than one image might be stored in a single file, or when we want to store a document or other complex object together with images in a file. Let's look at some ways to mix object types in one file.

4.5.5 Mixing Object Types in One File

Keywords   The FITS header (Fig. 4.15) illustrates an important technique, described earlier, for identifying fields and records: the use of *keywords*. In the case of FITS headers, we do not know what fields are going to be contained in any given header, so we identify each field using a "*keyword = value*" format.

Why does this format work for FITS files, whereas it was inappropriate for our address file? For the address file we saw that the use of keywords demanded a high price in terms of space, possibly even doubling the size of the file. In FITS files the amount of overhead introduced by keywords is quite small. When the image is included, the FITS file in the example contains approximately 2 megabytes. The keywords in the header occupy a total of about 400 bytes, or about 0.02% of the total file space.

Tags   With the addition via keywords of file structure information and metadata to a header, we see that a file can be more than just a collection of repeated fields and records. Can we extend this notion beyond the header to other, more elaborate objects? For example, suppose an astronomer would like to store *several* FITS images of different sizes in a file, together with the usual metadata, plus perhaps lab notes describing what the scientist learned from the image (Fig. 4.16). Now we can think of our file as a mixture of objects that may be very different in content—a view that our previous file structures do not handle well. Maybe we need a new kind of file structure.

There are many ways to address this new file design problem. One would be simply to put each type of object into a variable-length record and

FIGURE 4.16 Information that an astronomer wants to include in a file.

write our file processing programs so they know what each record looks like: The first record is a header for the first image; the second record is the image; the third record is a document; the fourth is a header for the second image; and so forth.

This solution is workable and simple, but it has some familiar drawbacks:

☐ Objects must be accessed sequentially, making access to individual images in large files time consuming.

☐ The file must contain exactly the objects that are described, in exactly the order indicated. We could not, for instance, leave out the notebook for some of the images (or in some cases leave out the notebook altogether) without rewriting all programs that access the file to reflect the changes in the file's structure.

A solution to these problems is hinted at in the FITS header: Each line begins with a keyword that identifies the metadata field that follows in the line. Why not use keywords to identify *all* objects in the file—not just the fields in the headers, but the headers themselves, as well as the images and any other objects we might need to store? Unfortunately, the "keyword = data" format makes sense in a FITS header—it is short and fits easily in an 80-byte line—but it doesn't work at all for objects that vary enormously in size and content. Fortunately, we can generalize the keyword idea to address these problems by making two changes:

☐ Lift the restriction that each record be 80 bytes, and let it be big enough to hold the object that is referenced by the keyword.

☐ Place the keywords in an index table, together with the byte offset of the actual metadata (or data) and a length indicator that indicates how many bytes the metadata (or data) occupies in the file.

The term *tag* is commonly used in place of *keyword* in connection with this type of file structure. The resulting structure is illustrated in Fig. 4.17. In it, we encounter two important conceptual tools for file design: (1) the use of an *index table* to hold descriptive information about the primary data, and (2) the use of *tags* to distinguish different types of objects. These tools allow us to store in one file a mixture of objects—objects that can vary from one another in structure and content.

Tag structures are common among standard file formats in use today. For example, a structure called TIFF (Tagged Image File Format) is a very popular tagged file format used for storing images. HDF (Hierarchical Data Format) is a standard tagged structure used for storing many different kinds of scientific data, including images. In the world of document storage and retrieval, SGML (Standard General Markup Language) is a *language* for

Index table
with tags:

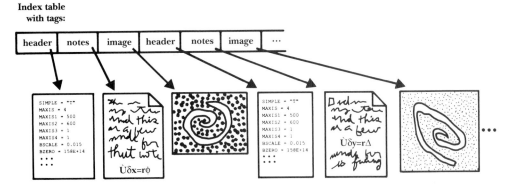

FIGURE 4.17 Same as Fig. 4.16, except with tags identifying the objects.

describing document structures and for defining tags used to mark up that structure. Like FITS, each of these provides an interesting study in file design and standardization. References to further information on each are provided at the end of this chapter, in "Further Readings."

Accessing Files with Mixtures of Data Objects   The idea of allowing files to contain widely varying objects is compelling, especially for applications that require large amounts of metadata or unpredictable mixes of different kinds of data, for it frees us of the requirement that all records be fundamentally the same. As usual, we must ask what this freedom costs us. To gain some insight into the costs, imagine that you want to write a program to access objects in such a file. You now have to read and write tags as well as data, and the structure and format for different data types are likely to be different. Here are some questions you will have to answer almost immediately:

□   When we want to read an object of a particular type, how do we search for the object?
□   When we want to store an object in the file, how and where do we store its tag, and where exactly do we put the object?
□   Given that different objects will have very different appearances within a file, how do we determine the correct method for storing or retrieving the object?

The first two questions have to do with accessing the table that contains the tags and pointers to the objects. Solutions to this problem are dealt with in detail in Chapter 6, so we defer their discussion until then. The third question, how to determine the correct methods for accessing objects, has implications that we briefly touch on here.

4.5.6 Object-oriented File Access

We have used the term *abstract data model* to describe the view that an application has of a data object. This is essentially an in-RAM, application-oriented view of an object, one that ignores the physical format of objects as they are stored in files. Taking this view of objects buys our software two things:

☐ It delegates to separate modules the responsibility of translating to and from the physical format of the object, letting the application modules concentrate on the task at hand. (For example, an image processing program that can operate in RAM on 8-bit images should not have to worry about the fact that a particular image comes from a file that uses the 32-bit FITS format.)

☐ It opens up the possibility of working with objects that at some level fit the same abstract data model, even though they are stored in different formats. The in-RAM representations of the images could be identical, even though they come from files with quite different formats.)

File access that exploits these possibilities could be called *object-oriented access,* emphasizing the parallels between it and the well-known object-oriented programming paradigm.

As an example that illustrates both points, suppose you have an image processing application program (we'll call it *find_star*) that operates in RAM on 8-bit images, and you need to process a collection of images. Some are stored in FITS files in a FITS format and some in TIFF files in a different format. An object-oriented approach (Fig. 4.18) would provide the application program with a routine (let's call it *read_image( )*) for reading images into RAM in the expected 8-bit form, letting the application concentrate on the image processing task. For its part, the routine *read_image( ),* given a file to get an image from, determines the format of the image within the file, invokes the proper procedure to read the image in that format, and converts it from that format into the 8-bit RAM format that the application needs.

Tagged file formats are one way to implement this conceptual view of file organization and file access. The specification of a tag can be accompanied by a specification of methods for reading, writing, and

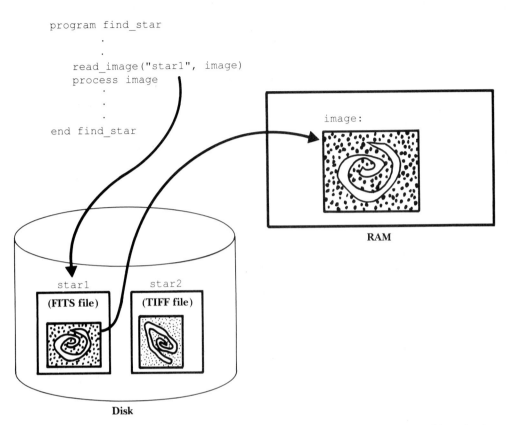

FIGURE 4.18 Example of object-oriented access. The program *find_star* knows nothing about the file format of the image that it wants to read. The routine *read_image* has methods to convert the image from whatever format it is stored in on disk into the 8-bit in-RAM format required by *find_star*.

otherwise manipulating the corresponding data object according to the needs of an application. Indeed, any specification that separates the definition of the abstract data model from that of the corresponding file format lends itself to the object-oriented approach.

4.5.7 Extensibility

One of the advantages of using tags to identify objects within files is that we do not have to know *a priori* what all of the objects will look like that our software may eventually have to deal with. We have just seen that if our program is to be able to access a mixture of objects in a file, it must have methods for reading and writing each object. Once we build into our software a mechanism for choosing the appropriate methods for a given type of object, it is easy to imagine extending, at some future time, the types of objects that our software can support. Every time we encounter a new type of object that we would like to accommodate in our files, we can implement methods for reading and writing that object and add those methods to the repertoire of methods available to our file processing software.

4.6   Portability and Standardization

A recurring theme in several of the examples that we have just seen is the idea that people often want to share files. Sharing files means making sure that they are accessible on all of the different computers that they might turn up on, and that they are somehow compatible with all of the different programs that will access them. In this final section, we look at two complementary topics that affect the sharability of files: portability and standardization.

4.6.1 Factors Affecting Portability

Imagine that you work for a company that wishes to share simple data files such as our address file with some other business. You get together with the other business to agree on a common field and record format, and you discover that your business does all of its programming and computing in C on a Sun computer and the other business uses Turbo Pascal on an IBM PC. What sorts of issues would you expect to arise?

Differences among Operating Systems   In Chapter 2 in the section "Unexpected Characters in Files," we saw that MS-DOS adds an extra linefeed character every time it encounters a carriage return character, whereas on most other file systems this is not the case. This means that every time our address file has a byte with hex value 0x0d, whether or not that byte is meant to be a carriage return, the file is extended by an extra 0x0a byte.

This example illustrates the fact that *the ultimate physical format of the same logical file can vary depending on differences among operating systems.*

Differences among Languages   Earlier in this chapter, when discussing header records, we chose to make our C header 32 bytes, but we were forced to make our Pascal header 64 bytes. C allows us to mix and match fixed record lengths according to our needs, but Pascal requires that all records in a nontext file be the same size.

This illustrates a second factor impeding portability among files: *The physical layout of files produced with different languages may be constrained by the way the languages let you define structures within a file.*

Differences in Machine Architectures Consider again the header record that we produce in the C version of our address file. The hex dump of the file (Fig. 4.13), which was generated using C on a Sun 3 computer, shows this header record in the first line:

```
0000000   0020 0000 0000 0000 0000 0000 0000 0000
```

The first two bytes contain the number of records in the file, in this case 20_{16}, or 32_{10}. If the same C program is compiled and executed on an IBM PC or a VAX, the hex dump of the header record will look like this:

```
0000000   2000 0000 0000 0000 0000 0000 0000 0000
```

Why are the bytes reversed in this version of the program? The answer is that in both cases the numbers were written to the file exactly as they appeared in RAM, and the two different machines represent two-byte integers differently—the Sun stores the high-order byte, followed by the low-order byte; the IBM PC and VAX store the low-order byte, followed by the high-order byte.

This reverse order also applies to four-byte integers on these machines. For example, in our discussion of file dumps we saw that the hexadecimal value of $500,000,000_{10}$ is $1dcd6500_{16}$. If you write this value out to a file on an IBM PC, or some other reverse-order machine, a hex dump of the file created looks like this:

```
0000000   0065 cd1d
```

The problem of data representation is not restricted only to binary numbers. The way structures, such as C structs or Pascal records, are laid out in RAM can vary from machine to machine and compiler to compiler. For example, suppose you have a C program containing the following lines of code:

```
struct {
      int   cost;
      char ident[4];
} item
...
write (fd, &item, sizeof(item));
```

and you want to write files using this code on two different machines, a Cray 2 and a Sun 3. Because it likes to operate on 64-bit words, Cray's C compiler allocates a minimum of eight bytes for any element in a struct, so it allocates 16 bytes for the struct *item*. When it executes the write( ) statement, then, the Cray writes 16 bytes to the file. The same program compiled on a Sun 3 writes only eight bytes, as you probably would expect, and on most IBM PCs it writes six bytes: same exact program; same language; three different results.

Text is also encoded differently on different platforms. In this case the differences are primarily restricted to two different types of systems: those that use EBCDIC[†] and those that use ASCII. EBCDIC is a standard created by IBM, so machines that need to maintain compatibility with IBM must support EBCDIC. Most others support ASCII. A few support both. Hence, text written to a file from an EBCDIC-based machine may well not be readable by an ASCII-based machine.

Equally serious, when we go beyond simple English text, is the problem of representing different character sets from different national languages. This is an enormous problem for developers of text databases.

4.6.2 Achieving Portability

Differences among languages, operating systems, and machine architectures represent three major problems when we need to generate portable files. Achieving portability means determining how to deal with these differences. And the differences are often not just differences between two platforms, for many different platforms could be involved.

The most important requirement for achieving portability is to recognize that it is not a trivial matter and to take steps ahead of time to insure it. Here are some guidelines.

Agree on a Standard Physical Record Format and Stay with It A physical standard is one that is represented the same physically, no matter what language, machine, or operating system is used. FITS is a good example of a physical standard, for it specifies exactly the physical format of each header record, the keywords that are allowed, the order in which keywords may appear, and the bit pattern that must be used to represent the binary numbers that describe the image.

Unfortunately, once a standard is established, it is very tempting to "improve" on it by changing it in some way, thereby rendering it no longer a standard. If the standard is sufficiently extensible, this temptation can sometimes be avoided. FITS, for example, has been extended a few times over its lifetime to support data objects that were not anticipated in its

---

[†]EBCDIC stands for Extended Binary Coded Decimal Interchange Code.

original design, yet all additions have remained compatible with the original format.

One way to make sure that a standard has staying power is to make it simple enough that files can be written in the standard format from a wide range of machines, languages, and operating systems. FITS again exemplifies such a standard. FITS headers are ASCII 80-byte records in blocks of 36 records each, and FITS images are stored as one contiguous block of numbers, both very simple structures that are easy to read and write in most modern operating systems and languages.

Agree on a Standard Binary Encoding for Data Elements   The two most common types of basic data elements are text and numbers. In the case of text, ASCII and EBCDIC represent the most common encoding schemes, with ASCII standard on virtually all machines except IBM mainframes. Depending on the anticipated environment, one of these should be used to represent all text.[†]

The situation for binary numbers is a little cloudier. Although the number of different encoding schemes is not large, the likelihood of having to share data among machines that use different binary encodings can be quite high, especially when the same data is processed both on large mainframes and on smaller computers. Two standards efforts have helped diminish the problem, however: IEEE Standard formats, and External Data Representation (XDR).

IEEE has established standard format specifications for 32-bit, 64-bit, and 128-bit floating point numbers, and for 8-bit, 16-bit, and 32-bit integers. With a few notable exceptions (e.g., IBM mainframes, Cray, and Digital) most computer manufacturers have followed these guidelines in designing their machines. This effort goes a long way toward providing portable number encoding schemes.

XDR is an effort to go the rest of the way. XDR specifies not only a set of standard encodings for all files (the IEEE encodings), but provides for a set of routines for each machine for converting from its binary encoding when writing to a file, and vice versa (Fig. 4.19). Hence, when we want to store numbers in XDR, we can read or write them by replacing read and write routines in our program with XDR routines. The XDR routines take care of the conversions.[‡]

[†]Actually, there are different versions of both ASCII and EBCDIC. However, for most applications, and for the purposes of this text, it is sufficient to consider each as a single character set.

[‡]XDR is used for more than just number conversions. It allows a C programmer to describe arbitrary data structures in a machine-independent fashion. XDR originated as a Sun protocol for transmitting data that is accessed by more than one type of machine. For further information, see Sun (1986 or later).

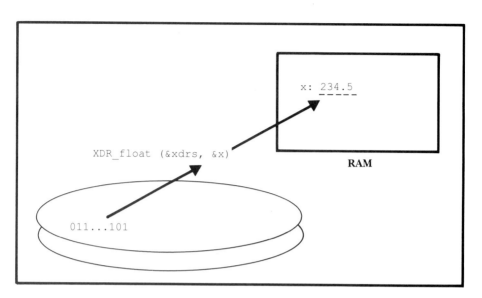

FIGURE 4.19 XDR specifies a standard external data representation for numbers stored in a file. XDR routines are provided for converting to and from the XDR representation to the encoding scheme used on the host machine. Here a routine called XDR_float( ) translates a 32-bit floating point number from its XDR representation on disk to that of the host machine.

Once again, FITS provides us with an excellent example: The binary numbers that constitute a FITS image must conform to the IEEE Standard. Any program written on a machine with XDR support can thus read and write portable FITS files.

Number and Text Conversion   Sometimes the use of standard data encodings is not feasible. For example, suppose you are working primarily on IBM mainframes with software that deals with floating point numbers and text. If you choose to store your data in IEEE Standard formats, every time your program reads or writes a number or character it must translate the number from the IBM format to the corresponding IEEE format. This is not only time-consuming but can result in loss of accuracy. It is probably better in this case to store your data in native IBM format in your files.

What happens, then, when you want to move your files back and forth between your IBM and a VAX, which uses a different native format for numbers and generally uses ASCII for text? You need a way to convert from the IBM format to the VAX format and back. One solution is to write (or borrow) a program that translates IBM numbers and text to their VAX equivalents, and vice versa. This simple solution is illustrated in Fig. 4.20(a).

But what if, in addition to IBM and VAX computers, you find that your data is likely to be shared among many different platforms that use different numeric encodings? One way to solve this problem is to write a program to convert from each of the representations to every other representation. This solution, illustrated in Fig. 4.20(b), can get rather complicated. In general, if you have n different encoding schemes, you will need $n(n - 1)$ different translators. (Why?) If n is large, this can be very messy. Not only do you need many translators, but you need to keep track, for each file, of where the file came from and/or where it is going in order to know which translator to use.

In this case, a better solution would probably be to agree on a standard intermediate format, such as XDR, and translate files into XDR whenever they are to be exported to a different platform. This solution is illustrated in Fig. 4.20(c). Not only does it cut down the number of translators from $n(n - 1)$ to $2n$, but it should be easy to find translators to convert from most platforms to and from XDR. One negative aspect of this solution is that it requires *two* conversions to go from any one platform to another, a cost that has to be weighed against the complexity of providing $n(n - 1)$ translators.

File Structure Conversion   Suppose you are a doctor and you have X-ray raster images of a particular organ taken periodically over several minutes. You want to look at a certain image in the collection using a program that lets you zoom in and out and detect special features in the image. You have another program that lets you animate the collection of images, showing how it changes over several minutes. Finally, you want to annotate the images and store them in a special X-ray archive, and you have another program for doing that. What do you do if each of these three programs requires that your image be in a different format?

The conversion problems that apply to atomic data encodings also apply to file structures for more complex objects, like images, but at a different level. Whereas character and number encodings are tied closely to specific platforms, more complex objects and their representations just as often are tied to specific *applications*.

For example, there are many software packages that deal with images, and very little agreement about a file format for storing them. When we look at this software, we find different solutions to this problem:

☐   Require that the user supply images in a format that is compatible with the one used by the package. This places the responsibility on the user to convert from one format to another. For such situations,

From: To:

(a) Converting between IBM and Vax native format
requires two conversion routines.

From: To:

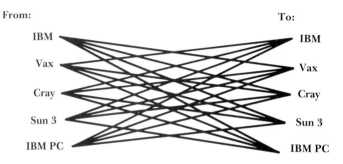

(b) Converting directly between five different native formats
requires 20 conversion routines.

To & From:

From: To:

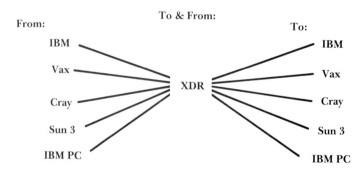

(c) Converting between five different native formats via an
intermediate standard format requires 10 conversion routines.

FIGURE 4.20 Direct conversion between n native machines formats requires $n(n-1)$ conversion routines, as illustrated in (a)
and (b). Conversion via an intermediate standard format requires
$2n$ conversion routines, as illustrated in (c).

it may be preferable to provide utility programs that translate from one format to another and that are invoked whenever translating.

☐   Process only images that adhere to some predefined standard format. This places the responsibility on a community of users and software developers for agreeing on and enforcing a standard. FITS is a good example of this approach.

☐   Include different sets of I/O methods capable of converting an image from several different formats into a standard RAM structure that the package can work with. This places the burden on the software developer to develop I/O methods for file object types that may be stored differently but for the purposes of an application are conceptually the same. You may recognize this approach as a variation on the concept of *object-oriented access* that we discussed earlier.

File System Differences   Finally, if you move files from one file system to another, chances are you will find differences in the way files are organized physically. For example, UNIX systems write files to tapes in 512-byte blocks, but non-UNIX systems often use different block sizes, such as 2,880-bytes—thirty-six 80-byte records. (Guess where the FITS blocking format comes from?) When transferring files between systems, you may need to deal with this problem.

UNIX and Portability   Recognizing problems such as the block-size problem just described, UNIX provides a utility called *dd*. Although *dd* is intended primarily for copying tape data to and from UNIX systems, it can be used to convert data from any physical source. The *dd* utility provides the following options, among others:

☐   Convert from one block size to another;
☐   Convert fixed-length records to variable length, or vice versa;
☐   Convert ASCII to EBCDIC, or vice versa;
☐   Convert all characters to lowercase (or to uppercase); and
☐   Swap every pair of bytes.

Of course, the greatest contribution UNIX makes to the problems discussed here is UNIX itself. By its simplicity and ubiquity, UNIX encourages the use of the same operating system, the same file system, the same views of devices, and the same general views of file organization, no matter what particular hardware platform you happen to be using.

For example, one of the authors works in an organization with a nationwide constituency that operates many different computers, including two Crays, a Connection Machine, and many Sun, Apple, IBM, Silicon Graphics, and Digital workstations. Because each runs some flavor of

UNIX, they all incorporate precisely the same view of all external storage devices, they all use ASCII, and they all provide the same basic programming environment and file management utilities. Files are not perfectly portable within this environment, for reasons that we have covered in this chapter, but the availability of UNIX goes a long way toward facilitating the rapid and easy transfer of files among the applications, programming environments, and hardware systems that the organization supports.

■ SUMMARY

The lowest level of organization that we normally impose on a file is a *stream of bytes*. Unfortunately, by storing data in a file merely as a stream of bytes, we lose the ability to distinguish among the fundamental informational units of our data. We call these fundamental pieces of information *fields*. Fields are grouped together to form *records*. Recognizing fields and recognizing records requires that we impose structure on the data in the file.

There are many ways to separate one field from the next and one record from the next:

- Fix the length of each field or record.
- Begin each field or record with a count of the number of bytes that it contains.
- Use delimiters to mark the divisions between entities.

In the case of fields, another useful technique is to use a "keyword = value" form to identify fields. In the case of records, another useful technique is to use a second, index file that tells where each record begins.

One higher level of organization, in which records are grouped into *blocks,* is also often imposed on files. This level is imposed to improve I/O performance rather than our logical view of the file.

In this chapter we use the record structure that uses a length indicator at the beginning of each record to develop programs for writing and reading a simple file of variable-length records containing names and addresses of individuals. We use buffering to accumulate the data in an individual record before we know its length to write it to the file. Buffers are also useful in allowing us to read in a complete record at one time. We represent the length field of each record as a binary number or as a sequence of ASCII digits. In the former case, it is useful to use a *file dump* to examine the contents of our file.

Sometimes we identify individual records by their *relative record numbers* (RRNs) in a file. It is also common, however, to identify a record by a *key* whose value is based on some of the record's content. Key values must occur in, or be converted to, some predetermined *canonical form* if they are to be recognized accurately and unambiguously by programs. If every record's key value is distinct from all others, the key can be used to identify and locate the unique record in the file. Keys that are used in this way are called *primary keys*.

In this chapter we look at the technique of searching sequentially through a file looking for a record with a particular key. Sequential search can perform poorly for long files, but there are times when sequential searching is reasonable. Record blocking can be used to improve the I/O time for a sequential search substantially. Two useful UNIX utilities that process files sequentially are *wc* and *grep*.

In our discussion of ways to separate records, it is clear that some of the methods provide a mechanism for looking up or calculating the *byte offset* of the beginning of a record. This, in turn, opens up the possibility of accessing the record *directly,* by RRN, rather than sequentially.

The simplest record formats for permitting direct access by RRN involve the use of fixed-length records. When the data itself actually comes in fixed-size quantities (e.g., zip codes), fixed-length records can provide good performance and good space utilization. If there is a lot of variation in the amount and size of data in records, however, the use of fixed-length records can result in expensive waste of space. In such cases the designer should look carefully at the possibility of using variable-length records.

Sometimes it is helpful to keep track of general information about files, such as the number of records they contain. A *header record,* stored at the beginning of the file it pertains to, is a useful tool for storing this kind of information.

It is important to be aware of the difference between *file access* and *file organization*. We try to organize files in such a way that they give us the types of access we need for a particular application. For example, one of the advantages of a fixed-length record *organization* is that it allows *access* that is either sequential or direct.

In addition to the traditional view of a file as a more or less regular collection of fields and records, we present a more purely logical view of the contents of files in terms of *abstract data models,* a view that lets applications ignore the physical structure of files altogether.

This view is often more appropriate to data objects such as sound, images, and documents. We call files *self-describing* when they do not require an application to reveal their structure, but provide that information themselves. Another concept that deviates from the traditional view is *metadata*, in which the file contains data that describe the primary data in the file. FITS files, used for storing astronomical images, contain extensive headers with metadata.

The use of abstract data models, self-describing files, and metadata makes it possible to mix a variety of different types of data objects in one file. When this is the case, file access is more *object oriented*. Abstract data models also facilitate *extensible* files—files whose structures can be extended to accommodate new kinds of objects.

Portability becomes increasingly important as files are used in more heterogeneous computing environments. Differences among operating systems, languages, and machine architectures all lead to the need for portability. One important way to foster portability is *standardization*, which means agreeing on physical formats, encodings for data elements, and file structures.

If a standard does not exist and it becomes necessary to convert from one format to another, it is still often much simpler to have one standard format that all converters convert into and out of. UNIX provides a utility called *dd* that facilitates data conversion. The UNIX environment itself supports portability simply by being commonly available on a large number of platforms.

■ KEY TERMS

Block. A collection of records stored as a physically contiguous unit on secondary storage. In this chapter, we use record blocking to improve I/O performance during sequential searching.

Byte count field. A field at the beginning of a variable-length record that gives the number of bytes used to store the record. The use of a byte count field allows a program to transmit (or skip over) a variable-length record without having to deal with the record's internal structure.

Canonical form. A standard form for a key that can be derived, by the application of well-defined rules, from the particular, nonstandard form of the data found in a record's key field(s) or provided in a search request supplied by a user.

Delimiter. One or more characters used to separate fields and records in a file.

Direct access. A file accessing mode that involves jumping to the exact location of a record. Direct access to a fixed-length record is usually accomplished by using its *relative record number* (RRN), computing its byte offset, and then seeking to the first byte of the record.

Extensibility. A characteristic of some file organizations that makes it possible to extend the types of objects that the format can accommodate without having to redesign the format. For example, tagged file formats lend themselves to extensibility, for they allow the addition of new tags for new data objects and associated new methods for accessing the objects.

Field. The smallest logically meaningful unit of information in a file. A record in a file is usually made up of several fields.

File-access method. The approach used to locate information in a file. In general, the two alternatives are *sequential access* and *direct access*.

File organization method. The combination of conceptual and physical structures used to distinguish one record from another and one field from another. An example of a kind of file organization is fixed-length records containing variable numbers of variable-length delimited fields.

Fixed-length record. A file organization in which all records have the same length. Records are padded with blanks, nulls, or other characters so they extend to the fixed length. Since all the records have the same length, it is possible to calculate the beginning position of any record, making *direct access* possible.

Header record. A record placed at the beginning of a file that is used to store information about the file contents and the file organization.

Key. An expression derived from one or more of the fields within a record that can be used to locate that record. The fields used to build the key are sometimes called the *key fields*. Keyed access provides a way of performing content-based retrieval of records, rather than retrieval based merely on a record's position.

Metadata. Data in a file that is not the primary data, but describes the primary data in a file. Metadata can be incorporated into any file whose primary data requires supporting information. If a file is going to be shared by many users, some of whom might not otherwise have easy access to its metadata, it may be most convenient to store the metadata in the file itself. A common place to store metadata in a file is the header record.

Object-oriented file access. A form of file access in which applications access data objects in terms of the applications' in-RAM view of the objects. Separate methods associated with the objects are responsible for translating to and from the physical format of the object, letting the application concentrate on the task at hand.

Portability. That characteristic of files that describes how amenable
they are to access on a variety of different machines, via a variety of
different operating systems, languages, and applications.

Primary key. A key that uniquely identifies each record and that is
used as the primary method of accessing the records.

Record. A collection of related fields. For example, the name, address,
etc. of an individual in a mailing list file would probably make up
one record.

Relative record number (RRN). An index giving the position of a
record relative to the beginning of its file. If a file has fixed-length
records, the RRN can be used to calculate the *byte offset* of a record
so the record can be accessed directly.

Self-describing files. Files that contain information such as the number
of records in the file and formal descriptions of the file's record
structure, which can be used by software in determining how to access the file. A file's header is a good place for this information.

Sequential access. Sequential access to a file means reading the file from
the beginning and continuing until you have read in everything that
you need. The alternative is direct access.

Sequential search. A method of searching a file by reading the file
from the beginning and continuing until the desired record has been
found.

Stream of bytes. Term describing the lowest-level view of a file. If we
begin with the basic *stream-of-bytes* view of a file, we can then impose
our own higher levels of order on the file, including field, record,
and block structures.

Variable-length record. A file organization in which the records have
no predetermined length. They are just as long as they need to be,
hence making better use of space than fixed-length records do. Unfortunately, we cannot calculate the byte offset of a variable-length
record by knowing only its relative record number.

■ EXERCISES

1. Find situations for which each of the four field structures described in
the text might be appropriate. Do the same for each of the record structures
described.

2. Discuss the appropriateness of using the following characters to delimit
fields or records: carriage return, linefeed, space, comma, period, colon,

escape. Can you think of situations in which you might want to use different delimiters for different fields?

3. Suppose you want to change the programs in section 4.1 to include a phone number field in each record. What changes need to be made?

4. Suppose you need to keep a file in which every record has both fixed- and variable-length fields. For example, suppose you want to create a file of employee records, using fixed-length fields for each employee's ID (primary key), sex, birthdate, and department, and using variable-length fields for each name and address. What advantages might there be to using such a structure? Should we put the variable-length portion first or last? Either approach is possible; how can each be implemented?

5. One record structure not described in this chapter is called *labeled*. In a labeled record structure each field that is represented is preceded by a label describing its contents. For example, if the labels LN, FN, AD, CT, ST, and ZP are used to describe the six fixed-length fields for a name and address record, it might appear as follows:

`LNAmesbbbbbbbFNJohnbbbbbbbAD123 MaplebbbbbbbCTStillwaterSTOKZP74075bbbb`

Under what conditions might this be a reasonable, even desirable, record structure?

6. Define the terms *stream of bytes, stream of fields,* and *stream of records.*

7. Find out what basic file structures are available to you in the programming language that you are currently using. For example, does your language recognize a sequence-of-bytes structure? Does it recognize lines of text? Record blocking? For those types of structures that your language does not recognize, describe how you might implement them using structures that your language does recognize.

8. Report on the basic field and record structures available in PL/I or COBOL.

9. Compare the use of ASCII characters to represent *everything* in a file with the use of binary and ASCII data mixed together.

10. If you list the contents of a file containing both binary and ASCII characters on your terminal screen, what results can you expect? What happens when you list a completely binary file on your screen? (*Warning:* If you actually try this, do so with a very small file. You could lock up or reconfigure your terminal, or even log yourself off!)

11. If a key in a record is already in canonical form and the key is the first field of the record, it is possible to search for a record by key without ever separating out the key field from the rest of the fields. Explain.

12. It has been suggested (Sweet, 1985) that primary keys should be "dataless, unchanging, unambiguous, and unique." These concepts are interrelated since, for example, a key that contains data runs a greater risk of changing than a dataless key. Discuss the importance of each of these concepts, and show by example how their absence can cause problems. The primary key used in our example file violates at least one of the criteria. How might you redesign the file (and possibly its corresponding information content) so primary keys satisfy these criteria?

13. How many comparisons would be required on average to find a record using sequential search in a 10,000-record disk file? If the record is not in the file, how many comparisons are required? If the file is blocked so 20 records are stored per block, how many disk accesses are required on average? What if only one record is stored per block?

14. In our evaluation of performance for sequential search, we assume that every read results in a seek. How do the assumptions change on a single-user machine with access to a magnetic disk? How do these changed assumptions affect the analysis of sequential searching?

15. Look up the differences between the UNIX commands grep, egrep, and fgrep. Why are they different? What motivates the differences?

16. Give a formula for finding the byte offset of a fixed-length record in which the RRN of the first record is 1 rather than 0.

17. Why is a variable-length record structure unworkable for the *update* program? Does it help if we have an index that points to the beginning of each variable-length record?

18. The *update* program lets the user change records, but not delete records. How must the file structure and access procedures be modified to allow for deletion if we do not care about reusing the space from deleted records? How do the file structures and procedures change if we do want to reuse the space?

19. In our discussion of the uses of relative record numbers (RRNs), we suggest that you can create a file in which there is a direct correspondence between a primary key, such as membership number, and RRN, so we can find a person's record by knowing just the name or membership number. What kinds of difficulties can you envision with this simple correspondence between membership number and RRN? What happens if we want to delete a name? What happens if we change the information in a record in a variable-length record file and the new record is longer?

20. The following file dump describes the first few bytes from a file of the type produced by the C version of *writrec,* but the right-hand column is not filled in. How long is the first record? What are its contents?

```
0000000  00264475  6D707C46  7265647C  38323120  ...............
0000020  4B6C7567  657C4861  636B6572  7C50417C  ...............
0000040  36353533  357C2E2E  48657861  64656369  ...............
```

21. Assume that we have a variable-length record file with long records (greater than 1,000 bytes each, on the average). Assume that we are looking for a record with a particular RRN. Describe the benefits of using the contents of a byte count field to skip sequentially from record to record to find the one we want. This is called *skip sequential* processing. Use your knowledge of system buffering to describe why this is useful only for long records. If the records are sorted in order by key and blocked, what information do you have to place at the start of each block to permit even faster skip sequential processing?

22. Suppose you have a fixed-length record with fixed-length fields, and the sum of the field lengths is 30 bytes. A record with a length of 30 bytes would hold them all. If we intend to store the records on a sectored disk with 512-byte sectors (see Chapter 3), we might decide to pad the record out to 32 bytes so we can place an integral number of records in a sector. Why would we want to do this?

23. Why is it important to distinguish between file access and file organization?

24. What is an abstract data model? Why did the early file processing programs not deal with abstract data models? What are the advantages of using abstract data models in applications? In what way does the UNIX concept of standard input and standard output conform to the notion of an abstract data model? (See "Physical and Logical Files in UNIX" in Chapter 2.)

25. What is metadata?

26. In the FITS header in Fig. 4.15, some metadata provides information about the files's structure, and some provides information about the scientific context in which the corresponding image was recorded. Give three examples of each.

27. In the FITS header in Fig. 4.15, there is enough information for a program to determine how to read the entire file. Assuming that the size of the block containing the header must be a multiple of 2,880 bytes, how large is the file? What proportion of the file contains header information?

28. In the discussion of field organization, we list the "keyword = value" construct as one possible type of field organization. How is this notion applied in tagged file structures? How does a tagged file structure support object-oriented file access? How do tagged file formats support extensibility?

29. List three factors that affect portability in files.

30. List three ways that portability can be achieved in files.

31. What is XDR? XDR is actually much more extensive than what we described in this chapter. If you have access to XDR documentation (see "Further Readings" at the end of this chapter), look up XDR and list the ways that it supports portability.

32. In Fig. 4.2, we see two possible record structures for our address file, one based on C and one based on Pascal. Discuss portability problems that might arise from using these record structures in a heterogeneous computing environment. (*Hint:* Some compilers allocate space for character fields starting on word boundaries, and others do not.)

Programming Exercises

33. Rewrite *writstrm* so it uses delimiters as field separators. The output of the new version of *writstrm* should be readable by *readstrm.c* or *readstrm.pas*.

34. Create versions of *writrec* and *readrec* that use the following fixed-field lengths rather than delimiters.

Last name:	15 characters
First name:	15 characters
Address:	30 characters
City:	20 characters
State:	2 characters
Zip:	5 characters

35. Write the program described in the preceding problem so it uses blocks. Make it store five records per block.

36. Implement the program *find*.

37. Rewrite the program *find* so it can find a record on the basis of its position in the file. For example, if requested to find the 547th record in a file, it would read through the first 546 records, then print the contents of the 547th record. Use skip sequential search (see exercise 21) to avoid reading the contents of unwanted records.

38. Write a program similar to *find,* but with the following differences. Instead of getting record keys from the keyboard, the program reads them from a separate transaction file that contains only the keys of the records to be extracted. Instead of printing the records on the screen, it writes them out to a separate output file. First, assume that the records are in no particular order. Then assume that both the main file and the transaction file are sorted by key. In the latter case, how can you make your program more efficient than *find?*

39. Make any or all of the following alterations to *update.pas* or *update.c.*
a. Let the user identify the record to be changed by name, rather than RRN.
b. Let the user change individual fields without having to change an entire record.
c. Let the user choose to view the entire file.

40. Modify *update.c* or *update.pas* to signal the user when a record exceeds the fixed-record length. The modification should allow the user to bring the record down to an acceptable size and input it again. What are some other modifications that would make the program more robust?

41. Change *update.c* or *update.pas* to a batch program that reads a transaction file in which each transaction record contains an RRN of a record that is to be updated, followed by the new contents of the record, and then makes the changes in a batch run. Although not necessary, it might be desirable to sort the transaction file by RRN. Why?

42. Write a program that reads a file and outputs the file contents as a file dump. The file dump should have a format similar to the one used in the examples in this chapter. The program should accept the name of the input file on the command line. Output should be to standard output (terminal screen).

43. Develop a set of rules for translating the dates August 7, 1949, Aug. 7, 1949, 8-7-49, 08-07-49, 8/7/49, and other, similar variations into a common canonical form. Write a function that accepts a string containing a date in one of these forms and returns the canonical form, according to your rules. Be sure to document the limitations of your rules and function.

44. Write a program to read in a FITS file and print
   a. The size of the image (e.g., 256 by 256)
   b. The title of the image
   c. The telescope used to make the image
   d. The date the image file was created
   e. The average pixel value in the image (use BSCALE and BZERO).

■ FURTHER READINGS

Many textbooks cover basic material on field and record structure design, but only a few go into the options and design considerations in much detail. Teorey and Fry (1982) and Wiederhold (1983) are two possible sources. Hanson's (1982) chapter, "Choice of File Organization," is excellent but is more meaningful after you read the material in the later chapters of this text. You can learn a lot about alternative types of file organization and access by studying descriptions of options available in certain languages and file management systems. PL/I offers a particularly rich set of alternatives, and Pollack and Sterling (1980) describe them thoroughly.

Sweet (1985) is a short but stimulating article on key field design. A number of interesting algorithms for improving performance in sequential searches are described in Gonnet (1984) and, of course, Knuth (1973b). Lapin (1987) provides a detailed coverage of portability in UNIX and C programming. For our coverage of XDR, we used the documentation in Sun (1986).

Our primary source of information on FITS is not formally printed text, but online materials. A good paper defining the original FITS format is Wells (1981). The FITS image and FITS header shown in this chapter, as well as the documentation of how FITS works, can (at the time of writing, at least) be found on an anonymous ftp server at the INTERNET address 128.183.10.4.

C Programs

The C programs listed in the following pages correspond to the programs discussed in the text. The programs are contained in the following files.

writstrm.c Writes out name and address information as a stream of consecutive bytes.

readstrm.c Reads a stream file as input and prints it to the screen.

writrec.c Writes a variable-length record file that uses a byte count at the beginning of each record to give its length.

readrec.c Reads through a file, record by record, displaying the fields from each of the records on the screen.

getrf.c Contains support functions for reading individual records or fields. These functions are needed by programs in *readrec.c* and *find.c*

find.c Searches sequentially through a file for a record with a particular key.

makekey.c Combines first and last names and converts them to a key in canonical form. Calls *strtrim( )* and *ucase( )*, found in *strfuncs.c.*

strfuncs.c Contains two string support functions: *strtrim( )* trims the blanks from the ends of strings; *ucase( )* converts alphabetic characters to uppercase.

update.c Allows new records to be added to a file or old records to be changed.

Fileio.h

All of the programs include a header file called *fileio.h* which contains some useful definitions. Some of these are system dependent. If the programs were to be run on a UNIX system *fileio.h* might look like this:

```
/*  fileio.h --- header file containing file I/O definitions
*/
```

(continued)

```
#include <stdio.h>
#include <fcntl.h>

#define PMODE      0755

#define DELIM_STR    "|"
#define DELIM_CHR    '|'

#define out_str(fd,s)  write((fd),(s),strlen(s));  \
                write((fd),DELIM_STR,1)

#define fld_to_recbuff(rb,fld) strcat(rb,fld); strcat(rb,DELIM_STR)

#define MAX_REC_SIZE 512
```

Writstrm.c

```
/* writstrm.c
    creates name and address file that is strictly a stream of
    bytes (no delimiters, counts, or other information to
    distinguish fields and records).

    A simple modification to the out_str macro:
        #define out_str(fd,s)   write((fd),(s),strlen(s)); \
                        write((fd),DELIM_STR,1);
    changes the program so that it creates delimited fields.
*/

#include "fileio.h"

#define  out_str(fd,s)          write((fd),(s),strlen(s))

main ( ) {

    char first[30], last[30], address[30], city[20];
    char state[15], zip[9];
    char filename[15];
    int fd;

    printf("Enter the name of the file you wish to create: ");
    gets(filename);

    if ((fd = creat(filename,PMODE)) < 0) {
        printf("file opening error --- program stopped\n");
        exit(1);
    }
```

```
printf("\n\nType in a last name (surname), or <CR> to exit\n>>>");
gets(last);
while (strlen(last) > 0)
{
     printf("\nFirst Name:");
     gets(first);
     printf("   Address:");
     gets(address);
     printf("      City:");
     gets(city);
     printf("     State:");
     gets(state);
     printf("       Zip:");
     gets(zip);

     /*output the strings to the buffer and then to the file*/
     out_str(fd,last);
     out_str(fd,first);
     out_str(fd,address);
     out_str(fd,city);
     out_str(fd,state);
     out_str(fd,zip);

     /* prepare for next entry */
     printf("\n\nType in a last name (surname), or <CR> to exit\n>>>");
     gets(last);
  }
  /* close the file before leaving */
  close(fd);
}
```

Readstrm.c

```
/* readstrm.c

     reads a stream of delimited fields
*/

#include "fileio.h"
int readfield(int fd, char s[]);

main( ) {

     int fd,n;
     char s[30];
     char filename[15];
     int fld_count;
```

(continued)

```
        printf("Enter name of file to read: ");
        gets(filename);
        if ((fd = open(filename,O_RDONLY)) < 0) {
            printf("file opening error --- program stopped\n");
            exit(1);
        }

        /* main program loop -- calls readfield( ) for as long
           as the function succeeds                                    */
        fld_count = 0;
        while ((n = readfield(fd,s)) > 0)
            printf("\tfield # %3d:   %s\n",++fld_count,s);

        close(fd);
}

int readfield(int fd, char s[])
{
        int i;
        char c;

        i = 0;
        while ( read(fd,&c,1) > 0  && c != DELIM_CHR)
            s[i++] = c;

        s[i] = '\0';        /* append null to end string */
        return (i);
}
```

Writrec.c

```
/* writrec.c
    creates name and address file using fixed length (2-byte)
    record length field ahead of each record
*/
#include "fileio.h"

char recbuff[MAX_REC_SIZE + 1];
char *prompt[] = {
    "Enter Last Name -- or <CR> to exit: ",
    "                        First name: ",
    "                           Address: ",
    "                              City: ",
    "                             State: ",
    "                               Zip: ",
    ""          /* null string to terminate the prompt loop */
};
```

```
main ( ) {

     char response[50];
     char filename[15];
     int fd,i;
     short rec_lgth;

     printf("Enter the name of the file you wish to create: ");
     gets(filename);

     if ((fd = creat(filename,PMODE)) < 0) {
         printf("file opening error --- program stopped\n");
         exit(1);
     }

     printf("\n\n%s",prompt[0]);
     gets(response);
     while (strlen(response) > 0)
     {
         recbuff[0] = '\0';
         fld_to_recbuff(recbuff,response);
         for (i=1; *prompt[i] != '\0' ; i++)
         {
           printf("%s",prompt[i]);
           gets(response);
             fld_to_recbuff(recbuff,response);
         }

         /* write out the record length and buffer contents */
         rec_lgth = strlen(recbuff);
         write(fd,&rec_lgth,sizeof(rec_lgth));
         write(fd,recbuff,rec_lgth);

         /* prepare for next entry */
         printf("\n\n%s",prompt[0]);
         gets(response);
     }
     /* close the file before leaving */
     close(fd);
}

/* question:

   How does the termination condition work in the for loop:
         for (i=1; *prompt[i] != '\0' ; i++)

   What does the "i" refer to?  Why do we need the "*"?
*/
```

Readrec.c

```
/* readrec.c ...

        reads through a file, record by record, displaying the
        fields from each of the records on the screen.
*/

#include "fileio.h"

main( )  {

        int fd, rec_count, fld_count;
        int scan_pos;
          short rec_lgth;
        char filename[15];
        char recbuff[MAX_REC_SIZE + 1];
        char field[MAX_REC_SIZE + 1];

        printf("Enter name of file to read: ");
        gets(filename);
        if ((fd = open(filename,O_RDONLY)) < 0) {
            printf("file opening error --- program stopped\n");
            exit(1);
        }

        rec_count = 0;
        scan_pos = 0;
        while  ((rec_lgth = get_rec(fd,recbuff)) > 0)
        {
            printf ("Record %d\n", ++rec_count);
            fld_count = 0;
            while ((scan_pos = get_fld(field,recbuff,scan_pos,
                                                    rec_lgth)) > 0
                printf ("\tField %d: %s\n",++fld_count,field);
        }

        close(fd);
}

/* question -- why can I assign 0 to scan_pos just once, outside
   of the while loop for records?  */
```

Getrf.c

```
/* getrf.c ...

        Two functions used by programs in readrec.c and find.c:

            get_rec( ) reads a variable length record from file fd
                       into the character array recbuff.
            get_fld( ) moves a field from recbuff into the character
                       array field, inserting a '\0' to make it a
                       string.
*/
#include "fileio.h"

get_rec(int fd, char recbuff[])
{
        short rec_lgth;

        if (read(fd, &rec_lgth, 2) == 0) /* get record length */
            return(0);                            /* return 0 if EOF */
        rec_lgth = read(fd, recbuff, rec_lgth);  /* read record */
        return(rec_lgth);
}

get_fld(char field[], char recbuff[], short scan_pos, short rec_lgth)
{
        short fpos = 0;        /* position in "field" array */

        if (scan_pos == rec_lgth) /*if no more fields to read,*/
            return(0);                /*return scan_pos of 0.*/

        /* scanning loop */
        while ( scan_pos < rec_lgth &&
                (field[fpos++] = recbuff[scan_pos++]) != DELIM_CHR)
            ;

        if (field[fpos -1] == DELIM_CHR)/*if last character is a field*/
            field[--fpos] = '\0'; /*delimiter, replace with null*/
        else
            field[fpos] = '\0'; /*otherwise, just ensure that
                                    the field is null-terminated*/
        return(scan_pos); /*return position of start of next field*/
}
```

Find.c

```
/* find.c ...
        searches sequentially through a file for a record with a
        particular key.
*/

#include "fileio.h"
#define   TRUE     1
#define   FALSE    0

main( )  {

        int fd, scan_pos;
          short rec_lgth;
        int matched;
        char search_key[30], key_found[30], last[30], first[30];
        char filename[15];
        char recbuff[MAX_REC_SIZE + 1];
        char field[MAX_REC_SIZE + 1];

        printf("Enter name of file to search: ");
        gets(filename);
        if ((fd = open(filename,O_RDONLY)) < 0) {
            printf("file opening error --- program stopped\n");
            exit(1);
        }

        printf("\n\nEnter last name: "); /* get search key */
        gets(last);
        printf("\nEnter first name: ");
        gets(first);
        makekey(last, first, search_key);

          matched = FALSE;
        while  (!matched && (rec_lgth = get_rec(fd,recbuff)) > 0 )
        {
            scan_pos = 0;
            scan_pos = get_fld(last, recbuff, scan_pos, rec_lgth);
            scan_pos = get_fld(first, recbuff, scan_pos, rec_lgth);
            makekey(last, first, key_found);
            if (strcmp (key_found, search_key) == 0)
                matched = TRUE;
        }

        /* if record found, print the fields */
        if (matched)
        {
```

```
        printf("\n\nRecord found:\n\n");
        scan_pos = 0;

        /* break out the fields */
        while((scan_pos=get_fld(field,recbuff,scan_pos,rec_lgth))>0)
          printf("\t%s\n",field);
    } else
        printf("\n\nRecord not found.\n");
}

/* questions:

    -why does scan_pos get set to zero inside the while loop here?

    -what would happen if we wrote the loop that reads records
     like this: while  ((rec_lgth = get_rec(fd,recbuff)) > 0 &&
     !matched )

*/
```

Makekey.c

```
/* makekey(last,first,s) ...

        function to make a key from the first and last names passed
        through the functions arguments.  Returns the key in
        canonical form through the address passed through the
        argument s.  Calling routine is responsible for ensuring
        that s is large enough to hold the return string.

        Value returned through the function name is the length of
        the string returned through s.

*/

makekey(char last[], char first[],char s[])
{
        int lenl,lenf;

        lenl = strtrim(last);   /* trim the last name */
        strcpy(s,last);              /* place it in the return string */
        s[lenl++] = ' ';   /* append a blank at the end */
        s[lenl] = '\0';
        lenf = strtrim(first);   /* trim the first name */
        strcat(s,first);   /* append it to the string */
        ucase(s,s);          /* convert everything to uppercase */
        return(lenl + lenf);
}
```

Strfuncs.c

```
/* strfuncs.c...

    module containing the following functions:

    strtrim(s) trims blanks from the end of the (null-terminated)
              string referenced by the string address s.  When
              done, the parameter s points to the trimmed string.
              The function returns the length of the trimmed
              string.

    ucase(si,so) converts all lowercase alphabetic characters in
              the string at address si into uppercase characters,
              returning the converted string through the address
              so.
*/

strtrim( char s[])
{
    int i;

    for (i = strlen(s)-1; i>=0 && s[i] == ' '; i--)
        ;
    /* now that the blanks are trimmed, reaffix null on the end
     to form a string */

    s[++i] = '\0';
    return(i);
}

ucase (char si[], char so[])
{
    while (*so++ = (*si >= 'a' && *si <= 'z') ? *si & 0x5f : *si)
        si++;
}
```

Update.c

```
/* update.c ...
    program to open or create a fixed length record file for
    updating.  Records may be added or changed.  Records to be
    changed must be accessed by relative record number

*/

#include "fileio.h"
#define REC_LGTH  64
```

```
static char *prompt[]= {"        Last Name: ",
                        "       First name: ",
                        "         Address: ",
                        "            City: ",
                        "           State: ",
                        "             Zip: ",
                        ""             };

static int fd;
static struct {
      short   rec_count;
      char    fill[30];
} head;

static menu( );
static ask_info(char recbuff[]);
static ask_rrn( );
static read_and_show( );
static change( );


main( ) {

   int i,menu_choice,rrn;
   int byte_pos;
   char filename[15];
   long lseek( );
   char recbuff[MAX_REC_SIZE + 1];/*buffer to hold a record*/

   printf("Enter the name of the file: ");
   gets(filename);
   if (( fd = open(filename, O_RDWR)) < 0) /*if OPEN fails*/
     {
       fd = creat(filename, PMODE);       /*then CREAT*/
       head.rec_count = 0;                /*initialize header */
       write(fd,&head,sizeof(head));      /*write header rec*/

     }
   else    /* existing file opened -- read in header */
       read(fd,&head,sizeof(head));
   /* main program loop -- call menu and then jump to options */
   while((menu_choice = menu( )) < 3)
     {
       switch(menu_choice)
       {
         case 1:               /* add a new record */
             printf("Input the information for the new record --\n\n");
             ask_info(recbuff);
             byte_pos = head.rec_count * REC_LGTH + sizeof(head);
             lseek(fd,(long) byte_pos,0);
```

(continued)

```
                    write(fd,recbuff,REC_LGTH);
                    head.rec_count++;
                    break;

            case 2:               /* update existing record */
                rrn = ask_rrn( );

                /* if rrn is too big, print error message ... */
                if (rrn >= head.rec_count) {
                    printf("Record Number is too large");
                    printf("... returning to menu ...");
                    break;
                }

                /* otherwise, seek to the record ... */
                byte_pos = rrn * REC_LGTH + sizeof(head);
                lseek(fd,(long) byte_pos,0);

                /* display it and ask for changes ... */
                read_and_show( );
                if (change( ))
                {
                    printf("\n\nInput the revised Values:\n\n");
                    ask_info(recbuff);
                    lseek(fd,(long) byte_pos,0);
                    write(fd,recbuff,REC_LGTH);
                }
                break;
        } /* end switch */
    } /* end while */

    /* rewrite correct record count to header before leaving */
    lseek(fd,0L,0);
    write(fd,&head,sizeof(head));
    close(fd);
}

/* menu( ) ...
     local function to ask user for next operation.
     Returns numeric value of user response
*/
static menu( ) {
    int choice;
    char response[10];

    printf("\n\n\n\n                        FILE UPDATING PROGRAM\n");
    printf("\n\nYou May Choose to:\n\n");
    printf("\t1.  Add a record to the end of the file\n");
    printf("\t2.  Retrieve a record for Updating\n");
    printf("\t3.  Leave the Program\n\n");
```

```
        printf("Enter the number of your choice: ");
        gets(response);
        choice = atoi(response);
        return(choice);
}

/* ask_info( ) ...
        local function to accept input of name and address fields,
        writing them to the buffer passed as a parameter
*/
static ask_info(char recbuff[])
{
        int field_count,i;
        char response[50];

        /* clear the record buffer */
        for (i = 0; i < REC_LGTH; recbuff[i++] = '\0')
                ;
        /* get the fields */
        for (i=0; *prompt[i] != '\0' ; i++)
        {
                printf("%s",prompt[i]);
                gets(response);
                fld_to_recbuff(recbuff,response);
        }
}

/* ask_rrn( ) ...
        local function to ask for the relative record number of the
        record that is to be updated.
*/
static ask_rrn( ) {

        int rrn;
        char response[10];

        printf("\n\nInput the Relative Record Number of the Record
        that\n");
        printf("\tyou want to update:  ");
        gets(response);
        rrn = atoi(response);
        return(rrn);
}

/* read_and_show( ) ...
        local function to read and display a record.  Note that this
        function does not include a seek -- reading starts at the
        current position in the file
*/
static read_and_show( )  {
```

(continued)

```
      char recbuff[MAX_REC_SIZE + 1],field[MAX_REC_SIZE + 1];
      int scan_pos, data_lgth;

      scan_pos = 0;
      read(fd,recbuff,REC_LGTH);

      printf("\n\n\n\nExisting Record Contents\n");
      recbuff[REC_LGTH] = '\0';   /* ensure that record ends with
      null */
      data_lgth = strlen(recbuff);
      while ((scan_pos = get_fld(field,recbuff,scan_pos,
                                                data_lgth)) > 0)

          printf ("\t%s\n",field);
}

/* change( ) ...
      local function to ask user whether or not he wants to change
      the record.  Returns 1 if the answer is yes, 0 otherwise
*/
static change( )  {
      char response[10];

      printf("\n\nDo you want to change this record?\n");
      printf("    Answer Y or N, followed by <CR> ==>");
      gets(response);
      ucase(response,response);
      return((response[0] == 'Y') ? 1 : 0);
}
```

Pascal Programs

The Pascal programs listed in the following pages correspond to the programs discussed in the text. Each program is organized into one or more files, as follows.

writstrm.pas	Writes out name and address information as a stream of consecutive bytes.
readstrm.pas	Reads a stream file as input and prints it to the screen.
writrec.pas	Writes a variable length record file that uses a byte count at the beginning of each record to give its length.
readrec.pas	Reads through a file, record by record, displaying the fields from each of the records on the screen.
get.prc	Supports functions for reading individual records or fields. These functions are needed by the program in *readrec.pas*.
find.pas	Searches sequentially through a file for a record with a particular key.
update.pas	Allows new records to be added to a file, or old records to be changed.
stod.prc	Support function for *update.pas*, which converts a variable of type *strng* to a variable of type *datarec*.

In addition to these files, there is a file called *tools.prc*, which contains the tools for operating on variables of type *strng*. A listing of *tools.prc* is contained in Appendix B at the end of the textbook.

We have added line numbers to some of these Pascal listings to assist the reader in finding specific program statements.

The files that contain Pascal functions or procedures but do not contain main programs are given the extension *.prc*, as in *get.prc* and *stod.prc*.

Writstrm.pas

Some things to note about *writstrm.pas:*

☐ The comment {$B-} on line 6 is a directive to the Turbo Pascal compiler, instructing it to handle keyboard input as a standard Pascal file. Without this directive we would not be able to handle the *len_str()* function properly in the WHILE loop on line 36.

☐ The comment {$I tools.prc} on line 24 is also a directive to the Turbo Pascal compiler, instructing it to include the file *tools.prc* in the compilation. The procedures *read_str, len_str,* and *fwrite_str* are in the file *tools.prc.*

☐ Although Turbo Pascal supports a special string type, we choose not to use that type here to come closer to conforming to standard Pascal. Instead, we create our own *strng* type, which is a packed array {0..MAX_REC_SIZE} of char. The length of the *strng* is stored in the zeroth byte of the array as a character value. If X is the character value in the zeroth byte of the array, then ORD(X) is the length of the string.

☐ The assign statement on line 31 is one that is nonstandard. It is a Turbo Pascal procedure, which, in this case, assigns *filename* to *outfile,* so all further operation on *outfile* will operate on the disk file.

```
1: PROGRAM writstrm (INPUT,OUTPUT);
2:
3: {    writes out name and address information as a stream of
4:      consecutive bytes }
5:
6: {$B-}    { Directive to the Turbo Pascal compiler, instructing it to
7:            handle keyboard input as a standard Pascal file }
8:
9: CONST
10:      DELIM_CHR   = '|';
11:      MAX_REC_SIZE = 255;
12:
13: TYPE
14:      strng       = packed array[0..MAX_REC_SIZE] of char;
15:      inp_list    = (last,first,address,city,state,zip);
16:      filetype    = packed array[1..40] of char;
17:
18: VAR
19:      response    : array [inp_list] of strng;
20:      resp_type   : inp_list;
21:      filename    : filetype;
22:      outfile     : text;
23:
```

```
24: {$I tools.prc}
25:  { Another directive, instructing the compiler to include the file
26:    tools.prc }
27:
28: BEGIN {main}
29:     write('Enter the name of the file: ');
30:     readln(filename);
31:     assign(outfile,filename);
32:     rewrite(outfile);
33:
34:     write('Type in a last name, or press <CR> to exit: ');
35:     read_str(response[last]);
36:     while (len_str(response[last]) > 0 ) DO
37:     BEGIN
38:         { get all the input for one person }
39:         write(' First Name: ');
40:         read_str(response[first]);
41:         write('    Address: ');
42:         read_str(response[address]);
43:         write('       City: ');
44:         read_str(response[city]);
45:         write('      State: ');
46:         read_str(response[state]);
47:         write('        Zip: ');
48:         read_str(response[zip]);
49:
50:         { write the responses to the file }
51:         for resp_type := last TO zip DO
52:             fwrite_str(outfile,response[resp_type]);
53:
54:         { start the next round of input }
55:         write('Type in a last name, or press <CR> to exit: ');
56:         read_str(response[last])
57:     END;
58:     close(outfile)
59: END.
```

Readstrm.pas

```
PROGRAM readstrm (INPUT,OUTPUT);

    { A program that reads a stream file (fields separated by
      delimiters) as input and prints it to the screen }

CONST
  DELIM_CHR = '|';
  MAX_REC_SIZE = 255;
```

(continued)

```
TYPE
   strng      = packed array [0..MAX_REC_SIZE] of char;
   filetype   = packed array [1..40] of char;

VAR
   filename  : filetype;
   infile    : text;
   fld_count : integer;
   fld_len   : integer;
   str       : strng;

{$I tools.prc}

FUNCTION readfield (VAR infile : text; VAR str : strng): integer;

{ Function readfield reads characters from file infile until it
  reaches end of file of a "|".  Readfield puts the characters in
  str and returns the length of str }

VAR
    i  : integer;
    ch : char;
BEGIN
  i  := 0;
  ch :=  ' ';
  while (not EOF(infile)) and (ch <> DELIM_CHR) DO
    BEGIN
      read (infile,ch);
      i := i + 1;
      str[i] := ch
    END;
i := i - 1;
str[0] := CHR(i);
readfield := i
END;

BEGIN {MAIN}
    write ('Enter the name of the file that you wish to open: ');
    readln (filename);
    assign(infile,filename);
    reset (infile);

    fld_count := 0;

    fld_len := readfield(infile,str);
    while (fld_len > 0) DO
      BEGIN
      fld_count := fld_count + 1
      write(' field #':10,fld_count:1,':':2);
      write_str(str);                    { write_str() is in tools.prc }
```

```
        fld_len := readfield(infile,str)
        END;
    close (infile)
END.
```

Writrec.pas

Note about *writrec.pas:* After writing the *rec_lgth* to outfile on line 69, we write a space to the file. This is because in Pascal values to be read into integer variables must be separated by spaces, tabs, or end-of-line markers.

```
 1: PROGRAM writrec (INPUT,OUTPUT);
 2:
 3: {$B-}
 4:
 5: CONST
 6:     DELIM_CHR = '|';
 7:     MAX_REC_SIZE = 255;
 8:
 9: TYPE
10:     strng = packed array [0..MAX_REC_SIZE] of char;
11:     filetype = packed array [1..40] of char;
12:
13: VAR
14:     filename : filetype;
15:     outfile  : text;
16:     response : strng;
17:     buffer   : strng;
18:     rec_lgth : integer;
19:
20: {$I tools.prc}
21:
22:
23: PROCEDURE fld_to_buffer(VAR buff: strng; s: strng);
24:
25: { This procedure concatenates s and a delimiter to end of
26:   buff }
27:
28: VAR
29:     d_str    : strng;
30: BEGIN
31:     cat_str(buff,s);
32:     d_str[0] := CHR(1);
33:     d_str[1] := DELIM_CHR;
34:     cat_str(buff,d_str)
35: END;
36:
```

(continued)

```
37:
38: BEGIN {main}
39:     write('Enter the name of the file you wish to create ');
40:     readln(filename);
41:     assign(outfile,filename);
42:     rewrite(outfile);
43:
44:     write('Enter Last Name -- or <CR> to exit: ');
45:     read_str(response);
46:     while (len_str(response) > 0) DO
47:         BEGIN
48:         buffer[0] := CHR(0);                    {Set length of string
49:                                                  in buffer to 0}
50:         fld_to_buffer(buffer,response);
51:         write('                        First name: ');
52:         read_str(response);
53:         fld_to_buffer(buffer,response);
54:         write('                           Address: ');
55:         read_str(response);
56:         fld_to_buffer(buffer,response);
57:         write('                              City: ');
58:         read_str(response);
59:         fld_to_buffer(buffer,response);
60:         write('                             State: ');
61:         read_str(response);
62:         fld_to_buffer(buffer,response);
63:         write('                               Zip: ');
64:         read_str(response);
65:         fld_to_buffer(buffer,response);
66:
67:         { write out the record length and buffer contents }
68:         rec_lgth := len_str(buffer);
69:         write(outfile,rec_lgth);
70:         write(outfile,' ');
71:         fwrite_str(outfile,buffer);
72:
73:         { prepare for next entry }
74:         write('Enter Last Name -- or <CR> to exit: ');
75:         read_str(response)
76:     END;
77:     close(outfile)
78: END.
```

Readrec.pas

```
PROGRAM readrec (INPUT,OUTPUT);

{ This program reads through a file, record by record, displaying
  the fields from each of the records on the screen. }
```

```
{$B-}

CONST
    input_size = 255;
    DELIM_CHR = '|';
    MAX_REC_SIZE = 255;

TYPE
    strng = packed array [0..input_size] of char;
    filetype = packed array [1..40] of char;

VAR
    filename   : filetype;
    outfile    : text;
    rec_count  : integer;
    scan_pos   : integer;
    rec_lgth   : integer;
    fld_count  : integer;
    buffer     : strng;
    field      : strng;
{$I tools.prc}
{$I get.prc}

BEGIN {main}
    write('Enter name of file to read: ');
    readln (filename);
    assign(outfile,filename);
    reset(outfile);

    rec_count := 1;
    scan_pos := 0;
    rec_lgth := get_rec(outfile,buffer);
    while rec_lgth > 0 DO
        BEGIN
        writeln('Record ',rec_count);
        rec_count := rec_count + 1;
        fld_count := 1;
        scan_pos := get_fld(field,buffer,scan_pos,rec_lgth);
        while scan_pos > 0 DO
            BEGIN
            write('     Field ',fld_count,': ');
            write_str(field);
            fld_count := fld_count + 1;
            scan_pos := get_fld(field,buffer,scan_pos,rec_lgth)
            END;
        rec_lgth := get_rec(outfile,buffer)
        END;

    close(outfile)

END.
```

Get.prc

```
FUNCTION get_rec(VAR fd: text; VAR buffer: strng); integer;

{ A function that reads a record and its length from file fd.
The function returns the length of the record. If EOF is
encountered get_rec() returns 0  }

VAR
    rec_lgth    : integer;
    space       : char;
BEGIN
    if EOF(fd) then
        get_rec := 0
    else
        BEGIN
        read(fd,rec_lgth);
        read(fd,space);
        fread_str(fd,buffer,rec_lgth);
        get_rec := rec_lgth
        END
END;

FUNCTION get_fld(VAR field:strng;buffer;strng;VAR scanpos: integer;
                 rec_lgth: integer): integer;

{ A function that starts reading at scanpos and reads characters
  from the buffer until it reaches a delimiter or the end of the
  record. It returns scanpos for use on the next call. }

VAR
    fpos    : integer;
BEGIN
    if scanpos = rec_lgth then
        get_fld := 0
    else
        BEGIN
        fpos := 1;
        scanpos := scanpos + 1;
        field[fpos] := buffer[scanpos];
        while (field[fpos] <> DELIM_CHR) and (scanpos < rec_lgth) DO
            BEGIN
            fpos := fpos + 1;
            scanpos := scanpos +1;
            field[fpos] := buffer[scanpos]
            END;
        if field[fpos] := DELIM_CHR then
            field[0] := CHR(fpos - 1)
```

```
        else
             field[0] := CHR(fpos);
        get_fld := scanpos
        END
END;
```

Find.pas

```pascal
PROGRAM find (INPUT,OUTPUT);

{ This program reads through a file, record by record, looking
  for a record with a particular key.  If a match occurs, when
  all the fields in the record are displayed.  Otherwise a message
  is displayed indicating that the record was not found. }

{$B-}

CONST
    MAX_REC_SIZE = 255;
    DELIM_CHR = '|';

TYPE
    strng = packed array [0..MAX_REC_SIZE] of char;
    filetype = packed array [1..40] of char;

VAR
    filename   : filetype;
    outfile    : text;
    last       : strng;
    first      : strng;
    search_key : strng;
    length     : integer;
    matched    : boolean;
    rec_lgth   : integer;
    buffer     : strng;
    scan_pos   : integer;
    key_found  : strng;
    field      : strng;

{$I tools.prc}
{$I get.prc}
BEGIN {main}
    write('Enter name of file to search: ');
    readln(filename);
    assign(outfile,filename);
    reset(outfile);
```

(continued)

```
write('Enter last name: ');
read_str(last);
write('Enter first name: ');
read_str(first);
makekey(last,first,search_key);

matched := FALSE;
rec_lgth := get_rec(outfile,buffer);
while ((not matched) and (rec_lgth > 0)) DO
    Begin
    scan_pos := 0;
    scan_pos := get_fld(last,buffer,scan_pos,rec_lgth);
    scan_pos := get_fld(first,buffer,scan_pos,rec_lgth);
    makekey(last,first,key_found);
    if cmp_str(key_found,search_key) = 0 then
        matched := TRUE
    else
        rec_lgth := get_rec(outfile,buffer);
    END;
close(outfile);
{ if record found, print the fields }
if matched then
    BEGIN
    writeln('Record found:');
    writeln;
    scan_pos := 0;

    { break out the fields }
    scan_pos := get_fld(field,buffer,scan_pos,rec_lgth);
    while scan_pos > 0 DO
        BEGIN
        write_str(field);
        scan_pos := get_fld(field,buffer,scan_pos,rec_lgth)
        END;
    END
else
    writeln(' Record not found.');
END.
```

Update.pas

Some things to note about *update.pas:*

□ In the procedure *ask_info()*, the name and address fields are read in as *strngs,* and procedure *fld_to_buffer()* writes the fields to *strbuff* (also of type *strng*). Writing *strbuff* to *outfile* would result in a type mismatch, since *outfile* is a file of type *datarec.* However, the procedure *stod(),* located in *stod.prc,* converts a variable of type *strng* to a variable of type *datarec* to write the buffer to the file. The calls to *stod()* are located on lines 210 and 237.

☐   The seek() statements on lines 212, 229, 239, and 250 are not standard; they are features of Turbo Pascal.

```
 1: PROGRAM update (INPUT,OUTPUT);
 2:
 3: {$B-}
 4:
 5: { A program to open or create a fixed length record file for
 6:   updating.  Records may be added or changed.  Records to be
 7:   changed must be accessed by relative record number }
 8:
 9: CONST
10:     MAX_REC_SIZE = 255;
11:     REC_LGTH     = 64;
12:     DELIM_CHR    = '|';
13:
14: TYPE
15:     strng    = packed array [0..MAX_REC_SIZE] of char;
16:     filetype = packed array [1..40] of char;
17:     datarec  = RECORD
18:                    len   : integer;
19:                    data  : packed array [1..REC_LGTH] of char
20:                END;
21:
22: VAR
23:     filename    : filetype;
24:     outfile     : file of datarec;
25:     response    : char;
26:     menu_choice : integer;
27:     strbuff     : strng;
28:     byte_pos    : integer;
29:     head        : datarec;
30:     rrn         : integer;
31:     drecbuff    : datarec;
32:     i           : integer;
33:     rec_count   : integer;
34: {$I tools.prc}
35: {$I stod.prc }
36: {$I get.prc  }
37:
38:
39: PROCEDURE fld_to_buffer(VAR buff: strng; s: strng);
40:
41: { fld_to_buffer concatenates strng s and a delimiter to the
42:   end of buff }
43:
```

(continued)

```
44: VAR
45:     d_str  : strng;
46: BEGIN
47:     cat_str(buff,s);
48:     d_str[0] := CHR(1);
49:     d_str[1] := DELIM_CHR;
50:     cat_str(buff,d_str)
51: END;
52:
53:
54: FUNCTION menu:integer;
55:
56: {local function to ask user for next operation. Returns numeric
57:  value of user response }
58:
59: VAR
60:     choice : integer:
61: BEGIN
62:     writeln;
63:     writeln('                        FILE UPDATING PROGRAM');
64:     writeln;
65:     writeln('You May Choose to: ');
66:     writeln;
67:     writeln('     1.  Add a record to the end of the file');
68:     writeln('     2.  Retrieve a record for updating');
69:     writeln('     3.  Leave the program');
70:     writeln;
71:     write('Enter the number of your choice: ');
72:     readln(choice);
73:     writeln;
74:     menu : = choice
75: END;
76: PROCEDURE ask_info(VAR strbuff: strng);
77:
78: {local procedure to accept input of name and address fields,
79:  writing them to the buffer passed as a parameter }
80:
81: VAR
82:     response  : strng;
83: BEGIN
84:     { clear the record buffer }
85:     clear_str(buff);
86:
87:     { get the fields }
88:     write('    Last Name: ');
89:     read_str(response);
90:     fld_to_buffer(strbuff,response);
91:     write('    First Name: ');
92:     read_str(response);
93:     fld_to_buffer(strbuff,response);
```

```
 94:      write('        Address: ');
 95:      read_str(response);
 96:      fld_to_buffer(strbuff,response);
 97:      write('          City: ');
 98:      read_str(response);
 99:      fld_to buffer(strbuff,response);
100:      write('         State: ');
101:      read_str(response);
102:      fld_to_buffer(strbuff,response);
103:      write('           Zip: ');
104:      read_str(response);
105:      fld'to'buffer(strbuff,response);
106:      writeln
107: END;
108:
109:
110: FUNCTION ask_rrn: integer;
111:
112: { function to ask for the relative record number of the record
113:   that is to be updated.  }
114:
115: VAR
116:      rrn     : integer;
117: BEGIN
118:      writeln('Input the relative record number of the record that');
119:      write('    you want to update: ');
120:      readln(rrn);
121:      writeln;
122:      ask_run := rrn
123: END;
124: PROCEDURE read_and_show;
125:
126 {procedure to read and display a record. This procedure does not
127:   include a seek -- reading starts at the current file position }
128:
129: VAR
130:      scan_pos    : integer;
131:      drecbuff    : datarec;
132:      i           : integer;
133:      data_lgth   : integer;
134:      field       : strng;
135:      strbuff     : strng;
136: BEGIN
137:      scan_pos := 0;
138:      read(outfile,drecbuff);
139:
140:      { convert drecbuff to type strng }
141:      strbuff[0] := CHR(drecbuff.len);
142:      for i := 1 to drecbuff.len DO
```

(continued)

```
143:            strbuff[i] := drecbuff.data[i];
144:
145:      writeln('Existing Record Contents');
146:      writeln;
147:
148:      data_lgth := len_str(strbuff);
149:      scan_pos := get_fld(field,strbuff,scan_pos,data_lgth);
150:      while scan_pos > 0 D)
151:            BEGIN
152:            write_str(field);
153:            scan_pos := get_fld(field,strbuff,scan:= pos,data:= lgth)
154:            END
155: END;
156:
157:
158: FUNCTION change: integer;
159:
160: { function to ask the user whether or not to change the
161:   record.  Returns 1 if the answer is yes, 0 otherwise.
162:
163: VAR
164:      response  : char;
165: BEGIN
166:      writeln('Do you want to change this record?');
167:      write('    Answer Y or N, followed by <CR> ==>');
168:      readln(response);
169:      writeln;
170:      if (response = 'Y') or (response = 'y') then
171:            change := 1
172:      else
173:            change := 0
174: END;
175: BEGIN {main}
176:      write('Enter the name of the file: ');
177:      readln(filename);
178:      assign(outfile,filename);
179:
180:      write('Does this file already exist? (respond Y or N): ');
181:      readln(response);
182:      writeln;
183:      if (response = 'Y') OR (response = 'y') then
184:            BEGIN
185:            reset(outfile);                { open outfile         }
186:            read(outfile,head);            { get header           }
187:            rec_count := head.len          { read in record count }
188:            END
189:      else
190:            BEGIN
191:            rewrite(outfile);              { create outfile          }
192:            rec_count := 0;                { initialize record count }
```

```
193:        head.len := rec_count;              { place in header record  }
194:        for i :=  1 to REC_LGTH DO
195:            head.data[i] := CHR(0);       { set header data to nulls}
196:        write(outfile,head)             { write header rec         }
197:        END;
198:
199:    { main program loop -- call menu and then jump to options }
200:    menu_choice := menu;
201:    while menu_choice < 3 DO
202:        BEGIN
203:        CASE menu_choice OF
204:            1 :                       { add a new record }
205:              BEGIN
206:              writeln('Input the information for the new record --');
207:              writeln;
208:              writeln;
209:              ask_info(strbuff);
210:              stod(drechbuff,strbuff); {convert strbuff to type datarec}
211:              rrn := rec_count + 1;
212:              seek(outfile,rrn);
213:              write(outfile,drecbuff);
214:              rec_count := rec_count + 1
215:              END;
216:            2 :                       { update existing record }
217:              BEGIN
218:              rrn := ask_rrn;
219:
220:              { if rrn is too big, print error message ... }
221:              if (rrn > rec_count) or (rrn < 1) then
222:                  BEGIN
223:                  write('Record Number is out of range');
224:                  writeln('...returning to menu...')
225:                  END
226:
227:              else                   { otherwise, seek to the record ... }
228:                  BEGIN
229:                  seek(outfile,rrn);
230:
231:                  { display it and ask for changes ... }
232:                  read_and_show;
233:                  if change = 1 then
234:                      BEGIN
235:                      writeln('Input the revised Values: ');
236:                      ask_info(strbuff);
237:                      stod(drecbuff,strbuff);  { convert strbuff to type
238:                                                    datarec }
239:                      seek(outfile,rrn);
240:                      write(outfile,drecbuff)
241:                      END
```

(continued)

```
242:                    END
243:                END
244:        END; { CASE }
245:        menu_choice := menu
246:        END; { while }
247:
248:        { rewrite correct record count to header before leaving }
249:        head.len := rec_ count;
250:        seek(outfile,0);
251:        write(outfile,head);
252:        close(outfile)
253: END.
```

Stod.prc

```
PROCEDURE stod (VAR drecbuff: datarec; strbuff; strng);

{ A procedure that converts a variable of type strng to a
  variable of type datarec }

VAR
    i : integer;
BEGIN
    drecbuff.len :=  min(REC_LGTH,len_str(strbuff));
    for i := 1 to drecbuff.len DO
        drecbuff.data[i] := strbuff[i];

    { Clear the rest of the buffer }
    while i < REC_LGTH DO
        BEGIN
        i := i + 1;
        drecbuff.data[i] := ' '
        END
END;
```

Organizing Files
for Performance

5

CHAPTER OBJECTIVES

- Look at several approaches to *data compression*.
- Look at *storage compaction* as a simple way of reusing space in a file.
- Develop a procedure for deleting fixed-length records that allows vacated file space to be reused dynamically.
- Illustrate the use of *linked lists* and *stacks* to manage an *avail list*.
- Consider several approaches to the problem of deleting variable-length records.
- Introduce the concepts associated with the terms *internal fragmentation* and *external fragmentation*.
- Outline some *placement strategies* associated with the re-use of space in a variable-length record file.
- Provide an introduction to the idea underlying a *binary search*.
- Undertake an examination of the limitations of binary searching.
- Develop a *keysort* procedure for sorting larger files; investigate the costs associated with keysort.
- Introduce the concept of a *pinned record*.

CHAPTER OUTLINE

We have already seen how important it is for the file system designer to consider how a file is to be accessed when deciding on how to create fields and records and other file structures. In this chapter we continue to focus on file organization, but the motivation is a little different. We look at ways to organize, or in some cases reorganize, files in direct response to the need to improve performance.

In the first section we look at how we organize files to make them smaller. Compression techniques let us make files smaller by encoding the basic information in the file.

Next we look at ways to reclaim unused space in files to improve performance. Compaction is a batch process that we can use to purge holes of unused space from a file that has undergone many deletions and updates. Then we investigate dynamic ways to maintain performance by reclaiming space made available by deletions and updates of records during the life of a file.

In the third section we examine the problem of reorganizing files by sorting them to support simple binary searching. Then, in an effort to find a better sorting method, we begin a conceptual line of thought that will continue throughout the rest of this text: We find a way to improve file performance by creating an external structure through which we can access the file.

5.1   Data Compression

In this section we look at some ways to make files smaller. There are many reasons for making files smaller. Smaller files

☐ Use less storage, resulting in cost savings;

☐ Can be transmitted faster, decreasing access time or, alternatively, allowing the same access time with a lower and cheaper bandwidth; and

☐ Can be processed faster sequentially.

Data compression involves encoding the information in a file in such a way as to take up less space. Many different techniques are available for compressing data. Some are very general and some are designed only for specific kinds of data, such as speech, pictures, text, or instrument data. The variety of data compression techniques is so large that we can only touch on the topic here, with a few examples.

5.1.1 Using a Different Notation

Remember our address file from Chapter 4? It had several fixed-length fields, including "state," "zip code," and "phone number." Fixed-length fields such as these are good candidates for compression. For instance, the "state" field in the address file required two ASCII bytes, 16 bits. How many bits are *really* needed for this field? Since there are only 50 states, we could represent all possible states with only six bits. (Why?) Thus, we could encode all state names in a single one-byte field, resulting in a space savings of one byte, or 50%, per occurrence of the state field.

This type of compression technique, in which we decrease the number of bits by finding a more *compact notation,*[†] is one of many compression techniques classified as *redundancy reduction.* The 10 bits that we were able to throw away were redundant in the sense that having 16 bits instead of 6 provided no extra information.

[†]Note that the original two-letter notation we used for "state" is itself a more compact notation for the full state name.

What are the costs of this compression scheme? In this case, there are many:

- ☐ By using a pure binary encoding, we have made the file unreadable by humans.
- ☐ We incur some cost in encoding time whenever we add a new state-name field to our file, and a similar cost for decoding when we need to get a readable version of state name from the file.
- ☐ We must also now incorporate the encoding and/or decoding modules in all software that will process our address file, increasing the complexity of the software.

With so many costs, is this kind of compression worth it? We can answer this only in the context of a particular application. If the file is already fairly small, if the file is often accessed by many different pieces of software, and if some of the software that will access the file cannot deal with binary data (e.g., an editor), then this form of compression is a bad idea. On the other hand, if the file contains several million records and is generally processed by one program, compression is probably a very good idea. Since the encoding and decoding algorithms for this kind of compression are extremely simple, the savings in access time is likely to exceed any processing time required for encoding or decoding.

5.1.2 Suppressing Repeating Sequences

Imagine an 8-bit image of the sky that has been processed so only objects above a certain brightness are identified and all other regions of the image are set to some background color represented by the pixel value 0. (See Fig. 5.1.)

Sparse arrays of this sort are very good candidates for compression of a sort called *run-length encoding,* which in this example works as follows. First, we choose one special, unused byte value to indicate that a run-length code follows. Then, the run-length encoding algorithm goes like this:

- ☐ Read through the pixels that make up the image, copying the pixel values to the file in sequence, except where the same pixel value occurs more than once in succession.
- ☐ Where the same value occurs more than once in succession, substitute the following three bytes, in order:

  - ☐ The special run-length code indicator;
  - ☐ The pixel value that is repeated; and
  - ☐ The number of times that the value is repeated (up to 256 times).

FIGURE 5.1 The empty space in this astronomical image is represented by repeated sequences of the same value and is thus a good candidate for compression. (This FITS image shows a radio continuum structure around the spiral galaxy NGC 891 as observed with the Westerbork Synthesis radio telescope in The Netherlands.)

For example, suppose we wish to compress an image using run–length encoding, and we find that we can omit the byte 0xff from the representation of the image. We choose the byte 0xff as our run–length code indicator. How would we encode the following sequence of hexadecimal byte values?

```
22 23 24 24 24 24 24 24 24 25 26 26 26 26 26 26 25 24
```

The first three pixels are to be copied in sequence. The runs of 24 and 26 are both run–length encoded. The remaining pixels are copied in sequence. The resulting sequence is

```
22 23 ff 24 07 25 ff 26 06 25 24
```

Run–length encoding is another example of redundancy reduction. (Why?) It can be applied to many kinds of data, including text, instrument data, and sparse matrices. Like the compact notation approach, the run–length encoding algorithm is a simple one whose associated costs rarely affect performance appreciably.

Unlike compact notation, run–length encoding does not guarantee any particular amount of space savings. A "busy" image with a lot of variation will not benefit appreciably from run–length encoding. Indeed, under some circumstances, the aforementioned algorithm could result in a "compressed" image that is larger than the original image. (Why? Can you prevent this?)

5.1.3 Assigning Variable-length Codes

Suppose you have two different symbols to use in an encoding scheme: a dot (".") and a dash ("-"). You have to assign combinations of dots and dashes to letters of the alphabet. If you are very clever, you might determine the most frequently occurring letters of the alphabet (*e* and *t*) and use a single dot for one and a single dash for the other. Other letters of the alphabet will be assigned two or more symbols, with the more frequently occurring letters getting fewer symbols.

Sound familiar? You may recognize this scheme as the oldest and most common of the *variable-length codes,* the Morse code. Variable-length codes, in general, are based on the principle that some values occur more frequently than others, so the codes for those values should take the least amount of space. Variable-length codes are another form of redundancy reduction.

A variation on the compact notation technique, the Morse code can be implemented using a table lookup, where the table never changes. In contrast, since many sets of data values do not exhibit a predictable frequency distribution, more modern variable-length coding techniques dynamically build the tables that describe the encoding scheme. One of the most successful of these is the *Huffman code,* which determines the probabilities of each value occurring in the data set, and then builds a binary tree in which the search path for each value represents the code for that value. More frequently occurring values are given shorter search paths in the tree. This tree is then turned into a table, much like a Morse code table, that can be used to encode and decode the data.

For example, suppose we have a data set containing only the seven letters shown in Fig. 5.2, and each letter occurs with the probability indicated. The third row in the figure shows the Huffman codes that would be assigned to the letters. Based on Fig. 5.2, the string "abde" would be encoded as "101000000001."

FIGURE 5.2 Example showing the Huffman encoding for a set of seven letters, assuming certain probabilities. (From Lynch, 1985.)

Letter:	a	b	c	d	e	f	g
Probability:	0.4	0.1	0.1	0.1	0.1	0.1	0.1
Code	1	010	011	0000	0001	0010	0011

In the example, the letter *a* occurs much more often than any of the others, so it is assigned the one-bit code 1. Notice that the minimum number of bits needed to represent these seven letters is three, yet in this case as many as four bits are required. This is a necessary trade-off to insure that the distinct codes can be stored together, without delimiters between them, and still be recognized.

5.1.4 Irreversible Compression Techniques

The techniques we have discussed so far preserve all information in the original data. In effect, they take advantage of the fact that the data, in its original form, contains redundant information that can be removed and then reinserted at a later time. Another type of compression, *irreversible compression,* is based on the assumption that some information can be sacrificed.[†]

An example of irreversible compression would be shrinking a raster image from, say, 400-by-400 pixels to 100-by-100 pixels. The new image contains one pixel for every 16 pixels in the original image, and there is no way, in general, to determine what the original pixels were from the one new pixel.

Irreversible compression is less common in data files than reversible compression, but there are times when the information that is lost is of little or no value. For example, speech compression is often done by *voice coding,* a technique that transmits a paramaterized description of speech, which can be synthesized at the receiving end with varying amounts of distortion.

5.1.5 Compression in UNIX

Both Berkeley and System V UNIX provide compression routines that are heavily used and quite effective. System V has routines called *pack* and *unpack,* which use Huffman codes on a byte-by-byte basis. Typically, pack achieves 25 to 40% reduction on text files, but appreciably less on binary files that have a more uniform distribution of byte values. When pack compresses a file, it automatically appends a ".z" to the end of the packed file, signalling to any future user that the file has been compressed using the standard compression algorithm.

Berkeley UNIX has routines called *compress* and *uncompress,* which use an effective dynamic method called Lempel-Ziv (Welch, 1984). Except for using different compression schemes, compress and uncompress behave

---

[†]Irreversible compression is sometimes called "entropy reduction" to emphasize that the average information (entropy) is reduced.

almost the same as pack and unpack.[†] Compress appends a ".Z" to the end of files it has compressed.

Since these routines are readily available on UNIX systems and are very effective general-purpose routines, it is wise to use them whenever there are not compelling reasons to use other techniques.

5.2 Reclaiming Space in Files

Suppose a record in a variable-length record file is modified in such a way that the new record is longer than the original record. What do you do with the extra data? You could append it to the end of the file and put a pointer from the original record space to the extension of the record. You could rewrite the whole record at the end of the file (unless the file needs to be sorted), leaving a hole at the original location of the record. Each solution has a drawback: In the former case, the job of processing the record is more awkward and slower than it was originally; in the latter case, the file contains wasted space.

In this section we take a close look at the way file organization deteriorates as a file is modified. In general, modifications can take any one of three forms:

☐ Record addition;
☐ Record updating; and
☐ Record deletion.

If the only kind of change to a file is record addition, there is no deterioration of the kind we cover in this chapter. It is only when variable-length records are updated, or when either fixed- or variable-length records are deleted, that maintenance issues become complicated and interesting. Since record updating can always be treated as a record deletion followed by a record addition, our focus is on the effects of record deletion. When a record has been deleted, we want to reuse the space.

5.2.1 Record Deletion and Storage Compaction

Storage compaction makes files smaller by looking for places in a file where there is no data at all, and then recovering this space. Since empty spaces occur in files when we delete records, we begin our discussion of compaction with a look at record deletion.

[†]Many implementations of System V UNIX also support compress and uncompress as Berkeley extensions.

Any record-deletion strategy must provide some way for us to recognize records as deleted. A simple and usually workable approach is to place a special mark in each deleted record. For example, in the name and address file developed in Chapter 4, we might place an asterisk as the first field in a deleted record. Figures 5.3(a) and 5.3(b) show a name and address file similar to the one in Chapter 4 before and after the second record is marked as deleted. (The dots at the ends of records 0 and 2 represent padding between the last field and the end of each record.)

Once we are able to recognize a record as deleted, the next question is how to reuse the space from the record. Approaches to this problem that rely on storage compaction do nothing at all to reuse the space for a while. The records are simply marked as deleted and left in the file for a period of time. Programs using the file must include logic that causes them to ignore records that are marked as deleted. One nice side effect of this approach is that it is usually possible to allow the user to "undelete" a record with very little effort. This is particularly easy if you keep the deleted mark in a special field, rather than destroy some of the original data, as in our example.

The reclamation of the space from the deleted records happens all at once. After deleted records have accumulated for some time, a special program is used to reconstruct the file with all the deleted records squeezed out (Fig. 5.3c). If there is enough space, the simplest way to do this compaction is through a file copy program that skips over the deleted records. It is also possible, though more complicated and time-consuming, to do the compaction in place. Either of these approaches can be used with both fixed- and variable-length records.

FIGURE 5.3 Storage requirements of sample file using 64-byte fixed-length records. (a) Before deleting the second record. (b) After deleting the second record. (c) After compaction—the second record is gone.

```
Ames¦John¦123 Maple¦Stillwater¦OK¦74075¦......................
Morrison¦Sebastian¦9035 South Hillcrest¦Forest Village¦OK¦74820¦
Brown¦Martha¦625 Kimbark¦Des Moines¦IA¦50311¦..................
```
(a)

```
Ames¦John¦123 Maple¦Stillwater¦OK¦74075¦......................
*¦rrison¦Sebastian¦9035 South Hillcrest¦Forest Village¦OK¦74820¦
Brown¦Martha¦625 Kimbark¦Des Moines¦IA¦50311¦..................
```
(b)

```
Ames¦John¦123 Maple¦Stillwater¦OK¦74075¦......................
Brown¦Martha¦625 Kimbark¦Des Moines¦IA¦50311¦..................
```
(c)

The decision about how often to run the storage compaction program can be based on either the number of deleted records or on the calendar. In accounting programs, for example, it often makes sense to run a compaction procedure on certain files at the end of the fiscal year or some other point associated with closing the books.

5.2.2 Deleting Fixed-length Records for Reclaiming Space Dynamically

Storage compaction is the simplest and most widely used of the storage reclamation methods we discuss. There are some applications, however, that are too volatile and interactive for storage compaction to be useful. In these situations we want to reuse the space from deleted records as soon as possible. We begin our discussion of such dynamic storage reclamation with a second look at fixed-length record deletion, since fixed-length records make the reclamation problem much simpler.

In general, to provide a mechanism for record deletion with subsequent reutilization of the freed space, we need to be able to guarantee two things:

☐ That deleted records are marked in some special way; and
☐ That we can find the space that deleted records once occupied so we can reuse that space when we add records.

We have already identified a method of meeting the first requirement: We mark records as deleted by putting a field containing an asterisk at the beginning of deleted records.

If you are working with fixed-length records and are willing to search sequentially through a file before adding a record, you can always provide the second guarantee if you have provided the first. Space reutilization can take the form of looking through the file, record by record, until a deleted record is found. If the program reaches the end of the file without finding a deleted record, then the new record can be appended at the end.

Unfortunately, this approach makes adding records an intolerably slow process if the program is an interactive one and the user has to sit at the terminal and wait as the record addition takes place. To make record reuse happen more quickly, we need

☐ A way to know immediately if there are empty slots in the file; and
☐ A way to jump directly to one of those slots if they exist.

Linked Lists The use of a *linked list* for stringing together all of the available records can meet both of these needs. A linked list is a data structure in which each element or *node* contains some kind of reference to its successor in the list. (See Fig. 5.4.)

FIGURE 5.4 A linked list.

If you have a head reference to the first node in the list, you can move through the list by looking at each node, and then at the node's pointer field, so you know where the next node is located. When you finally encounter a pointer field with some special, predetermined end-of-list value, you stop the traversal of the list. In Fig. 5.4 we use a −1 in the pointer field to mark the end of the list.

When a list is made up of deleted records that have become *available space* within the file, the list is usually called an *avail list*. When inserting a new record into a fixed-length record file, any one available record is just as good as any other. There is no reason to prefer one open slot over another since all the slots are the same size. It follows that there is no reason for ordering the avail list in any particular way. (As we see later, this situation changes for variable-length records.)

Stacks   The simplest way to handle a list is as a stack. A stack is a list in which all insertions and removals of nodes take place at one end of the list. So, if we have an avail list managed as a stack that contains relative record numbers (RRN) 5 and 2, and then add RRN 3, it looks like this before and after the addition of the new node:

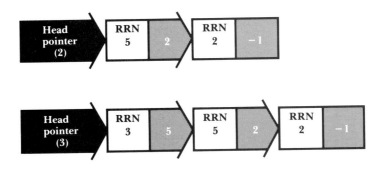

When a new node is added to the top or front of a stack, we say that it is *pushed* onto the stack. If the next thing that happens is a request for some available space, the request is filled by taking RRN 3 from the avail list.

This is called *popping* the stack. The list returns to a state in which it contains only records 5 and 2.

Linking and Stacking Deleted Records   Now we can meet the two criteria for rapid access to reusable space from deleted records. We need

□   A way to know immediately if there are empty slots in the file; and
□   A way to jump directly to one of those slots if they exist.

Placing the deleted records on a stack meets both criteria. If the pointer to the top of the stack contains the end-of-list value, then we know that there are not any empty slots and that we have to add new records by appending them to the end of the file. If the pointer to the stack top contains a valid node reference, then we know not only that a reusable slot is available, but also exactly where to find it.

Where do we keep the stack? Is it a separate list, perhaps maintained in a separate file, or is it somehow embedded within the data file? Once again, we need to be careful to distinguish between *physical* and *conceptual* structures. The deleted, available records are not actually moved anywhere when they are pushed onto the stack. They stay right where we need them, located in the file. The stacking and linking is done by arranging and rearranging the links used to make one available record slot point to the next. Since we are working with fixed-length records in a disk file, rather than with memory addresses, the pointing is not done with *pointer* variables in the formal sense, but through relative record numbers (RRNs).

Suppose we are working with a fixed-length record file that once contained seven records (RRNs 0–6). Furthermore, suppose that records 3 and 5 have been deleted, *in that order,* and that deleted records are marked by replacing the first field with an asterisk. We can then use the second field of a deleted record to hold the link to the next record on the avail list. Leaving out the details of the valid, in-use records, Fig. 5.5(a) shows how the file might look.

Record 5 is the first record on the avail list (top of the stack) since it is the record that is most recently deleted. Following the linked list, we see that record 5 points to record 3. Since the *link field* for record 3 contains −1, which is our end–of–list marker, we know that record 3 is the last slot available for reuse.

Figure 5.5(b) shows the same file after record 1 is also deleted. Note that the contents of all the other records on the avail list remain unchanged. Treating the list as a stack results in a minimal amount of list reorganization when we push and pop records to and from the list.

If we now add a new name to the file, it is placed in record 1, since RRN 1 is the first available record. The avail list would return to the

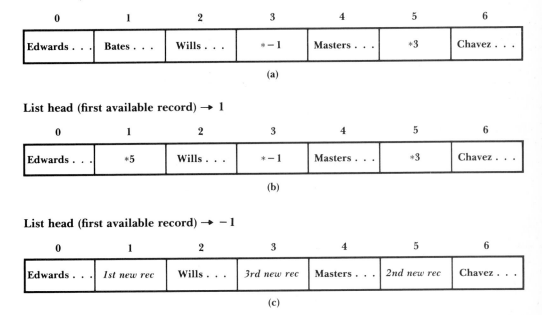

FIGURE 5.5 Sample file showing linked lists of deleted records. (a) After deletion of records 3 and 5, in that order. (b) After deletion of records 3, 5, and 1, in that order. (c) After insertion of three new records.

configuration shown in Fig. 5.5(a). Since there are still two record slots on the avail list, we could add two more names to the file without increasing the size of the file. After that, however, the avail list would be empty (Fig. 5.5c). If yet another name is added to the file, the program knows that the avail list is empty and that the name requires the addition of a new record at the end of the file.

Implementing Fixed-length Record Deletion Implementing mechanisms that place deleted records on a linked avail list and that treat the avail list as a stack is relatively straightforward. We need a suitable place to keep the RRN of the first available record on the avail list. Since this is information that is specific to the data file, it can be carried in a header record at the start of the file.

When we delete a record we must be able to mark the record as deleted, and then place it on the avail list. A simple way to do this is to place an '*' (or some other special mark) at the beginning of the record as a deletion mark, followed by the RRN of the next record on the avail list.

Once we have a list of available records within a file, we can reuse the space previously occupied by deleted records. For this we would write a single function that returns either (1) the RRN of a reusable record slot, or (2) the RRN of the next record to be appended if no reusable slots are available.

5.2.3 Deleting Variable-length Records

Now that we have a mechanism for handling an avail list of available space once records are deleted, let's apply this mechanism to the more complex problem of reusing space from deleted variable-length records. We have seen that to support record reuse through an avail list, we need

☐   A way to link the deleted records together into a list (i.e., a place to put a link field);

☐   An algorithm for adding newly deleted records to the avail list; and

☐   An algorithm for finding and removing records from the avail list when we are ready to use them.

An Avail List of Variable-length Records   What kind of file structure do we need to support an avail list of variable-length records? Since we will want to delete whole records and then place records on an avail list, we need a structure in which the record is a clearly defined entity. The file structure in which we define the length of each record by placing a byte count of the record contents at the beginning of each record will serve us well in this regard.

We can handle the contents of a deleted variable-length record just as we did with fixed-length records. That is, we can place a single asterisk in the first field, followed by a binary link field pointing to the next deleted record on the avail list. The avail list itself can be organized just as it was with fixed-length records, but with one difference: We cannot use relative record numbers (RRNs) for *links*. Since we cannot compute the byte offset of variable-length records from their RRNs, the links must contain the byte offsets themselves.

To illustrate, suppose we begin with a variable-length record file containing the three records for Ames, Morrison, and Brown introduced earlier. Figure 5.6(a) shows what the file looks like (minus the header) before any deletions, and Fig. 5.6(b) shows what it looks like after the deletion of the second record. The periods in the deleted record signify discarded characters.

```
    HEAD.FIRST_AVAIL: -1

40 Ames¦John¦123 Maple¦Stillwater¦OK¦74075¦64 Morrison¦Sebastian
¦9035 South Hillcrest¦Forest Village¦OK¦74820¦45 Brown¦Martha¦62
5 Kimbark¦Des Moines¦IA¦50311¦
                              (a)


    HEAD.FIRST_AVAIL: 43 ─────────────────┐
                                          │
                                          ▼
40 Ames¦John¦123 Maple¦Stillwater¦OK¦74075¦64 *¦ -1............
.........................................45 Brown¦Martha¦62
5 Kimbark¦Des Moines¦IA 50311¦
                              (b)
```

FIGURE 5.6 A sample file for illustrating variable-length record deletion. (a) Original sample file stored in variable-length format with byte count (header record not included). (b) Sample file after deletion of the second record (periods show discarded characters).

Adding and Removing Records Let's address the questions of adding and removing records to and from the list together, since they are clearly related. With fixed-length records we could access the avail list as a stack because one member of the avail list is just as usable as any other. That is not true when the record slots on the avail list differ in size, as they do in a variable-length record file. We now have an extra condition that must be met before we can reuse a record: The record must be the right size. For the moment we define *right size* as "big enough." Later we find that it is sometimes useful to be more particular about the meaning of *right size*.

It is possible, even likely, that we need to *search through* the avail list for a record slot that is the right size. We can't just pop the stack and expect the first available record to be big enough. Finding a proper slot on the avail list now means traversing the list until a record slot is found that is big enough to hold the new record that is to be inserted.

For example, suppose the avail list contains the deleted record slots shown in Fig. 5.7(a), and a record that requires 55 bytes is to be added. Since the avail list is not empty, we traverse the records whose sizes are 47 (too small), 38 (too small), and 72 (big enough). Having found a slot big enough to hold our record, we remove it from the avail list by creating a new link that jumps over the record (Fig. 5.7b). If we had reached the end of the avail list before finding a record that was large enough, we would have appended the new record at the end of the file.

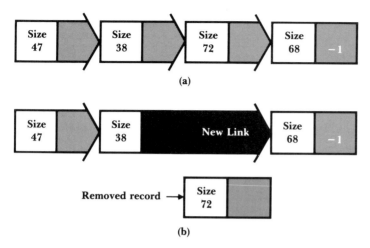

FIGURE 5.7 Removal of a record from an avail list with variable-length records. (a) Before removal. (b) After removal.

Since this procedure for finding a reusable record looks through the entire avail list if necessary, we do not need a sophisticated method for putting newly deleted records onto the list. If a record of the right size is somewhere on this list, our get-available-record procedure eventually finds it. It follows that we can continue to push new members onto the front of the list, just as we do with fixed-length records.

Development of algorithms for adding and removing avail list records is left to you as part of the exercises found at the end of this chapter.

5.2.4 Storage Fragmentation

Let's look again at the fixed-length record version of our three-record file (Fig. 5.8). The dots at the ends of the records represent characters we use as padding between the last field and the end of the records. The padding is wasted space; it is part of the cost of using fixed-length records. Wasted space *within* a record is called *internal fragmentation*.

Clearly, we want to minimize internal fragmentation. If we are working with fixed-length records, we attempt such minimization by

FIGURE 5.8 Storage requirements of sample file using 64-byte fixed-length records.

```
Ames¡John¡123 Maple¡Stillwater¡OK¡74075¡.........................
Morrison¡Sebastian¡9035 South Hillcrest¡Forest Village¡OK¡74820¡
Brown¡Martha¡625 Kimbark¡Des Moines¡IA¡50311¡...................
```

```
40 Ames¦John¦123 Maple¦Stillwater¦OK¦74075¦64 Morrison¦Sebastian
¦9035 South Hillcrest¦Forest Village¦OK¦74820¦45 Brown¦Martha¦62
5 Kimbark¦Des Moines¦IA¦50311¦
```

FIGURE 5.9 Storage requirements of sample file using variable-length records with a count field.

choosing a record length that is as close as possible to what we need for each record. But unless the actual data is fixed in length, we have to put up with a certain amount of internal fragmentation in a fixed-length record file.

One of the attractions of variable-length records is that they minimize wasted space by doing away with internal fragmentation. The space set aside for each record is exactly as long as it needs to be. Compare the fixed-length example with the one in Fig. 5.9, which uses the variable-length record structure—a byte count followed by delimited data fields. The only space (other than the delimiters) that is not used for holding data in each record is the count field. If we assume that this field uses two bytes, this amounts to only six bytes for the three-record file. The fixed-length record file wastes 24 bytes in the very first record.

But before we start congratulating ourselves for solving the problem of wasted space due to internal fragmentation, we should consider what happens in a variable-length record file after a record is deleted and replaced with a shorter record. If the shorter record takes less space than the original record, internal fragmentation results. Figure 5.10 shows how the problem

FIGURE 5.10 Illustration of fragmentation with variable-length records. (a) After deletion of the second record (unused characters in the deleted record are replaced by periods). (b) After the subsequent addition of the record for Al Ham.

```
       HEAD.FIRST_AVAIL: 43  ─────────────────┐
                                              │
                                              ▼
40 Ames¦John¦123 Maple¦Stillwater¦OK¦74075¦64 *¦ -1............
....................................................45 Brown¦Martha¦62
5 Kimbark¦Des Moines¦IA¦50311¦
```

(a)

```
       HEAD.FIRST_AVAIL: -1

40 Ames¦John¦123 Maple¦Stillwater¦OK¦74075¦64 Ham¦Al¦28 Elm¦Ada¦
OK¦70332¦.................................45 Brown¦Martha¦62
5 Kimbark¦Des Moines¦IA¦50311¦
```

(b)

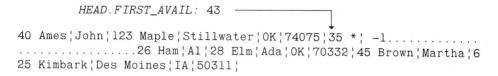

```
HEAD.FIRST_AVAIL: 43

40 Ames¦John¦123 Maple¦Stillwater¦OK¦74075¦35 *¦ -1............
.................26 Ham¦Al¦28 Elm¦Ada¦OK¦70332¦45 Brown¦Martha¦6
25 Kimbark¦Des Moines¦IA¦50311¦
```

FIGURE 5.11 Combatting internal fragmentation by putting the unused part of the deleted slot back on the avail list.

could occur with our sample file when the second record in the file is deleted and the following record is added:

Ham|Al|28 Elm|Ada|OK|70332|

It appears that escaping internal fragmentation is not so easy. The slot vacated by the deleted record is 37 bytes larger than is needed for the new record. Since we treat the extra 37 bytes as part of the new record, they are not on the avail list and are therefore unusable. But instead of keeping the 64-byte record slot intact, suppose we break it into two parts: one part to hold the new Ham record, and the other to be placed back on the avail list. Since we would take only as much space as necessary for the Ham record, there would be no internal fragmentation.

Figure 5.11 shows what our file looks like if we use this approach to insert the record for Al Ham. We steal the space for the Ham record *from the end* of the 64-byte slot and leave the first 35 bytes of the slot on the avail list. (The available space is 35 rather than 37 bytes because we need two bytes to form a new size field for the Ham record.)

The 35 bytes still on the avail list can be used to hold yet another record. Figure 5.12 shows the effect of inserting the following 25-byte record:

Lee|Ed|Rt 2|Ada|OK|74820|

As we would expect, the new record is carved out of the 35-byte record that is on the avail list. The data portion of the new record requires 25 bytes, and

FIGURE 5.12 Addition of the second record into the slot originally occupied by a single deleted record.

```
HEAD, FIRST_AVAIL: 43

40¦Ames¦John¦123 Maple¦Stillwater¦OK¦74075¦8 *¦ -1...25 Lee¦Ed¦
Rt 2¦Ada¦OK¦74820¦26 Ham¦Al¦28 Elm¦Ada¦OK¦70332¦45 Brown¦Martha¦6
25 Kimbark¦ Des Moines¦IA¦50311¦
```

then we need two more bytes for another size field. This leaves eight bytes in the record still on the avail list.

What are the chances of finding a record that can make use of these eight bytes? Our guess would be that the probability is close to zero. These eight bytes are not usable, even though they are not trapped inside any other record. This is an example of *external fragmentation*. The space is actually on the avail list rather than being locked inside some other record, but is too fragmented to be reused.

There are some interesting ways to combat external fragmentation. One way, which we discussed at the beginning of this chapter, is *storage compaction*. We could simply regenerate the file when external fragmentation becomes intolerable. Two other approaches are as follows:

☐ If two record slots on the avail list are physically adjacent, combine them to make a single, larger record slot. This is called *coalescing the holes* in the storage space.

☐ Try to minimize fragmentation before it happens by adopting a placement strategy that the program can use as it selects a record slot from the avail list.

Coalescing holes presents some interesting problems. The avail list is not kept in *physical* record order; if there are two deleted records that are physically adjacent, there is no reason to presume that they are linked adjacent to each other on the avail list. Exercise 15 at the end of this chapter provides a discussion of this problem along with a framework for developing a solution.

The development of better *placement strategies*, however, is a different matter. It is a topic that warrants a separate discussion, since the choice among alternative strategies is not as obvious as it might seem at first glance.

5.2.5 Placement Strategies

Earlier we discussed ways to add and remove variable-length records from an avail list. We add records by treating the avail list as a stack, putting deleted records at the front. When we need to remove a record slot from the avail list (to add a record to the file), we look through the list, starting at the beginning, until we either find a record slot that is big enough or reach the end of the list.

This is called a *first-fit* placement strategy. The least possible amount of work is expended when we place newly available space on the list, and we are not very particular about the closeness of fit as we look for a record slot to hold a new record. We accept the first available record slot that will do the job, regardless of whether the slot is 10 times bigger than what is needed or whether it is a perfect fit.

We could, of course, develop a more orderly approach for placing records on the avail list, keeping them in either ascending or descending sequence by size. Rather than always putting the newly deleted records at the front of the list, these approaches involve moving through the list, looking for the place to insert the record to maintain the desired sequence.

If we order the avail list in *ascending* order by size, what is the effect on the closeness of fit of the records that are retrieved from the list? Since the retrieval procedure searches sequentially through the avail list until it encounters a record that is big enough to hold the new record, the first record encountered is the *smallest* record that will do the job. The fit between the available slot and the new record's needs would be as close as we can make it. This is called a *best-fit* placement strategy.

A best-fit strategy is intuitively appealing. There is, of course, a price to be paid for obtaining this fit. We end up having to search through at least a part of the list not only when we get records from the list, but also when we put newly deleted records on the list. In a real-time environment the extra processing time could be significant.

A less obvious disadvantage of the best-fit strategy is related to the idea of finding the best possible fit: The free area left over after inserting a new record into a slot is as small as possible. Often this remaining space is too small to be useful, resulting in external fragmentation. Furthermore, the slots that are least likely to be useful are the ones that will be placed toward the beginning of the list, making first-fit searches increasingly long as time goes on.

These problems suggest an alternative strategy: What if we arrange the avail list so it is in *descending* order by size? Then the largest record slot on the avail list would always be at the head of the list. Since the procedure that retrieves records starts its search at the beginning of the avail list, it always returns the largest available record slot if it returns any slot at all. This is known as a *worst-fit* placement strategy. The amount of space in the record slot beyond what is actually needed is as large as possible.

A *worst-fit* strategy does not, at least initially, sound very appealing. But consider the following:

☐   The procedure for removing records can be simplified so it looks only at the first element of the avail list. If the first record slot is not large enough to do the job, none of the others will be.

☐   By extracting the space we need from the *largest* available slot, we are assured that the unused portion of the slot is as large as possible, decreasing the likelihood of external fragmentation.

What can you conclude from all of this? It should be clear that no one placement strategy is superior for all circumstances. The best you can do is formulate a series of general observations and then, given a particular design situation, try to select the strategy that seems most appropriate. Here are some suggestions. The judgment will have to be yours.

- ☐ Placement strategies make sense only with regard to volatile, variable-length record files. With fixed-length records, placement is simply not an issue.
- ☐ If space is lost due to *internal fragmentation,* then the choice is between first fit and best fit. A worst-fit strategy truly makes internal fragmentation worse.
- ☐ If the space is lost due to *external fragmentation,* then one should give careful consideration to a worst-fit strategy.

5.3   Finding Things Quickly: An Introduction to Internal Sorting and Binary Searching

This text begins with a discussion of the cost of accessing secondary storage. You may remember that the magnitude of the difference between accessing RAM and seeking information on a fixed disk is such that, if we magnify the time for a RAM access to 20 seconds, a similarly magnified disk access would take 58 days.

So far we have not had to pay much attention to this cost. This section, then, marks a kind of turning point. Once we move from fundamental organizational issues to the matter of searching a file for a particular piece of information, the cost of a seek becomes a major factor in determining our approach. And what is true for searching is all the more true for sorting. If you have studied sorting algorithms, you know that even a good sort involves making many comparisons. If each of these comparisons involves a seek, the sort is agonizingly slow.

Our discussion of sorting and searching, then, goes beyond simply getting the job done. We develop approaches that minimize the number of disk accesses and that therefore minimize the amount of time expended. This concern with minimizing the number of seeks continues to be a major focus throughout the rest of this text. This is just the beginning of a quest for ways to order and find things quickly.

5.3.1 Finding Things in Simple Field and Record Files

All of the programs we have written up to this point, despite any other strengths they offer, share a major failing: The only way to retrieve or find a record with any degree of rapidity is to look for it by relative record number (RRN). If the file has fixed-length records, knowing the RRN lets us compute the record's byte offset and jump to it using direct access.

But what if we do not know the byte offset or RRN of the record we want? How likely is it that a question about this file would take the form, "What is the record stored in RRN 23?" Not very likely, of course. We are much more likely to know the identity of a record by its key, and the question is more likely to take the form, "What is the record for Bill Kelly?"

Given the methods of organization developed so far, access by key implies a sequential search. What if there is no record containing the requested key? Then we would have to look through the entire file. What if we suspect that there might be more than one record that contains the key, and we want to find them all? Once again, we would be doomed to looking at every record in the file. Clearly, we need to find a better way to handle keyed access. Fortunately, there are many better ways.

5.3.2 Search by Guessing: Binary Search

Suppose we are looking for a record for Bill Kelly in a file of 1,000 fixed-length records, and suppose the file is sorted so the records appear in ascending order by key. We start by comparing KELLY BILL (the canonical form of the search key) with the middle key in the file, which is the key whose RRN is 500. The result of the comparison tells us which half of the file contains Bill Kelly's record. Next, we compare KELLY BILL with the middle key among records in the selected half of the file to find out which quarter of the file Bill Kelly's record is in. This process is repeated until either Bill Kelly's record is found or we have narrowed the number of potential records to zero.

This kind of searching is called binary searching. An algorithm for binary searching is shown in Fig. 5.13. Binary searching takes at most 10 comparisons to find Bill Kelly's record, if it is in the file, or to determine that it is not in the file. Compare this with a sequential search for the record. If there are 1,000 records, then it takes at most 1,000 comparisons to find a given record (or establish that it is not present); on the average, 500 comparisons are needed.

5.3.3 Binary Search versus Sequential Search

In general, a binary search of a file with n records takes at most

$$\lfloor \log n \rfloor + 1 \text{ comparisons}^{\dagger}$$

---

†In this text, log x refers to the logarithm function to the base 2. When any other base is intended, it is so indicated.

```
/* function to perform a binary search in the file associated with the
   logical name INPUT. Assumes that INPUT contains RECORD_COUNT records.
   Searches for the key KEY_SOUGHT. Returns RRN of record containing
   key if the key is found; otherwise returns -1
*/

FUNCTION: bin_search(INPUT, KEY_SOUGHT, RECORD_COUNT)

    LOW := 0                       /* initialize lower bound for searching   */
    HIGH := RECORD_COUNT - 1    /* intialize high bound -- we   subtract 1
                                   from the count since RRNs start from 0 */

    while (LOW <= HIGH)
        GUESS := (LOW + HIGH) / 2     /* find  midpoint                     */

        read record with RRN of GUESS
        place canonical form of key from record GUESS into KEY_FOUND

        if (KEY_SOUGHT < KEY_FOUND)            /* GUESS is too high        */
            HIGH := GUESS - 1                  /* so reduce upper  bound */
        else if (KEY_SOUGHT > KEY_FOUND)       /* GUESS is too low         */
            LOW  := GUESS + 1                  /* increase lower  bound   */
        else
            return(GUESS)                      /* match -- return the RRN  */
    endwhile

    return (-1)  /* if loop completes, then key was not  found             */
```

FIGURE 5.13 The *bin_search( )* function in pseudocode.

and on average approximately

$$\lfloor \log n \rfloor + \frac{1}{2} \text{ comparisons.}$$

A binary search is therefore said to be $O(\log n)$. In contrast, you may recall that a sequential search of the same file requires at most n comparisons, and on average $\frac{1}{2} n$, which is to say that a sequential search is $O(n)$.

The difference between a binary search and a sequential search becomes even more dramatic as we increase the size of the file to be searched. If we double the number of records in the file, we double the number of comparisons required for sequential search; when binary search is used, doubling the file size adds only one more guess to our worst case. This makes sense, since we know that each guess eliminates half of the possible choices. So, if we tried to find Bill Kelly's record in a file of 2,000 records, it would take at most

$$1 + \lfloor \log 2{,}000 \rfloor = 11 \text{ comparisons,}$$

whereas a sequential search would average

$$\frac{1}{2}n = 1,000 \text{ comparisons,}$$

and could take up to 2,000 comparisons.

Binary searching is clearly a more attractive way to find things than is sequential searching. But, as you might expect, there is a price to be paid before we can use binary searching: Binary searching works only when the list of records is ordered in terms of the key we are using in the search. So, to make use of binary searching, we have to be able to sort a list on the basis of a key.

Sorting is a very important part of file processing. Next, we look at some simple approaches to sorting files in RAM, at the same time introducing some important new concepts in file structure design. In Chapter 7 we take a second look at sorting, when we deal with some tough problems that occur when files are too large to sort in RAM.

5.3.4 Sorting a Disk File in RAM

Consider the operation of any internal sorting algorithm with which you are familiar. The algorithm requires multiple passes over the list that is to be sorted, comparing and reorganizing the elements. Some of the items in the list are moved a long distance from their original positions in the list. If such an algorithm were applied directly to data stored on a disk, it is clear that there would be a lot of jumping around, seeking, and rereading of data. This would be a very slow operation—unthinkably slow.

If the entire contents of the file can be held in RAM, a very attractive alternative is to read the entire file from the disk into memory, and then do the sorting there, using an *internal sort*. We still have to access the data on the disk, but this way we can access it sequentially, sector after sector, without having to incur the cost of a lot of seeking and the cost of multiple passes over the disk.

This is one instance of a general class of solutions to the problem of minimizing disk usage: Force your disk access into a sequential mode, performing the more complex, direct accesses in RAM.

Unfortunately, it is often not possible to use this simple kind of solution, but when you can, you should take advantage of it. In the case of sorting, internal sorts are increasingly viable as the amount of RAM space increases. A good illustration of an internal sort is the UNIX *sort* utility, which sorts files in RAM if it can find enough space. This utility is described in Chapter 7.

5.3.5 The Limitations of Binary Searching and Internal Sorting

Let's look at three problems associated with our "sort, then binary search" approach to finding things.

Problem 1: Binary Searching Requires More than One or Two Accesses   In the average case, a binary search requires approximately $\lfloor \log n \rfloor + \frac{1}{2}$ comparisons. If each comparison requires a disk access, a series of binary searches on a list of 1,000 items requires, on the average, 9.5 accesses per request. If the list is expanded to 100,000 items, the average search length extends to 16.5 accesses. Although this is a tremendous improvement over the cost of a sequential search for the key, it is also true that 16 accesses, or even 9 or 10 accesses, is not a negligible cost. The cost of this seeking is particularly noticeable, and objectionable, if we are doing a large enough number of repeated accesses by key.

When we access records by relative record number (RRN) rather than by key, we are able to retrieve a record with a single access. That is an order of magnitude of improvement over the 10 or more accesses that binary searching requires with even a moderately large file. Ideally, we would like to approach RRN retrieval performance, while still maintaining the advantages of access by key. In the following chapter, on the use of index structures, we begin to look at ways to move toward this ideal.

Problem 2: Keeping a File Sorted Is Very Expensive   Our ability to use a binary search has a price attached to it: We must keep the file in sorted order by key. Suppose we are working with a file to which we add records as often as we search for existing records. If we leave the file in unsorted order, doing sequential searches for records, then on the average each search requires reading through half the file. Each record addition, however, is very fast, since it involves nothing more than jumping to the end of the file and writing a record.

If, as an alternative, we keep the file in sorted order, we can cut down substantially on the cost of searching, reducing it to a handful of accesses. But we encounter difficulty when we add a record, since we want to keep all the records in sorted order. Inserting a new record into the file requires, on the average, that we not only read through half the records, but that we also shift the records to open up the space required for the insertion. We are actually doing more work than if we simply do sequential searches on an unsorted file.

The costs of maintaining a file that can be accessed through binary searching are not always as large as in this example involving frequent record addition. For example, it is often the case that searching is required much more frequently than is record addition. In such a circumstance, the benefits of faster retrieval can more than offset the costs of keeping the file sorted. As another example, there are many applications in which record additions can be accumulated in a transaction file and made in a batch mode. By sorting the list of new records before adding them to the main file, it is possible to merge them with the existing records. As we see in Chapter 7, such merging is a sequential process, passing only once over each record in the file. This can be an efficient, attractive approach to maintaining the file.

So, despite its problems, there are situations in which binary searching appears to be a useful strategy. However, knowing the costs of binary searching also lets us see what the requirements will be for better solutions to the problem of finding things by key. Better solutions will have to meet at least one of the following conditions:

☐ They will not involve reordering of the records in the file when a new record is added; and

☐ They will be associated with data structures that allow for substantially more rapid, efficient reordering of the file.

In the chapters that follow we develop approaches that fall into each of these categories. Solutions of the first type can involve the use of simple indexes. They can also involve hashing. Solutions of the second type can involve the use of tree structures, such as a B-tree, to keep the file in order.

Problem 3: An Internal Sort Works Only on Small Files Our ability to use binary searching is limited by our ability to sort the file. An internal sort works only if we can read the entire contents of a file into the computer's electronic memory. If the file is so large that we cannot do that, then we need a different kind of sort.

In the following section we develop a variation on internal sorting called a *keysort*. Like internal sorting, keysort is limited in terms of how large a file it can sort, but its limit is larger. More importantly, our work on keysort begins to illuminate a new approach to the problem of finding things that will allow us to avoid the sorting of records in a file.

5.4 Keysorting

Keysort, sometimes referred to as *tag sort,* is based on the idea that when we sort a file in RAM the only things that we really need to sort are the record keys; therefore, we do not need to read the whole file into RAM during the sorting process. Instead, we read the keys from the file into RAM, sort them, and then rearrange the records in the file according to the new ordering of the keys.

Since keysort never reads the complete set of records into memory, it can sort larger files than a regular internal sort, given the same amount of RAM.

5.4.1 Description of the Method

To keep things simple, we assume that we are dealing with a fixed-length record file of the kind developed in Chapter 4, with a count of the number records stored in a header record. We begin by reading the keys into an array of identically sized character fields, with each row of the array containing a key. We call this array KEYNODES[], and we call the key field KEYNODES[].KEY. Figure 5.14 illustrates the relationship between the array KEYNODES[] and the actual file at the time that the keysort procedure begins.

There must, of course, be some way of relating the keys back to the records from which they have been extracted. Consequently, each node of the array KEYNODES[] has a second field KEYNODES[].RRN that contains the RRN of the record associated with the corresponding key.

The actual sorting process simply sorts the KEYNODES[] array according to the KEY field. This produces an arrangement like that shown

FIGURE 5.14 Conceptual view of KEYNODES array to be used in RAM by internal sort routine, and record array on secondary store.

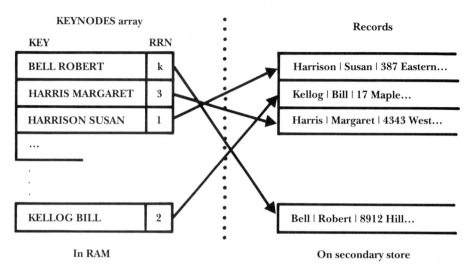

FIGURE 5.15 Conceptual view of KEYNODES array and file after sorting keys in RAM.

in Fig. 5.15. The elements of KEYNODES[] are now sequenced in such a way that the first element has the RRN of the record that should be moved to the first position in the file, the second element identifies the record that should be second, and so forth.

Once KEYNODES[] is sorted, we are ready to reorganize the file according to this new ordering. This process can be described as follows:

for i: = 1 to number of records

Seek in the input file to the record whose RRN is KEYNODES[i].RRN.

Read this record into a buffer in RAM.

Write the contents of the buffer out to output file.

Figure 5.16 outlines the keysort procedure in pseudocode. This procedure works much the same way that a normal internal sort would work, but with two important differences:

☐ Rather than read entire records into a RAM array, we simply read each record into a temporary buffer, extract the key, and then discard it; and

☐ When we are writing the records out in sorted order, we have to read them in a second time, since they are not all stored in RAM.

```
PROGRAM: keysort
     open input file as IN_FILE
     create output file as OUT_FILE

     read header record from IN_FILE and write a copy to OUT_FILE
     REC_COUNT := record count from header record

     /* read in records; set up KEYNODES array */
     for i := 1 to REC_COUNT
          read record from IN_FILE into BUFFER
          extract canonical key and place it in KEYNODES[i].KEY
          KEYNODES[i].RRN = i

     /* sort KEYNODES[].KEY, thereby ordering RRNs correspondingly */
     sort (KEYNODES, REC_COUNT)

     /* read in records according to sorted order, and write them  */
     /* out in this order                                          */
     for i := 1 to REC_COUNT
          seek in IN_FILE to record with RRN of KEYNODES[i].RRN
          read the record into BUFFER from IN_FILE
          write BUFFER contents to OUT_FILE
     close IN_FILE and OUT_FILE
end PROGRAM
```

FIGURE 5.16 Pseudocode for *keysort.*

5.4.2 Limitations of the Keysort Method

At first glance, keysorting appears to be an obvious improvement over sorts performed entirely in RAM; it might even appear to be a case of getting something for nothing. We know that sorting is an expensive operation and that we want to do it in RAM. Keysorting allows us to achieve this objective without having to hold the entire file in RAM at once.

But, while reading about the operation of writing the records out in sorted order, even a casual reader probably senses a cloud on this apparently bright horizon. In keysort we need to read in the records a second time before we can write out the new sorted file. Doing something twice is never desirable. But the problem is worse than that.

Look carefully at the *for* loop that reads in the records before writing them out to the new file. You can see that we are not reading through the input file sequentially. Instead, we are working in sorted order, moving from the sorted KEYNODES[] to the RRNs of the records. Since we have to seek to each record and read it in before writing it back out, creating the sorted file requires as many random seeks into the input file as there are records. As we have noted a number of times, there is an enormous difference between the time required to read all the records in a file sequentially and the time required to read those same records if we must seek to each record separately. What is worse, we are performing all of these accesses in alternation with write statements to the output file. So, even the writing of the output file, which would otherwise appear to be sequential, in most cases involves seeking. The disk drive must move the head back and forth between the two files as it reads and writes.

The getting-something-for-nothing aspect of keysort has suddenly evaporated. Even though keysort does the hard work of sorting in RAM, it turns out that creating a sorted version of the file from the map supplied by the KEYNODES[] array is not at all a trivial matter when the only copies of the records are kept on secondary store.

5.4.3 Another Solution: Why Bother to Write the File Back?

The fundamental idea behind keysort is an attractive one: Why work with an entire record when the only parts of interest, as far as sorting and searching are concerned, are the fields used to form the key? There is a compelling parsimony behind this idea, and it makes keysorting look promising. The promise fades only when we run into the problem of rearranging all the records in the file so they reflect the new, sorted order.

It is interesting to ask whether we can avoid this problem by simply not bothering with the task that is giving us trouble: What if we just skip the time-consuming business of writing out a sorted version of the file? What if, instead, we simply write out a copy of the array of canonical key nodes? If we do without writing the records back in sorted order, writing out the contents of our KEYNODES[] array instead, we will have written a program that outputs an *index* to the original file. The relationship between the two files is illustrated in Fig. 5.17.

This is an instance of one of our favorite categories of solutions to computer science problems: If some part of a process begins to look like a bottleneck, consider skipping it altogether. Can you do without it? Instead of creating a new, sorted copy of the file to use for searching, we have created a second kind of file, an index file, that is to be used in conjunction with the original file. If we are looking for a particular record, we do our binary search on the index file, then use the RRN stored in the index file record to find the corresponding record in the original file.

There is much to say about the use of index files, enough to fill several chapters. The next chapter is about the various ways we can use simple indexes, which is the kind of index we illustrate here. In later chapters we

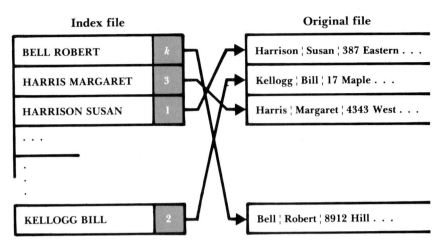

FIGURE 5.17 Relationship between the index file and the data file.

talk about different ways of organizing the index to provide more flexible access and easier maintenance.

5.4.4 Pinned Records

In section 5.2 we discussed the problem of updating and maintaining files. Much of that discussion revolved around the problems of deleting records and keeping track of the space vacated by deleted records so it can be reused. An avail list of deleted record slots is created by linking all of the available slots together. This linking is done by writing a link field into each deleted record that points to the next deleted record. This link field gives very specific information about the exact physical location of the next available record.

When a file contains such references to the physical locations of records, we say that these records are *pinned*. You can gain an appreciation for this particular choice of terminology if you consider the effects of sorting one of these files containing an avail list of deleted records. A pinned record is one that cannot be moved. Other records in the same file or in some other file (such as an index file) contain references to the physical location of the record. If the record is moved, these references no longer lead to the record; they become what are called *dangling pointers*, pointers leading to incorrect, meaningless locations in the file.

Clearly, the use of pinned records in a file can make sorting more difficult and sometimes impossible. But what if we want to support rapid access by key, while still reusing the space made available by record deletion? One solution is to use an index file to keep the sorted order of the records, while keeping the actual data file in its original order. Once again, the problem of finding things leads to the suggestion that we need to take a close look at the use of indexes, which, in turn, leads us to the next chapter.

■ SUMMARY

In this chapter we look at ways to organize or reorganize files to improve performance in some way.

Data compression methods are used to make files smaller by re-encoding data that goes into a file. Smaller files use less storage, take less time to transmit, and can often be processed faster sequentially.

The notation used for representing information can often be made more compact. For instance, if a two-byte field in a record can take on only 50 values, the field can be encoded using only 6 bits instead of 16. Another form of compression called *run-length encoding* encodes sequences of repeating values, rather than writing all of the values in the file.

A third form of compression assigns variable-length codes to values depending on how frequently the values occur. Values that occur often are given shorter codes, so they take up less space. *Huffman codes* are an example of variable-length codes.

Some compression techniques are *irreversible* in that they lose information in the encoding process. The UNIX utilities *compress, uncompress, pack,* and *unpack* provide good compression in UNIX.

A second way to save space in a file is to recover space in the file after it has undergone changes. A volatile file, one that undergoes many changes, can deteriorate very rapidly unless measures are taken to adjust the file organization to the changes. One result of making changes to files is storage fragmentation.

Internal fragmentation occurs when there is wasted space within a record. In a fixed-length record file, internal fragmentation can result when variable-length records are stored in fixed slots. It can also occur in a variable-length record file when one record is replaced by another record of a smaller size. *External fragmentation* occurs when holes of unused space between records are created, normally because of record deletions.

There are a number of ways to combat fragmentation. The simplest is *storage compaction,* which squeezes out unused space caused by external fragmentation by sliding all of the undeleted records together. Compaction is generally done in a batch mode.

Fragmentation can be dealt with *dynamically* by reclaiming deleted space when records are added. The need to keep track of the space to be reused makes this approach more complex than compaction.

We begin with the problem of deleting fixed-length records. Since finding the first field of a fixed-length record is very easy, deleting a record can be accomplished by placing a special mark in the first field.

Since all records in a fixed-length record file are the same size, the reuse of deleted records need not be complicated. The solution we adopt consists of collecting all the available record slots into an *avail list*. The avail list is created by stringing together all the deleted records to form a *linked list* of deleted record spaces.

In a fixed-length record file, any one record slot is just as usable as any other slot; they are interchangeable. Consequently, the simplest way to maintain the linked avail list is to treat it as a *stack*. Newly available records are added to the avail list by *pushing* them onto the front of the list; record slots are removed from the avail list by *popping* them from the front of the list.

Next, we consider the matter of deleting variable-length records. We still form a linked list of available record slots, but with variable-length records we need to be sure that a record slot is the right size to hold the new record. Our initial definition of *right size* is simply in terms of being big enough. Consequently, we need a procedure that can search through the avail list until it finds a record slot that is big enough to hold the new record. Given such a function, and a complementary function that places newly deleted records on the avail list, we can implement a system that deletes and reuses variable-length records.

We then consider the amount and nature of fragmentation that develops inside a file due to record deletion and reuse. Fragmentation can happen *internally* if the space is lost because it is locked up inside a record. We develop a procedure that breaks a single, large, variable-length record slot into two or more smaller ones, using exactly as much space as is needed for a new record, leaving the remainder on the avail list. We see that, although this could decrease the amount of wasted space, eventually the remaining fragments are too small to be useful. When this happens, the space is lost to *external fragmentation*.

There are a number of things that one can do to minimize external fragmentation. They include (1) *compacting* the file in a batch mode when the level of fragmentation becomes excessive; (2) *coalescing* adjacent record slots on the avail list to make larger, more generally useful slots; and (3) adopting a *placement strategy* to select slots for reuse in a way that minimizes fragmentation. Development of algorithms for coalescing holes is left as part of the exercises at the end of this chapter. Placement strategies need more careful discussion.

The placement strategy used up to this point by the variable-length record deletion and reuse procedures is a *first-fit* strategy. This strategy is simply, "If the record slot is big enough, use it." By keeping the avail list in sorted order, it is easy to implement either of two other placement strategies:

- *Best fit,* in which a new record is placed in the smallest slot that is still big enough to hold it. This is an attractive strategy for variable-length record files in which the fragmentation is *internal.* It involves more overhead than other placement strategies.
- *Worst fit,* in which a new record is placed in the largest record slot available. The idea is to have the left-over portion of the slot be as large as possible.

There is no firm rule for selecting a placement strategy; the best one can do is use informed judgment based on a number of guidelines.

In the third major section of this chapter, we look at ways to find things quickly in a file through the use of a key. In preceding chapters it was not possible to access a record rapidly without knowing its physical location or relative record number. Now we explore some of the problems and opportunities associated with keyed direct access.

This chapter develops only one method of finding records by key—binary searching. Binary searching requires $O (\log n)$ comparisons to find a record in a file with n records, and hence is far superior to sequential searching. Since binary searching works only on a sorted file, a sorting procedure is an absolute necessity. The problem of sorting is complicated by the fact that we are sorting files on secondary storage rather than vectors in RAM. We need to develop a sorting procedure that does not require seeking back and forth over the file.

Three disadvantages are associated with sorting and binary searching as developed up to this point:

- Binary searching is an enormous improvement over sequential searching, but it still usually requires more than one or two accesses per record. The need for fewer disk accesses becomes especially acute in applications where a large number of records are to be accessed by key.
- The requirement that the file be kept in sorted order can be expensive. For active files to which records are added frequently, the cost of keeping the file in sorted order can outweigh the benefits of binary searching.
- A RAM sort can be used only on relatively small files. This limits the size of the files that we could organize for binary searching, given our sorting tools.

The third problem can be solved partially by developing more powerful sorting procedures, such as a keysort. This approach to sorting resembles a RAM sort in most respects, but does not use RAM to hold the entire file. Instead, it reads in only the keys from the records, sorts the keys, and then uses the sorted list of keys to rearrange the records on secondary storage so they are in sorted order.

The disadvantage to a keysort is that rearranging a file of n records requires n random seeks out to the original file, which can take much more time than does a sequential reading of the same number of records. The inquiry into keysorting is not wasted, however. Keysorting naturally leads to the suggestion that we merely write the sorted list of keys off to secondary storage, setting aside the expensive matter of rearranging the file. This list of keys, coupled with RRN tags pointing back to the original records, is an example of an index. We look at indexing more closely in Chapter 6.

This chapter closes with a discussion of another, potentially hidden, cost of sorting and searching. Pinned records are records that are referenced elsewhere (in the same file or in some other file) according to their physical position in the file. Sorting and binary searching cannot be applied to a file containing pinned records, since the sorting, by definition, is likely to change the physical position of the record. Such a change causes other references to this record to become inaccurate, creating the problem of dangling pointers.

■ KEY TERMS

Avail list. A list of the space, freed through record deletion, that is available for holding new records. In the examples considered in this chapter, this list of space took the form of a linked list of deleted records.

Best fit. A placement strategy for selecting the space on the avail list used to hold a new record. Best-fit placement finds the available record slot that is closest in size to what is needed to hold the new record.

Binary search. A binary search algorithm locates a key in a sorted list by repeatedly selecting the middle element of the list, dividing the list in half, and forming a new, smaller list from the half that contains the key. This process is continued until the selected element is the key that is sought.

Coalescence. If two deleted, available records are physically adjacent, they can be combined to form a single, larger available record space. This process of combining smaller available spaces into a larger one is known as *coalescing holes.* Coalescence is a way to counteract the problem of external fragmentation.

Compaction. A way of getting rid of all *external fragmentation* by sliding all the records together so there is no space lost between them.

Data compression. Encoding information in a file in such a way as to take up less space.

External fragmentation. A form of fragmentation that occurs in a file when there is unused space outside or between individual records.

First fit. A placement strategy for selecting a space from the avail list. First-fit placement selects the first available record slot large enough to hold the new record.

Fragmentation. The unused space within a file. The space can be locked within individual records *(internal fragmentation)* or outside or between individual records *(external fragmentation).*

Huffman code. A variable-length code in which the lengths of the codes are based on their probability of occurrence.

Internal fragmentation. A form of fragmentation that occurs when space is wasted in a file because it is locked up, unused, inside of records. Fixed-length record structures often result in internal fragmentation.

Irreversible compression. Compression in which information is lost.

Keysort. A method of sorting a file that does not require holding the entire file in memory. Only the keys are held in memory, along with pointers that tie these keys to the records in the file from which they are extracted. The keys are sorted, and the sorted list of keys is used to construct a new version of the file that has the records in sorted order. The primary advantage of a keysort is that it requires less RAM than does a RAM sort. The disadvantage is that the process of constructing a new file requires a lot of seeking for records.

Linked list. A collection of nodes that have been organized into a specific sequence by means of references placed in each node that point to a single successor node. The *logical* order of a linked list is often different than the actual physical order of the nodes in the computer's memory.

Pinned record. A record is pinned when there are other records or file structures that refer to it by its physical location. It is pinned in the sense that we are not free to alter the physical location of the record: doing so destroys the validity of the physical references to the record. These references become useless dangling pointers.

Placement strategy. As used in this chapter, a placement strategy is a mechanism for selecting the space on the avail list that is to be used to hold a new record added to the file.

Redundancy reduction. Any form of compression that does not lose information.

Run-length encoding. A compression method in which runs of repeated codes are replaced by a count of the number of repetitions of the code, followed by the code that is repeated.

Stack. A kind of list in which all additions and deletions take place at the same end.

Variable-length encoding. Any encoding scheme in which the codes are of different lengths. More frequently occurring codes are given shorter lengths than are frequently occurring codes. Huffman encoding is an example of variable-length encoding.

Worst fit. A placement strategy for selecting a space from the avail list. Worst-fit placement selects the largest record slot, regardless of how small the new record is. Insofar as this leaves the largest possible record slot for reuse, worst fit can sometimes help minimize *external fragmentation*.

■ EXERCISES

1. In our discussion of compression, we show how we can compress the "state name" field from 16 bits to 6 bits, yet we say that this gives us a space savings of 50%, rather than 62.5%, as we would expect. Why is this so? What other measures might we take to achieve the full 62.5% savings?

2. What is redundancy reduction? Why is run-length encoding an example of redundancy reduction?

3. What is the maximum run length that can be handled in the run-length encoding described in the text? If much longer runs were common, how might you handle them?

4. Encode each of the following using run-length encoding. Discuss the results, and indicate how you might improve the algorithm.

(a) 01 01 01 01 01 01 01 01 01 02 03 03 03 03 03 03 03 04 05 06 06 07
(b) 01 01 02 02 03 03 04 05 06 06 05 05 04 04

5. From Fig. 5.2, determine the Huffman code for the sequence "daeab".

6. What is the difference between internal and external fragmentation? How can compaction affect the amount of internal fragmentation in a file? What about external fragmentation?

7. In-place compaction purges deleted records from a file without creating a separate new file. What are the advantages and disadvantages of in-place compaction compared to compaction in which a separate compacted file is created?

8. Why is a worst-fit placement strategy a bad choice if there is significant loss of space due to internal fragmentation?

9. Conceive of an inexpensive way to keep a continuous record of the amount of fragmentation in a file. This fragmentation measure could be used to trigger the batch processes used to reduce fragmentation.

10. Suppose a file must remain sorted. How does this affect the range of placement strategies available?

11. Develop a pseudocode description of a procedure for performing in-place compaction in a variable-length record file that contains size fields at the start of each record.

12. Consider the process of updating rather than deleting a variable-length record. Outline a procedure for handling such updating, accounting for the update possibly resulting in either a longer or shorter record.

13. In section 5.3, we raised the question of where to keep the stack containing the list of available records. Should it be a separate list, perhaps maintained in a separate file, or should it be embedded within the data file? We choose the latter organization for our implementation. What advantages and disadvantages are there to the second approach? What other kinds of file structures can you think of to facilitate various kinds of record deletion?

14. In some files, each record has a delete bit that is set to 1 to indicate that the record is deleted. This bit can also be used to indicate that a record is inactive rather than deleted. What is required to reactivate an inactive record? Could reactivation be done with the deletion procedures we have used?

15. In this chapter we outlined three general approaches to the problem of minimizing storage fragmentation: (a) implementation of a placement strategy; (b) coalescing of holes; and (c) compaction. Assuming an interactive programming environment, which of these strategies would be used "on the fly," as records are added and deleted? Which strategies would be used as batch processes that could be run periodically?

16. Why do placement strategies make sense only with variable-length record files?

17. Compare the average case performance of binary search with sequential search for records, assuming

☐   That the records being sought are guaranteed to be in the file;
☐   That half of the time the records being sought are not in the file; and
☐   That half of the time the records being sought are not in the file and that missing records must be inserted.

Make a table showing your performance comparisons for files of 1,000, 2,000, 4,000, 8,000, and 16,000 records.

18. If the records in exercise 17 are blocked with 20 records per block, how does this affect the performance of the binary and sequential searches?

19. An internal sort works only with files small enough to fit in RAM. Some computing systems provide users with an almost unlimited amount of RAM with a memory management technique called *virtual storage*. Discuss the use of internal sorting to sort large files on systems that use virtual storage.

20. Our discussion of keysorting covers the considerable expense associated with the process of actually creating the sorted output file, given the sorted vector of pointers to the canonical key nodes. The expense revolves around two primary areas of difficulty:

☐   Having to jump around in the input file, performing many seeks to retrieve the records in their new, sorted order; and
☐   Writing the output file at the same time we are reading the input file; jumping back and forth between the files can involve seeking.

Design an approach to this problem that uses buffers to hold a number of records, therefore mitigating these difficulties. If your solution is to be viable, obviously the buffers must use less RAM than would a sort taking place entirely within electronic memory.

Programming Exercises

21. Rewrite the program *update.c* or *update.pas* so it can delete and add records to a fixed-length record file using one of the replacement procedures discussed in this chapter.

22. Write a program similar to the one described in the preceding exercise, but that works with variable-length record files.

23. Develop a pseudocode description of a variable-length record deletion procedure that checks to see if the newly deleted record is contiguous with any other deleted records. If there is contiguity, coalesce the records to make a single, larger available record slot. Some things to consider as you address this problem are as follows:

a. The avail list does not keep records arranged in physical order; the next record on the avail list is not necessarily the next deleted record in the physical file. Is it possible to merge these two views of the avail list, the physical order and the logical order, into a single list? If you do this, what placement strategy will you use?

b. Physical adjacency can include records that precede as well as follow the newly deleted record. How will you look for a deleted record that precedes the newly deleted record?

c. Maintaining two views of the list of deleted records implies that as you discover physically adjacent records you have to rearrange links to update the nonphysical avail list. What additional complications would we encounter if we were combining the coalescing of holes with a best-fit or worst-fit strategy?

24. Implement the *bin_search()* function in either C or Pascal. Write a driver program named *search* to test the function *bin_search()*. Assume that the files are created with the *update* program developed in Chapter 4, and then sorted. Include enough debug information in the *search* driver and *bin_search()* function to watch the binary searching logic as it makes successive guesses about where to place the new record.

25. Modify the *bin_search()* function so if the key is not in the file, it returns the relative record number that the key would occupy were it in the file. The function should also continue to indicate whether the key was found or not.

26. Rewrite the *search* driver from exercise 24 so it uses the new *bin_search()* function developed in exercise 25. If the sought-after key is in the file, the program should display the record contents. If the key is not found, the program should display a list of the keys that surround the position that the key would have occupied. You should be able to move backward or forward through this list at will. Given this modification, you do not have to remember an entire key to retrieve it. If, for example, you know that you are looking for someone named Smith, but cannot remember the person's first name, this new program lets you jump to the area where all the Smith records are stored. You can then scroll back and forth through the keys until you recognize the right first name.

27. Write an internal sort that can sort a variable-length record file of the kind produced by the *writrec* programs in Chapter 4.

■ FURTHER READINGS

A thorough treatment of data compression techniques can be found in Lynch (1985). The Lempel-Ziv method is described in Welch (1984). Huffman encoding is covered in many data structures texts, and also in Knuth (1973a).

Somewhat surprising, the literature concerning storage fragmentation and reuse often does not consider these issues from the standpoint of secondary storage. Typically, storage fragmentation, placement strategies, coalescing of holes, and garbage collection are considered in the context of reusing space within electronic random access memory (RAM). As you read this literature with the idea of applying the concepts to secondary storage, it is necessary to evaluate each strategy in light of the cost of accessing secondary storage. Some strategies that are attractive when used in electronic RAM are too expensive on secondary storage.

Discussions about space management in RAM are usually found under the heading "Dynamic Storage Allocation." Knuth (1973a) provides a good, though technical, overview of the fundamental concerns associated with dynamic storage allocation, including placement strategies. Much of Knuth's discussion is reworked and made more approachable by Tremblay and Sorenson (1984). Standish (1980) provides a more complete overview of the entire subject, reviewing much of the important literature on the subject.

This chapter only touches the surface of issues relating to searching and sorting files. A large part of the remainder of this text is devoted to exploring the issues in more detail, so one source for further reading is the present text. But there is much more that has been written about even the relatively simple issues raised in this chapter. The classic reference on sorting and searching is Knuth (1973b). Knuth provides an excellent discussion of the limitations of keysort methods. He also develops a very complete discussion of binary searching, clearly bringing out the analogy between binary searching and the use of binary trees. Baase (1978) provides a clear, understandable analysis of binary search performance.

Indexing

6

CHAPTER OBJECTIVES

- Introduce concepts of *indexing* that have broad applications in the design of file systems.
- Introduce the use of a *simple linear index* to provide rapid access to records in an entry-sequenced, variable-length record file.
- Investigate the implications of the use of indexes for file maintenance.
- Describe the use of indexes to provide access to records by more than one key.
- Introduce the idea of an *inverted list,* illustrating *Boolean operations* on lists.
- Discuss the issue of *when to bind* an index key to an address in the data file.
- Introduce and investigate the implications of *self-indexing* files.

CHAPTER OUTLINE

6.1   What Is an Index?

The last few pages of many books contain an index. Such an index is a table containing a list of topics (keys) and numbers of pages where the topics can be found (reference fields).

All indexes are based on the same basic concept—keys and reference fields. The types of indexes we examine in this chapter are called *simple indexes* because they are represented using *simple arrays* of structures that contain the keys and reference fields. In later chapters we look at indexing schemes that use more complex data structures, especially trees. In this chapter, however, we want to emphasize that indexes can be very simple and still provide powerful tools for file processing.

The index to a book provides a way to find a topic quickly. If you have ever had to use a book without a good index, you already know that an index is a desirable alternative to scanning through the book sequentially to find a topic. In general, indexing is another way to handle the problem that we explored in Chapter 5: An index is a way to find things.

Consider what would happen if we tried to apply the previous chapter's methods, sorting and binary searching, to the problem of finding things in a book. Rearranging all the words in the book so they were in alphabetical order certainly would make finding any particular term easier but would obviously have disastrous effects on the meaning of the book. In a sense, the terms in the book are pinned records. This is an absurd example, but it clearly underscores the power and importance of the index as a conceptual tool. Since it works by indirection, *an index lets you impose order on a file without actually rearranging the file*. This not only keeps us from disturbing pinned records, but also makes matters such as record addition much less expensive than they are with a sorted file.

Take, as another example, the problem of finding books in a library. We want to be able to locate books by a specific author, by their titles, or by subject areas. One way of achieving this is to have three copies of each book and three separate library buildings. All of the books in one building would be sorted by author's name, another building would contain books arranged by title, and the third would have them ordered by subject. Again, this is an absurd example, but one that underscores another important advantage of indexing. Instead of using multiple arrangements, a library uses a card catalog. The card catalog is actually a set of three indexes, each using a different *key field,* and all of them using the same catalog number as a *reference field.* Another use of indexing, then, is to provide *multiple access paths* to a file.

We also find that indexing gives us *keyed access to variable-length record files.* Let's begin our discussion of indexing by exploring this problem of access to variable-length records and the simple solution that indexing provides.

6.2 A Simple Index with an Entry-Sequenced File

Suppose we own an extensive collection of musical recordings and we want to keep track of the collection through the use of computer files. For each recording, we keep the information shown in Fig. 6.1. The data file records are variable length. Figure 6.2 illustrates such a collection of data records. We refer to this data record file as *Datafile.*

There are a number of approaches that could be used to create a variable-length record file to hold these records; the record addresses used in Fig. 6.2 suggest that each record be preceded by a size field that permits skip sequential access and easier file maintenance. This is the structure we use.

Suppose we formed a *primary key* for these records consisting of the initials for the record company label combined with the record company's

Identification number
Title
Composer or composers
Artist or artists
Label (publisher)

FIGURE 6.1 Contents of a data record.

Rec. addr.	Label	ID number	Title	Composer(s)	Artist(s)
32†	LON	2312	Romeo and Juliet	Prokofiev	Maazel
77	RCA	2626	Quartet in C Sharp Minor	Beethoven	Julliard
132	WAR	23699	Touchstone	Corea	Corea
167	ANG	3795	Symphony No. 9	Beethoven	Giulini
211	COL	38358	Nebraska	Springsteen	Springsteen
256	DG	18807	Symphony No. 9	Beethoven	Karajan
300	MER	75016	Coq d'or Suite	Rimsky-Korsakov	Leinsdorf
353	COL	31809	Symphony No. 9	Dvorak	Bernstein
396	DG	139201	Violin Concerto	Beethoven	Ferras
442	FF	245	Good News	Sweet Honey in the Rock	Sweet Honey in the Rock

†Assume there is a header record that uses the first 32 bytes.

FIGURE 6.2 Sample contents of *Datafile*.

ID number. This will make a good primary key since it should provide a *unique* key for each entry in the file. We call this key the *Label ID*. The canonical form for the Label ID consists of the uppercase form of the Label field followed immediately by the ASCII representation of the ID number. For example,

```
LON2312
```

How could we organize the file to provide rapid keyed access to individual records? Could we sort the file and then use binary searching? Unfortunately, binary searching depends on being able to jump to the middle record in the file. This is not possible in a variable-length record file because direct access by relative record number is not possible—there is no way to know where the middle record is in any group of records.

An alternative to sorting is to construct an index for the file. Figure 6.3 illustrates such an index. On the right is the data file containing information about our collection of recordings, with one variable-length data record per recording. Only four fields are shown (Label, ID number, Title, and Composer), but it is easy to imagine the other information filling out each record.

On the left is the index file, each record of which contains a 12-character *key* (left justified, blank filled) corresponding to a certain Label ID in the data file. Each key is associated with a *reference field* giving the address of the

Indexfile *data pointer*		Datafile	
Key	*Reference field*	*Address of record*	*Actual data record*
ANG3795	167	32	LON ¦ 2312 ¦ Romeo and Juliet ¦ Prokofiev . . .
COL31809	353	77	RCA ¦ 2626 ¦ Quartet in C Sharp Minor . . .
COL38358	211	132	WAR ¦ 23699 ¦ Touchstone ¦ Corea . . .
DG139201	396	167	ANG ¦ 3795 ¦ Symphony No. 9 ¦ Beethoven . . .
DG18807	256	211	COL ¦ 38358 ¦ Nebraska ¦ Springsteen . . .
FF245	442	256	DG ¦ 18807 ¦ Symphony No. 9 ¦ Beethoven . . .
LON2312	32	300	MER ¦ 75016 ¦ Coq d'or Suite ¦ Rimsky . . .
MER75016	300	353	COL ¦ 31809 ¦ Symphony No. 9 ¦ Dvorak . . .
RCA2626	77	396	DG ¦ 139201 ¦ Violin Concerto ¦ Beethoven . . .
WAR23699	132	442	FF ¦ 245 ¦ Good News ¦ Sweet Honey In The . . .

FIGURE 6.3 Sample index with corresponding data file.

first byte of the corresponding data record. ANG3795, for example, corresponds to the reference field containing the number 167, meaning that the record containing full information on the recording with Label ID ANG3795 can be found starting at byte number 167 in the record file.

The structure of the index file is very simple. It is a fixed-length record file in which each record has two fixed-length fields: a key field and a byte–offset field. There is one record in the index file for every record in the data file.

Note also that the index is sorted, whereas the data file is not. Consequently, although Label ID ANG3795 is the first entry in the index; it is not necessarily the first entry in the data file. In fact, the data file is *entry sequenced,* which means that the records occur in the order that they are entered into the file. As we see soon, the use of an entry-sequenced file can make record addition and file maintenance much simpler than is the case with a data file that is kept sorted by some key.

```
PROCEDURE retrieve_record(KEY)

    find position of KEY in Indexfile   /* Probably using binary search */
    look up the BYTE_OFFSET of the corresponding record in Datafile
    use SEEK() and the byte_offset to move to the data record
    read the record from Datafile

end PROCEDURE
```

FIGURE 6.4 *Retrieve_record(): a procedure to retrieve a single record from Datafile through Indexfile.*

Using the index to provide access to the data file by Label ID is a simple matter. The steps needed to retrieve a single record with key KEY from *Datafile* are shown in the procedure *retrieve_record( )* in Fig. 6.4. Although this retrieval strategy is relatively straightforward, it contains some features that deserve comment:

- We are now dealing with two files—the index file and the data file. The index file is considerably easier to work with than the data file because it uses fixed-length records (which is why we can search it with a binary search) and because it is likely to be much smaller than the data file.
- By requiring that the index file have fixed-length records, we impose a limit on the sizes of our keys. In this example we assume that the primary key field is long enough to retain every key's unique identity. The use of a small, fixed key field in the index could cause problems if a key's uniqueness is truncated away as it is placed in the fixed index field.
- In the example, the index carries no information other than the keys and the reference fields, but this need not be the case. We could, for example, keep the length of each *Datafile* record in *Indexfile*.

6.3 Basic Operations on an Indexed, Entry-Sequenced File

We have noted that the process of keeping files sorted to permit binary searching for records can be very expensive. One of the great advantages of using a simple index with an entry-sequenced data file is that record addition can take place much more quickly than with a sorted data file as long as the index is small enough to be held entirely in memory. If the index record length is short, this is not a difficult condition to meet for small files consisting of no more than a few thousand records. For the moment our discussions assume that the condition is met and that the index is read from secondary storage into an array of structures called INDEX[ ]. Later we consider what should be done when the index is too large to fit into memory.

Keeping the index in memory as the program runs also lets us find records by key more quickly with an indexed file than with a sorted one since the binary searching can be performed entirely in memory. Once the byte offset for the data record is found, then a single seek is all that is required to retrieve the record. The use of a sorted data file, on the other hand, requires a seek for each step of the binary search.

The support and maintenance of an entry-sequenced file coupled with a simple index requires the development of procedures to handle a number of different tasks. Besides the *retrieve_record( )* algorithm described previously, other procedures used to find things by means of the index include the following:

□   Create the original empty index and data files;
□   Load the index file into memory before using it;
□   Rewrite the index file from memory after using it;
□   Add records to the data file and index;
□   Delete records from the data file; and
□   Update records in the data file.

Creating the Files   Both the index file and the data file are created as empty files, with header records and nothing else. This can be accomplished quite easily by creating the files and writing headers to both files.

Loading the Index into Memory   We assume that the index file is small enough to fit into primary memory, so we define an array *INDEX[ ]* to hold the index records. Each array element has the structure of an index record. Loading the index file into memory, then, is simply a matter of reading in and saving the index header record and then reading the records from the index file into the INDEX[ ] array. Since this will be a sequential read, and since the records are short, the procedure should be written so it reads a large number of index records at once, rather than one record at a time.

Rewriting the Index File from Memory   When processing of an indexed file is completed, it is necessary to rewrite INDEX[ ] back into the index file if the array has been changed in any way. In Fig. 6.5, the procedure *rewrite_index( )* describes the steps for doing this.

```
PROCEDURE rewrite_index()

    check a status flag that tells whether the INDEX[] array
        has been changed in any way.

    if there were changes, then
        open the index file as a new empty file
        update the header record and rewrite the header
        write the index out to the newly created file

    close the index file

end PROCEDURE
```

FIGURE 6.5 The *rewrite_index()* procedure.

It is important to consider what happens if this rewriting of the index does not take place, or takes place incompletely. Programs do not always run to completion. A program designer needs to guard against power failures, against the operator turning the machine off at the wrong time, and other such disasters. One of the serious dangers associated with reading an index into memory and then writing it out when the program is over is that the copy of the index on disk will be out of date and incorrect if the program is interrupted. It is imperative that a program contain at least the following two safeguards to protect against this kind of error:

☐   There should be a mechanism that permits the program to know when the index is out of date. One possibility involves setting a status flag as soon as the copy of the index in memory is changed. This status flag could be written into the header record of the index file on disk as soon as the index is read into memory, and then subsequently cleared when the index is rewritten. All programs could check the status flag before using an index. If the flag is found to be set, then the program would know that the index is out of date.

☐   If a program detects that an index is out of date, the program must have access to a procedure that reconstructs the index from the data file. This should happen automatically, taking place before any attempt is made to use the index.

Record Addition   Adding a new record to the data file requires that we also add a record to the index file. Adding to the data file itself is easy. The exact procedure depends, of course, on the kind of variable-length file organization being used. In any case, when we add a data record we should know the starting *byte_offset* of the file location at which we wrote the record. This information, along with the canonical form of the record's key, must be placed in the INDEX[ ] array.

Since the INDEX[ ] array is kept in sorted order by key, insertion of the new index record probably requires some rearrangement of the index. In a way, the situation is similar to the one we face as we add records to a sorted data file. We have to shift or slide all the records that have keys that come in order after the key of the record we are inserting. The shifting opens up a space for the new record. The big difference between the work we have to do on the index records and the work required for a sorted data file is that the INDEX[ ] array is contained *wholly in memory*. All of the index rearrangement can be done without any file access.

Record Deletion   In Chapter 5 we describe a number of approaches to deleting records in variable-length record files that allow for the reuse of the space occupied by these records. These approaches are completely viable for our data file since, unlike a sorted data file, the records in this file need not be moved around to maintain an ordering on the file. This is one of the great advantages of an indexed file organization: We have rapid access to individual records by key without disturbing pinned records. In fact, the indexing itself pins all the records.

Of course, when we delete a record from the data file we must also delete the corresponding entry from our index file. Since the index is contained in an array during program execution, deleting the index record and shifting the other records to close up the space may not be an overly expensive operation. Alternatively, we could simply mark the index record as deleted, just as we might mark the corresponding data record.

Record Updating   Record updating falls into two categories:

☐   *The update changes the value of the key field*. This kind of update can bring about a reordering of the index file as well as the data file. Conceptually, the easiest way to think of this kind of change is as a deletion followed by an addition. This delete/add approach can be implemented while still providing the program user with the view that he or she is merely changing a record.

☐   *The update does not affect the key field*. This second kind of update does not require rearrangement of the index file, but may well involve re-ordering of the data file. If the record size is unchanged or decreased by the update, the record can be written directly into its old space, but if the record size is increased by the update, a new slot for the record will have to be found. In the latter case the starting address of the rewritten record must replace the old address in the *byte_offset* field of the corresponding index record.

6.4   Indexes That Are Too Large to Hold in Memory

The methods we have been discussing, and, unfortunately, many of the advantages associated with them, are tied to the assumption that the index file is small enough to be loaded into memory in its entirety. If the index is too large for this approach to be practical, then index access and maintenance must be done on secondary storage. With simple indexes of the kind we have been discussing, accessing the index on a disk has the following disadvantages:

☐ Binary searching of the index requires several seeks rather than tak- ing place at electronic memory speeds. Binary searching of an index on secondary storage is not substantially faster than the binary searching of a sorted file.

☐ Index rearrangement due to record addition or deletion requires shift- ing or sorting records on secondary storage. This is literally millions of times more expensive than the cost of these same operations when performed in electronic memory.

Although these problems are no worse than those associated with the use of any file that is sorted by key, they are severe enough to warrant the consideration of alternatives. Any time a simple index is too large to hold in memory, you should consider using

☐ A *hashed* organization if access speed is a top priority; or

☐ A *tree-structured* index, such as a *B-tree,* if you need the flexibility of both keyed access and ordered, sequential access.

These alternative file organizations are discussed at length in the chapters that follow. But, before writing off the use of simple indexes on secondary storage altogether, we should note that they provide some important advantages over the use of a data file sorted by key even if the index cannot be held in memory:

☐ A simple index makes it possible to use a binary search to obtain keyed access to a record in a variable-length record file. The index provides the service of associating a fixed-length and therefore bi- nary-searchable record with each variable-length data record.

☐ If the index records are substantially smaller than the data file records, sorting and maintaining the index can be less expensive than would be sorting and maintaining the data file. This is simply because there is less information to move around in the index file.

☐ If there are pinned records in the data file, the use of an index lets us rearrange the keys without moving the data records.

There is another advantage associated with the use of simple indexes, one that we have not yet discussed. It, in itself, can be reason enough to use simple indexes even if they do not fit into memory. Remember the analogy between an index and a library card catalog? The card catalog provides multiple views or arrangements of the library's collection, even though there is only one set of books arranged in a single order. Similarly, we can use multiple indexes to provide multiple views of a data file.

6.5   Indexing to Provide Access by Multiple Keys

One question that might reasonably arise at this point is, "All this indexing business is pretty interesting, but who would ever want to find a record using a key such as DG18807? What I want is the Symphony No. 9 record by Beethoven."

Let's return to our analogy between our index and a library card catalog. Suppose we think of our primary key, the Label ID, as a kind of catalog number. Like the catalog number assigned to a book, we have taken care to make our Label ID unique. Now, in a library it is very unusual to begin by looking for a book with a particular catalog number (e.g., "I am looking for a book with a catalog number QA331T5 1959."). Instead, one generally begins by looking for a book on a particular subject, with a particular title, or by a particular author (e.g., "I am looking for a book on functions," or "I am looking for *The Theory of Functions* by Titchmarsh."). Given the subject, author, or title, one looks in the card catalog to find the *primary key,* the catalog number.

Similarly, we could build a catalog for our record collection consisting of entries for album title, composer, and artist. These fields are *secondary key fields.* Just as the library catalog relates an author entry (secondary key) to a card catalog number (primary key), so can we build an index file that relates Composer to Label ID, as illustrated in Fig. 6.6.

Along with the similarities, there is an important difference between this kind of secondary key index and the card catalog in a library. In a library, once you have the catalog number you can usually go directly to the

Composer index

Secondary key	Primary key
BEETHOVEN	ANG3795
BEETHOVEN	DG139201
BEETHOVEN	DG18807
BEETHOVEN	RCA2626
COREA	WAR23699
DVORAK	COL31809
PROKOFIEV	LON2312
RIMSKY-KORSAKOV	MER75016
SPRINGSTEEN	COL38358
SWEET HONEY IN THE R	FF245

FIGURE 6.6 Secondary key index organized by composer.

stacks to find the book since the books are arranged in order by catalog number. In other words, the books are sorted by primary key. The actual data records in our file, on the other hand, are *entry sequenced*. Consequently, after consulting the composer index to find the Label ID, you must consult one additional index, our primary key index, to find the actual byte offset of the record that has this particular Label ID. The procedure is summarized in Fig. 6.7.

Clearly it is possible to relate secondary key references (e.g., Beethoven) directly to a byte offset (211) rather than to a primary key (DG18807). However, there are excellent reasons for postponing this binding of a secondary key to a specific address for as long as possible. These reasons become clear as we discuss the way that fundamental file operations such as record deletion and updating are affected by the use of secondary indexes.

Record Addition   When a secondary index is present, adding a record to the file means adding a record to the secondary index. The cost of doing this

```
PROCEDURE search_on_secondary(KEY)

    search for KEY in the secondary index

    once the correct secondary index record is found, set LABEL_ID
        to the primary key value in the record's reference field

    call retrieve_record(LABEL_ID) to get the data record

end PROCEDURE
```

FIGURE 6.7 *Search_on_secondary:* an algorithm to retrieve a single record from *Datafile* through a secondary key index.

is very similar to the cost of adding a record to the primary index: Either records must be shifted or a vector of pointers to structures needs to be rearranged. As with primary indexes, the cost of doing this decreases greatly if the secondary index can be read into electronic memory and changed there.

Note that the key field in the secondary index file is stored in canonical form (all of the composers' names are capitalized), since this is the form that we want to use when we are consulting the secondary index. If we want to print out the name in normal, mixed upper- and lowercase form, we can pick up that form from the original data file. Also note that the secondary keys are held to a fixed length, which means that sometimes they are truncated. The definition of the canonical form should take this length restriction into account if searching the index is to work properly.

One important difference between a secondary index and a primary index is that a secondary index can contain duplicate keys. In the sample index illustrated in Fig. 6.6, there are four records with the key BEETHOVEN. Duplicate keys are, of course, grouped together. Within this group, they should be ordered according to the values of the reference fields. In this example, that means placing them in order by Label ID. The reasons for this second level of ordering become clear a little later, as we discuss retrieval based on combinations of two or more secondary keys.

Record Deletion   Deleting a record usually implies removing all references to that record in the file system. So, removing a record from the data file would mean removing not only the corresponding record in the primary index, but also all of the records in the secondary indexes that refer to this primary index record. The problem with this is that secondary indexes, like the primary index, are maintained in sorted order by key.

Consequently, deleting a record would involve rearranging the remaining records to close up the space left open by deletion.

This delete-all-references approach would indeed be advisable if the secondary index referenced the data file directly. If we did not delete the secondary key references, and if the secondary keys were associated with actual byte offsets in the data file, it could be difficult to tell when these references were no longer valid. This is another instance of the pinned-record problem. The reference fields associated with the secondary keys would be pointing to byte offsets that could, after deletion and subsequent space reuse in the data file, be associated with different data records.

But we have carefully avoided referencing actual addresses in the secondary key index. After we search to find the secondary key, we do another search, this time on primary key. Since the primary index *does* reflect changes due to record deletion, a search for the primary key of a record that has been deleted will fail, returning a record-not-found condition. In a sense, the updated primary key index acts as a kind of final check, protecting us from trying to retrieve records that no longer exist.

Consequently, one option that is open to us when we delete a record from the data file is to modify and rearrange only the primary key index. We could safely leave intact the references to the deleted record that exist in the secondary key indexes. Searches starting from a secondary key index that lead to a deleted record are caught when we consult the primary key index.

If there are a number of secondary key indexes, the savings that result from not having to rearrange all of these indexes when a record is deleted can be substantial. This is especially important when the secondary key indexes are kept on secondary storage. It is also important in an interactive system, where the user is waiting at a terminal for the deletion operation to complete.

There is, of course, a cost associated with this short cut: Deleted records take up space in the secondary index files. With a file system that undergoes few deletions, this is not usually a problem. With a somewhat more volatile file structure, it is possible to address the problem by periodically removing from the secondary index files all records that contain references that are no longer in the primary index. If a file system is so volatile that even periodic purging is not adequate, it is probably time to consider another index structure, such as a B-tree, which allows for deletion without having to rearrange a lot of records.

Record Updating   In our discussion of record deletion, we find that the primary key index serves as a kind of protective buffer, insulating the secondary indexes from changes in the data file. This insulation extends to record updating as well. If our secondary indexes contain references directly to byte offsets in the data file, then updates to the data file that result in changing a record's physical location in the file also require updating the secondary indexes. But, since we are confining such detailed information to the primary index, data file updates affect the secondary index only when they change either the primary or the secondary key. There are three possible situations:

- □ *Update changes the secondary key:* If the secondary key is changed, then we may have to rearrange the secondary key index so it stays in sorted order. This can be a relatively expensive operation.
- □ *Update changes the primary key:* This kind of change has a large impact on the primary key index, but often requires only that we update the affected reference field (*Label_id* in our example) in all the secondary indexes. This involves searching the secondary indexes (on the unchanged secondary keys) and rewriting the affected fixed-length field. It does not require reordering of the secondary indexes unless the corresponding secondary key occurs more than once in the index. If a secondary key does occur more than once, there may be some local reordering, since records having the same secondary key are ordered by the reference field (primary key).
- □ *Update confined to other fields:* All updates that do not affect either the primary or secondary key fields do not affect the secondary key index, even if the update is substantial. Note that if there are several secondary key indexes associated with a file, updates to records often affect only a subset of the secondary indexes.

6.6 Retrieval Using Combinations of Secondary Keys

One of the most important applications of secondary keys involves using two or more of them in combination to retrieve special subsets of records from the data file. To provide an example of how this can be done, we will extract another secondary key index from our file of recordings. This one uses the recording's *title* as the key, as illustrated in Fig. 6.8. Now we can respond to requests such as

- □ Find the record with Label ID COL38358 (primary key access);
- □ Find all the recordings of Beethoven's work (secondary key—composer); and

Title index

Secondary key	*Primary key*
COQ D'OR SUITE	MER75016
GOOD NEWS	FF245
NEBRASKA	COL38358
QUARTET IN C SHARP M	RCA2626
ROMEO AND JULIET	LON2312
SYMPHONY NO. 9	ANG3795
SYMPHONY NO. 9	COL31809
SYMPHONY NO. 9	DG18807
TOUCHSTONE	WAR23699
VIOLIN CONCERTO	DG139201

FIGURE 6.8 Secondary key index organized by recording title.

☐   Find all the recordings titled "Violin Concerto" (secondary key—title).

What is more interesting, however, is that we can also respond to a request that *combines* retrieval on the composer index with retrieval on the title index, such as: Find all recordings of Beethoven's Symphony No. 9. Without the use of secondary indexes, this kind of request requires a sequential search through the entire file. Given a file containing thousands, or even just hundreds, of records, this is a very expensive process. But, with the aid of secondary indexes, responding to this request is simple and quick.

We begin by recognizing that this request can be rephrased as a *Boolean AND* operation, specifying the intersection of two subsets of the data file:

```
Find all data records with:
    composer = "BEETHOVEN" AND title = "SYMPHONY NO. 9"
```

We begin our response to this request by searching the composer index for the list of Label IDs that identify records with Beethoven as the composer. (An exercise at the end of this chapter describes a binary search procedure that can be used for this kind of retrieval.) This yields the following list of Label IDs:

```
ANG3795
DG139201
DG18807
RCA2626
```

Next we search the title index for the Label IDs associated with records that have SYMPHONY NO. 9 as the title key:

```
ANG3795
COL31809
DG18807
```

Now we perform the Boolean AND, which is a match operation, combining the lists so only the members that appear in *both* lists are placed in the output list.

```
Composers            Titles                Matched list
ANG3795 ──────────→ ANG3795 ────────────→ ANG3795
DG139201             COL31809          ┌─→ DG18807
DG18807 ──────────→ DG18807 ──────────┘
RCA2626
```

We give careful attention to algorithms for performing this kind of match operation in Chapter 7. Note that this kind of matching is much easier if the lists that are being combined are in sorted order. That is the reason why, when we have more than one entry for a given secondary key, the records are ordered by the primary key reference fields.

Finally, once we have the list of primary keys occurring in both lists, we can proceed to the primary key index to look up the addresses of the data file records. Then we can retrieve the records:

```
ANG ¦ 3795 ¦ Symphony No. 9 ¦ Beethoven ¦ Guilini
DG ¦ 18807 ¦ Symphony No. 9 ¦ Beethoven ¦ Karajan
```

This is the kind of operation that makes computer-indexed file systems useful in a way that far exceeds the capabilities of manual systems. We have only one copy of each data file record, and yet, working through the secondary indexes, we have multiple views of these records: We can look at them in order by title, by composer, or by any other field that interests us.

Using the computer's ability to combine sorted lists rapidly, we can even combine different views, retrieving *intersections* (Beethoven AND Symphony No. 9) or *unions* (Beethoven OR Prokofiev OR Symphony No. 9) of these views. And since our data file is entry sequenced, we can do all of this without having to sort data file records, confining our sorting to the smaller index records which can often be held in electronic memory.

Now that we have a general idea of the design and uses of secondary indexes, we can look at ways to improve these indexes so they take less space and require less sorting.

6.7 Improving the Secondary Index Structure: Inverted Lists

The secondary index structures that we have developed so far result in two distinct difficulties:

☐ We have to rearrange the index file *every time* a new record is added to the file, even if the new record is for an existing secondary key. For example, if we add another recording of Beethoven's Symphony No. 9 to our collection, both the composer and title indexes would have to be rearranged, even though both indexes already contain entries for secondary keys (but not the Label IDs) that are being added.

☐ If there are duplicate secondary keys, the secondary key field is repeated for each entry. This wastes space, making the files larger than necessary. Larger index files are less likely to be able to fit in electronic memory.

6.7.1 A First Attempt at a Solution

One simple response to these difficulties is to change the secondary index structure so it associates an *array* of references with each secondary key. For example, we might use a record structure that allows us to associate up to four Label ID reference fields with a single secondary key, as in

BEETHOVEN	ANG3795	DG139201	DG18807	RCA2626

Figure 6.9 provides a schematic example of how such an index would look if used with our sample data file.

Revised composer index

Secondary key	Set of primary key references			
BEETHOVEN	**ANG3795**	**DG139201**	**DG18807**	**RCA2626**
COREA	**WAR23699**			
DVORAK	**COL31809**			
PROKOFIEV	**LON2312**			
RIMSKY-KORSAKOV	**MER75016**			
SPRINGSTEEN	**COL38358**			
SWEET HONEY IN THE R	**FF245**			

FIGURE 6.9 Secondary key index containing space for multiple references for each secondary key.

The major contribution of this revised index structure is toward the solution of our first difficulty: the need to rearrange the secondary index file every time a new record is added to the data file. Looking at Fig. 6.9, we can see that the addition of another recording of a work by Prokofiev does not require the addition of another record to the index. For example, if we add the recording

```
ANG  36193  Piano Concertos 3 and 5  Prokofiev  Francois
```

we need to modify only the corresponding secondary index record by inserting a second Label ID:

PROKOFIEV	**ANG36193**	**LON2312**

Since we are not adding another record to the secondary index, there is no need to rearrange any records. All that is required is a rearrangement of the fields in the existing record for Prokofiev.

Although this new structure helps avoid the need to rearrange the secondary index file so often, it does have some problems. For one thing, it provides space for only four Label IDs to be associated with a given key. In the very likely case that more than four Label IDs will go with some key, we need a mechanism for keeping track of the extra Label IDs.

A second problem has to do with space usage. Although the structure does help avoid the waste of space due to the repetition of identical keys, this space savings comes at a potentially high cost. By extending the fixed length of each of the secondary index records to hold more reference fields, we might easily lose more space to internal fragmentation than we gained by not repeating identical keys.

Since we don't want to waste any more space than we have to, we need to ask whether we can improve on this record structure. Ideally, what we would like to do is develop a new design, a revision of our revision, that

☐ Retains the attractive feature of not requiring reorganization of the secondary indexes for every new entry to the data file;

☐ Allows more than four Label IDs to be associated with each secondary key; and

☐ Does away with the waste of space due to internal fragmentation.

6.7.2 A Better Solution: Linking the List of References

Files such as our secondary indexes, in which a secondary key leads to a set of one or more primary keys, are called *inverted lists*. The sense in which the list is inverted should be clear if you consider that we are working our way backward from a secondary key to the primary key to the record itself.

The second word in the term inverted list also tells us something important: that we are, in fact, dealing with a *list* of primary key references. Our revised secondary index, which collects together a number of Label IDs for each secondary key, reflects this list aspect of the data more directly than did our initial secondary index. Another way of conceiving of this list aspect of our inverted list is illustrated in Fig. 6.10.

As Fig. 6.10 shows, an ideal situation would be to have each secondary key point to a different list of primary key references. Each of these lists could grow to be just as long as it needs to be. If we add the new Prokofiev record, the list of Prokofiev references becomes

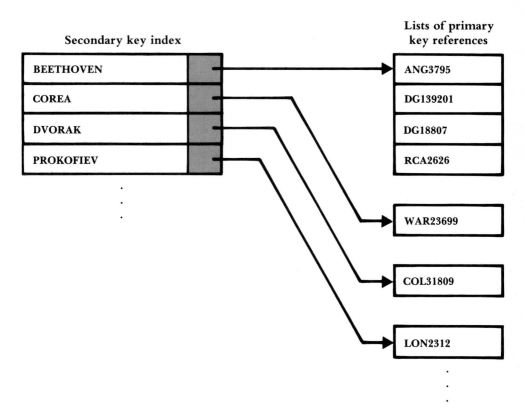

FIGURE 6.10 Conceptual view of the primary key reference fields as a series of lists.

Similarly, adding two new Beethoven recordings adds just two additional elements to the list of references associated with the Beethoven key. Unlike our record structure that allocates enough space for four Label IDs for each secondary key, the lists could contain hundreds of references, if needed, while still requiring only one instance of a secondary key. On the other hand, if a list requires only one element, then no space is lost to internal fragmentation. Most important of all, we need to rearrange only the file of secondary keys if a new composer is added to the file.

How can we set up an unbounded number of different lists, each of varying length, without creating a large number of small files? The simplest way is through the use of linked lists. We could redefine our secondary index so it consists of records with two fields—a secondary key field, and a field containing the relative record number of the first corresponding primary key reference (Label ID) in the inverted list. The actual primary key references associated with each secondary key would be stored in a separate, entry-sequenced file.

Given the sample data we have been working with, this new design would result in a secondary key file for composers and an associated Label ID file that are organized as illustrated in Fig. 6.11. Following the links for the list of references associated with Beethoven helps us see how the Label ID List file is organized. We begin, of course, by searching the secondary key index of composers for Beethoven. The record that we find points us to relative record number (RRN) 3 in the Label ID List file. Since this is a fixed-length file, it is easy to jump to RRN 3 and read in its Label ID (ANG3795). Associated with this Label ID is a link to a record with RRN 8. We read in the Label ID for that record, adding it to our list (ANG379 DG139201). We continue following links and collecting Label IDs until the list looks like this:

```
ANG3795      DG139201      DG18807      RCA2626
```

The link field in the last record read from the Label ID List file contains a value of −1. As in our earlier programs, this indicates end-of-list, so we know that we now have all the Label ID references for Beethoven records.

To illustrate how record addition affects the Secondary Index and Label ID List files, we add the Prokofiev recording mentioned earlier:

```
ANG  36193  Piano Concertos 3 and 5  Prokofiev  Francois
```

You can see (Fig. 6.11) that the Label ID for this new recording is the last one in the Label ID List file, since this file is entry sequenced. Before this record is added, there is only one Prokofiev recording. It has a Label ID of LON2312. Since we want to keep the Label ID Lists in order by ASCII character values, the new recording is inserted in the list for Prokofiev so it logically precedes the LON2312 recording.

Associating the Secondary Index file with a new file containing linked lists of references provides some advantages over any of the structures considered up to this point:

☐ The only time we need to rearrange the Secondary Index file is when a new composer's name is added or an existing composer's name is changed (e.g., it was misspelled on input). Deleting or adding recordings for a composer who is already in the index involves changing only the Label ID List file. Deleting *all* the recordings for a composer could be handled by modifying the Label ID List file, while leaving the entry in the Secondary Index file in place, using a value

Improved revision of the composer index

	Secondary Index file				Label ID List file	
0	BEETHOVEN	3		0	LON2312	−1
1	COREA	2		1	RCA2626	−1
2	DVORAK	7		2	WAR23699	−1
3	PROKOFIEV	10		3	ANG3795	8
4	RIMSKY-KORSAKOV	6		4	COL38358	−1
5	SPRINGSTEEN	4		5	DG18807	1
6	SWEET HONEY IN THE R	9		6	MER75016	−1
				7	COL31809	−1
				8	DG139201	5
				9	FF245	−1
				10	ANG36193	0

FIGURE 6.11 Secondary key index referencing linked lists of primary key references.

of −1 in its reference field to indicate that the list of entries for this composer is empty.

□ In the event that we do need to rearrange the Secondary Index file, the task is quicker now since there are fewer records and each record is smaller.

□ Since there is less need for sorting, it follows that there is less of a penalty associated with keeping the Secondary Index files off on secondary storage, leaving more room in RAM for other data structures.

□ The Label ID List file is entry sequenced. That means that it *never* needs to be sorted.

□ Since the Label ID List file is a fixed-length record file, it would be very easy to implement a mechanism for reusing the space from deleted records, as described in Chapter 5.

There is also at least one potentially significant disadvantage to this kind of file organization: The Label IDs associated with a given composer are no longer guaranteed to be physically grouped together. The technical term for such "togetherness" is *locality;* with a linked, entry-sequenced structure such as this, it is less likely that there will be locality associated with the logical groupings of reference fields for a given secondary key. Note, for example, that our list of Label IDs for Prokofiev consists of the very last and the very first records in the file. This lack of locality means that picking up the references for a composer that has a long list of references could involve a large amount of *seeking* back and forth on the disk. Note that this kind of seeking would not be required for our original Secondary Index file structure.

One obvious antidote to this seeking problem is to keep the Label ID List file in memory. This could be expensive and impractical, given many secondary indexes, except for the interesting possibility of using the same Label ID List file to hold the lists for a number of Secondary Index files. Even if the file of reference lists were too large to hold in memory, it might be possible to obtain a performance improvement by holding only a part of the file in memory at a time, paging sections of the file in and out of memory as they are needed.

Several exercises at the end of the chapter explore these possibilities more thoroughly. These are very important problems, since the notion of dividing the index into pages is fundamental to the design of B-trees and other methods for handling large indexes on secondary storage.

6.8   Selective Indexes

Another interesting feature of secondary indexes is that they can be used to divide a file into parts, providing a selective view. For example, it is possible to build a *selective index* that contains only the titles of classical recordings in the record collection. If we have additional information about the recordings in the data file, such as the date the recording was released, we could build selective indexes such as "recordings released prior to 1970" and "recordings since 1970." Such selective index information could be combined into Boolean AND operations to respond to requests such as, "List all the recordings of Beethoven's Ninth Symphony released since 1970." Selective indexes are sometimes useful when the contents of a file fall naturally and logically into several broad categories.

6.9   Binding

A recurrent and very important question that emerges in the design of file systems that utilize indexes is: *At what point in time is the key bound to the physical address of its associated record?*

In the file system we are designing in the course of this chapter, the *binding* of our primary keys to an address takes place *at the time the files are constructed.* The secondary keys, on the other hand, are bound to an address *at the time that they are actually used.*

Binding at the time of the file construction results in faster access. Once you have found the right index record, you have in hand the byte offset of the data record you are seeking. If we elected to bind our secondary keys to their associated records at the time of file construction, so when we find the DVORAK record in the composer index we would know immediately that the data record begins at byte 353 in the data file, secondary key retrieval would be simpler and faster. The improvement in performance is particularly noticeable if both the primary and secondary index files are used on secondary storage rather than in memory. Given the arrangement we designed, we would have to perform a binary search of the composer index and then a binary search of the primary key index before being able to jump to the data record. Binding early, at file construction time, does away entirely with the need to search on the primary key.

The disadvantage of binding directly in the file, of *binding tightly,* is that reorganizations of the data file must result in modifications to all bound index files. This reorganization cost can be very expensive, particularly with simple index files in which modification would often mean shifting records. By postponing binding until execution time, when the records are actually being used, we are able to develop a secondary key system that involves a minimal amount of reorganization when records are added or deleted.

Another important advantage of postponing binding until a record is actually retrieved is that this approach is safer. As we see in the system that we set up, associating the secondary keys with reference fields consisting of primary keys allows the primary key index to act as a kind of final check of whether a record is really in the file. The secondary indexes can afford to be wrong. This situation is very different if the secondary index keys are tightly bound, containing addresses. We would then be jumping directly from the secondary key into the data file; the address would need to be right.

This brings up a related safety aspect: It is always more desirable to have to make important changes in one place, rather than having to make them in many places. With a bind-at-retrieval-time scheme such as we developed, we need to remember to make a change in only one place, the primary key index, if we move a data record. With a more tightly bound system, we have to make many changes successfully to keep the system internally consistent, braving power failures, user interruptions, and so on.

When designing a new file system, it is better to deal with this question of binding *intentionally* and *early* in the design process, rather than letting the binding just happen. In general, tight, in-the-data binding is most attractive when

☐   The data file is static or nearly so, requiring little or no adding, deleting, and updating of records; and

☐   Rapid performance during actual retrieval is a high priority.

For example, tight binding is desirable for file organization on a mass-produced, read-only optical disk. The addresses will never change since no new records can ever be added; consequently, there is no reason not to obtain the extra performance associated with tight binding.

For file applications in which record addition, deletion, and updating do occur, however, binding at retrieval time is usually the more desirable option. Postponing binding for as long as possible usually makes these operations simpler and safer. If the file structures are carefully designed, and, in particular, if the indexes use more sophisticated organizations such as B-trees, retrieval performance is usually quite acceptable, even given the additional work required by a bind-at-retrieval system.

■ SUMMARY

We began this chapter with the assertion that indexing is an alternative to sorting as a way of structuring a file so records can be found *by key*. Unlike sorting, indexing permits us to perform *binary searches* for keys in variable-length record files. If the index can be held in memory, record addition, deletion, and retrieval can be done much more quickly with an indexed, entry-sequenced file than with a sorted file.

Indexes can do much more than merely improve on access time: They can provide us with new capabilities that are inconceivable with access methods based on sorted data records. The most exciting new capability involves the use of multiple secondary indexes. Just as a library card catalog allows us to regard a collection of books in author order, title order, or subject order, so index files allow us to maintain different views of the records in a data file. We find that we cannot only use secondary indexes to obtain different views of the file, but that we can also combine the associated lists of primary key references and thereby combine particular views.

In this chapter we address the problem of how to rid our secondary indexes of two liabilities:

- The need to repeat duplicate secondary keys; and
- The need to rearrange the secondary indexes every time a record is added to the data file.

A first solution to these problems involves associating a fixed-size *vector* of reference fields with each secondary key. This solution results in an overly large amount of internal fragmentation but serves to illustrate the attractiveness of handling the reference fields associated with a particular secondary key as a group, or *list*.

Our next iteration of solutions to our secondary index problems is more successful and much more interesting. We can treat the primary key references themselves as an entry-sequenced file, forming the necessary lists through the use of *link fields* associated with each primary record entry. This allows us to create a secondary index file that, in the case of the composer index, needs rearrangement only when we add new composers to the data file. The entry-sequenced file of linked reference lists never requires sorting. We call this kind of secondary index structure an *inverted list*.

There are also, of course, disadvantages associated with our new solution. The most serious disadvantage is that our file demonstrates less locality: Lists of associated records are less likely to be physically adjacent. A good antidote to this problem is to hold the file of linked lists in memory. We note that this is made more plausible because a single file of primary references can link the lists for a number of secondary indexes.

As indicated by the length and breadth of our consideration of secondary indexing, multiple keys, and inverted lists, these topics are among the most interesting aspects of indexed access to files. The concepts of secondary indexes and inverted lists become even more powerful later, as we develop index structures that are themselves more powerful than the simple indexes that we consider here. But, even so, we already see that for small files consisting of no more than a few thousand records, approaches to inverted lists that rely merely on simple indexes can provide a user with a great deal of capability and flexibility.

■ KEY TERMS

Binding. Binding takes place when a key is associated with a particular physical record in the data file. In general, binding can take place either during the preparation of the data file and indexes or during program execution. In the former case, which is called *tight binding,* the indexes contain explicit references to the associated physical data record. In the latter case, the connection between a key and a particular physical record is postponed until the record is actually retrieved in the course of program execution.

Entry-sequenced file. A file in which the records occur in the order that they are entered into the file.

Index. An index is a tool for finding records in a file. It consists of a *key field* on which the index is searched and a *reference field* that tells where to find the data file record associated with a particular key.

Inverted list. The term *inverted list* refers to indexes in which a key may be associated with a *list* of reference fields pointing to documents that contain the key. The secondary indexes developed toward the end of this chapter are examples of inverted lists.

Key field. The key field is the portion of an index record that contains the canonical form of the key that is being sought.

Locality. Locality exists in a file when records that will be accessed in a given temporal sequence are found in physical proximity to each other on the disk. Increased locality usually results in better performance, since records that are in the same physical area can often be brought into memory with a single *read* request to the disk.

Reference field. The reference field is the portion of an index record that contains information about where to find the data record containing the information listed in the associated key field of the index.

Selective index. A selective index contains keys for only a portion of the records in the data file. Such an index provides the user with a view of a specific subset of the file's records.

Simple index. All the index structures discussed in this chapter are simple indexes insofar as they are all built around the idea of an ordered, linear sequence of index records. All these simple indexes share a common weakness: Adding records to the index is expensive. As we see later, tree-structured indexes provide an alternate, more efficient solution to this problem.

■ EXERCISES

1. Until now, it was not possible to perform a binary search on a variable-length record file. Why does indexing make binary search possible? With a fixed-length record file it *is* possible to perform a binary search. Does this mean that indexing need not be used with fixed-length record files?

2. Why is *title* not used as a primary key in the data file described in this chapter? If it were used as a secondary key, what problems would have to be considered in deciding on a canonical form for titles?

3. What is the purpose of keeping an out-of-date-status flag in the header record of an index? In a multiprogramming environment, this flag might be found to be set by one program because another program is in the process of reorganizing the index. How should the first program respond to this situation?

4. Explain how the use of an index pins the data records in a file.

5. When a record in a data file is updated, corresponding primary and secondary key indexes may or may not have to be altered, depending on whether the file has fixed- or variable-length records, and depending on the type of change made to the data record. Make a list of the different updating situations that can occur, and explain how each affects the indexes.

6. Discuss the problem that occurs when you add the following recording to the recordings file, assuming that the composer index shown in Fig. 6.9 is used. How might you solve the problem without substantially changing the secondary key index structure?

    LON   1259   Fidelio   Beethoven   Maazel

7. What is an inverted list, and when is it useful?

8. How are the structures in Fig. 6.11 changed by the addition of the recording

    LON   1259   Fidelio   Beethoven   Maazel

9. Suppose you have the data file described in this chapter, greatly expanded, with a primary key index and secondary key indexes organized by composer, artist, and title. Suppose that an inverted list structure is used to organize the secondary key indexes. Give step-by-step descriptions of how a program might answer the following queries:
   a. List all recordings of Bach or Beethoven; and
   b. List all recordings by Perleman of pieces by Mozart or Joplin.

10. One possible antidote to the problem of diminished locality when using inverted lists is to use the same Label ID List file to hold the lists for several of the secondary index files. This increases the likelihood that the secondary indexes can be kept in primary memory. Draw a diagram of a single Label ID List file that can be used to hold references for both the secondary index of composers and the secondary index of titles. How would you handle the difficulties that this arrangement presents with regard to maintaining the Label ID List file?

11. Discuss the following structures as antidotes to the possible loss of locality in a secondary key index:

☐ Leave space for multiple references for each secondary key (Fig. 6.9).
☐ Allocate variable-length records for each secondary key value, where each record contains the secondary key value, followed by the Label IDs, followed by free space for later addition of new Label IDs. The amount of free space left could be fixed, or it could be a function of the size of the original list of Label IDs.

12. The method and timing of binding affect two important attributes of a file system—speed and flexibility. Discuss the relevance of these attributes, and the effect of binding time on them, for a hospital patient information system designed to provide information about current patients by patient name, patient ID, location, medication, doctor or doctors, and illness.

Programming and Design Exercises

13. Implement the *retrieve_record( )* procedure outlined in Fig. 6.4.

14. In solving the preceding problem, you have to create a mechanism for deciding how many bytes to read from the *Datafile* for each record. At least four options are open to you:

a. Jump to the *byte_offset,* read the size field, then use this information to read the record.

b. Build an index file that contains a record size field that reflects the *true* size of the data record, including the size field carried in the *Datafile*. Use the size field carried in the index file to decide how many bytes to read.

c. Follow much the same strategy as in option (b), except use a *Datafile* that does not contain internal size fields.

d. Jump to the *byte_offset* and read a fixed, overly large number of bytes (e.g., 512 bytes). Once these bytes are read into a memory buffer, use the size field at the start of the buffer to decide how many bytes to break out of the buffer.

Evaluate each of these options, listing the advantages and disadvantages of each.

15. Implement procedures to read in and to write back the *INDEX[ ]* array to the index file.

16. When searching secondary indexes that contain multiple records for some of the keys, we do not want to find just *any* record for a given secondary key; we want to find the *first* record containing that key. Finding the first record allows us to read ahead, sequentially, extracting all of the records for the given key. Write a variation of a binary search function that returns the relative record number of the *first* record containing the given key. The function should return a negative value if the key cannot be found.

17. If a Label ID List file such as the one shown in Fig. 6.11 is too large to be held in memory in its entirety, it might still be possible to improve performance by retaining a number of blocks of the file in memory. These blocks are called *pages*. Since the records in the Label ID List file are each 16 bytes long, a page might consist of 32 records (512 bytes). Write a function that would hold the most recently used eight pages in memory. Calls for a specific record from the Label ID List file would be routed through this function. It would check to see if the record exists in one of the pages that is already in memory. If so, the function would return the values of the record fields immediately. If not, the function would read in the page containing the desired record, either writing out or dumping the page that was used least recently. Clearly, if a page has been changed, it needs to be written out rather than dumped. When the program is over, all pages still in memory must be checked to see if they should be written out.

18. Assuming the use of a paged index as described in the preceding problem, and given that the Label ID List file is entry sequenced, is there any particular order of data entry (initial file loading) that tends to give better performance than other methods? How does the use of an organization method such as that described in problem 10, which combines the linked lists from several secondary indexes into a single file, affect your answer about performance?

19. The Label ID List file is entry sequenced. Development of paging schemes is simpler for entry-sequenced files than for files that are kept in sorted order. List the additional difficulties involved in the design of a paging system for a sorted index, such as the primary key index. Accepting the possibility that there will be a number of pages that are only partially full, design such a paging system. How will you handle the insertion of a new key when the page in which it belongs is full?

■ FURTHER READINGS

We have much more to say about indexing in later chapters, where we take up the subjects of tree-structured indexes and of indexed sequential file organizations. The topics developed in the current chapter, particularly those relating to secondary indexes and inverted files, are also covered by many other file and data structure texts. The few texts that we list here are of interest because they either develop certain topics in more detail or present the material from a different viewpoint.

Wiederhold (1983) provides a survey of many of the index structures we discuss, along with a number of others. His treatment is more mathematical than that provided in our text. Users interested in looking at indexed files in the context of PL/I and of large IBM mainframes will want to see Bradley (1982). A brief, readable overview of a number of different file organizations is provided in J. D. Ullman (1980).

Tremblay and Sorenson (1984) provide a comparison of inverted list structures with an alternative organization called *multilist* files. M. E. S. Loomis (1983) provides a similar discussion, along with some examples oriented toward COBOL users. Salton and McGill (1983) discuss inverted lists in the context of their application in information retrieval systems.

Cosequential Processing and the Sorting of Large Files

7

CHAPTER OBJECTIVES

▨ Describe a class of frequently used processing activities known as *cosequential processes.*

▨ Provide a general model for implementing all varieties of cosequential processes.

▨ Illustrate the use of the model to solve a number of different kinds of cosequential processing problems, including problems other than simple merges and matches.

▨ Introduce *heapsort* as an approach to overlapping I/O with sorting in RAM.

▨ Show how merging provides the basis for sorting very large files.

▨ Examine the costs of K-way merges on disk and find ways to reduce those costs.

▨ Introduce the notion of *replacement selection.*

▨ Examine some of the fundamental concerns associated with sorting large files using tapes rather than disks.

▨ Introduce UNIX utilities for sorting, merging, and cosequential processing.

CHAPTER OUTLINE

Cosequential operations involve *the coordinated processing of two or more sequential lists to produce a single output list*. Sometimes the processing results in a *merging*, or union, of the input lists; sometimes the goal is a *matching*, or intersection, of the lists; and other times the operation is a combination of matching and merging. These kinds of operations on sequential lists are the basis of a great deal of file processing.

In the first half of this chapter we develop a general model for doing cosequential operations, illustrate its use for simple matching and merging operations, and then apply it to the development of a more complex general ledger program. Next we apply the model to multiway merging, which is an essential component of external sort-merge operations. We conclude the chapter with a discussion of external sort-merge procedures, strategies, and trade-offs, paying special attention to performance considerations.

7.1   A Model for Implementing Cosequential Processes

Cosequential operations usually appear to be simple to construct; given the information that we provide in this chapter, this appearance of simplicity can be turned into reality. However, it is also true that approaches to cosequential processing are often confused, poorly organized, and incorrect. These examples of bad practice are by no means limited to student programs; the problems also arise in commercial programs and in textbooks. The difficulty with these incorrect programs is usually that they are not organized around a single, clear model for cosequential processing. Instead, they seem to deal with the various exception conditions and problems in a cosequential process in an *ad hoc* rather than systematic way.

This section addresses such lack of organization head on. We present a single, simple model that can be the basis for the construction of any kind of cosequential process. By understanding and adhering to the design principles inherent in the model, you will be able to write cosequential procedures that are simple, short, and robust.

7.1.1 Matching Names in Two Lists

Suppose we want to output the names common to the two lists shown in Fig. 7.1. This operation is usually called a *match operation,* or an *intersection.* We assume, for the moment, that we will not allow duplicate keys within a list, and that the lists are sorted in ascending order.

We begin by reading in the initial name from each list, and we find that they match. We output this first name as a member of the *match set,* or *intersection set.* We then read in the next name from each list. This time the name in List 2 is less than the name in List 1. When we are processing these lists visually, as we are now, we remember that we are trying to match the name CARTER from List 1, and scan down List 2 until we either find it or jump beyond it. In this case, we eventually find a match for CARTER, so we output it, read in the next name from each list, and continue the process. Eventually we come to the end of one of the lists. Since we are looking for names common to both lists, we know we can stop at this point.

Although the match procedure appears to be quite simple, there are a number of matters that have to be dealt with to make it work reasonably well.

List 1	List 2
ADAMS	ADAMS
CARTER	ANDERSON
CHIN	ANDREWS
DAVIS	BECH
FOSTER	BURNS
GARWICK	CARTER
JAMES	DAVIS
JOHNSON	DEMPSEY
KARNS	GRAY
LAMBERT	JAMES
MILLER	JOHNSON
PETERS	KATZ
RESTON	PETERS
ROSEWALD	ROSEWALD
TURNER	SCHMIDT
	THAYER
	WALKER
	WILLIS

FIGURE 7.1 Sample input lists for cosequential operations.

- ☐ *Initializing:* We need to arrange things in such a way that the procedure gets going properly.
- ☐ *Synchronizing:* We have to make sure that the current name from one list is never so far ahead of the current name on the other list that a match will be missed. Sometimes this means reading the next name from List 1, sometimes from List 2, sometimes from both lists.
- ☐ *Handling end-of-file conditions:* When we get to the end of either file 1 or file 2, we need to halt the program.
- ☐ *Recognizing errors:* When an error occurs in the data (e.g., duplicate names or names out of sequence) we want to detect it and take some action.

Finally, we would like our algorithm to be reasonably efficient, simple, and easy to alter to accommodate different kinds of data. The key to accomplishing these objectives in the model we are about to present lies in the way we deal with the second item in our list—synchronization.

At each step in the processing of the two lists, we can assume that we have two names to compare: a *current name* from List 1 and a current name from List 2. Let's call these two current names NAME_1 and NAME_2. We can compare the two names to determine whether NAME_1 is less than, equal to, or greater than NAME_2:

□ If NAME_1 is *less than* NAME_2, we read the next name from
List 1;
□ If NAME_1 is *greater than* NAME_2, we read the next name from
List 2; and
□ If the names are the same, we output the name and read the next
names from the two lists.

It turns out that this can be handled very cleanly with a single loop
containing one three-way conditional statement, as illustrated in the
algorithm in Fig. 7.2. The key feature of this algorithm is that *control always
returns to the head of the main loop after every step of the operation.* This means
that no extra logic is required within the loop to handle the case when List
1 gets ahead of List 2, or List 2 gets ahead of List 1, or the end-of-file

FIGURE 7.2 Cosequential match procedure based on a single loop.

```
PROGRAM: match

        call initialize() procedure to:
            - open input files LIST_1 and LIST_2
            - create output file OUT_FILE
            - set MORE_NAMES_EXIST to TRUE
            - initialize sequence checking variables

        call input() to get NAME_1 from LIST_1
        call input() to get NAME_2 from LIST_2

        while (MORE_NAMES_EXIST)

            if (NAME_1 < NAME_2)
                call input() to get NAME_1 from LIST_1

            else if (NAME_1 > NAME_2)
                call input() to get NAME_2 from LIST_2

            else   /* match -- names are the same */
                write NAME_1 to OUT_FILE
                call input() to get NAME_1 from LIST_1
                call input() to get NAME_2 from LIST_2
            endif
        endwhile
        finish_up()

end PROGRAM
```

condition is reached on one list before it is on the other. Since each pass through the main loop looks at the next pair of names, the fact that one list may be longer than the other does not require any special logic. Nor does the end-of-file condition—the while statement simply checks the MORE_NAMES_EXIST flag on every cycle.

The logic inside the loop is equally simple. Only three possible conditions can exist after reading a name; the *if . . . else* logic handles all of them. Since we are implementing a match process here, output occurs only when the names are the same.

Note that the main program does not concern itself with such matters as sequence checking and end-of-file detection. Since their presence in the main loop would only obscure the main synchronization logic, they have been relegated to subprocedures.

Since the end-of-file condition is detected during input, the setting of the MORE_NAMES_EXIST flag is done in the *input( )* procedure. The *input( )* procedure can also be used to check the condition that the lists be in strictly ascending order (no duplicate entries within a list). The algorithm in Fig. 7.3 illustrates one method of handling these tasks. This "filling out"

FIGURE 7.3 Input routine for match procedure.

```
PROCEDURE: input()     /* input routine for MATCH procedure */

    input arguments:
      INP_FILE            : file descriptor for input file to be used
                            (could be LIST_1 OR LIST_2)
      PREVIOUS_NAME       : last name read from this list

    arguments used to return values:
      NAME                : name to be returned from input procedure
      MORE_NAMES_EXIST    : flag used by main loop to halt processing

      read next NAME from INP_FILE

      /* check for end of file, duplicate names, names out of order    */
      if (EOF)
          MORE_NAMES_EXIST := FALSE     /* set flag to end processing */

      else if (NAME <= PREVIOUS_NAME)
          issue sequence check error
          abort processing
      endif

      PREVIOUS_NAME := NAME

end PROCEDURE
```

```
PROCEDURE: initialize( )

    arguments used to return values:
      PREV_1, PREV_2   : previous name variables for the 2 lists
      LIST_1, LIST_2   : file descriptors for input files to be used
      MORE_NAMES_EXIST : flag used by main loop to halt processing


        /* set both the previous_name variables (one for each list) to
           a value that is guaranteed to be less than any input value */
        PREV_1 := LOW_VALUE
        PREV_2 := LOW_VALUE

        open file for List 1 as LIST_1
        open file for List 2 as LIST_2

        if (both open statements succeed)
           MORE_NAMES_EXIST := TRUE

end PROCEDURE
```

FIGURE 7.4 Initialization procedure for cosequential processing.

of the *input()* procedure also indicates the arguments that the procedure would use.

All we need now to complete the logic is a description of the *initialize( )* procedure that begins the main cosequential match procedure. The *initialize( )* procedure, shown in Fig. 7.4, performs three tasks:

1. It opens the input and output files.
2. It sets the MORE_NAMES_EXIST flag to TRUE.
3. It sets the *previous_name* variables (one for each list) to a value that is guaranteed to be less than any input value. The effect of setting PREV_1 and PREV_2 to LOW_VALUE is that the procedure *input()* does not need to treat the reading of the first two records in any special way.

Given these program fragments, you should be able to work through the two lists provided in Fig. 7.1, following the pseudocode, and demonstrate to yourself that these simple procedures can handle the various resynchronization problems that these sample lists present.

7.1.2 Merging Two Lists

The three-way test, single-loop model for cosequential processing can easily be modified to handle *merging* of lists as well as matching, as

```
PROGRAM: merge

    call initialize() procedure to:
        - open input files LIST_1 and LIST_2
        - create output file OUT_FILE
        - set MORE_NAMES_EXIST to TRUE
        - initialize sequence checking variables

    call input() to get NAME_1 from LIST_1
    call input() to get NAME_2 from LIST_2

    while (MORE_NAMES_EXIST)

        if (NAME_1 < NAME_2)
            write NAME_1 to OUT_FILE
            call input() to get NAME_1 from LIST_1

          else if (NAME_1 > NAME_2)
            write NAME_2 to OUT_FILE
            call input() to get NAME_2 from LIST_2

        else   /* match -- names are the same */
            write NAME_1 to OUT_FILE
            call input() to get NAME_1 from LIST_1
            call input() to get NAME_2 from LIST_2
        endif
    endwhile
    finish_up()

end PROGRAM
```

FIGURE 7.5 Cosequential merge procedure based on a single loop.

illustrated in Fig. 7.5. Note that we now produce output for every case of
the *if . . . else* construction since a merge is a *union* of the list contents.

An important difference between matching and merging is that with
merging we must read *completely* through each of the lists. This necessi-
tates a change in our *input( )* procedure, since the version used for matching sets the MORE_NAMES_EXIST flag to FALSE as soon as we
detect end-of-file for one of the lists. We need to keep this flag set to
TRUE as long as there are records in *either* list. At the same time, we must
recognize that one of the lists has been read completely, and we should
avoid trying to read from it again. Both of these goals can be achieved if

we simply set the NAME variable for the completed list to some value that

☐ Cannot possibly occur as a legal input value; and
☐ Has a *higher* collating sequence value than any possible legal input value. In other words, this special value would come *after* all legal input values in the file's ordered sequence.

We refer to this special value as HIGH_VALUE. The pseudocode in Fig. 7.6 shows how HIGH_VALUE can be used to ensure that both input files are read to completion. Note that we have to add the argument OTHER_LIST_NAME to the argument list so the function knows whether the other input list has reached its end.

FIGURE 7.6 Input routine for merge procedure.

```
PROCEDURE: input()      /* input routine for MERGE procedure */

    input arguments
      INP_FILE            : file descriptor for input file to be used
                            (could be LIST_1 OR LIST_2)
      PREVIOUS_NAME       : last name read from this list
      OTHER_LIST_NAME     : most recent name read from the other list

    arguments used to return values:
      NAME                : name to be returned from input procedure
      MORE_NAMES_EXIST    : flag used by main loop to halt processing

        read next NAME from INP_FILE

        if (EOF) and (OTHER_LIST_NAME == HIGH_VALUE)
            MORE_NAMES_EXIST := FALSE      /* end of both lists    */

        else if (EOF)
            NAME := HIGH_VALUE             /* just this list ended */

        else if (NAME <= PREVIOUS_NAME)    /* sequence check       */
            issue sequence check error
            abort processing
        endif

        PREVIOUS_NAME := NAME

end PROCEDURE
```

Once again, you should use this logic to work, step by step, through the lists provided in Fig. 7.1 to see how the resynchronization is handled and how the use of the HIGH_VALUE forces the procedure to finish both lists before terminating. Note that the version of *input( )* incorporating the HIGH_VALUE logic can also be used for *matching* procedures, producing correct results. The only disadvantage to doing so is that the matching procedure would no longer terminate as soon as one list is completely processed, but would go through the extra work of reading all the way through the unmatched entries at the end of the other list.

With these two examples, we have covered all of the pieces of our model. Now let us summarize the model before adapting it to a more complex problem.

7.1.3 Summary of the Cosequential Processing Model

Generally speaking, the model can be applied to problems that involve the performance of set operations (union, intersection, and more complex processes) on two or more sorted input files to produce one or more output files. In this summary of the cosequential processing model, we assume that there are only two input files and one output file. It is important to understand that the model makes certain general assumptions about the nature of the data and type of problem to be solved. Here is a list of the assumptions, together with clarifying comments.

Assumptions	Comments
Two or more input files are to be processed in a parallel fashion to produce one or more output files.	In some cases an output file may be the same file as one of the input files.
Each file is sorted on one or more key fields, and all files are ordered in the same ways on the same fields.	It is not necessary that all files have the same record structures.
In some cases, there must exist a high key value that is greater than any legitimate record key, and a low key value that is less than any legitimate record key.	The use of a high key value and a low key value is not absolutely necessary, but can help avoid the need to deal with beginning-of-file and end-of-file conditions as special cases, hence decreasing complexity.
Records are to be processed in logical sorted order.	The *physical* ordering of records is irrelevant to the model, but in practice it may be very important to the way the model is implemented. Physical ordering can have a large impact on processing efficiency.

Assumptions	Comments
For each file there is only one current record. This is the record whose key is accessible within the main synchronization loop.	The model does not prohibit looking ahead or looking back at records, but such operations should be restricted to subprocedures and should not be allowed to affect the structure of the main synchronization loop.
Records can be manipulated only in internal memory.	A program cannot alter a record in place on secondary storage.

Given these assumptions, here are the essential components of the model.

1. Initialization. Current records for all files are read from the first logical records in the respective files. *Previous_key* values for all files are set to the low value.
2. One main synchronization loop is used, and the loop continues as long as relevant records remain.
3. Within the body of the main synchronization loop is a selection based on comparison of the record keys from respective input file records. If there are two input files, the selection takes a form such as

```
if (current_file1_key > current_file2_key) then
        .
        .
else if (current_file1_key < current_file2_key) then
        .
        .
else       /* current keys equal */
        .
        .
endif
```

4. Input files and output files are sequence checked by comparing the *previous_key* value with the *current_key* value when a record is read in. After a successful sequence check, *previous_key* is set to *current_key* to prepare for the next input operation on the corresponding file.
5. High values are substituted for actual key values when end-of-file occurs. The main processing loop terminates when high values have occurred for all relevant input files. The use of high values eliminates the need to add special code to deal with each end-of-file condition. (This step is not needed in a pure match procedure, since a match procedure halts when the first end-of-file condition is encountered.)

6. All possible I/O and error detection activities are to be relegated to subprocesses, so the details of these activities do not obscure the principal processing logic.

This three-way test, single-loop model for creating cosequential processes is both simple and robust. You will find very few applications requiring the coordinated sequential processing of two files that cannot be handled neatly and efficiently with the model. We now look at a problem that is much more complex than a simple match or merge, but that nevertheless lends itself nicely to solution by means of the model.

7.2 Application of the Model to a General Ledger Program

7.2.1 The Problem

Suppose we are given the problem of designing a general ledger program as part of an accounting system. The system includes a journal file and a ledger file. The ledger contains the month-by-month summaries of the values associated with each of the bookkeeping accounts. A sample portion of the

FIGURE 7.7 Sample ledger fragment containing checking and expense accounts.

Acct. no.	Account title	Jan	Feb	Mar	Apr
101	Checking account #1	1032.57	2114.56	5219.23	
102	Checking account #2	543.78	3094.17	1321.20	
505	Advertising expense	25.00	25.00	25.00	
510	Auto expenses	195.40	307.92	501.12	
515	Bank charges	0.00	5.00	5.00	
520	Books and publications	27.95	27.95	87.40	
525	Interest expense	103.50	255.20	380.27	
530	Legal expense				
535	Miscellaneous expense	12.45	17.87	23.87	
540	Office expense	57.50	105.25	138.37	
545	Postage and shipping	21.00	27.63	57.45	
550	Rent	500.00	1000.00	1500.00	
555	Supplies	112.00	167.50	241.80	
560	Travel and entertainment	62.76	198.12	307.74	
565	Utilities	84.89	190.60	278.48	

Acct. no.	Check no.	Date	Description	Debit/ credit
101	1271	04/02/86	Auto expense	− 78.70
510	1271	04/02/86	Tune up and minor repair	78.70
101	1272	04/02/86	Rent	− 500.00
550	1272	04/02/86	Rent for April	500.00
101	1273	04/04/86	Advertising	− 87.50
505	1273	04/04/86	Newspaper ad re: new product	87.50
102	670	04/07/86	Office expense	− 32.78
540	670	04/07/86	Printer ribbons (6)	32.78
101	1274	04/09/86	Auto expense	− 12.50
510	1274	04/09/86	Oil change	12.50

FIGURE 7.8 Sample journal entries.

ledger, containing only checking and expense accounts, is illustrated in Fig. 7.7.

The journal file contains the monthly transactions that are ultimately to be posted to the ledger file. Figure 7.8 shows what these journal transactions look like. Note that the entries in the journal file are paired. This is because every check involves both subtracting an amount from the checking account balance and adding an amount to at least one expense account. The accounting program package needs procedures for creating this journal file interactively, probably outputting records to the file as checks are keyed in and then printed.

Once the journal file is complete for a given month, which means that it contains all of the transactions for that month, the journal must be posted to the ledger. *Posting* involves associating each transaction with its account in the ledger. For example, the printed output produced for accounts 101, 102, 505, and 510 during the posting operation, given the journal entries in Fig. 7.8, might look like the output illustrated in Fig. 7.9.

How is the posting process implemented? Clearly, it uses the account number as a *key* to relate the journal transactions to the ledger records. One possible solution involves building an index for the ledger, so we can work through the journal transactions, using the account number in each journal entry to look up the correct ledger record. But this solution involves seeking back and forth across the ledger file as we work through the journal. Moreover, this solution does not really address the issue of creating the output list, in which all the journal entries relating to an account are collected together. Before we could print out the ledger balances and collect journal entries for even the first account, 101, we would have to proceed all

```
101  Checking Account #1
     1271  04/02/86  Auto expense                    -  78.70
     1272  04/02/86  Rent                            - 500.00
     1273  04/04/86  Advertising                     -  87.50
     1274  04/09/86  Auto expense                    -  12.50
                          Prev. bal: 5219.23   New bal: 4540.53

102  Checking account #2
      670  04/07/86  Office expense                  -  32.78
                          Prev. bal: 1321.20   New bal: 1288.42

505  Advertising expense
     1273  04/04/86  Newspaper ad re: new product       87.50
                          Prev. bal:   25.00   New bal:  112.50

510  Auto expenses
     1271  04/02/86  Tune up and minor repair           78.70
     1274  04/09/86  Oil change                         12.50
                          Prev. bal:  501.12   New bal:  592.32
```

FIGURE 7.9 Sample ledger printout showing the effect of posting from the journal.

the way through the journal list. Where would we save the transactions for account 101 as we collect them during this complete pass through the journal?

A much better solution is to begin by collecting all the journal transactions that relate to a given account. This involves sorting the journal transactions by account number, producing a list ordered as in Fig. 7.10.

FIGURE 7.10 List of journal transactions sorted by account number.

Acct. no.	Check no.	Date	Description	Debit/ credit
101	1271	04/02/86	Auto expense	- 78.70
101	1272	04/02/86	Rent	- 500.00
101	1273	04/04/86	Advertising	- 87.50
101	1274	04/09/86	Auto expense	- 12.50
102	670	04/07/86	Office expense	- 32.78
505	1273	04/04/86	Newspaper ad re: new product	87.50
510	1271	04/02/86	Tune up and minor repair	78.70
510	1274	04/09/86	Oil change	12.50
540	670	04/07/86	Printer ribbons (6)	32.78
550	1272	04/02/86	Rent for April	500.00

Ledger list		Journal list		
101	Checking account #1	101	1271	Auto expense
		101	1272	Rent
		101	1273	Advertising
		101	1274	Auto expense
102	Checking account #2	102	670	Office expense
505	Advertising expense	505	1273	Newspaper ad re: new product
510	Auto expenses	510	1271	Tune up and minor repair
		510	1274	Oil change

FIGURE 7.11 Conceptual view of cosequential matching of the ledger and journal files.

Now we can create our output list by working through both the ledger and the sorted journal *cosequentially,* meaning that we process the two lists sequentially and in parallel. This concept is illustrated in Fig. 7.11. As we start working through the two lists, we note that we have an initial match on account number. We know that multiple entries are possible in the journal file, but not in the ledger, so we move ahead to the next entry in the journal. The account numbers still match. We continue doing this until the account numbers no longer match. We then *resynchronize* the cosequential action by moving ahead in the ledger list.

This matching process seems simple, as it in fact is, as long as every account in one file also appears in another. But there will be ledger accounts for which there is no journal entry, and there can be typographical errors that create journal account numbers that do not actually exist in the ledger. Such situations can make resynchronization more complicated and can result in erroneous output or infinite loops if the programming is done in an *ad hoc* way. By using the cosequential processing model, we can guard against these problems. Let us now apply the model to our ledger problem.

7.2.2 Application of the Model to the Ledger Program

The ledger program must perform two tasks:

- ☐ It needs to update the ledger file with the correct balance for each account for the current month.
- ☐ It must produce a printed version of the ledger that not only shows the beginning and current balance for each account, but also lists all the journal transactions for the month.

We focus on the second task since it is the most difficult. Let's look again at the form of the printed output, this time extending the output to

```
101   Checking account #1
        1271  04/02/86   Auto expense              -  78.70
        1272  04/02/86   Rent                      - 500.00
        1273  04/04/86   Advertising               -  87.50
        1274  04/09/86   Auto expense              -  12.50
                              Prev. bal: 5219.23   New bal: 4540.53

102   Checking account #2
         670  04/07/86   Office expense            -  32.78
                              Prev. bal: 1321.20   New bal: 1288.42

505   Advertising expense
        1273  04/04/86   Newspaper ad re: new product       87.50
                              Prev. bal:   25.00   New bal:  112.50

510   Auto expenses
        1271  04/02/86   Tune up and minor repair          78.70
        1274  04/09/86   Oil change                        12.50
                              Prev. bal:  501.12   New bal:  592.32

515   Bank charges
                              Prev. bal:    5.00   New Bal:    5.00

520   Books and publications
                              Prev. bal:   87.40   New bal:   87.40
```

FIGURE 7.12 Sample ledger printout for the first six accounts.

include a few more accounts as shown in Fig. 7.12. As you can see, the printed output from the ledger program shows the balances of all ledger accounts, whether or not there were transactions for the account. From the point of view of the ledger accounts, the process is a *merge,* since even unmatched ledger accounts appear in the output.

What about unmatched journal accounts? The ledger accounts and journal accounts are not equal in authority. The ledger file *defines* the set of legal accounts; the journal file contains entries that are to be *posted* to the accounts listed in the ledger. The existence of a journal account that does not match a ledger account indicates an error. From the point of view of the journal accounts, the posting process is strictly one of *matching.* Our procedure needs to implement a kind of combined merging/matching algorithm while simultaneously handling the chores of printing account title lines, individual transactions, and summary balances.

Another difference between the ledger posting operation and the straightforward matching and merging algorithms is that the ledger procedure must accept duplicate entries for account numbers in the journal while still treating a duplicate entry in the ledger as an error. Recall that our earlier matching and merging routines accept keys only in strict ascending order, rejecting all duplicates.

The inherent simplicity of the three-way test, single-loop model works in our favor as we make these modifications. First, let's look at the input functions that we use for the ledger and journal files, identifying the variables that we need for use in the main loop. Figure 7.13 presents pseudocode for the procedure that accepts input from the ledger. We have treated individual variables within the ledger record as return values to draw attention to these variables; in practice the procedure would probably return the entire ledger record to the calling routine so that other procedures could have access to things such as the account title as they print the ledger. We are overlooking such matters here, focusing instead on the variables that are

FIGURE 7.13 Input routine for ledger file.

```
PROCEDURE: ledger_input()

    input arguments:
      L_FILE                 : file descriptor for ledger file
      J_ACCT                 : current value of journal account number

    arguments used to return values:
      L_ACCT                 : account number of new ledger record
      L_BAL                  : balance for this ledger record
      MORE_RECORDS_EXIST     : flag used by main loop to halt processing

    static, local variable that retains its value between calls
      PREV_L_ACCT            : last acct number read from ledger file

      read next record from L_FILE, assigning values to L_ACCT and L_BAL

      if (EOF) and (J_ACCT == HIGH_VALUE)
          MORE_RECORDS_EXIST := FALSE          /* end of both files       */

      else if (EOF)
          L_ACCT := HIGH_VALUE                 /* just ledger is done     */

      else if (L_ACCT <= PREV_L_ACCT)          /* sequence check          */
          issue sequence check error           /* (permit no duplicates)  */
          abort processing
      endif

      PREV_L_ACCT := L_ACCT

end PROCEDURE
```

involved in the cosequential logic. Note that since this function is strictly for use with ledger entries, we can keep track of the previous ledger account number locally within the procedure rather than pass this value in as an argument.

Figure 7.14 outlines the logic for the procedure used to accept input from the journal file. It is similar to the *ledger_input()* procedure in most respects, including that it returns values for individual variables, even though a working implementation would probably return the entire journal record. Note, however, that the sequence-checking logic is different in *journal_input()*. In this procedure we need to accept records that have the same account number as previous records. Given these input procedures,

FIGURE 7.14 Input routine for journal file.

```
PROCEDURE: journal_input()

    input arguments:
      J_FILE               : file descriptor for journal file
      L_ACCT               : current value of ledger account number

    arguments used to return values:
      J_ACCT               : account number of new journal record
      TRANS_AMT            : amount of this journal transaction
      MORE_RECORDS_EXIST   : flag used by main loop to halt processing

    static, local variable that retains its value between calls
      PREV_J_ACCT          : last acct number read from journal file

        read next record from J_FILE, assigning values to J_ACCT
            and TRANS_AMT

        if (EOF) and (L_ACCT == HIGH_VALUE)
            MORE_RECORDS_EXIST := FALSE       /* end of both files      */

        else if (EOF)
            J_ACCT := HIGH_VALUE              /* just ledger is done    */

        else if (J_ACCT < PREV_J_ACCT)        /* sequence check         */
            issue sequence check error        /* (permit duplicates)    */
            abort processing
        endif

        PREV_J_ACCT := J_ACCT

end PROCEDURE
```

```
PROGRAM: ledger

    call initialize() procedure to:
        - open input files L_FILE and J_FILE
        - set MORE_RECORDS_EXIST to TRUE

    call ledger_input()
    PREV_L_BAL := L_BAL                /* set starting ledger balance
                                          for this first ledger account */
    call journal_input()

    while (MORE_RECORDS_EXIST)

        if (L_ACCT < J_ACCT)          /* we have read all the journal
                                         entries for this account       */
            print PREV_L_BAL and L_BAL
            call ledger_input()
            if (L_ACCT < HIGH_VALUE)
                print account number and title for new ledger account
                PREV_L_BAL := L_BAL
            endif

        else if (L.ACCT > J.ACCT)    /* bad journal account number    */
            print error message
            call journal_input()

        else            /* match -- add journal transaction amount    */
                        /* to ledger balance for this account         */
            L_BAL := L_BAL + TRANS_AMT
                output the transaction to the printed ledger
            call journal_input()
        endif
    endwhile

end PROGRAM
```

FIGURE 7.15 Cosequential procedure to process ledger and journal files to produce printed ledger output.

we can handle our cosequential processing and output as illustrated in Fig. 7.15.

The reasoning behind the three-way test is as follows:

1. If the ledger account is less than the journal account, then there are no more transactions to add to this ledger account (perhaps there were none at all), so we print out the ledger account balances and read in the next ledger account. If the account exists (value <

HIGH_VALUE), we print the title line for the new account and update the PREV_BAL variable.

2. If the journal account is less than the ledger account, then it is an unmatched journal account, perhaps due to an input error. We print an error message and continue.

3. If the account numbers match, then we have a journal transaction that is to be posted to the current ledger account. We add the transaction amount to the account balance, print the description of the transaction, and then read in the next journal entry. Note that unlike the match case in either the matching or merging algorithms, we do not read in a new entry from both accounts. This is a reflection of our acceptance of more than one journal entry for a single ledger account.

The development of this ledger posting procedure from our basic cosequential processing model illustrates how the simplicity of the model contributes to its adaptability. We can also generalize the model in an entirely different direction, extending it to enable cosequential processing of more than two input files at once. To illustrate this, we now extend the model to include multiway merging.

7.3   Extension of the Model to Include Multiway Merging

The most common application of cosequential processes requiring more than two input files is a *K-way merge,* in which we want to merge K input lists to create a single, sequentially ordered output list. K is often referred to as the *order* of a K-way merge.

7.3.1 A *K*-way Merge Algorithm

Recall the synchronizing loop we use to handle a two-way merge of two lists of names (Fig. 7.5). This merging operation can be viewed as a process of deciding which of two input names has the *minimum* value, outputting that name, and then moving ahead in the list from which that name is taken. In the event of duplicate input entries, we move ahead in each list.

Given a *min()* function that returns the name with the lowest collating sequence value, there is no reason to restrict the number of input names to two. The procedure could be extended to handle three (or more) input lists as shown in Fig. 7.16.

Clearly, the expensive part of this procedure is the series of tests to see in which lists the name occurs and which files therefore need to be read.

```
while (MORE_NAMES_EXIST)

    OUT_NAME = min(NAME_1, NAME_2, NAME_3, ... NAME_K)
    write OUT_NAME to OUT_FILE

    if (NAME_1 == OUT_NAME)
        call input() to get NAME_1 from LIST_1

    if (NAME_2 == OUT_NAME)
        call input() to get NAME_2 from LIST_2

    if (NAME_3 == OUT_NAME)
        call input() to get NAME_3 from LIST_3
    .
    .
    .
    if (NAME_K == OUT_NAME)
        call input() to get NAME_K from LIST_K

endwhile
```

FIGURE 7.16 *K*-way merge loop, accounting for duplicate names.

Note that since the name can occur in several lists, every one of these *if* tests must be executed on every cycle through the loop. However, it is often possible to guarantee that a single name, or key, occurs in only one list. In this case, the procedure becomes much simpler and more efficient. Suppose we reference our lists through a vector of list names

```
        list[1], list[2], list[3], ... list[K]
```

and suppose we reference the names (or keys) that are being used from these lists at any given point in the cosequential process through another vector:

```
        name[1], name[2], name[3], ... name[K]
```

Then the procedure shown in Fig. 7.17 can be used, assuming once again that the *input()* procedure attends to the MORE_NAMES_EXIST flag.

This procedure clearly differs in many ways from our initial three-way test, single-loop procedure that merges two lists. But, even so, the single-loop parentage is still evident: There is no looping within a list. We determine which list has the key with the lowest value, output that key, move ahead one key in that list, and loop again. The procedure is as simple as it is powerful.

7.3.2 A Selection Tree for Merging Large Numbers of Lists

The *K*-way merge described in Fig. 7.17 works nicely if *K* is no larger than 8 or so. When we begin merging a larger number of lists, the set of sequential comparisons to find the key with the minimum value becomes noticeably expensive. We see later that for practical reasons it is rare to want to merge more than eight files at one time, so the use of sequential comparisons is normally a good strategy. If there is a need to merge considerably more than eight lists, we could replace the loop of comparisons with a *selection tree*.

Use of a selection tree is an example of the classic time versus space trade-off that we so often encounter in computer science. We reduce the time required to find the key with the lowest value by using a data structure to save information about the relative key values across cycles of the procedure's main loop. The concept underlying a selection tree can be readily communicated through a diagram such as that in Fig. 7.18. Here we have used lists in which the keys are numbers rather than names.

The selection tree is a kind of *tournament* tree in which each higher-level node represents the "winner" (in this case the *minimum* key value) of the

FIGURE 7.17 *K*-way merge loop, assuming no duplicate names.

```
/* initialize the process by reading in a name from each list   */
for i := 1 to K
    call input() to get name[i] from list[i]
next i

/* now start the K-way merge */
while (MORE_NAMES_EXIST)

    /* find subscript of name that has the lowest collating
       sequence value among the names available on the K lists   */
    LOWEST := 1
    for i := 2 to K
        if (name[i] < name[LOWEST])
            LOWEST := i
    next i

    write name[LOWEST] to OUT_FILE

    /* now replace the name that was written out               */
    call input() to get name[LOWEST] from list[LOWEST]
endwhile
```

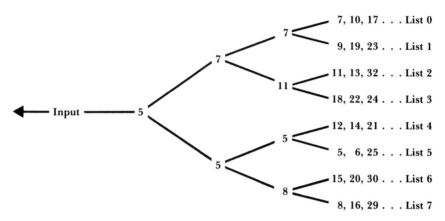

FIGURE 7.18 Use of a selection tree to assist in the selection of a key with minimum value in a *K*-way merge.

comparison between the two descendent keys. The minimum value is always at the root node of the tree. If each key has an associated reference to the list from which it came, it is a simple matter to take the key at the root, read the next element from the associated list, and then run the tournament again. Since the tournament tree is a binary tree, its depth is

$$\lceil \log_2 K \rceil$$

for a merge of *K* lists. The number of comparisons required to establish a new tournament winner is, of course, related to this depth, rather than being a linear function of *K*.

7.4   A Second Look at Sorting in RAM

In Chapter 5 we considered the problem of sorting a disk file that is small enough to fit in RAM. The operation we described involves three separate steps:

1. Read the entire file from disk into RAM.
2. Sort the records using a standard sorting procedure, such as Shell-sort.
3. Write the file back to disk.

The total time taken for sorting the file is the sum of the times for the three steps. We see that this procedure is much faster than sorting the file in place, on the disk, because both reading and writing are sequential.

Can we improve on the time that it takes for this RAM sort? If we assume that we are reading and writing the file as efficiently as possible, and we have chosen the best internal sorting routine available, it would seem not. Fortunately, there is one way that we might speed up an algorithm that has several parts, and that is to perform some of those parts in parallel.

Of the three operations involved in sorting a file that is small enough to fit into RAM, is there any way to perform some of them in parallel? If we have only one disk drive, clearly we cannot overlap the reading and writing operations, but how about doing either the reading or writing (or both) at the same time that we sort the file?

7.4.1 Overlapping Processing and I/O: Heapsort

Most of the time when we use an internal sort we have to wait until we have the whole file in memory before we can start sorting. Is there an internal sorting algorithm that is reasonably fast and that can begin sorting numbers immediately as they are read in, rather than waiting for the whole file to be in memory? In fact, there is, and we have already seen part of it in this chapter. It is called *heapsort,* and it is loosely based on the same principle as the selection tree.

Recall that the selection tree compares keys as it encounters them. Each time a new key arrives, it is compared to the others, and if it is the largest key it goes to the front of the tree. This is very useful for our purposes because it means that we can begin sorting keys as they arrive in RAM, rather than waiting until the entire file is loaded before we start sorting. That is, sorting can occur in parallel with reading.

Unfortunately, in the case of the selection tree, each time a new largest key is found it is output to the file. We cannot allow this to happen if we want to sort the whole file because we cannot begin outputting records until we know which one comes first, second, etc., and we won't know this until we have seen all of the keys.

Heapsort solves this problem by keeping all of the keys in a structure called a *heap.* A heap is a binary tree with these properties:

1. Each node has a single key, and that key is less than or equal to the key at its parent node.
2. It is a *complete* binary tree, which means that all of its leaves are on no more than two levels, and all of the keys on the lowest level are in the leftmost position.
3. Because of properties 1 and 2, storage for the tree can be allocated sequentially as an array in such a way that the indices of the left and right children of node i are 2i and 2i + 1, respectively. Conversely, the index of the parent of node j is $\lfloor j/2 \rfloor$.

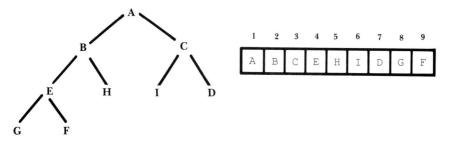

FIGURE 7.19 A heap in both its tree form and as it would be stored in an array.

Figure 7.19 shows a heap in both its tree form and as it would be stored in an array. Note that this is only one of many possible heaps for the given set of keys. In practice, each key has an associated record that is either stored in the array with the key or pointed to by a pointer stored with the key.

Property 3 is very useful for our purposes, because it means that a heap is just an array of keys, where the positions of the keys in the array are sufficient to impose an ordering on the entire set of keys. There is no need for pointers or other dynamic data structuring overhead to create and maintain the heap. (As we pointed out earlier, there may be pointers associating each key with its corresponding record, but this has nothing to do with maintaining the heap itself.)

7.4.2 Building the Heap while Reading in the File

The algorithm for heapsort has two parts. First we build the heap, and then we output the keys in sorted order. The first stage can occur at virtually the same time that we read in the data, so in terms of computer time it comes essentially free. The basic steps in the algorithm for building the heap are shown in Fig. 7.20. Figure 7.21 contains a sample application of this algorithm.

This describes how we build the heap, but it doesn't tell how to make the input overlap with the heap-building procedure. To solve that problem,

FIGURE 7.20 Procedure for building a heap.

```
For i := 1 to RECORD_COUNT
    Read in the next record and append it to the end of the
        array; call its key K
    While K is less than the key of its parent:
        Exchange the record with key K with its parent
next i
```

FDCGHIBEA

New key to be inserted	Heap, after insertion of the new key	Selected heaps in tree form
F	1 2 3 4 5 6 7 8 9 F	
D	1 2 3 4 5 6 7 8 9 D F	
C	1 2 3 4 5 6 7 8 9 C F D	
G	1 2 3 4 5 6 7 8 9 C F D G	
H	1 2 3 4 5 6 7 8 9 C F D G H	
I	1 2 3 4 5 6 7 8 9 C F D G H I	
B	1 2 3 4 5 6 7 8 9 B F C G H I D	
E	1 2 3 4 5 6 7 8 9 B E C F H I D G	
A	1 2 3 4 5 6 7 8 9 A B C E H I D G F	

FIGURE 7.21 Sample application of the heap-building algorithm. The keys F, D, C, G, H, I, B, E, and A are added to the heap in the order shown.

we need to look at how we perform the read operation. For starters, we are not going to do a seek every time we want a new record. Instead, we read a block of records at a time into an input buffer, and then operate on all of the records in the block before going on to the next block. In terms of RAM storage, the input buffer for each new block of keys can be part of the RAM area that is set up for the heap itself. Each time we read in a new block, we just append it to the end of the heap (i.e., the input buffer "moves" as the heap gets larger). The first new record is then at the end of the heap array, as required by the algorithm (Fig. 7.20). Once that record is absorbed into the heap, the next new record is at the end of the heap array, ready to be absorbed into the heap, and so forth.

Use of an input buffer avoids doing an excessive number of seeks, but it still doesn't let input occur at the same time that we build the heap. We saw in Chapter 3 that the way to make processing overlap with I/O is to use more than one buffer. With multiple buffering, as we process the keys in one block from the file, we can simultaneously be reading in later blocks from the file. If we use multiple buffers, how many should we use, and where should we put them? We already answered these questions when we decided to put each new block at the end of the array. Each time we add a new block, the array gets bigger by the size of that block, in effect creating a new input buffer for each block in the file. So the number of buffers is the number of blocks in the file, and they are located in sequence in the array itself.

Figure 7.22 illustrates the technique that we have just described, where we append each new block of records to the end of the heap, thereby employing a RAM-sized set of input buffers. Now we read in new blocks as fast as we can, never having to wait for processing before reading in a new block. On the other hand, processing (heap building) cannot occur on a given block until the block to be processed is read in, so there *may* be some delay in processing if processing speeds are faster than reading speeds.

7.4.3 Sorting while Writing out to the File

The second and final step involves writing out the heap in sorted order. Again, it is possible to overlap I/O (in this case writing) with processing. First, let's look at the algorithm for outputting the sorted keys (Fig. 7.23).

Again, there is nothing inherent in this algorithm that lets it overlap with I/O, but we can take advantage of certain features of the algorithm to make overlapping happen. First, we see that we know immediately which record will be written first in the sorted file; next, we know what will come second; and so forth. So as soon as we have identified a block of records, we can write out that block, and while we are writing out that block we can be identifying the next block, and so forth.

Furthermore, each time we identify a block to write out, we make the heap smaller by exactly the size of a block, freeing that space for a new output buffer. So just as was the case when building the heap, we can have as many output buffers as there are blocks in the file. Again, a little coordination is required between processing and output, but the conditions exist for the two to overlap almost completely.

A final point worth making about this algorithm is that all I/O that it performs is essentially sequential. All records are read in in the order in which they occur in the file to be sorted, and all records are written out in sorted order. The technique could work equally well if the file were kept on tape or disk. More importantly, since all I/O is sequential, we know that it can be done with a minimum amount of seeking.

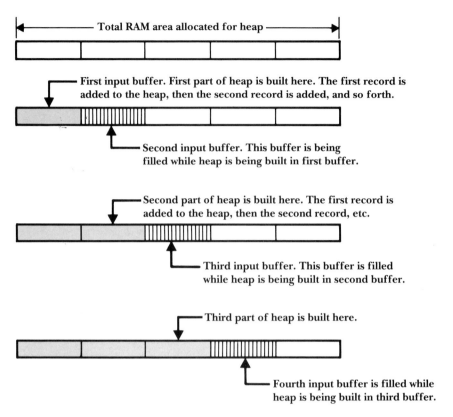

FIGURE 7.22 Illustration of the technique described in the text for overlapping input with heap building in RAM. First read in a block into the first part of RAM. The first record is the first record in the heap. Then extend the heap to include the second record, and incorporate that record into the heap, and so forth. While the first block is being processed, read in the second block. When the first block is a heap, extend it to include the first record in the second block, incorporate that record into the heap, and go on to the next record. Continue until all blocks are read in and the heap is completed.

FIGURE 7.23 Procedure for outputting the contents of a heap in sorted order.

```
For i := 1 to RECORD_COUNT
        Output the record in the first position in the array (this
            record has the smallest key).
        Move the key in the last position in the array (call it K)
            to the first position, and define the heap as having one
            fewer member than it previously had.
        While K is larger than both keys of its children:
                Exchange K with the smaller of its two children's keys.
next i
```

7.5 Merging as a Way of Sorting Large Files on Disk

In Chapter 5 we ran into problems when we needed to sort files that were too large to be wholly contained in RAM. The chapter offered a partial, but ultimately unsatisfactory, solution to this problem in the form of a *keysort,* in which we needed to hold only the keys in RAM, along with pointers to each key's corresponding record. Keysort had two shortcomings:

☐   Once the keys were sorted, we then had to bear the substantial cost of seeking to each record in sorted order, reading each record in and then writing it out into the new, sorted file.

☐   With keysorting, the size of the file that can be sorted is limited by the number of key/pointer pairs that can be contained in RAM. Consequently, we still cannot sort really large files.

As an example of the kind of file we cannot sort with either a RAM sort or a keysort, suppose we have a file with 800,000 records, each of which is 100 bytes long and contains a key field that is 10 bytes long. The total length of this file is about 80 megabytes. Let us further suppose that we have one megabyte of RAM available as a work area, not counting RAM used to hold the program, operating system, I/O buffers, and so forth. Clearly, we cannot sort the whole file in RAM. We cannot even sort all the keys in RAM.

The multiway merge algorithm discussed in section 7.3 provides the beginning of an attractive solution to the problem of sorting large files such as this one. Since RAM sorting algorithms such as heapsort can work in place, using only a small amount of overhead for maintaining pointers and some temporary variables, we can create a sorted subset of our full file by reading records into RAM until the RAM work area is almost full, sorting the records in this work area, and then writing the sorted records back to disk as a sorted subfile. We call such a sorted subfile a *run.* Given the memory constraints and record size in our example, a run could contain approximately

$$\frac{1,000,000 \text{ bytes of RAM}}{100 \text{ bytes per record}} = 10,000 \text{ records.}$$

Once we create the first run, we then read in a new set of records, once again filling RAM, and create another run of 10,000 records. In our example, we repeat this process until we have created 80 runs, with each run containing 10,000 sorted records.

Once we have the 80 runs in 80 separate files on disk, we can perform an 80-way merge of these runs, using the multiway merge logic outlined in

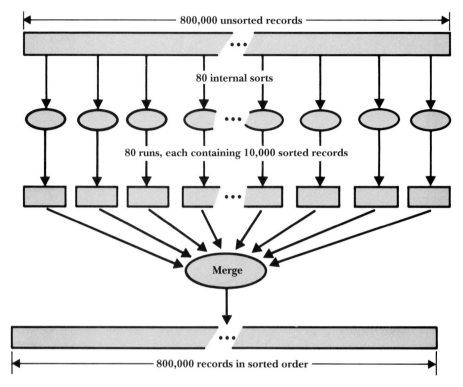

FIGURE 7.24 Sorting through the creation of runs (sorted subfiles) and subsequent merging of runs.

section 7.3, to create a completely sorted file containing all the original records. A schematic view of this run creation and merging process is provided in Fig. 7.24.

This solution to our sorting problem has the following features:

☐ It can, in fact, sort large files, and can be extended to files of any size.

☐ Reading of the input file during the run creation step is sequential, and hence is much faster than input that requires seeking for every record individually (as in a keysort).

☐ Reading through each run during merging and writing out the sorted records is also sequential. Random accesses are required only as we switch from run to run during the merge operation.

☐ If a heapsort is used for the in-RAM part of the merge, as described
in section 7.4, we can overlap these operations with I/O, so the in-
RAM part does not add appreciably to the total time for the merge.

☐ Since I/O is largely sequential, tapes can be used if necessary for both
input and output operations.

7.5.1 How Much Time Does a Merge Sort Take?

This general approach to the problem of sorting large files looks promising.
To compare this approach to others, we now look at how much time it
takes. We do this by taking our 800,000-record example file and seeing how
long it takes to do a merge sort on the hypothetical disk drive whose
specifications are listed in Table 3.2. (Please note that our intention here is
not to derive time estimates that mean anything in any environment other
than the hypothetical environment we have posited. Nor do we want to
overwhelm you with numbers or provide you with magic formulas for
determining how long a particular sort on a real system will *really* take.
Rather, our goal in this section is to derive some benchmarks that we can
use to compare several variations on the basic merge sort approach to
sorting external files.)

We can simplify matters by making the following assumptions about
the computing environment:

☐ Entire files are always stored in contiguous areas on disk (extents),
and a single cylinder-to-cylinder seek takes no time. Hence, *only one
seek is required for any single sequential access.*

☐ Extents that span more than one track are physically staggered in
such a way that *only one rotational delay is required per access.*

We see in Fig. 7.24 that there are four times when I/O is performed:

☐ During the sort phase:
    ☐ Reading all records into RAM for sorting and forming runs; and
    ☐ Writing sorted runs out to disk.

☐ During the merge phase:
    ☐ Reading sorted runs into RAM for merging; and
    ☐ Writing sorted file out to disk.

Let's look at each of these in order.

Step 1: Reading Records into RAM for Sorting and Forming Runs
Since we sort the file in one-megabyte chunks, we read in one megabyte at
a time from the file. In a sense, RAM is a one-megabyte input buffer that

we fill up 80 times to form the 80 runs. In computing the total time to input each run, we need to include the amount of time it takes to *access* each block (seek time + rotational delay), plus the amount of time it takes to *transfer* each block. We keep these two times separate because, as we see later in our calculations, the role that each plays can vary significantly depending on the approach used.

From Table 3.2 we see that seek and rotational delay times are 18 msec[†] and 8.3 msec, respectively, so total time per seek is 26.3 msec.[‡] The transmission rate is approximately 1,229 bytes per msec. Total input time for the sort phase consists of the time required for 80 seeks, plus the time required to transfer 80 megabytes:

Access: 80 seeks × 26.3 msec =   2 seconds
Transfer: 80 megabytes @ 1,229 bytes/msec = 65 seconds
_____
Total: 67 seconds.

Step 2: Writing Sorted Runs out to Disk   In this case, writing is just the reverse of reading — the same number of seeks and the same amount of data to transfer. So it takes another 67 seconds to write out the 80 sorted runs.

Step 3: Reading Sorted Runs into RAM for Merging   Since we have one megabyte of RAM for storing runs, we divide one megabyte into 80 parts for buffering the 80 runs. In a sense, we are reallocating our one megabyte of RAM as 80 input buffers. Each of the 80 buffers then holds 1/80th of a run (12,500 bytes), so we have to access *each* run 80 times to read all of it. Since there are 80 runs, to complete the merge operation (Fig. 7.25) we end up making

80 runs × 80 seeks = 6,400 seeks.

Total seek and rotation time is then $6,400 \times 26.3$ msec = 168 seconds. Since 80 megabytes is still transferred, transfer time is still 65 seconds.

[†]Unless the computing environment has many active users pulling the read/write head to other parts of the disk, seek time is actually likely to be less than the average, since many of the blocks that make up the file are probably going to be physically adjacent to one another on the disk. Many will be on the same cylinder, requiring no seeks at all. However, for simplicity we assume the average seek time.

[‡]For simplicity, we use the term *seek* even though we really mean *seek and rotational delay*. Hence, the time we give for a seek is the time that it takes to perform an average seek followed by an average rotational delay.

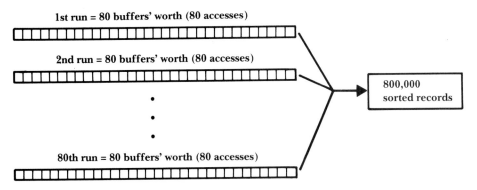

FIGURE 7.25 Effect of buffering on the number of seeks required, where each run is as large as the available work area in RAM.

Step 4: Writing Sorted File out to Disk   To compute the time for writing out the file, we need to know how big our output buffers are. Unlike steps 1 and 2, where our big RAM sorting space doubled as our I/O buffer, we are now using that RAM space for storing the data from the runs *before* it is actually merged. To keep matters simple, let us assume that we can allocate two 20,000-byte output buffers.[†] With 20,000-byte buffers, we need to make

$$\frac{80,000,000 \text{ bytes}}{20,000 \text{ bytes per seek}} = 4,000 \text{ seeks}.$$

Total seek and rotation time is then $4,000 \times 26.3$ msec $= 105$ seconds. Transfer time is still 65 seconds.

The time estimates for the four steps are summarized in the first row in Table 7.1. The total time for this merge sort is 537 seconds, or 8 minutes, 57 seconds. The sort phase takes 134 seconds, and the merge phase takes 403 seconds.

To gain an appreciation of the improvement that this merge sort approach provides us, we need only look at how long it would take us to do one part of a nonmerging method like the keysort method described in

---

[†]We use two buffers to allow double buffering; we use 20,000 bytes per buffer because that is approximately the size of a track on our hypothetical disk drive.

TABLE 7.1   Time estimates for merge sort of 80-megabyte file, assuming use of hypothetical disk drive described in Table 3.2. The total time for the sort phase (steps 1 and 2) is 134 seconds, and the total time for the merge phase is 403 seconds.

	Number of Seeks	Amount Transferred (Megabytes)	Seek + Rotation Time (Seconds)	Transfer Time (Seconds)	Total Time (Seconds)
Sort: reading	80	80	2	65	67
Sort: writing	80	80	2	65	67
Merge: reading	6,400	80	168	65	233
Merge: writing	4,000	80	105	65	170
Totals	10,560	320	277	260	537

Chapter 5. The last part of the keysort algorithm (Fig. 5.17) consists of this *for* loop:

```
/* read in records according to sorted order, and write them   */
/* out in this order                                           */
for i := 1 to REC_COUNT
    seek in IN_FILE to record with RRN of KEYNODES[i].RRN
    read the record into BUFFER from IN_FILE
    write BUFFER contents to OUT_FILE
```

This *for* loop requires us to do a separate seek for every record in the file. That is 800,000 seeks. At 26.3 msec per seek, the total time required to perform that one operation works out to 21,040 seconds, or 5 hours, 50 minutes, 40 seconds!

Clearly, for large files the merge sort approach in general is the best option of any that we have seen. Does this mean that we have found the best technique for sorting large files? If sorting is a relatively rare event and files are not too large, the particular approach to merge sorting that we have just looked at produces acceptable results. Let's see how those results stand up as we change some of the parameters of our sorting example.

7.5.2 Sorting a File That Is Ten Times Larger

The first question that comes to mind when we ask about the general applicability of a computing technique is, What happens when we make the problem bigger? In this instance, we need to ask how this approach stands up as we scale up the size of the file.

Before we look at how a bigger file affects the performance of our merge sort, it will help to examine the *kinds* of I/O that are being done in the two different phases, the sort phase and the merge phase. We will see that for the purposes of finding ways to improve on our original approach, we need pay attention only to one of the two phases.

A major difference between the sort phase and the merge phase is in the amount of sequential (vs. random) access that each performs. By using heapsort to create runs during the sort phase, we guarantee that all I/O is, in a sense, sequential.[†] Since sequential access implies minimal seeking, we cannot *algorithmically* speed up I/O during the sort phase. No matter what we do with the records in the file, we have to read them and write them all at least once. Since we cannot improve on this phase by changing the way we do the sort or merge, we ignore the sort phase in the analysis that follows.

The merge phase is a different matter. In particular, the *reading step* of the merge phase is different. Since there is a RAM buffer for each run, and these buffers get loaded and reloaded at unpredictable times, the read step of the merge phase is to a large extent one in which random accesses are the norm. Furthermore, the number and size of the RAM buffers that we read the run data into determine the number of times we have to do random accesses. If we can somehow reconfigure these buffers in ways that reduce the number of random accesses, we can speed up I/O correspondingly. So, if we are going to look for ways to improve performance in a merge sort algorithm, *our best hope is to look for ways to cut down on the number of random accesses that occur while reading runs during the merge phase.*

What about the write step of the merge phase? Like the steps of the sort phase, this step is not influenced by differences in the way we organize runs. Improvements in the way we organize the merge sort do not affect this step. On the other hand, we will see later that it is helpful to include this phase when we measure the results of changes in the organization of the merge sort.

To sum up, since the merge phase is the only one in which we can improve performance by improving the method, we concentrate on it from now on. Now let's get back to the question that we started this section with: What happens when we make the problem bigger? How, for instance, is the time for the merge phase affected if our file is 8,000,000 records rather than 800,000?

[†]It is *not* sequential in the sense that in a multiuser environment there will be other users pulling the read/write head to other parts of the disk between reads and writes, possibly forcing the disk to do a seek each time it reads or writes a block.

TABLE 7.2   Time estimates for merge sort of 800-megabyte file, assuming use of hypothetical disk drive described in Table 3.2. The total time for the merge phase is 19,186 seconds, or 5 hours, 19 minutes, 22 seconds.

	Number of Seeks	Amount Transferred (Megabytes)	Seek + Rotation Time (Seconds)	Transfer Time (Seconds)	Total Time (Seconds)
Merge: Reading	640,000	800	16,832	651	17,483
Merge: Writing	40,000	800	1,050	651	1,703
Totals	680,000	1,600	17,882	1,302	19,186

If we increase the size of our file by a factor of 10 without increasing the RAM space, we clearly need to create more runs. Instead of 80 initial 10,000-record runs, we now have 800 runs. This means we have to do an 800-way merge in our one megabyte of RAM space. This, in turn, means that during the merge phase we must divide RAM into 800 buffers. Each of the 800 buffers holds 1/800th of a run, so we would end up making 800 seeks per run, and

$$800 \text{ runs} \times 800 \text{ seeks/run} = 640,000 \text{ seeks altogether.}$$

The times for the merge phase are summarized in Table 7.2. Note that the total time is over 5 hours and 19 minutes, almost 50 times greater than for the 80-megabyte file. By increasing the size of our file, we have gotten ourselves back into the situation we had with keysort, where we can't do the job we need to do without doing a huge amount of seeking. In this instance, by increasing the order of the merge from 80 to 800, we made it necessary to divide our one-megabyte RAM area into 800 tiny buffers for doing I/O, and because the buffers are tiny each requires many seeks to process its corresponding run.

If we want to improve performance, clearly we need to look for ways to improve on the amount of time spent getting to the data during the merge phase. We will do this shortly, but first let us generalize what we have just observed.

7.5.3 The Cost of Increasing the File Size

Obviously, the big difference between the time it took to merge the 8-megabyte file and the 800-megabyte file was due to the difference in total seek and rotational delay times. You probably noticed that the number of seeks for the larger file is 100 times the number of seeks for the first file, and 100 is the square of the difference in size between the two files. We can formalize this relationship as follows: In general, for a K-way merge of K runs where each run is as large as the RAM space available, the buffer size for each of the runs is

$$\left(\frac{1}{K}\right) \times \text{size of RAM space} = \left(\frac{1}{K}\right) \times \text{size of each run,}$$

so K seeks are required to read in all of the records in each individual run. Since there are K runs altogether, the merge operation requires K^2 seeks. Hence, measured in terms of seeks, our sort merge is an $O(K^2)$ operation. Since K is directly proportional to N (if we increase the number of records from 800,000 to 8,000,000, K increases from 80 to 800) it also follows that our sort merge is an $O(N^2)$ operation, measured in terms of seeks.

This brief, formal look establishes the principle that as files grow large, we can expect the time required for our merge sort to increase rapidly. It would be very nice if we could find some ways to reduce this time. Fortunately, there are several:

☐ Allocate more hardware, such as disk drives, RAM, and I/O channels;
☐ Perform the merge in more than one step, reducing the order of each merge and increasing the buffer size for each run;
☐ Algorithmically increase the lengths of the initial sorted runs; and
☐ Find ways to overlap I/O operations.

In the following sections we look at each of these in detail, beginning with the first: Invest in more hardware.

7.5.4 Hardware-based Improvements

We have seen that changes in our sorting algorithm can improve performance. Likewise, there are changes that we can make in our hardware that will also improve performance. In this section we look at three possible changes to a system configuration that could lead to substantial decreases in sort time:

☐ Increasing the amount of RAM;
☐ Increasing the number of disk drives; and
☐ Increasing the number of I/O channels.

Increasing the Amount of RAM   It should be clear now that when we have to divide limited buffer space into many small buffers, we increase seek and rotation times to the point where they overwhelm all other sorting operations. Roughly speaking, the increase in the number of seeks is proportional to the square of the increase in file size, given a fixed amount of total buffer space.

It stands to reason, then, that increasing RAM space ought to have a substantial effect on total sorting time. A larger RAM size means longer and fewer initial runs during the sort phase, and it means fewer seeks per run during the merge phase. The product of fewer runs and fewer seeks per run means a substantial reduction in total seeks.

Let's test this conclusion with our 8,000,000-record file, which took about 5 hours, 20 minutes using one megabyte of RAM. Suppose we are able to obtain 4 megabytes of RAM buffer space for our sort. Each of the initial runs would increase from 10,000 records to 40,000 records, resulting in 200 40,000-record runs. For the merge phase, the internal buffer space would be divided into 200 buffers, each capable of holding 1/200th of a run, meaning that there would be $200 \times 200 = 40,000$ seeks. Using the same time estimates that we used for the previous two cases, the total time for this merge is 56 minutes, 45 seconds, nearly a sixfold improvement.

Increasing the Number of Dedicated Disk Drives If we could have a separate read/write head for every run and no other users contending for use of the same read/write heads, there would be no delay due to seek time after the original runs are generated. The primary source of delay would now be rotational delays and transfers, which would occur every time a new block had to be read in.

For example, if each run is on a separate, dedicated drive, our 800-way merge calls for only 800 seeks (one seek per run), down from 640,000, and cutting the total seek and rotation times from 11,500 seconds to 14 seconds. Of course we can't configure 800 separate disk drives every time we want to do a sort, but perhaps something short of this is possible. For instance, if we had two disk drives to dedicate for the merge, we could assign one to input and the other to output, so reading and writing could overlap whenever they occurred simultaneously. (This approach takes some clever buffer management, however. We discuss this later in this chapter.)

Increasing the Number of I/O Channels If there is only one I/O channel, then no two transmissions can occur at the same time, and the total transmission time is the one we have computed. But if there is a separate I/O channel for each disk drive, I/O can overlap completely.

For example, if for our 800-way merge there are 800 channels from 800 disk drives, then transmissions can overlap completely. Practically speaking, it is unlikely that 800 channels and 800 disk drives are available, and even if they were, it is unlikely that all transmissions would overlap because all buffers would not need to be refilled at one time. Nevertheless, increasing the number of I/O channels could improve transmission time substantially.

So we see that there are ways to improve performance if we have some control over how our hardware is configured. In those environments in which external sorting occupies a large percentage of computing time, we are likely to have at least some such control. On the other hand, many times we are not able to expand a system specifically to meet sorting needs that we might have. When this is the case, we need to look for algorithmic ways to improve performance, and this is what we do now.

7.5.5 Decreasing the Number of Seeks Using Multiple-step Merges

One of the hallmarks of a solution to a file structure problem, as opposed to the solution of a mere data structure problem, is the attention given to the enormous difference in cost between accessing information on disk and accessing information in RAM. If our merging problem involved only RAM operations, the relevant measure of work, or expense, would be the number of *comparisons* required to complete the merge. The *merge pattern* that would minimize the number of comparisons for our sample problem, in which we want to merge 800 runs, would be the 800-way merge considered. Looked at from a point of view that ignores the cost of seeking, this K-way merge has the following desirable characteristics:

- ☐   Each record is read only once.
- ☐   If a selection tree is used for the comparisons performed in the merging operation, as described in section 7.3, then the number of comparisons required for a K-way merge of N records (total) is a function of $N \cdot \log K$.
- ☐   Since K is directly proportional to N, this is an $O(N \cdot \log N)$ operation (measured in numbers of comparisons), which is to say that it is reasonably efficient even as N grows large.

This would all be very good news were we working exclusively in RAM, but the very purpose of this *merge sort* procedure is to be able to sort files that are too large to fit into RAM. Given the task at hand, the costs associated with disk seeks are orders of magnitude greater than the costs of operations in RAM. Consequently, if we can sacrifice the advantages of an 800-way merge, trading them for savings in access time, we may be able to obtain a net gain in performance.

We have seen that one of the keys to reducing seeks is to reduce the number of runs that we have to merge, thereby giving each run a bigger share of available buffer space. In the previous section we accomplished this by adding more memory. Multiple-step merging provides a way for us to apply the same principle without having to go out and buy more memory.

In multiple-step merging, we do not try to merge all runs at one time. Instead, we break the original set of runs into small groups and merge the runs in these groups separately. On each of these smaller merges, more buffer space is available for each run, and hence, fewer seeks are required per run. When all of the smaller merges are completed, a second pass merges the new set of merged runs.

It should be clear that this approach will lead to fewer seeks on the first pass, but now there is a second pass. Not only are a number of seeks required for reading and writing on the second pass, but extra transmission time is used in reading and writing all records in the file. Do the advantages of the two-pass approach outweigh these extra costs? Let's revisit the merge step of our 8-million record sort to find out.

Recall that we began with 800 runs of 10,000 records each. Rather than merging all 800 runs at once, we could merge them as, say, 25 sets of 32 runs each, followed by a 25-way merge of the intermediate runs. This scheme is illustrated in Fig. 7.26.

When compared to our original 800-way merge, this approach has the disadvantage of requiring that we read every record twice: once to form the

FIGURE 7.26 Two-step merge of 800 runs.

intermediate runs and then again to form the final sorted file. But, since each step of the merge is reading from 25 input files at a time, we are able to use larger buffers and avoid a large number of disk seeks. When we analyzed the seeking required for the 800-way merge, disregarding seeking for the output file, we calculated that the 800-way merge involved 640,000 seeks between the input files. Let's perform similar calculations for our multistep merge.

First Merge Step   For each of the 32-way merges of the initial runs, each input buffer can hold $\frac{1}{32}$ run, so we end up making $32 \times 32 = 1,024$ seeks. For all 25 of the 32-way merges, we make $25 \times 1,024 = 25,600$ seeks. Each of the resulting runs is 320,000 records, or 32 megabytes.

Second Merge Step   For each of the 25 final runs, $\frac{1}{25}$ of the total buffer space is allocated, so each input buffer can hold 400 records, or $\frac{1}{800}$ run. Hence, in this step there are 800 seeks per run, so we end up making $25 \times 800 = 20,000$ seeks, and

The total number of seeks for the two steps $= 25,600 + 20,000 = 45,600$.

So, by accepting the cost of processing each record twice, we reduce the number of seeks for reading in from 640,000 to 45,600, and we haven't spent a penny for extra RAM.

But what about the *total* time for the merge? We save on access times for inputting data, but there are costs. We now have to transmit all of the records four times instead of two, so transmission time increases by 651 seconds. Also, we write the records out twice, rather than once, requiring an extra 40,000 seeks. When we add in these extra operations, the total time for the merge is 5,907 seconds, or about 1 hour, 38 minutes, compared to 5 hours, 20 minutes for the single-step merge. These results are summarized in Table 7.3.

Once more, note that the essence of what we have done is to find a way to increase the available buffer space for each run. We trade extra passes over the data for a dramatic decrease in random accesses. In this case the trade is certainly a profitable one.

If we can achieve such an improvement with a two-step merge, can we do even better with three steps? Perhaps, but it is important to note in Table 7.3 that we have reduced total seek and rotation times to the point where transmission times are about as expensive. Since a three-step merge would require yet another pass over the file, we may have reached a point of diminishing returns.

We also could have chosen to distribute our initial runs differently. How would the merge perform if we did 400 two-way merges, followed by

TABLE 7.3 Time estimates for two-step merge sort of 800-megabyte file, assuming use of hypothetical disk drive described in Table 3.2. The total time is 1 hour, 31 minutes.

	Number of Seeks	Amount Transferred (Megabytes)	Seek + Rotation Time (Seconds)	Transfer Time (Seconds)	Total Time (Seconds)
1st Merge: Reading	25,600	800	673	651	1,324
1st Merge: Writing	40,000	800	1,052	651	1,703
2nd Merge: Reading	20,000	800	526	651	1,177
2nd Merge: Writing	40,000	800	1,052	651	1,703
Totals	125,600	3,200	3,303	2,604	5,907

one 400-way merge, for instance? A rigorous analysis of the trade-offs between seek and rotation time and transmission time, accounting for different buffer sizes, is beyond the scope of our treatment of the subject.[†] Our goal is simply to establish the importance of the interacting roles of the major costs in performing merge sorts: seek and rotation time, transmission time, buffer size, and number of runs. In the next section we focus on the pivotal role of the last of these—the number of runs.

7.5.6 Increasing Run Lengths Using Replacement Selection

What would happen if we could somehow increase the size of the initial runs? Consider, for example, our earlier sort of 8,000,000 records in which each record was 100 bytes. Our initial runs were limited to approximately 10,000 records because the RAM work area was limited to one megabyte. Suppose we are somehow able to create runs of twice this length, containing 20,000 records each. Then, rather than needing to perform an 800-way merge, we need to do only a 400-way merge. The available RAM is divided into 400 buffers, each holding 1/800th of a run. (Why?) Hence, the number of seeks required per run is 800, and the total number of seeks is

$$800 \text{ seeks/run} \times 400 \text{ runs} = 320,000 \text{ seeks},$$

half the number required for the 800-way merge of 10,000-byte runs.

[†]For more rigorous and detailed analyses of these issues, consult the references cited at the end of this chapter, especially Knuth (1973b) and Salzberg (1988, 1990).

In general, if we can somehow increase the size of the initial runs, we decrease the amount of work required during the merge step of the sorting process. A longer initial run means fewer total runs, which means a lower-order merge, which means bigger buffers, which means fewer seeks. But how, short of buying twice as much memory for the computer, can we create initial runs that are twice as large as the number of records that we can hold in RAM? The answer, once again, involves sacrificing some efficiency in our in-RAM operations in return for decreasing the amount of work to be done on disk. In particular, the answer involves the use of an algorithm known as *replacement selection*.

Replacement selection is based on the idea of always *selecting* the key from memory that has the lowest value, outputting that key, and then *replacing* it with a new key from the input list. Replacement selection can be implemented as follows:

1. Read in a collection of records and sort them using heapsort. This creates a heap of sorted values. Call this heap the *primary heap*.
2. Instead of writing out the entire primary heap in sorted order (as we do in a normal heapsort), write out only the record whose key has the lowest value.
3. Bring in a new record and compare the value of its key with that of the key that has just been output.
   a. If the new key value is higher, insert the new record into its proper place in the primary heap along with the other records that are being selected for output. (This makes the new record part of the run that is being created, which means that the run being formed will actually be larger than the number of keys that can be held in memory at one time.)
   b. If the new record's key value is lower, place the record in a *secondary heap* of records with key values lower than those already written out. (It cannot be put into the primary heap, because it cannot be included in the run that is being created.)
4. Repeat step 3 as long as there are records left in the primary heap and there are records to be read in. When the primary heap is empty, make the secondary heap into the primary heap and repeat steps 2 and 3.

To see how this works, let's begin with a simple example, using an input list of only six keys and a memory work area that can hold only three keys. As Fig. 7.27 illustrates, we begin by reading into RAM the three keys that fit there and use heapsort to sort them. We select the key with the minimum value, which happens to be 5 in this example, and output that key. We now have room in the heap for another key, so we read one from

Input:
21, 67, 12, 5, 47, 16
      ↑
     └─ Front of input string

Remaining input	Memory ($P = 3$)			Output run	
21, 67, 12	5	47	16		–
21, 67	12	47	16		5
21	67	47	16		12, 5
–	67	47	21		16, 12, 5
–	67	47	–		21, 16, 12, 5
–	67	–	–		47, 21, 16, 12, 5
–	–	–	–		67, 47, 21, 16, 12, 5

FIGURE 7.27 Example of the principle underlying replacement selection.

the input list. The new key, which has a value of 12, now becomes a member of the set of keys to be sorted into the output run. In fact, since it is smaller than the other keys in RAM, 12 is the next key that is output. A new key is read into its place, and the process continues. When the process is complete, it produces a sorted list of six keys while using only three memory locations.

In this example the entire file is created using only one heap, but what happens if the fourth key in the input list is 2 rather than 12? This key arrives in memory too late to be output into its proper position relative to the other keys: The 5 has already been written to the output list. Step 3b in the algorithm handles this case by placing such values in a second heap, to be included in the next run. Figure 7.28 illustrates how this process works. During the first run, when keys are brought in that are too small to be included in the primary heap, we mark them with parentheses, indicating that they have to be held for the second run.

It is interesting to use this example to compare the action of replacement selection to the procedure we have been using up to this point, namely that of reading keys into RAM, sorting them, and outputting a run that is the size of the RAM space. In this example our input list contains 13 keys. A series of successive RAM sorts, given only three memory locations, results in five runs. The replacement selection procedure results in only two runs. Since the disk accesses during a multiway merge can be a major expense, replacement selection's ability to create longer, and therefore fewer, runs can be an important advantage.

Two questions emerge at this point:

Input:

33, 18, 24, 58, 14, 17, 7, 21, 67, 12, 5, 47, 16

⌐— **Front of input string**

Remaining input	Memory (P = 3)	Output run
33, 18, 24, 58, 14, 17, 7, 21, 67, 12	5 47 16	—
33, 18, 24, 58, 14, 17, 7, 21, 67	12 47 16	5
33, 18, 24, 58, 14, 17, 7, 21	67 47 16	12, 5
33, 18, 24, 58, 14, 17, 7	67 47 21	16, 12, 5
33, 18, 24, 58, 14, 17	67 47 (7)	21, 16, 12, 5
33, 18, 24, 58, 14	67 (17) (7)	47, 21, 16, 12, 5
33, 18, 24, 58	(14) (17) (7)	67, 47, 21, 16, 12, 5

First run complete; start building the second

33, 18, 24, 58	14 17 7	—
33, 18, 24	14 17 58	7
33, 18	24 17 58	14, 7
33	24 18 58	17, 14, 7
—	24 33 58	18, 17, 14, 7
—	— 33 58	24, 18, 17, 14, 7
—	— — 58	33, 24, 18, 17, 14, 7
	—	58, 33, 24, 18, 17, 14, 7

FIGURE 7.28 Step-by-step operation of replacement selection working to form two sorted runs.

1. Given P locations in memory, how long a run can we expect replacement selection to produce, on the average?
2. What are the costs of using replacement selection?

Average Run Length for Replacement Selection   The answer to the first question is that, on the average, we can expect a run length of $2P$, given P memory locations. Knuth (1973b)[†] provides an excellent description of an intuitive argument for why this is so:

> A clever way to show that $2P$ is indeed the expected run length was discovered by E. F. Moore, who compared the situation to a snowplow on a circular track [U.S. Patent 2983904 (1961), Cols. 3–4]. Consider the situation shown [below]; flakes of snow are falling uniformly on a circular

[†]From Donald Knuth, *The Art of Computer Programming*, 1973, Addison-Wesley, Reading, Mass. Pages 254–55 and Figs. 64 and 65. Reprinted with permission.

road, and a lone snowplow is continually clearing the snow. Once the snow has been plowed off the road, it disappears from the system. Points on the road may be designated by real numbers x, $0 \leq x < 1$; a flake of snow falling at position x represents an input record whose key is x, and the snowplow represents the output of replacement selection. The ground speed of the snowplow is inversely proportional to the height of the snow that it encounters, and the situation is perfectly balanced so that the total amount of snow on the road at all times is exactly P. A new run is formed in the output whenever the plow passes point 0.

After this system has been in operation for awhile, it is intuitively clear that it will approach a stable situation in which the snowplow runs at constant speed (because of the circular symmetry of the track). This means that the snow is at constant height when it meets the plow, and the height drops off linearly in front of the plow as shown [below]. It follows that the volume of snow removed in one revolution (namely the run length) is twice the amount present at any one time (namely P).

So, given a random ordering of keys, we can expect replacement selection to form runs that contain about twice as many records as we can hold in memory at one time. It follows that replacement selection creates half as many runs as does a series of RAM sorts of memory contents, assuming that the replacement selection and the RAM sort have access to the same amount of memory. (As we see in a moment, the replacement selection does, in fact, have to make do with less memory than does the RAM sort.)

It is actually often possible to create runs that are substantially longer than $2P$. In many applications, the order of the records is *not* wholly random; the keys are often already partially in ascending order. In these cases replacement selection can produce runs that, on the average, exceed $2P$. (Consider what would happen if the input list is already sorted.) Replacement selection becomes an especially valuable tool for such partially ordered input files.

The Costs of Using Replacement Selection   Unfortunately, the no-free-lunch rule applies to replacement selection, as it does to so many other areas of file structure design. In the worked-by-hand examples we have looked at up to this point, we have been inputting records into memory one at a time. We know, in fact, that the cost of seeking out to disk for every single input record is prohibitive. Instead, we want to buffer the input, which means, in turn, that we are not able to use *all* of the memory for the operation of replacement selection. Some of it has to be used for input and output buffering. This cost, and the affect it has on available space for sorting, is illustrated in Fig. 7.29.

To see the effects of this need for buffering during the replacement selection step, let's return to our example in which we sort 8 million records, given a memory area that can hold 10,000 records.

```
+---------------------------------------------------+
|              heapsort area                        |
+---------------------------------------------------+
```

(a) In-RAM sort: all available space used for the sort.

FIGURE 7.29 In-RAM sort versus replacement selection, in terms of their use of available RAM for sorting operation.

```
+-------------+-------------------------------------+
| i/o buffer  |          heapsort area              |
+-------------+-------------------------------------+
```

(b) Replacement selection: some of available space is used for i/o.

For the RAM sorting methods such as heapsort, which simply read records into memory until it is full, we can perform sequential reads of 10,000 records at a time, until 800 runs have been created. This means that the sort step requires 1,600 seeks: 800 for reading and 800 for writing.

For replacement selection we might use an input/output buffer that can hold, for example, 2,500 records, leaving enough space to hold 7,500 records for the actual replacement selection process. If the I/O buffer holds 2,500 records, we can perform sequential reads of 2,500 records at a time, so it takes 8,000,000/2,500 = 3,200 seeks to access all records in the file. This means that the sort step for replacement selection requires 6,400 seeks: 3,200 for reading and 3,200 for writing.

If the records occur in a random key sequence, the average run length using replacement selection will be 2 × 7,500 = 15,000 records, and there will be about 8,000,000/15,000 = 534 such runs produced. For the merge step we divide the one megabyte of RAM into 534 buffers, which hold an average of 18.73 records, so we end up making 15,000/18.73 = 801 seeks per run, and

$$801 \text{ seeks per run} \times 534 \text{ runs} = 427,734 \text{ seeks altogether.}$$

Table 7.4 compares the access times required to sort the 8 million records using both a RAM sort and replacement selection. The table includes our initial 800-way merge and two replacement selection examples. The second replacement selection example, which produces runs of 40,000 records while using only 7,500 record storage locations in memory, assumes that there is already a good deal of sequential ordering within the input records.

It is clear that, given randomly distributed input data, replacement selection can substantially reduce the number of runs formed. Even though replacement selection requires four times as many seeks to form the runs, the reduction in the amount of seeking effort required to merge the runs more than offsets the extra amount of seeking that is required to form the runs. And when the original data is assumed to possess enough order to make the runs 40,000 records long, replacement selection produces less than one third as many seeks as RAM sorting.

7.5.7 Replacement Selection Plus Multistep Merging

While these comparisons highlight the advantages of replacement selection over RAM sorting, we would probably not in reality choose the one-step merge patterns shown in Table 7.4. We have seen that two-step merges can result in much better performance than one-step merges. Table 7.5 shows how these same three sorting schemes compare when two-step merges are

TABLE 7.4 Comparison of access times required to sort 8 million records using both RAM sort and replacement selection. Merge order is equal to the number of runs formed.

Approach	Number of Records per Seek to Form Runs	Size of Runs Formed	Number of Runs Formed	Number of Seeks Required to Form Runs	Merge Order Used	Total Number of Seeks	Total Seek and Rotational Delay Time (hr)	(min)
800 RAM sorts followed by an 800-way merge	10,000	10,000	800	1,600	800	681,600	4	58
Replacement selection followed by 534-way merge (records in random order)	2,500	15,000	534	6,400	534	521,134	3	48
Replacement selection followed by 200-way merge (records partially ordered)	2,500	40,000	200	6,400	200	206,400	1	30

TABLE 7.5 Comparison of access times required to sort 8 million records using both RAM sort and replacement selection, each followed by a two-step merge.

Approach	Number of Records per Seek to Form Runs	Size of Runs Formed	Number of Runs Formed	Merge Pattern Used	Number of Seeks in Merge Phases	Total Number of Seeks	Total Seek and Rotational Delay Times (hr)	(min)
800 RAM sorts	10,000	10,000	800	25 × 32-way then 25-way	25,600 20,000	127,200	0	56
Replacement selection (records in random order)	2,500	15,000	534	19 × 28-way then 19-way	22,876 15,162	124,438	0	55
Replacement selection (records partially ordered)	2,500	40,000	200	20 × 10-way then 20-way	8,000 16,000	110,400	0	48

used. From Table 7.5 we see that the total number of seeks is dramatically less in every case than it was for the one-step merges. Clearly, the method used to form runs is not nearly as important as the use of multistep, rather than one-step, merges.

Furthermore, since the number of seeks required for the merge steps is much smaller in all cases, while the number of seeks required to form runs remains the same, the latter have a bigger effect *proportionally* on the final total, and the differences between the RAM-sort based method and replacement selection are diminished.

The differences between the one-step and two-step merges are exaggerated by the results in Table 7.5, because they don't take into account the amount of time spent transmitting the data. The two-step merges require that we transfer the data between RAM and disk two more times than do the one-step merges. Table 7.6 shows the results after adding transmission time to our results. The two-step merges are still better, and replacement selection still wins, but the results are less dramatic.

7.5.8 Using Two Disk Drives with Replacement Selection

Interestingly, and fortunately, replacement selection offers an opportunity to save on both transmission and seek times in ways that RAM sort methods do not. As usual, this is at a cost, but if sorting time is expensive, it could well be worth the cost.

Suppose that we have two disk drives available that we can assign the separate dedicated tasks of reading and writing during replacement selection. One drive, which contains the original file, does only input, and the other does only output. This has two very nice results: (1) It means that input and output can overlap, reducing transmission time by as much as 50%; and (2) seeking is virtually eliminated.

If we have two disks at our disposal, we should also configure memory to take advantage of them. We configure memory as follows: We allocate two buffers each for input and output, permitting double buffering, and allocate the rest of memory for forming the selection tree. This arrangement is illustrated in Fig. 7.30.

Let's see how the merge sort process might proceed to take advantage of this configuration.

First, the sort phase. We begin by reading in enough records to fill up the heap-sized part of memory, and form the heap. Next, as we move records from the heap into one of the output buffers, we replace those records with records from one of the input buffers, adjusting the tree in the usual manner. While we empty one input buffer into the tree, we can be filling the other one from the input disk. This permits processing and input

TABLE 7.6 Comparison of sort merges illustrated in Tables 7.4 and 7.5, taking transmission times into account.

Approach	Number of Records per Seek to Form Runs	Merge Pattern Used	Number of Seeks for Sorts and Merges	Seek + Rotational Delay Time (min)	Total Passes over the File	Total Trans- mission Time (min)	Total of Seek, Rotation, and Transmission Times (min)
800 RAM sorts followed by an 800-way merge	10,000	800-way	681,700	298	4	43	341
Replacement selection followed by a 534-way merge (records in random order)	2,500	534-way	521,134	228	4	43	271
Replacement selection followed by a 200-way merge (records partially ordered)	2,500	200-way	206,400	90	4	43	133
800 RAM sorts followed by a two-step merge	10,000	25 × 32-way one 25-way	127,200	56	6	65	121
Replacement selection followed by a two-step merge (records in random order)	2,500	19 × 28-way one 19-way	124,438	55	6	65	120
Replacement selection followed by a two-step merge (records partially ordered)	2,500	20 × 10-way one 20-way	110,400	48	6	65	113

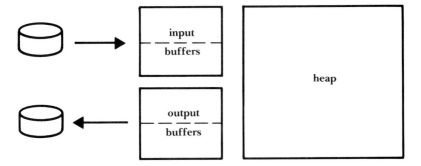

FIGURE 7.30 Memory organization for replacement selection.

to overlap. Similarly, at the same time that we are filling one of the output buffers from the tree, we can be transmitting the contents of the other to the output disk. In this way, run selection and output can overlap.

During the merge phase, the output disk becomes the input disk, and vice versa. Since the runs are all on the same disk, seeking will occur on the input disk. But output is still sequential, since it goes to a dedicated drive.

Because of the overlapping of so many parts of this procedure, it is difficult to estimate the amount of time the procedure is likely to take. But it should be clear that by substantially reducing seeking and transmission time, we are attacking those parts of the sort merge that are the most costly.

7.5.9 More Drives? More Processors?

If two drives can improve performance, why not three, or four, or more? Isn't it true that the more drives we have to hold runs during the merge phase, the faster we can perform I/O? Up to a point this is true, but of course the number and speed of I/O processors must be sufficient to keep up with the data streaming in and out. And there will also be a point at which I/O becomes so fast that processing can't keep up with it.

But who is to say that we can use only one processor? A decade ago, it would have been far-fetched to imagine doing sorting with more than one processor, but it is very common now to be able to dedicate more than one processor to a single job. Possibilities include the following:

☐ Mainframe computers, many of which spend a great deal of their time sorting, commonly come with two or more processors that can simultaneously work on different parts of the same problem.

☐ Vector and array processors can be programmed to execute certain kinds of algorithms orders of magnitude faster than scalar processors.

□   Massively parallel machines provide thousands, even millions, of
    processors that can operate independently and at the same time com-
    municate in complex ways with one another.

□   Very fast local area networks and communication software make it
    relatively easy to parcel out different parts of the same process to
    several different machines.

It is not appropriate, in this text, to cover in detail the implications of
these newer architectures for external sorting. But just as the changes over
the past decade in the availability and performance of RAM and disk storage
have altered the way we look at external sorting, we can expect it to change
many more times as the current generation of new architectures becomes
commonplace.

7.5.10 Effects of Multiprogramming

In our discussions of external sorting on disk we are, of course, making tacit
assumptions about the computing environment in which this merging is
taking place. We are assuming, for example, that the merge job is running
in a dedicated environment (no multiprogramming). If, in fact, the
operating system is multiprogrammed, as it normally is, the total time for
the I/O might be longer, as our job waits for other jobs to perform their
I/O.

On the other hand, one of the reasons for multiprogramming is to
allow the operating system to find ways to increase the efficiency of the
overall system by overlapping processing and I/O among different jobs. So
the system could be performing I/O for our job while it was doing CPU
processing on others, and vice versa, diminishing any delays caused by
overlap of I/O and CPU processing within our job.

Effects such as these are very hard to predict, even when you have
much information about your system. Only experimentation can determine
what real performance will be like on a busy, multiuser system.

7.5.11 A Conceptual Toolkit for External Sorting

We can now list many tools that can improve external sorting performance.
It should be our goal to add these various tools to our conceptual toolkit for
designing external sorts and to pull them out and use them whenever they
are appropriate. A full listing of our new set of tools would include the
following:

□   For in-RAM sorting, use heapsort for forming the original list of
    sorted elements in a run. With it and double buffering, we can over-
    lap input and output with internal processing.
□   Use as much RAM as possible. It makes the runs longer and pro-
    vides bigger and/or more buffers during the merge phase.
□   If the number of initial runs is so large that total seek and rotation
    time is much greater than total transmission time, use a multistep
    merge. It increases the amount of transmission time but can decrease
    the number of seeks enormously.
□   Consider using replacement selection for initial run formation, espe-
    cially if there is a possibility that the runs will be partially ordered.
□   Use more than one disk drive and I/O channel so reading and writ-
    ing can overlap. This is especially true if there are not other users on
    the system.
□   Keep in mind the fundamental elements of external sorting and their
    relative costs, and look for ways to take advantage of new architec-
    tures and systems, such as parallel processing and high-speed local
    area networks.

7.6   Sorting Files on Tape

There was a time when it was usually faster to perform large external sorts
on tape than on disk, but this is much less the case now. Nevertheless, tape
is still used in external sorting, and we would be remiss if we did not
consider sort merge algorithms designed for tape.

There are a large number of approaches to sorting files on tape. After
approximately 100 pages of closely reasoned discussion of different
alternatives for tape sorting, Knuth (1973b) summarizes his analysis in the
following way:

> **Theorem A.** It is difficult to decide which merge pattern is best in a
> given situation.

Because of the complexity and number of alternative approaches and
because of the way that these alternatives depend so closely on the specific
characteristics of the hardware at a particular computer installation, our
objective here is merely to communicate some of the fundamental issues
associated with tape sorting and merging. For a more comprehensive
discussion of specific alternatives we recommend Knuth's (1973b) work as
a starting point.

Viewed from a general perspective, the steps involved in sorting on tape resemble those that we discussed with regard to sorting on disk:

1. Distribute the unsorted file into sorted *runs;* and
2. Merge the runs into a single sorted file.

Replacement selection is almost always a good choice as a method for creating the initial runs during a tape sort. You will remember that the problem with replacement selection when we are working on disk is that the amount of seeking required during run creation more than offsets the advantage of creating longer runs. This seeking problem disappears when the input is from tape. So, for a tape-to-tape sort, it is almost always advisable to take advantage of the longer runs created by replacement selection.

7.6.1 The Balanced Merge

Given that the question of how to create the initial runs has such a straightforward answer, it is clear that it is in the merging process that we encounter all of the choices and complexities implied by Knuth's tongue-in-cheek theorem. These choices begin with the question of how to *distribute* the initial runs on tape and extend into questions about the process of merging from this initial distribution. Let's look at some examples to show what we mean.

Suppose we have a file that, after the sort phase, has been divided into 10 runs. We look at a number of different methods for merging these runs on tape, assuming that our computer system has four tape drives. Since the initial, unsorted file is read from one of the drives, we have the choice of initially distributing the 10 runs on two or three of the other drives. We begin with a method called *two-way balanced merging,* which requires that the initial distribution be on two drives, and that at each step of the merge, except the last, the output be distributed on two drives. Balanced merging is the simplest tape merging algorithm that we look at; it is also, as you will see, the slowest.

The balanced merge proceeds according to the pattern illustrated in Fig. 7.31.

This balanced merge process is expressed in an alternate, more compact form in Fig. 7.32. The numbers inside the table are the run lengths measured in terms of the number of initial runs included in each merged run. For example, in step 1 all the input runs consist of a single initial run. By step 2 the input runs each consist of a pair of initial runs. At the start of step 3, tape drive T1 contains one run consisting of four initial runs followed by a run consisting of two initial runs. This method of illustration

Tape	Contains runs				
T1	R1	R3	R5	R7	R9
T2	R2	R4	R6	R8	R10
T3	—				
T4	—				
T1	—				
T2	—				
T3	R1–R2	R5–R6	R9–R10		
T4	R3–R4	R7–R8			
T1	R1–R4	R9–R10			
T2	R5–R8				
T3	—				
T4	—				
T1	—				
T2	—				
T3	R1–R8				
T4	R9–R10				
T1	R1–R10				
T2	—				
T3	—				
T4	—				

Step 1 (T1–T4), Step 2 (T1–T4), Step 3 (T1–T4), Step 4 (T1–T4), Step 5 (T1–T4)

FIGURE 7.31 Balanced four-tape merge of 10 runs.

more clearly shows the way some of the intermediate runs combine and grow into runs of lengths 2, 4, and 8, whereas the one run that is copied again and again stays at length 2 until the end. The form used in this illustration is used throughout the following discussions on tape merging.

Since there is no seeking, the cost associated with balanced merging on tape is measured in terms of how much time is spent transmitting the data. In the example, we passed over all of the data four times during the merge phase. In general, given some number of initial runs, how many passes over the data will a two-way balanced merge take? That is, if we start with N runs, how many passes are required to reduce the number of runs to 1?

	T1	**T2**	**T3**	**T4**
Step 1	1 1 1 1 1	1 1 1 1 1	—	—
				Merge ten runs
Step 2	—	—	2 2 2	2 2
				Merge ten runs
Step 3	4 2	4	—	—
				Merge ten runs
Step 4	—	—	8	2
				Merge ten runs
Step 5	10	—	—	—

FIGURE 7.32 Balanced four-tape merge of 10 runs expressed in a more compact table notation.

Since each step combines two runs, the number of runs after each step is half the number for the previous step. If p is the number of passes, then we can express this relationship as follows:

$$(\tfrac{1}{2})^p \cdot N \le 1,$$

from which it can be shown that

$$p = \lceil \log_2 N \rceil.$$

In our simple example, $N = 10$, so four passes over the data were required. Recall that for our partially sorted 800-megabyte file there were 200 runs, so $\lceil \log_2 200 \rceil = 8$ passes are required for a balanced merge. If reading and writing overlap perfectly, each pass takes about 11 minutes,[†] so the total time is 1 hour, 28 minutes. This time is not competitive with our disk-based merges, even when a single disk drive is used. The transmission times far outweigh the savings in seek times.

7.6.2 The K-way Balanced Merge

If we want to improve on this approach, it is clear that we must find ways to reduce the number of passes over the data. A quick look at the formula tells us that we can reduce the number of passes by increasing the order of

---

[†]This assumes the 6,250 bpi tape used in the examples in Chapter 3. If the transports speed is 200 inches per second, the transmission rate is 1,250 Kbytes per second, assuming no blocking. At this rate an 800-megabyte file takes 640 seconds, or 10.67 minutes to read.

each merge. Suppose, for instance, that we have 20 tape drives, 10 for input and 10 for output, at each step. Since each step combines 10 runs, the number of runs after each step is one tenth the number for the previous step. Hence, we have

$$(\tfrac{1}{10})^p \cdot N \leq 1$$

and

$$p = \lceil \log_{10} N \rceil.$$

In general, A *k-way balanced merge* is one in which the order of the merge at each step (except possibly the last) is k. Hence, the number of passes required for a k-way balanced merge with N initial runs is

$$p = \lceil \log_k N \rceil.$$

For a 10-way balanced merge of our 800-megabyte file with 200 runs, $\lceil \log_{10} 200 \rceil = 3$, so three passes are required. The best estimated time now is reduced to a more respectable 42 minutes. Of course, the cost is quite high: We must keep 20 working tape drives on hand for the merge.

7.6.3 Multiphase Merges

The balanced merging algorithm has the advantage of being very simple; it is easy to write a program to perform this algorithm. Unfortunately, one reason it is simple is that it is "dumb" and cannot take advantage of opportunities to save work. Let's see how we can improve on it.

We can begin by noting that when we merge the extra run with empty runs in steps 3 and 4, we don't really accomplish anything. Figure 7.33 shows how we can dramatically reduce the amount of work that has to be done by simply not copying the extra run during step 3. Instead of merging this run with a dummy run, we simply stop tape T3 where it is. Tapes T1 and T2 now each contains a single run made up of four of the initial runs. We rewind all the tapes but T3 and then perform a three-way merge of the runs on tapes T1, T2, and T3, writing the final result on T4. Adding this intelligence to the merging procedure reduces the number of initial runs that must be read and written from 40 down to 28.

The example in Fig. 7.33 clearly indicates that there are ways to improve on the performance of balanced merging. It is important to be able to state, in general terms, what it is about this second merging pattern that saves work:

☐ We use a higher-order merge. In place of two two-way merges, we use one three-way merge.

	T1	**T2**	**T3**	**T4**
Step 1	1 1 1 1 1	1 1 1 1 1	—	—
				Merge ten runs
Step 2	—	—	2 2 2	2 2
				Merge eight runs
Step 3	4	4	. . 2	—
				Merge ten runs
Step 4	—	—	—	10

FIGURE 7.33 Modification of balanced four-tape merge that does not rewind between steps 2 and 3 to avoid copying runs.

☐   We extend the merging of runs from one tape over several steps. Specifically, we merge some of the runs from T3 in step 3 and some in step 4. We could say that we merge the runs from T3 in two *phases.*

These ideas, the use of higher-order merge patterns and the merging of runs from a tape in *phases,* are the basis for two well-known approaches to merging called *polyphase merging* and *cascade merging.* In general, these merges share the following characteristics:

☐   The initial distribution of runs is such that at least the initial merge is a $J-1$-way merge, where J is the number of available tape drives.
☐   The distribution of the runs across the tapes is such that the tapes often contain different numbers of runs.

Figure 7.34 illustrates how a polyphase merge can be used to merge 10 runs distributed on four tape drives. This merge pattern reduces the number of initial runs that must be read and written from 40 (for a balanced two-way merge) to 25. It is easy to see that this reduction is a consequence of the use of several three-way merges in place of two-way merges. It should also be clear that the ability to do these operations as three-way merges is related to the uneven nature of the initial distribution. Consider, for example, what happens if the initial distribution of runs is 4−3−3 rather than 5−3−2. We can perform three three-way merges to open up space on T3, but this also clears all the runs off of T2 and leaves only a single run on T1. Obviously, we are not able to perform another three-way merge as a second step.

Several questions arise at this point:

1. How does one choose an initial distribution that leads readily to an efficient merge pattern?

	T1	**T2**	**T3**	**T4**
Step 1	1 1 1 1 1	1 1 1	1 1	—
Step 2	. . 1 1 1	. . 1	—	3 3
Step 3	. . . 1 1	—	5	. 3
Step 4	 1	4	5	—
Step 5	—	—	—	10

Merge six runs (after Step 1)
Merge five runs (after Step 2)
Merge four runs (after Step 3)
Merge ten runs (after Step 4)

FIGURE 7.34 Polyphase four-tape merge of 10 runs.

2. Are there algorithmic descriptions of the merge patterns, given an initial distribution?
3. Given N runs and J tape drives, is there some way to compute the *optimal* merging performance so we have a yardstick against which to compare the performance of any specific algorithm?

Precise answers to these questions are beyond the scope of this text; in particular, the answer to question 3 requires a more mathematical approach to the problem than the one we have taken here. Readers wanting more than an intuitive understanding of how to set up initial distributions should consult Knuth (1973b).

7.6.4 Tapes versus Disks for External Sorting

A decade ago 100 K of RAM was considered a substantial amount of memory to allocate to any single job, and extra disk drives were very costly. This meant that many of the disk sorting techniques to decrease seeking that we have seen were not available to us or were very limited.

Suppose, for instance, that we want to sort our 800-megabyte file, and there is only 100 K of RAM available, instead of one megabyte. The approach that we used for allocating memory for replacement selection would provide 25 K for buffering, and 75 K for our selection tree. From this we can expect 5,334 runs of 1,500 records each, versus 534 when there is a megabyte of RAM. For a one-step merge, this 10-fold increase in the number of runs results in a 100-fold increase in the number of seeks. What took three hours with one megabyte of memory now takes 300 hours, just for the seeks! No wonder tapes, which are basically sequential and require no seeking, were preferred.

But now RAM is much more readily available. Runs can be longer and fewer, and seeks are much less of a problem. Transmission time is now more important. The best way to decrease transmission time is to reduce the number of passes over the data, and we can do this by increasing the order of the merge. Since disks are random-access devices, very large order merges can be performed, even if there is only one drive. Tapes, however, are not random-access devices; we need an extra tape drive for every extra run we want to merge. Unless a large number of drives is available, we can only perform low-order merges, and that means large numbers of passes over the data. Disks are better.

7.7   Sort-Merge Packages

Many very good utility programs are available for users who need to sort large files. Often the programs have enough intelligence to choose from one of several strategies, depending on the nature of the data to be sorted and the available system configuration. They also often allow users to exert some control (if they want it) over the organization of data and strategies used. Consequently, even if you are using a commercial sort package rather than designing your own sorting procedure, it is useful to be familiar with the variety of different ways to design merge sorts. It is especially important to have a good general understanding of the most important factors and trade-offs influencing performance.

7.8   Sorting and Cosequential Processing in UNIX

UNIX has a number of utilities for performing cosequential processing. It also has sorting routines, but nothing at the level of sophistication that you find in production sort-merge packages. In the following discussion we introduce some of these utilities. For full details, consult the UNIX documentation.

7.8.1 Sorting and Merging in UNIX

Because UNIX is not an environment in which one expects to do frequent sorting of large files of the type we discuss in this chapter, sophisticated sort-merge packages are not generally available on UNIX systems. Still, the sort routines you find in UNIX are quick and flexible and quite adequate for the types of applications that are common in a UNIX environment. We can divide UNIX sorting into two categories: (1) the *sort* command, and (2) callable sorting routines.

The UNIX *sort* Command The *sort* command has many different options, but the simplest one is to sort the lines in an ASCII file in ascending lexical order. (A line is any sequence of characters ending with the new-line character '\n'.) By default the *sort* utility takes its input file name from the command line and writes the sorted file to standard output. If the file to be sorted is too large to fit in RAM, *sort* performs a merge sort. If more than one file is named on the input line, *sort* sorts and merges the files.

As a simple example, suppose we have an ASCII file called *team* with names of members of a basketball team, together with their classes and their scoring averages:

```
Jean Smith Senior 7.8
Chris Mason Junior 9.6
Pat Jones Junior 3.2
Leslie Brown Sophomore 18.2
Pat Jones Freshman 11.4
```

To sort the file, enter

```
$ sort team
Chris Mason Junior 9.6
Jean Smith Senior 7.8
Leslie Brown Sophomore 18.2
Pat Jones Freshman 11.4
Pat Jones Junior 3.2
```

Notice that by default *sort* considers an entire line as the sort key. Hence, of the two players named "Pat Jones," the freshman occurs first in the output because "Freshman" is lexically smaller than "Junior." The assumption that the key is an entire line can be overridden by sorting on specified key fields. For *sort* a keyfield is assumed to be any sequence of characters delimited by spaces or tabs. You can indicate which key fields to use for sorting by giving their positions:

```
+pos1 [-pos2]
```

where *pos1* tells how many fields to skip before starting the key, and *pos2* tells which field to end with. If *pos2* is omitted, the key extends to the end of the line. Hence, entering

```
$ sort +1 -2 team
```

causes the file *team* to be sorted according to the last names. (There is also a form of *pos1* and *pos2* that allows you to specify the character within a field to start a key with.)

The following options, among others, allow you to override the default ASCII ordering used by *sort:*

-d   Use "dictionary" ordering: Only letters, digits, and blanks are significant in comparisons.

-f   "Fold" lowercase letters into uppercase. (This is the canonical form that we defined in Chapter 4.)

-r   "Reverse" the sense of comparison: Sort in descending ASCII order.

Notice that *sort* sorts lines, and within lines it compares groups of characters delimited by white space. In the language of Chapter 4, records are lines, and fields are groups of characters delimited by white space. This is consistent with the most common UNIX view of fields and records within UNIX text files.

The *qsort* Library Routine   The UNIX library routine *qsort( )* is a general sorting routine. Given a table of data, *qsort( )* sorts the elements in the table in place. A table could be the contents of a file, loaded into RAM, where the elements of the table are its records. In C, *qsort()* is defined as follows:

```
qsort(char *base, int nel, int width, int (*compar()) )
```

The argument *base* is a pointer to the base of the data, *nel* is the number of elements in the table, and *width* is the size of each element. The last argument, *compar( ),* is the name of a user-supplied comparison function that *qsort( )* uses to compare keys. *Compar( )* must have two parameters, which are pointers to elements that are to be compared. When *qsort( )* needs to compare two elements, it passes to *compar( )* pointers to these elements, and *compar( )* compares them, returning an integer that is less than, equal to, or greater than zero, depending on whether the first argument is considered less than, equal to, or greater than the second argument. A full explanation of how to use *qsort( )* is beyond the scope of this text. Consult the UNIX documentation for details.

7.8.2 Cosequential Processing Utilities in UNIX

UNIX provides a number of utilities for cosequential processing. The *sort* utility, when used to merge files, is one example. In this section we introduce three others: *diff, cmp,* and *comm.*

cmp   Suppose you find in your computer that you have two team files, one called *team* and the other called *myteam.* You think that the two files are the same, but you are not sure. You can use the command *cmp* to find out.

cmp compares two files. If they differ, it prints the byte and line number where they differ; otherwise it does nothing. If all of one file is identical to the first part of another, it reports that end-of-file was reached on the shorter file before any differences were found.

For example, suppose the file *team* and *myteam* have the following contents:

team	myteam
Jean Smith Senior 7.8	Jean Smith Senior 7.8
Chris Mason Junior 9.6	Stacy Fox Senior 1.6
Pat Jones Junior 3.2	Chris Mason Junior 9.6
Leslie Brown Sophomore 18.2	Pat Jones Junior 5.2
Pat Jones Freshman 11.4	Leslie Brown Sophomore 18.2
	Pat Jones Freshman 11.4

cmp tells you where they differ:

```
$ cmp team myteam
team myteam differ: char 23 line 2
```

Since *cmp* simply compares files on a byte-by-byte basis until it finds a difference, it makes no assumptions about fields or records. It works with both text and nontext files.

diff *cmp* is useful if you just want to know if two files are different, but it doesn't tell you much about how they differ. The command *diff* gives fuller information. *diff* tells what lines must be changed in two files to bring them into agreement. For example:

```
$ diff team myteam
1a2
> Stacy Fox Senior 1.6
3c4
< Pat Jones Junior 3.2
---
> Pat Jones Junior 5.2
```

The "1a2" indicates that after line 1 in the first file, we need to *add* line 2 from the second file to make them agree. This is followed by the line from the second file that would need to be added. The "3c4" indicates that we need to *change* line 3 in the first file to make it look like line 4 in the second file. This is followed by a listing of the two differing lines, where the leading "<" indicates that the line is from the first file, and the ">" indicates that it is from the second file.

One other indicator that could appear in *diff* output is "d", meaning that a line in the first file has been *deleted* in the second file. For example, "12d15" means that line 12 in the first file appears to have been deleted from being right after line 15 in the second file. Notice that *diff*, like *sort*, is designed to work with lines of text. It would not work well with non-ASCII text files.

comm   Whereas *diff* tells what is different about two files, *comm* compares two files, which must be ordered in ASCII collating sequence, to see what they have in common. The syntax for *comm* is the following:

```
comm [-123] file1 file2
```

comm produces three columns of output. Column 1 lists the lines that are in *file1* only; column 2 lists lines in *file2* only, and column 3 lists lines that are in both files. For example,

```
$ sort team >ts
$ sort myteam >ms
$ comm ts ms
                        Chris Mason Junior 9.6
                        Jean Smith Senior 7.8
                        Leslie Brown Sophomore 18.2
                        Pat Jones Freshman 11.4
    Pat Jones Junior 3.2
                    Pat Jones Junior 5.2
                    Stacy Fox Senior 1.6
```

Selecting any of the flags 1, 2, or 3 allows you to print only those columns you are interested in.

The *sort, diff, comm,* and *cmp* commands (and the *qsort()* function) are representative of what is available in UNIX for sorting and cosequential processing. As we have said, they have many useful options that we don't cover and that you will be interested in reading about.

■ SUMMARY

In the first half of this chapter, we develop a cosequential processing model and apply it to two common problems—updating a general ledger and merge sorting. In the second half of the chapter we identify the most important factors influencing performance in merge-sorting operations and suggest some strategies for achieving good performance.

The cosequential processing model can be applied to problems that involve operations such as matching and merging (and combinations of these) on two or more sorted input files. We begin the chapter by illustrating the use of the model to perform a simple match of the elements common to two lists, and a merge of two lists. The procedures we develop to perform these two operations embody all the basic elements of the model.

In its most complete form, the model depends on certain assumptions about the data in the input files. We enumerate these assumptions in our formal description of the model. Given these assumptions, we can describe the processing components of the model.

The real value of the cosequential model is that it can be adapted to more substantial problems than simple matches or merges without too much alteration. We illustrate this by using the model to design a general ledger accounting program.

All of our early sample applications of the model involve only two input files. We next adapt the model to a multiway merge to show how the model might be extended to deal with more than two input lists. The problem of finding the minimum key value during each pass through the main loop becomes more complex as the number of input files increases. Its solution involves replacing the three-way selection statement with either a multiway selection or a procedure that keeps current keys in a list structure that can be processed more conveniently.

We see that the application of the model to k-way merging performs well for small values of k, but that for values of k greater than eight or so, it is more efficient to find the minimum key value by means of a selection tree.

After discussing multiway merging, we shift our attention to a problem that we encountered in a previous chapter—how to sort large files. We begin with files that are small enough to fit into RAM and introduce an efficient sorting algorithm, *heapsort,* which makes it possible to overlap I/O with the sorting process.

The generally accepted solution when a file is too large for in-RAM sorts is some form of *merge sort.* A merge sort involves two steps:

1. Break the file into two or more sorted subfiles, or runs, using internal sorting methods; and
2. Merge the runs.

Ideally, we would like to keep every run in a separate file so we can perform the merge step with one pass through the runs. Unfortunately, practical considerations sometimes make it difficult to do this effectively.

The critical elements when merging many files on disk are seek and rotational delay times and transmission times. These times depend largely on two interrelated factors: the number of different runs being merged and the amount of internal buffer space available to hold parts of the runs. We can reduce seek and rotational delay times in two ways:

- By performing the merge in more than one step; and/or
- By increasing the sizes of the initial sorted runs.

In both cases, the order of each merge step can be reduced, increasing the sizes of the internal buffers and allowing more data to be processed per seek.

Looking at the first alternative, we see how performing the merge in several steps can decrease the number of seeks dramatically, though it also means that we need to read through the data more than once (increasing total data transmission time).

The second alternative is realized through use of an algorithm called *replacement selection*. Replacement selection, which can be implemented using the selection tree mentioned earlier, involves selecting the key from memory that has the lowest value, outputting that key, and replacing it with a new key from the input list.

With randomly organized files, replacement selection can be expected to produce runs twice as long as the number of internal storage locations available for performing the algorithms. Although this represents a major step toward decreasing the number of runs needing to be merged, it carries with it an additional cost. The need for a large buffer for performing the replacement selection operation leaves relatively little space for the I/O buffer, which means that many more seeks are involved in forming the runs than are needed when the sort step uses an in-RAM sort. If we compare the total number of seeks required by the two different approaches, we find that replacement selection can actually require more seeks; it performs substantially better only when there is a great deal of order in the initial file.

Next we turn our attention to file sorting on tapes. Since file I/O with tapes does not involve seeking, the problems and solutions associated with tape sorting can differ from those associated with disk sorting, although the fundamental goal of working with fewer, longer runs remains. With tape sorting, the primary measure of performance is the number of times each record must be transmitted. (Other factors, such as tape rewind time, can also be important, but we do not consider them here.)

Since tapes do not require seeking, replacement selection is almost always a good choice for creating initial runs. Since the number of drives available to hold run files is limited, the next question is how to distribute the files on the tapes. In most cases, it is necessary to put several runs on each of several tapes, reserving one or more other tapes for the results. This generally leads to merges of several steps, with the total number of runs being decreased after each merge step. Two approaches to doing this are *balanced merges* and *multiphase merges*. In a *k*-way balanced merge, all input tapes contain approximately the same number of runs, there are the same number of output tapes as there are input tapes, and the input tapes are read through entirely during each step. The number of runs is decreased by a factor of *k* after each step.

A multiphase merge (such as a *polyphase merge* or a *cascade merge*) requires that the runs initially be distributed unevenly among all but one of the available tapes. This increases the order of the merge and as a result can decrease the number of times each record has to be read. It turns out that the initial distribution of runs among the first set of input tapes has a major effect on the number of times each record has to be read.

Next, we discuss briefly the existence of sort-merge utilities, which are available on most large systems and can be very flexible and effective. We conclude the chapter with a listing of UNIX utilities used for sorting and cosequential processing.

■ KEY TERMS

Balanced merge. A multistep merging technique that uses the same number of input devices as output devices. A two-way balanced merge uses two input tapes, each with approximately the same number of runs on it, and produces two output tapes, each with approximately half as many runs as the input tapes. A balanced merge is suitable for merge sorting with tapes, though it is not generally the best method (see *multiphase merging*).

cmp. A UNIX utility for determining whether two files are identical. Given two files, it reports the first byte where the two files differ, if they differ.

comm. A UNIX utility for determining what lines two files have in common. Given two files, it reports the lines they have in common, the lines that are in the first file and not in the second, and the lines that are in the second file and not in the first.

Cosequential operations. Operations applied to problems that involve the performance of union, intersection, and more complex set operations on two or more sorted-input files to produce one or more output files built from some combination of the elements of the input files. Cosequential operations commonly occur in matching, merging, and file-updating problems.

diff. A UNIX utility for determining all the lines that differ between two files. It reports the lines that need to be added to the first file to make it like the second, the lines that need to be deleted from the second file to make it like the first, and the lines that need to be changed in the first file to make it like the second.

heapsort. A sorting algorithm especially well suited for sorting large files that fit in RAM because its execution can overlap with I/O. A variation of heapsort is used to obtain longer runs in the replacement selection algorithm.

HIGH_VALUE. A value used in the cosequential model that is greater than any possible key value. By assigning HIGH_VALUE as the current key value for files for which an end-of-file condition has been encountered, extra logic for dealing with end-of-file conditions can be simplified.

***k*-way merge.** A merge in which *k* input files are merged to produce one output file.

LOW_VALUE. A value used in the cosequential model that is less than any possible key value. By assigning LOW_VALUE as the previous key value during initialization, the need for certain other special start-up code is eliminated.

Match. The process of forming a sorted output file consisting of all the elements common to two or more sorted input files.

Merge. The process of forming a sorted output file that consists of the union of the elements from two or more sorted input files.

Multiphase merge. A multistep tape merge in which the initial distribution of runs is such that at least the initial merge is a $J-1$-way merge (J is the number of available tape drives), and in which the distribution of runs across the tapes is such that the merge performs efficiently at every step. (See *polyphase merge.*)

Multistep merge. A merge in which not all runs are merged in one step. Rather, several sets of runs are merged separately, each set producing one long run consisting of the records from all of its runs. These new, longer sets are then merged, either all together or in several sets. After each step, the number of runs is decreased and the length of the runs is increased. The output of the final step is a single run consisting of the entire file. (Be careful not to confuse our use of the term *multistep merge* with *multiphase merge.*) Although a multistep merge is theoretically more time-consuming than is a single-step merge, it can involve much less seeking when performed on a disk, and it may be the only reasonable way to perform a merge on tape if the number of tape drives is limited.

Order of a merge. The number of different files, or runs, being merged. For example, the 100 is the order of a 100-way merge.

Polyphase merge. A multiphase merge in which, ideally, the merge order is maximized at every step.

qsort. A general-purpose UNIX library routine for sorting files that employs a user-defined comparison function.

Replacement selection. A method of creating initial runs based on the idea of always *selecting* the record from memory whose key has the lowest value, outputting that record, and then *replacing* it in memory with a new record from the input list. When new records are brought in whose keys are greater than those of the most recently output records, they eventually become part of the run being created. When new records have keys that are less than those of the most recently output records, they are held over for the next run. Replacement selection generally produces runs that are substantially longer than runs that can be created by in-RAM sorts, and hence can help improve performance in merge sorting. When using replacement selection with merge sorts on disk, however, one must be careful that the extra seeking required for replacement selection does not outweigh the benefits of having longer runs to merge.

Run. A sorted subset of a file resulting from the sort step of a sort merge or one of the steps of a multistep merge.

Selection tree. A binary tree in which each higher-level node represents the winner of the comparison between the two descendent keys. The minimum (or maximum) value in a selection tree is always at the root node, making the selection tree a good data structure for merging several lists. It is also a key structure in replacement selection algorithms, which can be used for producing long runs for merge sorts. (*Tournament sort,* an internal sort, is also based on the use of a selection tree.)

Sequence checking. Checking that records in a file are in the expected order. It is recommended that all files used in a cosequential operation be sequence checked.

sort. A UNIX utility for sorting and merging files.

Synchronization loop. The main loop in the cosequential processing model. A primary feature of the model is to do all synchronization within a single loop, rather than in multiple nested loops. A second objective is to keep the main synchronization loop as simple as possible. This is done by restricting the operations that occur within the loop to those that involve current keys, and by relegating as much special logic as possible (such as error checking and end-of-file checking) to subprocedures.

Theorem A (Knuth). It is difficult to decide which merge pattern is best in a given situation.

▮ EXERCISES

1. Write an output procedure to go with the procedures described in section 7.1 for doing cosequential matching. As a defensive measure, it is a good idea to have the output procedure do sequence checking in the same manner as the input procedure does.

2. Consider the cosequential initialization routine in Fig. 7.4. If PREV_1 and PREV_2 were not set to LOW_VALUE in this routine, how would *input()* have to be changed? How would this affect the adaptability of *input()* for use in other cosequential processing algorithms?

3. Consider the cosequential merge procedures described in section 7.1. Comment on how they handle the following situations. If they do not correctly handle a situation, indicate how they might be altered to do so.
   a. List 1 empty and List 2 not empty
   b. List 1 not empty and List 2 empty
   c. List 1 empty and List 2 empty

4. In the ledger procedure example in section 7.2, modify the procedure so it also updates the ledger file with the new account balances for the month.

5. Use the k-way merge example as the basis for a procedure that is a k-way match.

6. Figure 7.17 shows a loop for doing a k-way merge, assuming that there are no duplicate names. If duplicate names are allowed, one could add to the procedure a facility for keeping a *list* of subscripts of duplicate lowest names. Alter the procedure to do this.

7. In section 7.3, two methods are presented for choosing the lowest of k keys at each step in a k-way merge: a linear search and use of a selection tree. Compare the performances of the two approaches in terms of numbers of comparisons for $k = 2, 4, 8, 16, 32,$ and 100. Why do you think the linear approach is recommended for values of k less than 8?

8. Suppose you have 8 megabytes of RAM available for sorting the 800,000-record file described in section 7.5.1.
   a. How long does it take to sort the file using the merge sort algorithm described in section 7.5.1?

b. How long does it take to sort the file using the keysort algorithm described in Chapter 5?

c. Why will keysort not work if there is one megabyte of RAM available for the sorting phase?

9. How much seek time is required to perform a one-step merge such as the one described in section 7.5 if the time for an average seek is 50 msec and the amount of available internal buffer space is 500 K? 100 K?

10. Performance in sorting is often measured in terms of the number of comparisons. Explain why the number of comparisons is not adequate for measuring performance in sorting large files.

11. In our computations involving the merge sorts, we made the simplifying assumption that only one seek and one rotational delay are required for any single sequential access. If this were not the case, a great deal more time would be required to perform I/O. For example, for the 80-megabyte file used in the example in section 7.5.1, for the input step of the sort phase ("reading all records into RAM for sorting and forming runs"), each individual run could require many accesses. Now let's assume that the extent size for our hypothetical drive is 20,000 bytes (approximately one track), and that all files are stored in track-sized blocks that must be accessed *separately* (one seek and one rotational delay per block).

a. How many seeks does step 1 now require?

b. How long do steps 1, 2, 3, and 4 now take?

c. How does increasing the file size by a factor of 10 now affect the total time required for the merge sort?

12. Derive two formulas for the number of seeks required to perform the merge step of a one-step k-way sort merge of a file with r records divided into k runs, where the amount of available RAM is equivalent to M records. If an internal sort is used for the sort phase, you can assume that the length of each run is M, but if replacement selection is used, you can assume that the length of each run is about $2M$. Why?

13. Assume a quiet system with four separately addressable disk drives, each of which is able to hold several hundred megabytes. Assume that the 80-megabyte file described in section 7.5 is already on one of the drives. Design a sorting procedure for this sample file that uses the separate drives to minimize the amount of seeking required. Assume that the final sorted file is written off to tape and that buffering for this tape output is handled invisibly by the operating system. Is there any advantage to be gained by using replacement selection?

14. Use replacement selection to produce runs from the following files, assuming $P = 4$.
   a. 23 29 5 17 9 55 41 3 51 33 18 24 11 47
   b. 3 5 9 11 17 18 23 24 29 33 41 47 51 55
   c. 55 51 47 41 33 29 24 23 18 17 11 9 5 3

15. Suppose you have a disk drive that has 10 read/write heads per surface, so 10 cylinders may be accessed at any one time without having to move the actuator arm. If you could control the *physical* organization of runs stored on disk, how might you be able to exploit this arrangement in performing a sort merge?

16. Assume we need to merge 14 runs on four tape drives. Develop merge patterns starting from each of these initial distributions:
   a. 8–4–2
   b. 7–4–3
   c. 6–5–3
   d. 5–5–4.

17. A four-tape polyphase merge is to be performed to sort the list 24 36 13 25 16 45 29 38 23 50 22 19 43 30 11 27 47. The original list is on tape 4. Initial runs are of length 1. After initial sorting, tapes 1, 2, and 3 contain the following runs (a slash separates runs):

Tape 1: 24 / 36 / 13 / 25
Tape 2: 16 / 45 / 29 / 38 / 23 / 50
Tape 3: 22 / 19 / 43 / 30 / 11 / 27 / 47
   a. Show the contents of tape 4 after one merge phase.
   b. Show the contents of all four tapes after the second and fourth phases.
   c. Comment on the appropriateness of the original 4–6–7 distribution for performing a polyphase merge.

18. Obtain a copy of the manual for one or more commercially available sort-merge packages. Identify the different kinds of choices available to users of the packages. Relate the options to the performance issues discussed in this chapter.

Programming Exercises

19. Implement the cosequential match procedures described in section 7.1 in C or Pascal.

20. Implement the cosequential merge procedures described in section 7.1 in C or Pascal.

21. Implement a complete program corresponding to the solution to the general ledger problem presented in section 7.2.

22. Design and implement a program to do the following:
   a. Examine the contents of two sorted files M1 and M2.
   b. Produce a third file COMMON containing a copy of records from the original two files that are identical.
   c. Produce a fourth file DIFF that contains all records from the two files that are not identical.

■ FURTHER READINGS

The subject matter treated in this chapter can be divided into two separate topics: the presentation of a model for cosequential processing, and discussion of external merging procedures on tape and disk. Although most file processing texts discuss cosequential processing, they usually do it in the context of specific applications, rather than presenting a general model that can be adapted to a variety of applications. We found this useful and flexible model through Dr. James VanDoren, who developed this form of the model himself for presentation in the file structures course that he teaches. We are not aware of any discussion of the cosequential model elsewhere in the literature.

Quite a bit of work has been done toward developing simple and effective algorithms to do sequential file updating, which is an important instance of cosequential processing. The results deal with some of the same problems the cosequential model deals with, and some of the solutions are similar. See Levy (1982) and Dwyer (1981) for more.

Unlike cosequential processing, external sorting is a topic that is covered widely in the literature. The most complete discussion of the subject, by far, is in Knuth (1973b). Students interested in the topic of external sorting must, at some point, familiarize themselves with Knuth's definitive summary of the subject. Knuth also describes replacement selection, as evidenced by our quoting from his book in this chapter.

Salzberg (1987) provides an excellent analytical treatment of external sorting, and Salzberg (1990) describes an approach that takes advantage of replacement selection, parallelism, distributed computing, and large amounts of memory. Lorin (1975) spends several chapters on sort-merge techniques. Bradley (1982) provides a good treatment of replacement selection and multiphase merging, including some interesting comparisons of processing time on different devices. Tremblay and Sorenson (1984) and Loomis (1983) also have chapters on external sorting.

Since the sorting of large files accounts for a large percentage of data processing time, most systems have sorting utilities available. IBM's DFSORT (described in IBM, 1985) is a flexible package for handling sorting and merging applications. A VAX sort utility is described in Digital (1984).

B-Trees and Other Tree-structured File Organizations

8

CHAPTER OUTLINE

8.1 Introduction: The Invention of the B-Tree

Computer science is a young discipline. As evidence of this youth, consider that at the start of 1970, after astronauts had twice travelled to the moon, B-trees did not yet exist. Today, only 15 years later, it is hard to think of a major, general-purpose file system that is not built around a B-tree design.

Douglas Comer, in his excellent survey article, "The Ubiquitous B-Tree" [1979], recounts the competition among computer manufacturers and independent research groups that developed in the late 1960s. The goal was the discovery of a general method for storing and retrieving data in large file systems that would provide rapid access to the data with minimal overhead cost. Among the competitors were R. Bayer and E. McCreight, who were working for Boeing Corporation at that time. In 1972 they published an article, "Organization and Maintenance of Large Ordered

Indexes," which announced B-trees to the world. By 1979, when Comer published his survey article, B-trees had already become so widely used that Comer was able to state that "the B-tree is, *de facto,* the standard organization for indexes in a database system."

We have reprinted the first few paragraphs of the 1972 Bayer and McCreight article[†] because it so concisely describes the facets of the problem that B-trees were designed to solve: how to access and maintain efficiently an index that is too large to hold in memory. You will remember that this is the same problem that is left unresolved in Chapter 6, on simple index structures. It will be clear as you read Bayer and McCreight's introduction that their work goes straight to the heart of the issues we raise back in the indexing chapter.

> In this paper we consider the problem of organizing and maintaining an index for a dynamically changing random access file. By an *index* we mean a collection of index elements which are pairs *(x, a)* of fixed size physically adjacent data items, namely a key *x* and some associated information *a.* The key *x* identifies a unique element in the index, the associated information is typically a pointer to a record or a collection of records in a random access file. For this paper the associated information is of no further interest.
>
> We assume that the index itself is so voluminous that only rather small parts of it can be kept in main store at one time. Thus the bulk of the index must be kept on some backup store. The class of backup stores considered are *pseudo random access devices* which have rather long access or wait time—as opposed to a true random access device like core store—and a rather high data rate once the transmission of physically sequential data has been initiated. Typical pseudo random access devices are: fixed and moving head disks, drums, and data cells.
>
> Since the data file itself changes, it must be possible not only to search the index and to retrieve elements, but also to delete and to insert keys—more accurately index elements—economically. The index organization described in this paper allows retrieval, insertion, and deletion of keys in time proportional to $\log_k I$ or better, where I is the size of the index, and k is a device dependent natural number which describes the page size such that the performance of the maintenance and retrieval scheme becomes near optimal.

Exercises 17, 18, and 19 at the end of Chapter 6 introduced the notion of a paged index. Bayer and McCreight's statement that they have developed a scheme with retrieval time proportional to $\log_k I$, where k is related to the page size, is very significant. As we will see, the use of a B-tree

---

[†]From *Acta-Informatica,* 1:173–189, © 1972, Springer Verlag, New York. Reprinted with permission.

with a page size of 64 to index a file with a million records results in being able to find the key for any record in no more than four seeks to the disk. A binary search on the same file can require as many as 20 seeks. Moreover, we are talking about getting this kind of performance from a system that requires only minimal overhead as keys are inserted and deleted.

Before looking in detail at Bayer and McCreight's solution, let's first return to a more careful look at the problem, picking up where we left off in Chapter 6. We will also look at some of the data and file structures that were routinely used to attack the problem before the invention of B-trees. Given this background, it will be easier to appreciate the contribution made by Bayer and McCreight's work.

One last matter before we begin: Why the name *B-tree?* Comer (1979) provides this footnote:

> The origin of "B-tree" has never been explained by [Bayer and Mc-Creight]. As we shall see, "balanced," "broad," or "bushy" might apply. Others suggest that the "B" stands for Boeing. Because of his contributions, however, it seems appropriate to think of B-trees as "Bayer"-trees.

8.2 Statement of the Problem

The fundamental problem with keeping an index on secondary storage is, of course, that accessing secondary storage is slow. This fundamental problem can be broken down into two more specific problems:

☐ *Binary searching requires too many seeks.* Searching for a key on a disk often involves seeking to different disk tracks. Since seeks are expensive, a search that has to look in more than three or four locations before finding the key often requires more time than is desirable. If we are using a binary search, four seeks is only enough to differentiate between 15 items. An average of about 9.5 seeks is required to find a key in an index of 1,000 items using a binary search. We need to find a way to home in on a key using fewer seeks.

☐ *It can be very expensive to keep the index in sorted order so we can perform a binary search.* As we saw in Chapter 6, if inserting a key involves moving a large number of the other keys in the index, index maintenance is very nearly impractical on secondary storage for indexes consisting of only a few hundred keys, much less thousands of keys. We need to find a way to make insertions and deletions that have only local effects in the index, rather than requiring massive reorganization.

| AX | CL | DE | FB | FT | HN | JD | KF | NR | PA | RF | SD | TK | WS | YJ |

FIGURE 8.1 Sorted list of keys.

These were the two critical problems that confronted Bayer and McCreight in 1970. They serve as guideposts for steering our discussion of the use of tree structures for secondary storage retrieval.

8.3   Binary Search Trees as a Solution

Let's begin by addressing the second of these two problems, looking at the cost of keeping a list in sorted order so we can perform binary searches. Given the sorted list in Fig. 8.1, we can express a binary search of this list as a *binary search tree,* as shown in Fig. 8.2.

Using elementary data structure techniques, it is a simple matter to create nodes that contain right and left link fields so the binary search tree can be constructed as a linked structure. Figure 8.3 illustrates a linked representation of the first two levels of the binary search tree shown in Fig. 8.2. In each node, the left and right links point to the left and right *children* of the node.

If each node is treated as a fixed-length record in which the link fields contain relative record numbers (RRNs) pointing to other nodes, then it is possible to place such a tree structure on secondary storage. Figure 8.4 illustrates the contents of the 15 records that would be required to form the binary tree depicted in Fig. 8.2.

Note that over half of the link fields in the file are empty because they are leaf nodes, with no children. In practice, leaf nodes need to contain some special character, such as −1, to indicate that the search through the tree has

FIGURE 8.2 Binary search tree representation of the list of keys.

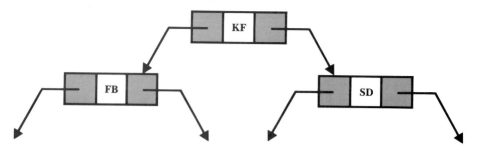

FIGURE 8.3 Linked representation of part of a binary search tree.

reached the leaf level and that there are no more nodes on the search path. We leave the fields blank in this figure to make them more noticeable, illustrating the potentially substantial cost in terms of space utilization incurred by this kind of linked representation of a tree.

But to focus on the costs and not the advantages is to miss the important new capability that this tree structure gives us: We no longer have to sort the file to be able to perform a binary search. Note that the records in the file illustrated in Fig. 8.4 appear in random rather than sorted

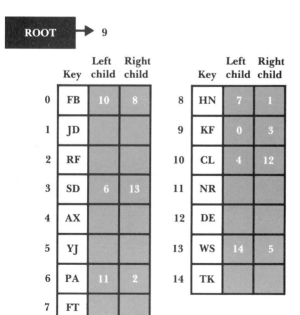

FIGURE 8.4 Record contents for a linked representation of the binary tree in Fig. 8.2.

ROOT → 9

	Key	Left child	Right child
0	FB	10	8
1	JD		
2	RF		
3	SD	6	13
4	AX		
5	YJ		
6	PA	11	2
7	FT		

	Key	Left child	Right child
8	HN	7	1
9	KF	0	3
10	CL	4	12
11	NR		
12	DE		
13	WS	14	5
14	TK		

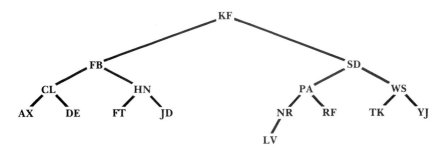

FIGURE 8.5 Binary search tree with LV added.

order. The sequence of the records in the file has no necessary relation to the structure of the tree; all the information about the logical structure is carried in the link fields. The very positive consequence that follows from this is that if we add a new key to the file, such as *LV, we need only link it to the appropriate leaf node to create a tree that provides search performance that is as good as we would get with a binary search on a sorted list.* The tree with LV added is illustrated in Fig. 8.5.

Search performance on this tree is still good because the tree is in a *balanced* state. By balanced we mean that the height of the shortest path to a leaf does not differ from the height of the longest path by more than one level. For the tree in Fig. 8.5, this difference of one is as close as we can get to *complete balance,* where all the paths from root to leaf are exactly the same length.

Consider what happens if we go on to enter the following eight keys to the tree in the sequence in which they appear:

NP MB TM LA UF ND TS NK

Just searching down through the tree and adding each key at its correct position in the search tree results in the tree shown in Fig. 8.6.

The tree is now out of balance. This is a typical result for trees built by placing keys into the tree as they occur without rearrangement. The resulting disparity between the length of various search paths is undesirable in any binary search tree, but is especially troublesome if the nodes of the tree are being kept on secondary storage. There are now keys that require seven, eight, or nine seeks for retrieval. A binary search on a sorted list of these 24 keys requires only five seeks in the worst case. Although the use of a tree lets us avoid sorting, we are paying for this convenience in terms of extra seeks at retrieval time. For trees with hundreds of keys, in which an out-of-balance search path might extend to 30, 40, or more seeks, this price is too high.

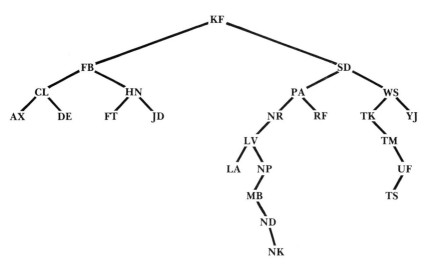

FIGURE 8.6 Binary search tree showing the effect of added keys.

8.4   AVL Trees

Earlier we said that there is no *necessary* relationship between the order in which keys are entered and the structure of the tree. We stress the word *necessary* because it is clear that order of entry is, in fact, important in determining the structure of the sample tree illustrated in Fig. 8.6. The reason for this sensitivity to the order of entry is that, so far, we have just been linking the newest nodes at the leaf levels of the tree. This approach can result in some very undesirable tree organizations. Suppose, for example, that our keys consist of the letters A–G, and that we receive these keys in alphabetical order. Linking the nodes together as we receive them

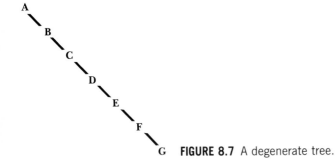

FIGURE 8.7 A degenerate tree.

FIGURE 8.8 AVL trees.

produces a degenerate tree that is, in fact, nothing more than a linked list, as illustrated in Fig. 8.7.

The solution to this problem is somehow to reorganize the nodes of the tree as we receive new keys, maintaining a near optimal tree structure. One elegant method for handling such reorganization results in a class of trees known as *AVL trees,* in honor of the pair of Russian mathematicians, G. M. Adel'son-Vel'skii and E. M. Landis, who first defined them. An AVL tree is a *height-balanced* tree. This means that there is a limit placed on the amount of difference that is allowed between the heights of any two subtrees sharing a common root. In an AVL tree the maximum allowable difference is 1. An AVL tree is therefore called a *height-balanced 1-tree* or *HB(1) tree*. It is a member of a more general class of height-balanced trees known as *HB(k)* trees, which are permitted to be *k* levels out of balance.

The trees illustrated in Fig. 8.8 have the AVL, or HB(1) property. Note that no two subtrees of any root differ by more than one level. The trees in Fig. 8.9 are *not* AVL trees. In each of these trees, the root of the subtree that is not in balance is marked with an X.

The two features that make AVL trees important are as follows:

☐ By setting a maximum allowable difference in the height of any two subtrees, AVL trees guarantee a certain minimum level of performance in searching; and

☐ Maintaining a tree in AVL form as new nodes are inserted involves the use of one of a set of four possible rotations. Each of the rota-

FIGURE 8.9 Trees that are not AVL trees.

FIGURE 8.10 A completely balanced search tree.

tions is confined to a single, local area of the tree. The most complex of the rotations requires only five pointer reassignments.

AVL trees are an important class of data structure. The operations used to build and maintain AVL trees are described in Knuth (1973b), Standish (1980), and elsewhere. AVL trees are not themselves directly applicable to most file structure problems because, like all strictly *binary* trees, they have too many levels—they are too *deep*. However, in the context of our general discussion of the problem of accessing and maintaining indexes that are too large to fit in memory, AVL trees are interesting because they suggest that it is possible to define procedures that maintain height balance.

The fact that an AVL tree is height-balanced guarantees that search performance approximates that of a *completely balanced* tree. For example, the completely balanced form of a tree made up from the input keys

BCGEFDA

is illustrated in Fig. 8.10, and the AVL tree resulting from the same input keys, arriving in the same sequence, is illustrated in Fig. 8.11.

For a completely balanced tree, the worst-case search to find a key, given N possible keys, looks at

$$\log_2 (N + 1)$$

levels of the tree. For an AVL tree, the worst-case search could look at

$$1.44 \log_2 (N + 2)$$

levels. So, given 1,000,000 keys, a completely balanced tree requires seeking to 20 levels for some of the keys, but never to 21 levels. If the tree is an AVL tree, the maximum number of levels increases to only 28. This

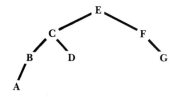

FIGURE 8.11 A search tree constructed using AVL procedures.

is a very interesting result, given that the AVL procedures guarantee that a single reorganization requires no more than five pointer reassignments. Empirical studies by VanDoren and Gray (1974), among others, have shown that such local reorganizations are required for approximately every other insertion into the tree and for approximately every fourth deletion. So height balancing using AVL methods guarantees that we will obtain a reasonable approximation to optimal binary tree performance at a cost that is acceptable in most applications using primary, random-access memory.

When we are using secondary storage, a procedure that requires more than five or six seeks to find a key is less than desirable; 20 or 28 seeks is unacceptable. Returning to the two problems that we identified earlier in this chapter:

☐   Binary searching requires too many seeks; and
☐   Keeping an index in sorted order is expensive,

we can see that height-balanced trees provide an acceptable solution to the second problem. Now we need to turn our attention to the first problem.

8.5   Paged Binary Trees

Once again we are confronting what is perhaps the most critical feature of secondary storage devices: It takes a relatively long time to seek to a specific location, but once the read head is positioned and ready, reading or writing a stream of contiguous bytes proceeds rapidly. This combination of slow seek and fast data transfer leads naturally to the notion of paging. In a paged system, you do not incur the cost of a disk seek just to get a few bytes. Instead, once you have taken the time to seek to an area of the disk, you read in an entire page from the file. This page might consist of a great many individual records. If the next bit of information you need from the disk is in the page that was just read in, you have saved the cost of a disk access.

Paging, then, is a potential solution to our searching problem. By dividing a binary tree into pages and then storing each page in a block of contiguous locations on disk, we should be able to reduce the number of seeks associated with any search. Figure 8.12 illustrates such a paged tree. In this tree we are able to locate any one of the 63 nodes in the tree with no more than two disk accesses. Note that every page holds seven nodes and can branch to eight new pages. If we extend the tree to one additional level of paging, we add 64 new pages; we can then find any one of 511 nodes in only three seeks. Adding yet another level of paging lets us find any one of 4,095 nodes in only four seeks. A binary search of a list of 4,095 items can take as many as 12 seeks.

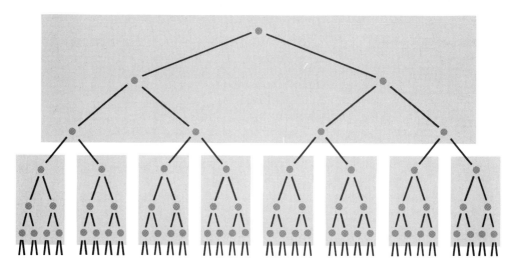

FIGURE 8.12 Paged binary tree.

Clearly, breaking the tree into pages has the potential to result in faster searching on secondary storage, providing us with much faster retrieval than any other form of keyed access that we have considered up to this point. Moreover, our use of a page size of seven in Fig. 8.12 is dictated more by the constraints of the printed page than by anything having to do with secondary storage devices. A more typical example of a page size might be 8 kilobytes capable of holding 511 key/reference field pairs. Given this page size, and assuming that each page contains a completely balanced, full tree, and that the pages themselves are organized as a completely balanced, full tree, it is then possible to find any one of 134,217,727 keys with only three seeks. That is the kind of performance we are looking for. Note that, while the number of seeks required for a worst-case search of a completely full, balanced binary tree is

$$\log_2 (N + 1)$$

where N is the number of keys in the tree, the number of seeks required for the *paged* versions of a completely full, balanced tree is

$$\log_{k+1} (N + 1)$$

where N is, once again, the number of keys. The new variable, $k,$ is the number of keys held in a single page. The second formula is actually a generalization of the first, since the number of keys in a page of a purely binary tree is 1. It is the logarithmic effect of the page size that makes the impact of paging so dramatic:

$$\log_2 (134{,}217{,}727 + 1) = 27 \text{ seeks}$$

$$\log_{511+1} (134{,}217{,}727 + 1) = 3 \text{ seeks.}$$

The use of large pages does not come free. Every access to a page requires the transmission of a large amount of data, most of which is not used. This extra transmission time is well worth the cost, however, because it saves so many seeks, which are far more time-consuming than the extra transmissions. A much more serious problem, which we look at next, has to do with keeping the paged tree organized.

8.6 The Problem with the Top-down Construction of Paged Trees

Breaking a tree into pages is a strategy that is well suited to the physical characteristics of secondary storage devices such as disks. The problem, once we decide to implement a paged tree, is how to build it. If we have the entire set of keys in hand before the tree is built, the solution to the problem is relatively straightforward: We can sort the list of keys and build the tree from this sorted list. Most importantly, if we plan to start building the tree from the root, we know that the middle key in the sorted list of keys should be the *root key* within the *root page* of the tree. In short, we know where to begin and are assured that this beginning point will divide the set of keys in a balanced manner.

Unfortunately, the problem is much more complicated if we are receiving keys in random order and inserting them as soon as we receive them. Assume that we must build a paged tree as we receive the following sequence of single-letter keys:

C S D T A M P I B W N G U R K E H O L J Y Q Z F X V

We will build a paged binary tree that contains a maximum of three keys per page. As we insert the keys, we rotate them within a page as necessary to keep each page as balanced as possible. The resulting tree is illustrated in Fig. 8.13. Evaluated in terms of the depth of the tree (measured in pages), this tree does not turn out too badly. (Consider, for example, what happens if the keys arrive in alphabetical order.)

Even though this tree is not dramatically misshapen, it clearly illustrates the difficulties inherent in building a paged binary tree from the top down. When you start from the root, the initial keys must, of necessity, go into the root. In this example at least two of these keys, C and D, are not keys that

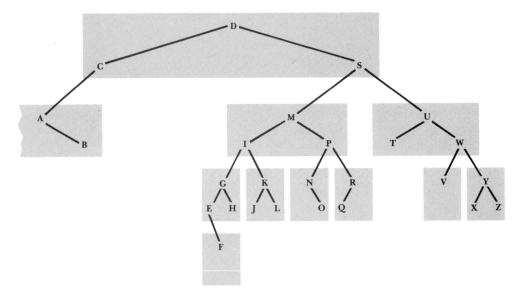

FIGURE 8.13 Paged tree constructed from keys arriving in random input sequence.

we want there. They are adjacent in sequence and tend toward the beginning of the total set of keys. Consequently, they force the tree out of balance.

Once the wrong keys are placed in the root of the tree (or in the root of any subtree further down the tree), what can you do about it? Unfortunately, there is no easy answer to this. We cannot simply rotate entire pages of the tree in the same way that we would rotate individual keys in an unpaged tree. If we rotate the tree so the initial root page moves down to the left, moving the C and D keys into a better position, then the S key is out of place. So we must break up the pages. This opens up a whole world of possibilities and difficulties. Breaking up the pages implies rearranging them to create new pages that are both internally balanced and well arranged relative to other pages. Try creating a page rearrangement algorithm for the simple, three-keys-per-page tree from Fig. 8.13. You will find it very difficult to create an algorithm that has only local effects, rearranging just a few pages. The tendency is for rearrangements and adjustments to spread out through a large part of the tree. This situation grows even more complex with larger page sizes.

So, although we have determined that the idea of collecting keys into pages is a very good one from the standpoint of reducing seeks to the disk, we have not yet found a way to collect the right keys. We are still confronting at least two unresolved questions:

☐ How do we ensure that the keys in the root page turn out to be good *separator* keys, dividing up the set of other keys more or less evenly?

☐ How do we avoid grouping keys, such as *C, D,* and *S* in our example, that should not share a page?

There is, in addition, a third question that we have not yet had to confront because of the small page size of our sample tree:

☐ How can we guarantee that each of the pages contains at least some minimum number of keys? If we are working with a larger page size, such as 8,191 keys per page, we want to avoid situations in which a large number of pages each contains only a few dozen keys.

Bayer and McCreight's 1972 B-tree article provides a solution directed precisely toward these questions.

8.7 B-Trees: Working up from the Bottom

A number of the elegant, powerful ideas used in computer science have grown out of looking at a problem from a different viewpoint. B-trees are an example of this viewpoint-shift phenomenon.

The key insight required to make the leap from the kinds of trees we have been considering to a new solution, B-trees, is that we can choose to *build trees upward from the bottom instead of downward from the top.* So far, we have assumed the necessity of starting construction from the root as a given. Then, as we found that we had the wrong keys in the root, we tried to find ways to repair the problem with rearrangement algorithms. Bayer and McCreight recognized that the decision to work down from the root was, of itself, the problem. Rather than finding ways to undo a bad situation, they decided to avoid the difficulty altogether. With B-trees, you allow the root to *emerge,* rather than set it up and then find ways to change it.

8.8 Splitting and Promoting

In a B-tree, a page, or *node,* consists of an ordered sequence of keys and a set of pointers. There is no explicit tree within a node, as with the paged trees shown previously; there is just an ordered list of keys and some pointers. The number of pointers always exceeds the number of keys by

FIGURE 8.14 Initial leaf of a B-tree with a page size of seven.

one. The maximum number of pointers that can be stored in a node is called the *order* of the B-tree. For example, suppose we have an order-eight B-tree. Each page can hold at most seven keys and eight pointers. Our initial *leaf* of the tree might have a structure like that illustrated in Fig. 8.14 after the insertion of the letters

B C G E F D A

The starred (*) fields are the pointer fields. In this leaf, as in any other leaf node, the value of all the pointers is set to indicate end-of-list. By definition, a leaf node has no children in the tree; consequently, the pointers do not lead to other pages in the tree. We assume that the pointers in the leaf pages usually contain an invalid pointer value, such as −1. Note, incidentally, that this *leaf* is also our *root*.

In a real-life application there is also usually some other information stored with the key, such as a reference to a record containing data that are associated with the key. Consequently, additional pointer fields in each page might actually lead to some associated data records that are stored elsewhere. But, paraphrasing Bayer and McCreight, for our present purposes, "the associated information is of no further interest."

Building the first page is easy enough. As we insert new keys, we use a single disk access to read the page into memory and, working in memory, insert the key into its place in the page. Since we are working in electronic memory, this insertion is relatively inexpensive compared to the cost of additional disk accesses.

But what happens as additional keys come in? Suppose we want to add the key *J* to the B-tree. When we try to insert the *J* we find that our leaf is full. We then *split* the leaf into two leaves, distributing the keys as evenly as we can between the old leaf node and the new one, as shown in Fig. 8.15.

Since we now have two leaves, we need to create a higher level in the tree to enable us to choose between the leaves when searching. In short, we

FIGURE 8.15 Splitting the leaf to accommodate the new *J* key.

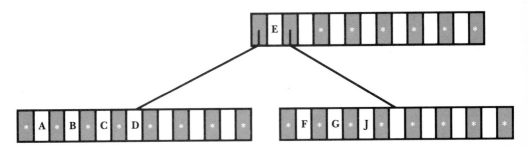

FIGURE 8.16 Promotion of the *E* key into a root node.

need to create a new root. We do this by *promoting* a key that *separates* the leaves. In this case, we promote the *E* from the first position in the second leaf, as illustrated in Fig. 8.16.

In this example we describe the splitting and the promotion operations in two steps to make the procedure as clear as possible; in practice, splitting and promotion are handled in a single operation.

Let's see how a B-tree grows given the key sequence that produces the paged binary tree illustrated in Fig. 8.13. The sequence is

C S D T A M P I B W N G U R K E H O L J Y Q Z F X V

We use an order-four B-tree (four pointer fields and three key fields per page), since this corresponds to the page size of the paged binary tree. Using such a small page size has the additional advantage of causing pages to split more frequently, providing us with more examples of splitting and promotion. We omit explicit indication of the pointer fields so we can fit a larger tree on the printed page.

Figure 8.17 illustrates the growth of the tree up to the point at which the root node is about to split. Figure 8.18 shows the tree after the splitting of the root node. The figure also shows how the tree continues to grow as the remaining keys in the sequence are added. We number each of the tree's pages (upper left corner of each node) so you can distinguish the newly added pages from the ones already in the tree.

Note that the tree is always perfectly balanced with regard to height; the path from the root to any leaf is the same as the path from the root to any other leaf. Also note that the keys that are promoted upward into the tree are necessarily the kind of keys we want in a root: keys that are good separators. By working up from the leaf level, splitting and promoting as pages fill up, we overcome the problems that plague our earlier paged binary tree efforts.

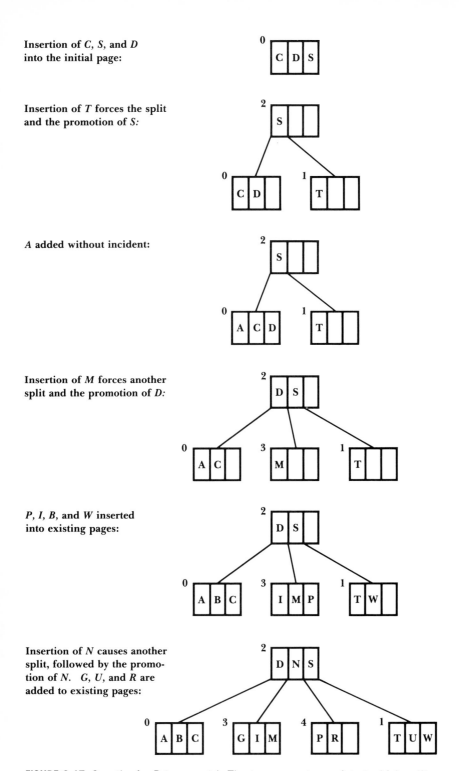

Insertion of C, S, and D
into the initial page:

Insertion of T forces the split
and the promotion of S:

A added without incident:

Insertion of M forces another
split and the promotion of D:

P, I, B, and W inserted
into existing pages:

Insertion of N causes another
split, followed by the promotion of N. G, U, and R are
added to existing pages:

FIGURE 8.17 Growth of a B-tree, part I. The tree grows to a point at which splitting of the root is imminent.

Insertion of *K* causes a split at leaf level, followed by the promotion of *K*. This causes a split of the root. *N* is promoted to become the new root. *E* is added to a leaf:

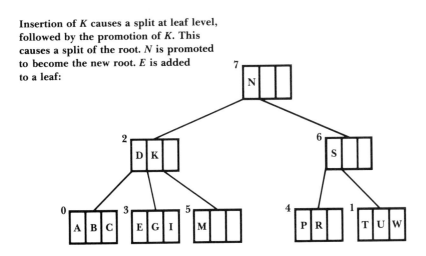

Insertion of *H* causes a leaf to split. *H* is promoted. *O*, *L*, and *J* are added:

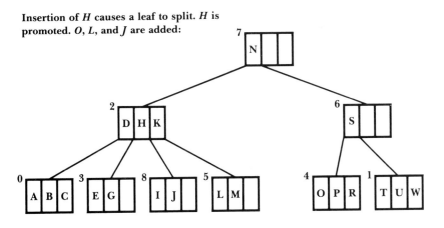

Insertion of *Y* and *Q* force two more leaf splits and promotions. Remaining letters are added:

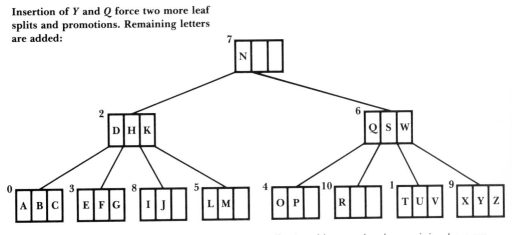

FIGURE 8.18 Growth of a B-tree, part II. The root splits to add a new level; remaining keys are inserted.

8.9   Algorithms for B-Tree Searching and Insertion

Now that we have had a brief look at how B-trees work on paper, let's outline the structures and algorithms required to make them work in a computer. Most of the code that follows is pseudocode. C and Pascal implementations of the algorithms can be found at the end of this chapter.

Page Structure   We begin by defining one possible form for the page used by a B-tree. As you see later in this chapter and in the following chapter, there are many different ways to construct the page of a B-tree. We start with a simple one in which each key is a single character. If the maximum number of keys and children allowed on a page is MAXKEYS and MAXCHILDREN, respectively, then the following structures expressed in C and Pascal describe a page called PAGE.

In C:

```
struct BTPAGE {
     short    KEYCOUNT;          /* number of keys stored in PAGE */
     char     KEY[MAXKEYS];      /* the actual keys               */
     short    CHILD[MAXKEYS+1];  /* RRNs of children              */
} PAGE;
```

In Pascal:

```
TYPE
    BTPAGE = RECORD
                KEYCOUNT: integer;
                KEY      : array[1..MAXKEYS] of char;
                CHILD    : array[1..MAXCHILDREN] of integer
             END;
VAR
    PAGE : BTPAGE;
```

Given this page structure, the file containing the B-tree consists of a set of fixed-length records. Each record contains one page of the tree. Since the keys in the tree are single letters, this structure uses an array of *characters* to hold the keys. More typically, the key array is a vector of strings rather than just a vector of characters. The variable PAGE.KEYCOUNT is useful when the algorithms must determine whether a page is full or not. The PAGE.CHILD[] array contains the RRNs of PAGE's children, if there are any. When there is no descendent, the corresponding element of PAGE. CHILD[] is set to a nonaddress value, which we call NIL. Figure 8.19 shows two pages in a B-tree of order four.

Part of a B-tree:

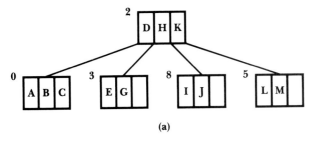

(a)

Contents of PAGE for pages 2 and 3:

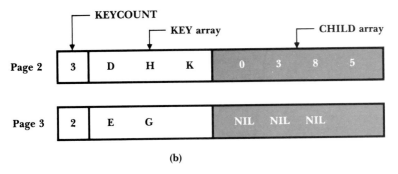

(b)

FIGURE 8.19 A B-tree of order four. (a) An internal node and some leaf nodes. (b) Nodes 2 and 3, as we might envision them in the structure PAGE.

Searching   The first B-tree algorithms we examine are a tree-*searching* procedure. Searching is a good place to begin because it is relatively simple yet still illustrates the characteristic aspects of most B-tree algorithms:

☐ They are recursive; and
☐ They work in two stages, operating alternatively on entire pages and then *within* pages.

The searching procedure calls itself recursively, seeking to a page and then searching through the page, looking for the key at successively lower levels of the tree until it either finds the key or finds that it cannot descend further, having reached beyond the leaf level. Figure 8.20 contains a description of the searching procedure in pseudocode.

```
FUNCTION: search (RRN, KEY, FOUND_RRN , FOUND_POS)

    if RRN == NIL then    /* stopping condition for the recursion */
        return NOT FOUND
    else
        read page RRN into PAGE
        look through PAGE for KEY, setting POS equal to the
            position where KEY occurs or should occur.
        if KEY was found then
            FOUND_RRN := RRN      /* current RRN contains the key */
            FOUND_POS := POS
            return FOUND
        else /* follow CHILD reference to next level down  */
            return(search(PAGE.CHILD[POS], KEY, FOUND_RRN, FOUND_POS))
        endif
    endif

end FUNCTION
```

FIGURE 8.20 Function *search (RRN, KEY, FOUND_RRN, FOUND_POS)* searches recursively through the B-tree to find KEY. Each invocation searches the page referenced by RRN. The arguments FOUND_RRN and FOUND_POS identify the page and position of the key, if it is found. If *search()* finds the key, it returns FOUND. If it goes beyond the leaf level without finding the key, it returns NOT FOUND.

Let's work through the function by hand, searching for the key K in the tree illustrated in Fig. 8.21. We begin by calling the function with the RRN argument equal to the RRN of the root (2). This RRN is not NIL, so the function reads the root into PAGE, then searches for K among the elements of PAGE.KEY[]. The K is not found. Since K should go between D and N, POS identifies position 1[†] in the root as the position of the pointer to where the search should proceed. So *search()* calls itself, this time using the RRN stored in PAGE.CHILD[1]. The value of this RRN is 3.

On the next call, *search()* reads the page containing the keys G, I, and M. Once again the function searches for K among the keys in PAGE.KEY[]. Again, K is not found. This time PAGE.CHILD[2] indicates where the search should proceed. *Search()* calls itself again, this time using the RRN stored in PAGE.CHILD[2].

Since this call is from a leaf node, PAGE.CHILD[2] is NIL, so the call to *search()* fails immediately. The value NOT FOUND is passed back through the various levels of *return* statements until the program that originally calls *search()* receives the information that the key is not found.

[†]We will use zero origin indexing in these examples, so the leftmost key in a page is PAGE.KEY[0], and the RRN of the leftmost child is PAGE.CHILD[0].

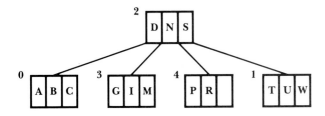

FIGURE 8.21 B-tree used for the search example.

Now let's use *search()* to look for *M,* which *is* in the tree. It follows the same downward path that it did for *K,* but this time it finds the *M* in position 2 of page 3. It stores the values 3 and 2 in *FOUND_RRN* and *FOUND_POS,* respectively, indicating that *M* can be found in the position 2 of page 3, and returns the value FOUND.

Insertion, Splitting, and Promotion   There are two important observations we can make about the insertion, splitting, and promotion process.

☐   It begins with a search that proceeds all the way down to the leaf level; and
☐   After finding the insertion location at the leaf level, the work of insertion, splitting, and promotion proceeds upward from the bottom.

Consequently, we can conceive of our recursive procedure as having three phases:

1. A search-page step that, as in the *search()* function, takes place before the recursive call;
2. The recursive call itself, which moves the operation down through the tree as it searches for either the key or the place to insert it; and
3. Insertion, splitting, and promotion logic that are executed after the recursive call, the action taking place on the upward return path following the recursive descent.

We need an example of an insertion so we can watch the insertion procedure work through these phases. Let's insert the $ character into the tree shown in the top half of Fig. 8.22, which contains all of the letters of the alphabet. Since the ASCII character sequence places the $ character ahead of the character *A,* the insertion is into the page with an RRN of 0. This page and its parent are both already full, so the insertion causes splitting and promotion that result in the tree shown in the bottom half of Fig. 8.22.

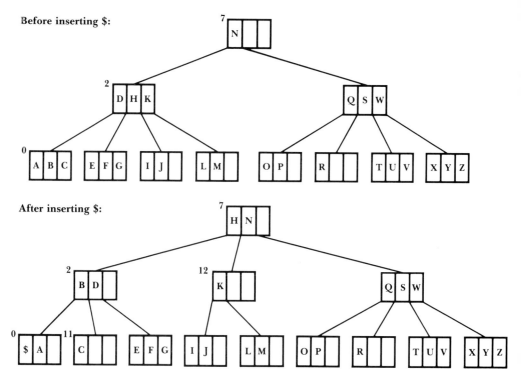

FIGURE 8.22 The effect of adding $ to the tree constructed in Fig. 8.18.

Now let's see how the *insert()* function performs this splitting and promotion. Since the function operates recursively, it is important to understand how the function arguments are used on successive calls. The *insert()* function that we are about to describe uses four arguments:

CURRENT_RRN	The RRN of the B-tree page that is currently in use. As the function recursively descends and ascends the tree, all the RRNs on the search and insertion path are used.
KEY	The key that is to be inserted.
PROMO_KEY	Argument used only to carry back the return value. If the insertion results in a split and the promotion of a key, PROMO_KEY contains the promoted key on the ascent back up the tree.
PROMO_R_CHILD	This is another return value argument. If there is a split, higher levels of the calling sequence must not only insert the promoted key value,

but also the RRN of the new page created in
the split. When PROMO_KEY is inserted,
PROMO_R_CHILD is the right child pointer
inserted with it.

In addition to the values returned via the arguments PROMO_KEY
and PROMO_R_CHILD, *insert()* returns the value PROMOTION if it
makes a promotion, NO PROMOTION if an insertion is done and
nothing is promoted, and ERROR if the insertion cannot be made.

Figure 8.23 illustrates the way the values of these arguments change as
the *insert()* function is called and calls itself to perform the insertion of the
$ character. The figure makes a number of important points:

☐   During the search step part of the insertion, only CURRENT_RRN
    changes as the function calls itself, descending the tree. This search
    path of successive calls includes every page of the tree that can be af-
    fected by splitting and promotion on the return path.
☐   The search step ends when CURRENT_RRN is NIL. There are no
    further levels to search.
☐   As each recursive call returns, we execute the insertion and splitting
    logic at that level. If the lower-level function returns the value PRO-
    MOTION, then we have a key to insert at this level. Otherwise, we
    have no work to do and can just return. For example, we are able to
    insert *H* at the highest (root) level of the tree without splitting, and
    therefore return NO PROMOTION from this level. That means
    that the PROMO_KEY and PROMO_R_CHILD from this level
    have no meaning.

Given this introduction to the *insert()* function's operation, we are ready
to look at an algorithm for the function shown in Fig. 8.24. We have already
described *insert()*'s arguments. There are several important local variables as
well:

PAGE	The page that *insert()* is currently examining.
NEWPAGE	New page created if a split occurs.
POS	The position in PAGE where the key occurs (if it is present) or would occur (if inserted).
P_B_RRN	The relative record number promoted *from below up to this level*. If a split occurs at the next lower level, P_B_RRN contains the relative record number of the new page created during the split. P_B_RRN is the right child that is inserted with P_B_KEY into PAGE.
P_B_KEY	The key promoted from below up to this level. This key, along with P_B_RRN, is inserted into PAGE.

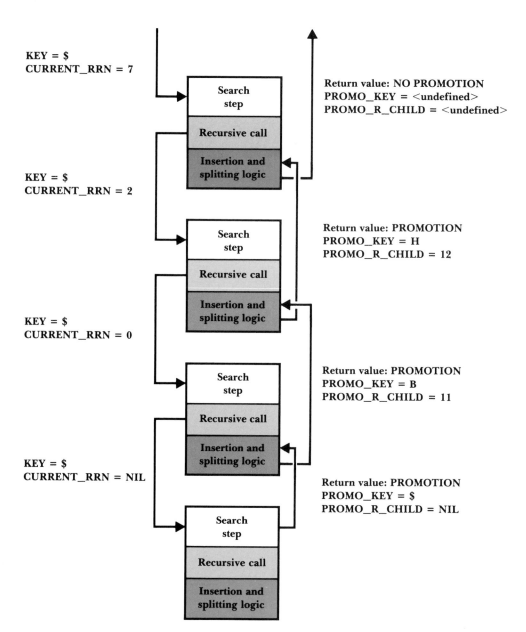

FIGURE 8.23 Pattern of recursive calls to insert $ into the B-tree as illustrated in Fig. 8.22.

```
FUNCTION: insert (CURRENT_RRN, KEY, PROMO_R_CHILD, PROMO_KEY)

    if CURRENT_RRN = NIL then      /* past bottom of tree */
        PROMO_KEY := KEY
        PROMO_R_CHILD := NIL
        return PROMOTION       /* promote original key and NIL */
    else
        read page at CURRENT_RRN into PAGE
        search for KEY in PAGE.
        let POS := the position where KEY occurs or should occur.

    if KEY found then
        issue error message indicating duplicate key
        return ERROR

    RETURN_VALUE := insert(PAGE.CHILD[POS], KEY, P_B_RRN, P_B_KEY)

    if RETURN_VALUE == NO PROMOTION or ERROR then
        return RETURN_VALUE

    elseif there is space in PAGE for P_B_KEY then
        insert P_B_KEY and P_B_RRN (promoted from below) in PAGE
        return NO PROMOTION
    else
        split(P_B_KEY, P_B_RRN, PAGE,PROMO_KEY, PROMO_R_CHILD, NEWPAGE)
        write PAGE to file at CURRENT_RRN
        write NEWPAGE to file at rrn PROMO_R_CHILD
        return PROMOTION   /* promoting PROMO_KEY and PROMO_R_CHILD */
    endif

end FUNCTION
```

FIGURE 8.24 Function *insert (CURRENT_RRN, KEY, PROMO_R_CHILD, PROMO_KEY)* inserts a KEY in a B-tree. The insertion attempt starts at the page with relative record number CURRENT_RRN. If this page is not a leaf page, the function calls itself recursively until it finds KEY in a page or reaches a leaf. If it finds KEY, it issues an error message and quits, returning ERROR. If there is space for KEY in PAGE, KEY is inserted. Otherwise, PAGE is split. A split assigns the value of the middle key to PROMO_KEY and the relative record number of the newly created page to PROMO_R_CHILD so insertion can continue on the recursive ascent back up the tree. If a promotion does occur, *insert()* indicates this by returning PROMOTION. Otherwise, it returns NO PROMOTION.

```
PROCEDURE: split (I_KEY, I_RRN, PAGE, PROMO_KEY, PROMO_R_CHILD, NEWPAGE)

    copy all keys and pointers from PAGE into a working page that
        can hold one extra key and child.

    insert I_KEY and I_RRN into their proper places in the working page.

    allocate and initialize a new page in the B-tree file to hold NEWPAGE.

    set PROMO_KEY to value of middle key, which will be promoted after
        the split.

    set PROMO_R_CHILD to RRN of NEWPAGE.

    copy keys and child pointers preceding PROMO_KEY from the working
        page to PAGE.

    copy keys and child pointers following PROMO_KEY from the working
        page to NEWPAGE.

end PROCEDURE
```

FIGURE 8.25 *Split (I_KEY, I_RRN, PAGE, PROMO_KEY, PROMO_R_CHILD, NEWPAGE)*, a procedure that inserts I_KEY and I_RRN, causing overflow, creates a new page called NEWPAGE, distributes the keys between the original PAGE and NEWPAGE, and determines which key and RRN to promote. The promoted key and RRN are returned via the arguments PROMO_KEY and PROMO_R_CHILD.

When coded in a real language, *insert()* uses a number of support functions. The most obvious one is *split()*, which creates a new page, distributes the keys between the original page and the new page, and determines which key and RRN to promote. Figure 8.25 contains a description of a simple *split()* procedure, which is also encoded in C and Pascal at the end of this chapter.

You should pay careful attention to how *split()* moves data. Note that only the *key* is promoted from the working page—*all* of the CHILD RRNs are transferred back to PAGE and NEWPAGE. The *RRN* that is promoted is the RRN of NEWPAGE, since NEWPAGE is the right descendent from the promoted key. Figure 8.26 illustrates the working page activity among PAGE, NEWPAGE, the working page, and the function arguments.

The version of *split()* described here is less efficient than might sometimes be desirable, since it moves more data than it needs to. In Exercise 17 you are asked to implement a more efficient version of *split()*.

The Top Level We need a routine to tie together our *insert()* and *split()* procedures and to do some things that are not done by the lower-level routines. Our driver must be able to do the following:

□   Open or create the B-tree file, and identify or create the root page.
□   Read in keys to be stored in the B-tree, and call *insert()* to put the keys in the tree.
□   Create a new root node when *insert()* splits the current root page.

The routine *driver* shown in Fig. 8.27 carries out these top-level tasks. It is assumed that the RRN of the root node is stored in the B-tree file itself,

FIGURE 8.26 The movement of data in *split()*.

Contents of **PAGE** are copied to the working page.

```
MAIN PROCEDURE: driver

    if the B-tree file exists, then
        open B-tree file
    else
        create a B-tree file and place the first key in the root
    get RRN of root page from file and store it in ROOT
    get a key and store it in KEY
    while keys exist
        if (insert(ROOT, KEY, PROMO_R_CHILD, PROMO_KEY) == PROMOTION) then
            create a new root page with key := PROMO_KEY, left
                child := ROOT, and right child := PROMO_R_CHILD
            set ROOT to RRN of new root page
        get next key and store it in KEY
    endwhile
    write RRN stored in ROOT back to B-tree file
    close B-tree file

end MAIN PROCEDURE
```

FIGURE 8.27 *Driver* for building a B-tree.

if the file exists. If the file does exist, *driver* opens it and gets the RRN of the root node. If it does not exist, *driver* must create the file and build an original root page. Since a root must contain at least one key, this involves getting the first key to be inserted in the tree and placing it in the root. Next, *driver* reads in the keys to be inserted, one at a time, and calls *insert()* to insert the keys into the B-tree file. If *insert()* splits the root node, it promotes a key and right child in PROMO_KEY and PROMO_R_CHILD, and *driver* uses these to create a new root.

8.10   B-Tree Nomenclature

Before moving on to discuss B-tree performance and variations on the basic B-tree algorithms, we need to formalize our B-tree terminology. Providing careful definitions of terms such as *order* and *leaf* enables us to state precisely the properties that must be present for a data structure to qualify as a B-tree. This definition of B-tree properties, in turn, informs our discussion of matters such as the procedure for deleting keys from a B-tree.

Unfortunately, the literature on B-trees is not uniform in its use of terms relating to B-trees. Reading that literature and keeping up with new developments therefore require some flexibility and some background: The reader needs to be aware of the different usages of some of the fundamental terms.

For example, Bayer and McCreight (1972), Comer (1979), and a few others refer to the *order* of a B-tree as the *minimum* number of *keys* that can be in a page of a tree. So, our initial sample B-tree (Fig. 8.16), which can hold a *maximum* of seven keys per page, has an *order* of three, using Bayer and McCreight's terminology. The problem with this definition of order is that it becomes clumsy when you try to account for pages that hold a maximum number of keys that is *odd*. For example, consider the following question: Within the Bayer and McCreight framework, is the page of an order three B-tree full when it contains six keys or when it contains seven keys?

Knuth (1973b) and others have addressed the odd/even confusion by defining the *order* of a B-tree to be the *maximum* number of *descendents* that a page can have. This is the definition of *order* that we use in this text. Note that this definition differs from Bayer and McCreight's in two ways: It references a *maximum*, not a *minimum*, and it counts *descendents* rather than *keys*.

Use of Knuth's definition must be coupled with the fact that the number of keys in a B-tree page is always one less than the number of descendents from the page. Consequently, a B-tree of order 8 has a maximum of seven keys per page. In general, given a B-tree of order m, the maximum number of keys per page is $m - 1$.

When you split the page of a B-tree, the descendents are divided as evenly as possible between the new page and the old page. Consequently, every page except the root and the leaves has at *least* $m/2$ descendents. Expressed in terms of a ceiling function, we can say that the minimum number of descendents is $\lceil m/2 \rceil$. It follows that the *minimum* number of *keys* per page is $\lceil m/2 \rceil - 1$, so our initial sample B-tree has an order of eight, which means that it can hold no more than seven keys per page and that all of the pages except the root and leaves contain at least three keys.

The other term that is used differently by different authors is *leaf*. Bayer and McCreight refer to the lowest level of keys in a B-tree as the leaf level. This is consistent with the nomenclature we have used in this text. Other authors, including Knuth, consider the leaves of a B-tree to be one level *below* the lowest level of keys. In other words, they consider the leaves to be the actual data records that might be pointed to by the lowest level of keys in the tree. We do *not* use this definition, sticking instead with the notion of leaf as the lowest level of keys in the B-tree.

8.11   Formal Definition of B-Tree Properties

Given these definitions of order and leaf, we can formulate a precise statement of the properties of a B-tree of order m:

1. Every page has a maximum of m descendents.
2. Every page, except for the root and the leaves, has at least $\lceil m/2 \rceil$ descendents.
3. The root has at least two descendents (unless it is a leaf).
4. All the leaves appear on the same level.
5. A nonleaf page with k descendents contains $k - 1$ keys.
6. A leaf page contains at least $\lceil m/2 \rceil - 1$ keys and no more than $m - 1$ keys.

8.12   Worst-case Search Depth

It is important to have a quantitative understanding of the relationship between the page size of a B-tree, the number of keys to be stored in the tree, and the number of levels that the tree can extend. For example, you might know that you need to store 1,000,000 keys and that, given the nature of your storage hardware and the size of your keys, it is reasonable to consider using a B-tree of order 512 (maximum of 511 keys per page). Given these two facts, you need to be able to answer the question, "In the worst case, what will be the maximum number of disk accesses required to locate a key in the tree?" This is the same as asking how deep the tree will be.

We can answer this question by beginning with the observation that the number of descendents from any level of a B-tree is one greater than the number of keys contained at that level and all the levels above it. Figure 8.28 illustrates this relation for the tree we constructed earlier in this chapter. This tree contains 27 keys (all the letters of the alphabet and $). If you count the number of potential descendents trailing from the leaf level, you see that there are 28 of them.

Next we need to observe that we can use the formal definition of B-tree properties to calculate the *minimum* number of descendents that can extend from any level of a B-tree of some given order. This is of interest because we are interested in the *worst-case* depth of the tree. The worst case occurs when every page of the tree has only the minimum number of descendents. In such a case the keys are spread over a *maximal height* for the tree and a *minimal breadth*.

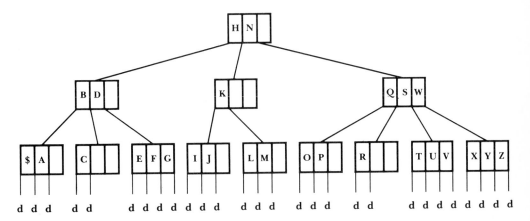

FIGURE 8.28 A B-tree with *N* keys can have (*N* + 1) descendents from the leaf level.

For a B-tree of order *m*, the minimum number of descendents from the root page is two, so the second level of the tree contains only two pages. Each of these pages, in turn, has at least $\lceil m/2 \rceil$ descendents. The third level, then, contains

$$2 \times \lceil m/2 \rceil$$

pages. Since each of these pages, once again, has a minimum of $\lceil m/2 \rceil$ descendents, the general pattern of the relation between depth and the minimum number of descendents takes the following form:

Level	Minimum number of descendents
1 (root)	2
2	$2 \times \lceil m/2 \rceil$
3	$2 \times \lceil m/2 \rceil \times \lceil m/2 \rceil$ or $2 \times \lceil m/2 \rceil^2$
4	$2 \times \lceil m/2 \rceil^3$
.	.
.	.
.	.
d	$2 \times \lceil m/2 \rceil^{d-1}$

So, in general, for any level *d* of a B-tree, the *minimum* number of descendents extending from that level is

$$2 \times \lceil m/2 \rceil^{d-1}.$$

We know that a tree with N keys has $N + 1$ descendents from its leaf level. Let's call the depth of the tree at the leaf level d. We can express the relationship between the $N + 1$ descendents and the minimum number of descendents from a tree of height d as

$$N + 1 \geq 2 \times \lceil m/2 \rceil^{d-1}$$

since we know that the number of descendents from any tree cannot be less than the number for a worst-case tree of that depth. Solving for d, we arrive at the following expression:

$$d \leq 1 + \log_{\lceil m/2 \rceil} ((N + 1)/2).$$

This expression gives us an *upper bound* for the depth of a B-tree with N keys. Let's find the upper bound for the hypothetical tree that we describe at the start of this section: a tree of order 512 that contains 1,000,000 keys. Substituting these specific numbers into the expression, we find that

$$d \leq 1 + \log_{256} 500000.5,$$

or

$$d \leq 3.37.$$

So we can say that given 1,000,000 keys, a B-tree of order 512 has a depth of no more than three levels.

8.13 Deletion, Redistribution, and Concatenation

Indexing 1,000,000 keys in no more than three levels of a tree is precisely the kind of performance we are looking for. As we have just seen, this performance is predicated on the B-tree properties we describe earlier; in particular, the ability to guarantee that B-trees are broad and shallow rather than narrow and deep is coupled to the rules that state the following:

☐ Every page except for the root and the leaves has at least $\lceil m/2 \rceil$ descendents;

☐ A nonleaf page with k descendents contains $k - 1$ keys; and

☐ A leaf page contains at least $\lceil m/2 \rceil - 1$ keys and no more than $m - 1$ keys.

We have already seen that the process of page splitting guarantees that these properties are maintained when new keys are inserted into the tree. We need to develop some kind of equally reliable guarantee that these properties are maintained when keys are *deleted* from the tree.

Working through some simple deletion situations by hand helps us demonstrate that the deletion of a key can result in several different situations. Figure 8.29 illustrates each of these situations and the associated response in the course of several deletions from an order six B-tree.

The simplest situation is illustrated in case 1. Deleting the key J does not cause the contents of page 5 to drop below the minimum number of keys. Consequently, deletion involves nothing more than removing the key from the page and rearranging the keys *within* the page to close up the space.

Deleting the M (case 2) is more complicated. If we simply remove the M from the root, it becomes very difficult to reorganize the tree to maintain its B-tree structure. Since this problem can occur whenever we delete a key from a nonleaf page, we always delete keys only from leaf pages. If a key to be deleted is not in a leaf, there is an easy way to get it into a leaf: We swap it with its immediate successor, which is guaranteed to be in a leaf, then delete it immediately from the leaf. In our example, we can swap the M with the N in page 6, then delete the M from page 6. This simple operation does not put the N out of order, since all keys in the subtree of which N is a part must be greater than N. (Can you see why this is the case?)

In case 3 we delete R from page 7. If we simply remove R and do nothing more, the page that it is in has only one key. The minimum number of keys for the leaf page of an order six tree is

$$\lceil 6/2 \rceil - 1 = 2.$$

Therefore, we have to take some kind of action to correct this underflow condition. Since the neighboring page 8 (called a *sibling* since it has the same parent) has more than the minimum number of keys, the corrective action consists of redistributing the keys between the pages. *Redistribution* must also result in a change in the key that is in the parent page so it continues to act as a separator between the lower-level pages. In the example, we move the U and V into page 7, and move W into the separator position in page 2.

The deletion of A in case 4 results in a situation that cannot be resolved by redistribution. Addressing the underflow in page 3 by moving keys from page 4 only transfers the underflow condition. There are not enough keys to share between two pages. The solution to this is *concatenation,* combining the two pages and the key from the parent page to make a single full page.

Concatenation is essentially the reverse of splitting. Like splitting, it can propagate upward through the B-tree. Just as splitting promotes a key, concatenation must involve demotion of keys, and this can in turn cause underflow in the parent page. This is just what happens in our example. Our concatenation of pages 3 and 4 pulls the key D from the parent page down to the leaf level, leading to case 5: The loss of the D from the parent page causes it, in turn, to underflow. Once again, redistribution does not solve the problem, so concatenation must be used.

Case 1: No action.
Delete *J* from page 5. Since page 5 has more
than the minimum number of keys,
J can be removed without reorganization.

Case 2: Swap with immediate successor.
Delete *M*. Swap *M* (page 0) with *N* (page 6),
and then delete *M* from page 6.

Case 3: Redistribution.
Delete *R*. Underflow occurs. Redistribute keys
among pages 2, 7, and 8 to restore balance
between leaves.

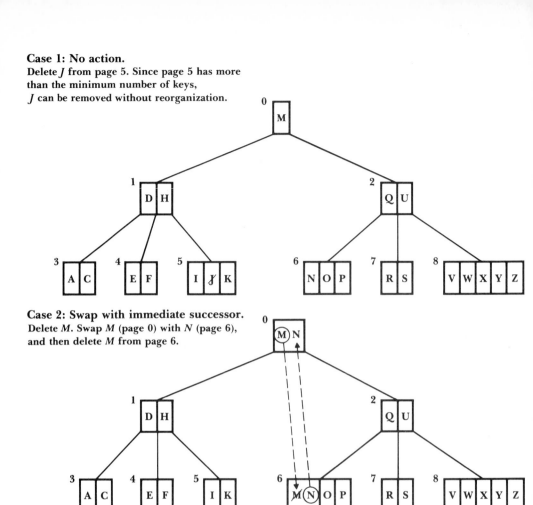

Promote *W*
move *U* and *V*
into page 7.

FIGURE 8.29 Six situations that can occur during deletions.

Case 4: Concatenation.
Delete *A*. Underflow occurs, but it cannot be addressed by redistribution. Concatenate the keys from pages 3 and 4, plus the *D* from page 1 into one page.

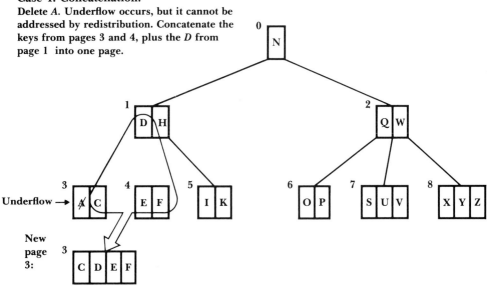

Case 5: Underflow propagates upward.
Now page 1 has underflow. Again, we cannot redistribute, so we concatenate.

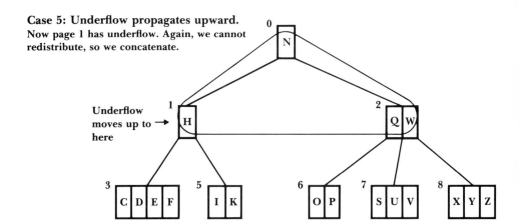

Case 6: Height of tree decreased.
Since the root contains only one key, it is absorbed into the new root.

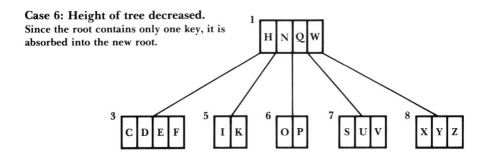

Note that the propagation of the underflow condition does not necessarily imply the propagation of concatenation. If page 2 (Q and W) had contained another key, then redistribution, not concatenation, would be used to resolve the underflow condition at the second level of the tree.

Case 6 shows what happens when concatenation propagates all the way to the root. The concatenation of pages 1 and 2 absorbs the only key in the root page, decreasing the height of the tree by one level.

The steps involved in deleting keys from a B-tree can be summarized as follows:

1. If the key to be deleted is not in a leaf, swap it with its immediate successor, which is in a leaf.
2. Delete the key.
3. If the leaf now contains at least the minimum number of keys, no further action is required.
4. If the leaf now contains one too few keys, look at the left and right siblings.
   a. If a sibling has more than the minimum number of keys, redistribute.
   b. If neither sibling has more than the minimum, concatenate the two leaves *and* the median key from the parent into one leaf.
5. If leaves are concatenated, apply steps 3–6 to the *parent*.
6. If the last key from the root is removed, then the height of the tree decreases.

8.13.1 Redistribution

Unlike concatenation, which is a kind of reverse split, redistribution is a new idea. Our insertion algorithm does not involve operations analogous to redistribution.

Redistribution differs from both splitting and concatenation in that it does not propagate. It is guaranteed to have strictly local effects. Note that the term *sibling* implies that the pages have the same parent page. If there are two nodes at the leaf level that are logically adjacent but do not have the same parent (for example, IJK and NOP in the tree at the top of Fig. 8.29), these nodes are not siblings. Redistribution algorithms are generally written so they do not consider moving keys between nodes that are not siblings, even when they are logically adjacent. Can you see the reasoning behind this restriction?

Another difference between redistribution on the one hand and concatenation and splitting on the other is that there is no necessary, fixed prescription for how the keys should be rearranged. A single deletion in a properly formed B-tree cannot cause an underflow of more than one key. Therefore, redistribution can restore the B-tree properties by moving only one key from a sibling into the page that has underflowed, even if the distribution of the keys between the pages is very uneven. Suppose, for example, that we are managing a B-tree of order 101. The minimum number of keys that can be in a page is 50, the maximum is 100. Suppose we have one page that contains the minimum and a sibling that contains the maximum. If a key is deleted from the page containing 50 keys, an underflow condition occurs. We can correct the condition through redistribution by moving one key, 50 keys, or any number of keys that falls between 1 and 50. The usual strategy is to divide the keys as evenly as possible between the pages. In this instance that means moving 25 keys.

8.14 Redistribution during Insertion: A Way to Improve Storage Utilization

As you may recall, B-tree insertion does not require an operation analogous to redistribution; splitting is able to account for all instances of overflow. This does not mean, however, that it is not *desirable* to use redistribution during insertion as an *option,* particularly since a set of B-tree maintenance algorithms must already include a redistribution procedure to support deletion. Given that a redistribution procedure is already present, what advantage might we gain by using it as an alternative to node splitting?

Redistribution during insertion is a way of avoiding, or at least postponing, the creation of new pages. Rather than splitting a full page and creating two approximately half-full pages, redistribution lets us place some of the overflowing keys into another page. The use of redistribution in place of splitting should therefore tend to make a B-tree more efficient in terms of its utilization of space.

It is possible to quantify this efficiency of space utilization by viewing the amount of space used to store information as a percentage of the total amount of space required to hold the B-tree. After a node splits, each of the two resulting pages is about half full. So, in the worst case, space utilization in a B-tree using two-way splitting is around 50%. Of course, the actual degree of space utilization is better than this worst-case figure. Yao (1978) has shown that, for large trees of relatively large order, space utilization approaches a theoretical average of about 69% if insertion is handled through two-way splitting.

The idea of using redistribution as an alternative to splitting when possible, splitting a page only when both of its siblings are full, is introduced in Bayer and McCreight's original paper (1972). The paper includes some experimental results that show that two-way splitting results in a space utilization of 67% for a tree of order 121 after 5,000 random insertions. When the experiment was repeated, using redistribution when possible, space utilization increased to over 86%. Subsequent empirical testing by Davis (1974) (B-tree of order 49) and Crotzer (1975) (B-tree of order 303) also resulted in space utilization exceeding 85% when redistribution was used. These findings and others suggest that any serious application of B-trees to even moderately large files should implement insertion procedures that handle overflow through redistribution when possible.

8.15   B* Trees

In his review and amplification of work on B-trees in 1973, Knuth (1973b) extends the notion of redistribution during insertion to include new rules for splitting. He calls the resulting variation on the fundamental B-tree form a *B* * tree.

Consider a system in which we are postponing splitting through redistribution, as outlined in the preceding section. If we are considering any page other than the root, we know that when it finally is time to split, the page has at least one sibling that is also full. This opens up the possibility of a two-to-three split rather than the usual one-to-two or two-way split. Figure 8.30 illustrates such a split.

The important aspect of this two-to-three split is that it results in pages that are each about two-thirds full rather than just half full. This makes it possible to define a new kind of B-tree, called a B* tree, which has the following properties:

1. Every page has a maximum of m descendents.
2. *Every page except for the root and the leaves has at least $(2m - 1)/3$ descendents.*
3. The root has at least two descendents (unless it is a leaf).
4. All the leaves appear on the same level.
5. A nonleaf page with k descendents contains $k - 1$ keys.
6. *A leaf page contains at least $\lfloor (2m - 1)/3 \rfloor$ keys and no more than $m - 1$ keys.*

The critical changes between this set of properties and the set we define for a conventional B-tree are in rules 2 and 6: a B* tree has pages that contain a minimum of $\lfloor (2m - 1)/3 \rfloor$ keys. This new property, of course, affects procedures for deletion and redistribution.

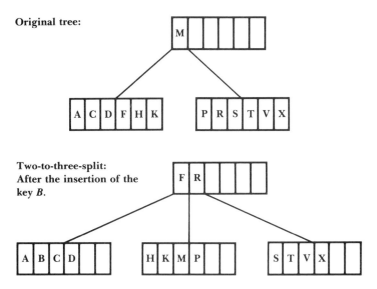

FIGURE 8.30 A two-to-three split.

To implement B∗ tree procedures, one must also deal with the question of splitting the root, which, by definition, never has a sibling. If there is no sibling, no two-to-three split is possible. Knuth suggests allowing the root to grow to a size larger than the other pages so, when it does split, it can produce two pages that are each about two-thirds full. This suggestion has the advantage of ensuring that all pages below the root level adhere to B∗ tree characteristics. However, it has the disadvantage of requiring that the procedures be able to handle a page that is larger than all the others. Another solution is to handle the splitting of the root as a conventional one-to-two split. This second solution avoids any special page-handling logic. On the other hand, it complicates deletion, redistribution, and other procedures that must be sensitive to the minimum number of keys allowed in a page. Such procedures would have to be able to recognize that pages descending from the root might legally be only half full.

8.16 Buffering of Pages: Virtual B-Trees

We have seen that, given some additional refinements, the B-tree can be a very efficient, flexible storage structure that maintains its balanced properties after repeated deletions and insertions and that provides access to any key with just a few disk accesses. However, focusing on just the structural aspects, as we have so far, can cause us inadvertently to overlook ways of using this structure to full advantage. For example, the fact that a B-tree has a depth of three levels does not at all mean that we need to do three disk accesses to retrieve keys from pages at the leaf level. We can do much better than that.

Obtaining better performance from B-trees involves looking in a precise way at our original problem. We needed to find a way to make efficient use of indexes that are too large to be held *entirely* in RAM. Up to this point we have approached this problem in an all-or-nothing way: An index has been either held entirely in RAM, organized as a list or binary tree, or has been accessed entirely on secondary store, using a B-tree structure. But, stating that we cannot hold *ALL* of an index in RAM does not imply that we cannot hold *some* of it there.

For example, assume we have an index that contains a megabyte of records and that we cannot reasonably use more than 256 K of RAM for index storage at any given time. Given a page size of 4 K, holding around 64 keys per page, our B-tree can be contained in three levels. We can reach any one of our keys in no more than three disk accesses. That is certainly acceptable, but why should we settle for this kind of performance? Why not try to find a way to bring the average number of disk accesses per search down to one disk access or less?

Thinking of the problem strictly in terms of physical storage structures, retrieval averaging one disk access or less sounds impossible. But, remember, our objective was to find a way to manage our megabyte of index within 256 K of RAM, not within the 4 K required to hold a single page of our tree.

We know that every search through the tree requires access to the root page. Rather than accessing the root page again and again at the start of every search, we could read the root page into RAM and just keep it there. This strategy increases our RAM requirement from 4 K to 8 K, since we need 4 K for the root and 4 K for whatever other page we read in, but this is still much less than the 256 K that are available. This very simple strategy reduces our worst-case search to two disk accesses, and the average search to under two accesses (keys in the root require *no* disk access; keys at the first level require one access).

This simple, keep-the-root strategy suggests an important, more general approach: Rather than just holding the root page in RAM, we can create a *page buffer* to hold some number of B-tree pages, perhaps 5, 10, or more. As we read pages in from the disk in response to user requests, we fill up the buffer. Then, when a page is requested, we access it from RAM if we can, thereby avoiding a disk access. If the page is not in RAM, then we read it into the buffer from secondary storage, replacing one of the pages that was previously there. A B-tree that uses a RAM buffer in this way is sometimes referred to as a *virtual B-tree*.

8.16.1 LRU Replacement

Clearly, such a buffering scheme works only if we are more likely to request a page that is in the buffer than one that is not. The process of accessing the disk to bring in a page that is *not* already in the buffer is called a *page fault*. There are two causes of page faults:

1. We have never used the page.
2. It was once in the buffer but has since been replaced with a new page.

The first cause of page faults is unavoidable: If we have not yet read in and used a page, there is no way it can already be in the buffer. But the second cause is one we can try to minimize through buffer management. The critical management decision arises when we need to read a new page into a buffer that is already full: Which page do we decide to replace?

One common approach is to replace the page that was least recently used; this is called *LRU* replacement. Note that this is different from replacing the page that was *read into* the buffer least recently. Since the root page is always read in first, simply replacing the oldest page results in replacing the root, which is an undesirable outcome. Instead, the LRU method keeps track of the actual *requests* for pages. Since the root is requested on every search, it seldom, if ever, is selected for replacement. The page to be replaced is the one that has gone the longest time without a request for use.

Some research by Webster (1980) shows the effect of increasing the number of pages that can be held in the buffer area under an LRU replacement strategy. Table 8.1 summarizes a small but representative

TABLE 8.1 Effect of using more buffers with a simple LRU replacement strategy

Buffer Count	1	5	10	20
Average Accesses per Search	3.00	1.71	1.42	0.97

Number of keys = 2,400
Total pages = 140
Tree height = 3 levels

portion of Webster's results. It lists the average number of disk accesses per search given different numbers of page buffers. These results are obtained using a simple LRU replacement strategy without accounting for page height.

Webster's study was conducted using B^+ trees rather than simple B-trees. In the next chapter, where we look closely at B^+ trees, you see that the nature of B^+ trees accounts for the fact that, given one buffer, the average search length is 3.00. With B^+ trees, all searches must go all the way to the leaf level every time. The fact that Webster used B^+ trees, however, does not detract from the usefulness of his results as an illustration of the positive impact of page buffering. Keeping less than 15% of the tree in RAM (20 pages out of the total 140) reduces the average number of accesses per search to less than one. The results are even more dramatic with a simple B-tree, since not all searches have to proceed to the leaf level.

Note that the decision to use LRU replacement is based on the assumption that we are more likely to need a page that we have used recently than we are to need a page that we have never used or one that we used some time ago. If this assumption is not valid, then there is absolutely no reason to preferentially retain pages that were used recently. The term for this kind of assumption is *temporal locality*. We are assuming that there is a kind of *clustering* of the use of certain pages over time. The hierarchical nature of a B-tree makes this kind of assumption reasonable.

For example, during redistribution after overflow or underflow, we access a page and then access its sibling. Because B-trees are hierarchical, accessing a set of sibling pages involves repeated access to the parent page in rapid succession. This is an instance of temporal locality; it is easy to see how it is related to the tree's hierarchy.

8.16.2 Replacement Based on Page Height

There is another, more direct way to use the hierarchical nature of the B-tree to guide decisions about page replacement in the buffers. Our simple, keep-the-root strategy exemplifies this alternative: Always retain the pages that occur at the highest levels of the tree. Given a larger amount of buffer space, it might be possible to retain not only the root, but also all of the pages at the second level of a tree.

Let's explore this notion by returning to a previous example in which we have access to 256 K of RAM and a 1-megabyte index. Since our page size is 4 K, we could build a buffer area that holds 64 pages within the RAM area. Assume that our 1 megabyte worth of index requires around 1.2 megabytes of storage on disk (storage utilization = 83%). Given the 4 K page size, this 1.2 megabytes requires slightly more than 300 pages. We assume that, on the average, each of our pages has around 30 descendents. It follows that our three-level tree has, of course, a single page at the root level, followed by 9 or 10 pages at the second level, with all the remaining pages at the leaf level. Using a page replacement strategy that always retains the higher-level pages, it is clear that our 64-page buffer eventually contains the root page and all the pages at the second level. The approximately 50 remaining buffer slots are used to hold leaf-level pages. Decisions about which of these pages to replace can be handled through an LRU strategy. For many searches, all of the pages required are already in the buffer; the search requires no disk accesses. It is easy to see how, given a sizable buffer, it is possible to bring the average number of disk accesses per search down to a number that is less than one.

Webster's research (1980) also investigates the effect of taking page height into account, giving preference to pages that are higher in the tree when it comes time to decide which pages to keep in the buffers. Augmenting the LRU strategy with a weighting factor that accounts for page height reduces the average number of accesses, given a 10-page buffer, from 1.42 accesses per search down to 1.12 accesses per search.

8.16.3 Importance of Virtual B-Trees

It is difficult to overemphasize the importance of including a page buffering scheme into any implementation of a B-tree index structure. Because the B-tree structure itself is so interesting and powerful, it is easy to fall into the trap of thinking that the B-tree organization is itself a sufficient solution to the problem of accessing large indexes that must be maintained on secondary storage. As we have emphasized, to fall into that trap is to lose sight of the original problem: to find a way to *reduce* the amount of memory required to handle large indexes. We did not, however, need to reduce the amount of memory to the amount required for a single index page. It is usually possible to find enough memory to hold a number of pages. Doing so can dramatically increase system performance.

8.17 Placement of Information Associated with the Key

Early in this chapter we focused on the B-tree index itself, setting aside any consideration of the actual information associated with the keys. We paraphrased Bayer and McCreight and stated that "the associated information is of no further interest."

But, of course, in any actual application the associated information is, in fact, the true object of interest. Rarely do we ever want to index keys just to be able to find the keys themselves. It is usually the information associated with the key that we really want to find. So, before closing our discussion of B-tree indexes, it is important to turn to the question of where and how to store the information indexed by the keys in the tree. Fundamentally, we have two choices. We can

☐ Store the information in the B-tree along with the key; or
☐ Place the information in a separate file: within the index we couple the key with a relative record number or byte address pointer that references the location of the information in that separate file.

The distinct advantage that the first approach has over the second is that once the key is found, no more disk accesses are required. The information is right there with the key. However, if the amount of information associated with each key is relatively large, then storing the information with the key reduces the number of keys that can be placed in a page of the B-tree. As the number of keys per page is reduced, the order of the tree is reduced, and the tree tends to become taller since there are fewer descendents from each page. So, the advantage of the second method is that, given associated information that has a long length relative to the length of a key, placing the associated information elsewhere allows us to build a higher-order and therefore possibly shallower tree.

For example, assume we need to index 1,000 keys and associated information records. Suppose that the length required to store a key and its associated information is 128 bytes. Furthermore, suppose that if we store the associated information elsewhere, we can store just the key and a pointer to the associated information in only 16 bytes. Given a B-tree page that had 512 bytes available for keys and associated information, the two fundamental storage alternatives translate into the following orders of B-trees:

☐ *Information stored with key:* four keys per page—order five tree; and
☐ *Pointer stored with key:* 32 keys per page—order 33 tree.

Using the formula for finding the worst-case depth of B-trees developed earlier:

$$d_{(\text{info w/key})} \leq 1 + \log_3 500.5 = 6.66$$
$$d_{(\text{info elsewhere})} \leq 1 + \log_{17} 500.5 = 3.19$$

So, if we store the information with the keys, the tree has a worst-case depth of six levels. If we store the information elsewhere, we end up reducing the height of the worst-case tree to three. Even though the additional indirection associated with the second method costs us one disk access, the second method still reduces the total number of accesses to find a record in the worst case.

In general, then, the decision about where to store the associated information should be guided by some calculations that compare the depths of the trees that result. The critical factor that influences these calculations is the ratio of overall record length to the length of just a key and pointer. If you can put many key/pointer pairs in the area required for a single, full key/record pair, it is probably advisable to remove the associated information from the B-tree and put it in a separate file.

8.18 Variable-length Records and Keys

In many applications the information associated with a key varies in length. Secondary indexes referencing inverted lists are an excellent example of this. One way to handle this variability is to place the associated information in a separate, variable-length record file; the B-tree would contain a reference to the information in this other file. Another approach is to allow a variable number of keys and records in a B-tree page.

Up to this point we have regarded B-trees as being of some order *m*. Each page has a fixed maximum and minimum number of keys that it can legally hold. The notion of a variable-length record, and, therefore, a variable number of keys per page, is a significant departure from the point of view we have developed so far. A B-tree with a variable number of keys per page clearly has no single, fixed order.

The variability in length can also extend to the keys themselves as well as to entire records. For example, in a file in which people's names are the keys, we might choose to use only as much space as required for a name, rather than allocate a fixed-size field for each key. As we saw in earlier chapters, implementing a structure with variable-length fields can allow us to put many more names in a given amount of space since it does away with internal fragmentation. If we can put more keys in a page, then we have a larger number of descendents from a page and, very probably, a tree with fewer levels.

Accommodating this variability in length means using a different kind of page structure. We look at page structures appropriate for use with variable-length keys in detail in the next chapter, where we discuss B^+ trees. We also need a different criterion for deciding when a page is full and when it is in an underflow condition. Rather than use a maximum and minimum number of keys per page, we need to use a maximum and minimum number of bytes.

Once the fundamental mechanisms for handling variable-length keys or records are in place, interesting new possibilities emerge. For example, we might consider the notion of biasing the key promotion mechanism so the shortest variable-length keys (or key/record pairs) are promoted upward in preference to longer keys. The idea is that we want to have pages with the largest numbers of descendents up high in the tree, rather than at the leaf level. Branching out as broadly as possible as high as possible in the tree tends to reduce the overall height of the tree. McCreight (1977) explores this notion in the article, "Pagination of B* Trees with Variable-Length Records."

The principal point we want to make with these examples of variations on B-tree structures is that this chapter introduces only the most basic forms of this very useful, flexible file structure. Actual implementations of B-trees do not slavishly follow the textbook form of B-trees. Instead, they use many of the other organizational techniques we study in this book, such as variable-length record structures, in combination with the fundamental B-tree organization to make new, special-purpose file structures uniquely suited to the problems at hand.

■ SUMMARY

We begin this chapter by picking up the problem we left unsolved at the end of Chapter 6: Simple, linear indexes work well if they are held in electronic RAM memory, but are expensive to maintain and search if they are so big that they must be held on secondary storage. The expense of using secondary storage is most evident in two areas:

- Sorting of the index; and
- Searching, since even binary searching required more than just two or three disk accesses.

We first address the question of structuring an index so it can be kept in order without sorting. We use tree structures to do this, discovering that we need a *balanced* tree to ensure that the tree does not become overly deep after repeated random insertions. We see that AVL trees provide a way of balancing a binary tree with only a small amount of overhead.

Next we turn to the problem of reducing the number of disk accesses required to search a tree. The solution to this problem involves dividing the tree into pages, so a substantial portion of the tree can be retrieved with a single disk access. Paged indexes let us search through very large numbers of keys with only a few disk accesses.

Unfortunately, we find that it is difficult to combine the idea of *paging* of tree structures with the *balancing* of these trees by AVL methods. The most obvious evidence of this difficulty is associated with the problem of selecting the members of the root page of a tree or subtree when the tree is built in the conventional top-down manner. This sets the stage for introducing Bayer and McCreight's work on B-trees, which solves the paging and balancing dilemma by starting from the leaf level, promoting keys upward as the tree grows.

Our discussion of B-trees begins with examples of searching, insertion, splitting, and promotion to show how B-trees grow while maintaining balance in a paged structure. Next we formalize our description of B-trees. This formal definition permits us to develop a formula for estimating worst-case B-tree depth. The formal description also motivates our work on developing deletion procedures that maintain the B-tree properties when keys are removed from a tree.

Once the fundamental structure and procedures for B-trees are in place, we begin refining and improving on these ideas. The first set of improvements involves increasing the storage utilization within B-trees. Of course, increasing storage utilization can also result in a decrease in the height of the tree, and therefore in improvements in performance. We find that by sometimes redistributing keys during insertion, rather than splitting pages, we can improve storage utilization in B-trees so it averages around 85%. Carrying our search for increased storage efficiency even farther, we find that we can combine redistribution during insertion with a different kind of splitting to ensure that the pages are about two-thirds full rather than only one-half full after the split. Trees using this combination of redistribution and two-to-three splitting are called $B*$ trees.

Next we turn to the matter of buffering pages, creating a *virtual B-tree*. We note that the use of memory is not an all-or-nothing choice: Indexes that are too large to fit into memory do not have to be accessed *entirely* from secondary storage. If we hold pages that are likely to be reused in RAM, then we can save the expense of reading these pages in from the disk again. We develop two methods of guessing which pages are to be reused. One method uses the height of the page in the tree to decide which pages to keep. Keeping the root has the highest priority, the root's descendents have the next priority, and so on. The second method for selecting pages to keep in RAM is based on recentness of use: We always replace the least-recently-used (LRU) page, retaining the pages used most recently. We see that it is possible to combine these methods, and that doing so can result in the ability to find keys while using an average of less than one disk access per search.

We then turn to the question of where to place the information associated with a key in the B-tree index. Storing it with the key is attractive because, in that case, finding the key is the same as finding the information; no additional disk accesses are required. However, if the associated information takes up a lot of space, it can reduce the order of the tree, thereby increasing the tree's height. In such cases it is often advantageous to store the associated information in a separate file.

We close the chapter with a brief look at the use of variable-length records within the pages of a B-tree, noting that significant savings in space and consequent reduction in the height of the tree can result from the use of variable-length records. The modification of the basic textbook B-tree definition to include the use of variable-length records is just one example of the many variations on B-trees that are used in real-world implementations.

■ KEY TERMS

AVL tree. A height-balanced (HB(1)) binary tree in which insertions and deletions can be performed with minimal accesses to local nodes. AVL trees are interesting because they keep branches from getting overly long after many random insertions.

B-tree of order *m*. A multiway search tree with these properties:

1. Every node has a maximum of *m* descendents.
2. Every node except the root and the leaves has at least $\lceil m/2 \rceil$ descendents.
3. The root has at least two descendents (unless it is a leaf).
4. All of the leaves appear on the same level.
5. A nonleaf page with *k* descendents contains *k* − 1 keys.
6. A leaf page contains at least $\lceil m/2 \rceil - 1$ keys and no more than *m* − 1 keys.

B-trees are built upward from the leaf level, so creation of new pages always starts at the leaf level.

The power of B-trees lies in the facts that they are balanced (no overly long branches); they are shallow (requiring few seeks); they accommodate random deletions and insertions at a relatively low cost while remaining in balance; and they guarantee at least 50% storage utilization.

B∗ tree. A special B-tree in which each node is at least two-thirds full. B∗ trees generally provide better storage utilization than do B-trees.

Concatenation. When a B-tree node underflows (becomes less than 50% full), it sometimes becomes necessary to combine the node with an adjacent node, thus decreasing the total number of nodes in the tree. Since concatenation involves a change in the number of nodes in the tree, its effects can require reorganization at many levels of the tree.

Height-balanced tree. A tree structure with a special property: For each node there is a limit to the amount of difference that is allowed among the heights of any of the node's subtrees. An *HB(k)* tree allows subtrees to be *k* levels out of balance. (See *AVL tree.*)

Leaf of a B-tree. A page at the lowest level in a B-tree. All leaves in a B-tree occur at the same level.

Order of a B-tree. The maximum number of descendents that a node in the B-tree can have.

Paged index. An index that is divided into blocks, or pages, each of which can hold many keys. The use of paged indexes allows us to search through very large numbers of keys with only a few disk accesses.

Promotion of a key. The movement of a key from one node into a higher-level node (creating the higher-level node, if necessary) when the original node becomes overfull and must be split.

Redistribution. When a B-tree node underflows (becomes less than 50% full), it may be possible to move keys into the node from an adjacent node with the same parent. This helps ensure that the 50%-full property is maintained. When keys are redistributed, it becomes necessary to alter the contents of the parent as well. Redistribution, as opposed to *concatenation,* does not involve creation or deletion of nodes—its effects are entirely local. Redistribution can also often be used as an alternative to splitting.

Splitting. Creation of two nodes out of one because the original node becomes overfull. Splitting results in the need to promote a key to a higher-level node to provide an index separating the two new nodes.

Virtual B-tree. A B-tree index in which several pages are kept in RAM in anticipation of the possibility that one or more of them will be needed by a later access. Many different strategies can be applied to replacing pages in RAM when virtual B-trees are used, including the least-recently-used strategy and height-weighted strategies.

■ EXERCISES

1. Balanced binary trees can be effective index structures for RAM-based indexing, but they have several drawbacks when they become so large that part or all of them must be kept on secondary storage. The following questions should help bring these drawbacks into focus, and thus reinforce the need for an alternative structure such as the B-tree.

  a. There are two major problems with using binary search to search a simple sorted index on secondary storage: The number of disk accesses is larger than we would like; and the time it takes to keep the index sorted is substantial. Which of the problems does a binary search tree alleviate?

b. Why is it important to keep search trees balanced?

c. In what way is an AVL tree better than a simple binary search tree?

d. Suppose you have a file with 1,000,000 keys stored on disk in a completely full, balanced binary search tree. If the tree is not paged, what is the maximum number of accesses required to find a key? If the tree is paged in the manner illustrated in Fig. 8.12, but with each page able to hold 15 keys and to branch to 16 new pages, what is the maximum number of accesses required to find a key? If the page size is increased to hold 511 keys with branches to 512 nodes, how does the maximum number of accesses change?

e. Consider the problem of balancing the three-key-per-page tree in Fig. 8.13 by rearranging the pages. Why is it difficult to create a tree-balancing algorithm that has only local effects? When the page size increases to a more likely size (such as 512 keys), why does it become difficult to guarantee that each of the pages contains at least some minimum number of keys?

f. Explain the following statement: B-trees are built upward from the bottom, whereas binary trees are built downward from the top.

g. Although B-trees are generally considered superior to binary search trees for external searching, binary trees are still commonly used for internal searching. Why is this so?

2. Describe the *necessary* parts of a leaf node of a B-tree. How does a leaf node differ from an internal node?

3. Since leaf nodes never have children, it might be possible to use the pointer fields in a leaf node to point to data records. This could eliminate the need for pointer fields to data records in the internal nodes. Why? What are the implications of doing this in terms of storage utilization and retrieval time?

4. Show the B-trees of order four that result from loading the following sets of keys in order.
   a. C G J X
   b. C G J X N S U O A E B H I
   c. C G J X N S U O A E B H I F
   d. C G J X N S U O A E B H I F K L Q R T V U W Z

5. Figure 8.23 shows the pattern of recursive calls involved in inserting a $ into the B-tree in Fig. 8.22. Suppose that subsequent to this insertion, the character [is inserted *after* the Z. (The ASCII code for [is greater than the ASCII code for Z.) Draw a figure similar to Fig. 8.23 which shows the pattern of recursive calls required to perform this insertion.

6. Given a B-tree of order 256
   a. What is the maximum number of descendents from a page?
   b. What is the minimum number of descendents from a page (excluding the root and leaves)?
   c. What is the minimum number of descendents from the root?
   d. What is the minimum number of descendents from a leaf?
   e. How many keys are there on a nonleaf page with 200 descendents?
   f. What is the maximum depth of the tree if it contains 100,000 keys?

7. Using a method similar to that used to derive the formula for worst-case depth, derive a formula for best case, or minimum depth, for an order m B-tree with N keys. What is the minimum depth of the tree described in the preceding question?

8. Suppose you have a B-tree index for an unsorted file containing N data records, where each key has stored with it the RRN of the corresponding record. The depth of the B-tree is d. What are the maximum and minimum numbers of disk accesses required to
   a. Retrieve a record;
   b. Add a record;
   c. Delete a record; and
   d. Retrieve all records from the file in sorted order.
   Assume that page buffering is *not* used. In each case, indicate how you arrived at your answer.

9. Show the trees that result after each of the keys A, B, Q, and R is deleted from the following B-tree of order five.

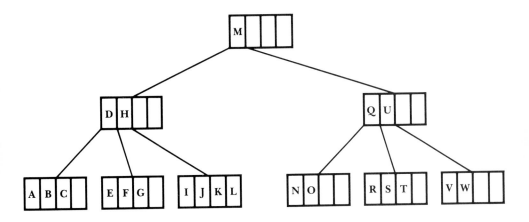

10. A common belief about B-trees is that a B-tree cannot grow deeper unless it is 100% full. Discuss this.

11. Suppose you want to delete a key from a node in a B-tree. You look at the right sibling and find that redistribution does not work; concatenation would be necessary. You look to the left and see that redistribution is an option here. Do you choose to concatenate or redistribute?

12. What is the difference between a B∗ tree and a B-tree? What improvement does a B∗ tree offer over a B-tree, and what complications does it introduce? How does the minimum depth of an order *m* B∗ tree compare with that of an order *m* B-tree?

13. What is a virtual B-tree? How can it be possible to average fewer than one access per key when retrieving keys from a three-level virtual B-tree? Write a pseudocode description for an LRU replacement scheme for a 10-page buffer used in implementing a virtual B-tree.

14. Discuss the trade-offs between storing the information indexed by the keys in a B-tree with the key and storing the information in a separate file.

15. We noted that, given variable-length keys, it is possible to optimize a tree by building in a bias toward promoting shorter keys. With fixed-order trees we promote the middle key. In a variable-order, variable-length key tree, what is the meaning of "middle key"? What are the trade-offs associated with building in a bias toward shorter keys in this selection of a key for promotion? Outline an implementation for this selection and promotion process.

Programming Exercises

16. Implement the programs at the end of this chapter and add a recursive procedure that performs a parenthesized symmetric traversal of a B-tree created by the program. As an example, here is the result of a parenthesized traversal of the tree shown in Fig. 8.18:

(((A,B,C)D(E,F,G)H(I,J)K(L,M))N((O,P)Q(R)S(T,U,V)W(X,Y,Z)))

17. The *split()* routine in the B-tree programs is not very efficient. Rewrite it to make it more efficient.

18. Write a program that searches for a key in a B-tree.

19. Write an interactive program that allows a user to find, insert, and delete keys from a B-tree.

20. Write a B-tree program that uses keys that are strings, rather than single characters.

21. Write a program that builds a B-tree index for a data file in which records contain more information than just a key.

■ FURTHER READINGS

Currently available textbooks on file and data structures contain surprisingly brief discussions on B-trees. These discussions do not, in general, add substantially to the information presented in this chapter and the following chapter. Consequently, readers interested in more information about B-trees must turn to the articles that have appeared in journals over the past 15 years.

The article that introduced B-trees to the world is Bayer and McCreight's "Organization and Maintenance of Large Ordered Indexes" (1972). It describes the theoretical properties of B-trees and includes empirical results concerning, among other things, the effect of using redistribution in addition to splitting during insertion. Readers should be aware that the notation and terminology used in this article differ from that used in this text in a number of important respects.

Comer's (1979) survey article, "The Ubiquitous B-tree," provides an excellent overview of some important variations on the basic B-tree form. Knuth's (1973b) discussion of B-trees, although brief, is an important resource, in part because many of the variant forms such as B∗ trees were first collected together in Knuth's discussion. McCreight (1977) looks specifically at operations on trees that use variable-length records and that are therefore of variable order. Although this article speaks specifically about B∗ trees, the consideration of variable-length records can be applied to many other B-tree forms. In "Time and Space Optimality on B-trees," Rosenberg and Snyder (1981) analyze the effects of initializing B-trees with the minimum number of nodes. In "Analysis of Design Alternatives for Virtual Memory Indexes," Murayama and Smith (1977) look at three factors that affect the cost of retrieval: choice of search strategy, whether or not pages in the index are structured, and whether or not keys are compressed. Zoellick (1986) discusses the use of B-tree–like structures on optical discs.

Since B-trees in various forms have become a standard file organization for databases, a good deal of interesting material on applications of B-trees can be found in the database literature. Ullman (1986) Held and Stonebraker (1978), and Snyder (1978) discuss the use of B-trees in database systems generally. Ullman (1986) covers the problem of dealing with applications in which several programs have access to the same database concurrently and identifies literature concerned with concurrent access to B-tree.

Uses of B-trees for secondary key access are covered in many of the previously cited references. There is also a growing literature on multidimensional dynamic indexes, including a B-tree–like structure called a *k-d* B-tree. *K-d* B-trees are described in papers by Ouskel and Scheuermann (1981) and Robinson (1981). Other approaches to secondary indexing include the use of *tries* and *grid files.* Tries are covered in many texts on files and data structures, including Knuth (1973b) and Loomis (1983). Grid files are covered thoroughly in Nievergelt et al. (1984).

An interesting early paper on the use of dynamic tree structures for processing files is "The Use of Tree Structures for Processing Files," by Sussenguth (1963). Wagner (1973) and Keehn and Lacy (1974) examine the index design considerations that led to the development of VSAM. VSAM uses an index structure very similar to a B-tree, but appears to have been developed independently of Bayer and McCreight's work. Readers interested in learning more about AVL trees will find a good, approachable discussion of the algorithms associated with these trees in Standish (1980). Knuth (1973b) takes a more rigorous, mathematical look at AVL tree operations and properties.

C Programs to Insert Keys into a B-Tree

The C program that follows implements the insert program described in the text. The only difference between this program and the one in the text is that this program builds a B-tree of order five, whereas the one in the text builds a B-tree of order four. Input characters are taken from standard I/O, with *q* indicating end of data.

The program requires the use of functions from several files:

driver.c	Contains the main program, which parallels the driver program described in the text very closely.
insert.c	Contains *insert()*, the recursive function that finds the proper place for a key, inserts it, and supervises splitting and promotions.
btio.c	Contains all support functions that directly perform I/O. The header files *fileio.h* and *stdio.h* must be available for inclusion in *btio.c*.
btutil.c	Contains the rest of the support functions, including the function *split()* described in the text.

All the programs include the header file called *bt.h*.

```
/* bt.h...
      header file for btree programs
*/


#define   MAXKEYS   4
#define   MINKEYS   MAXKEYS/2
#define   NIL       (-1)
#define   NOKEY     '@'
#define   NO        0
#define   YES       1

typedef struct {
    short  keycount;              /* number of keys in page      */
    char   key[MAXKEYS];          /* the actual keys             */
    short  child[MAXKEYS+1];      /* ptrs to rrns of descendants */
} BTPAGE;
```

(continued)

```
#define PAGESIZE   sizeof(BTPAGE)

extern short  root;      /* rrn of root page */
extern int btfd;  /* file descriptor of btree file */
extern int infd;  /* file descriptor of input file */

/* prototypes */
btclose();
btopen();
btread(short rrn, BTPAGE *page_ptr);
btwrite(short rrn, BTPAGE *page_ptr);
create_root(char key, short left, short right);
short create_tree();
short getpage();
short getroot();
insert (short rrn, char key, short *promo_r_child, char *promo_key);
ins_in_page(char key, short r_child, BTPAGE *p_page);
pageinit (BTPAGE *p_page);
putroot(short root);
search_node(char key, BTPAGE *p_page, short *pos);
split(char key, short r_child, BTPAGE *p_oldpage, char *promo_key,
                    short *promo_r_child, BTPAGE *p_newpage);
```

Driver.c

```
/* driver.c...
      Driver for btree tests:

            Opens or creates b-tree file.
            Gets next key and calls insert to insert key in tree.
            If necessary, creates a new root.
*/
#include <stdio.h>
#include "bt.h"

main()
{
   int    promoted; /* boolean: tells if a promotion from below */
   short root,      /* rrn of root page                         */
       promo_rrn;   /* rrn promoted from below                  */
   char  promo_key,/* key promoted from below                   */
       key;         /* next key to insert in tree               */

   if (btopen())          /* try to open btree.dat and get root */
       root = getroot();
   else                   /* if btree.dat not there, create it  */
       root = create_tree();
```

```
        while ((key = getchar()) != 'q') {
            promoted = insert(root, key, &promo_rrn, &promo_key);
            if (promoted)
                root = create_root(promo_key, root, promo_rrn);
        }
        btclose();
}
```

Insert.c

```
/* insert.c...
        Contains insert() function to insert a key into a btree.
        Calls itself recursively until bottom of tree is reached.
        Then inserts key in node.
        If node is out of room,
            - calls split() to split node
            - promotes middle key and rrn of new node
*/
#include "bt.h"

/* insert() ...
Arguments:
        rrn:            rrn of page to make insertion in
        *promo_r_child: child promoted up from here to next level
        key:            key to be inserted here or lower
        *promo_key:     key promoted up from here to next level
*/
insert(short rrn, char key, short *promo_r_child, char *promo_key)
{
        BTPAGE page,            /* current page                        */
                newpage;        /* new page created if split occurs    */
        int found, promoted; /* boolean values                        */
        short   pos,
                p_b_rrn;        /* rrn promoted from below             */
        char    p_b_key;        /* key promoted from below             */

        if (rrn == NIL) {           /* past bottom of tree... "promote"*/
            *promo_key = key;       /* original key so that it will be */
            *promo_r_child = NIL;/* inserted at leaf level             */
            return (YES);
        }
        btread(rrn, &page);
        found = search_node(key, &page, &pos);
        if (found) {
          printf("Error: attempt to insert duplicate key: %c \n\007", key);
          return (0);
        }
```

(continued)

```
    promoted = insert(page.child[pos], key, &p_b_rrn, &p_b_key);
    if (!promoted)
      return (NO);  /* no promotion */
    if (page.keycount < MAXKEYS) {
      ins_in_page(p_b_key, p_b_rrn, &page);/* OK to insert key and */
      btwrite(rrn, &page);                 /* pointer in this page. */
      return (NO);  /* no promotion */
    }
    else {
      split(p_b_key,p_b_rrn,&page,promo_key,promo_r_child,&newpage);
      btwrite(rrn, &page);
      btwrite(*promo_r_child, &newpage);
      return (YES);   /* promotion */
    }
}
```

Btio.c

```
/* btio.c...
    Contains btree functions that directly involve file i/o:

    btopen() -- open file "btree.dat" to hold the btree.
    btclose() -- close "btree.dat"
    getroot() -- get rrn of root node from first two bytes of btree.dat
    putroot() -- put rrn of root node in first two bytes of btree.dat
    create_tree() -- create "btree.dat" and root node
    getpage() -- get next available block in "btree.dat" for a new page
    btread() -- read page number rrn from "btree.dat"
    btwrite() -- write page number rrn to "btree.dat"
*/
#include "stdio.h"
#include "bt.h"
#include "fileio.h"

int btfd;      /* global file descriptor for "btree.dat"  */

btopen()
{
    btfd = open("btree.dat", O_RDWR);
    return(btfd > 0);
}

btclose()
{
    close(btfd);
}

short getroot()
{
```

```
    short root;
    long lseek();

    lseek(btfd, 0L, 0);
    if (read(btfd, &root, 2) == 0) {
        printf("Error: Unable to get root.\007\n");
        exit(1);
    }
    return (root);
}

putroot(short root)
{
    lseek(btfd, 0L, 0);
    write(btfd, &root, 2);
}

short create_tree()
{
    char key;

    btfd = creat("btree.dat",PMODE);
    close(btfd);        /* Have to close and reopen to insure  */
    btopen();           /* read/write access on many systems.  */
    key = getchar();    /* Get first key.  */
    return (create_root(key, NIL, NIL));
}

short getpage()
{
    long lseek(), addr;
    addr = lseek(btfd, 0L, 2) - 2L;
    return ((short) addr / PAGESIZE);
}

btread(short rrn, BTPAGE *page_ptr)
{
    long lseek(), addr;

    addr = (long)rrn * (long)PAGESIZE + 2L;
    lseek(btfd, addr, 0);
    return ( read(btfd, page_ptr, PAGESIZE) );
}

btwrite(short rrn, BTPAGE *page_ptr)
{
    long lseek(), addr;
    addr = (long) rrn * (long) PAGESIZE + 2L;
    lseek(btfd, addr, 0);
    return (write(btfd, page_ptr, PAGESIZE));
}
```

Btutil.c

```
/* btutil.c...
    Contains utility functions for btree program:

    create_root() -- get and initialize root node and insert one key
    pageinit() -- put NOKEY in all "key" slots and NIL in "child" slots
    search_node() -- return YES if key in node, else NO. In either case,
                    put key's correct position in pos.
    ins_in_page() -- insert key and right child in page
    split() -- split node by creating new node and moving half of keys to
                    new node. Promote middle key and rrn of new node.
 */
#include "bt.h"

create_root(char key, short left, short right)
{
    BTPAGE page;
    short rrn;
    rrn = getpage();
    pageinit(&page);
    page.key[0] = key;
    page.child[0] = left;
    page.child[1] = right;
    page.keycount = 1;
    btwrite(rrn,&page);
    putroot(rrn);
    return(rrn);
}

pageinit(BTPAGE *p_page)    /* p_page: pointer to a page  */
{
    int j;

    for (j = 0; j < MAXKEYS; j++) {
        p_page->key[j] = NOKEY;
        p_page->child[j] = NIL;
    }
    p_page->child[MAXKEYS] = NIL;
}

search_node(char key, BTPAGE *p_page, short *pos)
                /* pos: position where key is or should be inserted  */
{
    int i;
    for (i = 0;  i < p_page->keycount  &&   key > p_page->key[i] ; i++ )
        ;
    *pos = i;
```

```
    if (  *pos < p_page->keycount  &&  key == p_page->key[*pos] )
        return (YES);  /* key is in page */
    else
        return (NO);   /* key is not in page */
}


ins_in_page(char key, short r_child, BTPAGE *p_page)
{
    int i;
    for (i = p_page->keycount; key < p_page->key[i-1] && i > 0; i--) {
        p_page->key[i] = p_page->key[i-1];
        p_page->child[i+1] = p_page->child[i];
    }
    p_page->keycount++;
    p_page->key[i] = key;
    p_page->child[i+1] = r_child;
}


/* split ()
Arguments:
      key:            key to be inserted
      promo_key:      key to be promoted up from here
      r_child:        child rrn to be inserted
      promo_r_child:  rrn to be promoted up from here
      p_oldpage:      pointer to old page structure
      p_newpage:      pointer to new page structure
*/
split(char key, short r_child, BTPAGE *p_oldpage, char *promo_key,
                            short *promo_r_child, BTPAGE *p_newpage)
{
    int   i;
    short mid;                     /* tells where split is to occur       */
    char  workkeys[MAXKEYS+1];/* temporarily holds keys, before split    */
    short workch[MAXKEYS+2];  /* temporarily holds children, before split*/

    for (i=0; i < MAXKEYS; i++) {         /* move keys and children from  */
      workkeys[i] = p_oldpage->key[i];    /* old page into work arrays     */
      workch[i] = p_oldpage->child[i];
    }
    workch[i] = p_oldpage->child[i];
    for (i=MAXKEYS; key < workkeys[i-1] && i > 0; i--) {/* insert new key */
        workkeys[i] = workkeys[i-1];
        workch[i+1] = workch[i];
    }
    workkeys[i] = key;
    workch[i+1] = r_child;

    *promo_r_child = getpage();               /* create new page for split,  */
    pageinit(p_newpage);                      /* and promote rrn of new page */
```
                                                            (continued)

```
    for (i = 0; i < MINKEYS; i++) {        /* move first half of keys and  */
       p_oldpage->key[i] = workkeys[i];    /* children to old page, second */
       p_oldpage->child[i] = workch[i];    /*  half to new page            */
       p_newpage->key[i] = workkeys[i+1+MINKEYS];
       p_newpage->child[i] = workch[i+1+MINKEYS];
       p_oldpage->key[i+MINKEYS] = NOKEY;    /* mark second half of old  */
       p_oldpage->child[i+1+MINKEYS] = NIL;  /* page as empty            */
    }
    p_oldpage->child[MINKEYS] = workch[MINKEYS];
    p_newpage->child[MINKEYS] = workch[i+1+MINKEYS];
    p_newpage->keycount = MAXKEYS - MINKEYS;
    p_oldpage->keycount = MINKEYS;
    *promo_key = workkeys[MINKEYS];             /* promote middle key */
}
```

Pascal Programs to Insert Keys into a B-Tree

The Pascal program that follows implements the insert program described in the text. The only difference between this program and the one in the text is that this program builds a B-tree of order five, whereas the one in the text builds a B-tree of order four. Input characters are taken from standard I/O, with *q* indicating end of data.

The main program includes three nonstandard compiler directives:

```
{$B-}
{$I btutil.prc}
{$I insert.prc}
```

The $B− instructs the Turbo Pascal compiler to handle keyboard input as a standard Pascal file.

The $I directives instruct the compiler to include the files *btutil.prc* and *insert.prc* in the main program. These two files contain functions needed by the main program. So the B-tree program requires the use of functions from three files:

driver.pas	Contains the main program, which closely parallels the driver program described in the text.
insert.prc	Contains *insert()*, the recursive function that finds the proper place for a key, inserts it, and supervises splitting and promotions.
btutil.prc	Contains all other support functions, including the function *split()* described in the text.

Driver.pas

```
PROGRAM btree (INPUT,OUTPUT);
{
        Driver for B-tree tests:
```

(continued)

```
                   Opens or creates btree file
                   Gets next key and calls insert to insert key in tree.
                   If necessary, creates a new root.
}

{$B-}

CONST
    MAXKEYS = 4;        {maximum number of keys in page}
    MAXCHLD = 5;        {maximum number of children in page}
    MAXWKEYS = 5;       {maximum number of keys in working space}
    MAXWCHLD = 6;       {maximum number of children in working space}
    NOKEY = '@'         {symbol to indicate no key}
    NO = FALSE;
    YES = TRUE;
    NULL = -1;

TYPE
    BTPAGE = RECORD
      keycount : integer;                        {number of keys in page      }
      key : array [1..MAXKEYS] of char;          {the actual keys             }
      child : array [1..MAXCHLD] of integer; {ptrs to RRNs of descendents}
    END;

VAR
    promoted  : boolean;                    {tells if a promotion from below}
    root,                                   {RRN of root                    }
    promo_rrn : integer;                    {RRN promoted from below         }
    promo_key,                              {key promoted from below         }
    key       : char;                       {next key to insert in tree      }
    btfd      : file of BTPAGE;             {global file descriptor for      }
                                            {"btree.dat"                     }
    MINKEYS   : integer;                    {min. number of keys in a page   }
    PAGESIZE  : integer;                    {size of a page                  }

{$I btutil.prc}
{$I insert.prc}

BEGIN {main}
    MINKEYS := MAXKEYS DIV 2;
    PAGESIZE := sizeof(BTPAGE);

    if btopen then                 {try to open btree.dat and get root}
        root := getroot
    else                           {if btree.dat not there, create it}
        root := create_tree;

    read(key);
    WHILE (key <> 'q') DO
        BEGIN
```

```
    promoted := insert(root,key,promo_rrn,promo_key);
    if promoted then
        root := create_root(promo_key,root,promo_rrn);
    read(key)
    END;

    btclose
END
```

Insert.prc

```
FUNCTION insert (rrn: integer;key: char;VAR promo_r_child: integer;
                VAR promo_key: char): boolean;

{   Function to insert a key into a B-tree:

        Calls itself recursively until the bottom of the tree is reached.
        Then inserts the key in the node.
        If node is out of room, then it calls split() to split the node and
            promotes the middle key and RRN of new node.
}

VAR
    page,                   {current page                           }
    newpage : BTPAGE;       {new page created if split occurs       }
    found,                  {tells if key is already in B-tree      }
    promoted : boolean;     {tells if key is promoted               }
    pos,                    {position that key is to go in          }
    p_b_rrn : integer;      {RRN promoted from below                }
    p_b_key : char;         {key promoted from below                }

BEGIN
    if (rrn = NULL) then            {past bottom of tree... "promote" }
        BEGIN                       {original key so that it will be   }
        promo_key := key;           {inserted at leaf level            }
        promo_r_child := NULL;
        insert := YES
        END
    else
        BEGIN
        btread(rrn,page);
        found := search_node(key,page,pos);
        if (found) then
            BEGIN
            writeln('Error: attempt to insert duplicate key: ',key);
            insert := NO
            END
```

(continued)

```
    else            {insert key at lower level}
        BEGIN
        promoted := insert(page.child[pos],key,p_b_rrn,p_b_key);
        if (NOT promoted) then
            insert := NO       {no promotion}
        else
            BEGIN
            if (page,keycount < MAXKEYS) then
                BEGIN                                    {OK to insert key      }
                ins_in_page(p_b_key,p_b_rrn,page); {and pointer in this }
                btwrite(rrn,page);                       {page.                 }
                insert := NO    {no promotion}
                END
            else
                BEGIN
                split(p_b_key,p_b_rrn,page,promo_key,
                        promo_r_child,newpage);
                btwrite(rrn,page);
                btwrite(promo_r_child,newpage);
                insert := YES        {promotion}
                END
            END
        END
    END
END:
```

Btutil.prc

```
FUNCTION btopen : BOOLEAN;
{Function to open "btree.dat" if it already exists. Otherwise
 it returns false}
VAR
    response : char;
BEGIN
    assign(btfd,'btree.dat');
    write('Does btree.dat already exist? (respond Y or N): ');
    readln(response);
    writeln;
    if (response = 'Y') OR (response = 'y') then
        BEGIN
        reset(btfd);
        btopen := TRUE
        END
    else
        btopen := FALSE
END;
```

```
PROCEDURE btclose;
{Procedure to close "btree.dat"}
BEGIN
    close (btfd);
END;


FUNCTION getroot : integer;
{Function to get the RRN of the root node from first record of btree.dat}
VAR
    root : BTPAGE;
BEGIN
    seek(btfd,0);
    if (not EOF) then
        BEGIN
        read(btfd,root);
        getroot := root.keycount
        END
    else
        writeln('Error: Unable to get root.')
END;


FUNCTION getpage : integer;
{Function that gets the next available block in "btree.dat" for a new page}
BEGIN
    getpage := filesize(btfd)
END;

PROCEDURE pageinit (VAR p_page : BTPAGE);
{puts NOKEY in all "key" slots and NULL in "child" slots}
VAR
    j : integer;
BEGIN
    for j := 1 to MAXKEYS  DO
        BEGIN
        p_page.key[j] := NOKEY;
        p_page.child[j] := NULL;
        END;
    p_page.child[MAXKEYS+1] := NULL
END;

PROCEDURE putroot (root: integer);
{Puts RRN of root node in the keycount of the first record of btree.dat }
VAR
    rootrrn : BTPAGE;
BEGIN
    seek(btfd,0);
    rootrrn.keycount := root;
```

(continued)

```
    pageinit (rootrrn);
    write(btfd,rootrrn)
END;

PROCEDURE btread (rrn : integer; VAR page_ptr : BTPAGE);
{reads page number RRN from btree.dat}
BEGIN
    seek (btfd,rrn);
    read(btfd,page_ptr);
END;


PROCEDURE btwrite (rrn : integer; page_ptr : BTPAGE);
{writes page number RRN to btree.dat}
BEGIN
    seek(btfd,rrn);
    write(btfd,page_ptr);
END;

FUNCTION create_root (key :char; left,right : integer): integer;
{get and initialize root node and insert one key}
VAR
    page : BTPAGE;
    rrn : integer;
BEGIN
    rrn := getpage;
    pageinit(page);
    page.key[1] := key;
    page.child[1] := left;
    page.child[2] := right;
    page.keycount := 1;
    btwrite(rrn,page);
    putroot(rrn);
    create_root := rrn
END;

FUNCTION create_tree : integer;
{creates "btree.dat" and the root node}
VAR
    rootrrn : integer;
BEGIN
    rewrite(btfd);
    read(key);
    rootrrn := getpage;
    putroot(rootrrn);
    create_tree := create_root(key,NULL,NULL);
END;
```

```
FUNCTION search_node(key:char; p_page:BTPAGE; VAR pos:integer): boolean;
{returns YES if key in node, else NO. In either case, put key's correct
 position in pos}
VAR
    i : integer;
BEGIN
    i := 1;
    while ((i <= p_page.keycount) AND (key > p_page.key[i])) DO
        i := i + 1;
    pos := i;
    if ((pos <= p_page.keycount) AND (key = p_page.key[pos])) then
        search_node := YES
    else
        search_node := NO
END;


PROCEDURE ins_in_page (key: char;r_child: integer; VAR p_page: BTPAGE);
{insert key and right child in page}
VAR
    i : integer;
BEGIN
    i := p_page.keycount + 1;
    while ((key < p_page.key[i-1]) AND (i > 1)) DO
        BEGIN
        p_page.key[i] := p_page.key[i-1];
        p_page.child[i+1] := p_page.child[i];
        i := i - 1
        END;
    p_page.keycount := p_page.keycount + 1;
    p_page.key[i] := key;
    p_page.child[i+1] := r_child
END;



PROCEDURE split (key: char; r_child: integer; VAR p_oldpage: BTPAGE;
                 VAR promo_key: char; VAR promo_r_child: integer;
                 VAR p_newpage: BTPAGE);

{split node by creating new node and moving half of keys to new node.
 Promote middle key and RRN of new node.}
VAR
    i : integer;
    workkeys : array [1..MAXWKEYS] of char;   {temporarily holds keys,}
                                              { before split}
    workch : array [1..MAXWCHLD] of integer;  {temporarily holds children, }
                                              { before split }
```

(continued)

```
BEGIN
    for i := 1 to MAXKEYS  DO                    {move keys and children from }
        BEGIN                                    {old page into work arrays   }
        workkeys[i] := p_oldpage.key[i];
        workch[i] := p_oldpage.child[i]
        END;
    workch[MAXKEYS+1] := p_oldpage.child[MAXKEYS+1];


    i := MAXKEYS + 1;
    while ((key < workkeys[i-1])  AND  (i > 1)) DO
        BEGIN
        workkeys[i] := workkeys[i-1];            {insert new key }
        workch[i+1] := workch[i];
        i := i - 1
        END;
    workkeys[i] := key;
    workch[i+1] := r_child;


    promo_r_child := getpage;                    {create new page for split   }
    pageinit(p_newpage);                         {and promote RRN of new page }
    for i := 1 TO MINKEYS DO                      {move first half of keys and }
        BEGIN                                    {children to old page,       }
        p_oldpage.key[i] := workkeys[i];         {second half to new page.    }
        p_oldpage.child[i] := workch[i];
        p_newpage.key[i] := workkeys[i+1+MINKEYS];
        p_newpage.child[i] := workch[i+1+MINKEYS];
        p_oldpage.key[i+MINKEYS] := NOKEY;       {mark second half of old }
        p_oldpage.child[i+1+MINKEYS] := NULL     {page as empty           }
        END;
    p_oldpage.child[MINKEYS+1] := workch[MINKEYS+1];

    if odd(MAXKEYS)
        then begin
                p_newpage.key[MINKEYS+1] := workkeys[MAXWKEYS];
                p_newpage.child[MINKEYS+2] := workch[MAXWCHLD];
                p_newpage.child[MINKEYS+1] := workch[MAXWCHLD=1];
            end
        else
            p_newpage.child[MINKEYS+1] := workch[MAXWCHLD];
            p_newpage.keycount := MAXKEYS - MINKEYS;
            p_oldpage.keycount := MINKEYS;
            promo_key := workkeys[MINKEY S+1]             {promote middle key }
END;
```

The B$^+$ Tree Family and Indexed Sequential File Access

9

CHAPTER OBJECTIVES

- Introduce *indexed sequential* files.
- Describe operations on a *sequence set* of blocks that maintains records in order by key.
- Show how an *index set* can be built on top of the sequence set to produce an indexed sequential file structure.
- Introduce the use of a B-tree to maintain the index set, thereby introducing *B$^+$ trees* and *simple prefix B$^+$ trees*.
- Illustrate how the B-tree index set in a simple prefix B$^+$ tree can be of variable order, holding a variable number of separators.
- Compare the strengths and weaknesses of B$^+$ trees, simple prefix B$^+$ trees, and B-trees.

9.1 Indexed Sequential Access

Indexed sequential file structures provide a choice between two alternative views of a file:

☐ *Indexed:* The file can be seen as a set of records that is *indexed* by key; or

☐ *Sequential:* The file can be accessed sequentially (physically contiguous records—no seeking), returning records in order by key.

The idea of having a single organizational method that provides both of these views is a new one. Up to this point we have had to choose between them. As a somewhat extreme, though instructive, example of the potential divergence of these two choices, suppose that we have developed a file structure consisting of a set of entry-sequenced records indexed by a separate B-tree. This structure can provide excellent *indexed* access to any individual record by key, even as records are added and deleted. Now let's suppose that we also want to use this file as part of a cosequential merge. In cosequential processing we want to retrieve all the records in order by key. Since the actual records in this file system are *entry sequenced,* rather than physically sorted by key, the only way to retrieve them in order by key is through the index. For a file of N records, following the N pointers from the index into the entry sequenced set requires N essentially random seeks into the record file. This is a *much* less efficient process than the sequential reading of physically adjacent records—so much so that it is unacceptable for any situation in which cosequential processing is a frequent occurrence.

On the other hand, our discussions of indexing show us that a file consisting of a set of records sorted by key, though ideal for cosequential processing, is an unacceptable structure when we want to access, insert, and delete records by key in random order.

What if an application involves both interactive random access and cosequential batch processing? There are many examples of such dual-mode applications. Student record systems at universities, for example, require keyed access to individual records while also requiring a large amount of batch processing, as when grades are posted or when fees are paid during registration. Similarly, credit card systems require both batch processing of charge slips and interactive checks of account status. Indexed sequential access methods were developed in response to these kinds of needs.

9.2   Maintaining a Sequence Set

We set aside, for the moment, the indexed part of indexed sequential access, focusing on the problem of keeping a set of records in physical order by key as records are added and deleted. We refer to this ordered set of records as a *sequence set*. We will assume that once we have a good way of maintaining a sequence set, we will find some way to index it as well.

9.2.1 The Use of Blocks

We can immediately rule out the idea of sorting and resorting the entire sequence set as records are added and deleted, since we know that sorting an entire file is an expensive process. We need instead to find a way to *localize* the changes. One of the best ways to restrict the effects of an insertion or deletion to just a part of the sequence set involves a tool we first encountered in chapters 3 and 4: We can collect the records into *blocks*.

When we block records, the block becomes the basic unit of input and output. We read and write entire blocks at once. Consequently, the size of the buffers we use in a program is such that they can hold an entire block. After reading in a block, all the records in a block are in RAM, where we can work on them or rearrange them much more rapidly.

An example helps illustrate how the use of blocks can help us keep a sequence set in order. Suppose we have records that are keyed on last name and collected together so there are four records in a block. We also include *link fields* in each block that point to the preceding block and the following block. We need these fields because, as you will see, consecutive blocks are not necessarily physically adjacent.

As with B-trees, the insertion of new records into a block can cause the block to *overflow*. The overflow condition can be handled by a block-splitting process that is analogous to, but not the same as, the block-splitting process used in a B-tree. For example, Fig. 9.1(a) shows what our blocked sequence set looks like before any insertions or deletions take place. We show only the forward links. In Fig. 9.1(b) we have inserted a new record with the key CARTER. This insertion causes block 2 to split. The second half of what was originally block 2 is found in block 4 after the split. Note that this block-splitting process operates differently than the splitting we encountered in B-trees. In a B-tree a split results in the *promotion* of a record. Here things are simpler: We just divide the records between two blocks and rearrange the links so we can still move through the file in order by key, block after block.

Deletion of records can cause a block to be less than half full and therefore to *underflow*. Once again, this problem and its solutions are analogous to what we encounter when working with B-trees. Underflow in a B-tree can lead to either of two solutions:

☐ If a neighboring node is also half full, we can *concatenate* the two nodes, freeing one up for reuse.
☐ If the neighboring nodes are more than half full, we can *redistribute* records between the nodes to make the distribution more nearly even.

Underflow within a block of our sequence set can be handled through the same kinds of processes. As with insertion, the process for the sequence set is simpler than the process for B-trees since the sequence set is *not* a tree and there are therefore no keys and records in a parent node. In Fig. 9.1(c) we show the effects of deleting the record for DAVIS. Block 4 underflows and is then concatenated with its successor in *logical* sequence, which is block 3. The concatenation process frees up block 3 for reuse. We do not show an example in which underflow leads to redistribution, rather than concatenation, since it is easy to see how the redistribution process works. Records are simply moved between logically adjacent blocks.

Given the separation of records into blocks, along with these fundamental block-splitting, concatenation, and redistribution operations, we can keep a sequence set in order by key without ever having to sort the entire set of records. As always, nothing comes free; consequently, there are costs associated with this avoidance of sorting:

☐ Once insertions are made, our file takes up more space than an un-blocked file of sorted records because of internal fragmentation

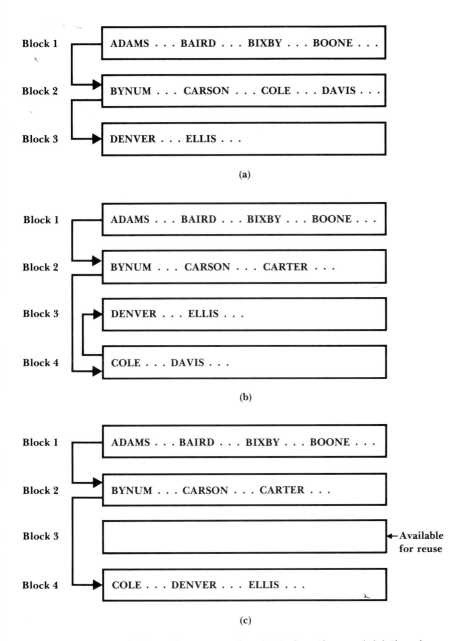

FIGURE 9.1 Block splitting and concatenation due to insertions and deletions in the sequence set. (a) Initial blocked sequence set. (b) Sequence set after insertion of CARTER record—block 2 splits, and the contents are divided between blocks 2 and 4. (c) Sequence set after deletion of DAVIS record—block 4 is less than half full, so it is concatenated with block 3.

within a block. However, we can apply the same kinds of strategies used to increase space utilization in a B-tree (e.g., the use of redistribution in place of splitting during insertion, two-to-three splitting, and so on). Once again, the implementation of any of these strategies must account for the fact that the sequence set *is not a tree* and that there is therefore no promotion of records.

☐ The order of the records is not necessarily *physically* sequential throughout the file. The maximum guaranteed extent of physical sequentiality is within a block.

This last point leads us to the important question of selecting a block size.

9.2.2 Choice of Block Size

As we work with our sequence set, a block is the basic unit for our I/O operations. When we read data from the disk, we never read less than a block; when we write data, we always write at least one block. A block is also, as we have said, the maximum *guaranteed* extent of physical sequentiality. It follows that we should think in terms of *large* blocks, with each block holding many records. So the question of block size becomes one of identifying the *limits* on block size: Why not make the block size so big we can fit the entire file in a single block?

One answer to this is the same as the reason why we cannot always use a RAM sort on a file: We usually do not have enough RAM available. So our first consideration regarding an upper bound for block size is as follows:

Consideration 1: The block size should be such that we can hold several blocks in RAM at once. For example, in performing a block split or concatenation, we want to be able to hold at least two blocks in RAM at a time. If we are implementing two-to-three splitting to conserve disk space, we need to hold at least three blocks in RAM at a time.

Although we are presently focusing on the ability to access our sequence set *sequentially,* we eventually want to consider the problem of randomly accessing a single record from our sequence set. We have to read in an entire block to get at any one record within that block. We can therefore state a second consideration:

Consideration 2: Reading in or writing out a block should not take very long. Even if we had an unlimited amount of RAM, we would want to place an upper limit on the block size so we would not end up reading in the entire file just to get at a single record.

This second consideration is more than a little imprecise: How long is very long? We can refine this consideration by factoring in some of our knowledge of the performance characteristics of disk drives:

Consideration 2   The block size should be such that we can access a
(redefined):   block without having to bear the cost of a disk seek
                          within the block read or block write operation.

This is not a *mandatory* limitation, but it is a sensible one: We are interested in a block because it contains records that are physically adjacent, so let's not extend blocks beyond the point at which we can guarantee such adjacency. And where is that?

When we discussed sector formatted disks back in Chapter 3, we introduced the term *cluster*. A cluster is the minimum number of sectors allocated at a time. If a cluster consists of eight sectors, then a file containing only one byte still uses up eight sectors on the disk. The reason for clustering is that it guarantees a minimum amount of physical sequentiality. As we move from cluster to cluster in reading a file, we may incur a disk seek, but within a cluster the data can be accessed without seeking.

One reasonable suggestion for deciding on a block size, then, is to make each block equal to the size of a cluster. Often the cluster size on a disk system has already been determined by the system administrator. But what if you are configuring a disk system for a particular application and can therefore choose your own cluster size? Then you need to consider the issues relating to cluster size raised in Chapter 3, along with the constraints imposed by the amount of RAM available and the number of blocks you want to hold in RAM at once. As is so often the case, the final decision will probably be a compromise between a number of divergent considerations. The important thing is that the compromise be a truly *informed* decision, based on knowledge of how I/O devices and file structures work, rather than just a guess.

If you are working with a disk system that is not sector oriented, but that allows you to choose the block size for a particular file, a good starting point is to think of a block as an entire track of the disk. You may want to revise this downward, to half a track, for instance, depending on memory constraints, record size, and other factors.

9.3   Adding a Simple Index to the Sequence Set

We have created a mechanism for maintaining a set of records so we can access them sequentially in order by key. It is based on the idea of grouping the records into blocks and then maintaining the blocks, as records are

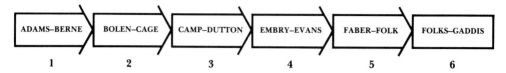

FIGURE 9.2 Sequence of blocks showing the range of keys in each block.

added and deleted, through splitting, concatenation, and redistribution. Now let's see whether we can find an efficient way to locate some specific block containing a particular record, given the record's key.

We can view each of our blocks as containing a *range* of records, as illustrated in Fig. 9.2. This is an outside view of the blocks (we have not actually read any blocks and so do not know *exactly* what they contain), but it is sufficiently informative to allow us to choose which block *might* have the record we are seeking. We can see, for example, that if we are looking for a record with the key BURNS, we want to retrieve and inspect the second block.

It is easy to see how we could construct a simple, single-level index for these blocks. We might choose, for example, to build an index of fixed-length records that contain the key for the last record in each block, as shown in Fig. 9.3.

The combination of this kind of index with the sequence set of blocks provides complete indexed sequential access. If we need to retrieve a specific record, we consult the index and then retrieve the correct block; if we need sequential access we start at the first block and read through the linked list of blocks until we have read them all. As simple as this approach is, it is in fact a very workable one as long as the entire index can be held in electronic RAM memory. The requirement that the index be held in RAM is important for two reasons:

☐ Since this is a simple index of the kind we discussed in Chapter 6, we find specific records by means of a binary search of the index.

FIGURE 9.3 Simple index for the sequence set illustrated in Fig. 9.2.

Key	Block number
BERNE	1
CAGE	2
DUTTON	3
EVANS	4
FOLK	5
GADDIS	6

Binary searching works well if the searching takes place in RAM, but, as we saw in the previous chapter on B-trees, it requires too many seeks if the file is on a secondary storage device.

☐ As the blocks in the sequence set are changed through splitting, concatenation, and redistribution, the index has to be updated. Updating a simple, fixed-length record index of this kind works well if the index is relatively small and contained in RAM. If, however, the updating requires seeking to individual index records on disk, the process can become very expensive. Once again, this is a point we discussed more completely in earlier chapters.

What do we do, then, if the file contains so many blocks that the block index does not conveniently fit into RAM? In the preceding chapter we found that we could divide the index structure into *pages,* much like the *blocks* we are discussing here, handling several pages, or blocks, of the index in RAM at a time. More specifically, we found that B-trees are an excellent file structure for handling indexes that are too large to fit entirely in RAM. This suggests that we might organize the index to our sequence set as a B-tree.

The use of a B-tree index for our sequence set of blocks is, in fact, a very powerful notion. The resulting hybrid structure is known as a B^+ *tree,* which is appropriate since it is a B-tree index *plus* a sequence set that holds the actual records. Before we can fully develop the notion of a B^+ tree, we need to think more carefully about what it is we need to keep in the index.

9.4 The Content of the Index: Separators Instead of Keys

The purpose of the index we are building is to assist us when we are searching for a record with a specific key. The index must guide us to the block in the sequence set that contains the record, if it exists in the sequence set at all. The index serves as a kind of roadmap for the sequence set. We are interested in the content of the index only insofar as it can assist us in getting to the correct block in the sequence set; the index set does not itself contain answers, it contains only information about where to go to get answers.

Given this view of the index set as a roadmap, we can take the very important step of recognizing that *we do not need to have actual keys in the index set.* Our real need is for *separators.* Figure 9.4 shows one possible set of separators for the sequence set in Fig. 9.2.

Note that there are many potential separators capable of distinguishing between two blocks. For example, all of the strings shown between blocks 3 and 4 in Fig. 9.5 are capable of guiding us in our choice between the blocks as we search for a particular key. If a string comparison between the key and

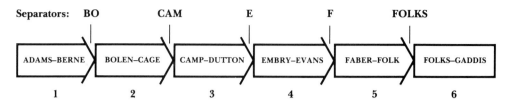

FIGURE 9.4 Separators between blocks in the sequence set.

any of these separators shows that the key precedes the separator, we look for the key in block 3. If the key follows the separator, we look in block 4.

If we are willing to treat the separators as variable-length entities within our index structure (we talk about how to do this later), we can save space by placing the *shortest separator* in the index structure. Consequently, we use *E* as the separator to guide our choice between blocks 3 and 4. Note that there is not always a unique shortest separator. For example, BK, BN, and BO are separators that are all the same length and that are equally effective as separators between blocks 1 and 2 in Fig. 9.4. We choose BO and all of the other separators contained in Fig. 9.4 by using the logic embodied in the C function shown in Fig. 9.6 and in the Pascal procedure listed in Fig. 9.7.

Note that these functions can produce a separator that is the same as the second key. This situation is illustrated in Fig. 9.4 by the separator between blocks 5 and 6, which is the same as the first key contained in block 6. It follows that, as we use the separators as a roadmap to the sequence set, we must decide to retrieve the block that is to the right of the separator or the one that is to the left of the separator according to the following rule:

Relation of Search Key and Separator	Decision
Key < separator	Go left
Key = separator	Go right
Key > separator	Go right

FIGURE 9.5 A list of potential separators.

```
/* find_sep(key1,key2,sep) ...

        finds shortest string that serves as a separator between key1 and
        key2.  Returns this separator through the address provided by
        the "sep" parameter

        the function assumes that key2 follows key1 in collating sequence
*/

find_sep(key1,key2,sep)
        char key1[], key2[], sep[];
{
        while ( (*sep++ = *key2++) == *key1++)
              ;
        *sep='\0';    /* ensure that separator string is null terminated */
}
```

FIGURE 9.6 C function to find a shortest separator.

FIGURE 9.7 Pascal procedure to find a shortest separator.

```
PROCEDURE find_sep (key1, key2 : strng ; VAR sep : strng);
{ finds the shortest string that serves as a separator between key1 and
  key2.  Returns the separator through the variable sep.  Strings are
  handled as character arrays in which the length of the string is stored
  in the 0th position of the array.  The type "strng" is used for strings.

  Assumes that key2 follows key1 in collating sequence.

  Uses two functions defined in the Appendix:
      len_str(s) -- returns the length of the string s.
      min(i,j)   -- compares i and j and returns the smallest value
}
VAR
    i, minlgth  : integer;
BEGIN
    minlgth := min(len_str(key1),len_str(key2));
    i := 1;
    while (key1[i] = key2[i]) and (i <= minlgth) DO
    BEGIN
        sep[i] := key2[i];
        i := i + 1
    END;
    sep[i] := key2[i];
    sep[0] := CHR(i)              { set length indicator in separator array }
END;
```

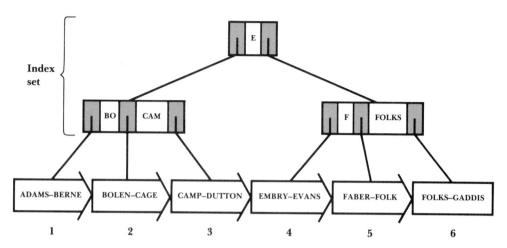

FIGURE 9.8 A B-tree index set for the sequence set, forming a simple prefix B⁺ tree.

9.5   The Simple Prefix B⁺ Tree

Figure 9.8 shows how we can form the separators identified in Fig. 9.4 into a B-tree index of the sequence set blocks. The B-tree index is called the *index set*. Taken together with the sequence set, it forms a file structure called a *simple prefix B⁺ tree*. The modifier *simple prefix* indicates that the index set contains shortest separators, or *prefixes* of the keys rather than copies of the actual keys. Our separators are simple because they are, simply, prefixes: They are actually just the initial letters within the keys. More complicated (not simple) methods of creating separators from key prefixes remove unnecessary characters from the front of the separator as well as from the rear. (See Bayer and Unterauer, 1977, for a more complete discussion of prefix B⁺ trees.)[†]

Note that since the index set is a B-tree, a node containing *N* separators branches to *N* + 1 children. If we are searching for the record with the key EMBRY, we start at the root of the index set, comparing EMBRY to the separator E. Since EMBRY comes after E, we branch to the right, retrieving the node containing the separators F and FOLKS. Since EMBRY

[†]The literature on B⁺ trees and simple prefix B⁺ trees is remarkably inconsistent in the nomenclature used for these structures. B⁺ trees are sometimes called B∗ trees; simple prefix B⁺ trees are sometimes called simple prefix B-trees. Comer's important article in *Computing Surveys* in 1979 has reduced some of the confusion by providing a consistent, standard nomenclature which we use here.

comes before even the first of these separators, we follow the branch that is to the left of the F separator, which leads us to block 4, the correct block in the sequence set.

9.6   Simple Prefix B⁺ Tree Maintenance

9.6.1 Changes Localized to Single Blocks in the Sequence Set

Let's suppose that we want to delete the records for EMBRY and FOLKS, and let's suppose that neither of these deletions results in any concatenation or redistribution within the sequence set. Since there is no concatenation or redistribution, the effect of these deletions on the *sequence set* is limited to changes *within* blocks 4 and 6. The record that was formerly the second record in block 4 (let's say that its key is ERVIN) is now the first record. Similarly, the former second record in block 6 (we assume it has a key of FROST) now starts that block. These changes can be seen in Fig. 9.9.

The more interesting question is what effect, if any, these deletions have on the *index set*. The answer is that since the number of sequence set blocks is unchanged, and since no records are moved between blocks, the index set can also remain unchanged. This is easy to see in the case of the EMBRY deletion: E is still a perfectly good separator for sequence set blocks 3 and 4, so there is no reason to change it in the index set. The case

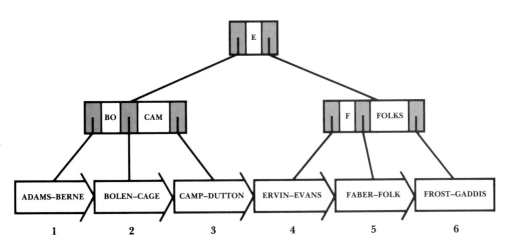

FIGURE 9.9 The deletion of the EMBRY and FOLKS records from the sequence set leaves the index set unchanged.

of the FOLKS deletion is a little more confusing since the string FOLKS appears both as a key in the deleted record and as a separator within the index set. To avoid confusion, remember to distinguish clearly between these two uses of the string FOLKS: FOLKS can continue to serve as a separator between blocks 5 and 6 even though the FOLKS record is deleted. (One could argue that although we do not *need* to replace the FOLKS separator, we should do so anyway because it is now possible to construct a *shorter* separator. However, the cost of making such a change in the index set usually outweighs the benefits associated with saving a few bytes of space.)

The effect of inserting into the sequence set new records that do not cause block splitting is much the same as the effect of these deletions that do not result in concatenation: The index set remains unchanged. Suppose, for example, that we insert a record for EATON. Following the path indicated by the separators in the index set, we find that we will insert the new record into block 4 of the sequence set. We assume, for the moment, that there is room for the record in the block. The new record becomes the first record in block 4, but no change in the index set is necessary. This is not surprising since we decided to insert the record into block 4 on the basis of the existing information in the index set. It follows that the existing information in the index set is sufficient to allow us to find the record again.

9.6.2 Changes Involving Multiple Blocks in the Sequence Set

What happens when the addition and deletion of records to and from the sequence set *does* change the number of blocks in the sequence set? Clearly, if we have more blocks, we need additional separators in the index set, and if we have fewer blocks, we need fewer separators. Changing the number of separators certainly has an effect on the index set, where the separators are stored.

Since the index set for a simple prefix B⁺ tree is actually just a normal B-tree, the changes to the index set are handled according to the familiar rules for B-tree insertion and deletion.[†] In the following examples, we assume that the index set is a B-tree of order three, which means that the maximum number of separators we can store in a node is two. We use this small node size for the index set to illustrate node splitting and concatenation while using only a few separators. As you will see later, actual implementations of simple prefix B⁺ trees place a much larger number of separators in a node of the index set.

[†]As you study the material here, you may find it helpful to refer back to Chapter 8, where we discuss B-tree operations in much more detail.

We begin with an insertion into the sequence set shown in Fig. 9.9. Specifically, let's assume that there is an insertion into the first block, and that this insertion causes the block to split. A new block (block 7) is brought in to hold the second half of what was originally the first block. This new block is linked into the correct position in the sequence set, following block 1 and preceding block 2 (these are the *physical* block numbers). These changes to the sequence set are illustrated in Fig. 9.10.

Note that the separator that formerly distinguished between blocks 1 and 2, the string BO, is now the separator for blocks 7 and 2. We need a new separator, with a value of AY, to distinguish between blocks 1 and 7. As we go to place this separator into the index set, we find that the node into which we want to insert it, containing BO and CAM, is already full. Consequently, insertion of the new separator causes a split and promotion, according to the usual rules for B-trees. The promoted separator, BO, is placed in the root of the index set.

Now let's suppose we delete a record from block 2 of the sequence set that causes an underflow condition and consequent concatenation of blocks 2 and 3. Once the concatenation is complete, block 3 is no longer needed in the sequence set, and the separator that once distinguished between blocks 2 and 3 must be removed from the index set. Removing this separator, CAM, causes an underflow in an index set node. Consequently, there is

FIGURE 9.10 An insertion into block 1 causes a split and the consequent addition of block 7. The addition of a block in the sequence set requires a new separator in the index set. Insertion of the AY separator into the node containing BO and CAM causes a node split in the index set B-tree and consequent promotion of BO to the root.

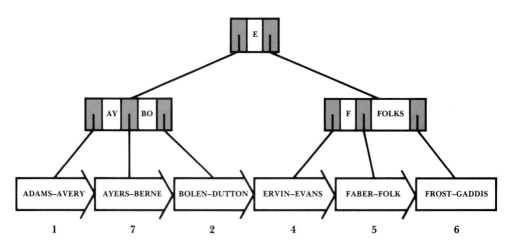

FIGURE 9.11 A deletion from block 2 causes underflow and the consequent concatenation of blocks 2 and 3. After the concatenation, block 3 is no longer needed and can be placed on an avail list. Consequently, the separator CAM is no longer needed. Removing CAM from its node in the index set forces a concatenation of index set nodes, bringing BO back down from the root.

another concatenation, this time in the index set, that results in the demotion of the BO separator from the root, bringing it back down into a node with the AY separator. Once these changes are complete, the simple prefix B⁺ tree has the structure illustrated in Fig. 9.11.

Although in these examples a block split in the sequence set results in a node split in the index set, and a concatenation in the sequence set results in a concatenation in the index set, there is not always this correspondence of action. Insertions and deletions in the index set are handled as standard B-tree operations; whether there is splitting or a simple insertion, concatenation or a simple deletion, depends entirely on how full the index set node is.

Writing procedures to handle these kinds of operations is a straightforward task if you remember that the changes take place *from the bottom up*. Record insertion and deletion *always* take place in the sequence set, since that is where the records are. If splitting, concatenation, or redistribution is necessary, perform the operation just as you would *if there were no index set at all*. Then, after the record operations in the sequence set are complete, make changes as necessary in the index set:

☐   If blocks are split in the sequence set, a new separator must be inserted into the index set;

□   If blocks are concatenated in the sequence set, a separator must be removed from the index set; and

□   If records are redistributed between blocks in the sequence set, the
value of a separator in the index set must be changed.

Index set operations are performed according to the rules for B-trees.
This means that node splitting and concatenation *propagate* up through the
higher levels of the index set. We see this in our examples as the BO
separator moves in and out of the root. Note that the operations on the
sequence set do not involve this kind of propagation. That is because the
sequence set is a linear, linked list, whereas the index set is a tree. It is easy
to lose sight of this distinction and think of an insertion or deletion in terms
of a *single* operation on the *entire* simple prefix B^+ tree. This is a good way
to become confused. Remember: Insertions and deletions happen in the
sequence set since that is where the records are. Changes to the index set are
secondary; they are a byproduct of the fundamental operations on the
sequence set.

9.7   Index Set Block Size

Up to this point we have ignored the important issues of the size and
structure of the index set nodes. Our examples have used extremely small
index set nodes and have treated them as fixed-order B-tree nodes, even
though the separators are variable in length. We need to develop more
realistic, useful ideas about the size and structure of index set nodes.

The physical size of a node for the index set is usually the same as the
physical size of a block in the sequence set. When this is the case, we speak
of index set *blocks,* rather than *nodes,* just as we speak of sequence set blocks.
There are a number of reasons for using a common block size for the index
and sequence sets:

□   The block size for the sequence set is usually chosen because there is
a good fit between this block size, the characteristics of the disk
drive, and the amount of memory available. The choice of an index
set block size is governed by consideration of the same factors; therefore, the block size that is best for the sequence set is usually best for
the index set.

□   A common block size makes it easier to implement a buffering
scheme to create a *virtual* simple prefix B^+ tree, similar to the virtual
B-trees discussed in the preceding chapter.

□   The index set blocks and sequence set blocks are often mingled
within the same file to avoid seeking between two separate files

while accessing the simple prefix B^+ tree. Use of one file for both kinds of blocks is simpler if the block sizes are the same.

9.8   Internal Structure of Index Set Blocks: A Variable-order B-Tree

Given a large, fixed-size block for the index set, how do we store the separators within it? In the examples considered so far, the block structure is such that it can contain only a fixed number of separators. The entire motivation behind the use of *shortest* separators is the possibility of packing more of them into a node. This motivation disappears completely if the index set uses a fixed-order B-tree in which there is a fixed number of separators per node.

We want each index set block to hold a variable number of variable-length separators. How should we go about searching through these separators? Since the blocks are probably large, any single block can hold a large number of separators. Once we read a block into RAM for use, we want to be able to do a binary rather than sequential search on its list of separators. We therefore need to structure the block so it can support a binary search, despite the fact that the separators are of variable length.

In Chapter 6, which covers indexing, we see that the use of a separate index can provide a means of performing binary searches on a list of variable-length entities. If the index itself consists of fixed-length references, we can use binary searching on the index, retrieving the actual variable-length records or fields through indirection. For example, suppose we are going to place the following set of separators into an index block:

As, Ba, Bro, C, Ch, Cra, Dele, Edi, Err, Fa, Fle.

(We are using lowercase letters, rather than all uppercase letters, so you can find the separators more easily when we concatenate them.) We could concatenate these separators and build an index for them, as shown in Fig. 9.12.

If we are using this block of the index set as a roadmap to help us find the record in the sequence set for "Beck", we perform a binary search on the index to the separators, retrieving first the middle separator, "Cra", which starts in position 10. Note that we can find the length of this separator by looking at the starting position of the separator that follows. Our binary search eventually tells us that "Beck" falls between the separators "Ba" and "Bro". Then what do we do?

The purpose of the index set roadmap is to guide us downward through the levels of the simple prefix B^+ tree, leading us to the sequence set block

FIGURE 9.12 Variable-length separators and corresponding index.

we want to retrieve. Consequently, the index set block needs some way to store references to its children, to the blocks descending from it in the next lower level of the tree. We assume that the references are made in terms of a relative block number (RBN), which is analogous to a relative record number except that it references a fixed-length block rather than a record. If there are N separators within a block, the block has $N + 1$ children, and therefore needs space to store $N + 1$ RBNs in addition to the separators and the index to the separators.

There are many ways to combine the list of separators, index to separators, and list of RBNs into a single index set block. One possible approach is illustrated in Fig. 9.13. In addition to the vector of separators, the index to these separators, and the list of associated block numbers, this block structure includes:

□ *Separator count:* We need this to help us find the middle element in the index to the separators so we can begin our binary search.

□ *Total length of separators:* The list of concatenated separators varies in length from block to block. Since the index to the separators begins at the end of this variable-length list, we need to know how long the list is so we can find the beginning of our index.

Let's suppose, once again, that we are looking for a record with the key "Beck" and that the search has brought us to the index set block pictured in Fig. 9.13. The total length of the separators and the separator count allows

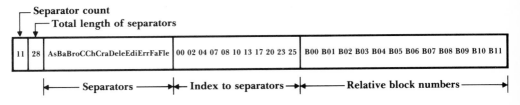

FIGURE 9.13 Structure of an index set block.

Separator subscript:	0		1		2		3		4		5		6		7		8		9		10	

B00	As	B01	Ba	B02	Bro	B03	C	B04	Ch	B05	Cra	B06	Dele	B07	Edi	B08	Err	B09	Fa	B10	Fle	B11

FIGURE 9.14 Conceptual relationship of separators and relative block numbers.

us to find the beginning, the end, and consequently the middle of the index to the separators. As in the preceding example, we perform a binary search of the separators through this index, finally concluding that the key "Beck" falls between the separators "Ba" and "Bro". *Conceptually,* the relation between the keys and the RBNs is as illustrated in Fig. 9.14. (Why isn't this a good *physical* arrangement?)

As Fig. 9.14 makes clear, discovering that the key falls between "Ba" and "Bro" allows us to decide that the *next* block we need to retrieve has the RBN stored in the B02 position of the RBN vector. This next block could be another index set block, and thus another block of the roadmap, or it could be the sequence set block that we are looking for. In either case, the quantity and arrangement of information in the current index set block is sufficient to let us conduct our binary search *within* the index block and then proceed to the next block in the simple prefix B⁺ tree.

There are many alternate ways to arrange the fundamental components of this index block. (For example, would it be easier to build the block if the vector of keys were placed at the end of the block? How would you handle the fact that the block consists of both *character* and *integer* entities with no constant, fixed dividing point between them?) For our purposes here, the specific implementation details for this particular index block structure are not nearly as important as the block's *conceptual structure.* This kind of index block structure illustrates two important points.

The first point is that a block is not just an arbitrary chunk cut out of a homogeneous file; it can be more than just a set of records. A block can have a sophisticated internal structure all its own, including its own internal index, a collection of variable-length records, separate sets of fixed-length records, and so forth. This idea of building more sophisticated data structures inside of each block becomes increasingly attractive as the block size increases. With very large blocks it becomes imperative that we have an efficient way of processing all of the data within a block once it has been read into RAM. This point applies not only to simple prefix B⁺ trees, but to any file structure using a large block size.

The second point is that a node within the B-tree index set of our simple prefix B$^+$ tree is of variable order, since each index set block contains a variable number of separators. This variability has interesting implications:

□   The number of separators in a block is directly limited by block size rather than by some predetermined *order* (as in an *order M* B-tree). The index set will have the maximum *order,* and therefore the minimum depth, that is possible given the degree of compression used to form the separators.

□   Since the tree is of *variable order,* operations such as determining when a block is full, or half full, are no longer a simple matter of comparing a separator count against some fixed maximum or minimum. Decisions about when to split, concatenate, or redistribute become more complicated.

The exercises at the end of this chapter provide opportunities for exploring variable-order trees more thoroughly.

9.9   Loading a Simple Prefix B$^+$ Tree

In the previous description of the simple prefix B$^+$ tree, we focus first on building a sequence set, and subsequently present the index set as something that is added or built on top of the sequence set. It is not only possible to *conceive* of simple prefix B$^+$ trees this way, as a sequence set with an added index, but one can also *build* them this way.

One way of building a simple prefix B$^+$ tree, of course, is through a series of successive insertions. We would use the procedures outlined in section 9.6, where we discuss the maintenance of simple prefix B$^+$ trees, to split or redistribute blocks in the sequence set and in the index set as we added blocks to the sequence set. The difficulty with this approach is that splitting and redistribution are relatively expensive. They involve searching down through the tree for each insertion and then reorganizing the tree as necessary on the way back up. These operations are fine for tree *maintenance* as the tree is updated, but when we are loading the tree we do not have to contend with a *random-order* insertion and therefore do not need procedures that are so powerful, flexible, and expensive. Instead, we can begin by sorting the records that are to be loaded. Then we can guarantee that the next record we encounter is the next record we need to load.

Working from a sorted file, we can place the records into sequence set blocks, one by one, starting a new block when the one we are working with fills up. As we make the transition between two sequence set blocks, we can

Next separator: CAT

Next sequence set block: CATCH–CHECK

FIGURE 9.15 Formation of the first index set block as the sequence set is loaded.

determine the shortest separator for the blocks. We can collect these separators into an index set block that we build and hold in RAM until it is full.

To develop an example of how this works, let's assume that we have sets of records associated with terms that are being compiled for a book index. The records might consist of a list of the occurrences of each term. In Fig. 9.15 we show four sequence set blocks that have been written out to the disk and one index set block that has been built in RAM from the shortest separators derived from the sequence set block keys. As you can

FIGURE 9.16 Simultaneous building of two index set levels as the sequence set continues to grow.

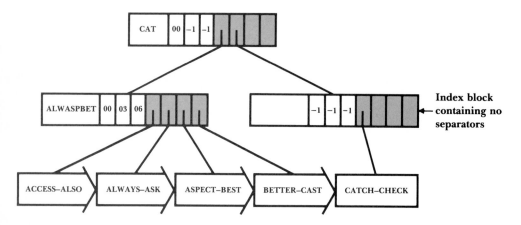

Index block containing no separators

see, the next sequence set block consists of a set of terms ranging from CATCH through CHECK, and therefore the next separator is CAT. Let's suppose that the index set block is now full. We write it out to disk. Now what do we do with the separator CAT?

Clearly, we need to start a new index block. But we cannot place CAT into another index block at the same level as the one containing the separators ALW, ASP, and BET since we cannot have two blocks at the same level without having a parent block. Instead, we promote the CAT separator to a higher-level block. However, the higher-level block cannot point directly to the sequence set; it must point to the lower-level index blocks. This means that we will now be building *two* levels of the index set in RAM as we build the sequence set. Figure 9.16 illustrates this working-on-two-levels phenomenon: The addition of the CAT separator requires us to start a new, root-level index block as well as a lower-level index block. (Actually, we are working on *three* levels at once since we are also constructing the sequence set blocks in RAM.) Figure 9.17 shows what the index looks like after even more sequence set blocks are added. As you can see, the lower-level index block that contained no separators when we added CAT to the root has now filled up. To establish that the tree works, do a search for the term CATCH. Then search for the two terms CASUAL and CATALOG. How can you tell that these terms are not in the sequence set?

It is instructive to ask what would happen if the last record were CHECK, so the construction of the sequence sets and index sets would stop with the configuration shown in Fig. 9.16. The resulting simple prefix B$^+$ tree would contain an index set node that holds no separators. This is not an isolated, one-time possibility. If we use this sequential loading method to build the tree, there will be many points during the loading process at which there is an empty or nearly empty index set node. If the index set grows to more than two levels, this empty node problem can occur at even higher levels of the tree, creating a potentially severe out-of-balance problem. Clearly, these empty node and nearly empty node conditions violate the B-tree rules that apply to the index set. However, once a tree is loaded and goes into regular use, the very fact that a node is violating B-tree conditions can be used to guarantee that the node will be corrected through the action of normal B-tree maintenance operations. It is easy to write the procedures for insertion and deletion so a redistribution procedure is invoked when an underfull node is encountered.

The advantages of loading a simple prefix B$^+$ tree in this way, as a sequential operation following a sort of the records, almost always outweigh the disadvantages associated with the possibility of creating

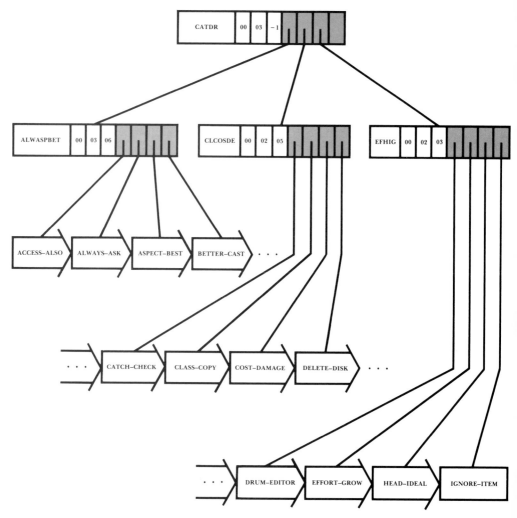

FIGURE 9.17 Continued growth of index set built up from the sequence set.

blocks that contain too few records or too few separators. The principal advantage is that the loading process goes more quickly since

☐ The output can be written sequentially;

☐ We make only one pass over the data, rather than the many passes associated with random order insertions; and

☐ No blocks need to be reorganized as we proceed.

There are two additional advantages to using a separate loading process such as the one we have described. These advantages are related to performance *after* the tree is loaded rather than performance during loading:

- ☐ Random insertion produces blocks that are, on the average, between 67% and 80% full. In the preceding chapter, as we discussed B-trees, we increased this storage utilization by mechanisms such as using redistribution during insertion rather than using just block splitting. But, still, we never had the option of filling the blocks completely so we had 100% utilization. The sequential loading process changes this. If we want, we can load the tree so it starts out with 100% utilization. This is an attractive option if we do not expect to add very many records to the tree. On the other hand, if we do anticipate many insertions, sequential loading allows us to select any other degree of utilization that we want. Sequential loading gives us much more control over the amount and placement of empty space in the newly loaded tree.

- ☐ In the loading example presented in Fig. 9.16, we write out the first four sequence set blocks, then write out the index set block containing the separators for these sequence set blocks. If we use the same file for both sequence set and index set blocks, this process guarantees that an index set block starts out in *physical proximity* to the sequence set blocks that are its descendents. In other words, our sequential loading process is creating a degree of *spatial locality* within our file. This locality can minimize seeking as we search down through the tree.

9.10   B⁺ Trees

Our discussions up to this point have focused primarily on simple prefix B⁺ trees. These structures are actually a variant of an approach to file organization known simply as a *B⁺ Tree*. The difference between a simple prefix B⁺ tree and a plain B⁺ tree is that the latter structure does not involve the use of prefixes as separators. Instead, the separators in the index set are simply copies of the actual keys. Contrast the index set block shown in Fig. 9.18, which illustrates the initial loading steps for a B⁺ tree, with the index block that is illustrated in Fig. 9.15, where we are building a simple prefix B⁺ tree.

The operations performed on B⁺ trees are essentially the same as those discussed for simple prefix B⁺ trees. Both B⁺ trees and simple prefix B⁺ trees consist of a set of records arranged in key order in a sequence set,

FIGURE 9.18 Formation of the first index set block in a B⁺ tree without the use of shortest separators.

coupled with an index set that provides rapid access to the block containing any particular key/record combination. The only difference is that in the simple prefix B⁺ tree we build an index set of shortest separators formed from key prefixes.

One of the reasons behind our decision to focus first on simple prefix B⁺ trees, rather than on the more general notion of a B⁺ tree, is that we want to distinguish between the role of the *separators* in the index set and *keys* in the sequence set. It is much more difficult to make this distinction when the separators are exact copies of the keys. By beginning with simple prefix B⁺ trees, we have the pedagogical advantage of working with separators that are clearly different than the keys in the sequence set.

But another reason for starting with simple prefix B⁺ trees revolves around the fact that they are quite often a more desirable alternative than the plain B⁺ tree. We want the index set to be as shallow as possible, which implies that we want to place as many separators into an index set block as we can. Why use anything longer than the simple prefix in the index set? In general, the answer to this question is that we do not, in fact, want to use anything longer than a simple prefix as a separator; consequently, simple prefix B⁺ trees are often a good solution. There are, however, at least two factors that might argue in favor of using a B⁺ tree that uses full copies of keys as separators:

☐   The reason for using shortest separators is to pack more of them into an index set block. As we have already said, this implies, ineluctably, the use of variable-length fields within the index set blocks. For some applications the cost of the extra overhead required to maintain and use this variable-length structure outweighs the benefits of shorter separators. In these cases one might choose to build a straightforward B$^+$ tree using fixed-length copies of the keys from the sequence set as separators.

☐   Some key sets do not show much compression when the simple prefix method is used to produce separators. For example, suppose the keys consist of large, consecutive alphanumeric sequences such as 34C18K756, 34C18K757, 34C18K758, and so on. In this case, to enjoy appreciable compression, we need to use compression techniques that remove redundancy from the *front* of the key. Bayer and Unterauer (1977) describe such compression methods. Unfortunately, they are more expensive and complicated than simple prefix compression. If we calculate that tree height remains acceptable with the use of full copies of the keys as separators, we might elect to use the no-compression option.

9.11   B-Trees, B$^+$ Trees, and Simple Prefix B$^+$ Trees in Perspective

In this chapter and the preceding chapter we have looked at a number of "tools" used in building file structures. These tools—B-trees, B$^+$ trees, and simple prefix B$^+$ trees—have similar-sounding names and a number of common features. We need a way to differentiate these tools so we can reliably choose the most appropriate one for a given file structure job.

Before addressing this problem of differentiation, however, we should point out that these are not the only tools in the toolbox. Because B-trees, B$^+$ trees, and their relatives are such powerful, flexible file structures, it is easy to fall into the trap of regarding them as the answer to all problems. This is a serious mistake. Simple index structures of the kind discussed in Chapter 6, which are maintained wholly in RAM, are a much simpler, neater solution when they suffice for the job at hand. As we saw at the beginning of this chapter, simple RAM indexes are not limited to direct access situations. This kind of index can be coupled with a sequence set of blocks to provide effective indexed sequential access as well. It is only when the index grows so large that we cannot economically hold it in RAM that we need to turn to paged index structures such as B-trees and B$^+$ trees.

In the chapter that follows we encounter yet another tool, known as *hashing*. Like simple RAM-based indexes, hashing is an important alternative to B-trees, B$^+$ trees, and so on. In many situations, hashing can provide faster access to a very large number of records than can the use of a member of the B-tree family.

So, B-trees, B^+ trees, and simple prefix B^+ trees are not a panacea. However, they do have broad applicability, particularly for situations that require the ability to access a large file both sequentially, in order by key, and through an index. All three of these different tools share the following characteristics:

□   They are all paged index structures, which means that they bring entire blocks of information into RAM at once. As a consequence, it is possible to choose between a great many alternatives (e.g., the keys for hundreds of thousands of records) with just a few seeks out to disk storage. The shape of these trees tends to be broad and shallow.

□   All three approaches maintain height-balanced trees. The trees do not grow in an uneven way, which would result in some potentially long searches for certain keys.

□   In all cases the trees grow from the bottom up. Balance is maintained through block splitting, concatenation, and redistribution.

□   With all three structures it is possible to obtain greater storage efficiency through the use of two-to-three splitting and of redistribution in place of block splitting when possible. These techniques are described in Chapter 8.

□   All three approaches can be implemented as virtual tree structures in which the most recently used blocks are held in RAM. The advantages of virtual trees were described in Chapter 8.

□   Any of these approaches can be adapted for use with variable-length records using structures inside a block similar to those outlined in this chapter.

For all of this similarity, there are some important differences. These differences are brought into focus through a review of the strengths and unique characteristics of each of these three file structures.

B-Trees   B-trees contain information that is grouped as a set of *pairs*. One member of each pair is the *key;* the other member is the *associated information*. These pairs are distributed over *all* the nodes of the B-tree. Consequently, we might find the information we are seeking at any level of the B-tree. This differs from B^+ trees and simple prefix B^+ trees, which require all searches to proceed all the way down to the lowest, sequence set level of the tree. Because the B-tree itself contains the actual keys and associated information, and there is therefore no need for additional storage to hold separators, a B-tree can take up less space than does a B^+ tree.

Given a large enough block size and an implementation that treats the tree as a virtual B-tree, it is possible to use a B-tree for ordered sequential access as well as for indexed access. The ordered sequential access is obtained through an in-order traversal of the tree. The implementation as a virtual tree is necessary so this traversal does not involve seeking as it returns to the next highest level of the tree. This use of a B-tree for indexed sequential access works only when the record information is actually stored within the B-tree. If the B-tree merely contains pointers to records that are in entry sequence off in some other file, then indexed sequential access is not workable because of all the seeking required to retrieve the actual record information.

B-trees are most attractive when the key itself comprises a large part of each record stored in the tree. When the key is only a small part of the record, it is possible to build a broader, shallower tree using B$^+$ tree methods.

B$^+$ Trees   The primary difference between the B$^+$ tree and the B-tree is that in the B$^+$ tree all the key and record information is contained in a linked set of blocks known as the *sequence set*. The key and record information is *not* in the upper-level, tree-like portion of the B$^+$ tree. Indexed access to this sequence set is provided through a conceptually (though not necessarily physically) separate structure called the *index set*. In a B$^+$ tree the index set consists of copies of the keys that represent the boundaries between sequence set blocks. These copies of keys are called *separators* since they separate a sequence set block from its predecessor.

There are two significant advantages that the B$^+$ tree structure provides over the B-tree:

☐   The sequence set can be processed in a truly linear, sequential way, providing efficient access to records in order by key; and

☐   The use of separators, rather than entire records, in the index set often means that the number of *separators* that can be placed in a single index set block in a B$^+$ tree substantially exceeds the number of *records* that could be placed in an equal-sized block in a B-tree. Separators (copies of keys) are simply smaller than the key/record pairs stored in a B-tree. Since you can put more of them in a block of given size, it follows that the number of other blocks descending from that block can be greater. As a consequence, a B$^+$ tree approach can often result in a shallower tree than would a B-tree approach.

In practice, the latter of these two advantages is often the more important one. The impact of the first advantage is lessened by the fact that it is often possible to obtain acceptable performance during an in-order traversal of a B-tree through the page buffering mechanism of a virtual B-tree.

Simple Prefix B⁺ Trees   We just indicated that the primary advantage of using a B⁺ tree instead of a B-tree is that a B⁺ tree sometimes allows us to build a shallower tree because we can obtain a higher branching factor out of the upper-level blocks of the tree. The simple prefix B⁺ tree builds on this advantage by making the separators in the index set *smaller* than the keys in the sequence set, rather than just using copies of these keys. If the separators are smaller, then we can fit more of them into a block to obtain an even higher branching factor out of the block. In a sense, the simple prefix B⁺ tree takes one of the strongest features of the B⁺ tree one step farther.

The price we have to pay to obtain this separator compression and consequent increase in branching factor is that we must use an index set block structure that supports variable-length fields. The question of whether this price is worth the gain is one that has to be considered on a case-by-case basis.

■ SUMMARY

We begin this chapter by presenting a new problem. In previous chapters we provided either indexed access or sequential access in order by key, but without finding an efficient way to provide both of these kinds of access. This chapter explores one class of solutions to this problem, a class based on the use of a blocked sequence set and an associated index set.

The sequence set holds all of the file's data records in order by key. Since all insertion or deletion operations on the file begin with modifications to the sequence set, we start our study of indexed sequential file structures with an examination of a method for managing sequence set changes. The fundamental tools used to insert and delete records while still keeping everything in order within the sequence set are ones that we encountered in Chapter 8: block splitting, block concatenation, and redistribution of records between blocks. The critical difference between the use made of these tools for B-trees and the use made here is that there is no promotion of records or keys during block splitting in a sequence set. A sequence set is just a linked list of blocks, not a tree; therefore there is no place to promote anything to. So, when a block splits, *all* the records are divided between blocks at the same level; when blocks are concatenated there is no need to bring anything down from a parent node.

In this chapter, we also discuss the question of how large to make sequence set blocks. There is no precise answer we can give to this question since conditions vary between applications and environments. In general a block should be large, but not so large that we cannot hold several blocks in RAM or cannot read in a block without incurring the cost of a seek. In practice, blocks are often the size of a cluster (on sector-formatted disks) or the size of a single disk track.

Once we are able to build and maintain a sequence set, we turn to the matter of building an index for the blocks in the sequence set. If the index is small enough to fit in RAM, one very satisfactory solution is to use a simple index that might contain, for example, the key for the last record in every block of the sequence set.

If the index set turns out to be too large to fit in RAM, we recommend the use of the same strategy we developed in the preceding chapter when a simple index outgrows the available RAM space: We turn the index into a B-tree. This combination of a sequence set with a B-tree index set is our first encounter with the structure known as a B^+ *tree*.

Before looking at B^+ trees as complete entities, we take a closer look at the makeup of the index set. The index set does not hold any information that we would ever seek for its own sake. Instead, an index set is used only as a roadmap to guide searches into the sequence set. The index set consists of *separators* that allow us to choose between sequence set blocks. There are many possible separators for any two sequence set blocks, so we might as well choose the *shortest separator*. The scheme we use to find this shortest separator consists of finding the common prefix of the two keys on either side of a block boundary in the sequence set, and then going one letter beyond this common prefix to define a true separator. A B^+ tree with an index set made up of separators formed in this way is called a *simple prefix* B^+ *tree*.

We study the mechanism used to maintain the index set as insertions and deletions are made in the sequence set of a B^+ tree. The principal observation we make about all of these operations is that the primary action is within the *sequence set,* since that is where the records are. Changes to the index set are secondary; they are a byproduct of the fundamental operations on the sequence set. We add a new separator to the index set only if we form a new block in the sequence set; we delete a separator from the index set only if we remove a block from the sequence set through concatenation. Block overflow and underflow in the index set differ from the operations on the sequence set in that the index set is potentially a *multilevel* structure and is therefore handled as a B-tree.

The size of blocks in the index set is usually the same as the size chosen for the sequence set. To create blocks containing variable numbers of variable-length separators while at the same time supporting binary searching, we develop an internal structure for the block that consists of block header fields (for the separator count and total separator length), the variable-length separators themselves, an index to these separators, and a vector of relative block numbers (RBNs) for the blocks descending from the index set block. This illustrates an important general principle about large blocks within file structures: They are more than just a slice out of a homogeneous set of records; blocks often have a sophisticated internal structure of their own, apart from the larger structure of the file.

We turn next to the problem of loading a B^+ tree. We find that if we start with a set of records sorted by key, we can use a single-pass, sequential process to place these records into the sequence set. As we move from block to block in building the sequence set, we can extract separators and build the blocks of the index set. Compared to a series of successive insertions that work down from the top of the tree, this sequential loading process is much more efficient. Sequential loading also lets us choose the percentage of space utilized, right up to a goal of 100%.

The chapter closes with a comparison of B-trees, B^+ trees, and simple prefix B^+ trees. The primary advantages that B^+ trees offer over B-trees are:

- They support true indexed sequential access; and
- The index set contains only separators, rather than full keys and records, so it is often possible to create a B^+ tree that is shallower than a B-tree.

We suggest that the second of these advantages is often the more important one, since treating a B-tree as a virtual tree provides acceptable indexed sequential access in many circumstances. The simple prefix B^+ tree takes this second advantage and carries it farther, compressing the separators and potentially producing an even shallower tree. The price for this extra compression in a simple prefix B^+ tree is that we must deal with variable-length fields and a variable-order tree.

■ KEY TERMS

B^+ **tree.** A B^+ tree consists of a *sequence set* of records that are ordered sequentially by key, along with an *index set* that provides indexed access to the records. All of the records are stored in the sequence set. Insertions and deletions of records are handled by splitting, concatenating, and redistributing blocks in the sequence set. The index set, which is used only as a finding aid to the blocks in the sequence set, is managed as a B-tree.

Index set. The index set consists of *separators* that provide information about the boundaries between the blocks in the sequence set of a B^+ tree. The index set can locate the block in the sequence set that contains the record corresponding to a certain key.

Indexed sequential access. Indexed sequential access is not actually a single-access method, but rather a term used to describe situations in which a user wants both sequential access to records, ordered by key, and indexed access to those same records. B^+ trees are just one method for providing indexed sequential access.

Separator. Separators are derived from the keys of the records on either side of a block boundary in the sequence set. If a given key is in one of the two blocks on either side of a separator, the separator reliably tells the user which of the two blocks holds the key.

Sequence set. The sequence set is the base level of an indexed sequential file structure, such as B^+ tree. It contains all of the records in the file. When read in logical order, block after block, the sequence set lists all of the records in order by key.

Shortest separator. Many possible separators can be used to distinguish between any two blocks in the sequence set. The class of shortest separators consists of those separators that take the least space, given a particular compression strategy. We looked carefully at a compression strategy that consists of removing as many letters as possible from the rear of the separators, forming the shortest simple prefix that can still serve as a separator.

Simple prefix B^+ tree. A B^+ tree in which the index set is made up of *shortest separators* that are simple prefixes, as described in the definition for *shortest separator*.

Variable order. A B-tree is of variable order when the number of direct descendents from any given node of the tree is variable. This occurs when the B-tree nodes contain a variable number of keys or separators. This form is most often used when there is variability in the *lengths* of the keys or separators. Simple prefix B^+ trees always make use of a variable-order B-tree as an index set so it is possible to take advantage of the compression of separators and place more of them in a block.

▉ EXERCISES

1. Describe file structures that permit each of the following types of access: (a) sequential access only; (b) direct access only; (c) indexed sequential access.

2. A B$^+$ tree structure is generally superior to a B-tree for indexed sequential access. Since B$^+$ trees incorporate B-trees, why not use a B$^+$ tree whenever a hierarchical indexed structure is called for?

3. Consider the sequence set shown in Fig. 9.1(b). Show the sequence set after the keys DOVER and EARNEST are added; then show the sequence set after the key DAVIS is deleted. Did you use concatenation or redistribution for handling the underflow?

4. What considerations affect your choice of a block size for constructing a sequence set? If you know something about expected patterns of access (primarily sequential versus primarily random versus an even division between the two), how might this affect your choice of block size? On a sector-oriented drive, how might sector size and cluster size affect your choice of a block size?

5. It is possible to construct an indexed sequential file without using a tree-structured index. A simple index like the one developed in Chapter 6 could be used. Under what conditions might one consider using such an index? Under what conditions might it be reasonable to use a binary tree (such as an AVL tree) rather than a B-tree for the index?

6. The index set of a B$^+$ tree is just a B-tree, but unlike the B-trees discussed in Chapter 8, the separators do not have to be keys. Why the difference?

7. How does block splitting in the sequence set of a simple prefix B$^+$ tree differ from block splitting in the index set?

8. If the key BOLEN in the simple prefix B$^+$ tree in Fig. 9.8 is deleted from the sequence set node, how is the separator BO in the parent node affected?

9. Consider the simple prefix B$^+$ tree shown in Fig. 9.8. Suppose a key added to block 5 results in a split of block 5 and the consequent addition of block 8, so blocks 5 and 8 appear as follows:

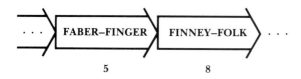

a. What does the tree look like after the insertion?
b. Suppose that, subsequent to the insertion, a deletion causes under-

flow and the consequent concatenation of blocks 4 and 5. What does the tree look like after the deletion?

c. Describe a case in which a deletion results in redistribution, rather than concatenation, and show the effect it has on the tree.

10. Why is it often a good idea to use the same block size for the index set and the sequence set in a simple prefix B^+ tree? Why should the index set nodes and the sequence set nodes usually be kept in the same file?

11. Show a conceptual view of an index set block, similar to the one illustrated in Fig. 9.12, that is loaded with the separators

Ab Arch Astron B Bea

Also show a more detailed view of the index block, as illustrated in Fig. 9.13.

12. If the initial set of records is sorted by key, the process of loading a B^+ tree can be handled by using a single-pass sequential process, instead of randomly inserting new records into the tree. What are the advantages of this approach?

13. Show how the simple prefix B^+ tree in Fig. 9.17 changes after the addition of the node

ITEMIZE–JAR

Assume that the index set node containing the separators EF, H, and IG does not have room for the new separator but that there is room in the root.

14. Use the data stored in the simple prefix B^+ tree in Fig. 9.17 to construct a B^+ tree. Assume that the index set of the B^+ tree is of order four. Compare the resulting B^+ tree with the simple prefix B^+ tree.

15. The use of variable-length separators and/or key compression changes some of the rules about how we define and use a B-tree and how we measure B-tree performance.

a. How does it affect our definition of the order of a B-tree?

b. Suggest criteria for deciding when splitting, concatenation, and redistribution should be performed.

c. What difficulties arise in estimating simple prefix B^+ tree height, maximum number of accesses, and space?

16. Make a table comparing B-trees, B^+ trees, and simple prefix B^+ trees in terms of the criteria listed below. Assume that the B-tree nodes do not contain data records, but only keys and corresponding RRNs of data records. In some cases you will be able to give specific answers based on a tree's height or the number of keys in the tree. In other cases, the answers will depend on unknown factors, such as patterns of access or average separator length.

    a. The number of accesses required to retrieve a record from a tree of height h (average, best case, and worst case).

    b. The number of accesses required to insert a record (best and worst cases).

    c. The number of accesses required to delete a record (best and worst cases).

    d. The number of accesses required to process a file of n keys sequentially, assuming that each node can hold a maximum of k keys and a minimum of $k/2$ keys (best and worst cases).

    e. The number of accesses required to process a file of n keys sequentially, assuming that there are $h + 1$ node-sized buffers available.

17. Some commercially available indexed sequential file organizations are based on block interval splitting approaches very similar to those used with B⁺ trees. IBM's VSAM offers the user several file access modes, one of which is called *key-sequenced* access and which results in a file being organized much like a B⁺ tree. Look up a description of VSAM and report on how its key-sequenced organization relates to a B⁺ tree, and also how it offers the user file handling capabilities well beyond those of a straightforward B⁺ tree implementation. (See the Further Readings section of this chapter for articles and books on VSAM.)

18. Although B⁺ trees provide the basis for most indexed sequential access methods now in use, this was not always the case. A method called ISAM (see Further Readings for this chapter) was once very common, especially on large computers. ISAM uses a rigid tree-structured index consisting of at least two and at most three levels. Indexes at these levels are tailored to the specific disk drive being used. Data records are organized by track, so the lowest level of an ISAM index is called the *track index*. Since the track index points to the track on which a data record can be found, there is one track index for each cylinder. When the addition of data records causes a track to overflow, the track is not split. Instead, the extra records are put into a separate overflow area and chained together in logical order. Hence, every entry in a track index may contain a pointer to the overflow area, in addition to its pointer to the home track.

    The essential difference between the ISAM organization and B⁺ tree–like organizations is in the way overflow records are handled. In the case of ISAM, overflow records are simply added to a chain of overflow records—the index structure is not altered. In the B^+ tree case, overflow records are not tolerated. When overflow occurs, a block is split and the index structure is altered to accommodate the extra data block.

Can you think of any advantages of using the more rigid index structure of ISAM, with separate overflow areas to handle overflow records? Why do you think B^+ tree–like approaches are replacing those that use overflow chains to hold overflow records? Consider the two approaches in terms of both sequential and direct access, as well as addition and deletion of records.

Programming Exercises

We begin this chapter by discussing operations on a sequence set, which is just a linked list of blocks containing records. Only later do we add the concept of an index set to provide faster access to the blocks in the sequence set. The following programming problems echo this approach, requiring you first to write a program that builds a sequence set, then to write functions that maintain the sequence set, and finally to write programs and functions to add an index set to the sequence set, creating a B^+ tree. These programs can be implemented in either C or Pascal.

19. Write a program that accepts a file of strings as input. The input file should be sorted so the strings are in ascending order. Your program should use this input file to build a sequence set with the following characteristics:

☐   The strings are stored in 15-byte records;

☐   A sequence set block is 128 bytes long;

☐   Sequence set blocks are doubly linked;

☐   The first block in the output file is a header block containing, among other things, a reference to the RRN of the first block in the sequence set;

☐   Sequence set blocks are loaded so they are as full as possible; and

☐   Sequence set blocks contain other fields (other than the actual records containing the strings) as needed.

20. Write an update program that accepts strings input from the keyboard, along with an instruction either to search, add, or delete the string from the sequence set. The program should have the following characteristics:

☐   Strings in the sequence set must, of course, be kept in order;

☐   Response to the search instruction should be either found or not found;

☐   A string should not be added if it is already in the sequence set;

□ Blocks in the sequence set should never be allowed to be less than half full; and

□ Splitting, redistribution, and concatenation operations should be written as separate procedures so they can be used in subsequent program development.

21. Write a program that traverses the sequence set created in the preceding exercises and that builds an index set in the form of a B-tree. You may assume that the B-tree index will never be deeper than two levels. The resulting file should have the following characteristics:

□ The index set and the sequence set, taken together, should constitute a B^+ tree;

□ Do not compress the keys as you form the separators for the index set;

□ Index set blocks, like sequence set blocks, should be 128 bytes long; and

□ Index set blocks should be kept in the same file as the sequence set blocks. The header block should contain a reference to the root of the index set as well as the already existing reference to the beginning of the sequence set.

22. Write a new version of the update program that acts on the entire B^+ tree that you created in the preceding exercise. Search, add, and delete capabilities should be supported, as they are in the earlier update program. B-tree characteristics should be maintained in the index set; the sequence set should, as before, be maintained so blocks are always at least half full.

23. Consider the block structure illustrated in Fig. 9.13, in which an index to separators is used to permit binary searching for a key in an index page. Each index set block contains three variable length sets of items: a set of separators, an index to the separators, and a set of relative block numbers. Develop code in Pascal or C for storing these items in an index block and for searching the block for a separator. You need to answer such questions as:

□ Where should the three sets be placed relative to one another?

□ Given the data types permitted by the language you are using, how can you handle the fact that the block consists of *both* character and integer data with no fixed dividing point between them?

□ As items are added to a block, how do you decide when a block is too full to insert another separator?

■ FURTHER READINGS

The initial suggestion for the B^+ tree structure appears to have come from Knuth (1973b), although he did not name or develop the approach. Most of the literature that discusses B^+ trees in detail (as opposed to describing specific implementations such as VSAM) is in the form of articles rather than textbooks. Comer (1979) provides what is perhaps the best brief overview of B^+ trees. Bayer and Unterauer (1977) offer a definitive article describing techniques for compressing separators. The article includes consideration of simple prefix B^+ trees as well as a more general approach called a *prefix B^+ tree*. McCreight (1977) describes an algorithm for taking advantage of the variation in the lengths of separators in the index set of a B^+ tree. McCreight's algorithm attempts to ensure that short separators, rather than longer ones, are promoted as blocks split. The intent is to shape the tree so blocks higher up in the tree have a greater number of immediate descendents, thereby creating a shallower tree.

Rosenberg and Snyder (1981) study the effects of initializing a compact B-tree on later insertions and deletions. The use of batch insertions and deletions to B-trees, rather than individual updates, is proposed and analyzed in Lang et al. (1985). B^+ trees are compared with more rigid indexed sequential file organizations (such as ISAM) in Batory (1981) and in IBM's *VSAM Planning Guide*.

There are many commercial products that use methods related to the B^+ tree operations described in this chapter, but detailed descriptions of their underlying file structures are scarce. An exception to this is IBM's Virtual Storage Access Method (VSAM), one of the most widely used commercial products providing indexed sequential access. Wagner (1973) and Keehn and Lacy (1974) provide interesting insights into the early thinking behind VSAM. They also include considerations of key maintenance, key compression, secondary indexes, and indexes to multiple data sets. Good descriptions of VSAM can be found in several sources, and from a variety of perspectives, in IBM's *VSAM Planning Guide,* Bohl (1981), Comer (1979) (VSAM as an example of a B^+ tree), Bradley (1982) (emphasis on implementation in a PL/I environment), and Loomis (1983) (with examples from COBOL).

VAX-11 Record Management Services (RMS), Digital's file and record access subsystem of the VAX/VMS operating system, uses a B^+ tree−like structure to support indexed sequential access (Digital, 1979). Many microcomputer implementations of B^+ trees can be found, including dBase III and Borland's Turbo Toolbox (Borland, 1984).

Hashing

10

CHAPTER OBJECTIVES

- Introduce the concept of *hashing*.
- Examine the problem of choosing a good *hashing algorithm*, present a reasonable one in detail, and describe some others.
- Explore three approaches for *reducing collisions:* randomization of addresses, use of extra memory, and storage of several records per address.
- Develop and use mathematical tools for analyzing performance differences resulting from the use of different hashing techniques.
- Examine problems associated with *file deterioration* and discuss some solutions.
- Examine effects of *patterns of record access* on performance.

445

10.1 Introduction

$O(1)$ access to files means that no matter how big the file grows, access to a record always takes the same, small number of seeks. By contrast, sequential searching gives us $O(N)$ access, wherein the number of seeks grows in proportion to the size of the file. As we saw in the preceding chapters, B-trees improve on this greatly, providing $O(\log_k N)$ access; the number of seeks increases as the logarithm to the base k of the number of records, where k is a measure of the leaf size. $O(\log_k N)$ access can provide very good retrieval performance, even for very large files, but it is still not $O(1)$ access.

In a sense, $O(1)$ access has been the Holy Grail of file structure design. Everyone agrees that $O(1)$ access is what we want to achieve, but until about 10 years ago it was not clear that one could develop a general class of $O(1)$ access strategies that would work on dynamic files that change greatly in size.

In this chapter we begin with a description of static hashing techniques. They provide us with $O(1)$ access but are not extensible as the file increases in size. Static hashing was the state of the art until about 1980. In the following chapter we show how research and design work during the 1980s has begun to find ways to extend hashing, and $O(1)$ access, to files that are dynamic and increase in size over time.

10.1.1 What is Hashing?

A *hash function* is like a black box that produces an address every time you drop in a key. More formally, it is a function $h(K)$ that transforms a key K into an address. The resulting address is used as the basis for storing and retrieving records.In Fig. 10.1, the key LOWELL is transformed by the hash function to the address 4. That is, $h(LOWELL) = 4$. Address 4 is said to be the *home address* of LOWELL.

Hashing is like indexing in that it involves associating a key with a relative record address. Hashing differs from indexing in two important ways:

☐   With hashing, the addresses generated appear to be random—there is no immediately obvious connection between the key and the location of the corresponding record, even though the key is used to determine the location of the record. For this reason, hashing is sometimes referred to as *randomizing*.

☐   With hashing, two different keys may be transformed to the same address so two records may be sent to the same place in the file. When this occurs, it is called a *collision* and some means must be found to deal with it.

Consider the following simple example. Suppose you want to store 75 records in a file, where the key to each record is a person's name. Suppose also that you set aside space for 1,000 records. The key can be hashed by taking two numbers from the ASCII representations of the first two characters of the name, multiplying these together, then using the rightmost three digits of the result for the address. Table 10.1 shows how three names would produce three addresses. Note that even though the names are listed in alphabetical order, there is no apparent order to the addresses. They appear to be in *random* order.

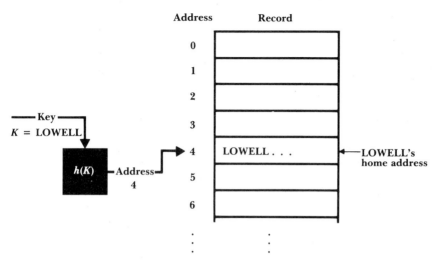

FIGURE 10.1 Hashing the key LOWELL to address 4.

10.1.2 Collisions

Now suppose there is a key in the sample file with the name OLIVIER. Since the name OLIVIER starts with the same two letters as the name LOWELL, they produce the same address (004). There is a *collision* between the record for OLIVIER and the record for LOWELL. We refer to keys that hash to the same address as *synonyms*.

Collisions cause problems. We cannot put two records in the same space, so we must resolve collisions. We do this in two ways: by choosing hashing algorithms partly on the basis of how few collisions they are likely to produce, and by playing some tricks with the ways we store records.

TABLE 10.1 A simple hashing scheme

Name	ASCII Code for First Two Letters	Product	Home Address
BALL	66 65	66 × 65 = 4,290	290
LOWELL	76 79	76 × 79 = 6,004	004
TREE	84 82	84 × 82 = 6,888	888

The ideal solution to collisions is to find a transformation algorithm that avoids collisions altogether. Such an algorithm is called a *perfect hashing algorithm*. It turns out to be much more difficult to find a perfect hashing algorithm than one might expect, however. Suppose, for example, that you want to store 4,000 records among 5,000 available addresses. It can be shown (Hanson, 1982) that of the huge number of possible hashing algorithms for doing this, only one out of $10^{120,000}$ avoids collisions altogether. Hence, it is usually not worth trying.[†]

A more practical solution is to reduce the number of collisions to an acceptable number. For example, if only one out of 10 searches for a record results in a collision, then the *average* number of disk accesses required to retrieve a record remains quite low. There are several different ways to reduce the number of collisions, including the following three:

☐ *Spread out the records.* Collisions occur when two or more records compete for the same address. If we could find a hashing algorithm that distributes the records fairly randomly among the available addresses, then we would not have large numbers of records clustering around certain addresses. Our sample hash algorithm, which uses only two letters from the key, is not good on this account because certain combinations of two letters are quite common in starting names, while others are uncommon (e.g., compare the number of names that start with "JO" with the number that start with "XZ"). We need to find a hashing algorithm that distributes records more randomly.

☐ *Use extra memory.* It is easier to find a hash algorithm that avoids collisions if we have only a few records to distribute among many addresses than if we have about the same number of records as addresses. Our sample hashing algorithm is very good on this account since there are 1,000 possible addresses and only 75 addresses (corresponding to the 75 records) will be generated. The obvious disadvantage to spreading out the records is that storage space is wasted. (In the example, 7.5% of the available record space is used, and the remaining 92.5% is wasted.) There is no simple answer to the question of how much empty space should be tolerated to get the best hashing performance, but some techniques are provided later in this

---

[†]It is not unreasonable to try to generate perfect hashing functions for small (less than 500), stable sets of keys, such as might be used to look up reserved words in a programming language. But files generally contain more than a few hundred keys, or they contain sets of keys that change frequently, so they are not normally considered candidates for perfect hashing functions. See Knuth (1973b), Sager (1985), Chang (1984), and Chichelli (1980) for more on perfect hashing functions.

chapter for measuring the relative gains in performance for different amounts of free space.

□ *Put more than one record at a single address.* Up to now we have assumed tacitly that each physical record location in a file could hold exactly one record, but there is usually no reason why we cannot create our file in such a way that every file address is big enough to hold several records. If, for example, each record is 80 bytes long, and we create a file with 512-byte physical records, we can store up to six records at each file address. Each address is able to tolerate five synonyms. Addresses that can hold several records in this way are sometimes called *buckets*.

In the following sections we elaborate on these collision-reducing methods, and as we do so we present some programs for managing hashed files.

10.2 A Simple Hashing Algorithm

One goal in choosing any hashing algorithm should be to spread out records as uniformly as possible over the range of addresses available. The use of the term *hash* for this technique suggests what is done to achieve this. Our dictionary reminds us that the verb *to hash* means "to chop into small pieces . . . muddle or confuse." The algorithm used previously chops off the first two letters and then uses the resulting ASCII codes to produce a number that is in turn chopped to produce the address. It is not very good at avoiding clusters of synonyms because so many names begin with the same two letters.

One problem with the algorithm is that it does not really do very much hashing. It uses only two letters of the key and it does not do much with the two letters. Now let us look at a hash function that does much more randomizing, primarily because it uses more of the key. It is a reasonably good basic algorithm and is likely to give good results no matter what kinds of keys are used. It is also an algorithm that is not too difficult to alter in case a specific instance of the algorithm does not work well.

This algorithm has three steps:

1. Represent the key in numerical form.
2. Fold and add.
3. Divide by a prime number and use the remainder as the address.

Step 1. Represent the Key in Numerical Form   If the key is already a number, then this step is already accomplished. If it is a string of characters, we take the ASCII code of each character and use it to form a number. For example,

$$\text{LOWELL} = \begin{array}{cccccccccccc} 76 & 79 & 87 & 69 & 76 & 76 & 32 & 32 & 32 & 32 & 32 & 32 \\ L & O & W & E & L & L & \multicolumn{6}{c}{\longleftarrow \text{ Blanks } \longrightarrow} \end{array}$$

In this algorithm we use the entire key, rather than just the first two letters. By using more parts of a key, we increase the likelihood that differences among the keys cause differences in addresses produced. The extra processing time required to do this is usually insignificant when compared to the potential improvement in performance.

Step 2. Fold and Add   *Folding and adding* means chopping off pieces of the number and adding them together. In our algorithm we chop off pieces with two ASCII numbers each:

$$76\ 79\ \vert\ 87\ 69\ \vert\ 76\ 76\ \vert\ 32\ 32\ \vert\ 32\ 32\ \vert\ 32\ 32$$

These number pairs can be thought of as integer variables (rather than character variables, which is how they started out) so we can do arithmetic on them. If we can treat them as integer variables, then we can add them. This is easy to do in C because C allows us to do arithmetic on characters. In Pascal, we can use the *ord()* function to obtain the integer position of a character within the computer's character set.

Before we add the numbers, we have to mention a problem caused by the fact that in most cases the sizes of numbers we can add together are limited. On some microcomputers, for example, integer values that exceed 32,767 (15 bits) cause overflow errors or become negative. For example, adding the first five of the foregoing numbers gives

$$7679 + 8769 + 7676 + 3232 + 3232 = 30588.$$

Adding in the last 3,232 would, unfortunately, push the result over the maximum 32,767 (30,588 + 3,232 = 33,820), causing an overflow error. Consequently, we need to make sure that each successive sum is less than 32,767. We can do this by first identifying the largest single value we will ever add in our summation, and then making sure after each step that our intermediate result differs from 32,767 by that amount.

In our case, let us assume that keys consist only of blanks and uppercase alphabetic characters, so the largest addend is 9,090, corresponding to ZZ. Suppose we choose 19,937 as our largest allowable intermediate result. This differs from 32,767 by much more than 9,090, so we can be confident (in this example) that no new addition will cause overflow. We can ensure in our algorithm that no intermediate sum exceeds 19,937 by using the *mod* operator, which returns the remainder when one integer is divided by another:

$$
\begin{aligned}
7679 + 8769 &\rightarrow 16448 \rightarrow 16448 \bmod 19937 \rightarrow 16448 \\
16448 + 7676 &\rightarrow 24124 \rightarrow 24124 \bmod 19937 \rightarrow 4187 \\
4187 + 3232 &\rightarrow 7419 \rightarrow 7419 \bmod 19937 \rightarrow 7419 \\
7419 + 3232 &\rightarrow 10651 \rightarrow 10651 \bmod 19937 \rightarrow 10651 \\
10651 + 3232 &\rightarrow 13883 \rightarrow 13883 \bmod 19937 \rightarrow 13883
\end{aligned}
$$

The number 13,883 is the result of the fold-and-add operation.

Why did we use 19,937 as our upper bound rather than, say, 20,000? Because the division and subtraction operations associated with the *mod* operator are more than just a way of keeping the number small; they are part of the transformation work of the hash function. As we see in the discussion for the next step, division by a prime number usually produces a more random distribution than does transformation by a nonprime. The number 19,937 is prime.

Step 3. Divide by the Size of the Address Space   The purpose of this step is to cut down to size the number produced in step 2 so it falls within the range of addresses of records in the file. This can be done by dividing that number by a number that is the address size of the file, and then taking the remainder. The remainder will be the home address of the record.

We can represent this operation symbolically as follows: If s represents the sum produced in step 2 (13,820 in the example), n represents the divisor (the number of addresses in the file), and a represents the address we are trying to produce, we apply the formula

$$a = s \bmod n.$$

The remainder produced by the mod operator will be a number between 0 and $n - 1$.

Suppose, for example, that we decide to use the 100 addresses 0–99 for our file. In terms of the preceding formula,

$$
\begin{aligned}
a &= 13820 \bmod 100 \\
&= 20.
\end{aligned}
$$

Since the number of addresses allocated for the file does not have to be any specific size (as long as it is big enough to hold all of the actual records to be stored in the file), we have a great deal of freedom in choosing the divisor n. It is a good thing that we do, because the choice of n can have a major effect on how well the records are spread out.

A *prime* number is usually used for the divisor because primes tend to distribute remainders much more uniformly than do nonprimes. A nonprime can work well in many cases, however, especially if it has no

```
FUNCTION hash(KEY,MAXAD)

    set SUM to 0
    set J to 0

    while (J < 12)
        set SUM to (SUM + 100*KEY[J] + KEY[J + 1]) mod 19937
        increment J by 2
    endwhile

    return (SUM mod MAXAD)

end FUNCTION
```

FIGURE 10.2 Function *hash(KEY,MAXAD)* uses folding and prime number division to compute a hash address.

prime divisors less than 20 (Hanson, 1982). Since the remainder is going to be the address of a record, we choose a number as close as possible to the desired size of the address space. This number actually determines the size of the address space. For a file with 75 records, a good choice might be 101, which would leave the file 74.3% full (74/101 = 0.743).

If 101 is the size of the address space, the home address of the record in the example becomes

$$a = 13820 \bmod 101$$
$$= 84.$$

Hence, *the record whose key is LOWELL is assigned to record number 84 in the file.*

The procedure described previously can be carried out with a function that we call *hash()*, described mostly in pseudocode in Fig. 10.2. Procedure *hash()* takes two inputs: *KEY,* which must be an array of ASCII codes for at least 12 characters, and *MAXAD,* which has the address size. The value returned by *hash()* is the address.

10.3 Hashing Functions and Record Distributions

Of the two hash functions we have so far examined, one spreads out records pretty well, and one does not spread them out well at all. In this section we look at ways to describe distributions of records in files. Understanding distributions makes it easier to discuss other hashing methods.

10.3.1 Distributing Records among Addresses

Figure 10.3 illustrates three different distributions of seven records among 10 addresses. Ideally, a hash function should distribute records in a file so there are no collisions, as illustrated by distribution (a). Such a distribution is called *uniform* because the records are spread out uniformly among the addresses. We pointed out earlier that completely uniform distributions are so hard to find that it is generally not considered worth trying to find them.

Distribution (b) illustrates the worst possible kind of distribution. All records share the same home address, resulting in the maximum number of collisions. The more a distribution looks like this one, the more collisions will be a problem.

Distribution (c) illustrates a distribution in which the records are somewhat spread out, but with a few collisions. This is the most likely case if we have a function that distributes keys *randomly*. If a hash function is random, then for a given key every address has the same likelihood of being chosen as every other address. The fact that a certain address is chosen for one key neither diminishes nor increases the likelihood that the same address will be chosen for another key.

It should be clear that if a random hash function is used to generate a large number of addresses from a large number of keys, then simply *by chance* some addresses are going to be generated more often than others. If you have, for example, a random hash function that generates addresses between 0 and 99, and you give the function 100 keys, you would expect

FIGURE 10.3 Different distributions. (a) No synonyms (uniform). (b) All synonyms (worst case). (c) A few synonyms.

some of the 100 addresses to be chosen more than once and some to be chosen not at all.

Although a random distribution of records among available addresses is not ideal, it is an acceptable alternative, given that it is practically impossible to find a function that gives a uniform distribution. Uniform distributions may be out of the question, but there are times when we can find distributions that are better than random in the sense that, while they do generate a fair number of synonyms, they spread out records among addresses more uniformly than does a random distribution.

10.3.2 Some Other Hashing Methods

It would be nice if there were a hash function that guaranteed a better-than-random distribution in all cases, but there is not. The distribution generated by a hashing function depends on the set of keys that are actually hashed. Therefore, the choice of a proper hashing function should involve some intelligent consideration of the keys to be hashed, and perhaps some experimentation. The approaches to choosing a reasonable hashing function covered in this section are ones that have been found to work well, given the right circumstances. Further details on these and other methods can be found in Knuth (1973b), Maurer (1975), Hanson (1982), and Sorenson et al. (1978).

Here are some methods that are potentially better than random:

☐ *Examine keys for a pattern.* Sometimes keys fall in patterns that naturally spread themselves out. This is more likely to be true of numeric keys than of alphabetic keys. For example, a set of employee identification numbers might be ordered according to when the employees entered an organization. This might even lead to *no* synonyms. If some *part* of a key shows a usable underlying pattern, a hash function that extracts that part of the key can also be used.

☐ *Fold parts of the key.* Folding is one stage in the method discussed earlier. It involves extracting digits from part of a key and adding the extracted parts together. This method destroys the original key patterns but in some circumstances may preserve the separation between certain *subsets* of keys that naturally spread themselves out.

☐ *Divide the key by a number.* Division by the address size and use of the remainder usually is involved somewhere in a hash function since the purpose of the function is to produce an address within a certain range. Division preserves consecutive key sequences, so you can take advantage of sequences that effectively spread out keys. However, if there are *several* consecutive key sequences, division by a number that has many small factors can result in many collisions. Research has shown that numbers with no divisors less than 19 generally avoid this problem. Division by a *prime* is even more likely than division by a nonprime to generate different results from different consecutive sequences.

The preceding methods are designed to take advantage of natural orderings among the keys. The next two methods should be tried when, for some reason, the better-than-random methods do not work. In these cases, randomization is the goal.

- ☐ *Square the key and take the middle.* This popular method (often called the *mid-square* method) involves treating the key as a single large number, squaring the number, and extracting whatever number of digits is needed from the middle of the result. For example, suppose you want to generate addresses between 0 and 99. If the key is the number 453, its square is 205,209. Extracting the middle two digits yields a number between 0 and 99, in this case 52. As long as the keys do not contain many leading or trailing zeros, this method usually produces fairly random results. One unattractive feature of this method is that it often requires multiple precision arithmetic.
- ☐ *Radix transformation.* This method involves converting the key to some number base other than the one you are working in, and then taking the result modulo the maximum address as the hash address. For example, suppose you want to generate addresses between 0 and 99. If the key is the decimal number 453, its base 11 equivalent is 382; 382 mod 99 = 85, so 85 is the hash address.

Radix transformation is generally more reliable than the mid-square method for approaching true randomization, though mid-square has been found to give good results when applied to some sets of keys.

10.3.3 Predicting the Distribution of Records

Given that it is nearly impossible to achieve a uniform distribution of records among the available addresses in a file, it is important to be able to predict how records are likely to be distributed. If we know, for example, that a large number of addresses is likely to have far more records assigned to them than they can hold, then we know that there are going to be a lot of collisions.

Although there are no nice mathematical tools available for predicting collisions among distributions that are better than random, there are mathematical tools for understanding just this kind of behavior when records are distributed randomly. If we assume a random distribution (knowing that very likely it will be better than random), we can use these tools to obtain conservative estimates of how our hashing method is likely to behave.

The Poisson Distribution[†]   We want to predict the number of collisions that are likely to occur in a file that can hold only one record at an address. We begin by concentrating on what happens to a single given address when a hash function is applied to a key. We would like to answer the following questions. When all of the keys in a file are hashed, what is the likelihood that

- ☐ None will hash to the given address?
- ☐ Exactly one key will hash to the address?
- ☐ Exactly two keys will hash to the address (two synonyms)?
- ☐ Exactly three, four (and so on) keys will hash to the address?
- ☐ All keys in the file will hash to the same given address?

Which of these outcomes would you expect to be fairly likely, and which quite unlikely? Suppose there are N addresses in a file. When a single key is hashed, there are two possible outcomes with respect to the given address:

A—The address is not chosen; or

B—The address is chosen.

How do we express the probabilities of the two outcomes? If we let both $p(A)$ and a stand for the probability that the address is not chosen, and $p(B)$ and b stand for the probability that the address is chosen, then

$$p(B) = b = \frac{1}{N},$$

since the address has one chance in N of being chosen, and

$$p(A) = a = \frac{N-1}{N} = 1 - \frac{1}{N}$$

[†]This section develops a formula for predicting the ways in which records will be distributed among addresses in a file if a random hashing function is used. The discussion assumes knowledge of some elementary concepts of probability and combinatorics. You may want to skip the development and go straight to the formula, which is introduced in the next section.

since the address has $N - 1$ chances in N of not being chosen. If there are 10 addresses $(N = 10)$, the probability of our address being chosen is $b = 1/10 = 0.1$, and the probability of the address not being chosen is $a = 1 - 0.1 = 0.9$.

Now suppose *two* keys are hashed. What is the probability that both keys hash to our given address? Since the two applications of the hashing function are independent of one another, the probability that both will produce the given address is a *product:*

$$p(BB) = b \times b = \frac{1}{N} \times \frac{1}{N} \qquad \text{for } N = 10: b \times b = 0.1 \times 0.1 = 0.01.$$

Of course, other outcomes are possible when two keys are hashed. For example, the second key could hash to an address other than the given address. The probability of this is the product

$$p(BA) = b \times a = \frac{1}{N} \times \left(1 - \frac{1}{N}\right) \qquad \text{for } N = 10: b \times a = 0.1 \times 0.9 = 0.09.$$

In general, when we want to know the probability of a certain sequence of outcomes, such as *BABBA,* we can replace each A and B by a and b, respectively, and compute the indicated product:

$$p(BABBA) = b \times a \times b \times b \times a = a^2b^3 \qquad \text{for } N = 10: a^2b^3 = (0.9)^2(0.1)^3.$$

This example shows how to find the probability of three Bs and two As, where the Bs and As occur in the order shown. We want to know the probability that there are a certain number of Bs and As, but *without regard to order.* For example, suppose we are hashing four keys and we want to know how likely it is that exactly two of the keys hash to our given address. This can occur in six ways, all six ways having the same probability:

Outcome	Probability	For $N = 10$
BBAA	$bbaa = b^2a^2$	$(0.1)^2(0.9)^2 = 0.0036$
BABA	$baba = b^2a^2$	$(0.1)^2(0.9)^2 = 0.0036$
BAAB	$baab = b^2a^2$	$(0.1)^2(0.9)^2 = 0.0036$
ABBA	$abba = b^2a^2$	$(0.1)^2(0.9)^2 = 0.0036$
ABAB	$abab = b^2a^2$	$(0.1)^2(0.9)^2 = 0.0036$
AABB	$aabb = b^2a^2$	$(0.1)^2(0.9)^2 = 0.0036$

Since these six sequences are independent of one another, the probability of two Bs and two As is the sum of the probabilities of the individual outcomes:

$$p(BBAA) + p(BABA) + \ldots + p(AABB) = 6b^2a^2 = 6 \times 0.0036 = 0.0216.$$

The 6 in the expression $6b^2a^2$ represents the number of ways two Bs and two As can be distributed among four places.

In general, the event "r trials result in $r - x$ As and x Bs" can happen in as many ways as $r - x$ letters A can be distributed among r places. The probability of each such way is

$$a^{r-x}b^x$$

and the number of such ways is given by the formula

$$C = \frac{r!}{(r - x)!x!}.$$

This is the well-known formula for the number of ways of selecting x items out of a set of r items. It follows that when r keys are hashed, the probability that an address will be chosen x times and not chosen $r - x$ times can be expressed as

$$p(x) = Ca^{r-x}b^x.$$

Furthermore, if we know that there are N addresses available, we can be precise about the individual probabilities of A and B, and the formula becomes

$$p(x) = C\left(1 - \frac{1}{N}\right)^{r-x}\left(\frac{1}{N}\right)^x,$$

where C has the definition given previously.

What does this *mean*? It means that if, for example, $x = 0$, we can compute the probability that a given address will have 0 records assigned to it by the hashing function using the formula

$$p(0) = C\left(1 - \frac{1}{N}\right)^{r-0}\left(\frac{1}{N}\right)^0.$$

If $x = 1$, this formula gives the probability that *one* record will be assigned to a given address:

$$p(1) = C\left(1 - \frac{1}{N}\right)^{r-1}\left(\frac{1}{N}\right)^1.$$

This expression has the disadvantage that it is awkward to compute. (Try it for 1,000 addresses and 1,000 records: $N = r = 1,000$.) Fortunately, for large values of N and r, there is a function that is a very good approximation for $p(x)$ and is much easier to compute. It is called the *Poisson function*.

The Poisson Function Applied to Hashing   The Poisson function, which we also denote by $p(x)$, is given by

$$p(x) = \frac{(r/N)^x e^{-(r/N)}}{x!},$$

where N, r, x, and $p(x)$ have exactly the same meaning they have in the previous section. That is, if

N = the number of available addresses;

r = the number of records to be stored; and

x = the number of records assigned to a given address,

then $p(x)$ *gives the probability that a given address will have had x records assigned to it after the hashing function has been applied to all n records.*

Suppose, for example, that there are 1,000 addresses $(N = 1,000)$ and 1,000 records whose keys are to be hashed to the addresses $(r = 1,000)$. Since $r/N = 1$, the probability that a given address will have *no* keys hashed to it $(x = 0)$ becomes

$$p(0) = \frac{1^0 e^{-1}}{0!} = 0.368.$$

The probabilities that a given address will have exactly one, two, or three keys, respectively, hashed to it are

$$p(1) = \frac{1^1 e^{-1}}{1!} = 0.368$$

$$p(2) = \frac{1^2 e^{-1}}{2!} = 0.184$$

$$p(3) = \frac{1^3 e^{-1}}{3!} = 0.061.$$

If we can use the Poisson function to estimate the probability that a given address will have a certain number of records, we can also use it to predict the number of addresses that will have a certain number of records assigned.

For example, suppose there are 1,000 addresses $(N = 1,000)$ and 1,000 records $(r = 1,000)$. Multiplying 1,000 by the probability that a *given* address will have x records assigned to it gives the expected *total* number of addresses with x records assigned to them. That is, $1,000p(x)$ gives the number of addresses with x records assigned to them.

In general, if there are N addresses, then the expected number of addresses with x records assigned to them is

$$Np(x).$$

This suggests another way of thinking about $p(x)$. Rather than thinking about $p(x)$ as a measure of probability, *we can think of $p(x)$ as giving the proportion of addresses having x logical records assigned by hashing.*

Now that we have a tool for predicting the expected proportion of addresses that will have zero, one, two, etc. records assigned to them by a random hashing function, we can apply this tool to predicting numbers of collisions.

10.3.4 Predicting Collisions for a Full File

Suppose you have a hashing function that you believe will distribute records randomly, and you want to store 10,000 records in 10,000 addresses. How many addresses do you expect to have no records assigned to them?

Since $r = 10,000$ and $N = 10,000$, $r/N = 1$. Hence the proportion of addresses with 0 records assigned should be

$$p(0) = \frac{1^0 e^{-1}}{0!} = 0.3679.$$

The *number* of addresses with no records assigned is

$$10,000 \times p(0) = 3,679.$$

How many addresses should have one, two, and three records assigned, respectively?

$$10,000 \times p(1) = 0.3679 \times 10,000 = 3,679$$

$$10,000 \times p(2) = 0.1839 \times 10,000 = 1,839$$

$$10,000 \times p(3) = 0.0613 \times 10,000 = 613.$$

Since the 3,679 addresses corresponding to $x = 1$ have exactly one record assigned to them, their records have no synonyms. The 1,839 addresses with two records apiece, however, represent potential trouble. If each such address has space only for one record, and two records are assigned to them, there is a collision. This means that 1,839 records will fit into the addresses, but another 1,839 will not fit. There will be 1,839 *overflow* records.

Each of the 613 addresses with three records apiece has an even bigger problem. If each address has space for only one record, there will be two overflow records per address. Corresponding to these addresses will be a total of 2 × 613 = 1,226 overflow records. This is a bad situation. We have thousands of records that do not fit into the addresses assigned by the hashing function. We need to develop a method for handling these overflow records. But first, let's try to reduce the *number* of overflow records.

10.4 How Much Extra Memory Should Be Used?

We have seen the importance of choosing a good hashing algorithm to reduce collisions. A second way to decrease the number of collisions (and thereby decrease the average search length) is to use extra memory. The tools developed in the previous section can be used to help us determine the effect of the use of extra memory on performance.

10.4.1 Packing Density

The term *packing density* refers to the ratio of the number of records to be stored (r) to the number of available spaces (N):[†]

$$\frac{\text{Number of records}}{\text{Number of spaces}} = \frac{r}{N} = \text{packing density.}$$

For example, if there are 75 records $(n = 75)$ and 100 addresses $(N = 100)$, the packing density is

$$\frac{75}{100} = 0.75 = 75\%.$$

The packing density gives a measure of the amount of space in a file that is actually used, and it is the only such value needed to assess performance in a hashing environment, assuming that the hash method used gives a reasonably random distribution of records. The raw size of a file and its address space do not matter; what is important is the relative sizes of the two, which are given by the packing density.

Think of packing density in terms of tin cans lined up on a 10-foot length of fence. If there are 10 tin cans and you throw a rock, there is a certain likelihood that you will hit a can. If there are 20 cans on the same length of fence, the fence has a higher packing density and your rock is more likely to hit a can. So it is with records in a file. The more records

---

[†]We assume here that only one record can be stored at each address. In fact, that is not necessarily the case, as we see later.

there are packed into a given file space, the more likely it is that a collision will occur when a new record is added.

We need to decide how much space we are willing to waste to reduce the number of collisions. The answer depends in large measure on particular circumstances. We want to have as few collisions as possible, but not, for example, at the expense of requiring the file to use two disks instead of one.

10.4.2 Predicting Collisions for Different Packing Densities

We need a quantitative description of the effects of changing the packing density. In particular, we need to be able to predict the number of collisions that are likely to occur for a given packing density. Fortunately, the Poisson function provides us with just the tool to do this.

You may have noted already that the formula for packing density (r/N) occurs twice in the Poisson formula

$$p(x) = \frac{(r/N)^x e^{-r/N}}{x!}.$$

Indeed, the numbers of records (r) and addresses (N) always occur together as the *ratio* r/N. They never occur independently. An obvious implication of this is that the way records are distributed depends partly on the ratio of the number of records to the number of available addresses, and *not* on the absolute numbers of records or addresses. The same behavior is exhibited by 500 records distributed among 1,000 addresses as by 500,000 records distributed among 1,000,000 addresses.

Suppose that 1,000 addresses are allocated to hold 500 records in a randomly hashed file, and that each address can hold one record. The packing density for the file is

$$\frac{r}{N} = \frac{500}{1,000} = 0.5.$$

Let us answer the following questions about the distribution of records among the available addresses in the file:

☐ How many addresses should have no records assigned to them?
☐ How many addresses should have exactly one record assigned (no synonyms)?
☐ How many addresses should have one record *plus* one or more synonyms?
☐ Assuming that only one record can be assigned to each home address, how many overflow records can be expected?
☐ What percentage of records should be overflow records?

1. *How many addresses should have no records assigned to them?* Since $p(0)$ gives the *proportion* of addresses with no records assigned, the number of such addresses is

$$Np(0) = 1,000 \times \frac{(0.5)^0 e^{-0.5}}{0!}$$
$$= 1,000 \times 0.607$$
$$= 607.$$

2. *How many addresses should have exactly one record assigned (no synonyms)?*

$$Np(1) = 1,000 \times \frac{(0.5)^1 e^{-0.5}}{1!}$$
$$= 1,000 \times 0.303$$
$$= 303.$$

3. *How many addresses should have one record plus one or more synonyms?* The values of $p(2)$, $p(3)$, $p(4)$, and so on give the proportions of addresses with one, two, three, and so on synonyms assigned to them. Hence the sum

$$p(2) + p(3) + p(4) + \ \cdots$$

gives the proportion of all addresses with at least one synonym. This may appear to require a great deal of computation, but it doesn't since the values of $p(x)$ grow quite small for x larger than 3. This should make intuitive sense. Since the file is only 50% loaded, one would not expect very many keys to hash to any one address. Therefore, the number of addresses with more than about three keys hashed to them should be quite small. We need only compute the results up to $p(5)$ before they become insignificantly small:

$$p(2) + p(3) + p(4) + p(5) = 0.0758 + 0.0126 + 0.0016 + 0.0002$$
$$= 0.0902.$$

The *number* of addresses with one or more synonyms is just the product of N and this result:

$$N[p(2) + p(3) + \ \cdots \ ] = 1,000 \times 0.0902$$
$$= 90.$$

4. *Assuming that only one record can be assigned to each home address, how many overflow records could be expected?* For each of the addresses represented by $p(2)$, one record can be stored at the address and one must be an overflow record. For each address represented by $p(3)$, one record can be stored at the address, *two* are overflow records,

and so on. Hence, the expected number of overflow records is given by

$$1 \times N \times p(2) + 2 \times N \times p(3) + 3 \times N \times p(4) + 4 \times N \times p(5)$$
$$= N \times [1 \times p(2) + 2 \times p(3) + 3 \times p(4) + 4 \times p(5)]$$
$$= 1{,}000 \times [1 \times 0.0758 + 2 \times 0.0126 + 3 \times 0.0016 + 4 \times 0.0002]$$
$$= 107.$$

5. *What percentage of records should be overflow records?* If there are 107 overflow records and 500 records in all, then the proportion of over-flow records is

$$\frac{107}{500} = 0.214 = 21.4\%.$$

Conclusion: If the packing density is 50% and each address can hold only one record, we can expect about 21% of all records to be stored somewhere other than at their home addresses.

Table 10.2 shows the proportion of records that are not stored in their home addresses for several different packing densities. The table shows that if the packing density is 10%, then about 5% of the time we try to access a record, there is already another record there. If the density is 100%, then about 37% of all records collide with other records at their home addresses. The 4.8% collision rate that results when the packing density is 10% looks

TABLE 10.2 Effect of packing density on the proportion of records not stored at their home addresses

Packing Density (%)	Synonyms as % of Records
10	4.8
20	9.4
30	13.6
40	17.6
50	21.4
60	24.8
70	28.1
80	31.2
90	34.1
100	36.8

very good until you realize that for every record in your file there will be nine unused spaces!

The 36.8% that results from 100% usage looks good when viewed in terms of 0% unused space. Unfortunately, 36.8% doesn't tell the whole story. If 36.8% of the records are not at their home addresses, then they are somewhere else, probably in many cases using addresses that are home addresses for other records. The more homeless records there are, the more contention there is for space with other homeless records. After a while, clusters of overflow records can form, leading in some cases to extremely long searches for some of the records. Clearly, the placement of records that collide is an important matter. Let us now look at one simple approach to placing overflow records.

10.5 Collision Resolution by Progressive Overflow

Even if a hashing algorithm is very good, it is likely that collisions will occur. Therefore, any hashing program must incorporate some method for dealing with records that cannot fit into their home addresses. There are a number of techniques for handling overflow records, and the search for

FIGURE 10.4 Collision resolution with progressive overflow.

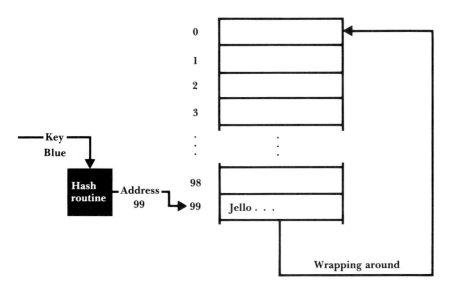

FIGURE 10.5 Searching for an address beyond the end of a file.

ever-better techniques continues to be a lively area of research. We examine several approaches, but we concentrate on a very simple one that often works well. The technique has various names, including *progressive overflow* and *linear probing*.

10.5.1 How Progressive Overflow Works

An example of a situation in which a collision occurs is shown in Fig. 10.4. In the example, we want to store the record whose key is York in the file. Unfortunately, the name York hashes to the same address as the name Rosen, whose record is already stored there. Since York cannot fit in its home address, it is an overflow record. If progressive overflow is used, the next several addresses are searched in sequence until an empty one is found. The first free address becomes the address of the record. In the example, address 9 is the first record found empty, so the record pertaining to York is stored in address 9.

Eventually we need to find York's record in the file. Since York still hashes to 6, the search for the record begins at address 6. It does not find York's record there, so it proceeds to look at successive records until it gets to address 9, where it finds York.

An interesting problem occurs when there is a search for an open space or for a record at the *end* of the file. This is illustrated in Fig. 10.5, in which it is assumed that the file can hold 100 records in addresses 0–99. Blue is hashed to record number 99, which is already occupied by Jello. Since the file holds only 100 records, it is not possible to use 100 as the next address. The way this is handled in progressive overflow is to wrap around the address space of the file by choosing address 0 as the next address. Since, in this case, address 0 is not occupied, Blue gets stored in address 0.

What happens if there is a search for a record but the record was never placed in the file? The search begins, as before, at the record's home address, and then proceeds to look for it in successive locations. Two things can happen:

☐   If an open address is encountered, the searching routine might as-sume this means that the record is not in the file; or

☐   If the file is full, the search comes back to where it began. Only then is it clear that the record is not in the file. When this occurs, or even when we approach filling our file, searching can become intolerably slow, whether or not the record being sought is in the file.

The greatest strength of progressive overflow is its simplicity. In many cases, it is a perfectly adequate method. There are, however, collision-handling techniques that perform better than progressive overflow, and we examine some of them later in this chapter. Now let us look at the effect of progressive overflow on performance.

10.5.2 Search Length

The reason to avoid overflow is, of course, that extra searches (hence, extra disk accesses) have to occur when a record is not found in its home address. If there are a lot of collisions, there are going to be a lot of overflow records taking up spaces where they ought not to be. Clusters of records can form, resulting in the placement of records a long way from home, so many disk accesses are required to retrieve them.

Consider the following set of keys and the corresponding addresses produced by some hash function.

Key	Home Address
Adams	20
Bates	21
Cole	21
Dean	22
Evans	20

Actual address		Home address	Number of accesses needed to retrieve
0			
. . .	. . .		
20	Adams . . .	20	1
21	Bates . . .	21	1
22	Cole . . .	21	2
23	Dean . . .	22	2
24	Evans . . .	20	5
25			
. . .	. . .		

FIGURE 10.6 Illustration of the effects of clustering of records. As keys are clustered, the number of accesses required to access later keys can become large.

If these records are loaded into an empty file, and progressive overflow is used to resolve collisions, only two of the records will be at their home addresses. All the others require extra accesses to retrieve. Figure 10.6 shows where each key is stored, together with information on how many accesses are required to retrieve it.

The term *search length* refers to the number of accesses required to retrieve a record from secondary memory. In the context of hashing, the search length for a record increases every time there is a collision. If a record is a long way from its home address, the search length may be unacceptable. A good measure of the extent of the overflow problem is *average search length*. The average search length is just the average number of times you can expect to have to access the disk to retrieve a record. A rough estimate of average search length may be computed by finding the *total search length* (the sum of the search lengths of the individual records) and dividing this by the number of records:

$$\text{Average search length} = \frac{\text{total search length}}{\text{total number of records}}.$$

In the example, the average search length for the five records is

$$\frac{1 + 1 + 2 + 2 + 5}{5} = 2.2.$$

With no collisions at all, the average search length is 1, since only one access is needed to retrieve any record. (We indicated earlier that an algorithm that distributes records so evenly that no collisions occur is appropriately called a *perfect* hashing algorithm, and that, unfortunately, such an algorithm is almost impossible to construct.) On the other hand, if a large number of the records in a file results in collisions, the average search length becomes quite long. There are ways to estimate the expected average search length, given various file specifications, and we discuss them in a later section.

It turns out that, using progressive overflow, the average search length goes up very rapidly as the packing density increases. The curve in Fig. 10.7, adapted from Peterson (1957), illustrates the problem. If the packing density is kept as low as 60%, the average record takes fewer than two tries to access, but for a much more desirable packing density of 80% or more, it increases very rapidly.

Average search lengths of greater than 2.0 are generally considered unacceptable, so it appears that it is usually necessary to use less than 40% of your storage space to get tolerable performance. Fortunately, we can

FIGURE 10.7 Average search length versus packing density in a hashed file in which one record can be stored per address, progressive overflow is used to resolve collisions, and the file has just been loaded.

Average search length

Packing density

improve on this situation substantially by making one small change to our hashing program. The change involves putting more than one record at a single address.

10.6 Storing More Than One Record per Address: Buckets

Recall that when a computer receives information from a disk, it is just about as easy for the I/O system to transfer several records as it is to transfer a single record. Recall too that sometimes it might be advantageous to think of records as being grouped together in *blocks* rather than stored individually. Therefore, why not extend the idea of a record address in a file to an address of a *group* of records? The word *bucket* is sometimes used to describe a block of records that is retrieved in one disk access, especially when those records are seen as sharing the same address. On sector-addressing disks, a bucket typically consists of one or more sectors; on block-addressing disks, a bucket might be a block.

Consider the following set of keys, which is to be loaded into a hash file.

Key	Home Address
Green	30
Hall	30
Jenks	32
King	33
Land	33
Marx	33
Nutt	33

Figure 10.8 illustrates part of a file into which the records with these keys are loaded. Each address in the file identifies a bucket capable of holding the records corresponding to three synonyms. Only the record corresponding to Nutt cannot be accommodated in a home address.

When a record is to be stored or retrieved, its home *bucket address* is determined by hashing. The entire bucket is loaded into primary memory. An in-RAM search through successive records in the bucket can then be used to find the desired record. When a bucket is filled, we still have to worry about the record overflow problem (as in the case of Nutt), but this occurs much less often when buckets are used than when each address can hold only one record.

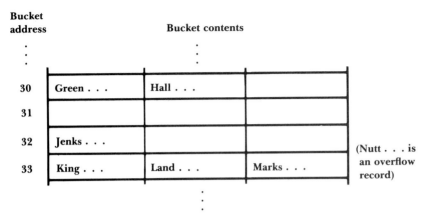

FIGURE 10.8 An illustration of buckets. Each bucket can hold up to three records. Only one synonym (Nutt) results in overflow.

10.6.1 Effects of Buckets on Performance

When buckets are used, the formula used to compute packing density is changed slightly since each bucket address can hold more than one record. To compute how densely packed a file is, we need to consider both the number of addresses (buckets) and the number or records we can put at each address (bucket size). If N is the number of addresses and b is the number of records that fit in a bucket, then bN is the number of available locations for records. If r is still the number of records in the file, then

$$\text{Packing density} = \frac{r}{bN}.$$

Suppose we have a file in which 750 records are to be stored. Consider the following two ways we might organize the file.

☐ We can store the 750 data records among 1,000 locations, where each location can hold one record. The packing density in this case is

$$\frac{750}{1,000} = 75\%.$$

☐ We can store the 750 records among 500 locations, where each location has a bucket size of 2. There are still 1,000 places (2 × 500) to store the 750 records, so the packing density is still

$$\frac{r}{bN} = 0.75 = 75\%.$$

Since the packing density is not changed, we might at first not expect the use of buckets in this way to improve performance, but in fact it does improve performance dramatically. The key to the improvement is that, although there are fewer addresses, each individual address has more room for variation in the number of records assigned to it.

Let's calculate the difference in performance for these two ways of storing the same number of records in the same amount of space. The starting point for our calculations is the fundamental description of each file structure.

	File without Buckets	File with Buckets
Number of records	$r = 750$	$r = 750$
Number of addresses	$N = 1,000$	$N = 500$
Bucket size	$b = 1$	$b = 2$
Packing density	0.75	0.75
Ratio of records to addresses	$r/N = 0.75$	$r/N = 1.5$

To determine the number of overflow records that are expected in the case of each file, recall that when a random hashing function is used, the Poisson function

$$p(x) = \frac{(r/N)^x e^{-r/N}}{x!}$$

gives the expected proportion of addresses assigned x records. Evaluating the function for the two different file organizations, we find that records are assigned to addresses according to the distributions shown in Table 10.3.

We see from the table that when buckets are not used, 42.3% of the addresses have no records assigned, whereas when two-record buckets are used, only 22.3% of the addresses have no records assigned. This should make intuitive sense—since in the two-record case there are only half as many addresses to choose from, it stands to reason that a greater proportion of the addresses are chosen to contain at least one record.

Note that the bucket column in Table 10.3 is longer than the nonbucket column. Does this mean that there are more synonyms in the bucket case than in the nonbucket case? Indeed it does, but half of those synonyms do not result in overflow records because each bucket can hold two records. Let us examine this further by computing the exact number of overflow records likely to occur in the two cases.

TABLE 10.3 Poisson distributions for two different file organizations

p(x)	File without Buckets (r/N = 0.75)	File with Buckets (r/N = 1.5)
p(0)	0.472	0.223
p(1)	0.354	0.335
p(2)	0.133	0.251
p(3)	0.033	0.126
p(4)	0.006	0.047
p(5)	0.001	0.014
p(6)	—	0.004
p(7)	—	0.001

In the case of the file with bucket size one, any address that is assigned exactly one record does not have any overflow. Any address with more than one record does have overflow. Recall that the expected number of overflow records is given by

$$N \times [1 \times p(2) + 2 \times p(3) + 3 \times p(4) + 4 \times p(5) + \ldots]$$

which, for $r/N = 0.75$ and $N = 1{,}000$, is approximately

$$1{,}000 \times [1 \times 0.1328 + 2 \times 0.0332 + 3 \times 0.0062 + 4 \times 0.0009 + 5 \times 0.0001] = 222.$$

The 222 overflow records represent 29.6% overflow.

In the case of the bucket file, any address that is assigned either one *or* two records does not have overflow. The value of $p(1)$ (with $r/N = 1.5$) gives the proportion of addresses assigned exactly one record, and $p(2)$ (with $r/N = 1.5$) gives the proportion of addresses assigned exactly two records. It is not until we get to $p(3)$ that we encounter addresses for which there are overflow records. For each address represented by $p(3)$, two records can be stored at the address, and one must be an overflow record. Similarly, for each address represented by $p(4)$, there are two overflow records, and so forth. Hence, the expected number of overflow records in the bucket file is

$$N \times [1 \times p(3) + 2 \times p(4) + 3 \times p(5) + 4 \times p(6) + \ldots],$$

which for $r/N = 1.5$ and $N = 500$ is approximately

$$500 \times [1 \times 0.1255 + 2 \times 0.0471 + 3 \times 0.0141 + 4 \times 0.0035 + 5 \times 0.0008] = 140.$$

The 140 overflow records represent 18.7% overflow.

We have shown that with one record per address and a packing density of 75%, the expected number of overflow records is 29.6%. When 500 buckets are used, each capable of holding two records, the packing density remains 75%, but the expected number of overflow records drops to 18.7%. That is about a 37% decrease in the number of times the program is going to have to look elsewhere for a record. As the bucket size gets larger, performance continues to improve.

Table 10.4 shows the proportions of collisions that occur for different packing densities and for different bucket sizes. We see from the table, for example, that if we keep the packing density at 75% and increase the bucket size to 10, record accesses result in overflow only 4% of the time.

It should be clear that the use of buckets can improve hashing performance substantially. One might ask, "How big should buckets be?" Unfortunately, there is no simple answer to this question because it depends very much on a number of different characteristics of the system, including

TABLE 10.4 Synonyms causing collisions as a percent of records for different packing densities and different bucket sizes

Packing Density (%)	Bucket Size				
	1	2	5	10	100
10	4.8	0.6	0.0	0.0	0.0
20	9.4	2.2	0.1	0.0	0.0
30	13.6	4.5	0.4	0.0	0.0
40	17.6	7.3	1.1	0.1	0.0
50	21.3	10.4	2.5	0.4	0.0
60	24.8	13.7	4.5	1.3	0.0
70	28.1	17.0	7.1	2.9	0.0
75	29.6	18.7	8.6	4.0	0.0
80	31.2	20.4	10.3	5.3	0.1
90	34.1	23.8	13.8	8.6	0.8
100	36.8	27.1	17.6	12.5	4.0

the sizes of buffers the operating system can manage, sector and track capacities on disks, and access times of the hardware (seek, rotation, and data transfer times).

As a rule, it is probably not a good idea to use buckets larger than a track (unless records are very large). Even a track, however, can sometimes be too large when one considers the amount of time it takes to transmit an entire track, as compared to the amount of time it takes to transmit a few sectors. Since hashing almost always involves retrieving only one record per search, any extra transmission time resulting from the use of extra large buckets is essentially wasted.

In many cases a single cluster is the best bucket size. For example, suppose that a file with 200-byte records is to be stored on a disk system that uses 1,024-byte clusters. One could consider each cluster as a bucket, store five records per cluster, and let the remaining 24 bytes go unused. Since it is no more expensive, in terms of seek time, to access a five-record cluster than it is to access a single record, the only losses from the use of buckets are the extra transmission time and the 24 unused bytes.

The obvious question now is, "How do improvements in the number of collisions affect the average search time?" The answer depends in large measure on characteristics of the drive on which the file is loaded. If there are a large number of tracks in each cylinder, there will be very little seek time because overflow records will be unlikely to spill over from one cylinder to another. If, on the other hand, there is only one track per cylinder, seek time could be a major consumer of search time.

A less exact measure of the amount of time required to retrieve a record is average search length, which we introduced earlier. In the case of buckets, average search length represents the average number of buckets that must be accessed to retrieve a record. Table 10.5 shows the expected average search lengths for files with different packing densities and bucket sizes, given that progressive overflow is used to handle collisions. Clearly, the use of buckets seems to help a great deal in decreasing the average search length. The bigger the bucket, the shorter the search length.

10.6.2 Implementation Issues

In the early chapters of this text, we paid quite a bit of attention to issues involved in producing, using, and maintaining random-access files with fixed-length records that are accessed by relative record number (RRN). Since a hashed file is a fixed-length record file whose records are accessed by RRN, you should already know much about implementing hashed files. Hashed files differ from the files we discussed earlier in two important respects, however:

TABLE 10.5 Average number of accesses required in a successful search by progressive overflow

Packing Density (%)	Bucket Sizes				
	1	**2**	**5**	**10**	**50**
10	1.06	1.01	1.00	1.00	1.00
30	1.21	1.06	1.00	1.00	1.00
40	1.33	1.10	1.01	1.00	1.00
50	1.50	1.18	1.03	1.00	1.00
60	1.75	1.29	1.07	1.01	1.00
70	2.17	1.49	1.14	1.04	1.00
80	3.00	1.90	1.29	1.11	1.01
90	5.50	3.15	1.78	1.35	1.04
95	10.50	5.6	2.7	1.8	1.1

Adapted from Donald Knuth, *The Art of Computer Programming,* Vol. 3, ©1973, Addison-Wesley, Reading, Mass. Page 536. Reprinted with permission.

1. Since a hash function depends on there being a fixed number of available addresses, the logical size of a hashed file must be fixed before the file can be populated with records, and it must remain fixed as long as the same hash function is used. (We use the phrase *logical size* to leave open the possibility that physical space be allocated as needed.)

2. Since the home RRN of a record in a hashed file is uniquely related to its key, any procedures that add, delete, or change a record must do so without breaking the bond between a record and its home address. If this bond is broken, the record is no longer accessible by hashing.

We must keep these special needs in mind when we write programs to work with hashed files.

Bucket Structure   The only difference between a file with buckets and one in which each address can hold only one key is that with a bucket file each address has enough space to hold more than one logical record. All records that are housed in the same bucket share the same address. Suppose, for example, that we want to store as many as *five* names in one bucket. Here are three such buckets with different numbers of records.

An empty bucket:	0	/ / / / /	/ / / / /	/ / / / /	/ / / / /	/ / / / /

Two entries:	2	JONES	ARNSWORTH	/ / / / /	/ / / / /	/ / / / /

A full bucket:	5	JONES	ARNSWORTH	STOCKTON	BRICE	THROOP

Each bucket contains a *counter* that keeps track of how many records it has stored in it. Collisions can occur only when the addition of a new record causes the counter to exceed the number of records a bucket can hold.

The counter tells us how many data records are stored in a bucket, but it does not tell us which slots are used and which are not. We need a way to tell whether or not a record slot is empty. One simple way to do this is to use a special marker to indicate an empty record, just as we did with deleted records earlier. We use the key value ///// to mark empty records in the preceding illustration.

Initializing a File for Hashing   Since the *logical* size of a hashed file must remain fixed, it makes sense in most cases to allocate physical space for the file before we begin storing data records in it. This is generally done by creating a file of empty spaces for all records, and then filling the slots as they are needed with the data records. (It is not necessary to construct a file of empty records before putting data in it, but doing so increases the likelihood that records will be stored close to one another on the disk, avoids the error that occurs when an attempt is made to read a missing record, and makes it easy to process the file sequentially, without having to treat the empty records in any special way.)

Loading a Hash File   A program that loads a hash file is similar in many ways to earlier programs we use for populating fixed-length record files, with two differences. First, the program uses the function *hash()* to produce a home address for each key. Second, the program looks for a free space for the record by starting with the bucket stored at its home address and then, if the home bucket is full, continuing to look at successive buckets until one is found that is not full. The new record is inserted in this bucket, which is rewritten to the file at the location from which it is loaded.

If, as it searches for an empty bucket, a loading program passes the maximum allowable address, it must wrap around to the beginning address. A potential problem occurs in loading a hash file when so many records have been loaded into the file that there are no empty spaces left. A naive search for an open slot can easily result in an infinite loop. Obviously, we want to prevent this from occurring by having the program make sure that there is space available for each new record somewhere in the file.

Another problem that often arises when adding records to files occurs when an attempt is made to add a record that is already stored in the file. If there is a danger of duplicate keys occurring, and duplicate keys are not allowed in the file, some mechanism must be found for dealing with this problem.

10.7 Making Deletions

Deleting a record from a hashed file is more complicated than adding a record for two reasons:

☐   The slot freed by the deletion must not be allowed to hinder later searches; and

☐   It should be possible to reuse the freed slot for later additions.

When progressive overflow is used, a search for a record terminates if an open address is encountered. Because of this, we do not want to leave open addresses that break overflow searches improperly. The following example illustrates the problem.

Adams, Jones, Morris, and Smith are stored in a hash file in which each address can hold one record. Adams and Smith both are hashed to address 5, and Jones and Morris are hashed to address 6. If they are loaded in alphabetical order using progressive overflow for collisions, they are stored in the locations shown in Fig. 10.9.

A search for Smith starts at address 5 (Smith's home address), successively looks for Smith at addresses 6, 7, and 8, then finds Smith at 8. Now suppose Morris is deleted, leaving an empty space, as illustrated in Fig. 10.10. A search for Smith again starts at address 5, and then looks at addresses 6 and 7. Since address 7 is now empty, it is reasonable for the program to conclude that Smith's record is not in the file.

Record	Home address	Actual address
Adams	5	5
Jones	6	6
Morris	6	7
Smith	5	8

<table>
<tr><td>4</td><td></td></tr>
<tr><td>5</td><td>Adams . . .</td></tr>
<tr><td>6</td><td>Jones . . .</td></tr>
<tr><td>7</td><td>Morris . . .</td></tr>
<tr><td>8</td><td>Smith . . .</td></tr>
</table>

FIGURE 10.9 File organization before deletions.

10.7.1 Tombstones for Handling Deletions

In Chapter 5 we discussed techniques for dealing with the deletion problem. One simple technique we use for identifying deleted records involves replacing the deleted record (or just its key) with a marker indicating that a record once lived there but no longer does. Such a marker is sometimes

<table>
<tr><td>4</td><td></td></tr>
<tr><td>5</td><td>Adams . . .</td></tr>
<tr><td>6</td><td>Jones . . .</td></tr>
<tr><td>7</td><td></td></tr>
<tr><td>8</td><td>Smith . . .</td></tr>
</table>

FIGURE 10.10 The same organization as in Fig. 10.9, with Morris deleted.

5	Adams . . .
6	Jones . . .
7	######
8	Smith . . .

FIGURE 10.11 The same file as in Fig. 10.9 after the insertion of a tombstone for Morris.

referred to as a *tombstone* (Wiederhold, 1983). The nice thing about the use of tombstones is that it solves both of the problems described previously:

☐ The freed space does not break a sequence of searches for a record; and
☐ The freed space is obviously available and may be reclaimed for later additions.

Figure 10.11 illustrates how the sample file might look after the tombstone *######* is inserted for the deleted record. Now a search for Smith does *not* halt at the empty record number 7. Instead, it uses the *######* as an indication that it should continue the search.

It is not necessary to insert tombstones every time a deletion occurs. For example, suppose in the preceding example that the record for Smith is to be deleted. Since the slot following the Smith record is empty, nothing is lost by marking Smith's slot as empty rather than inserting a tombstone. Indeed, it is actually unwise to insert a tombstone where it is not needed. (If, after putting an unnecessary tombstone in Smith's slot, a new record is added at address 9, how would a subsequent unsuccessful search for Smith be affected?)

10.7.2 Implications of Tombstones for Insertions

With the introduction of the use of tombstones, the *insertion* of records becomes slightly more difficult than our earlier discussions imply. Whereas programs that perform initial loading simply search for the first occurrence of an empty record slot (signified by the presence of the key /////), it is now permissible to insert a record where either ///// or ###### occurs as the key.

This new feature, which is desirable because it yields a shorter average search length, brings with it a certain danger. Consider, for example, the earlier example in which Morris is deleted, giving the file organization shown in Fig. 10.11. Now suppose you want a program to insert Smith into the file. If the program simply searches until it encounters a ######, it never notices that Smith is already in the file. We almost certainly don't want to put a second Smith record into the file, since doing so means that later searches would never find the older Smith record. To prevent this from occurring, the program must examine the entire cluster of contiguous keys and tombstones to ensure that no duplicate key exists, and then go back and insert the record in the first available tombstone, if there is one.

10.7.3 Effects of Deletions and Additions on Performance

The use of tombstones enables our search algorithms to work and helps in storage recovery, but one can still expect some deterioration in performance after a number of deletions and additions occur within a file.

Consider, for example, our little four-record file of Adams, Jones, Smith, and Morris. After deleting Morris, Smith is one slot further from its home address than it needs to be. If the tombstone is never to be used to store another record, every retrieval of Smith requires one more access than is absolutely necessary. More generally, after a large number of additions and deletions, one can expect to find many tombstones occupying places that could be occupied by records whose home records precede them but that are stored after them. In effect, each tombstone represents an unexploited opportunity to reduce by one the number of locations that must be scanned while searching for these records.

Some experimental studies show that after a 50% to 150% turnover of records, a hashed file reaches a point of equilibrium, so average search length is as likely to get better as it is to get worse (Bradley, 1982; Peterson, 1957). By this time, however, search performance has deteriorated to the point that the average record is three times as far (in terms of accesses) from its home address as it would be after initial loading. This means, for example, that if after original loading the average search length is 1.2, it will be about 1.6 after the point of equilibrium is reached.

There are three types of solutions to the problem of deteriorating average search lengths. One involves doing a bit of local reorganizing every time a deletion occurs. For example, the deletion algorithm might examine the records that follow a tombstone to see if the search length can be shortened by moving the record backward toward its home address. Another solution involves completely reorganizing the file after the average search length reaches an unacceptable value. A third type of solution involves using an altogether different collision resolution algorithm.

10.8 Other Collision Resolution Techniques

Despite its simplicity, randomized hashing using progressive overflow with reasonably sized buckets generally performs well. If it does not perform well enough, however, there are a number of variations that may perform even better. In this section we discuss some refinements that can often improve hashing performance when using external storage.

10.8.1 Double Hashing

One of the problems with progressive overflow is that if many records hash to buckets in the same vicinity, clusters of records can form. As the packing density approaches one, this clustering tends to lead to extremely long searches for some records. One method for avoiding clustering is to store overflow records a long way from their home addresses by *double hashing*. With double hashing, when a collision occurs, a second hash function is applied to the key to produce a number c that is relatively prime to the number of addresses.[†] The value c is added to the home address to produce the overflow address. If the overflow address is already occupied, c is added to it to produce another overflow address. This procedure continues until a free overflow address is found.

Double hashing does tend to spread out the records in a file, but it suffers from a potential problem that is encountered in several improved overflow methods: It violates locality by deliberately moving overflow records some distance from their home addresses, increasing the likelihood that the disk will need extra time to get to the new overflow address. If the file covers more than one cylinder, this could require an expensive extra head movement. Double hashing programs can solve this problem if they are able to generate overflow addresses in such a way that overflow records are kept on the same cylinder as home records.

[†]If N is the number of addresses, then c and N are relatively prime if they have no common divisors.

10.8.2 Chained Progressive Overflow

Chained progressive overflow is another technique designed to avoid the problems caused by clustering. It works in the same manner as progressive overflow, except that synonyms are linked together with pointers. That is, each home address contains a number indicating the location of the next record with the same home address. The next record in turn contains a pointer to the following record with the same home address, and so forth. The net effect of this is that for each set of synonyms there is a linked list connecting their records, and it is this list that is searched when a record is sought.

The advantage of chained progressive overflow over simple progressive overflow is that only records with keys that are synonyms need to be accessed in any given search. Suppose, for example, that the set of keys shown in Fig. 10.12 is to be loaded in the order shown into a hash file with bucket size one, and progressive overflow is used. A search for Cole involves an access to Adams (a synonym) and Bates (not a synonym). Flint, the worst case, requires six accesses, only two of which involve synonyms.

Since Adams, Cole, and Flint are synonyms, a chaining algorithm forms a linked list connecting these three names, with Adams at the head of the list. Since Bates and Dean are also synonyms, they form a second list. This arrangement is illustrated in Fig. 10.13. The average search length decreases from 2.5 to

$$\frac{1 + 1 + 2 + 2 + 1 + 3}{6} = 1.7.$$

The use of chained progressive overflow requires that we attend to some details that are not required for simple progressive overflow. First, a *link field* must be added to each record, requiring the use of a little more

FIGURE 10.12 Hashing with progressive overflow.

Key	Home address	Actual address	Search length
Adams	20	20	1
Bates	21	21	1
Cole	20	22	3
Dean	21	23	3
Evans	24	24	1
Flint	20	25	6

Average search length = (1 + 1 + 3 + 3 + 1 + 6)/6 = 2.5

Home address	Actual address	Data	Address of next synonym	Search length
		. . .		
20	20	Adams . . .	22	1
21	21	Bates . . .	23	1
20	22	Cole . . .	25	2
21	23	Dean . . .	−1	2
24	24	Evans . . .	−1	1
20	25	Flint . . .	−1	3
		. . .		

FIGURE 10.13 Hashing with chained progressive overflow. Adams, Cole, and Flint are synonyms; Bates and Dean are synonyms.

storage. Second, a chaining algorithm must guarantee that it is possible to get to any synonym by starting at its home address. This second requirement is not a trivial one, as the following example shows.

Suppose that in the example Dean's home address is 22 instead of 21. Since, by the time Dean is loaded, address 22 is already occupied by Cole, Dean still ends up at address 23. Does this mean that Cole's pointer should point to 23 (Dean's actual address) or to 25 (the address of Cole's synonym Flint)? If the pointer is 25, the linked list joining Adams, Cole, and Flint is kept intact, but Dean is lost. If the pointer is 23, Flint is lost.

The problem here is that a certain address (22) that *should* be occupied by a home record (Dean) is occupied by a different record. One solution to the problem is to require that every address that qualifies as a home address for some record in the file actually hold a home record. The problem can be handled easily when a file is first loaded by using a technique called two-pass loading.

Two-pass loading, as the name implies, involves loading a hash file in two passes. On the first pass, only home records are loaded. All records that are not home records are kept in a separate file. This guarantees that no potential home addresses are occupied by overflow records. On the second pass, each overflow record is loaded and stored in one of the free addresses according to whatever collision resolution technique is being used.

Two-pass loading guarantees that every potential home address actually is a home address, so it solves the problem in the example. It does not guarantee that later deletions and additions will not re-create the same problem, however. As long as the file is used to store both home records and overflow records, there remains the problem of overflow records displacing new records that hash to an address occupied by an overflow record.

The methods used for handling these problems after initial loading are somewhat complicated and can, in a very volatile file, require many extra disk accesses. (For more information on techniques for maintaining pointers, see Knuth, 1973b and Bradley, 1982.) It would be nice if we could somehow altogether avoid this problem of overflow lists bumping into one another, and that is what the next method does.

10.8.3 Chaining with a Separate Overflow Area

One way to keep overflow records from occupying home addresses where they should not be is to move them all to a separate overflow area. Many hashing schemes are variations of this basic approach. The set of home addresses is called the *prime data area,* and the set of overflow addresses is called the *overflow area.* The advantage of this approach is that it keeps all unused but potential home addresses free for later additions.

In terms of the file we examined in the preceding section, the records for Cole, Dean, and Flint could have been stored in a separate overflow area rather than potential home addresses for later-arriving records (Fig. 10.14). Now no problem occurs when a new record is added. If its home address has room, it is stored there. If not, it is moved to the overflow file, where it is added to the linked list that starts at the home address.

If the bucket size for the primary file is large enough to prevent excessive numbers of overflow records, the overflow file can be a simple entry-sequenced file with a bucket size of one. Space can be allocated for overflow records only when it is needed.

The use of a separate overflow area simplifies processing somewhat and would seem to improve performance, especially when many additions and deletions occur. However, this is not always the case. If the separate overflow area is on a different cylinder than is the home address, every search for an overflow record will involve a very costly head movement. Studies show that actual access time is generally worse when overflow records are stored in a separate overflow area than when they are stored in the prime overflow area (Lum, 1971).

One situation in which a separate overflow area is *required* occurs when the packing density is greater than one—there are more records than home

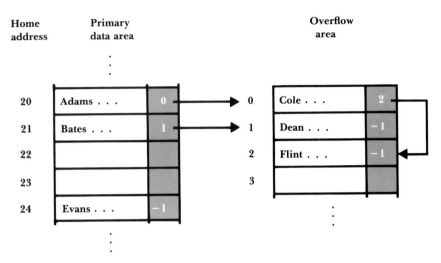

FIGURE 10.14 Chaining to a separate overflow area. Adams, Cole, and Flint are synonyms; Bates and Dean are synonyms.

addresses. If, for example, it is anticipated that a file will grow beyond the capacity of the initial set of home addresses and that rehashing the file with a larger address space is not reasonable, then a separate overflow area must be used.

10.8.4 Scatter Tables: Indexing Revisited

Suppose you have a hash file that contains no records, only pointers to records. The file is obviously just an index that is searched by hashing rather than by some other method. The term *scatter table* (Severance, 1974) is often applied to this approach to file organization. Figure 10.15 illustrates the organization of a file using a scatter table.

The scatter table organization provides many of the same advantages simple indexing generally provides, with the additional advantage that the search of the index itself requires only one access. (Of course, that one access is one more than other forms of hashing require, unless the scatter table can be kept in primary memory.) The data file can be implemented in many different ways. For example, it can be a set of linked lists of synonyms (as shown in Fig. 10.15), a sorted file, or an entry-sequenced file. Also, scatter table organizations conveniently support the use of variable-length records. For more information on scatter tables, see Severance (1974) and Teorey and Fry (1982).

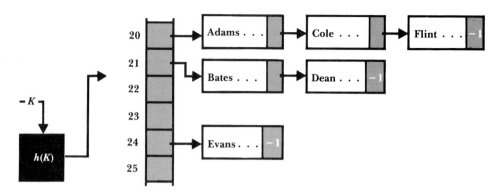

FIGURE 10.15 Example of a scatter table structure. Because the hashed part is an index, the data file may be organized in any way that is appropriate.

10.9   Patterns of Record Access

> Twenty percent of the fishermen catch 80 percent of the fish.
> Twenty percent of the burglars steal 80 percent of the loot.
>
> *L. M. Boyd*

The use of different collision resolution techniques is not the only nor necessarily the best way of improving performance in a hashed file. If we know something about the patterns of record access, for example, then it is often possible to use simple progressive overflow techniques and still achieve very good performance.

Suppose you have a grocery store with 10,000 different categories of grocery items, and you have on your computer a hashed inventory file with a record for each of the 10,000 items that your company handles. Every time an item is purchased, the record that corresponds to that item must be accessed. Since the file is hashed, it is reasonable to assume that the 10,000 records are distributed randomly among the available addresses that make up the file. Is it equally reasonable to assume that the distribution of *accesses* to the records in the inventory are randomly distributed? Probably not. Milk, for example, will be retrieved very frequently, brie seldom.

There is a principle used by economists called the Pareto Principle, or The Concept of the Vital Few and the Trivial Many, which in file terms says that a small percentage of the records in a file account for a large percentage of the accesses. A popular version of the Pareto Principle is the 80/20 Rule of Thumb: 80% of the accesses are performed on 20% of the records. In our groceries file, milk would be among the 20% high-activity items, brie among the rest.

We cannot take advantage of the 80/20 principle in a file structure unless we know something about the probable distribution of record accesses. Once we have this information, we need to find a way to place the high-activity items where they can be found with as few accesses as possible. If, when items are loaded into a file, they can be loaded in such a way that the 20% (more or less) that are most likely to be accessed are loaded at or near their home addresses, then most of the transactions will access records that have short search lengths, so the *effective* average search length will be shorter than the nominal average search length that we defined earlier.

For example, suppose our grocery store's file handling program keeps track of the number of times each item is accessed during a one-month period. It might do this by storing with each record a counter that starts at zero and is incremented every time the item is accessed. At the end of the month the records for all the items in the inventory are dumped onto a file that is sorted in descending order according to the number of times they have been accessed. When the sorted file is rehashed and reloaded, the first records to be loaded are the ones that, according to the previous month's experience, are most likely to be accessed. Since they are the first ones loaded, they are also the ones most likely to be loaded into their home addresses. If reasonably sized buckets are used, there will be *very few*, if any, high-activity items that are not in their home addresses and therefore retrievable in one access.

■ SUMMARY

There are three major modes for accessing files: *sequentially,* which provides $O(N)$ performance, through *tree structures,* which can produce $O(\log_k N)$ performance, and *directly.* Direct access provides $O(1)$ performance, which means that the number of accesses required to retrieve a record is constant and independent of the size of the file. Hashing is the primary form of organization used to provide direct access.

Hashing can provide faster access than most of the other organizations we study, usually with very little storage overhead, and it is adaptable to most types of primary keys. Ideally, hashing makes it possible to find any record with only one disk access, but this ideal is rarely achieved. The primary disadvantage of hashing is that hashed files may not be sorted by key.

Hashing involves the application of a hash function $h(K)$ to a record key K to produce an address. The address is taken to be the *home address* of the record whose key is K, and it forms the basis for searching for the record. The addresses produced by hash functions generally appear to be random.

When two or more keys hash to the same address, they are called *synonyms*. If an address cannot accommodate all of its synonyms, *collisions* result. When collisions occur, some of the synonyms cannot be stored in the home address and must be stored elsewhere. Since searches for records begin with home addresses, searches for records that are not stored at their home addresses generally involve extra disk accesses. The term *average search length* is used to describe the average number of disk accesses that are required to retrieve a record. An average search length of 1 is ideal.

Much of the study of hashing deals with techniques for decreasing the number and effects of collisions. In this chapter we look at three general approaches to reducing the number of collisions:

- Spreading out the records;
- Using extra memory; and
- Using buckets.

Spreading out the records involves choosing a hashing function that distributes the records at least randomly over the address space. A *uniform distribution* spreads out records evenly, resulting in no collisions. A *random* or nearly random distribution is much easier to achieve and is usually considered acceptable.

In this chapter a simple hashing algorithm is developed to demonstrate the kinds of operations that take place in a hashing algorithm. The three steps in the algorithm are:

1. Represent the key in numerical form;
2. Fold and add; and
3. Divide by the size of the address space, producing a valid address.

When we examine several different types of hashing algorithms, we see that sometimes algorithms can be found that produce *better-than-random* distributions. Failing this, we suggest some algorithms that generally produce distributions which are approximately random.

The *Poisson distribution* provides a mathematical tool for examining in detail the effects of a random distribution. Poisson functions can be used to predict the numbers of addresses likely to be assigned 0, 1, 2, and so on, records, given the number of records to be hashed and the number of available addresses. This allows us to predict the number of collisions likely to occur when a file is hashed, the number of overflow records likely to occur, and sometimes the average search length.

Using extra memory is another way to avoid collisions. When a fixed number of keys is hashed, the likelihood of synonyms occurring decreases as the number of possible addresses increases. Hence, a file organization that allocates many more addresses than are likely to be used has fewer synonyms than one that allocates few extra addresses. The term *packing density* describes the proportion of available address space that actually holds records. The Poisson function is used to determine how differences in packing density influence the percentage of records that are likely to be synonyms.

Using buckets is the third method for avoiding collisions. File addresses can hold one or more records, depending on how the file is organized by the file designer. The number of records that can be stored at a given address, called *bucket size,* determines the point at which records assigned to the address will overflow. The Poisson function can be used to explore the effects of variations in bucket sizes and packing densities. Large buckets, combined with a low packing density, can result in very small average search lengths.

Although we can reduce the number of collisions, we need some means to deal with collisions when they do occur. We examined one simple collision resolution technique in detail—*progressive overflow*. If an attempt to store a new record results in a collision, progressive overflow involves searching through the addresses that follow the record's home address in order until one is found to hold the new record. If a record is sought and is not found in its home address, successive addresses are searched until either the record is found or an empty address is encountered.

Progressive overflow is simple and sometimes works very well. Progressive overflow creates long search lengths, however, when the packing density is high and the bucket size is low. It also sometimes produces clusters of records, creating very long search lengths for new records whose home addresses are in the clusters.

Three problems associated with record deletion in hashed files are

1. The possibility that empty slots created by deletions will hinder later searches for overflow records;
2. The need to recover space made available when records are deleted; and
3. The deterioration of average search lengths caused by empty spaces keeping records further from home than they need be.

The first two problems can be solved by using *tombstones* to mark spaces that are empty (and can be reused for new records) but should not halt a search for a record. Solutions to the deterioration problem include local reorganization, complete file reorganization, and the choice of a collision-resolving algorithm that does not cause deterioration to occur.

Because overflow records have a major influence on performance, many different overflow handling techniques have been proposed. Four such techniques that are appropriate for file applications are discussed briefly:

1. *Double hashing* reduces local clustering but may place some overflow records so far from home that they require extra seeks.
2. *Chained progressive overflow* reduces search lengths by requiring that only synonyms be examined when a record is being sought. For chained overflow to work, every address that qualifies as a home record for some record in the file must hold a home record. Mechanisms for making sure that this occurs are discussed.
3. *Chaining with a separate overflow area* simplifies chaining substantially and has the advantage that the overflow area may be organized in ways more appropriate to handling overflow records. A danger of this approach is that it might lose locality.
4. *Scatter tables* combine indexing with hashing. This approach provides much more flexibility in organizing the data file. A disadvantage of using scatter tables is that, unless the index can be held in RAM, it requires one extra disk access for every search.

Since in many cases certain records are accessed more frequently than others (the *80/20 rule of thumb*), it is often worthwhile to take access patterns into account. If we can identify those records that are most likely to be accessed, we can take measures to make sure that they are stored closer to home than less frequently accessed records, thus decreasing the *effective* average search length. One such measure is to load the most frequently accessed records before the others.

KEY TERMS

Average search length. We define average search length as the *sum of the number of accesses required for each record in the file* divided by *the number of records in the file*. This definition does not take into account the number of accesses required for unsuccessful searches, nor does it account for the fact that some records are likely to be accessed more often than others. See *80/20 rule of thumb*.

Better-than-random. This term is applied to distributions in which the records are spread out more uniformly than they would be if the hash function distributed them randomly. Normally, the distribution produced by a hash function is a little bit better than random.

Bucket. An area of space on the file that is treated as a physical record for storage and retrieval purposes but that is capable of storing several *logical* records. By storing and retrieving logical records in buckets rather than individually, access times can, in many cases, be improved substantially.

Collision. Situation in which a record is hashed to an address that does not have sufficient room to store the record. When a collision occurs, some means has to be found to resolve the collision.

Double hashing. A collision resolution scheme in which collisions are handled by applying a second hash function to the key to produce a number c, which is added to the original address (modulo the number of addresses) as many times as necessary until either the desired record is located or an empty space is found. Double hashing helps avoid some of the clustering that occurs with progressive overflow.

The 80/20 rule of thumb. An assumption that a large percentage (e.g., 80%) of the accesses are performed on a small percentage (e.g., 20%) of the records in a file. When the 80/20 rule applies, the *effective* average search length is determined largely by the search lengths of the more active records, so attempts to make *these* search lengths short can result in substantially improved performance.

Fold and add. A method of hashing in which the encodings of fixed-sized parts of a key are extracted (e.g., every two bytes) and are added. The resulting sum can be used to produce an address.

Hashing. A technique for generating a unique home address for a given key. Hashing is used when rapid access to a key (or its corresponding record) is required. In this chapter applications of hashing involve direct access to records in a file, but hashing is also often used to access items in arrays in RAM. In indexing, for example, an index might be organized for hashing rather than for binary search if extremely fast searching of the index is desired.

Home address. The address generated by a hash function for a given key. If a record is stored at its home address, then the search length for the record is one because only one access is required to retrieve the record. A record not at its home address requires more than one access to retrieve or store.

Indexed hash. Instead of using the results of a hash to produce the address of a record, the hash can be used to identify a location in an index that in turn points to the address of the record. Although this approach requires one extra access for every search, it makes it possible to organize the actual data records in a way that facilitates other types of processing, such as sequential processing.

Mid-square method. A hashing method in which a representation of the key is squared and some digits from the middle of the result are used to produce the address.

Minimum hashing. Hashing scheme in which the number of addresses is exactly equal to the number of records. No storage space is wasted.

Open addressing. See *progressive overflow.*

Overflow. The situation that occurs when a record cannot be stored in its home address.

Packing density. The proportion of allocated file space that actually holds records. (Sometimes referred to as *load factor.*) If a file is half full, its packing density is 50%. The packing density and bucket size are the two most important measures in determining the likelihood of a collision occurring when searching for a record in a file.

Perfect hashing function. A hashing function that distributes records uniformly, minimizing the number of collisions. Perfect hashing functions are very desirable, but they are extremely difficult to find for large sets of keys.

Poisson distribution. Distribution generated by the Poisson function, which can be used to approximate the distribution of records among addresses if the distribution is random. A particular Poisson distribution depends on the ratio of the number of records to the number of available addresses. A particular instance of the Poisson function, $p(x)$, gives the proportion of addresses that will have x keys assigned to them. See *better-than-random.*

Prime division. Division of a number by a prime number and use of the remainder as an address. If the address size is taken to be a prime number p, a large number can be transformed into a valid address by dividing it by p. In hashing, division by primes is often preferred to division by nonprimes because primes tend to produce more random remainders.

Progressive overflow. An overflow handling technique in which collisions are resolved by storing a record in the next available address after its home address. Progressive overflow is not the most efficient overflow handling technique, but it is one of the simplest and is adequate for many applications.

Randomize. To produce a number (e.g., by hashing) that appears to be random.

Synonyms. Two or more different keys that hash to the same address. When each file address can hold only one record, synonyms always result in collisions. If buckets are used, several records whose keys are synonyms may be stored without collisions.

Tombstone. A special marker placed in the key field of a record to mark it as no longer valid. The use of tombstones solves two problems associated with the deletion of records: The freed space does not break a sequential search for a record, and the freed space is easily recognized as available and may be reclaimed for later additions.

Uniform. Term applied to a distribution in which records are spread out evenly among addresses. Algorithms that produce uniform distributions are better than randomizing algorithms in that they tend to avoid the numbers of collisions that would occur by chance from a randomizing algorithm.

■ EXERCISES

1. Use the function *hash(KEY, MAXAD)* described in the text to answer the following questions.

a. What is the value of *hash("Browns", 101)*?

b. Find two different words of more than four characters that are synonyms.

c. It is assumed in the text that the function *hash()* does not need to generate an integer greater than 19,937. This could present a problem if we have a file with addresses larger than 19,937. Suggest some ways to get around this problem.

2. In understanding hashing, it is important to understand the relationships between the size of the available memory, the number of keys to be hashed, the range of possible keys, and the nature of the keys. Let us give names to these quantities, as follows:

M = the number of memory spaces available (each capable of holding one record);

r = the number of records to be stored in the memory spaces;

n = the number of unique home addresses produced by hashing the r record keys; and

K = a key, which may be any combination of exactly five uppercase characters.

Suppose $h(K)$ is a hash function that generates addresses between 0 and $M - 1$.

a. How many unique keys are possible? (Hint: If K were one uppercase letter, rather than five, there would be 26 possible unique keys.)

b. How are n and r related?

c. How are r and M related?

d. If the function h were a minimum perfect hashing function, how would n, r, and M be related?

3. The following table shows distributions of keys resulting from three different hash functions on a file with 6,000 records and 6,000 addresses.

	Function A	Function B	Function C
$d(0)$	0.71	0.25	0.40
$d(1)$	0.05	0.50	0.36
$d(2)$	0.05	0.25	0.15
$d(3)$	0.05	0.00	0.05
$d(4)$	0.05	0.00	0.02
$d(5)$	0.04	0.00	0.01
$d(6)$	0.05	0.00	0.01
$d(7)$	0.00	0.00	0.00

a. Which of the three functions (if any) generates a distribution of records that is approximately random?

b. Which generates a distribution that is nearest to uniform?

c. Which (if any) generates a distribution that is worse than random?

d. Which function should be chosen?

4. There is a surprising mathematical result called *the birthday paradox* that says that if there are more than 23 people in a room, then there is a better than 50-50 chance that two of them have the same birthday. How is the birthday paradox illustrative of a major problem associated with hashing?

5. Suppose that 10,000 addresses are allocated to hold 8,000 records in a randomly hashed file and that each address can hold one record. Compute the following values:

a. The packing density for the file;

b. The expected number of addresses with no records assigned to them by the hash function;

c. The expected number of addresses with one record assigned (no synonyms);

d. The expected number of addresses with one record *plus* one or more synonyms;

e. The expected number of overflow records; and

f. The expected percentage of overflow records.

6. Consider the file described in the preceding exercise. What is the expected number of overflow records if the 10,000 locations are reorganized as

  a. 5,000 two-record buckets; and

  b. 1000 10-record buckets?

7. Make a table showing Poisson function values for $r/N = 0.1, 0.5, 0.8$, 1, 2, 5, and 10. Examine the table and discuss any features and patterns that provide useful information about hashing.

8. There is an overflow handling technique called *count-key progressive overflow* (Bradley, 1982) that works on block-addressable disks as follows. Instead of generating a relative record number from a key, the hash function generates an address consisting of three values: a cylinder, a track, and a block number. The corresponding three numbers constitute the home address of the record.

  Since block-organized drives (see Chapter 3) can often scan a track to find a record with a given key, there is no need to load a block into memory to find out whether or not it contains a particular record. The I/O processor can direct the disk drive to search a track for the desired record. It can even direct the disk to search for an empty record slot if a record is not found in its home position, effectively implementing progressive overflow.

  a. What is it about this technique that makes it superior to progressive overflow techniques that might be implemented on sector-organized drives?

  b. The main disadvantage of this technique is that it can be used only with a bucket size of 1. Why is this the case, and why is it a disadvantage?

9. In discussing implementation issues, we suggest initializing the data file by creating real records that are marked empty before loading the file with actual data. There are some good reasons for doing this. However, there might be some reasons not to do it this way. For example, suppose you want a hash file with a very low packing density and cannot afford to have the unused space allocated. How might a file management system be designed to work with a very large *logical* file, but allocate space only for those blocks in the file that actually contain data?

10. This exercise (inspired by an example in Wiederhold, 1983, p. 136) concerns the problem of deterioration. A number of additions and deletions are to be made to a file. Tombstones are to be used where necessary to preserve search paths to overflow records.

  a. Show what the file looks like after the following operations, and compute the average search length.

Operation	Home Address
Add Alan	0
Add Bates	2
Add Cole	4
Add Dean	0
Add Evans	1
Del Bates	
Del Cole	
Add Finch	0
Add Gates	2
Del Alan	
Add Hart	3

How has the use of tombstones caused the file to deteriorate?
What would be the effect of reloading the remaining items in the file in the order Dean, Evans, Finch, Gates, Hart?
b. What would be the effect of reloading the remaining items using two-pass loading?

11. Suppose you have a file in which 20% of the records account for 80% of the accesses, and that you want to store the file with a packing density of 0 and a bucket size of 5. When the file is loaded, you load the active 20% of the records first. After the active 20% of the records are loaded, and before the other records are loaded, what is the packing density of the partially filled file? Using this packing density, compute the percentage of the active 20% which would be overflow records. Comment on the results.

12. In our computations of average search lengths, we consider only the times it takes for *successful* searches. If our hashed file were to be used in such a way that searches were often made for items that are not in the file, it would be useful to have statistics on average search length for an *unsuccessful* search. If a large percentage of searches to a hashed file are unsuccessful, how do you expect this to affect overall performance if overflow is handled by
    a. Progressive overflow; or
    b. Chaining to a separate overflow area?
    (See Knuth, 1973b, pp. 535–539 for a treatment of these differences.)

13. Although hashed files are not generally designed to support access to records in any sorted order, there may be times when batches of transactions need to be performed on a hashed data file. If the data file is sorted (rather than hashed), these transactions are normally carried out by some sort of cosequential process, which means that the transaction file also has to be sorted. If the data file is hashed, the transaction file might also be presorted, but on the basis of the home addresses of its records rather than some more "natural" criterion.

Suppose you have a file whose records are usually accessed directly, but that is periodically updated from a transaction file. List the factors you would have to consider in deciding between using an indexed sequential organization and hashing. (See Hanson, 1982, pp. 280–285, for a discussion of these issues.)

14. We assume throughout this chapter that a hashing program should be able to tell correctly whether a given key is located at a certain address. If this were not so, there would be times when we would assume that a record exists when in fact it does not, a seemingly disastrous result. But consider what Doug McIlroy did in 1978 when he was designing a spelling checker program. He found that by letting his program allow one out of every 4,000 misspelled words to sneak by as valid (and using a few other tricks), he could fit a 75,000-word spelling dictionary into 64 K of RAM, thereby improving performance enormously.

McIlroy was willing to tolerate one undetected misspelled word out of every 4,000 because he observed that drafts of papers rarely contained more than 20 errors, so one could expect at most one out of every 200 runs of the program to fail to detect a misspelled word. Can you think of some other cases where it might be reasonable to report that a key exists when in fact it does not?

Jon Bentley (1985) provides an excellent account of McIlroy's program, plus several insights on the process of solving problems of this nature. D. J. Dodds (1982) discusses this general approach to hashing, called *check-hashing*. Read Bentley's and Dodds's articles, and report on them to your class. Perhaps they will inspire you to write a spelling checker.

Programming Exercises

15. Implement and test a version of the function *hash()*.

16. Create a hashed file with one record for every city in California. The key in each record is to be the name of the corresponding city. (For the purposes of this exercise, there need be no fields other than the key field.) Begin by creating a sorted list of the names of all of the cities and towns in California. (If time or space is limited, just make a list of names starting with the letter 'S'.)

a. Examine the sorted list. What patterns do you notice that might affect your choice of a hash function?

b. Implement the function *hash()* in such a way that you can alter the number of characters that are folded. Assuming a packing density of 1, hash the entire file several times, each time folding a different number of characters, and producing the following statistics for each run:

☐ The number of collisions; and
☐ The number of addresses assigned 0, 1, 2, . . . , 10, and 10-or-more records.

Discuss the results of your experiment in terms of the effects of folding different numbers of characters, and how they compare to the results you might expect from a random distribution.

c. Implement and test one or more of the other hashing methods described in the text, or use a method of your own invention.

17. Using some set of keys, such as the names of California towns, do the following:

a. Write and test a program for loading the keys into three different hash files using bucket sizes of 1, 2, and 5, respectively, and a packing density of 0.8. Use progressive overflow for handling collisions.

b. Have your program maintain statistics on the average search length, the maximum search length, and the percentage of records that are overflow records.

c. Assuming a Poisson distribution, compare your results with the expected values for average search length and the percentage of records that are overflow records.

18. Repeat exercise 17, but use double hashing to handle overflow.

19. Repeat exercise 17, but handle overflow using chained overflow into a separate overflow area. Assume that the packing density is the ratio of number of keys to available *home* addresses.

20. Write a program that can perform insertions and deletions in the file created in the previous problem using a bucket size of 5. Have the program keep running statistics on average search length. (You might also implement a mechanism to indicate when search length has deteriorated to a point where the file should be reorganized.) Discuss in detail the issues you have to confront in deciding how to handle insertions and deletions.

■ FURTHER READINGS

There are a number of good surveys of hashing and issues related to hashing generally, including Knuth (1973b), Severance (1974), Maurer (1975), and Sorenson, Tremblay, and Deutscher (1978). Textbooks concerned with file design generally contain substantial amounts of material on hashing, and they often provide extensive references for further study. Each of the following can be useful:

☐ Hanson (1982) is filled with analytical and experimental results exploring all of the issues we introduce, and many more, and also contains a good chapter on comparing different file organizations.

☐ Bradley (1982) covers file hashing generally but also includes much information on programming for hashed files using IBM PL/I.

☐ Loomis (1983) also covers hashing generally, with additional emphasis on programming for hashed files in COBOL.

☐ Teorey and Fry (1982) and Wiederhold (1983) will be useful to practitioners interested in analyses of trade-offs among the basic hashing methods.

One of the applications of hashing that has stimulated a great deal of interest recently is the development of *spelling checkers*. Because of special characteristics of spelling checkers, the types of hashing involved are quite different from the approaches we describe in this text. Papers by Bentley (1985) and Dodds (1982) provide entry into the literature on this topic. (See also exercise 14.)

Extendible Hashing

11

CHAPTER OBJECTIVES

- Describe the problem solved by extendible hashing and related approaches.

- Explain how extendible hashing works; show how it combines *tries* with conventional, static hashing.

- Show how to implement extendible hashing, including deletion.

- Review studies of extendible hashing performance.

- Examine alternative approaches to the same problem, including *dynamic hashing, linear hashing,* and hashing schemes that control splitting by allowing for overflow buckets.

CHAPTER OUTLINE

11.1 Introduction

In Chapter 8 we began with a historical review of the work that led up to B-trees. B-trees are such an effective solution to the problems that stimulated their development that it is easy to wonder if there is any more important thinking to be done about file structures. Work on extendible hashing during the late 1970s and early 1980s shows that the answer to that question is yes. This chapter tells the story of that work and describes some of the file structures that emerge from it.

B-trees do for secondary storage what AVL trees do for storage in memory: They provide a way of using tree structures that works well with *dynamic* data. By *dynamic* we mean that we add and delete records from the data set. The key feature of both AVL trees and B-trees is that they are self-adjusting structures that include mechanisms to maintain themselves. As we add and delete records, the tree structures use limited, local restructuring to ensure that the additions and deletions do not degrade performance beyond some predetermined level.

Robust, self-adjusting data and file structures are critically important to data storage and retrieval. Judging from the historical record, they are also hard to develop. It was not until 1963 that Adel'son-Vel'skii and Landis developed a self-adjusting structure for tree storage in memory, and it took another decade of work before computer scientists found, in B-trees, a dynamic tree structure that works well on secondary storage.

B-trees provide $O(\log_k N)$ access to the keys in a file. Hashing, when there is no overflow, provides access to a record with a single seek. But as a file grows larger, the need to look for records that overflow their buckets degrades performance. For dynamic files that undergo a lot of growth, the performance of a static hashing system such as we described in Chapter 10 is typically worse than the performance of a B-tree. So, by the late 1970s, after the initial burst of new research and design work revolving around B-trees was over, a number of researchers began to work on finding ways to modify hashing so that it, too, could be self-adjusting as files grow and shrink. As often happens when a number of groups are working on the same problem, several different, yet essentially similar, approaches emerged to extend hashing to dynamic files. We begin our discussion of the problem by looking closely at the approach called "extendible hashing" described by Fagin, Nievergelt, Pippenger, and Strong (1979). Later in this chapter we compare this approach with others that emerged over the last decade.

11.2   How Extendible Hashing Works

11.2.1 Tries

The key idea behind extendible hashing is to combine conventional hashing with another retrieval approach called the *trie*. (The word *trie* is pronounced so that it rhymes with *sky*.) Tries are also sometimes referred to as *radix searching* because the branching factor of the search tree is equal to the number of alternative symbols (the radix of the alphabet) that can occur in each position of the key. A few examples will illustrate how this works.

Suppose we want to build a trie that stores the keys *able, abrahms, adams, anderson, andrews,* and *baird.* A schematic form of the trie is shown in Fig. 11.1. As you can see, the searching proceeds letter by letter through the key. Since there are 26 symbols in the alphabet, the potential branching factor at every node of the search is 26. If we used the digits $0-9$ as our search alphabet, rather than the letters $a-z$, the radix of the search would be reduced to 10. A search tree using digits might look like the one shown in Fig. 11.2.

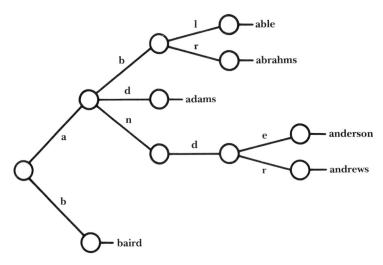

FIGURE 11.1 Radix 26 trie that indexes names according to the letters of the alphabet.

FIGURE 11.2 Radix 10 trie that indexes numbers according to the digits they contain.

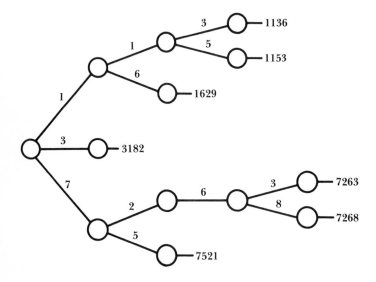

Notice that in searching a trie we sometimes use only a portion of the key. We use more of the key as we need more information to complete the search. This use-more-as-we-need-more capability is fundamental to the structure of extendible hashing.

11.2.2 Turning the Trie into a Directory

We use tries with a radix of two in our approach to extendible hashing: Search decisions are made on a bit-by-bit basis. Furthermore, since we are retrieving from secondary storage, we will not work in terms of individual keys, but in terms of *buckets* containing keys, just as in conventional hashing. Suppose we have bucket A containing keys that, when hashed, have hash addresses that begin with the bits *01*. Bucket B contains keys with hash addresses beginning with *10,* and bucket C contains keys with addresses that start with *11*. Figure 11.3 shows a trie that allows us to retrieve these buckets.

How should we represent the trie? If we represent it as a tree structure, we are forced to do a number of comparisons as we descend the tree. Even worse, if the trie becomes so large that it, too, is stored on disk, we are faced once again with all of the problems associated with storing trees on disk. We might as well go back to B-trees and forget about extendible hashing.

So, rather than representing the trie as a tree, we flatten it into an array of contiguous records, forming a directory of hash addresses and pointers to the corresponding buckets. The first step in turning a tree into an array involves extending it so it is a complete binary tree with all of its leaves at the same level as shown in Fig. 11.4(a). Even though the initial *0* is enough to select bucket A, the new form of the tree also uses the second address bit so both alternatives lead to the same bucket. Once we have extended the tree this way, we can collapse it into the directory structure shown in Fig. 11.4(b). Now we have a structure that provides the kind of direct access associated with hashing: Given an address beginning with the bits *10,* the 10_2^{th} directory entry gives us a pointer to the associated bucket.

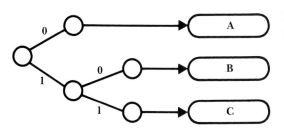

FIGURE 11.3 Radix 2 trie that provides an index to buckets.

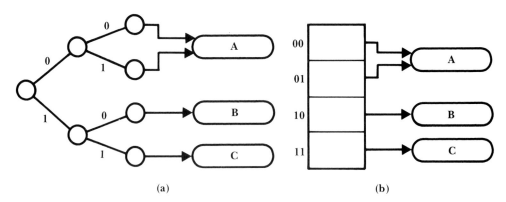

(a)   (b)

FIGURE 11.4 The trie from Fig. 11.3 transformed first into a complete binary tree, and then flattened into a directory to the buckets.

11.2.3 Splitting to Handle Overflow

A key issue in any hashing system is what happens when a bucket overflows. The goal in an *extendible* hashing system is to find a way to increase the address space in response to overflow, rather than responding by creating long sequences of overflow records and buckets that have to be searched linearly.

Suppose we insert records that cause bucket A in Fig. 11.4(b) to overflow. In this case the solution is simple: Since addresses beginning with *00* and *01* are mixed together in bucket A, we can split bucket A by putting all the *01* addresses in a new bucket D, while keeping only the *00* addresses in A. Put another way, we already have two bits of address information, but are throwing one away as we access bucket A. So, now that bucket A is overflowing, we must use the full two bits to divide the addresses between two buckets. We do not need to extend the address space; we simply make full use of the address information that we already have. Figure 11.5 shows the directory and buckets after the split.

Let's consider a more complex case. Starting once again with the directory and buckets in Fig. 11.4(b), suppose that bucket B overflows. How do we split bucket B and where do we attach the new bucket after the split? Unlike our previous example, we do not have additional, unused bits of address space that we can press into duty as we split the bucket. We now need to use three bits of the hash address in order to divide up the records that hash to bucket B. The trie illustrated in Fig. 11.6(a) makes the distinctions required to complete the split. Figure 11.6(b) shows what this trie looks like once it is extended into a completely full binary tree with all leaves at the same level, and Fig. 11.6(c) shows the collapsed, directory form of the trie.

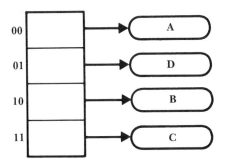

FIGURE 11.5 The directory
from Fig. 11.4(b) after bucket
A overflows.

FIGURE 11.6 The results of an overflow of bucket B in Fig. 11.4(b), represented first as a trie, then as a complete binary tree, and finally as a directory.

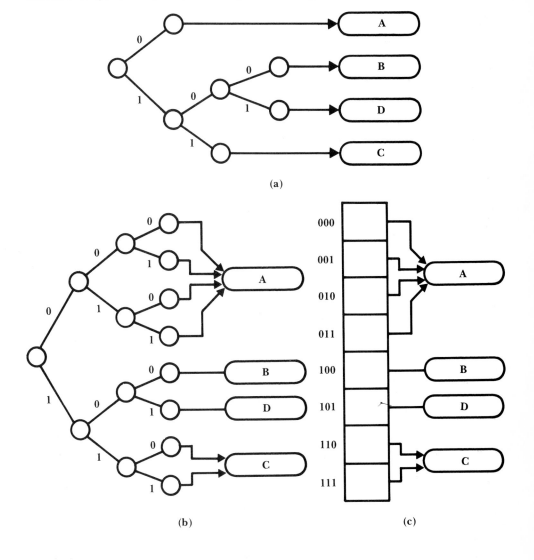

(a)

(b)   (c)

By building on the trie's ability to extend the amount of information used in a search, we have doubled the size of our address space (and, therefore, of our directory), extending it from 2^2 to 2^3 cells. This ability to grow (or shrink) the address space gracefully is what extendible hashing is all about.

We have been concentrating on the contribution that tries make to extendible hashing; one might well ask where the actual *hashing* comes into play. Why not just use the tries on the bits in the key itself, splitting buckets and extending the address space as necessary? The answer to this question grows out of hashing's most fundamental characteristic: A good hash function produces a nearly uniform distribution of keys across an address space. Notice that the trie shown in Fig. 11.6 is poorly balanced, resulting in a directory that is twice as big as it actually needs to be. If we had an uneven distribution of addresses that placed even more records in buckets *B* and *D* without using other parts of the address space, the situation would get even worse. By using a good hash function to create addresses with a nearly uniform distribution, we avoid this problem.

11.3   Implementation

11.3.1 Creating the Addresses

Now that we have a high-level overview of how extendible hashing works, let's look at pseudocode in Fig. 11.7 that describes the algorithms in more detail. The place to start is with the functions that create the addresses, since the notion of an extendible address underlies all other extendible hashing operations.

The hash function itself is a simple variation on the fold-and-add hashing algorithm we used in Chapter 10. The only difference is that we do not conclude the operation by returning the remainder of the folded address divided by the address space. We don't need to do that, since in extendible hashing we don't have a fixed address space, instead using as much of the address as we need. The division that we do perform in this function, when we take the sum of the folded character values modulo 19,937, is to make sure that the character summation stays within the range of a signed 16-bit integer. For machines that use 32-bit integers, we could divide by a larger number and create an even larger initial address.

Since extendible hashing uses more bits of the hashed address as they are needed to distinguish between buckets, we need a *make_address* function that extracts just a portion of the full hashed address. We also use the *make_address* function to reverse the order of the bits in the hashed address, making the lowest-order bit of the hash address the highest-order bit of the value used in extendible hashing. To see why this reversal of bit order is

```
FUNCTION hash(KEY)

    set SUM to 0
    set J to 0
    set LEN to the length of the key

    if LEN is odd, concatenate a blank to the key
         to make the length even

    while (J < LEN)
        SUM := (SUM + 100*KEY[J] + KEY[J+1]) mod 19937
        increment J by 2
    endwhile

    return SUM

end FUNCTION
```

FIGURE 11.7 Function *hash(KEY)* returns an integer hash value for KEY for a 15-bit address space.

desirable, look at Fig. 11.8, which is a set of keys and binary hash addresses produced by our *hash* function. Even a quick scan of these addresses reveals that the distribution of the least significant bits of these integer values tends to have more variation than the high-order bits. This is because many of the addresses do not make use of the upper reaches of our address space; the high-order bits often turn out to be zero.

By reversing the bit order, working from right to left, we take advantage of the greater variability of low-order bit values. For example, given a four-bit address space, we want to avoid having the addresses of *bill, lee,* and *pauline* turn out to be *0000, 0000,* and *0000.* If we work from right to left, starting with the low-order bit in each address, we get *0011* for *bill, 0001* for *lee,* and *1010* for *pauline,* which is a much more useful result.

The *make_address* function, described in Fig. 11.9, accomplishes this bit extraction and reversal. The DEPTH argument tells the function the number of address bits to return.

bill	0000 0011	0110 1100	
lee	0000 0100	0010 1000	
pauline	0000 1111	0110 0101	
alan	0100 1100	1010 0010	
julie	0010 1110	0000 1001	
mike	0000 0111	0100 1101	
elizabeth	0010 1100	0110 1010	
mark	0000 1010	0000 0111	

FIGURE 11.8 Output from the *hash* function for a number of keys.

```
FUNCTION make_address(KEY, DEPTH)

    set RETVAL to 0        /* to accumulate reversed
                              bit string            */
    set MASK to 1          /* 0...001 mask to extract
                              low bit from N         */
    HASH_VAL := hash(KEY)

    /*  Summary of loop logic:  Shift RETVAL one position
    **  left, to make room for a new low bit.  Then move
    **  HASH_VAL's low bit to RETVAL's low bit.  Then
    **  shift HASH_VAL in the opposite direction, to the
    **  right, so we can look at the next lowest bit.
    **  Keep doing this until we have moved as many bits
    **  as we need from HASH_VAL to RETVAL in reverse
    **  order.
    */
    for J := 1 to DEPTH
        RETVAL := RETVAL left shifted one position
        LOWBIT := HASH_VAL bitwise ANDed with MASK
        RETVAL := RETVAL bitwise ORed with LOWBIT
        HASH_VAL := HASH_VAL right shifted one position
    next J

    return RETVAL

end FUNCTION
```

FIGURE 11.9 Function *make_address (DEPTH)* gets a hashed address, reverses the order of the bits, and returns an address of *DEPTH* bits.

FIGURE 11.10 *BUCKET* and *DIR_CELL* record structures.

```
Record Type: BUCKET
    DEPTH        integer count of the number of bits used
                 "in common" by the keys in this bucket
    COUNT        integer count of the number of keys in
                 the bucket
    KEY[]        array [1..MAX_BUCKET_SIZE] of strings to
                 hold keys

Record Type: DIRECTORY_CELL
    BUCKET_REF   relative record number or other reference
                 to a specific BUCKET record on disk
```

11.3.2 Implementing the Top-level Operations

Our extendible hashing scheme consists of a set of buckets and a directory that references them. Each bucket is a record that contains the information shown in Fig. 11.10. These bucket records are stored in a file; we retrieve them as necessary.

Each cell in the directory consists of a reference to a BUCKET record. Because we use *direct access* to find directory records, we implement the directory as an array of these cells in RAM. The address values returned by *make_address* are treated as subscripts for this array, ranging from 0 to one less than the directory size.

From the high-level view of the driver function, use of the system consists of an initialization step that reads the directory into RAM from disk, a set of calls from the user to find or add keys, and a final, closing step that writes the possibly modified directory back to disk. Pseudocode for the driver, initialization, and close functions are shown in Fig. 11.11.

FIGURE 11.11 The *driver, ex_init,* and *ex_close* functions provide a high-level view of the extendible hashing program operation.

```
FUNCTION driver()
    ex_init()
    call op_add() and op_find() as directed by the user
    ex_close()
end FUNCTION


FUNCTION ex_init()
    open (or create, as necessary) the directory
        and bucket files
    if the hash file already exists
        read directory records into the array DIRECTORY
        DIR_DEPTH := log₂(size of DIRECTORY)
    else
        allocate an initial directory consisting of a
            single cell
        set DIR_DEPTH to 0
        allocate an initial bucket and assign its address
            to the directory cell
    endif
end FUNCTION


FUNCTION ex_close()
    write the directory back to disk
    close files
end FUNCTION
```

Note that the DIR_DEPTH is directly related to the size of the directory, since

$$2^{\text{DIR\_DEPTH}} = \text{the number of cells in DIRECTORY.}$$

If we are starting a new hash file, the DIR_DEPTH is zero, which means that we are using *no* bits to distinguish between addresses; all the keys go into the same bucket, no matter what their address. We get the address of the initial, everything-goes-here bucket and assign it to the single directory cell.

Given a way to open and close the file, we are ready to add records. The *op_add* and *op_find* functions are outlined in Fig. 11.12.

The *op_find* function turns the key into a directory address. Given this address, we do a direct lookup of the bucket location, retrieve the bucket and assign it to FOUND_BUCKET, and then search for the key. If FOUND_BUCKET contains the key, we return success; otherwise, we return FAILURE.

The *op_add* function begins by calling *op_find*. If the key already exists in the hash file, *op_add* returns immediately; if the key is not found, *op_add* calls *bk_add_key* to insert it.

11.3.3 Bucket and Directory Operations

When *op_add* calls *bk_add_key,* it passes a bucket and a key. If the bucket is not full, *bk_add_key* (Fig. 11.13) simply inserts it into the bucket. A full bucket, however, requires a split, which is where things start to get interesting.

What we do when we split a bucket depends on the relationship between the number of address bits used in the bucket and the number used in the directory as a whole. The two numbers are often not the same. To see this, look at Fig. 11.6(a). The directory uses *three* bits to define its address space (8 cells). The keys in bucket *A* are distinguished from keys in other buckets by having an initial *0* bit. All the other bits in the hashed key values in bucket *A* can be any value; it is only the first bit that matters. Bucket *A* is using only *one* bit.

The keys in bucket *C* all share a common first *two* bits; they all begin with *11*. The keys in buckets *B* and *D* use *three* bits to establish their identities and, therefore, their bucket locations. If you look at Fig. 11.6(c), you can see how using more or fewer address bits changes the relationship between the directory and the bucket. Buckets that do not use as many address bits as the directory have more than one directory cell pointing to them.

If we split one of the buckets that is using fewer address bits than the directory, and which therefore is referenced from more than one directory

```
FUNCTION: op_add (KEY)
    /* if we find the key, we do not add a second copy */
    if op_find(KEY, FOUND_BUCKET)
        return FAILURE

    /* otherwise, add the key to the bucket that op_find
    ** retrieved
    */
    bk_add_key(FOUND_BUCKET, KEY)
    return SUCCESS

end FUNCTION



FUNCTION: op_find (KEY, FOUND_BUCKET)

    /* uses DIR_DEPTH, the number of bits used to create
    ** the addresses in the directory
    */

    /* create an address based on directory depth */
    ADDRESS := make_address(KEY, DIR_DEPTH)

    /* get the bucket that will contain the key, if the
    ** key exists in the file
    */
    FOUND_BUCKET := bucket referenced by
                        DIRECTORY[ADDRESS].BUCKET_REF

    if FOUND_BUCKET contains the KEY
        return SUCCESS
    else
        return FAILURE

end FUNCTION
```

FIGURE 11.12 *op_add* and *op_find* functions.

```
FUNCTION bk_add_key(BUCKET, KEY)

    if (BUCKET.USED < MAX_BUCKET_SIZE)
        add the key
    else
        bk_split(BUCKET)
        op_add(KEY)
    endif

end FUNCTION
```

FIGURE 11.13 *bk_add_key* function adds the key to the existing bucket if there is room. If the bucket is full, it splits it and then adds the key.

```
FUNCTION bk_split(BUCKET)
   /* if the depth used for the BUCKET addresses is
   ** already the same as the address depth in the
   ** directory, we must first split the directory
   ** to double the directory address space
   */
   if (BUCKET.DEPTH == DIR_DEPTH)
      dir_double()

   allocate NEW_BUCKET

   /* find the range of directory entries for the new
   ** bucket, given the depth and keys in the old bucket
   */
   find_new_range(BUCKET, NEW_START, NEW_END)

   /* insert the new bucket over this range */
   dir_ins_bucket(NEW_BUCKET, NEW_START, NEW_END)

   /* change the address depths in the buckets to
   ** reflect the split
   */
   increment BUCKET.DEPTH
   NEW_BUCKET.DEPTH := BUCKET.DEPTH

   redistribute the keys between the two buckets

end FUNCTION
```

FIGURE 11.14 *bk_split* function divides keys between an existing bucket and a new bucket. If necessary, it doubles the size of the directory to accommodate the new bucket.

cell, we can use half of the directory cells to point to the new bucket after the split. Suppose, for example, that we split bucket *A* in Fig. 11.6(c). Before the split only one bit, the initial zero, is used to identify keys that belong in bucket *A*. After the split, we use two bits. Keys starting with *00* (directory cells *000* and *001*) go in bucket *A*; keys starting with *01* (directory cells *010* and *011*) go in the new bucket. We do not have to expand the directory because the directory already has the capacity to keep track of the additional address information required for the split.

If, on the other hand, we split a bucket that has the same address depth as the directory, such as buckets *B* or *D* in Fig. 11.6(c), then there are no additional directory entries that we can use to reference the new bucket. Before we can split the bucket, we have to double the size of the directory, creating a new directory entry for every one that is currently there, so we can accommodate the new address information.

Figure 11.14 shows the bucket-splitting logic in pseudocode. First we compare the number of bits used for the directory with the number used for the bucket to determine whether we need to double the directory. If the depths are the same, we double the directory before proceeding.

Next we get the new bucket that we need for the split. Then we find the range of directory addresses that we will use for the new bucket. For instance, when we split bucket *A* in Fig. 11.6(c), the range of directory addresses for the new bucket is from *010* to *011*. We attach the new bucket to the directory over this range, adjust the bucket address depth information in both buckets to reflect the use of an additional address bit, and then redistribute the keys from the original bucket across the two buckets.

The most complicated operation supporting the *bk_split* function is *find_new_range,* which finds the range of directory cells that should point to the new bucket instead of the old one after the split. It is described in pseudocode in Fig. 11.15. To see how it works, return, once again, to Fig.

FIGURE 11.15 *find_new_range* function finds the start and end directory addresses for the new bucket by using information from the old bucket.

```
FUNCTION find_new_range(OLD_BUCKET, NEW_START, NEW_END)

    /* find the shared address for the OLD bucket */
    SHARED_ADDRESS := make_address(any KEY from
        OLD_BUCKET, OLD_BUCKET.DEPTH)

    /* shift everything one bit to the left, then put
    ** a 1 in the lowest bit. This is the shared address
    ** for the new bucket. Fill the new shared address on
    ** the right with zero bits until we have reached the
    ** directory depth. This is the start of the range.
    ** Fill it with 1 bits -- this is the range's end.
    */
    NEW_SHARED := SHARED_ADDRESS left shifted 1 place
    NEW_SHARED := NEW_SHARED bitwise ORed with 1

    BITS_TO_FILL := DIR_DEPTH - (OLD_BUCKET.DEPTH + 1)
    set NEW_START and NEW_END to the NEW_SHARED value
    for J := 1 to BITS_TO_FILL
        NEW_START := NEW_START left shifted 1 place
        NEW_END := NEW_END left shifted 1 place
        NEW_END := NEW_END bitwise ORed with 1
    next J

end FUNCTION
```

11.6(c). Assume that we need to split bucket *A*, putting some of the keys into a new bucket *E*. Before the split, any address beginning with a *0* leads to *A*. In other words, the *shared address* of the keys in bucket *A* is *0*.

When we split bucket *A* we add another address bit to the path leading to the keys; addresses leading to bucket *A* now share an initial *00* while those leading to *E* share an *01*. So, the range of addresses for the new bucket is all directory addresses beginning with *01*. Since the directory addresses

FIGURE 11.16 Directory operations to support *bk_split:* the *dir_double* and *dir_ins_bucket* functions.

```
FUNCTION dir_double()
    /* calculate the current size and new size */
    CURRENT_SIZE := 2^DIR_DEPTH
    NEW_SIZE := 2 * CURRENT_SIZE

    allocate memory for the new, larger directory --
        temporarily call it NEW_DIR

    /* Transfer the bucket addresses from the old
    ** directory to the new one. Each cell in the
    ** original is copied into two cells of the
    ** expanded directory
    */
    for I := 0 to CURRENT_SIZE - 1
        NEW_DIR[2*I].BUCKET_REF :=
                        DIRECTORY[I].BUCKET_REF
        NEW_DIR[2*I+1].BUCKET_REF :=
                        DIRECTORY[I].BUCKET_REF
    next I

    free memory for old DIRECTORY
    rename NEW_DIR to DIRECTORY
    increment DIR_DEPTH

end FUNCTION



FUNCTION dir_ins_bucket(BUCKET_ADDRESS, START, LAST)
    for J := START to LAST
        DIRECTORY[J].BUCKET_REF := BUCKET_ADDRESS
    next J

end FUNCTION
```

use three bits, the new bucket is attached to the directory cells starting with *010* and ending with *011*.

Suppose that the directory used a five-bit address instead of a three-bit address. Then the range for the new bucket would start with *01000* and would end with *01111*. This range covers all five bit addresses that share *01* as the first two bits. The logic for finding the range of directory addresses for the new bucket, then, starts by finding *shared address* bits for the new bucket. It then fills the address out with zeroes until we have the number of bits used in the directory. This is the start of the range. Filling the address out with ones produces the end of the range.

The directory operations required to support *bk_split* are easy to implement. They are outlined in pseudocode in Fig. 11.16. The first, *dir_double,* simply calculates the new directory size, allocates the required memory, and writes the information from each old directory cell into two successive cells in the new directory. It finishes by freeing the old space associated with the name DIRECTORY, renaming the new space as the DIRECTORY, and increasing the DIR_DEPTH value to reflect the fact that the directory is now using an additional address bit.

The *dir_ins_bucket* function, used to attach a bucket address across a range of directory cells, is simply a loop that works through the cells to make the change.

11.3.4 Implementation Summary

Now that we have assembled all of the pieces necessary to add records to an extendible hashing system, let's see how the pieces work together.

The *op_add* function manages record addition. If the key already exists, *op_add* returns immediately. If the key does not exist, *op_add* calls *bk_add_key,* passing it the bucket into which the key is to be added. If *bk_add_key* finds that there is still room in the bucket, it adds the key and the operation is complete. If the bucket is full, *bk_add_key* calls *bk_split* to handle the task of splitting the bucket.

The *bk_split* function starts by determining whether the directory is large enough to accommodate the new bucket. If the directory needs to be larger, *bk_split* calls a function that doubles the directory size. The function then allocates a new bucket, attaches it to the appropriate directory cells, and divides the keys between the two buckets.

When *bk_add_key* regains control after *bk_split* has allocated a new bucket, it calls *op_add* to try to place the key into the new, revised directory structure. The *op_add* function, of course, calls *bk_add_key* again, recursively. This cycle continues until there is a bucket that can accommodate the new key.

11.4 Deletion

11.4.1 Overview of the Deletion Process

If extendible hashing is to be a truly *dynamic* system, like B-trees or AVL trees, it must be able to *shrink* files gracefully as well as grow them. When we delete a key, we need a way to see if we can decrease the size of the file system by combining buckets and, if possible, decreasing the size of the directory.

As with any dynamic system, the important question during deletion concerns the definition of the triggering condition: When do we combine buckets? This question, in turn, leads us to ask, Which buckets can be combined? For B-trees the answer involves determining whether buckets are *siblings* and whether they are at the leaf level of the tree. In extendible hashing we use a similar concept: buckets that are *buddy* buckets.

Look again at the trie in Fig. 11.6(b). Which buckets could be combined? Trying to combine anything with bucket *A* would mean collapsing everything else in the trie first. Similarly, there is no single bucket that could be combined with bucket *C*. But buckets *B* and *D* are in the same configuration as buckets that have just split. They are ready to be combined; they are buddy buckets. We will take a closer look at the question of finding buddy buckets as we consider implementation of the deletion procedure; for now let's assume that we combine buckets *B* and *D*.

After combining buckets, we examine the directory to see if we can make changes there. Looking at the directory form of the trie in Fig. 11.6(c), we see that once we combine buckets *B* and *D,* directory entries *100* and *101* both point to the same bucket. In fact, each of the buckets has at least a pair of directory entries pointing to it. In other words, none of the buckets requires the depth of address information that is currently available in the directory. That means that we can shrink the directory and reduce the address space to half its size.

Reducing the size of the address space restores the directory and bucket structure to the arrangement shown in Fig. 11.4, before the additions and splits that produced the structure in Fig. 11.6(c). Reduction consists of collapsing each adjacent pair of directory cells into a single cell. This is easy, since both cells in each pair point to the same bucket. Note that this is nothing more than a reversal of the directory splitting procedure that we use when we need to add new directory cells.

11.4.2 A Procedure for Finding Buddy Buckets

Given this overview of how deletion works, we begin by focusing on buddy buckets. Given a bucket, how do we find its buddy? Figure 11.17

```
FUNCTION bk_find_buddy(BUCKET)
    /* NOTE: this function uses DIR_DEPTH -- we
    ** assume this value is available globally or
    ** through a function call
    */

    /* There is no buddy if the DIR_DEPTH is 0 (there
    ** is just a single bucket)
    */
    if (DIR_DEPTH == 0)
        return NO_BUDDY

    /* unless the bucket has the same depth as the
    ** directory, there is no single bucket to pair with
    */
    if (BUCKET.DEPTH < DIR_DEPTH)
        return NO_BUDDY

    /* find the shared address for this bucket */
    SHARED_ADDRESS := make_address(any KEY from
        BUCKET, BUCKET.DEPTH)

    /* flip the last bit -- that is the address of the
    ** buddy bucket
    */
    BUDDY_ADDRESS := SHARED_ADDRESS exclusive ORed with 1

    return BUDDY_BUCKET found at BUDDY_ADDRESS

end FUNCTION
```

FIGURE 11.17 The *bk_find_buddy* function returns a buddy bucket or the special signal NO_BUDDY if none is found.

describes the procedure in pseudocode. The procedure works by checking to see whether it is possible for there to be a buddy bucket. Clearly, if the directory depth is zero, meaning that there is only a single bucket, there cannot be a buddy.

The next test compares the number of bits used by the bucket with the number of bits used in the directory address space. A pair of buddy buckets is a set of buckets that are immediate descendents of the same node in the trie. They are, in fact, pairwise siblings resulting from a split. Going back to Fig. 11.6(b), we see that asking whether the bucket uses all the address bits used in the directory is another way of asking whether the bucket is at the lowest level of the trie. It is only when a bucket is at the outer edge of the trie that it can have a single parent and a single buddy.

Once we determine that there is a buddy bucket, we need to find its address. First we find the address used to find the bucket we have at hand; this is the shared address of the keys in the bucket. Since we know that the buddy bucket is the other bucket that was formed from a split, we know that the buddy has the same address in all regards except for the last bit. Once again, this relationship is illustrated by buckets *B* and *D* in Fig. 11.6(b). So, to get the buddy address, we flip the last bit. We return the buddy bucket.

11.4.3 Collapsing the Directory

The other important support function used to implement deletion is the function that handles collapsing the directory. Downsizing the directory is one of the principal potential benefits of deleting records. In our implementation we use one function to check to see whether downsizing is possible and, if it is, to actually collapse the directory. Figure 11.18 shows pseudocode for this function, called *dir_try_collapse( )*.

The function begins by making sure that we are not at the lower limit of directory size. By treating the special case of a directory with a single cell here, at the start of the function, we simplify subsequent processing: With the exception of this case, all directory sizes are evenly divisible by two.

The actual test for the COLLAPSE_CONDITION consists of examining each pair of directory entries. We assume at the outset that we can collapse the directory and then look for a pair of directory cells that do not both point to the same bucket. As soon as we find such a pair, we know that we *cannot* collapse the directory. We set the value of the COLLAPSE_CONDITION to false and break out of the test loop. If we get all the way through the directory without encountering such a pair, then we can collapse the directory.

The actual collapsing operation consists of allocating space for a new directory that is half the size of the original and then copying the bucket references shared by each cell pair to a single cell in the new directory.

11.4.4 Implementing the Deletion Operations

Now that we have an approach to the two critical support operations for deletion, finding buddy buckets and collapsing the directory, we are ready to construct the higher levels of the deletion operation.

The highest-level deletion operation, *op_del,* is very simple. We first try to find the key to be deleted. If we cannot find it, we return failure; if we do find it, we call a service function to remove the key from the bucket. We

```
FUNCTION dir_try_collapse()
    /* the directory is already at minimum size when
    ** the depth is zero
    */
    if (DIR_DEPTH == 0)
        return FAILURE

    /* check each pair of directory cells to see whether
    ** each member references the same bucket -- if so,
    ** we can collapse the directory.
    */
    DIR_SIZE := 2^DIR_DEPTH
    COLLAPSE_CONDITION := TRUE;   /* assume the best, then
                                     try to disprove it */
    for J := 0 to DIR_SIZE - 1 by 2
        if (DIRECTORY[J].BUCKET_REF !=
                DIRECTORY[J+1].BUCKET_REF)
            COLLAPSE_CONDITION := FALSE
            break out of the loop
        endif
    next J by 2

    /* if we have a collapse condition, create a new
    ** directory that is half the size of the original,
    ** and transfer the bucket references
    */
    if (COLLAPSE_CONDITION)
        NEW_DIR_SIZE := DIR_SIZE / 2
        allocate memory for NEW_DIR

        for J := 0 to NEW_DIR_SIZE - 1
            NEW_DIR[J].BUCKET_REF :=
                    DIRECTORY[2*J].BUCKET_REF
        next J

        free memory for old DIRECTORY
        rename NEW_DIR to DIRECTORY
        decrement DIR_DEPTH
    endif

    return COLLAPSE_CONDITION

end FUNCTION
```

FIGURE 11.18 The *dir_try_collapse* function first tests to see whether the directory can be collapsed. If the test succeeds, the directory is collapsed.

```
FUNCTION: op_del (KEY)
    if (op_find(KEY, FOUND_BUCKET) == FAILURE)
        return FAILURE

    /* found it -- now delete it */
    return (bk_del_key(FOUND_BUCKET, KEY))

end FUNCTION



FUNCTION bk_del_key(BUCKET, KEY)
    set KEY_REMOVED to FALSE

    Look for KEY in BUCKET -- if found
        remove the KEY
        set KEY_REMOVED to TRUE
        decrement BUCKET.COUNT

    /* if a key was removed, see whether we can combine
    ** this bucket with its buddy bucket
    */
    if (KEY_REMOVED)
        bk_try_combine(BUCKET)
        return SUCCESS
    else
        return FAILURE
    endif

end FUNCTION
```

FIGURE 11.19 The *op_del* and *bk_del_key* functions.

return the value reported back from the service function. Figure 11.19 describes *op_del* and the service function, *bk_del_key,* in pseudocode.

The *bk_del_key* function does its work in two steps. The first step consists of finding the key and physically removing it from the bucket. The second step, which takes place only if a key is removed, consists of calling *bk_try_combine* to see if deleting the key has decreased the size of the bucket enough to allow us to combine it with its buddy.

Figure 11.20 shows the pseudocode for *bk_try_combine* and its service function, *bk_combine.* Note that when we combine buckets, we reduce the address depth associated with the bucket: Combining buckets means that we use one less address bit to differentiate keys.

After combining the buckets, we call *dir_try_collapse* to see if the decrease in the number of buckets enables us to decrease the size of the directory. If we do, in fact, collapse the directory (*dir_try_collapse* succeeds), *bk_try_combine* calls itself recursively. Collapsing the directory may have created a new buddy for the BUCKET; it may be possible to do even more combination and collapsing. Typically, this recursive combining and collapsing happens only when the directory has a number of *empty* buckets that are awaiting changes in the directory structure that finally produce a buddy to combine with.

FIGURE 11.20 The *bk_try_combine* function tests to see whether a bucket can be combined with its buddy. If the test succeeds, *bk_try_combine* calls *bk_combine* to do the actual combination.

```
FUNCTION bk_try_combine(BUCKET)
    /* If there is no buddy return right away */
    BUDDY := bk_find_buddy(BUCKET)
    if (BUDDY == NO_BUDDY)
        return

    /* see if we can combine buckets */
    if (BUDDY.COUNT + BUCKET.COUNT <= MAX_BUCKET_SIZE)

        bk_combine(BUCKET, BUDDY)

        free memory used by the BUDDY bucket

        reassign the DIRECTORY value for the BUDDY so
            that it now references the BUCKET

        /* see if we can collapse the directory -- if
        ** so, there may be a new buddy to combine with
        */
        if (dir_try_collapse())
            bk_try_combine(BUCKET)
    endif

end FUNCTION


FUNCTION bk_combine(BUCKET, BUDDY)
    for J := 1 to BUDDY.COUNT
        increment BUCKET.COUNT
        BUCKET[BUCKET.COUNT].KEY = BUDDY[J].KEY
    next J

    decrement BUCKET.DEPTH
end FUNCTION
```

11.4.5 Summary of the Deletion Operation

Deletion begins with a call to *op_del* that passes the key that is to be deleted. If the key cannot be found, there is nothing to delete. If the key is found, the bucket containing the key is passed to *bk_del_key*.

The *bk_del_key* function deletes the key and then passes the bucket on to *bk_try_combine* to see if the smaller size of the bucket will now permit combination with a buddy bucket. The *bk_try_combine* function first checks to see if there is a buddy bucket. If not, we are done. If there is a buddy, and if the sum of the keys in the bucket and its buddy is less than or equal to the size of a single bucket, we combine the buckets.

The elimination of a bucket through combination might enable collapsing of the directory to half its size. We investigate this possibility by calling *bk_try_collapse*. If collapsing succeeds, we may have a new buddy bucket, and so *bk_try_combine* calls itself again, recursively.

11.5   Extendible Hashing Performance

Extendible hashing is an elegant solution to the problem of extending and contracting the address space for a hash file as the file itself grows and shrinks. How well does it work? As always, the answer to this question must consider the trade-off between time and space.

The time dimension is easy to handle: If the directory for extendible hashing can be kept in RAM, a single access is all that is ever required to retrieve a record. If the directory is so large that it must be paged in and out of RAM, two accesses may be necessary. The important point is that extendible hashing provides $O(1)$ performance: Since there is no overflow, these access time values are truly independent of the size of the file.

Questions about space utilization for extendible hashing are more complicated than questions about access time. We need to be concerned about two uses of space: the space for the buckets and the space for the directory.

11.5.1 Space Utilization for Buckets

In their original paper describing extendible hashing, Fagin, Nievergelt, Pippenger, and Strong include analysis and simulation of extendible hashing performance. Both the analysis and simulation show that the space utilization is strongly periodic, fluctuating between values of 0.53 and 0.94. The analysis portion of their paper suggests that for a given number of records r and a block size of b, the average number of blocks N is approximated by the formula

$$N \approx \frac{r}{b \ln 2}.$$

Space utilization, or packing density, is defined as the ratio of the actual number of records to the total number of records that could be stored in the allocated space:

$$\text{Utilization} = \frac{r}{bN}.$$

Substituting the approximation for N gives us:

$$\text{Utilization} \approx \ln 2 = 0.69.$$

So, we expect *average* utilization of 69%. In Chapter 8, where we looked at space utilization for B-trees, we found that simple B-trees tend to have a utilization of about 67%, but this can be increased to over 85% by redistributing keys during insertion, rather than just splitting when a page is full. So, B-trees tend to use less space than simple extendible hashing, typically at a cost of requiring a few extra seeks.

The average space utilization for extendible hashing is only part of the story; the other part relates to the periodic nature of the variations in space utilization. It turns out that if we have keys with randomly distributed addresses, the buckets in the extendible hashing table tend to fill up at about the same time and therefore tend to split at the same time. This explains the large fluctuations in space utilization. As the buckets fill up, space utilization can reach past 90%. This is followed by a concentrated series of splits that reduce the utilization to below 50%. As these now nearly half-full buckets fill up again, the cycle repeats itself.

11.5.2 Space Utilization for the Directory

The directory used in extendible hashing grows by doubling its size. A prudent designer setting out to implement an extendible hashing system will want assurance that this doubling levels off for reasonable bucket sizes, even when the number of keys is quite large. Just how large a directory should we expect to have, given an expected number of keys?

Flajolet (1983) addressed this question in a lengthy, carefully developed paper that produces a number of different ways to estimate the directory size. Table 11.1, which is taken from Flajolet's paper, shows the expected value for the directory size for different numbers of keys and different bucket sizes.

TABLE 11.1   Expected directory size for a given bucket size *b* and total number of records *r*

b	5	10	20	50	100	200
r						
10^3	1.50 K	0.30 K	0.10 K	0.00 K	0.00 K	0.00 K
10^4	25.60 K	4.80 K	1.70 K	0.50 K	0.20 K	0.00 K
10^5	424.10 K	68.20 K	16.80 K	4.10 K	2.00 K	1.00 K
10^6	6.90 M	1.02 M	0.26 M	62.50 K	16.80 K	8.10 K
10^7	111.11 M	11.64 M	2.25 M	0.52 M	0.26 M	0.13 M

$1 \text{ K} = 10^3$, $1 \text{ M} = 10^6$.
From Flajolet, 1983.

Flajolet also provides the following formula for making rough estimates of the directory size for values that are not in this table. He notes that this formula tends to overestimate directory size by a factor of 2 to 4.

$$\text{Estimated directory size} \approx \frac{3.92}{b} r^{(1+1/b)}$$

11.6   Alternative Approaches

11.6.1   Dynamic Hashing

In 1978, before Fagin, Nievergelt, Pippenger, and Strong produced their paper on extendible hashing, Larson published a paper describing a scheme called *dynamic hashing*. Functionally, dynamic hashing and extendible hashing are very similar. Both use a directory to track the addresses of the buckets, and both extend the directory through the use of tries.

The key difference between the approaches is that dynamic hashing, like conventional, static hashing, starts with a hash function that covers an address space of a fixed size. As buckets within that fixed address space overflow, they split, forming the leaves of a trie that grows down from the original address node. Eventually, after enough additions and splitting, the buckets are addressed through a forest of tries that have been seeded out of the original static address space.

Let's look at an example. Figure 11.21(a) shows an initial address space of four, and four buckets descending from the four addresses in the

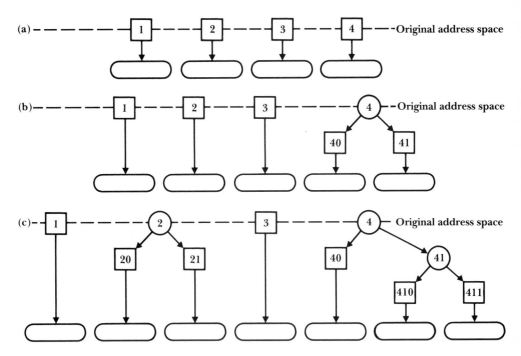

FIGURE 11.21 The growth of index in dynamic hashing.

directory. In Fig. 11.21(b) we have split the bucket at address *4.* We address
the two buckets resulting from the split as *40* and *41.* We change the shape
of the directory node at address *4* from a square to a circle because it has
changed from an external node, referencing a bucket, to an internal node
that points to two child nodes.

In Fig. 11.21(c) we split the bucket addressed by node *2,* creating the
new external nodes *20* and *21.* We also split the bucket addressed by *41,*
extending the trie downward to include *410* and *411.* Because the directory
node *41* is now an internal node rather than an external one, it changes from
a square to a circle. As we continue to add keys and split buckets, these
directory tries continue to grow.

Finding a key in a dynamic hashing scheme can involve the use of two
hash functions, rather than just one. First, there is the hash function that
covers the original address space. If you find that the directory node is an
external node, and therefore points to a bucket, the search is complete.
However, if the directory node is an internal node, then you need additional
address information to guide you through the ones and zeroes that form the

trie. Larson suggests using a second hash function on the key and using the result of this hashing as the seed for a random-number generator that produces a sequence of ones and zeroes for the key. This sequence describes the path through the trie.

It is interesting to compare dynamic hashing and extendible hashing. A brief, but illuminating, characterization of similarities and differences is that while both schemes extend the hash function locally, as a binary search trie, in order to handle overflow, dynamic hashing expresses the extended directory as a linked structure while extendible hashing expresses it as a perfect tree, which is in turn expressible as an array.

Because of this fundamental similarity, it is not surprising that the space utilization within the buckets is the same (69%) for both approaches. Moreover, since the directories are essentially equivalent, and are just expressed differently, it follows that the estimates of directory depth developed by Flajolet (1983) apply equally well to dynamic hashing and extendible hashing. (In section 11.5.2 we talk about estimates for the directory *size* for extendible hashing, but we know that in extendible hashing *directory depth* = $\log_2$ *directory size.*)

The primary difference between the two approaches is that dynamic hashing allows for slower, more gradual growth of the directory, whereas extendible hashing extends the directory by doubling it. However, because the directory nodes in dynamic hashing must be capable of holding pointers to children, the actual size of a node in dynamic hashing is larger than a directory cell in extendible hashing, probably by at least a factor of two. So, the directory for dynamic hashing will usually require more space in memory. Moreover, if the directory becomes so large that it requires use of virtual memory, extendible hashing offers the advantage of being able to access the directory with no more than a single page fault. Since dynamic hashing uses a linked structure for the directory, it may be necessary to incur more than one page fault to move through the directory.

11.6.2 Linear Hashing

The key feature of both extendible hashing and dynamic hashing is that they use a directory to direct access to the actual buckets containing the key records. This directory makes it possible to expand and modify the hashed address space without expanding the number of buckets: After expanding the directory, more than one directory node can point to the same bucket. However, the directory adds an additional layer of indirection which, if the directory must be stored on disk, can result in an additional seek.

Linear hashing, introduced by Litwin in 1980, does away with the directory. An example, developed in Fig. 11.22, shows how linear hashing

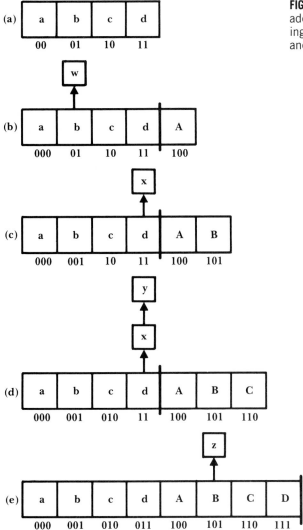

FIGURE 11.22 The growth of address space in linear hashing. Adapted from Enbody and Du (1988).

works. This example is adapted from a description of linear hashing by Enbody and Du (1988).

Linear hashing, like extendible hashing, uses more bits of hashed value as the address space grows. The example begins (Fig. 11.22a) with an address space of four, which means that we are using an address function that produces addresses with two bits of depth. In terms of the pseudocode that we developed earlier in this chapter, we are calling *make_address* with a key and a second argument of 2. For this example we will refer to this as the $h_2(k)$ address function. Note that the address space consists of four *buckets*, rather than four directory nodes that can point to buckets.

As we add records, bucket *b* overflows. The overflow forces a split. However, as Fig. 11.22(b) shows, it is not bucket *b* that splits, but bucket *a*. The reason for this is that we are extending the address space *linearly*, and bucket *a* is the next bucket that must split to create the next linear extension, which we call bucket *A*. A three-bit hash function, $h_3(k)$, is applied to buckets *a* and *A* to divide the records between them. Since bucket *b* was not the bucket that we split, the overflowing record is placed into an overflow bucket *w*.

We add more records, and bucket *d* overflows. Bucket *b* is the next one to split and extend the address space, so we use the $h_3(k)$ address function to divide the records from bucket *b* and its overflow bucket *w* between *b* and the new bucket *B*. The record overflowing bucket *d* is placed in an overflow bucket *x*. The resulting arrangement is illustrated in Fig. 11.22(c).

Figure 11.22(d) shows what happens when, as we add more records, bucket *d* overflows beyond the capacity of the overflow bucket *w*. Bucket *c* is the next in the extension sequence, so we use the $h_3(k)$ address function to divide the records between *c* and *C*.

Finally, assume that bucket *B* overflows. The overflow record is placed in the overflow bucket *z*. The overflow also triggers the extension to bucket *D*, dividing the contents of *d*, *x*, and *y* between buckets *d* and *D*. At this point all of the buckets use the $h_3(k)$ address function, and we have finished the expansion cycle. The pointer for the next bucket to be split returns to bucket *a* to get ready for a new cycle that will use an $h_4(k)$ address function to reach new buckets.

Since linear hashing uses two hash functions to reach the buckets during an expansion cycle, an $h_d(k)$ function for the buckets at the current address depth and an $h_{d+1}(k)$ function for the expansion buckets, finding a record requires knowing which function to use. If *p* is the pointer to the address of the next bucket to be split and extended, then the procedure for finding the address of the bucket containing a key *k* is as follows:

$$\text{if } h_d(k) > = p$$

$$address : = h_d(k)$$

else

$$address : = h_{d + 1}(k)$$

Litwin (1980) shows that the access time performance of linear hashing is quite good. There is no directory to access or maintain, and since we extend the address space through splitting every time there is overflow, the overflow chains do not become very large. Given a bucket size of 50, the average number of disk accesses per search approaches very close to one. Space utilization, on the other hand, is lower than it is for extendible hashing or dynamic hashing, averaging around only 60%.

11.6.3 Approaches to Controlling Splitting

We know from Chapter 8 that we can increase the storage capacity of B-trees by implementing measures that tend to postpone splitting, redistributing keys between pages rather than splitting pages. We can apply similar logic to the hashing schemes introduced in this chapter, placing records in chains of overflow buckets to postpone splitting.

Since linear hashing has the lowest storage utilization of the schemes introduced here, and since it already includes logic to handle overflow buckets, it is an attractive candidate for use of controlled splitting logic. In its uncontrolled-splitting form, linear hashing splits a bucket and extends the address space every time any bucket overflows. This choice of a triggering event for splitting is arbitrary, particularly when we consider that the bucket that splits is typically not the bucket that overflows. Litwin (1980) suggests using the overall load factor of the file as an alternative triggering event. Suppose we let the buckets overflow until the space utilization reaches some desired figure, such as 75%. Every time the utilization exceeds that figure, we split a bucket and extend the address space. Litwin simulated this kind of system and found that for load factors of 75% and even 85%, the average number of accesses for successful and unsuccessful searches still stays below 2.

We can also use overflow buckets to defer splitting and increase space utilization for dynamic hashing and extendible hashing. For these methods, which use directories to the buckets, deferring splitting has the additional attraction of keeping the directory size down. For extendible hashing it is particularly advantageous to chain to an overflow bucket and therefore avoid a split when the split would cause the directory to double in size. Consider the example that we used early in this chapter, where we split the bucket B in Fig. 11.4(b), producing the expanded directory and bucket structure shown in Fig. 11.6(c). If we had allowed bucket B to overflow instead, we could have retained the smaller directory. Depending on how much space we allocated for the overflow buckets, we might also have improved space utilization among the buckets. The cost of these improvements, of course, is a potentially greater search length due to the overflow chains.

Studies of the effects of different overflow bucket sizes and chaining mechanisms has supported a small industry of academic research during the early and mid-1980s. Larson (1978) suggested the use of deferred splitting in his original paper on dynamic hashing but found the results of some preliminary simulations of the idea to be disappointing. Scholl (1981) developed a refinement of this idea in which overflow buckets are shared. Master's thesis research by Chang (1985) tested Scholl's suggestions empirically and found that it was possible to achieve storage utilization of about 81% while maintaining search performance in the range of 1.1 seeks per search. Veklerov (1985) suggested using buddy buckets for overflow rather than allocating chains of new buckets. This is an attractive suggestion, since splitting buckets without buddies can never cause a doubling of the directory in extendible hashing. Veklerov obtained storage utilization of about 76% with a bucket size of 8.

■ SUMMARY

Conventional, static hashing does not adapt well to file structures that are *dynamic,* that grow and shrink over time. Extendible hashing is one of several hashing systems that allow the address space for hashing to grow and shrink along with the file. Because the size of the address space can grow as the file grows, it is possible for extendible hashing to provide hashed access without the need for overflow handling, even as files grow many times beyond their original expected size.

The key to extendible hashing is the idea of using more bits of the hashed value as we need to cover more address space. The model for extending the use of the hashed value is the *trie:* Every time we use another bit of the hashed value, we have added another level to the depth of a trie with a radix of two.

In extendible hashing we fill out all the leaves of the trie until we have a perfect tree, and then we collapse that tree into a one-dimensional array. The array forms a directory to the buckets, kept on disk, that actually hold the keys and records. The directory is managed in RAM, if possible.

If we add a record and there is no room for it in a bucket, we split the bucket. We use one additional bit from the hash values for the keys in the bucket to divide the keys between the old bucket and the new one. If the address space represented in the directory can cover the use of this new bit, no more changes are necessary. If, however, the address space is using fewer bits than are needed by our splitting buckets, then we double the address space to accommodate the use of the new bit.

Deletion reverses the addition process, recognizing that it is possible to combine the records for two buckets only if they are *buddy* buckets, which is to say that they are the pair of buckets that resulted from a split.

Access performance for extendible hashing is a single seek if the directory can be kept in RAM. If the directory must be paged off to disk, worst-case performance is two seeks. Space utilization for the buckets is approximately 69%. Tables and an approximation formula developed by Flajolet (1983) permit estimation of the probable directory size, given a bucket size and total number of records.

There are a number of other approaches to the problem solved by extendible hashing. *Dynamic hashing* uses a very similar approach but expresses the directory as a linked structure rather than as an array. The linked structure is more cumbersome but grows more smoothly. Space utilization and seek performance for dynamic hashing are the same as for extendible hashing.

Linear hashing does away with the directory entirely, extending the address space by adding new buckets in a linear sequence. Although the overflow of a bucket can be used to trigger extension of the address space in linear hashing, typically the bucket that overflows is not the one that is split and extended. Consequently, linear hashing implies maintaining overflow chains and a consequent degradation in seek performance. The degradation is slight, since the chains typically do not grow to be very long before they are pulled into a new bucket. Space utilization is about 60%.

Space utilization for extendible, dynamic, and linear hashing can be improved by postponing the splitting of buckets. This is easy to implement for linear hashing, since there are already overflow buckets. Using deferred splitting, it is possible to increase space utilization for any of the hashing schemes described here to 80% or better while still maintaining search performance averaging less than two seeks. Overflow handling for these approaches can use the sharing of overflow buckets.

■ KEY TERMS

Buddy bucket. Given a bucket with an address *uvwxy*, where *u*, *v*, *w*, *x*, and *y* have values of either *0* or *1*, the buddy bucket, if it exists, has the value *uvwxz*, such that

$$z = y \text{ XOR } 1.$$

Buddy buckets are important in deletion operations for extendible hashing since, if enough keys are deleted, the contents of buddy buckets can be combined into a single bucket.

Deferred splitting. It is possible to improve space utilization for *dynamic hashing, extendible hashing,* and *linear hashing* by postponing, or deferring, the splitting of buckets, placing records into overflow buckets instead. This is a classic space/time trade-off in which we accept diminished performance in return for more compact storage.

Directory. Conventional, static hashing schemes transform a key into a bucket address. Both *extendible hashing* and *dynamic hashing* introduce an additional layer of indirection, in which the key is hashed to a *directory address*. The directory, in turn, contains information about the location of the bucket. This additional indirection makes it possible to extend the address space by extending the directory, rather than having to work with an address space made up of buckets.

Dynamic hashing. Used in a generic sense, *dynamic hashing* can refer to any hashing system that provides for expansion and contraction of the address space for dynamic files where the number of records changes over time. In this chapter we use the term in a more specific sense to refer to a system initially described by Larson (1978). The system uses a directory to provide access to the buckets that actually contain the records. Entries in the directory can be used as root nodes of *trie* structures that accommodate greater numbers of buckets as buckets split.

Extendible hashing. Like *dynamic hashing, extendible hashing* is sometimes used to refer to any hashing scheme that allows the address space to grow and shrink so it can be used in dynamic file systems. Used more precisely, as it is used in this chapter, *extendible hashing* refers to an approach to hashed retrieval for dynamic files that was first proposed by Fagin, Nievergelt, Pippenger, and Strong (1979). Their proposal is for a system that uses a directory to represent the address space. Access to buckets containing the records is through the directory. The directory is handled as an array; the size of the array can be doubled or halved as the number of buckets changes.

Linear hashing. An approach to hashing for dynamic files that was first proposed by Litwin (1980). Unlike *extendible hashing* and *dynamic hashing,* linear hashing does not use a directory. Instead, the actual address space is extended one bucket at a time as buckets overflow. Because the extension of the address space does not necessarily correspond to the bucket that is overflowing, linear hashing necessarily involves the use of overflow buckets, even as the address space expands.

Splitting. The hashing schemes described in this chapter make room for new records by splitting buckets to form new buckets, and then extending the address space to cover these buckets. Conventional, static hashing schemes rely strictly on overflow buckets without extending the address space.

Trie. A search tree structure in which each successive character of the key is used to determine the direction of the search at each successive level of the tree. The branching factor (the *radix* of the trie) at any level is potentially equal to the number of values that the character can take.

■ EXERCISES

1. Briefly describe the differences between extendible hashing, dynamic hashing, and linear hashing. What are the strengths and weaknesses of each approach?

2. The tries that are the basis for the extendible hashing procedure described in this chapter have a radix of two. How does performance change if we use a larger radix?

3. In the *make_address* function, what would happen if we did not reverse the order of the bits but just extracted the required number of low-order bits in the same left-to-right order that they occur in the address? Think about the way the directory location would change as we extend the implicit trie structure to use yet another bit.

4. If the language that you are using to implement the *make_address* function does not support bit shifting and masking operations, how could you achieve the same ends, even if less elegantly and clearly?

5. In the *bk_split* function, we redistribute keys between the original bucket and a new one. Outline a possible implementation for this redistribution. How do you decide whether a key belongs in the new bucket or the original bucket?

6. Suppose the redistribution of keys in *bk_split* does not result in moving any keys into the new bucket. Under what conditions could such an event happen? How will the program handle this?

7. The *bk_try_combine* function is potentially recursive. In section 11.4.4 we described a situation in which there are empty buckets that can be combined with other buckets through a series of recursive calls to *bk_try_combine*. Describe two situations that could produce empty buckets in the hash structure.

8. Deletion occasionally results in collapsing the directory. Describe the conditions that must be met before the directory can collapse.

9. Deletion depends on finding *buddy buckets*. Why does the address depth for a bucket have to be the same as the address depth for the directory in order for a bucket to have a buddy?

10. In the extendible hashing procedure described in this chapter, the directory can occasionally point to empty buckets. Describe two situations that can produce empty buckets. How could we modify the procedures to avoid empty buckets?

11. If buckets are large, a bucket containing only a few records is not much less wasteful than an empty bucket. How could we minimize *nearly empty* buckets?

12. Linear hashing makes use of overflow records. Assuming an uncontrolled splitting implementation where we split and extend the address space as soon as we have an overflow, what is the effect of using different bucket sizes for the overflow buckets? For example, consider overflow buckets that are as large as the original buckets. Now consider overflow buckets that can only hold one record. How does this choice affect performance in terms of space utilization and access time?

13. In section 11.6.3 we described an approach to linear hashing that controls splitting. For a load factor of 85%, the average number of accesses for a successful search is 1.20 (Litwin, 1980). Unsuccessful searches require an average of 1.78 accesses. Why is the average search length greater for unsuccessful searches?

14. Because linear hashing splits one bucket at a time, in order, until it has reached the end of the sequence, the overflow chains for the last buckets in the sequence can become much longer than those for the earlier buckets. Read about Larson's approach to solving this problem through the use of "partial expansions," originally described in Larson (1980) and subsequently summarized in Enbody and Du (1988). Write a pseudocode description of linear hashing with partial expansions, paying particular attention to how addressing is handled.

15. In section 11.6.3 we discussed different mechanisms for deferring the splitting of buckets in extendible hashing in order to increase storage utilization. What is the effect of using smaller overflow buckets rather than larger ones? How does the use of smaller overflow buckets compare with the idea of sharing overflow buckets?

Programming Exercises

16. Write a version of the *make_address* function that prints out the input key, the hash value, and the extracted, reversed address. Build a driver that allows you to enter keys interactively for this function and see the results. Study the operation of the function on different keys.

17. Write a simplified version of the extendible hashing program described in pseudocode in this chapter. This simplified version should

☐   Keep the directory and buckets in RAM rather than on disk;
☐   Hold three keys per bucket;
☐   Find and add keys, but not delete them;
☐   Accept keys entered interactively; and
☐   Display the resulting directory structure and buckets so you can see how the directory references the buckets and can see which buckets contain which keys.

Once you build this program, play with it to see how the directory grows as buckets split. Use the program developed in exercise 16 to develop sequences of keys that all hash to the same bucket. Enter such sequences and watch what happens.

18. Extend exercise 17 to include deletion. Once again, experiment with the program to see how deletion works. Try deleting all the keys. Try to create situations where the directory will recursively collapse over more than one level.

19. Write an extendible hashing program that stores and retrieves buckets from disk rather than from RAM.

20. Using the information in Enbody and Du (1988) and Litwin (1980), implement a simple, RAM-based linear hashing program.

■ FURTHER READINGS

For information about hashing for dynamic files that goes beyond what we present here, you must turn to journal articles. The best summary of the different approaches is Enbody and Du's *Computing Surveys* article titled "Dynamic Hashing Schemes," which appeared in 1988.

The original paper on extendible hashing is "Extendible Hashing—A Fast Access Method for Dynamic Files" by Fagin, Nievergelt, Pippenger, and Strong (1979). Larson (1978) introduces dynamic hashing in an article titled "Dynamic Hashing." Litwin's initial paper on linear hashing is titled "Linear Hashing: A New Tool for File and Table Addressing" (1980). All three of these introductory articles are quite readable; Larson's paper and Fagin, Nievergelt, Pippenger, and Strong are especially recommended.

Michel Scholl's 1981 paper titled "New File Organizations Based on Dynamic Hashing" provides another readable introduction to dynamic hashing. It also investigates implementations that defer splitting by allowing buckets to overflow.

Papers analyzing the performance of dynamic or extendible hashing often derive results that apply to either of the two methods. Flajolet (1983) presents a careful analysis of directory depth and size. Mendelson (1982) arrives at similar results and goes on to discuss the costs of retrieval and deletion as different design parameters are changed. Veklerov (1985) analyzes the performance of dynamic hashing when splitting is deferred by allowing records to overflow into a buddy bucket. His results can be applied to extendible hashing as well.

After introducing dynamic hashing, Larson wrote a number of papers building on the ideas associated with linear hashing. His 1980 paper titled "Linear Hashing with Partial Expansions" introduces an approach to linear hashing that can avoid the uneven distribution of the lengths of overflow chains across the cells in the address space. He followed up with a performance analysis in a 1982 paper titled "Performance Analysis of Linear Hashing with Partial Expansions." A subsequent, 1985 paper titled "Linear Hashing with Overflow—Handling by Linear Probing" introduces a method of handling overflow that does not involve chaining.

Appendix A

 File Structures on CD-ROM

OBJECTIVES

■ Introduce the commercially important characteristics of CD-ROM storage.

■ Examine a storage medium with performance characteristics that are very different from those of magnetic disks; show how to apply good file structure design principles to develop solutions that are appropriate to this new medium.

■ Describe the directory structure of the CD-ROM file system and show how it grows from the characteristics of the medium.

OUTLINE

A.1 Using this Appendix

This appendix has two purposes. The first is to tell you about the performance characteristics of CD-ROM, a commercially important information distribution medium. The second is to use the problem of designing file structures for CD-ROM to review many of the design issues and techniques presented in the text.

We begin by introducing CD-ROM. We explain how CD-ROM works and enumerate the features that make file structure design for CD-ROM a different problem than file structure design for magnetic media.

Once we have examined CD-ROM's performance, we provide a high-level look at how this performance affects the design of tree structures, hashed indexes, and directory structures for CD-ROM. These discussions of trees and hashing do not present new information; they review material that has already been developed in detail. Since you already have the tools required to think through these design problems, we introduce exercises and questions throughout this discussion, rather than holding them to the end. We encourage you to stop at these blocks of questions, think carefully about the answers, and then compare results with the discussion that follows.

A.2 Introduction to CD-ROM

CD-ROM is an acronym for Compact Disc Read-Only Memory.[†] It is a CD audio disc that contains digital data rather than digital sound. CD-ROM is commercially interesting because it can hold a lot of data and can be reproduced cheaply. A single disc can hold over 600 megabytes of data. That is approximately 200,000 printed pages, enough storage to hold almost 400 books the size of this one. Replicates can be stamped from a master disc for about only a dollar a copy.

CD-ROM is read-only in the same sense as a CD audio disc: You cannot record on it. It is a publishing medium, used for distributing information to many users, rather than a data storage and retrieval medium like magnetic disks. Currently, CD-ROMs are often used to publish database information such as telephone directories, zip codes, and demographic information. There are also many CD-ROM products that deliver textual data, such as bibliographic indexes, abstracts, dictionaries, and encyclopedias, often in association with digitized images stored on the disc. They are also used to publish video information and, of course, digital audio.

A.2.1 A Short History of CD-ROM

CD-ROM is the offspring of videodisc technology developed in the late 1960s and early 1970s, before the advent of the home VCR. The goal was to store movies on disc. Different companies developed a number of methods for storing video signals, including one that used a needle to respond mechanically to grooves in a disc, much like a vinyl LP record does. The consumer products industry spent a great deal of money developing the different technologies, including several approaches to optical storage, and then spent years fighting over the question of which approach should become standard. The surviving format is one called LaserVision. By the time LaserVision emerged as the winner of these

---

[†]Usually we spell disk with a *k,* but the convention among optical disc manufacturers is to spell it with a *c.*

standards battles, the competing developers had not only spent enormous sums of money, but had also lost important market opportunities. These hard lessons were put to use in the subsequent development of CD audio and CD-ROM.

From the outset, there was interest in using LaserVision discs to do more than just record movies. The LaserVision format supports recording in both a CLV (Constant Linear Velocity) format that maximizes storage capacity, and a CAV (Constant Angular Velocity) format that enables fast seek performance. By using the CAV format to access individual video frames quickly, a number of organizations, including the MIT Media Lab, produced prototype interactive video discs that could be used to teach and entertain.

In the early 1980s, a number of firms began looking at the possibility of storing digital, textual information on LaserVision discs. LaserVision stores data in an analog form; it is, after all, storing an analog video signal. Different firms came up with different ways of encoding digital information in analog form so it could be stored on the disc. The capabilities demonstrated in the prototypes and early, narrowly distributed products were impressive. The videodisc has a number of performance characteristics that make it a technically more desirable medium than the CD-ROM; in particular, one can build drives that seek quickly and deliver information from the disc at a high rate of speed. But, reminiscent of the earlier disputes over the physical format of the videodisc, each of these pioneers in the use of LaserVision discs as computer peripherals had incompatible encoding schemes and error correction techniques. There was no standard format, and none of the firms was large enough to impose their format over the others through sheer marketing muscle. Potential buyers were frightened by the lack of a standard; consequently, the market never grew.

During this same period the Philips and Sony companies began work on a way to store music on optical discs. Rather than storing the music in the kind of analog form used on videodiscs, they developed a digital data format. Philips and Sony had learned hard lessons from the expensive standards battles over videodiscs. This time they worked with other players in the consumer products industry to develop a licensing system that resulted in the emergence of CD audio discs as a broadly accepted, standard format as soon as the first discs and players were introduced. CD audio appeared in the United States in early 1984. CD-ROM, which is a digital data format built on top of the CD audio standard, emerged shortly thereafter. The first commercially available CD-ROM drives appeared in 1985.

Not surprisingly, the firms that were delivering digital data on LaserVision discs first saw CD-ROM as a threat to their existence. They also recognized, however, that CD-ROM promised to provide what had always eluded them in the past: a standard physical format. Anyone with a CD-ROM drive was guaranteed that they could find and read a sector off of any disc manufactured by any firm. For a storage medium to be used in publishing, standardization at such a fundamental level is essential.

What happened next is remarkable in the history of standards and cooperation within an industry. The firms that had been working on products to deliver computer data from videodiscs recognized that a standard physical format, such as that provided by CD-ROM, was not enough. A standard physical format meant that everyone was guaranteed to be able to read sectors off of any disc. But computer applications do not work in terms of sectors; they store data in files. Having an agreement about finding sectors, without further agreement about how to organize the sectors into files, is like everyone's agreeing on an alphabet without having settled on how letters are to be organized into words on a page. In late 1985 the firms emerging from the videodisc/digital data industry, all of which were relatively small, called together many of the much larger firms moving into the CD-ROM industry to begin work on a standard file system to be built on top of the CD-ROM format. In a rare display of cooperation, the different firms, large and small, worked out the main features of a file system standard by early summer of 1986; that work has now emerged as an official international standard for organizing files on CD-ROM.

The CD-ROM industry is still young, though in the past two years it has begun to show mature signs of moving away from concentration on matters such as disc formats to a concern with CD-ROM applications; rather than focusing on the new medium in isolation, vendors are seeing it as an enabling mechanism for new systems. As it finds more uses in a broader array of applications, CD-ROM looks like an optical publishing technology that will be with us over the long term.

A.2.2 CD-ROM as a File Structure Problem

CD-ROM presents interesting file structure problems because it is a medium with great strengths and weaknesses. The strengths of CD-ROM include the fact that it has a lot of storage capacity, is inexpensive, and is durable. The key weakness is that seek performance on a CD-ROM is very slow, often taking from a half second to a second per seek. In the introduction to this textbook we compared RAM access and magnetic disk access and showed that if RAM access is analogous to your taking 20 seconds to look up something in the index to this textbook, the equivalent disk access would take 58 days, or almost two months. With a CD-ROM the analogy stretches the disc access to over *two and a half years!* This kind of performance, or lack of it, makes intelligent file structure design a critical concern for CD-ROM applications. CD-ROM provides an excellent test of our ability to integrate and adapt the principles we have developed in the preceding chapters of this book.

A.3   Physical Organization of CD-ROM

CD-ROM is the child of CD audio. In this instance, the impact of heredity is strong, with both positive and negative aspects. Commercially, the CD audio parentage is probably wholly responsible for CD-ROM's viability in the market. It is because of the enormous size of the CD audio market that it is possible to make CD-ROM discs so inexpensively. Similarly, advances in the design and decreases in the costs of making CD audio players affect performance and price of CD-ROM drives. Other optical disc media that have not enjoyed the benefits of this parentage have not experienced the commercial success of CD-ROM.

On the other hand, making use of the manufacturing capacity associated with CD audio means adhering to the fundamental physical organization of the CD audio disc. Audio discs are designed to play music, not to provide fast, random access to data. This difference in design objective biases CD toward having high storage capacity and moderate data transfer rates, but against decent seek performance. If an application requires good random-access performance, that performance has to emerge from our file structure design efforts; it won't come from anything inherent in the medium itself.

A.3.1 Reading Pits and Lands

CD-ROM discs are stamped from a master disc. The master is formed by using the digital data that we want to encode to turn a powerful laser on and off very quickly. The master disc, which is made of glass, has a coating that is changed by the laser beam. When the coating is developed, the areas hit by the laser beam turn into pits along the track followed by the beam. The smooth, unchanged areas between the pits are called *lands*. The copies formed from the master retain this pattern of pits and lands.

When we read the stamped copy of the disc, we focus a beam of laser light on the track as it moves under the optical pickup. The pits scatter the light, but the lands reflect most of it back to the pickup. This alternating pattern of high- and low-intensity reflected light is the signal used to reconstruct the original digital information. The encoding scheme used for this signal is not simply a matter of calling a pit a 1 and a land a 0. Instead, the 1s are represented by the transitions from pit to land and back again. Every time the light intensity changes, we get a 1. The zeroes are represented by the amount of time between transitions; the longer between transitions, the more zeroes we have.

If you think about this encoding scheme, you realize that it is not possible to have two adjacent 1s — 1s are always separated by zeroes. In fact, due to the limits of the resolution of the optical pickup, there must be at least two 0s between any pair of 1s. This means that the raw pattern of 1s and 0s has to be translated in order to get the 8-bit patterns of 1s and 0s that form the bytes of the original data. This translation scheme, which is done through a lookup table, turns the original 8 bits of data into 14 expanded bits that can be represented in the pits and lands on the disc; the reading process reverses this translation. Figure A.1 shows a portion of the lookup table values. Readers who have looked closely at the specifications for CD players may have encountered the term *EFM* encoding. *EFM* stands for "eight to fourteen modulation" and refers to this translation scheme.

It is important to realize that since we represent the zeroes in the EFM-encoded data by the *length of time* between transitions, our ability to read the data is dependent on moving the pits and lands under the optical pickup at a precise and constant speed. As we will see, this affects the CD-ROM drive's ability to seek quickly.

A.3.2 CLV Instead of CAV

Data on a CD-ROM is stored in a single, spiral track that winds for almost three miles from the center to the outer edge of the disc. This spiral pattern is part of the CD-ROM's heritage from CD audio. For audio data, which requires a lot of storage space, we want to pack the data on the disc as tightly as possible. Since we "play" audio data, often from start to finish

Decimal value	Original bits	Translated bits
0	00000000	01001000100000
1	00000001	10000100000000
2	00000010	10010000100000
3	00000011	10001000100000
4	00000100	01000100000000
5	00000101	00000100010000
6	00000110	00010000100000
7	00000111	00100100000000
8	00001000	01001001000000

FIGURE A.1 A portion of the EFM encoding table.

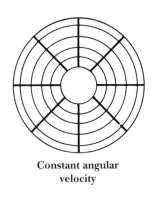

Constant angular
velocity

Constant linear
velocity

FIGURE A.2 CLV and CAV recording.

without interruption, seeking is not important. As Fig. A.2 shows, a spiral pattern serves these needs well. A sector toward the outer edge of the disc takes the same amount of space as a sector toward the center of the disc. This means that we can write all of the sectors at the maximum density permitted by the storage medium. Since reading the data requires that it pass under the optical pickup device at a constant rate, the constant data density implies that the disc has to spin more slowly when we are reading at the outer edges than when we are reading toward the center. This is why the spiral is a Constant Linear Velocity (CLV) format: As we seek from the center to the edge, we change the rate of rotation of the disc so the linear speed of the spiral past the pickup device stays the same.

By contrast, the familiar Constant Angular Velocity (CAV) arrangement shown in Fig. A.2, with its concentric tracks and pie-shaped sectors, writes data less densely in the outer tracks than in the tracks toward the center. We are wasting storage capacity in the outer tracks but have the advantage of being able to spin the disc at the same speed for all positions of the read head. Given the sector arrangement shown in the figure, one rotation reads eight sectors, no matter where we are on the disc. Furthermore, a timing mark placed on the disk makes it easy to find the start of a sector.

The CLV format is responsible, in large part, for the poor seeking performance of CD-ROM drives. The CAV format provides definite track boundaries and a timing mark to find the start of a sector. The CLV format, on the other hand, provides no straightforward way to jump to a specific location. Part of the problem is associated with the need to change rotational speed as we seek across the disc. To read the address information that is stored on the disc along with the user's data, we need to be moving the data under the optical pickup at the correct speed. But to know how to adjust the speed, we need to be able to read the address information so we know where we are. How does the drive's control mechanism break out of this loop? In practice, the answer often involves making guesses, finding the correct speed through trial and error. This takes time and slows down seek performance.

On the positive side, the CLV sector arrangement contributes to the CD-ROM's large storage capacity. Given a CAV arrangement, the CD-ROM would have only a little better than half its present capacity.

A.3.3 Addressing

The use of the CLV organization means that the familiar cylinder, track, sector way of identifying a sector address will not work on a CD-ROM. Instead, we use a sector-addressing scheme that is related to the CD-ROM's roots as an audio playback device. Each second of playing time on a CD is divided into 75 sectors, each of which holds 2 Kbytes of data. According to the original Philips/Sony standard, a CD disc, whether used for audio or CD-ROM, contains at least one hour of playing time. That means that the disc is capable of holding at least 540,000 Kbytes of data:

60 minutes × 60 seconds/minute × 75 sectors/second = 270,000 sectors.

In fact, since it is possible to put over 70 minutes of playing time on a CD, the capacity of the disk is over 600 Mbytes.

We address a given sector by referring to the minute, second, and sector of play. So, the 34th sector in the 22nd second in the 16th minute of play would be addressed with the three numbers 16:22:34.

A.3.4 Structure of a Sector

It is interesting to look at the way that the fundamental design of the CD disc, initially designed for delivering digital audio information, has been adapted for computer data storage. This investigation will also help answer the question, "If the disc is capable of storing a quarter of a million printed pages, why does it hold only an hour's worth of Roy Orbison?"

When we want to store sound, we need to convert a wave pattern into digital form. Figure A.3 shows a wave. At any given point in time, the wave has a specific amplitude. We digitize the wave by measuring the

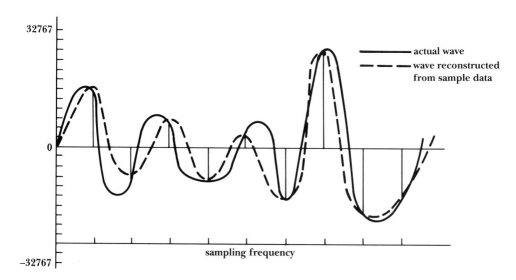

FIGURE A.3 Digital sampling of a wave.

amplitude at very frequent intervals and storing the measurements. So, the question of how much storage space we need to represent a wave digitally turns into two other questions: How much space does it take to store each amplitude sample, and how often do we take samples?

CD audio uses 16 bits to store each amplitude measurement; that means that our "ruler" that we use to measure the height of the wave has 65,536 different gradations. To accurately approximate a wave through digital sampling, we need to take the samples at a rate that is more than twice as frequent as the highest frequency that we want to capture. This makes sense if you look at the wave in Fig. A.4. You can see that if we sample at less than twice the frequency of the wave, we lose information about the variation in the wave pattern. The designers of CD audio selected a sampling frequency of 44.1 KHz, or 44,100 times per second, so they could record sounds with frequencies ranging up to 20 KHz (20,000 cycles per second), which is toward the upper bound of what people can hear.

So, if we are taking a 16-bit, or 2-byte sample 44,100 times per second, we need to store 88,200 bytes per second. Since we want to store stereo sound, we need double this, storing 176,400 bytes per second. You can see why storing an hour of Roy Orbison takes so much space.

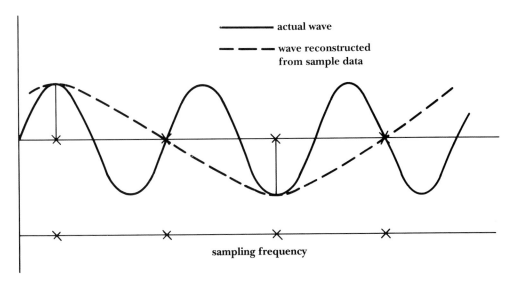

FIGURE A.4 The effect of sampling at less than twice the frequency of the wave.

If you divide the 176,400-byte-per-second storage capacity of the CD into 75 sectors per second, you have 2,352 bytes per sector. CD-ROM divides up this "raw" sector storage as shown in Fig. A.5 to provide 2 K of user data storage, along with addressing information, error detection, and error correction information. The error correction information is necessary because, although CD audio contains redundancy for error correction, it is not adequate to meet computer data storage needs. The audio error correction would result in an average of one incorrect byte for every two discs. The additional error correction information stored within the 2,352-byte sector decreases this error rate to one uncorrectable byte in every 20,000 discs.

FIGURE A.5 Structure of a CD-ROM sector.

12 bytes synch	4 bytes sector ID	2,048 bytes user data	4 bytes error detection	8 bytes null	276 bytes error correction

A.4   CD-ROM Strengths and Weaknesses

As we say throughout this book, good file design is responsive to the nature of the medium, making use of strengths and minimizing weaknesses. We begin, then, by cataloging the strengths and weaknesses of CD-ROM.

A.4.1 Seek Performance

The chief weakness of CD-ROM is the random-access performance. Current magnetic disk technology is such that the average time for a random data access, combining seek time and rotational delay, is about 30 msec. On a CD-ROM, this average access takes 500 msec, and can take up to a second or more. Clearly, our file design strategies must avoid seeks to an even greater extent than on magnetic disks.

A.4.2 Data Transfer Rate

A CD-ROM drive reads 75 sectors, or 150 Kbytes of data per second. This data transfer rate is part of the fundamental definition of CD-ROM; it can't be changed without leaving behind the commercial advantages of adhering to the CD audio standard. It is a modest transfer rate, about five times faster than the transfer rate for floppy disks, and an order of magnitude slower than the rate for good Winchester disks. The inadequacy of the transfer rate makes itself felt when we are loading large files, such as those associated with digitized images. On the other hand, the transfer rate is fast enough relative to the CD-ROM's seek performance that we have a design incentive to organize data into blocks, reading more data with each seek with the hope that we can avoid as much seeking as possible.

A.4.3 Storage Capacity

A CD-ROM holds more than 600 Mbytes of data. Although it is possible to use up this storage area very quickly, particularly if you are storing raster images, 600 Mbytes is big when it comes to text applications. If you decide to download 600 Mbytes of text with a 2,400-baud modem, it will take about three days of constant data transmission, assuming errorless transmission conditions. Many typical text databases and document collections published on CD-ROM use only a fraction of the disc's capacity.

The design benefit arising from such large capacity is that it enables us to build indexes and other support structures that can help overcome some of the limitations associated with CD-ROM's poor seek performance.

A.4.4 Read-Only Access

From a design standpoint, the fact that CD-ROM is a publishing medium, a storage device that cannot be changed after manufacture, provides significant advantages. We never have to worry about updating. This not only simplifies some of the file structures but also means that it is worthwhile to optimize our index structures and other aspects of file organization. We know that our efforts to optimize access will not be lost through later additions or deletions.

A.4.5 Asymmetric Writing and Reading

For most media, files are written and read using the same computer system. Often, reading and writing are both interactive and are therefore constrained by the need to provide quick response to the user. CD-ROM is different. We create the files to be placed on the disc once; then we distribute the disc and it is accessed thousands, even millions, of times. We are in a position to bring substantial computing power to the task of file organization and creation, even when the disc will be used on systems with much less capability. In fact, we can use extensive, batch-mode processing on large computers to try to provide systems that will perform well on small machines. We make the investment in intelligent, carefully designed file structures only once; users can enjoy the benefits of this investment again and again.

A.5   Tree Structures on CD-ROM

A.5.1 Design Exercises

Tree structures are a good way to organize indexes and data on CD-ROM. Chapters 8 and 9 took a close look at B-trees and B^+ trees. Before we discuss the effective use of trees on CD-ROM, think through these design questions:

1. How big should the block size be for B-trees and B^+ trees?
2. How far should you go in the direction of using virtual tree structures? How much memory should you set aside for buffering blocks?
3. How could you use special loading procedures to advantage in a B^+ tree implementation? Are there similar procedures that will assist in the loading of B-trees?
4. Suppose we have a primary index and several secondary indexes to a set of records. How should you organize these access mechanisms

for CD-ROM? Address the issues of binding and pinned records in your reply.

A.5.2 Block Size

Avoiding seeks is the key strategy in CD-ROM file structure design. Consequently, B-tree and B^+ tree structures are good choices for implementing index structures on CD-ROM. As we showed in Chapters 8 and 9, given a large enough block size, B-trees and B^+ trees can provide access to a large number of records in only a few seeks.

How large should the block size be? The answer, of course, depends on the application, but it is possible to provide some general guidelines. First, since the sector size of the CD-ROM is 2 Kbytes, the block size should not be less than 2 Kbytes. A sector is the smallest addressable unit on the disc; consequently, it does not make sense to read in anything less than a sector. Since the CD-ROM's sequential reading performance is moderately fast, especially when viewed relative to its seeking performance, it is usually attractive to use a block composed of several sectors. Once you have spent the better part of a second seeking for the sector and reading it, reading an additional 6 Kbytes to make an 8-Kbyte block takes only an additional 40 msec. If this added fraction of a second can contribute to avoiding another seek, it is time well spent.

Table A.1 shows the maximum number of 32-byte records that can be contained in a B-tree as the tree changes in height and block size. The dramatic effect of block size on the record counts for two- and three-level trees suggests that large tree structures should usually use at least an 8-Kbyte block.

TABLE A.1 The maximum number of 32-byte records that can be stored in a B-tree of given height and block size

	Tree Height		
	One Level	Two Levels	Three Levels
Block size = 2 K	64	4,224	274,624
Block size = 4 K	128	16,640	2,146,688
Block size = 8 K	256	66,048	16,974,592

A.5.3 Special Loading Procedures and Other Considerations

B^+ trees are commonly used in CD-ROM applications because they provide both indexed and sequential access to records. If, for example, you are building a telephone directory system for CD-ROM, you will need an index that can provide fast access to any one of the millions of names that appear on the disc. You will also want to provide sequential access so once users have found a name, they can browse through records with the same name, checking addresses, to make sure they have the right phone number.

B^+ trees are also attractive in CD-ROM applications because they can provide very shallow, broad indexes to a set of sequenced records. As we showed in Chapter 9, the content of the index part of a B^+ tree can consist of nothing more than the shortest separators required to provide access to lower levels of the tree and, ultimately, to the target records. If these shortest separators are only a few bytes long, as is frequently the case, it is often possible to provide access to millions of records with an index that is only two levels deep. An application can keep the root of this index in RAM, reducing the cost of searching the index part of the tree to a single seek. With one additional seek we are at the record in the sequence set.

Another attractive feature of B^+ trees is that it is easy to build a two-level index above the sequence set with a separate loading procedure that builds the tree from the bottom up. We described this operation in Chapter 9. The great advantage of this kind of loading procedure, as opposed to building the tree through a series of top-down insertions, is that we can pack the nodes and leaves of the tree as fully as we wish. With CD-ROM, where the cost of additional seeks is so high, and where there is absolutely no possibility that anyone will make additional insertions to the tree, we will want to pack the nodes and leaves of the tree so they are completely full. This is an example of a design decision that recognizes that the CD-ROM is a publishing medium that, once constructed, is used only for retrieval, and never for additional storage.

This kind of special, 100%-full loading procedure can also be designed for B-tree applications. The procedure for B-trees is usually somewhat more complex because the index will often consist of more than just a root node and one level of children. The loading procedure for B-trees has to manage more levels of the tree at a time.

This discussion of indexes, and the importance of packing them as tightly as possible, brings home one of the interesting paradoxes of CD-ROM design. The CD-ROM disc has a relatively large storage capacity that usually gives us a great deal of freedom with regard to how we store data on the disc; a few bytes here or there usually doesn't matter much when you have 600 Mbytes of capacity. But when we design the index structures for CD-ROM, we find ourselves counting bytes, sometimes even counting bits as we pack information into a single byte or integer. The reason for this is not, in most cases, that we are running out of space on the disc, but because packing the index tightly can often save us from making an additional seek. In CD-ROM file design the cost of seeks adds up very quickly; the designer needs to get as much information out of every seek as possible.

A.5.4 Virtual Trees and Buffering Blocks

Given the very high cost of seeking on CD-ROM, we will want to keep blocks in RAM for as long as they are likely to be useful. The tree's root node should always be buffered. As we indicated in our discussion of virtual trees in Chapter 8, buffering nodes below the root can sometimes contribute significantly to reducing seek time, particularly when the buffering is intelligent in selecting the node to replace in the buffer. Buffering is most useful when successive accesses to the tree tend to be clustered in one area.

Note that packing the tree as tightly as possible during loading, which we discussed earlier as a way to reduce tree height, also increases the likelihood that an index block in RAM will be useful on successive accesses to the data.

A.5.5 Trees as Secondary Indexes on CD-ROM

Typically, CD-ROM applications provide more than one access route to the data on the disc. For example, document retrieval applications usually give direct access to the documents, so you can page through them in sequence or call them up by name, chapter, or section while also providing access through an index of keywords or included terms. Similarly, in a telephone directory application you would have access to the database by name, but also by location (state, city, zip code, street address). As we described in Chapter 6, secondary indexes provide these multiple views of the data.

Chapter 5 raised the design issue of whether the secondary indexes should be tightly bound to the records they point to, or whether the binding should take place at retrieval time, through the use of a common key accessed through yet another index. Viewed another way, the issue is whether the target records should be pinned to a specific location through references in secondary indexes, or whether they should be left unpinned so they can be reorganized.

Records will never be reorganized on a CD-ROM; since it is a read-only disc, there is no disadvantage to having pinned records. Further, minimizing the number of seeks is the overriding design consideration on CD-ROM. Consequently, secondary index designs for CD-ROM should usually bind the indexes to the target records as tightly as possible, ensuring that once you have found the correct place in the index, you are ready to retrieve the target with, at most, one additional seek.

One objection to this bind-tightly approach to CD-ROM index design is that, although it is true that the indexes cannot be reorganized once written to the CD-ROM, they are, in fact, quite frequently reorganized between successive "editions" of the disc. Many CD-ROM publications are reissued to keep them up to date. The period between successive versions may be years, or may be as short as a week. So, although pinned records cause no problem on the finished disc, they may cause a great deal of difficulty in the files used to prepare the disc.

There are a number of approaches to resolving this tension between what is best on the published disc and what is best for the files used to produce it. One solution is to maintain loosely bound records in the source database, transforming them to tightly bound records for publication on CD-ROM. CD-ROM product designers often fail to realize that the file structures placed on the disc can, and often should, be different than the structures used to maintain the source data and produce the discs. Another solution, of course, is to trade off performance on the published disc for decreased costs in producing it. Production costs, time constraints, user acceptance, and competitive factors interact to determine which course is best. The key issue from the file designer's standpoint is to recognize that the alternatives exist, and then to be able to quantify the costs and benefits of each.

A.6   Hashed Files on CD-ROM

A.6.1 Design Exercises

Hashing, with its promise of single access retrieval, is an excellent way to organize indexes on CD-ROM. We begin with some design questions that intersect your knowledge of hashing with what you now know about CD-ROM. As you think through your answers, remember that your goal should be to avoid any additional seeking due to hash bucket overflow. As in any hashing design problem, the design parameters that you can manipulate are

- Bucket size;
- Packing density for the hashed index; and
- The hash function itself.

The following questions, which you should try to answer before you read on, encourage you to think about ways to use these parameters to build efficient CD-ROM applications.

1. What considerations go into choosing a bucket size?
2. How does the relatively large storage capacity of CD-ROM assist in developing efficient hashed retrieval?
3. Since a CD-ROM is read-only, you have a complete list of the keys to be hashed before you create the disc. How can this assist in reducing retrieval costs?

A.6.2 Bucket Size

In Chapter 10 we showed how to reduce overflow, and therefore retrieval time, by grouping records into *buckets,* so each hashed address references an entire bucket of records. Since any access to a CD-ROM always reads in a minimum of a 2-Kbyte sector, the bucket size should be a multiple of 2 Kbytes. Having the bucket be only a part of a sector would be counterproductive. As we described in Chapter 3, transferring anything less than a sector means first moving the data into a system buffer, and from there into the user's data area. With transfers of a complete sector, many operating systems can move the data directly into the user area.

How many sectors should go into a bucket? As with trees, it is a trade-off between seeking and sequential reading. In addition, larger buckets require more searching and comparing to find the record once the bucket is read into RAM. In Chapter 10 we provided tools to allow you to calculate the effect of bucket size on the probability of overflow. For CD-ROM applications, you will want to use these tools to reduce the probability of overflow to almost nothing.

A.6.3 How the Size of CD-ROM Helps

Packing a hashed file loosely is another way to avoid overflow and additional seeking. A good rule of thumb is that, even with only a moderate bucket size, keeping the packing density below 60% will tend to avoid overflow almost all the time. Consulting Tables 10.4 and 10.5 in Chapter 10, we see that for randomly distributed keys, a packing density of 60% and a bucket size of 10 will reduce the percentage of records that overflow to 1.3% and will reduce the average number of seeks required for a successful search to 1.01.

When there is unused space available on the disc, there is no disadvantage to expanding the size of the hashed index so overflow is virtually eliminated.

A.6.4 Advantages of CD-ROM's Read-Only Status

What if space is at a premium on the CD-ROM disc, and you need to find a way to pack your index so it is 90% full? Despite the relatively large capacity of CD-ROM discs, this situation is fairly common. Large text file collections often use most of the disc just for text. If the product is storing digitized images along with the text, the available space disappears even more quickly. Applications requiring the use of two discs at once are much harder to sell and deliver than a single disc application; when a disc is already nearly full of data, the index files are always a target for size reduction.

The calculations that we do to estimate the effects of bucket size and packing density assume a *random* distribution of keys across the address space. If we could find a hash function that would distribute the keys *uniformly,* rather than randomly, we could achieve 100% packing density and no overflow.

Once again, the fact that CD-ROM is read-only opens up possibilities that would not be available in a dynamic, read-write environment. When we produce a CD-ROM, we have all the keys that are to be hashed at hand. This means that we do not have to choose a hash function and then settle for whatever distribution of keys that it produces, hoping for the best, but expecting a distribution that is merely random. Instead, we can select a hash function that provides the performance we need, given the set of keys we have to hash. If our performance and space constraints require it, we can develop a hash function that produces no overflow even at very high packing densities. We identify the selected hash function on the disc, along with the data, so the retrieval software knows how to locate the keys. This relatively expensive and time-consuming function-fitting effort is worthwhile because of the asymmetric nature of writing and reading CD-ROMs; the one-time effort spent in making the disc is paid back many times as the disc is distributed to many users.

A.7   The CD-ROM File System

A.7.1 The Problem

When the firms involved in developing CD-ROM applications came together to begin work on a common file system in late 1985, they were confronted with an interesting file structures problem. The design goals and constraints included the following:

☐   Support hierarchical directory structures;

□ Find and open any one of thousands of files with only one or two seeks; and

□ Support the use of *generic* file names, as in "file∗.c", during directory access.

The usual way to support hierarchical directories is to treat the directories as nothing more than a special kind of file. If, using UNIX notation, you are looking for a file with the full path

```
/usr/home/mydir/filebook/cdrom/part3.txt
```

you look in the root directory (/) to find the directory file *usr*, then you open *usr* to find the location of the directory file *home*, you seek to *home* and open it to find *mydir*, and so on until you finally open the directory file named *cdrom*, where you find the location of the target file *part3.txt*. This is a very simple, flexible system; it is the approach used in MS-DOS, UNIX, VMS, and many other operating systems. The problem, from the standpoint of a CD-ROM developer, is that before we can find the location of *part3.txt*, we must seek to, open, and use six other files. At a half-second per seek on CD-ROM, such a directory structure results in a very unresponsive file system.

A.7.2 Design Exercise

At the time of the initial meetings to begin looking at a standard CD-ROM directory structure and file system, a number of vendors were using this treat-directories-as-files approach, literally replicating magnetic disc directory systems on CD-ROM. There were at least two alternative approaches that were commercially available and more specifically tailored to CD-ROM. One placed the entire directory structure in a single file, building a *left child, right sibling* tree to express the directory structure. Given the directory hierarchy in Fig. A.6, this system produced a file containing the tree shown in Fig. A.7. The other system created an index to the file locations by hashing the full path names of each file. The entries in the hash table for the directory structure in Fig. A.6 are shown in Fig. A.8.

Considering what you know about CD-ROM (slow seeking, read-only, and so on), think about these alternative file systems and try to answer the following questions. Keep in mind the design goals and constraints that were facing the committee (hierarchical structure, fast access to thousands of files, use of generic file names).

1. List the advantages and disadvantages of each system.
2. Try to come up with an alternative approach that combines the best features of the other systems while minimizing the disadvantages.

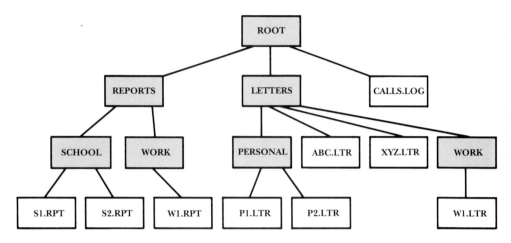

FIGURE A.6 A sample directory hierarchy.

FIGURE A.7 Left child, right sibling tree to express directory structure.

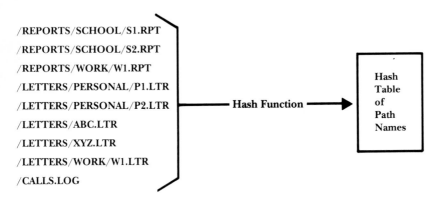

FIGURE A.8 Hashed index of file pathnames.

A.7.3 A Hybrid Design

Placing the entire directory structure into a single file, as with the left-child, right sibling tree, works well as long as the directory structure is small. If the file containing the tree fits into a few kilobytes, the entire directory structure can be held in RAM and can be accessed without any seeking at all. But if the directory structure is large, containing thousands of files, accessing the various parts of the tree can require multiple seeks, just as it does when each directory is a separate file.

Hashing the path names, on the other hand, provides single-seek access to any file but does a very poor job of supporting generic file and directory names, such as *prog*.c, or even a simple command such as *ls* or *dir* to list all the files in a given subdirectory. By definition, hashing randomizes the distribution of the keys, scattering them over the directory space. Finding all of the files in a given subdirectory, say the *letters* subdirectory for the tree shown in Fig. A.6, requires a sequential reading of the entire directory.

What about a hybrid approach, in which we build a conventional directory structure that uses a file for each directory and then supplement this by building a hashed index to all the files in all directories? This approach allows us to get to any subdirectory, and therefore to the information required to open a file, with a single seek. At the same time, it provides us with the ability to work with the files inside each directory, using generic file names and commands such as *ls* and *dir*. In short, we build a conventional directory structure to get all the advantages of that approach, and then solve the access problem by building an index for the subdirectories.

RRN		Parent
0	Root	-1
1	Reports	0
2	Letters	0
3	School	1
4	Work	1
5	Personal	2
6	Work	2

FIGURE A.9 Path index table of directories.

This is very close to the approach that the committee settled on. But they went one step further. Since the directory structure is a highly organized, hierarchical collection of files, the committee decided to use a special index that takes advantage of that hierarchy, rather than simply hashing the path names of the subdirectories. Figure A.9 shows what this index structure looks like when it is applied to the directory structure in Fig. A.6. Only the directories are listed in the index; access to the data files is through the directory files. The directories are ordered in the index so parents always appear before their children. Each child is associated with an integer that is a backward reference to the relative record number (RRN) of the parent. This allows us to distinguish between the WORK directory under REPORTS and the WORK directory under LETTERS. It also allows us to traverse the directory structure, moving both up and down with a command such as the *cd* command in DOS or UNIX, without having to access the actual directory files on the CD-ROM. It is a good example of a specialized index structure that makes use of the organization inherent in the data to produce a very compact, highly functional access mechanism.

Summary

CD-ROM is an electronic publishing medium that allows us to replicate and distribute large amounts of information very inexpensively. The primary disadvantage of CD-ROM is that seek performance is relatively slow. This is not a problem that can be solved simply by building better drives; the limits in seek performance grow directly from the fact that CD-ROM is built on top of the CD audio standard. Adherence to this standard, even given its limitations, is the basis for CD-ROM's success as a publishing medium. Consequently, CD-ROM application developers must look to careful file structure design to build fast, responsive retrieval software.

B-tree and B^+ tree structures work well on CD-ROM because of their ability to provide access to many keys with just a few seeks. Because the sector size on CD-ROM is 2 Kbytes, the block size used in a tree should be 2 Kbytes or an even multiple of this sector size. Because CD-ROM drives seek so slowly, it is usually advantageous to use larger blocks consisting of 8 Kbytes or more. Since no additions or deletions will be made to a tree once it is on CD-ROM, it is useful to build the trees from the bottom up so the blocks are completely filled. When using trees to create secondary indexes, the read-only nature of CD-ROM makes it possible to bind the indexes tightly to the target data, pinning the index records to reduce seeking and increase performance.

Hashed indexes are often a good choice for CD-ROM because they can provide single-seek access to target information. As with trees, the 2-Kbyte sector size affects the design of the hashed index: The bucket size should be one or more full sectors. Since CD-ROMs are large, there is often enough space on the disc to permit use of packing densities of 60% or less for the hashed index. Use of packing densities of less than 60%, combined with a bucket size of 10 or more records, results in single-seek access for almost all records. But it is not always possible to pack the index this loosely. Higher packing densities can be accommodated without loss of performance if we tailor the hash function to the records in the index, using a function that provides a more nearly uniform distribution. Since we know that there will be no deletions or additions to the index, and since time spent optimizing the index will result in benefits again and again as the discs are used, it is often worthwhile to invest the effort in finding the best of several hash functions. This is especially true when we need to support higher packing densities of 90% or more.

In 1985 companies trying to build the CD-ROM publishing market faced an interesting file structure problem. They realized that they needed a common directory structure and file system for CD-ROM. At the time, there were no directory structure designs in use on CD-ROM that provided nearly optimal performance across a wide variety of applications.

Directory structures are usually implemented as a series of files. Moving from a directory to a subdirectory beneath it means seeking to another file. This is not a good design for CD-ROM, since it could result in a wait of several seconds just to locate and open a single file. Simple alternatives, such as putting the entire directory structure in a single file, or hashing the path names of all the files on a disc, have other drawbacks. The committee charged with solving this problem emerged with a design that combined a conventional hierarchical directory of files with an index to the directory. The index makes use of the structure inherent in the directory hierarchy to provide a very compact, yet functional map of the directory structure. Typical of other CD-ROM indexing problems, this directory index illustrates the importance of building indexes very tightly on CD-ROM, despite the vast, often unused capacity of the CD-ROM disc. Tight, dense indexes work better on CD-ROM because they require fewer seeks to access. Avoiding seeks is the key consideration for all CD-ROM file structure design.

Appendix B

ASCII Table

	Dec.	Oct.	Hex.		Dec.	Oct.	Hex.		Dec.	Oct.	Hex.		Dec.	Oct.	Hex.
nul	0	0	0	sp	32	40	20	@	64	100	40	'	96	140	60
sol	1	1	1	!	33	41	21	A	65	101	41	a	97	141	61
stx	2	2	2	"	34	42	22	B	66	102	42	b	98	142	62
etx	3	3	3	#	35	43	23	C	67	103	43	c	99	143	63
eot	4	4	4	$	36	44	24	D	68	104	44	d	100	144	64
enq	5	5	5	%	37	45	25	E	69	105	45	e	101	145	65
ack	6	6	6	&	38	46	26	F	70	106	46	f	102	146	66
bel	7	7	7	'	39	47	27	G	71	107	47	g	103	147	67
bs	8	10	8	(	40	50	28	H	72	110	48	h	104	150	68
ht	9	11	9	)	41	51	29	I	73	111	49	i	105	151	69
nl	10	12	A	*	42	52	2A	J	74	112	4A	j	106	152	6A
vt	11	13	B	+	43	53	2B	K	75	113	4B	k	107	153	6B
np	12	14	C	,	44	54	2C	L	76	114	4C	l	108	154	6C
cr	13	15	D	–	45	55	2D	M	77	115	4D	m	109	155	6D
so	14	16	E	.	46	56	2E	N	78	116	4E	n	110	156	6E
si	15	17	F	/	47	57	2F	O	79	117	4F	o	111	157	6F
dle	16	20	10	0	48	60	30	P	80	120	50	p	112	160	70
dcl	17	21	11	1	49	61	31	Q	81	121	51	q	113	161	71
dc2	18	22	12	2	50	62	32	R	82	122	52	r	114	162	72
dc3	19	23	13	3	51	63	33	S	83	123	53	s	115	163	73
dc4	20	24	14	4	52	64	34	T	84	124	54	t	116	164	74
nak	21	25	15	5	53	65	35	U	85	125	55	u	117	165	75
syn	22	26	16	6	54	66	36	V	86	126	56	v	118	166	76
etb	23	27	17	7	55	67	37	W	87	127	57	w	119	167	77
can	24	30	18	8	56	70	38	X	88	130	58	x	120	170	78
em	25	31	19	9	57	71	39	Y	89	131	59	y	121	171	79
sub	26	32	1A	:	58	72	3A	Z	90	132	5A	z	122	172	7A
esc	27	33	1B	;	59	73	3B	[	91	133	5B	{	123	173	7B
fs	28	34	1C	<	60	74	3C	\	92	134	5C	|	124	174	7C
gs	29	35	1D	=	61	75	3D	]	93	135	5D	}	125	175	7D
rs	30	36	1E	>	62	76	3E	^	94	136	5E	~	126	176	7E
us	31	37	1F	?	63	77	3F	–	95	137	5F	del	127	177	7F

Appendix C

String Functions in Pascal: *tools.prc*

Functions and Procedures Used to Operate on *strng*

The following functions and procedures make up the tools for operating on variables that are declared as:

```
TYPE
    strng = packed array [0..MAX_REC_LGTH] of char;
```

The length of the *strng* is stored in the zeroth byte of the array as a character representative of the length. Note that the Pascal functions CHR() and ORD() are used to convert integers to characters and vice versa.

Functions include:

len_str(str)	Returns the length of *str*.
clear_str(str)	Clears *str* by setting its length to 0.
copy_str(str1,str2)	Copies contents of *str2* to *str1*.
cat_str(str1,str2)	Concatenates *str2* to end of *str1*. Puts result in *str1*.
read_str(str)	Reads *str* as input from the keyboard.
write_str(str)	Writes contents of *str* to the screen.
fread_str(fd,str,lgth)	Reads a *str* with length *lgth* from file *fd*.
fwrite_str(fd,str)	Writes contents of *str* to file *fd*.
trim_str(str)	Trims trailing blanks from *str*. Returns length of *str*.
ucase(str1,str2)	Converts *str1* to uppercase, storing result in *str2*.
makekey(last, first, key)	Combines *last* and *first* into key in canonical form, storing result in *key*.
min(int1,int2)	Returns the minimum of two integers.
cmp_str(str1,str2)	Compares *str1* to *str2*: If *str1* = *str2*, *cmp_str* returns 0. If *str1* < *str2*, returns a negative number. If *str1* > *str2*, returns a positive number

567

```
FUNCTION len_str (str: strng): integer;
{ len_str() returns the length of str }
BEGIN
    len_str := ORD(str[0]
END;


PROCEDURE clear_str(VAR str: strng);
{ A procedure that clears str by setting its length to 0 }
BEGIN
    str[0] := CHR(0)
END;

PROCEDURE copy_str(VAR str1: strng; str2: strng);
{ A procedure to copy str2 into str1 }
VAR
    i    : integer;
BEGIN
    for i := 1 to len_str(str2) DO
        str1[i] := str2[i];
    str1[0] := str2[0]
END;


PROCEDURE cat_str (VAR str1: strng; str2: strng);
{ cat_str() concatenates str2 to the end of str1 and stores
  the result in str1  }
VAR
    i    : integer;
BEGIN
    for i := 1 to len_str(str2) DO
        str1[(len_str(str1)+i)] := str2[i];
    str1[0] := CHR(len_str(str1) + len_str(str2))
END;


PROCEDURE read_str (VAR str: strng);
  A procedure that reads str as input from the keyboard }
VAR
    lgth    : integer;
BEGIN
    lgth := 0;
    while (not EOLN) and (lgth <= MAX_REC_SIZE) DO
    BEGIN
        lgth := lgth + 1;
        read (str[lgth])
    END;
    readln;
    str[0] := CHR(lgth)
END;
```

```
PROCEDURE write_str (VAR str: strng);
{ write_str() writes str to the screen }
VAR
    i  : integer
BEGIN
    for i := 1 to len_str(str) DO
        write(str[i]);
    writeln
END;




PROCEDURE fread_str (VAR fd: text; VAR str: strng; lgth: integer);
{ fread_str() reads a str with length lgth from fd }
VAR
    i  : integer;
BEGIN
    for i := 1 to lgth DO
        read(fd,str[i];
    str[0] := CHR(lgth)
END;




PROCEDURE fwrite_str (VAR fd: text; str : strng);
{ fwrite_str() writes str to file fd }
VAR
    i : integer;
BEGIN
    for i := 1 to len_str(str) DO
        write(fd,str[i])
END;




FUNCTION trim_str (VAR str: strng): integer;
{ trim_str() trims the blanks off the end of str and
 returns its new length }
VAR
    lgth  : integer;
BEGIN
    lgth := len_str(str);
    while str[lgth] = ' ' DO
        lgth := lgth - 1;
    str[0] := CHR(lgth);
    trim_str := lgth
END;
```

```
PROCEDURE ucase (str1: strng; VAR str2: strng);
{ ucase() converts str1 to uppercase letters and stores the
  capitalized string in str2 }
VAR
    i    :  integer;
BEGIN
for i := 1 to len_str(str1) DO
    BEGIN
    if (ORD(str1[i]) >= ORD('a')) AND (ORD(str1[i]) <= ORD('z')) then
        str2[i] := CHR(ORD(str1[i])- 32)
    else
        str2[i] := str1[i];
    END;
str2[0] := str1[0]
END;


PROCEDURE makekey (last: strng; first: strng; VAR key: strng);
{ makekey() trims the blanks off the ends of the strngs last and
  first,concatenates last and first together with a space
  separating them, and converts the letters to uppercase }
VAR
    lenl      : integer;
    lenf      : integer;
    blank_str: strng;
BEGIN
    lenl := trim_str(last);
    copy_str (key,last);
    blank_str[0] := CHR(1);
    blank_str[1] := ' ';
    cat_str(key,blank_str);
    lenf := trim_str(first);
    cat_str(key,first);
    ucase(key,key)
END;


FUNCTION min (int1,int2: integer): integer;
  min() returns the minimum of two integers }
BEGIN
    if int1 <= int2 then
        min := int1
    else
        min := int2
END;


FUNCTION cmp_str (str1: strng; str2: strng): integer;

{ A function that compares str1 to str2.  If str1 = str2, then
  cmp_str returns 0.  If str1 < str2, then cmp_str returns a
```

```
    negative number.  Or if str1 > str2, then cmp_str returns a
    positive number. }

VAR
    i        : integer;
    length : integer;
BEGIN
    if len_str(str1) = len_str(str2) then
        BEGIN
        i := 1;
        while str1[1] = str2[i] DO
            i := i + 1;
        if (i - 1) = len_str(str1) then
            cmp_str := 0
        else
            cmp_str := (ORD(str1[i])) - (ORD(str2[i]))
        END
    else   BEGIN
           length := min(len_str(str1),len_str(str2));
           i := 1;
           while (stri[i] = str2[i]) and (i <= length) DO
               i := i + 1;
           if i > length then
               cmp_str := len_str(str1) - len_str(str2)
           else
               cmp_str := (ORD(str1[i])) - (ORD(str2[i]))
           END
END;
```

Appendix D

Comparing Disk Drives

There are enormous differences among different types of drives in terms of the amount of data they hold, the time it takes them to access data, overall cost, cost per bit, and intelligence. Furthermore, disk devices and media are evolving so rapidly that the figures on speed, capacity, and intelligence that apply one month may very well be out of date the next month.

Access time, you will recall, is composed of seek time, rotational delay, and transfer time.

Seek times are usually described in two ways: *minimum seek time* and *average seek time*. Usually, but not always, minimum seek time includes the time it takes for the head to accelerate from a standstill, move one track, and settle to a stop. Sometimes the track-to-track seek time is given, with a separate figure for head settling time. One has to be careful with figures such as these since their meanings are not always stated clearly.

Average seek time is the average time it takes for a seek if the desired sector is as likely to be on any one cylinder as it is on any other. In a completely random accessing environment, it can be shown that the number of cylinders covered in an average seek is approximately one-third of the total number of cylinders (Pechura and Schoeffler, 1983). Estimates of average seek time are commonly based on this result.

Certain disk drives, called *fixed head disk drives,* require no seek time. Fixed head drives provide one or more read/write heads per track, so there is no need to move the heads from track to track. Fixed head disk drives are very fast, but also considerably more expensive than movable head drives.

There are generally no significant differences in *rotational delay* among similar drives. Most floppy disk drives rotate between 300 and 600 rpm. Hard disk drives generally rotate at approximately 3600 rpm, though this will increase as disks decrease in physical size. There is at least one drive that rotates at 5400 rpm, and speeds of 7200 rpm are possible. Floppy disks usually do not spin continuously, so intermittent accessing of floppy drives might involve an extra delay due to startup of a second or more. Strategies such as sector interleaving can mitigate the effects of rotational delay in some circumstances.

The volume of data to be transferred has increased enormously in recent years, thereby focusing much attention on *data transfer rate*. Data transfer rate from a single drive is constrained by rotation speed, recording density on the disk itself, and the speed at which the controller can pass data through to or from RAM. Since rotation speeds vary little, the main differences among drives are due to differences in recording density. In recent years there have been tremendous advances in improving recording densities on disks of all types. Differences in recording densities are usually expressed in terms of the number of *tracks per surface,* and the number of *bytes per track*. If data are organized by sector on a disk, and more than one sector is transferred at a time, the effective data transfer rate depends also on the method of sector interleaving used. The effect of interleaving can be substantial, of course, since logically adjacent sectors are often widely separated physically.

A different approach to increasing data transfer rate is to access data from different places simultaneously. A technology called *PTD* (parallel transfer disk) reads and writes data simultaneously from multiple read/write heads. The Seagate Sable PTD reaches a transfer rate of over 20 Mbytes per second using eight read/write heads.

Another promising technology for achieving high transfer rates is *RAID* (redundant arrays of inexpensive disks), in which a collection of small inexpensive disks function as one. RAIDs allow the use of several separate I/O controllers operating in parallel. These parallel accesses can be coordinated to satisfy a single logical I/O request, or can service several independent I/O requests simultaneously.

Although it is very possible that most of the figures in Table D.1 will be superseded during the time between the writing and the publication of this text, they should give you a basic idea of the magnitude and range of performance characteristics for disks. The fact that they *are* changing so rapidly should also serve to emphasize the importance of being aware of disk drive performance characteristics when you are in a position to choose among different drives.

Of course, in addition to the quantitative differences among drives, there are other important differences. The IBM 3380 drive, for example, has many built-in features, including separate actuator arms that allow it to perform two accesses simultaneously. It also has large local buffers and a great deal of local intelligence, enabling it to optimize many operations that, with less sophisticated drives, have to be monitored by the central computer.

TABLE D.1 Comparisons of disk drives

	3.5-inch Floppy	Small Sectored	Large Sectored (DEC RP07)	Large Blocked (IBM 3380 AE4)[†]	Large Blocked (Amdahl 6390)[‡]	CD-ROM	Solid State (Amdahl 6680)[★]
Speed							
Average Seek Time (msec)	70	28	23	17	10.7	400	.3
Rotational Delay (msec)	50	8.3	8.3	8.3	6.9	—	0.0
Transfer Rate (Mbyte/sec)	.2	1.25	2.2	3.0	1.5-4.5	0.15	1.5-4.5
Capacity							
Bytes/Track	9,200	18,434	25,600	47,476	56,664	NA	47,476
Tracks/Cylinder	2	4	16	15	15	NA	15
Cylinders/Drive	80	1,224	1,260	1,770	2,655	NA	1-182
Mbytes/Drive	1.4	90	516	2,520	1,890	600	256

[†]Basic configuration includes four drives, so the total capacity of a unit is 5,040 Mbytes. The transfer rate is the rate at which data is transferred between the drive and the IBM 3380 storage control.

[‡]Basic configuration includes 16 drives, so the total capacity of a unit is 30.24 Gbytes. Data transfer rate depends on the speed of the channel.

[★]Electronic storage configured permanently in the image of a disk drive. There is no seeking and no rotational delay. Seek times are actually "access times" provided in the specifications for the drive. The transfer of data goes through a normal disk channel, hence it is the same as for other Amdahl drives.

Bibliography

AT&T. *System V Interface Definition*. Indianapolis, IN: AT&T, 1986.

Baase, S. *Computer Algorithms: Introduction to Design and Analysis.* Reading, Mass.: Addison-Wesley, 1978.

Batory, D.S. "B$^+$ trees and indexed sequential files: A performance comparison." *ACM SIGMOD* (1981): 30–39.

Bayer, R., and E. McCreight. "Organization and maintenance of large ordered indexes." *Acta Informatica* 1, no. 3 (1972): 173–189.

Bayer, R., and K. Unterauer. "Prefix B-trees." *ACM Transactions on Database Systems* 2, no. 1 (March 1977): 11–26.

Bentley, J. "Programming pearls: A spelling checker." *Communications of the ACM* 28, no. 5 (May 1985): 456–462.

Bohl, M. *Introduction to IBM Direct Access Storage Devices.* Chicago: Science Research Associates, Inc., 1981.

Borland. *Turbo Toolbox Reference Manual.* Scott's Valley, Calif.: Borland International, Inc., 1984.

Bourne, S.R. *The Unix System.* Reading, Mass.: Addison-Wesley, 1984.

Bradley, J. *File and Data Base Techniques.* New York: Holt, Rinehart, and Winston, 1982.

Chaney, R., and B. Johnson. "Maximizing hard-disk performance." *Byte* 9, no. 5 (May 1984): 307–334.

Chang, C.C. "The study of an ordered minimal perfect hashing scheme." *Communications of the ACM* 27, no. 4 (April 1984): 384–387.

Chang, H. "A Study of Dynamic Hashing and Dynamic Hashing with Deferred Splitting." Unpublished Master's thesis, Oklahoma State University, December 1985.

Chichelli, R.J. "Minimal perfect hash functions made simple." *Communications of the ACM* 23, no. 1 (January 1980): 17–19.

Comer, D. "The ubiquitous B-tree." *ACM Computing Surveys* 11, no. 2 (June 1979): 121–137.

Cooper, D. *Standard Pascal User Reference Manual.* New York: W.W. Norton & Co., 1983.

Crotzer, A.D. "Efficacy of B-trees in an information storage and retrieval environment." Unpublished Master's thesis, Oklahoma State University, 1975.

Davis, W.S. "Empirical behavior of B-trees." Unpublished Master's thesis, Oklahoma State University, 1974.

Deitel, H. *An Introduction to Operating Systems.* Revised 1st Ed. Reading, Mass.: Addison-Wesley, 1984.

Digital. *Introduction to VAX-11 Record Management Services.* Order No. AA-DO24A-TE. Digital Equipment Corporation, 1978.

Digital. *Peripherals Handbook.* Digital Equipment Corporation, 1981.

Digital. *RMS-11 User's Guide.* Digital Equipment Corporation, 1979.

Digital. *VAX-11 SORT/MERGE User's Guide.* Digital Equipment Corporation, 1984.

Digital. *VAX Software Handbook.* Digital Equipment Corporation, 1982.

Dodds, D.J. "*Pracnique:* Reducing dictionary size by using a hashing technique." *Communications of the ACM* 25, no. 6 (June 1982): 368–370.

Dwyer, B. "One more time—how to update a master file." *Communications of the ACM* 24, no. 1 (January 1981): 3–8.

Enbody, R.J., and H.C. Du. "Dynamic Hashing Schemes." *ACM Computing Surveys* 20, no. 2 (June 1988): 85–113.

Fagin, R., J. Nievergelt, N. Pippenger, and H.R. Strong. "Extendible hashing—a fast access method for dynamic files." *ACM Transactions on Database Systems* 4, no. 3 (September 1979): 315–344.

Faloutsos, C. "Access methods for text." *ACM Computing Surveys* 17, no. 1 (March 1985): 49–74.

Flajolet, P. "On the Performance Evaluation of Extendible Hashing and Trie Searching." *Acta Informatica* 20 (1983): 345–369.

Flores, I. *Peripheral Devices.* Englewood Cliffs, N.J.: Prentice-Hall, 1973.

Gonnet, G.H. *Handbook of Algorithms and Data Structures.* Reading, Mass.: Addison-Wesley, 1984.

Hanson, O. *Design of Computer Data Files.* Rockville, Md.: Computer Science Press, 1982.

Held, G., and M. Stonebraker. "B-trees reexamined." *Communications of the ACM* 21, no. 2 (February 1978): 139–143.

Hoare, C.A.R. "The emperor's old clothes." The C.A.R. Turing Award address. *Communications of the ACM* 24, no. 2 (February 1981): 75–83.

IBM. *DFSORT General Information.* IBM Order No. GC33-4033-11.

IBM. *OS/VS Virtual Storage Access Method (VSAM) Planning Guide.* IBM Order No. GC26-3799.

Jensen, K., and N. Wirth. *Pascal User Manual and Report,* 2d Ed. Springer Verlag, 1974.

Keehn, D.G., and J.O. Lacy. "VSAM data set design parameters." *IBM Systems Journal* 13, no. 3 (1974): 186–212.

Kernighan, B., and R. Pike. *The UNIX Programming Environment.* Englewood Cliffs, N.J.: Prentice-Hall, 1984.

Kernighan, B., and D. Ritchie. *The C Programming Language.* Englewood Cliffs, N.J.: Prentice-Hall, 1978.

Kernighan, B., and D. Ritchie. *The C Programming Language*, 2nd Ed. Englewood Cliffs, N.J.: Prentice-Hall, 1988.

Knuth, D. *The Art of Computer Programming*. Vol. 1, *Fundamental Algorithms*. 2d Ed. Reading, Mass.: Addison-Wesley, 1973a.

Knuth, D. *The Art of Computer Programming*. Vol. 3, *Searching and Sorting*. Reading, Mass.: Addison-Wesley, 1973b.

Lang, S.D., J.R. Driscoll, and J.H. Jou. "Batch insertion for tree structured file organizations—improving differential database representation." CS-TR-85, Department of Computer Science, University of Central Florida, Orlando, Flor.

Lapin, J.E. *Portable C and UNIX System Programming*. Englewood Cliffs, N.J.: Prentice-Hall, 1987.

Larson, P. "Dynamic Hashing." *BIT* 18 (1978): 184–201.

Larson, P. "Linear Hashing with Overflow-handling by Linear Probing." *ACM Transactions on Database Systems* 10, no. 1 (March 1985): 75–89.

Larson, P. "Linear Hashing with Partial Expansions." *Proceedings of the 6th Conference on Very Large Databases*. (Montreal, Canada Oct 1–3, 1980) New York: ACM/IEEE: 224–233.

Larson, P. "Performance Analysis of Linear Hashing with Partial Expansions." *ACM Transactions on Database Systems* 7, no. 4 (December 1982): 566–587.

Laub, L. "What is CD-ROM?" In *CD-ROM: The New Papyrus*. S. Lambert and S. Ropiequet, eds. Redmond, WA: Microsoft Press, 1986: 47–71.

Leffler, S., M.K. McKusick, M. Karels, and J.S. Quarterman. *The Design and Implementation of the 4.3BSD UNIX Operating System*. Reading, Mass.: Addison-Wesley, 1989.

Levy, M.R. "Modularity and the sequential file update problem." *Communications of the ACM* 25, no. 6 (June 1982): 362–367.

Litwin, W. "Linear Hashing: A New Tool for File and Table Addressing." *Proceedings of the 6th Conference on Very Large Databases* (Montreal, Canada, Oct 1–3, 1980) New York: ACM/IEEE: 212–223.

Litwin, W. "Virtual Hashing: A Dynamically Changing Hashing." *Proceedings of the 4th Conference on Very Large Databases* (Berlin 1978) New York: ACM/IEEE: 517–523.

Loomis, M. *Data Management and File Processing*. Englewood Cliffs, N.J.: Prentice-Hall, 1983.

Lorin, H. *Sorting and Sort Systems*. Reading, Mass.: Addison-Wesley, 1975.

Lum, V.Y., P.S. Yuen, and M. Dodd. "Key-to-Address Transform Techniques, A Fundamental Performance Study on Large Existing Formatted Files." *Communications of the ACM* 14, no. 4 (April 1971): 228–39.

Lynch, T. *Data Compression Techniques and Applications*. New York: Van Nostrand Reinhold Company, Inc., 1985.

Madnick, S.E., and J.J. Donovan. *Operating Systems*. Englewood Cliffs, N.J.: Prentice-Hall, 1974.

Maurer, W.D., and T.G. Lewis. "Hash table methods." *ACM Computing Surveys* 7, no. 1 (March 1975): 5–19.

McCreight, E. "Pagination of B* trees with variable length records." *Communications of the ACM* 20, no. 9 (September 1977): 670–674.

McKusick, M.K., W.M. Joy, S.J. Leffler, and R.S. Fabry. "A fast file system for UNIX." *ACM Transactions on Computer Systems* 2, no. 3 (August 1984): 181–197.

Mendelson, H. "Analysis of Extendible Hashing." *IEEE Transactions on Software Engineering* 8, no. 6 (November 1982): 611–619.

Microsoft, Inc. *Disk Operating System. Version 2.00.* IBM Personal Computer Language Series. IBM, 1983.

Morgan, R., and H. McGilton. *Introducing UNIX System V.* New York: McGraw-Hill, 1987.

Murayama, K., and S.E. Smith. "Analysis of design alternatives for virtual memory indexes." *Communications of the ACM* 20, no. 4 (April 1977): 245–254.

Nievergelt, J., H. Hinterberger, and K. Sevcik. "The grid file: an adaptive symmetric, multikey file structure." *ACM Transactions on Database Systems* 9, no. 1 (March 1984): 38–71.

Ouskel, M., and P. Scheuermann. "Multidimensional B-trees: Analysis of dynamic behavior." *BIT* 21 (1981):401–418.

Pechura, M.A., and J.D. Schoeffler. "Estimating file access of floppy disks." *Communications of the ACM* 26, no. 10 (October 1983): 754–763.

Peterson, J.L., and A. Silberschatz. *Operating System Concepts,* 2nd Ed. Reading, Mass.: Addison-Wesley, 1985.

Peterson, W.W. "Addressing for random access storage." *IBM Journal of Research and Development* 1, no. 2(1957):130–146.

Pollack, S., and T. Sterling. *A Guide to Structured Programming and PL/I.* 3rd Ed. New York: Holt, Rinehart, and Winston, 1980.

Ritchie, B., and K. Thompson. "The UNIX time-sharing system." *Communications of the ACM* 17, no. 7 (July 1974): 365–375.

Ritchie, D. *The Unix I/O System.* Murray Hill, N.J.: AT&T Bell Laboratories, 1979.

Robinson, J.T. "The *K-d* B-tree: A search structure for large multidimensional dynamic indexes." *ACM SIGMOD 1981 International Conference on Management of Data.* April 29–May 1, 1981.

Rosenberg, A.L., and L. Snyder. "Time and space optimality in B-trees." *ACM Transactions on Database Systems* 6, no. 1 (March 1981): 174–183.

Sager, T.J. "A polynomial time generator for minimal perfect hash functions." *Communications of the ACM* 28, no. 5 (May 1985): 523–532.

Salton, G., and M. McGill. *Introduction to Modern Information Retrieval.* McGraw-Hill, 1983.

Salzberg, B. *File Structures.* Englewood Cliffs, N.J.: Prentice-Hall, 1988.

Salzberg, B., et al. "FastSort: A Distributed Single-Input, Single-Output Sort." *Proceedings of the 1990 ACM SIGMOD International Conference on Management of Data, SIGMOD RECORD,* Vol. 19, Issue 2, (June 1990): 94–101.

Scholl, M. "New file organizations based on dynamic hashing." *ACM Transactions on Database Systems* 6, no. 1 (March 1981): 194–211.

Severance, D.G. "Identifier search mechanisms: A survey and generalized model." *ACM Computing Surveys* 6, no. 3 (September 1974): 175–194.

Snyder, L. "On B-trees reexamined." *Communications of the ACM* 21, no. 7 (July 1978): 594.

Sorenson, P.G., J.P. Tremblay and R.F. Deutscher. "Key-to-Address Transformation Techniques." *INFOR* (Canada) Vol. 16, no. 1 (1978): 397–409.

Spector, A., and D. Gifford. "Case study: The space shuttle primary computer system." *Communications of the ACM* 27, no. 9 (September 1984): 872–900.

Standish, T.A. *Data Structure Techniques.* Reading, Mass.: Addison-Wesley, 1980.

Sun Microsystems. *Networking on the Sun Workstation.* Mountain View, CA: Sun Microsystems, Inc., 1986.

Sussenguth, E.H. "The use of tree structures for processing files." *Communications of the ACM* 6, no. 5 (May 1963): 272–279.

Sweet, F. "Keyfield design." *Datamation* (October 1, 1985): 119–120.

Teory, T.J., and J.P. Fry. *Design of Database Structures.* Englewood Cliffs, N.J.: Prentice-Hall, 1982.

The Joint ANSI/IEEE Pascal Standards Committee. "Pascal: Forward to the candidate extension library." *SIGPLAN Notices* 19, no. 7 (July 1984): 28–44.

Tremblay, J.P., and P.G. Sorenson. *An Introduction to Data Structures with Applications.* New York: McGraw-Hill, 1984.

Ullman, J. *Principles of Database Systems,* 2d Ed. Rockville, Md.: Computer Science Press, 1980.

Ullman, J.D. *Principles of Database Systems,* 3d Ed. Rockville, Md.: Computer Science Press, 1986.

U.C. Berkeley. *UNIX Programmer's Reference Manual.* University of California Berkeley, 1986.

VanDoren, J. "Some empirical results on generalized AVL trees." *Proceedings of the NSF-CBMS Regional Research Conference on Automatic Information Organization and Retrieval.* University of Missouri at Columbia (July 1973): 46–62.

VanDoren, J., and J. Gray. "An algorithm for maintaining dynamic AVL trees." In *Information Systems, COINS IV,* New York: Plenum Press, 1974: 161–180.

Veklerov, E. "Analysis of Dynamic Hashing with Deferred Splitting." *ACM Transactions on Database Systems* 10, no. 1 (March 1985): 90–96.

Wagner, R.E. "Indexing design considerations." *IBM Systems Journal* 12, no. 4 (1973): 351–367.

Wang, P. *An Introduction to Berkeley Unix.* Belmont, CA: Wadsworth Publishing Co., 1988.

Webster, R.E. "B$^+$ trees." Unpublished Master's thesis, Oklahoma State University, 1980.

Welch, T. "A Technique for High Performance Data Compression." *IEEE Computer,* Vol. 17, no. 6 (June 1984): 8–19.

Wells, D.C., E.W. Greisen and R.H. Harten. "FITS: A Flexible Image Transport System." *Astronomy and Astrophysics Supplement Series,* no. 44 (1981): 363–370.

Wiederhold, G. *Database Design,* 2d Ed. New York: McGraw-Hill, 1983.

Wirth, N. "An assessment of the programming language Pascal." *IEEE Transactions on Software Engineering* SE-1, no. 2 (June 1975).

Yao, A. Chi-Chih. "On random 2–3 trees." *Acta Informatica* 9, no. 2 (1978): 159–170.

Zoellick, B. "CD-ROM software development." *Byte* 11, no. 5 (May 1986): 173–188.

Zoellick, B. "File System Support for CD-ROM." In *CD-ROM: The New Papyrus*. S. Lambert and S. Ropiequet, eds. Redmond, WA: Microsoft Press, 1986: 103–128.

Zoellick, B. "Selecting an Approach to Document Retrieval." In *CD-ROM, Volume 2: Optical Publishing*. S. Ropiequet, ed. Redmond, WA: Microsoft Press, 1987: 63–82.

Index